MCDONALD INSTITUTE MONOGRAPHS

Stone knapping

the necessary conditions for a uniquely hominin behaviour

Edited by Valentine Roux & Blandine Bril

Published by:

McDonald Institute for Archaeological Research
University of Cambridge
Downing Street
Cambridge, UK
CB2 3ER
(0)(1223) 339336 (Publications Office)
(0)(1223) 333538 (General Office)
(0)(1223) 333536 (FAX)
dak12@cam.ac.uk
www.mcdonald.cam.ac.uk

Distributed by Oxbow Books
 United Kingdom: Oxbow Books, Park End Place, Oxford, OX1 1HN, UK.
  Tel: (0)(1865) 241249; Fax: (0)(1865) 794449; www.oxbowbooks.com
 USA: The David Brown Book Company, P.O. Box 511, Oakville, CT 06779, USA.
  Tel: 860-945-9329; Fax: 860-945-9468

ISBN: 1-902937-34-1
ISSN: 1363-1349 (McDonald Institute)

Edited for the Institute by Chris Scarre (*Series Editor*) and Dora A. Kemp (*Production Editor*).

Cover illustration: Dora Kemp, after an original idea of Gérard Monthel (CNRS, UMR 7055).

Printed and bound by Short Run Press, Bittern Rd, Sowton Industrial Estate, Exeter, EX2 7LW, UK.

CONTENTS

CONTRIBUTORS

NEZHA BENNIS
CNRS UMR 8119, UFR Biomédicale - Université René Descartes, 45 rue des Saint Pères, 75006 Paris, France.

ELENA V. BIRYUKOVA
Institute of Higher Nervous Activity and Neurophysiology, Russian Academy of Sciences, Butlerov str. 5A, 117845 Moscow, Russia.
Email: birds@orc.ru

RAOUL M. BONGERS
Center for Human Movement Sciences, University of Groningen, PO Box 196, 9700 AD Groningen, The Netherlands.
Email: r.m.bongers@ppsw.rug.nl

BLANDINE BRIL
Groupe de Recherche: Apprentissage et Contexte, École des Hautes Études en Sciences Sociales, 54 Bd Raspail, 75006 Paris, France.
Email: Blandine.Bril@ehess.fr

AMY E. BRUGGER
Psychology Department, Tufts University, 490 Boston Ave, Medford, MA 02155, USA.

EMILY W. BUSHNELL
Psychology Department, Tufts University, 490 Boston Ave, Medford, MA 02155, USA.
Email: emily.bushnell@tufts.edu

RICHARD W. BYRNE
Professor of Evolutionary Psychology, School of Psychology, The University of St Andrews, St Andrews, Fife, KY16 9JP, Scotland.
Email: rwb@st-andrews.ac.uk

DANIELA CORBETTA
Department of Health and Kinesiology and Department of Psychological Sciences, Purdue University, 800 West Stadium Ave, Lambert Fieldhouse, West Lafayette, IN 47907, USA.
Email: Dcorbetta@sla.purdue.edu

RALF F.A. COX
Behavioral Science Institute, Radboud University Nijmegen, Montessorilaan 3, PO Box 9104, 6500 HE Nijmegen, The Netherlands.
Email: r.cox@psych.ru.nl

SARAH E. CUMMINS-SEBREE
Behavioral Sciences Department, Raymond Walters College, University of Cincinnatti, 9555 Plainfield Road, Blue Ash, OH 45236-1096, USA.
Email: cumminsh@ucrwcu.rwc.uc.edu

EVA DAVID
UMR 7055, Préhistoire et Technologie, CNRS, Maison de l'Archéologie et de l'Ethnologie, 21 allée de l'Université, 92023 Nanterre cedex, France.

GILLES DIETRICH
UMRS/CNRS 2164, Aérodynamique et Biomécanique du Mouvement, Marseille, France.

JULIE FOUCART
EHESS, Groupe de Recherche «Apprentissage et Contexte» et INSERM 483, 54 Boulevard Raspail 75006 Paris, France.
Email: Julie.Foucart@ehess.fr

DOROTHY M. FRAGASZY
Department of Psychology, University of Georgia, Athens, GA 30602-3013, USA.
Email: doree@uga.edu

SATOSHI HIRATA
Hayashibara Great Ape Research Institute, Okayama, Japan.
E-mail: hirata@gari.be.to

M.K. HOLDER
Handedness Research Institute, and the Center for the Integrative Study of Animal Behavior, Indiana University, 402 N. Park Avenue, Bloomington, IN 47405, USA.
Email: primate@indiana.edu

CHIHARU HOUKI
Okayama University of Science, Japan.
E-mail: amero-chihare@mgb.biglobe.ne.jp

GALINA P. IVANOVA
Department of Biomechanics, P.F. Lesgaft State Academy of Physical Culture, Dekabristov str. 35, 193318, St Petersburg, Russia.
Email: ivanova@insar.org

STÉPHANE JACOBS
CNRS UMR 8119, UFR Biomédicale - Université René Descartes, 45 rue des Saint Pères, 75006 Paris, France.
Email: jacobs@biomedicale.univ-paris5.fr

PETER A. KIRKWOOD
Sobell Department of Motor Neuroscience and Movement Disorders, Institute of Neurology, University College London, Queen Square, London, WC1N 3BG, UK.
Email: pkirkwoo@ion.ucl.ac.uk

MIKHAIL A. KULIKOV
Institute of Higher Nervous Activity and Neurophysiology, Russian Academy of Sciences, Butlerov str. 5A, 117845 Moscow, Russia.

ROGER N. LEMON
Sobell Department of Motor Neuroscience and Movement
Disorders, Institute of Neurology, University College
London, Queen Square, London, WC1N 3BG, UK.
Email: rlemon@ion.ucl.ac.uk

JEFFREY J. LOCKMAN
Department of Psychology, 2007 Percival Stern Hall,
Tulane University, New Orleans, LA 70118, USA.
Email: lockman@tulane.edu

MARC A. MAIER
UMR-742 Inserm/UPMC, Université Pierre et Marie
Curie, 9 Quai St-Bernard, 75005 Paris, France.
Email: Marc.Maier@snv.jussieu.fr

LINDA F. MARCHANT
Department of Anthropology, Professor and Chair, Miami
University, 157 Upham Hall, Oxford OH 5056, USA.
Email: marchalf@muohio.edu

MARY W. MARZKE
Department of Anthropology, Arizona State University,
Tempe, AZ 85287-2402, USA.
Email: mary.marzke@asu.edu

TETSURO MATSUZAWA
Primate Research Institute, Kyoto University, Inuyama,
Japan.
E-mail: matsuzaw@pri.kyoto-u.ac.jp

WILLIAM C. MCGREW
Department of Biological Anthropology, University of
Cambridge, Pembroke Street, Cambridge, CB2 3DZ, UK.
Email: wcm21@cam.ac.uk

PETR E. MOLCHANOV
Department of Physics, Moscow State University,
Moscow.

NARUKI MORIMURA
Hayashibara Great Ape Research Institute, Okayama,
Japan.
E-mail: narukim@rc4.so-net.ne.jp

KATSUMI NAKAJIMA
Department of Biological Control Systems, Division
of System Neurophysiology, National Institute for
Physiological Sciences, Myodaiji, Okazaki 444-8585, Japan.
Email: nakajima@nips.ac.jp

JACQUES PELEGRIN
UMR 7055, CNRS, Maison de l'Archéologie et de
l'Ethnologie, 21 allée de l'Université, 92023 Nanterre
cedex, France.
Email: pelegrin@mae.u-paris10.fr

AGNÈS ROBY-BRAMI
CNRS UMR 8119, Neurophysique et Physiologie du
système moteur, UFR Biomédicale - Université René
Descartes, 45 rue des Saint Pères, 75270 Paris cedex 06,
France.
Email: agnes.roby-brami@univ-paris5.fr

HÉLÈNE ROCHE
UMR 7055, CNRS, Maison de l'Archéologie et de
l'Ethnologie, 21 allée de l'Université, 92023 Nanterre
cedex, France.
Email: roche@mae.u-paris10.fr

VALENTINE ROUX
UMR 7055, Préhistoire et Technologie, CNRS, Maison de
l'Archéologie et de l'Ethnologie, 21 allée de l'Université,
92023 Nanterre cedex, France.
Email: valentine.roux@mae.u-paris10.fr

JASON SIDMAN
Psychology Department, Tufts University, 490 Boston Ave,
Medford, MA 02155, USA.
Email: Jason.Sidman@tufts.edu

AD W. SMITSMAN
Behavioral Science Institute, Radboud University
Nijmegen, Montessorilaan 3, PO Box 9104, 6500 HE
Nijmegen, The Netherlands.
Email: smitsman@psych.ru.nl

JAMES STEELE
School of Humanities (Archaeology), University of
Southampton, Highfield, Southampton, SO17 1BJ, UK.
Email: tjms@soton.ac.uk

DIETRICH STOUT
Department of Anthropology, George Washington
University, 2110 G St, NW, Washington, DC 20052, USA.
Email: stout@gwu.edu

YOSHIKAZU UENO
Primate Research Institute, Kyoto University, Inuyama,
Japan.
E-mail: okuma@pri.kyoto-u.ac.jp

NATALIE UOMINI
School of Humanities (Archaeology), University of
Southampton, Highfield, Southampton, SO17 1BJ, UK.
Email: n.t.uomini@soton.ac.uk

VICKY WINTON
University of Oxford, The PADMAC Unit, The Donald
Baden-Powell Quaternary Research Centre, Pitt Rivers
Museum, Oxford, OX2 6PN, UK.
Email: victoria.winton@prm.ox.ac.uk

Figures

Tables

Preface

This volume originates in a workshop held in Pont-à-Mousson in November 2001 'Stone Knapping: a Uniquely Hominid Behaviour'. The origin of this workshop, organized by B. Bril and V. Roux, goes back to 1993. At that time, a research project was granted to V. Roux and B. Bril by the French Ministry of Research, Cognitive Science Department, to carry out a study on stone knapping in India (Khambhat, Gujarat). The archaeological question underlying this study was related to the archaeology of the Indus Civilization (third millennium BC). Numerous stone beads had been found on archaeological sites thus leading to the question as to what was the organization of the bead production given the different levels of expertise required for knapping. In order to investigate the skills involved in stone-bead knapping, a study was conducted in Khambhat, a town in Gujarat, where the traditional stone-bead industry is still very much alive. The main conclusion emphasized the difficulties of acquisition and mastery of the elementary knapping gesture. The results of this first study are reported in various papers (Roux *et al.* 1995; Bril *et al.* 2000).

A second four-year research project, granted in 1998 by the CNRS (French National Centre of Scientific Research) brought together a small group of French scientists to exchange ideas around the question of 'Technical skills among the early hominids'. Various fields of research were represented: archaeology with Valentine Roux, Hélène Roche and Jacques Pelegrin; primatology with Frederic Joulian; and movement science, with Elena Biryukova and Gilles Dietrich (both specializing in biomechanics), Agnès Roby-Brami (specializing in neuroscience) and Blandine Bril (specializing in psychology).

The main objective of this group was to construct a reference base for interpreting the stone-knapping action in terms of motor and cognitive skills. For this purpose, a second experiment was conducted in India. Numerous discussions followed focusing mainly on the specificity of the skills involved in actions like stone knapping. The final outcome of this group has been to expand the discussions at an international level through a workshop which was hosted by an illustrious seventeenth-century Abbey, *l'Abbaye des Prémontrés*, in Pont-à-Mousson (France) from the 21st to the 24th of November 2001. The abbey was a highly suitable location for a workshop which was the most rewarding way to conclude this four-year research program. The meeting was conceived as a place where everyone was free to expose and debate his/her own ideas about what could give insight into the question: *why do non-human primates not knap stone?* It represented a unique opportunity for confronting studies about complex motor actions, as led by anatomy, movement science, neurology, primatology and psychology, in order to assess tentatively what unique biological and/or cultural resources rendered possible the practice of this activity.

We are very glad to have addressed most of the topics debated during the workshop in this volume which, by bringing together scientists from various backgrounds, should encourage further research in the search for discovering who our ancestors were. We would like to express our gratitude to all the contributors of this volume who made possible this debate on the emergence of stone knapping among human primates. We hope that future workshops will permit further development of the different questions highlighted here which relate to the very roots of the history of humankind.

The editors, Nanterre, May 2004

Acknowledgements

The workshop was funded by the CNRS through the program OHLL (Origine de l'Homme, des langues et du langage). We are grateful to Jehanne Féblot-Augustins, Kimberly De Haan and Marcia-Anne Dobres for their help in editing and improving the English of the francophone papers. We would like to kindly thank anonymous reviewers and Thomas Wynn for critique, suggestions, and editorial comments. Our gratitude goes to Dora Kemp, Production Editor of the McDonald Institute, for her tireless help in the editing process.

References

Bril, B., V. Roux & G. Dietrich, 2000. Habiletés impliquées dans la taille des perles en calcédoine. Caractéristiques motrices et cognitives d'une action située complexe, in *Cornaline de l'Inde: des pratiques techniques de Cambay aux techno-systèmes de l'Indus*, ed. V. Roux. Paris: Editions de la MSH, 207–332. English CD-rom. www.epistemes.net/arkeotek/p_cornaline.htm.

Roux, V., B. Bril & G. Dietrich, 1995. Skills and learning difficulties involved in stone knapping: the case of stone bead knapping in Khambhat, India. *World Archaeology* 27(1), 63–87.

Chapter 1

General Introduction: a Dynamic Systems Framework for Studying a Uniquely Hominin Innovation

Valentine Roux & Blandine Bril

> The Oldowan lithic culture differs from anything known for free-ranging apes, but all of the capacities needed to make it are manifested in the non-lithic tools of chimpanzees (Wynn & McGrew 1989). The challenge is to find anything uniquely hominid in the capacities needed to make these artefacts (McGrew 1993, 165).

Evidence of stone knapping first occurs in East Africa during the late Pliocene, *c.* 2.6 million years ago (Myr). This is the beginning of a long technological story during which different genera (*Australopithecus* and *Homo*) and species coexisted and evolved. The technological story describes the development of more and more elaborate knapping processes, as reported by Jacques Pelegrin. Hélène Roche's recent research in Turkana, northern Kenya, however, reveals that Oldowan lithic assemblages (between 2.6 and 2.2 Myr) are not as homogeneous as previously supposed. They represent the legacy of both awkward opportunistic knappers and, on the contrary, skilled knappers who controlled the flaking process through careful core monitoring. Oldowan lithic variability raises the question not only of the genus and species assumed to be the tool-makers, but also of the reasons that might explain why some groups performed better than others. Could it be a question of differences in competence and/or performance? Might these differences in competence act as adaptive values in the selective process that underpin hominin evolution?

The tentative purpose of this book is to characterize the capacities involved in stone knapping. The question of their specificity remains a highly-controversial issue. Considered essential for a better understanding of what distinguishes early hominins from non-human primates, the specificity of stone knapping has been tentatively explored in numerous studies. The issue has been addressed either by assessing the non-human primate capacities involved in

tool use and tool-making (e.g. Boesch & Boesch 1990; 1992; 2000; McGrew 1992; 1993; Wynn & McGrew 1989), or by teaching stone knapping to primates (e.g. Schick *et al.* 1999; Savage-Rumbaugh & Lewin 1994; Toth *et al.* 1993; Wright 1972), or by interpreting lithic industries in terms of motor and cognitive skills in reference to neuropsychological concepts (e.g. Pelegrin this volume; 1993; Wynn 1985; 1991; 2002a; Roche & Texier 1996; Roche *et al.* 1999; Schlanger 1996). Primatologists contend that compared with non-human primates, Oldowan toolmakers do not display distinct motor or cognitive capacities (e.g. Joulian 1996; Wynn & McGrew 1989), even though they admit that it is problematic for chimpanzees to learn how to knap stone. In this respect, the experiments conducted with Kanzi (Savage-Rumbaugh & Lewin 1994) are very telling (Schick *et al.* 1999). Kanzi understands that producing flakes is a means of obtaining cutting edges. In addition, he understands that flakes can be obtained by breaking stones. Yet, after a few years of apprenticeship, Kanzi only manages to produce splinters, with accidental conchoidal pieces looking like 'flakes' (Pelegrin this volume). In other words, Kanzi has not succeeded in learning how to knap stone. He is definitely unable to control the conchoidal fracture. Savage-Rumbaugh suggested that: '... if Kanzi is limited in the quality of flaking through hard-hammer percussion, it is the result of biomechanical, not cognitive, constraints' (Savage-Rumbaugh & Lewin 1994, 219). The hypothesis that the specificity of stone knapping could pertain to motor skill has been taken up by a few archaeologists (e.g. Ambrose 2001). Few studies, however, have focused on this skill-related behavioural aspect of tool-making. Most of them focus on the cognitive capacities that one might infer from lithic industries (e.g. Gowlett 1992; Pelegrin 1993; Toth 1993; Wynn 2002a).

In order to renew the approach to the question of this uniquely hominin invention, the knapping

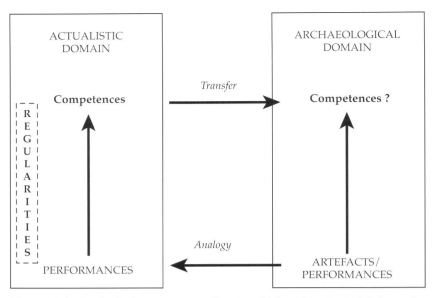

Figure 1.1. *Analogical process according to which archaeological data are interpreted in reference to actualistic regularities (after J.C. Gardin 1979).*

task is studied here in the light of other skilled activities and various disciplinary perspectives. As stated by Thomas Wynn (2002b, 718), 'all studies of skilled activity can provide potential analogues and ... more general accounts of human and non-human cognition can provide important insights'. These studies are mainly actualistic: they are psychological, biomechanical, anatomical, neurological, primatological and ethnoarchaeological. Indeed, the interpretation of artefacts requires that knowledge external to archaeology should be drawn upon (Gallay 1986). Prehistoric artefacts are interpreted following a reasoning by analogy and by transfer of attributes (Gardin 1979). In the case of lithic industries, performances are indicated by the objects themselves. They are deciphered through technological analyses, which enable prehistorians to reconstruct the entire evolution of lithic technology. On the contrary, the competences that underpin observable performances, as well as the conditions for the effectuation of these competences, are not 'given' by the artefacts themselves. They are necessarily interpreted in reference to actualistic data, which associate performances with competences. In other words, given that regularities between performance and competence are established in actualistic domains, prehistoric artefacts can be interpreted in terms of competence (Fig. 1.1). The regularities studied here refer to the competences that underpin skilled tool-related behaviour, to the bio-behavioural, anatomical and neuronal conditions needed for their development, and to the socio-cognitive conditions required for their actualization. They are highlighted through

comparative studies of human and non-human primate tool-related skills, in order to apply them to stone tools made by the early hominins for whom no analogues exist.

Following the principles of the analysis of technological change (Roux 2003), this volume is organized into three sections. The first section includes such papers as contribute to characterize stone knapping in terms of techniques and skills. The second section includes papers which contribute to the study of the mechanisms that underpin the effectuation of the skills involved in stone knapping. The study of these mechanisms should bring to light the essential prerequisites of stone knapping and help assess the extent to which the skills involved in stone knapping are specific to human primates, as compared to non-human primates. Finally, the third section presents the papers pertaining to the definition of the socio-cognitive conditions needed for the actualization of stone knapping, the focus shifting at this point from invention to innovation.

Invention and innovation are here clearly distinguished from one another. Invention is what happens locally, on an individual scale. It affects the evolution of the system when it becomes an innovation through being widely accepted (van der Leeuw & Torrence 1989). Innovation is a complex social and anthropological process characterized, like any complex system, by interactions between numerous non-hierarchically-ordered components which, in the present case, operate in and across the technological and the social domains (Roux 2003). The main components are the technical task, the subject and the environment. Innovation stems from interactions between the properties of these components (Fig. 1.2). An analysis of innovation thus requires the analysis, not only of the technical task, but also of the subject's intention(s), which are rooted in the socio-cultural arena and its collective representations, and of the environment. As a historical process, innovation corresponds to a local scenario (Gallay 1986), which has to be reconstructed on the basis of the archaeological data liable to provide information on the cultural specifics as expressed in the subject's intention(s), and on the basis of environmental data (the evidence of remains and theoretical modelling). The study of local scenarios and their related metaphoric explanations is beyond the scope of this book, which focuses mainly on the invention of stone knapping, a process that operates at the level of the technical task. It also, however, includes papers on the conditions required for the actualization of stone knapping as an innovation.

Stone knapping: characterizing a tool-related task

To begin with, it should be specified that the technical task, as one of the three components of the innovation process, refers on the one hand to the technique that allows the transformation of raw materials into objects, and on the other hand to the motor and cognitive skills that convert technique into action. It can be described independently of the cultural context within which it takes place. It is a sub-system that possesses its own dynamics and is supposed to become an emergent property of the technological system, but whose actualization proper depends on the dynamics of the technological system (the innovation process). Skills are at the heart of the mechanisms that underlie changes in technical tasks, since a new technical task necessarily requires new skills (Bril & Roux 2002). The skills that make a technological invention possible can be characterized as either continuous or discontinuous, depending on whether the individual has to acquire new capabilities or can build on pre-existing ones.

Because the study of a technical task requires that it be characterized in terms of techniques and skills, this first section comprises introductory studies presenting the techniques of stone knapping, followed by studies on the skills involved in tool-related tasks.

Stone knapping: a technical characterization
A technique is defined as the physical modality according to which raw material is transformed (Tixier 1967). As shown throughout prehistory, a technical task can be achieved using different techniques. Studying the invention of stone knapping implies a fine understanding of the physical modalities according to which the first lithic tools were made in order to characterize this task compared to other percussion tasks such as nut cracking. Indeed, nut cracking, as a percussive technique, has been often considered as the technical action from which stone technology (e.g. de Beaune 2004; Sugiyama & Koman 1979) or the intention to flake (e.g. Marchant & McGrew this volume) developed. As we shall see, however, nut

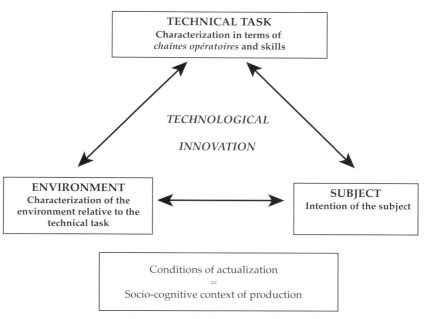

Figure 1.2. *The dynamic process of technological change (after Roux 2003).*

cracking and stone knapping call for different physical modalities by which nuts or stone are transformed. As underlined by Pelegrin, who summarizes the characteristics of stone knapping, these are not comparable techniques.

Stone knapping responds to the mechanism of conchoidal fracture. It must be distinguished from split breaking. Conchoidal fracture alone ensures that the transformation of the stone is controlled. Split breaking is caused by a forceful stroke, with no control over the fracture of the stone, which then breaks in unexpected ways. A conchoidal fracture refers to the Hertzian cone phenomenon. Detaching flakes by conchoidal fracturing implies the control of numerous parameters and requires, in particular, much more precision than split breaking, which allows for a large precision tolerance. In conchoidal fracturing, the stroke has to be applied near the edge and at no less than a 90° angle; precision of the stroke determines the geometric characteristics of the detached flake. Pelegrin's contribution is essential for understanding that the lithic production made by Kanzi is not obtained by controlled conchoidal fracturing and that, in this respect, Kanzi's technique for making splinters is comparable to the nut-cracking technique alone, that is, split breaking. Controlled conchoidal fracturing can be achieved according to different techniques. Techniques must be distinguished from methods. Methods relate to the organized reduction processes. Pelegrin recounts how stone-knapping methods became more and more elaborate during prehistory, testifying to what could be specifically human cognitive capacities.

Now, as reported by Roche, the earliest-known lithic industries provide clear evidence of conchoidal fracturing. These industries belong to late Pliocene archaeological sites (2.6 Myr to 2.2 Myr) from East Africa, where no fewer than five species grouped into two genera (*Australopithecus* and *Homo*) are present at the time. These industries may be characterized as heterogeneous. On the one hand, there is a type of flaking that can be qualified both as simple, given the limited succession of removals achieved, and as poorly skilled, as shown by percussive strokes whose points of impact sometimes lack precision (as at Gona and Lokalelei 1). On the other hand, there is a surprisingly well-organized debitage of flakes that testifies to a high degree of control over the percussion gestures, as specifically shown by the total absence of 'hammering' on the cores. This is the case at Lokalelei 2c. Refittings on 13 cobbles demonstrate a genuine monitoring of the cores. In one case, up to 73 flakes were detached from a single cobble. Evidence of such an organized debitage is not even attested in the Early Pleistocene. Roche emphasizes the fact that the Lokalelei 2c lithic assemblage testifies to an exceptional command of elementary gestures associated with a well-controlled unfolding of series of removals. Still, several hundreds of thousands of years will have to pass before prehistoric stone knappers are able to free themselves from the initial geometric characteristics of the raw material and give the stone the desired morphology. Roche also recounts this later part of the history of lithic technology, up to the moment when the genus *Homo* becomes predominant.

Stone knapping: characterizing the skills involved
Acting in everyday life presupposes the capacity to perform goal-directed actions, that is, the faculty to produce conclusive behavioural sequences that bring the agent nearer the objective. Tool use and tool making are complex actions that involve compound sequences of movements to carry out the task at hand. Tool use entails interacting — most often manually — with objects in the environment. This places significant challenges on the cognitivo-motor system. To address the issue of the nature of the skills involved in tool use it is common nowadays to contrast two different approaches to action.[1] One approach, referred to as the computational or cognitive approach, postulates that action depends upon an internal representation; action is guided by a pre-existing representation. This approach has been more concerned with the nature of the processes that precede action rather than with the way the action itself is carried out. This 'motor system approach' emphasizes an information-processing perspective, the existence of some kind of 'central re-

presentation', 'internal models', or 'motor commands'. Along this theoretical position, the agent activity is directly caused by some kind of planning that controls the production of behavioural sequences.

The second theoretical approach, referred to as the ecological approach, stresses the reciprocal role of the organism and the environment acting as a set of constraints from which behaviour emerges. This approach considers the agent as participating in the world, not as controlling it, and insists on the action as being the result of the functional coupling between the organism and the environment. This 'action system approach' considers itself to be more appropriate to the study of everyday life skills (Reed 1988).

Goal-oriented action: the 'motor system approach'
'Knowing how' and 'knowing that' are often considered when everyday life technical or tool-use skills are referred to. This distinction echoes two different types of knowledge, procedural and declarative knowledge (Anderson 1980), each implying two distinct encodings or representations (Annett 1996). Knowledge associated with motor actions is usually considered as procedural, which is implicit, hence unconscious. By contrast, 'knowing that' qualifies declarative knowledge, available to consciousness. As a result, it can be expressed verbally. A clear definition is given by Parker & Milbrath (1993), who consider that:

> knowing how 'to make a tool' is an example of procedural knowledge which also constitutes procedural planning. While preceded by intention, procedural plans are represented primarily in action schemes, which if interrupted can be modified on the spot. In contrast, planning based in declarative knowledge involves representation which in turn allows for anticipation of consequences and modification of planning sequences before plan execution. Declarative knowledge is more flexible . . . (Parker & Milbrath 1993, 315)

Miller *et al.*'s (1960) seminal definition of planning is often referred to:

> A plan is any hierarchical process in the organism that can control the order in which a sequence of operations is to be performed (Miller *et al.* 1960, 16)

Here emphasis is placed on the ability to structure the serial order of the organism's behaviour. This traditional view considers that the notion of plans addresses the question of structure. In other words, an action has the structure it does, because it arises through the execution of entities called plans, which have the same structure.

The problem becomes more difficult when simultaneously considering both a sequence of actions and the elementary actions that are called upon to carry out the global action. In both cases planning is called upon. Jeannerod (1997), among others, considers that simple actions are embedded in more complex actions; that is, elementary actions are sustained by higher-order factors, which refer to the final goal of the action. Here the main function of planning is to select, from a stock of available 'motor schemas', those

> which will have to be performed, relate them to the proper internal and external cues, and organize them into an appropriate sequence (Jeannerod 1997, 127).

Along this line, planning consists essentially in selecting stored elements — schemas, scripts — that will best satisfy the goal, and regulates their modality and time of expression. It is acknowledged, however, that the whole course of action need not require a complete representation of the detailed succession of elementary actions, and that part of the process may be carried out on-line. If difficulties arise, changes in planning will be made and search for other and more appropriate schema will be accessed and selected and accordingly more suitable action performed.

This view grants 'plan' as program a causal role. Plan as program determines the agent activity. Yet this theory does not offer a convincing account of how actions are adapted to their circumstances, how uncertainty is faced up to. As real life is characterized by the unfolding of continuous unpredictable events, behaviour must denote flexibility and adaptability. In this classical view, the 'homunculus' is asked to make an overwhelming number of decisions, which requires an overwhelming amount of information besides a huge repertoire of action schemas or action representations. In addition, the origin of these representations there remains a difficult question to deal with. The other puzzling issue difficult to meet concerns the processes that 'bridge the gap between ideas (or representation) and behaviour, a "miracle"', to use Kunde's (2001) words, often taken for granted. How can an abstract action plan be translated into a concrete motor behaviour? How is a single one chosen among the infinite number of equi-functional action/motor representations? One view developed by artificial intelligence is to give planning a smaller role. Agre & Chapman (1990) consider planning as a resource among others. The agent participates in the world, but does not control it. The 'plan as communication' as opposed to the 'plan as program' does not directly determine the agent's actions. A plan is a resource, i.e. a plan guides activity but does not give solution to problems (Agre & Chapman 1990). Here again, however, while this view does not ascribe behaviour to one main cause and emphasizes the multi-causal origin of action, it does not really elucidate the

guiding function of such a plan. In addition it works at the level of the sequence of actions, not at the level of the elementary action.

Goal-oriented action: the 'ecological' framework
To overcome these difficulties the ecological framework proposes a thoroughly different approach — one that has been adopted, to a certain extent by most of the contributors to this volume who are studying skills as a complex phenomenon (Bril *et al.*; Bushnell; Corbetta; Cummins-Sebree & Fragaszi; Jacobs *et al.*; Lockman; Roux & David; Smitsman; Stout). Originating in the association of Bernstein's (1967) view of motor control, which leaves 'as little as possible residing in the homunculus', and Gibson's (1977) perception/action overtures, the ecological framework offers new foundations for action apprehension. As the focus of this volume is not to give an exhaustive presentation of the ecological framework, we shall present the main features that we think are fundamental to understanding why this approach is presented here as an alternative to more cognitive views.

The main trait of the ecological perspective is to consider the organism (human or animal) as part of a larger system. More specifically it is the mutual relationship between the organism and the environment that is central to the analysis. The environment is described not in physical but in ecological terms, and behaviour is viewed as a solution a person engaged in a goal-oriented action has been able to perform, owing to the environmental constraints. Behaviour is then considered as an emergent phenomenon. Stable action modes emerge from the dynamics of the organism–environment system, which is in turn guided by the information produced by the ongoing action, and therefore specific to these dynamics (Warren 1990). Gibson (1986) expressed it in what has become a notorious maxim: 'We must perceive in order to move, but we must move in order to perceive' (Gibson 1986, 223).

Shaw & Wagman (2001) recently rephrased this idea that perception and action are mutually interacting, through an information field in the following way:

> Any adequate theory for perception and action linkage should satisfy an intentionality condition — that perceiving refers to acting, and acting refers back to perceiving. Similarly, ecological psychologists generally agree that a circular causality holds between perceiving and acting, where agents perceive how to act to reach a goal and then the acting updates the next goal-specific perceiving, which then updates the next goal-relevant acting, and so on until the goal is reached or the effort aborted. Goal-directed activities conform to a perceiving-acting 'cycle' wherein information and control reciprocate under mutually shared intentions (Shaw & Wagman 2001, 905).

Three concepts — constraints to action, degrees of freedom and affordances — are essential for understanding the ecological framework, and more specifically for understanding why this approach may be fruitful when discussing issues relating to stone knapping skills.

Constraints to action: Newell (1986; 1996) considers that three sources of constraints combine to provide the boundary conditions to carry out an action: the organism, the task at hand, and the environment. The organism embraces all the dimensions of a person (or a non-human primate): his/her physiological, biomechanical, neurological, as well as cognitive, and affective facets. The task properties refer to its functional properties, that is, to what the organism must produce to successfully reach the goal. Walking, for example, consists of displacing the body ahead, along the antero-posterio axis, by means of a succession of unipodal and bipodal stances, with the constraint of alternate left and right unipodal stances. To successfully reach the goal, one must produce forces that will 'cause' the intended gait movements. The environment comprises universal constraints experienced by all living organisms, such as gravity or temperature, and more specific and local constraints such as tools. Back to the example of walking, considering walking behaviour as emerging from these three sources of constraints focuses the analysis on the possible range of variation of the action, and more precisely 'on the emerging properties of the co-ordination modes of action, and to the resultant expression of skill' (Newell 1996, 405). The gait movements differ in toddlers and in adults, in visually impaired persons compared with persons with normal vision, or for the same person when walking on a flat surface, uphill or downhill. Exactly the same demonstration can be made for knapping movements.

Degrees of freedom: The degrees of freedom of a system refer to the number of independent dimensions to be controlled. The question of the degrees of freedom in movement has been to a large extent developed by Bernstein (1967; Turvey *et al.* 1982). Usually it is considered that the greater the number of degrees of freedom of a system, the more difficult the control. Depending on the level of analysis the number of degrees of freedom varies greatly. As far as joints are concerned, the upper limb for example has seven degrees of freedom (see Biryukova this volume), the whole body about 10^2, but at the level of muscles the number of degrees of freedom is as high as 10^3, and 10^{14}, if the level of neurons is considered.

Bernstein viewed the degrees of freedom question as central to the understanding of movement co-ordination and skill. Due to the large number of degrees of freedom of the human body there is an infinite number of ways to solve any 'everyday-life motor problem'. As a result it is this great number of possibilities of action that guarantees the flexibility needed to adapt action to local circumstances (Newell 1996; Jordan & Rosenbaum 1989). Depending on the level of analysis, the main question is then: how are these degrees of freedom controlled? How is a system, with an infinite number of possibilities that would be impossible to control, reduced to a controllable system? This question is beyond the scope of this book (for a recent review see Roby-Brami *et al.* 2005), but is of substantial importance to understanding technical skills. For Bernstein, learning a (motor) skill consists of progressively mastering the redundant degrees of freedom of the system, and 'exploiting' these degrees of freedom of the organism–tool system (see Biryukova this volume).

Affordances: The organism–environment mutuality has been expressed by Gibson (1977; 1986) through the concept of affordance, an original word coined by Gibson himself. An affordance is a relation between an organism — human or animal — and its environment, that has consequences for behaviour. In other words, affordances are properties of the environment that have consequences for the organism behaviour (Stoffregen 2000). The properties of the environment constitute affordances only when taken in reference to the action capabilities of the organism. Recent views about affordances insist on the functional utility of the environment (Flash & Smith 2000). In other words what is perceived of the environment is its potential for action, as well as the potential consequence of action. In return, the intention to perform a specific action constrains information detection. This means that the affordances of the environment may be different from one organism to another. Affordances, however, need to be perceived, and therefore learning to perceive the information from the environment constitutes a necessary stage.

In sum, according to this view, the mastering of a technical skill depends on the capacity of an organism to set up the constraints of the system according to the task demand, and to mobilize adaptively the degrees of freedom of the system. At a behavioural level, the unfolding of the action may be viewed as an emergent process, at the interface of information available to the organism (affordances) and the set of constraints associated with the task.

Contrary to what has often been said, the ecological perspective does not deny that some kind of 'representation', or planning could exist. As suggested by Shaw & Wagman (2001), however, the ecological framework stipulates that 'program or symbols should be used sparingly, and then only to set subtle boundaries on dynamical processes'. Along this line Agre & Chapman's (1990) proposal to consider planning as resources that guide the unfolding of the course of action is not incompatible.

Three sub-sections of this volume organize the studies of the skills involved in technical tasks. The first sub-section gathers together papers concerned with stone-knapping case studies, such as stone-bead knapping, a craft still practised in India, and a study of experimental handaxe knapping. In a second sub-section, the motor and cognitive skills involved in tool use and tool making are further considered. These studies allow the characteristics of the competencies underlying tool making to be assessed at a more general level. In a third sub-section, the skilled behaviour developed by non-human primates is examined. The results obtained enable us, by comparison, to characterize the tool-related skills developed by human primates.

Skills involved in stone knapping
The studies by Bril *et al.*, Biryukova *et al.*, and Roux & David report field experiments conducted at Khambhat (Gujarat, India), one of the very rare places in the world where the stone-knapping technique still adheres to the principles of the conchoidal fracture. The technique practised is indirect percussion by counter-blow and is used for making stone beads. This technique is a recent one in the history of techniques. Assuming, however, that similar skills are required for mastering the parameters of conchoidal fracture, the situation can be considered an appropriate referent for studying the skills involved in stone knapping. In order to characterize these skills, a program of field experiments was developed. A field experiment is a compromise between fieldwork and laboratory experimentation. The craftsmen should operate in a setting departing as little as possible from their usual work context, but the nature of the data obtained should also allow the analysis of parameters usually studied under laboratory conditions.

The first study to be carried out was Bril *et al.*'s. The experiment was designed to uncover the features enabling high-level experts to be distinguished from lower-level experts. The aim was to tentatively disentangle and characterize the different dimensions of expertise. Referring to the distinction between technique and method, the process of knapping a roughout to produce a preform was analyzed along three levels of action:
1. the *course of action*, which refers to the way each craftsman actualizes the method; it corresponds to the 'path' of sub-goals produced to transform a roughout into a preform;
2. the *sub-goals*, that is, the way the different functional operations are actualized; a sub-goal is generally carried out by means of a succession of elementary actions, i.e. of strokes;
3. the *elementary action*, that is the flake removal; it corresponds to the actualization of the technique and is carried out by performing a stroke.

An original technical set-up was developed which made it possible to simultaneously record data on the course of action and on the elementary action. The elementary action was analyzed through its main functional dimensions, that is, the movement of the hammer by means of an accelerometer stuck on its head. The rationale for the experiment was the introduction of glass, a new raw material to be knapped. An experimental paradigm based on the capacity for transfer and generalization was considered. It was assumed that the higher the dexterity of the craftsmen, the greater their capacity to transfer to new situations. The results very strongly suggest that expertise rests on the elementary action rather than on the course of action. High-level experts are more capable than low-level experts of adapting the acceleration of the hammer to the raw material and to the length of the flake they want to remove. They have a more flexible behaviour, better adapted to the task constraints. Rather than from *a priori* planning of the overall task (level of the method), expertise thus appears to stem from a command of the dynamics involved in the task (level of the technique), that is, the dynamic coupling between the craftsman, the stone, the hammer and the anvil. Becoming an expert, argue Bril *et al.*, consists of learning how to turn the properties of the system to best account in order to reach a given goal.

In this experiment the functional outcome of the percussive arm movement (i.e. the movement of the hammer) was analyzed. It was shown that high-level experts adapted the acceleration of the hammer in a more tuned manner than low-level experts. Once this tuning capacity was recognized as one dimension of high expertise, the next step was to try to understand how it is produced. For this purpose, a subsequent experiment aimed at qualifying kinematic arm synergies in craftsmen of different levels of expertise was carried out: craftsmen who participated in this experiment were high- and low-level experts, as well as high- and low-level learners. In addition to the accelerometer used in the Bril *et al.*'s experiment, an electromagnetic device was used to record the kinematics of the arm movement. The analysis led by Biryukova *et al.* is based on the fact that the human arm is kinematically redundant, which means that there are many ways to perform the same movement of the hammer using different combinations of rotations in the joints. The hypothesis was then that the peculiarities of the kinematic synergies should reflect the peculiarities of motor-control strategy in relation to the different levels of expertise. The comparative analysis of the kinematic synergies in high-level and low-level experts and in high-level and low-level learners led to the following conclusions. The low-level expert synergies are characterized by stereotyped kinematic patterns of both joint trajectories and hammer trajectories. On the contrary, the high-level expert synergies show flexible behaviours expressed in: 1) rich kinematic content of the synergies, i.e. large number of degrees of freedom, involved in the motion; and 2) a large repertory of motor synergies allowing the successful task completion. The analysis of the arm movement highlights the importance of a high degree of control over the elementary action, that is, over the technique.

In order to develop the relationship between the command of elementary movements and the course of action, Roux & David then studied the courses of action followed by craftsmen of different levels of expertise for transforming chalcedony pebbles into parallelepipedal roughouts. As far as planning is concerned, this knapping stage is supposed to be more informative than the transformation of roughouts into preforms because shapes and raw material are not standardized. The results obtained tend to confirm the previous conclusions, that is, that a knowledge of the methods is not sufficient for making high-quality roughouts. Methods are guidelines along which courses of action unfold. In this respect, they can be considered to represent pre-existing mental schemes. They are not sufficient, however, for the craftsman to act efficiently. Neither are adequate courses of action — which are the actualization of the methods — sufficient for making high-quality roughouts. Expert courses of action are mainly characterized by the use of efficient subgoals (typical removals) for rectifying delicate situations due to previous failed removals. The interesting point is that all the craftsmen know the subgoals required for making a roughout. Given that apprenticeship bears on the subgoals, that is, on the technique itself, rather than on the methods or the courses of action, the authors suggest that the effectuation of what could be called 'efficient' courses of action stem from the command of the technique. This hypothesis is borne out by the variability observed within and between craftsmen of different levels of expertise. Depending on how well the technique is mastered, knapping courses of action present an either flexible or rigid ordering of subgoals. Command of the techniques has implications for the perception of the

task, which also affects the variability of the courses of action. Roux & David conclude that expertise in planning is linked to the command of elementary movements, a result that has relevant implications for the study of the evolution of lithic industries.

The results of the Khambhat studies converge with those obtained by Winton in the course of an experimental study conducted with modern-day knappers, both novice and skilled. Her objective is to gain a better understanding not only of the lithic variability observed on prehistoric handaxes, but also of the skills that prehistoric knappers had to develop in order to become skilled practitioners and make well proportioned, serviceable handaxes. For this purpose, she examines the procedure followed by the different modern-day knappers to obtain handaxes, through a fine analysis of their production. She observes mainly that the tools produced by novice knappers tend to be smaller than those made by skilled knappers. These short proportions appear to be due to the inability to detach large flakes during the 'roughing out' stage. These are thinning flakes, which are necessary for defining both faces of the tool as well as proper angles for future thinning and shaping of the handaxe. This problem of controlling different types of flakes is recognized to be the major difficulty met by novice knappers. Winton also notes that the last reducing stage may be the easiest for learners to accomplish, since the morphology of the 'roughout' 'more closely resembles the end product than did the unmodified unit of raw material'. This observation tallies with the observations made in Khambhat, where owing to the difficulty of controlling the detachment of thinning flakes, bead knappers learn to knap preforms before roughouts.

Further considerations on the skills involved in tool use
Stone knapping implies a dexterity whose characterization can be highlighted through the analysis of other types of motor behaviour. The principles of production of efficient strokes, be they stone flaking or tennis strokes, are examined by Ivanova, whereas principles of planning in tool use are discussed by Smitsman. Their studies enable us to assess the extent to which the results obtained for stone knapping can be generalized to other contexts.

In the first place, the importance of the fine control of the moving segments in strokes, as shown by the Khambhat data, is also demonstrated by Ivanova in different complex coordinated strokes. To be successful, a stroke necessitates the consecutive involvement of all moving segments to provide the required final velocity of the working point, which is the racket for tennis stroke, the hand for volleyball stroke, the foot for the football stroke, or the head of the hammer for the hammer stroke. Ivanova analyzes the generation of the working point velocity through the impulse transmission. A comparison between experts and non-experts shows important differences in the way the impulse is transmitted from proximal to distal segments. Impulse transmission is much higher for experts than for non-experts. The dramatic differences in the process of impulse transmission illustrate the very high complexity of body-segment coordination needed to produce the adequate velocity of the working point, be it the tennis racket or the hammer. This example clearly illustrates how expertise in motor behaviour rests on common principles, which can be identified at the level of the elementary action.

Secondly, considering action at a more general level, Smitsman *et al.* similarly outline the importance of the elementary action in the dynamics of the course of action. The authors elaborate on the general capacities involved in tool use and tool making. Because these activities are primarily actions that have an important motor component, Smitsman *et al.* consider that the necessary capacities involved cannot be reduced to the cognitive component alone. They define the capacity to act as 'determined by opportunities and limitation of the body relative to a particular environment task'. Implementation of a tool extends the boundaries of action because it modifies the bodily resources that can be mobilized to perform a task. As a consequence, tool use implies taking advantage of the changes that occur within the scale of the individual's action system (body–task–environment). Taking full advantage of a modified system is a complicated task that may require years of practice. In order to understand how it operates, the authors study the relationship that exists between the constituents of a tool-use situation (tool, target and their surroundings). For this purpose, they develop a 'topological' approach that enables them to describe tool use and tool making in terms of the regulation of a set of relative geometrical and dynamical parameters (relative distance, orientation, size, shape, linear and rotational motion, inertial and material properties). As far as planning is concerned, Smitsman *et al.* conceive

> planning as being time-dependent, and order as emerging out of the complexity of the many mutual influences at the lower level of the activities themselves, and by internal, environmental and task constraints.

They argue that planning cannot be understood without considering its emergence. Study of its emergence highlights that planning is a 'dynamic affair', which consists in regulating a set of parameters, driven by attention, memory and perceptual input, and which

leads to ordered sequences of events. Smooth order is a question of constraints on topological parameters, and as a result, planning need not include all the phases of the action. In conclusion, the authors suppose that the evolution of the brain did not lead to mental representations of longer and more complex sequences of events, but to more stability and flexibility in the dynamics of planning, allowing humans to evolve tool use and technology.

Skills involved in object-related tasks in non-human primates

The specificity of the skills developed by the early hominins, as expressed in stone knapping, may be assessed by comparing these skills with the ones developed by non-human primates for tool-making and tool-using skills. In a way, non-human primate tool-related skills have already been the object of numerous studies (e.g. Beck 1980; Boesch *et al.* 1994; Inoue-Nakamura & Matsuzawa 1997; McGrew 1992; McGrew *et al.* 1997; Myowa-Yamakoshi & Matsuzawa 2000; Russon 1999; van Schaik *et al.* 1999; Westergaard & Fragaszy 1987). When it comes to comparing non-human and human primate tool-related skills, however, methodological questions arise relative to captive condition *versus* nature, recording procedures, object-related task *versus* tool-related task, inter-species comparison, intention, environment, etc. The studies presented here address some of these issues by conducting analyses of object-related tasks according to methodologies that echo the ones used for describing the tool-related skills developed by human primates. The apparatus for recording procedures of action is the same as that used with human primates (Foucart *et al.*). The analysis of action distinguishes between elementary movements and plan of action (Byrne; Cummins-Sebree & Fragaszy). The study of tool-related tasks is broadened to object-related tasks in order to have a large comparative body of data (Byrne). Moreover, not only apes, but also monkeys are considered in order to investigate convergent evolution of tool-using abilities (Cummins-Sebree & Fragaszy). As we shall see, the results obtained by the authors highlight that the differences between the skills developed by human and non-human primates are mainly a matter of degree, perceptible at the motor rather than at the cognitive level. In particular, non-human primates arguably lack the precision of human primates for the effectuation of the elementary gestures required for controlling the conchoidal fracture.

Let us first consider the study of nut cracking. This task is considered as the task *par excellence* to be compared with stone knapping, not only because it is a percussive technique but also because it implies a bimanual asymmetrical co-operative activity of the hands. This has led some authors to consider nut cracking as the starting point of human technology (Sugiyama & Koman 1979; Boesch & Boesch 1981). But how close is the connection between nut cracking and stone knapping? From a technical point of view, technologists have shown that these were not comparable techniques (Pelegrin this volume). Now what about the technical gestures involved? Indeed, the history of techniques abundantly shows that inventions may often result from a transfer of technical gestures (Haudricourt 1987). In order to assess whether the nut-cracking and stone-knapping gestures are comparable, Foucart *et al.* propose to analyze the movements performed to crack open a nut as well as the dynamics of the task as expressed by the succession of movements. The authors report an experiment carried out with a captive chimpanzee (Loi) from the Great Ape Research Institute (Okayama, Japan). In order to assess the capacity for flexibility and adaptation of Loi's movements, the task was based on two varieties of nuts and two different anvil-tools. Both sessions were entirely recorded with video cameras. A 3D reconstruction of the upper limb movements was performed. The action was described according to postural parameters, sequences of movements and elementary movements. Preliminary results clearly show that, at the level of the action, that is, the striking strategy and the succession of blows, the chimpanzee Loi shows a flexible behaviour adapted to the specificity of the task. The results are less clear concerning the adaptation of the movement, even though they tend to show that Loi has the capacity to finely adapt his movement to the situation. The authors conclude that the capacity for adaptation and flexibility in chimpanzees appears mainly at the level of the action. Even if more data are needed to assess chimpanzee capacity to adjust their movement to the properties of the hammer, Foucart *et al.* suppose that, in any case, nut cracking and stone knapping are basically different, the conchoidal fracture imposing more precise movements. Moreover, stone knapping requires an asymmetrical use of both hands, characterized by the simultaneous control of at least two variables (reciprocal orientation of the core and of the trajectory of the hammer, which keeps varying during the sequences of blows). That would be far beyond chimpanzee capacities.

Foucart *et al.*'s study focuses on movements, the smallest functional unit of action, and their chaining. Byrne proposes to consider not only the elementary gestures and their chaining, but also the courses of action within which they take place in order gain a better understanding of the specificity of the skills developed by early hominins. He compares the dif-ferent ways 'hard-to-process' plants are prepared for consumption in living great apes, since this object-directed manual skill is found inter-species and reveals the psychological capacities of apes when coping with complex tasks. A wide range of elementary movements has been recorded among apes. They are achieved in asymmetric bimanual hand action with manual role differentiation. They are characterized by important digit differentiation. They are hierarchically organized and are combined in many different ways, suggesting a quite outstanding feature, that is, generative skills. This latter feature is apparently rare or absent in monkey species. It suggests that apes do have the cognitive capacities to deal with complex manual tasks, which require flexible courses of action. Conversely, apes may not be able to achieve elementary movements that require both power and precision as in stone knapping. Indeed, Byrne argues that if population-level manual laterality is taken as reflecting difficulties in manual tasks, it appears that the more difficult tasks apes can achieve never combine power and precision, which are exerted in alternation. Byrne concludes that apes are not in a position to develop stone knapping, even though the intention were present as well as the required cognitive capacities, because of an inability to produce the requisite elementary movements.

Comparable conclusions are obtained by Cummins-Sebree & Fragaszy, who study the skills developed by capuchins in object-related tasks. The authors examine the extent to which the skills and psychological capacities necessary for stone knapping can be compared with those involved in the manual tasks exerted by capuchins in captive conditions and in nature. From the skill point of view, it appears that capuchins can apply force with one object to another object or a surface, even though this force is limited given their size and weight (capuchins weigh a mere 3 kg); they use a precision grip, including thumb-forefinger opposition; they exhibit differentiated roles for the two hands in bimanual manipulation; and last, they can develop strong manual preferences arising from practice with the task. These skills are fostered by the capuchins' postural stability while seated or standing bipedally, as well as by their terrestrial habits. Concerning their psychological capacities, observation and experimental data show that capuchins use stones as pounding tools and modify stones for making cutting tools. They have the cognitive capacities for exploring and discovering the properties of objects by managing multiple simultaneous dynamic spatial relations and planning actions accordingly. They also have the capacities for selecting appropriate tools according to their properties. Cummins-Sebree & Fragaszy conclude that capuchins display skills and psychological capacities that could, to a certain degree, be compared to those found in stone knapping. However, because difference in degree is determinant, capuchins will probably never knap stone: to begin with, the kinetic force of their blows will never reach that of humans; in addition, although capuchins may possess all the action capability relevant to stone knapping, humans are better at every single step. Lastly, and this is a central point, it is not certain whether capuchins can 'modulate actions of the two hands in an integrated task requiring precise positioning and production of force, as occurs in knapping' (p. 180).

Stone knapping: the necessary conditions for the required skills

Studies on skilled tool-related behaviour demonstrate that there are differences between the skills developed by human and non-human primates, even though it may only be a question of degree. These differences relate mainly to manipulative behaviour, and more precisely to bimanual elementary movements. Hence the following question: what enables human primates to develop such skilled behaviour that non-human primates acquire? In other words, given the importance of the elementary movements for stone knapping practices, what are the necessary conditions required for producing the elementary movements enabling the control of the conchoidal fracture? Defining these conditions should enable us to understand how stone knapping was possibly instantiated among human primates and why this is not the case among non-human primates.

Forty years ago, a novel hypothesis was developed by Leroi-Gourhan (1964) among other scholars. Leroi-Gourhan stressed the probable importance of the dynamics at work in-between the vertical posture, the freeing of the hand and the evolution of the brain. The debate is now well enriched with new empirical data established by researchers from different fields, particularly psychology, anatomy and neural sciences.

The conditions for developing the skills involved in stone knapping are here studied for the organism components at issue when exerting functional bimanual controlled movements, that is the bio-behavioural system, the hand anatomy and the neural substrate.

The bio-behavioural system
Such a favourable bio-behavioural system as the one developed by early hominins may represent the necessary conditions for the emergence of stone knapping. As demonstrated by Corbetta, this favourable bio-behavioural system is characterized by an erect posture, handedness and fine bimanual coordination. She argues

that to perform precise two-handed movements, such as stone knapping, stable dynamic interactions between a steady posture, handedness (stable division of labour between hands) and fine bimanual coordination between hands are necessary. As shown by findings with human infants and non-human primates, such stable interactions can be achieved following the emergence and adoption of the erect posture. Findings with human infants show, in particular, strong links between stability of the two-handed coordination and the lateral organization of the upper limbs, which change as infants learn to sit, crawl and walk. In particular, hand preferences and specialization stabilize only following the emergence of upright locomotion. Findings with non-human primates show that, if in an upright position, solving manual tasks leads to greater indexes of hand preference. Together, these data suggest that bipedal forms of locomotion facilitate stable lateralized fine bimanual coordination. From this body of evidence, Corbetta first argues that the emergence of bipedalism may have created bio-behavioural conditions for the development of manual specialization, given that the 'brain continuously changes and reorganizes itself, in particular, following novel sensory-motor experiences and motor skill learning'. In particular, emergence of bipedalism would have contributed to dissociating patterns of muscle activity for the arms from patterns of muscle activity specific to walking. It would have then favoured manual specialization and handedness. Handedness may have been an established behavioural trait when hominins stabilized their erect posture. Secondly, Corbetta argues that stone knapping may have developed only in hominins, because only hominins adopted a fully-erect posture.

The fact that an analogous bio-behavioural system has not been identified among non-human primates would thus explain why they never developed the skills required for stone knapping. More precisely non-human primates present a bio-behavioural system whose components would prevent them from developing stable dynamic interactions comparable to the ones necessary for stone knapping. These interactions may not be comparable because the behavioural components at stake are not developed to the same degree. They do occur, however, when non-human primates show interactions between handedness and asymmetric bimanual coordination, as observed for apes by Byrne, and interactions between postural stability and handedness, as elaborated by Holder and touched upon by Cummins-Sebree & Fragaszy.

More precisely, Holder investigates, according to a cost/benefit/milieu approach, how and why manual specialization is acquired by individual primates, and what is the link between manual specialization and postural stability. Manual specialization is defined as a motor skill acquired over time through repeated practice which 'requires the optimization of biomechanical potential for the task to be successfully performed' (p. 205). Most manual specializations are performed with a consistent manual preference since biomechanical optimization is then needed. Manual tasks, however, that do not require biomechanical optimization may be achieved with a consistent hand preference when routinely performed. In this case, benefits of hand preference derive from task automatization. At last, manual tasks can be performed by ambidexters. In the case of ambidexters who can perform half the manual tasks with one hand, and half with the other hand, strong manual specializations can develop. Manual specializations are acquired when the perceived benefits either balance or outweigh associated costs, within a given context. Describing how five species of wild African primates typically behave in their environment has enabled Holder to identify what factors other than presumed brain specialization might be capable of influencing manual asymmetry. Among these factors, one finds postural stability, development and injury. Directional hand preferences (right or left) have been identified at the individual, but not at the species level.

As shown by primatology, interactions at the bio-behavioural system level enable non-human primates to develop specific task-related skills. But their behavioural components do not present the same characteristics (posture, handedness and coordination) as human ones. Different outcomes in terms of skills ensue. The cornerstone is the erect posture. As demonstrated by Corbetta, bipedalism is determinant in the way both handedness and fine bimanual coordination develop among human primates. Among human primates, handedness occurs at the population level, contrary to non-human primates, even though Byrne reports that gorilla leaf-eating tasks show weak but statistically significant right-handedness. Importance of fine bimanual coordination, and *a fortiori* of stone knapping, for the development of handedness at the population level are reported by Steele & Uomini.

Steele & Uomini discuss the mechanisms liable to explain handedness as a population-level bias. They link handedness and stone knapping. The hypothesis is that there is an advantage for the dominant hand in tool use. This advantage is seen in the greater skill of the dominant hand. It relates to 'an underlying efficiency in information transfer rate in the contralateral hemisphere'. The practice of stone knapping would therefore have contributed to handedness as a behavioural trait. Handedness in tool use can be identified on skeletons, as shown by studies of

skeletons from modern times to prehistoric times populations. Predominant right-handedness appears to extend back in time to at least the early members of our own genus *Homo* (*Homo ergaster*). Archaeological evidence from tools and other artefacts can also be used to infer the evolution of human handedness. Steele & Uomini review the material-cultural markers of handedness including tool production (multiple flake analysis, knapping scatters, knapping gesture, lateral retouch, use and use-wear), cut marks on teeth and art (representations of lateral tool use, engravings, profile drawing, handprints and hand stencils). The authors' conclusion insists on the importance of the study of human handedness for addressing the issue of the evolution of human tool making and tool use, while acknowledging that this may only be part of the problem.

Somatic and neural substrate
In a recent paper entitled 'What's so special about human tool use?', Johnson-Frey (2003) emphasizes the growing number of research studies that provide evidence for homologous mechanisms involved in the control of prehension and in sensorimotor abilities among human and non-human primates. This view minimizes differences in the motor capacity of human and non-human primates to use tools. In this section, the different authors explore some aspect of the somatic and neural substrate of tool use in human and non-human primates. Manual dexterity is here considered as a prerequisite to optimal tool use. The data discussed show how both the hand anatomy and the neural system might contribute to the understanding of the precondition for dexterity and tool use. Markze examines the necessary conditions for a hand to be used by a tool maker, while Maier and colleagues address the question of the evolution of the neural structure that controls this apparatus (i.e. the hand). In the last two chapters, Stout and Jacobs and colleagues investigate the cerebral control of tool use.

In order to define the hand anatomical features necessary for stone knapping, Markze conducted a multi-level comparative study aimed at discovering specific tool-making patterns. The first step consisted of examining how modern human-hand morphology relates to the manipulative behaviour required by stone knapping. Systematic biomechanical studies were performed with modern stone knappers, enabling the author to characterize manipulative requirements for stone knapping in terms of forceful precision grips that resist large external forces. These grips are not shared by chimpanzees. The second step consisted of finding skeletal correlates of joint movements, stresses and muscle functions associated with human forceful precision grips and the power squeeze grips. Markze finds clear evidence throughout the human hand for a unique pattern of morphology 'that is both distinctive of humans and consistent with the movement capabilities and stresses associated with the manufacture of stone tools' (p. 249). This pattern is characterized by a set of features (including bone shape and internal structure, joint surface topography, muscle and tendon attachment areas) that is consistent with stone knapping when defined in terms of bimanual percussion using forceful precision grips. Looking at early hominin fossil bones, Markze proposes nut-pounding but not stone-knapping manipulative behaviour for *A. afarensis*. On the contrary, bones from Sterkfontein and Swartkrans are consistent with forceful manipulative behaviour. Drawing on a comparison with gorillas, who exert force in food retrieval and processing, the author suggests that such food activities may have fostered the evolution of features in ancestral hominin hands, predisposing them to subsequently exert forceful precision grips in tool making. Although not central to Markze's issue, the neurological requirements for manipulative behaviour are also touched upon.

The neurological basis of manual dexterity is developed by Maier *et al.* They examine the emergence of dexterity in relation with the phylogenetic development of the corticospinal track among different species. Dexterity is here considered in a more restricted way than Bernstein's definition (1967) as it refers exclusively to its neural basis. While acknowledging that crucial features of hand morphology are needed to provide the mechanical substrate for manual skills, Maier *et al.* underline the possibility that the evolution of hand morphology and of neural control may not have been concomitant. The key issue of their chapter is the assessment of which premotor system is most important for providing a high degree of manual dexterity. Considering that the neural basis of manual dexterity rests mainly on two neural systems, the corticospinal and propriospinal systems, the authors speculate on the relation between the evolution of these two systems, the growth of dexterity and the development of tool use and tool manufacturing. The corticospinal system, a direct pathway, allows for the ability to complete independent finger movements, the mark of dexterity. It may equally control some aspects of reaching needed to support distal grasp and manipulation. The propriospinal system that also contributes to dexterity is an indirect cortical pathway. The authors base their demonstration on an interspecies comparison of the phylogenetic development of manual dexterity and of the two neural systems in four species — cat, squirrel monkey, macaque monkey and

Homo. After an extensive discussion of what identifies dexterity, the authors develop a very detailed and rigorous analysis of published data, including their own, relating the index of dexterity and the efficacy of motoneurons excitation of corticospinal neurons (CM) and propriospinal (PN) systems. They show a clear qualitative relation between an increase in dexterity and efficacy of the CM system, and a negative relation between dexterity and efficacity of the PN systems. They conclude that phylogenetic development favours direct (corticospinal system) rather than indirect (propriospinal system) cortical control over motoneurons. The existence of direct cortico-motoneuronal connections appears as a necessary and sufficient precondition for a high degree of manual dexterity; they provide the necessary descending output system, but dexterity alone is not a sufficient condition for tool use and tool manufacturing. In this respect this conclusion is akin to Ivanova's view. In order to use manual dexterity for manipulation and consequently for tool use, other modalities are necessary, be it sensory modalities and/or cognitive modalities.

Studies by Stout and Jacobs and colleagues offer an insight into the neuroanatomical structures that are active during tool use and even more specifically during stone knapping.

Adopting a perception-action approach, Stout examines brain activation during simple Oldowan-style stone knapping using Positron Emission Tomography (PET). The theoretical position of Stout is novel in the sense that brain imaging is generally called upon in defence of a representational approach aiming to localize the neural substrata of complex cognitive processes. Stout reports results from an exploratory study and ongoing research with experimental stone knappers. If PET imagery does not explain how neuronal activity contributes to behaviour, it does indicate where this activity takes place. The spatial distribution of activation shows that stone knapping involves activation of a network of structures commonly associated with visuomotor performance (pericentral cortex, superior parietal lobe, occipital lobe and cerebellum) and no activation of the frontal association cortex involved in tasks that demand planning of complex goal-oriented actions, or of the temporal and/or parietal cortex possibly associated with internal models of object's physical properties. Stout's results make it clear that 'the most salient mental demands of [Oldowan-style stone] knapping have to do with execution rather than conceptualization' (p. 282). This conclusion challenges representational perspectives, which have been more concerned with how the individual conceives what he does than with what the individual actually does. It emphasizes the fact that stone knapping, including its earliest manifestation, is an especially demanding perceptual-motor task. Going one step further, Stout suggests the existence of microstructural adaptations relating to stone-knapping ability, for which evidence might be found in a 'uniquely human adaptation in the dorsal stream of cortical visual processing' (p. 283).

The clinical approach espoused by Jacobs, Bennis and Roby-Brami, inverts the rationale of Stout's study. While Stout takes stone knapping as his starting point and then focuses on the underlying brain activity, Jacobs and colleagues open with apraxis and brain damage patients and go on to consider the impairment in tool-use actions. Theirs is a major contribution, all the more since archaeologists sometimes refer to neuropsychology as a conceptual framework (Pelegrin 1993). Their well-articulated review of the neuropsychological theories about the control of complex gestures and actions raised by the study of apraxia echoes and helps to put into perspective the different accounts of motor theories discussed in several previous chapters. In spite of the enormous variety of cases encountered, or maybe because of this variety, the authors underline the fact that 'neuropsychological concepts such as *movement representations* ... remain an abstract "black box"' (p. 291). Commenting on this puzzling point, Jacobs and colleagues address, through the precise biomechanical description of tool-use movement in apraxis and healthy adults, the question of how the motor system concretely controls complex actions such as tool use. The analysis focuses on the working point of the tool (i.e. the head of the hammer in hammering), like that of Biryukova and colleagues. Their results are potentially, if indirectly, very informative for our understanding of stone-knapping skills. They demonstrate that left brain damage affects the capacity to anticipate and adapt the action to the mechanical properties of the task. More eloquent is the inability of patients to capitalize on the tool's mechanical properties to produce the most efficient movement possible. Jacobs and colleagues suggest that this behaviour might reflect a disability to integrate the tool's mechanical properties into the movement (see also Smitsman *et al.* this volume).

'Actualizing' conditions for innovation in stone knapping

Concerning the reasons causing innovation to occur at specific 'moments' in time, the dynamic systems framework suggests that the context in which qualitative innovation takes place should be investigated (Roux 2003). In technology, this context of innovation corresponds to the conditions actualizing the innovation, that is, the context of craft production in the broad

sense of the word, and more specifically here the context of stone-tool production (Fig. 1.2). This context encompasses social structure, sociability, apprenticeship, cultural transmission, cognitive capacities and technical traditions. These matters have received particular attention in a wide range of studies pertaining to the domain of tool-use traditions in primates (e.g. Boesch *et al.* 1994; Box & Gibson 1999; Byrne 1999; McGrew *et al.* 1997; McGrew 1992; Matsuzawa 2001; Tomasello 1999; van Schaik & Pradhan 2003; Whiten *et al.* 1999). Three aspects of such studies bearing on 'actualizing' conditions are developed in this third section: the psychological capacities required for discovering new tool actions, the social conditions required for learning and transmitting technical actions, and finally the technological context required for developing stone-knapping technology. The psychological conditions are found at the individual level, as opposed to the social and technological conditions, which are found at the collective level. Indeed, because the actualization of innovation connects real time (invention) and the *longue durée* of historical time (innovation), and because the most elementary components of a system can, over time, constrain its global structure or form (Aslin 1993), conditions for the actualization of innovation deal with both individual and collective conditions. More precisely, invention expresses individual cognitive activity, whereas innovation is expressed by the emergence of a new tradition, whose development and acceptance can be slow or rapid depending on the cultural context. It is the temporal course of these two interacting variables — the individual and the collective — that gives the system its faculty to adapt and bring about widespread technological change. As a result, conditions for the actualization of innovation are to be found at both the individual and the collective levels, which have to be dealt with as a whole.

Concerning the psychological conditions, found at the individual level, they can be considered as part of the supportive context necessary for invention to happen and be transformed into innovation. This supportive context should not be confused with the necessary conditions for exerting an action. It corresponds to individual capacities for producing new actions, which are made manifest through a specific transmission behaviour. Among these psychological conditions, causal understanding and future-oriented thinking are considered as central to making and using tools. To begin with, Bushnell *et al.* note that causal understanding, like future-oriented thinking, increases from monkeys to humans, as well as in the course of early child development. Among infants, however, as well as non-human primates, there are situations where tool action is performed without causal understanding. Bushnell *et al.* propose to study how causal understanding emerges, in order to define the favourable cognitive conditions for the coming into existence of stone knapping. They suggest that imitating the means might be a mechanism that could support early instances of means–ends behaviour without causal understanding. This capacity for imitating the means, rather than emulating the ends, governs motor transfer among infants. Transferring the means appears to be an intermediate step in the development of causal cognition. It would also be at the root of individual invention, the means being transferred to new objects even without full causal understanding. Reverting to prehistory, the authors suggest that the early hominins had the imitative capacities that enabled them to transfer the means, to discover the physical effect of these means, then to invent and, later, refine knapping techniques.

Lockman enlarges on the question of the favourable psychological capacities for developing elementary forms of tool use by focusing on the manipulative capacities of infants for discovering the properties of tools. The hypothesis is that a study of these capacities can lead to new insights into the foundations of tool use. Lockman adopts a Gibsonian perspective in the light of which he reassesses the discontinuous models of tool use according to which advanced representational or symbolic capacities are necessary for the emergence of tool use. Rather than implying that tool use represents a discontinuous cognitive advance, the Gibsonian perspective suggests 'that tool use is rooted in the perception–action routines that infants perform to explore and act on their surroundings' (p. 323) and is not the product of a sudden insight or newly-developed cognitive abilities. Lockman's own researches show that tool use develops from object manipulation and capacities to relate objects to substrates in their surroundings. In this respect, it seems that tool use may be considered to be a perceptuomotor achievement rather than a cognitive one, and that the emergence of tool use may not require sophisticated cognitive abilities.

Concerning the social transmission of knowledge about tools, considered by many as essential for the development of tool use and manual skills with objects, debates bear on the one hand on the mode of transmission at the caregiver level, and on the other hand on the social organization that permits different modes of transmission between caregivers and infants. Bushnell *et al.* and Lockman outline the importance of the learning context at the caregiver level for actualizing the favourable psychological capacities underlying the emergence of tool use. Lockman proposes that object manipulation itself may in part be 'a socially

mediated achievement'. Indeed, in a perception-action perspective, caregivers may highlight information available from objects and in so doing may promote mastery of object manipulation and tool use. The resulting rich learning environment is rarely observed in our living primate relatives and would therefore represent a quite unique feature of human primates, something also suggested by Byrne, who emphasizes that active teaching is very rare among apes.

Turning now to the favourable social organization for stone-knapping skill acquisition, Stout examines the role of the social and cultural context for learning stone knapping through a study of the stone adze-makers of Langda village in Indonesian Irian Jaya. He notices that the social and cultural context of adze-making in Langda provides an important scaffold for skill learning. The adze-makers structure the learning process by providing a learning schedule appropriate to the different difficulties that must be successively controlled over the years, and through continual interaction between experts and novices. Reverting to prehistory, Stout suggests that the skills involved in the making of lithic objects such as handaxes would have been long to acquire and would have similarly required social arrangements for supporting their progressive apprenticeship. As shown by the researches led by van Schaik *et al.* (1999) among modern ape populations, the degree of social tolerance seems to influence the distribution of tool use. This degree is assessed by 'the number of individuals in the social unit with whom the naive individual spends a significant amount of time in close proximity' (van Schaik & Pradhan 2003, 648). Hence, a high degree of social tolerance would have represented favourable conditions for the transmission of technical skills among early hominins. Such a degree of tolerance, however, would not have been sufficient for acquiring expertise, apprenticeship of which extends into the adult age and requires the kind of social support that ape populations do not develop. From this point of view, and according to Stout, comparative actualistic data suggest that the transmission of skills long to acquire, such as stone knapping, would have required meaningful social relationships, 'characterized by Tomasello (1999) as the key adaptation underlying the emergence of modern human cognitive sophistication' (p. 338).

Finally, Marchant & McGrew consider the technological context in which stone knapping could have appeared. They suggest as a favourable technological context one that would already have a complex percussive technology tradition. Following Matsuzawa, the complexity of a percussive technology is defined by the number of objects involved in the task. The authors review the different percussive technologies found in apes and present new data on percussive technology for cracking open baobab fruit found at Mont Assirik, Senegal. The issue concerned the way in which percussive technology was used (anvil only *versus* hammer and anvil). Anvil use only is suggested by both ethno-archaeological and behavioural data sets. The first type of data, involving indirect evidence, points to terrestrial smashing on stones, whereas the second, involving direct evidence, shows smashing on the trunks or branches of baobab trees. These data raise the question of a percussive technology used as an arboreal *versus* a terrestrial activity. On the strength of this, the authors develop an evolutionary scenario with, as a starting point, arboreal apes smashing big fruit on tree trunk; the next stage entailed a shift from arboreality to increasing terrestriality and the use of harder anvils, made from stone; in order to smash small fruit, such as nuts, the items involved in the task changed from two to three, that is, from the anvil alone to the hammer and anvil. All was then set for the transition to stone knapping, that is, the shift from accidental flaking by stone on stone percussion to goal directed percussion.

Concluding remarks

The field of investigation of this volume has been deliberately restricted to the skills involved in tool use and tool making in order to better understand the specificity of stone knapping, when considered as a uniquely hominin invention.

In relation to this goal, quite a few chapters focus specifically on the characteristics of object-related tasks defined in terms of techniques and skills. Studies based on new techniques and methods are reported in several of these chapters. We believe that such recording techniques will give new insights into the question of the nature of skilled behaviour, and consequently lead to relevant comparisons between human and non-human primates.

We are well aware, however, that numerous questions related to such an innovation as stone knapping are not dealt with or even touched upon in this volume. But the reconstruction of the historical process that underpins this innovation necessarily requires, as a preliminary step, the well-controlled analysis of the technical task in terms of techniques and skills, that is, the analysis of the invention of stone knapping itself. In the same way that invention and innovation are here distinguished, the distinction between innovation and the 'actualizing' conditions for innovation enables us to 'isolate' the context in which innovation takes place, and therefore to solve a major methodo-

logical problem when considering that technological facts are embedded in socio-cultural systems. Here again, only some aspects of this context are addressed in this volume. But as we shall see in the 'synthesis and speculations' final chapter, the array of papers presented in this volume all excellently contribute to shedding new light on the necessary conditions for a uniquely hominin invention, stone knapping.

Note

1. The controversy among researchers dedicated to complex movement behaviour has been reported very interestingly in a book published in 1988 and entitled *Complex Movement Behaviour: the Motor-action Controversy*. The aim of this book, edited by O.G. Meijer & K. Roth, was to debate the common ground of these theories as well as their points of departure.

References

Agre, P.E. & D. Chapman, 1990. What are plans for?, in *Designing Autonomous Agents: Theory and Practice from Biology to Engineering and Back*, ed. P. Maes. Cambridge (MA): The MIT Press, 17–34.
Ambrose, S.H., 2001. Paleolithic technology and human evolution. *Science* 291, 1748–53.
Anderson, J.R., 1980. *Cognitive Psychology and its Implications*. San Francisco (CA): Freeman.
Annett, J., 1996. On knowing how to do things: a theory of motor imagery. *Cognitive Brain Research* 3, 65–9.
Aslin, R.N., 1993. Commentary: the strange attractiveness of dynamic systems to development, in *A Dynamic Systems Approach to Development*, eds. L.B. Smith & E. Thelen. Cambridge (MA) & London: MIT Press, 385–400.
Beck, B.B., 1980. *Animal Tool Behaviour: the Use and Manufacture of Tools by Animals*. New York (NY): Garland.
Bernstein, N., 1967. *The Coordination and Regulation of Movements*. London: Pergamon Press.
Boesch, C. & H. Boesch, 1981. Sex differences in the use of natural hammers by wild chimpanzees: a preliminary report. *Journal of Human Evolution* 10(7), 585–93.
Boesch, C. & H. Boesch, 1990. Tool-use and tool-making in wild chimpanzees. *Folia Primatologica* 54, 86–99.
Boesch, C. & H. Boesch, 1992. Transmission aspects of tool-use in wild chimpanzees, in *Tools, Language and Cognition in Human Evolution*, eds. K.R. Gibson & T. Ingold. Cambridge: Cambridge University Press, 171–83.
Boesch, C. & H. Boesch-Achermann, 2000. *The Chimpanzees of the Taï Forest: Behavioural Ecology and Evolution*. Oxford: Oxford University Press.
Boesch, C., P. Marchesi, N. Marchesi, N. Fruth & F. Joulian, 1994. Is nut cracking in wild chimpanzees a cultural behaviour? *Journal of Human Evolution* 26, 325–38.
Box, H.O. & K.R. Gibson, 1999. *Mammalian Social Learning: Comparative and Ecological Perspectives*. Cambridge: Cambridge University Press.

Bril, B. & V. Roux (eds.), 2002. *Le Geste Technique: Réflexions Théoriques et Méthodologiques*. (Technologies/Idéologies/Pratiques.) Ramonville Saint-Agne: Édition Érès.

Byrne, R.W., 1999. Cognition in great ape ecology: skill learning ability opens up foraging opportunities, in *Mammalian Social Learning: Comparative and Ecological Perspectives*, eds. H.O. Box & K.R. Gibson. Cambridge: Cambridge University Press, 333–50.

de Beaune, S.A., 2004. The invention of technology: prehistory and cognition. *Current Anthropology* 45(2), 139–62.

Flash, J.M. & R.H. Smith, 2000. Right strategy, wrong tactic. *Ecological Psychology* 12(1), 43–52.

Gallay, A., 1986. *Une archéologie demain*. Paris: Belfond.

Gardin, J.C., 1979. *Une archéologie théorique*. Paris: Hachette.

Gibson, J.J., 1977. The theory of affordance, in *Perceiving, Acting, and Knowing*, eds. R.E. Shaw & J. Bransford. Hillsdale (NJ): Lawrence Erlbaum Associates, 67–82.

Gibson, J.J., 1986. *The Ecological Approach to Visual Perception*. Hillsdale (NJ): Lawrence Erlbaum Associates.

Gowlett, J.A.J., 1992. Early human mental abilities, in *The Cambridge Encyclopedia of Human Evolution*, eds. S. Bunney & S. Jones. Cambridge: Cambridge University Press, 341–5.

Haudricourt, A.G., 1987. *La technologie science humaine. Recherches d'histoire et d'ethnologie des techniques*. Paris: Éditions de la Maison des Sciences de l'Homme.

Inoue-Nakamura, N. & T. Matsuzawa, 1997. Development of stone tool use by wild chimpanzees (*Pan troglodytes*). *Journal of Comparative Psychology* 111(2), 159–73.

Jeannerod, M., 1997. *The Cognitive Neuroscience of Action*. Cambridge: Blackwell Publishers.

Johnson-Frey, S.H., 2003. What's so special about human tool use? *Neuron* 39, 201–4.

Jordan, M.I. & D.A. Rosenbaum, 1989. Action, in *Foundations of Cognitive Science*, ed. M.I. Posner. Cambridge: A Bradford Book, 728–67.

Joulian, F., 1996. Comparing chimpanzee and early hominid techniques: some contributions to cultural and cognitive questions, in *Modelling the Early Human Mind*, eds. P. Mellars & K. Gibson. (McDonald Institute Monographs.) Cambridge: The McDonald Institute for Archaeological Research, 173–89.

Kunde, W., 2001. Exploring the hyphen in ideo-motor action. Commentary on Hommel *et al.*: Theory of event coding. *Behavioral and Brain Sciences* 24, 891–2.

Leroi-Gourhan, A., 1964. *Le geste et la parole: Technique et langage*. Paris: Éditions Albin Michel.

Matsuzawa, T., 2001. Primate foundations of human intelligence: a view of tool use in non-human primates and fossil hominids, in *Primate Origins of Human Cognition and Behaviour*, ed. T. Matsuzawa. New York (NY): Springer-Verlag Publishing, 3–25.

McGrew, W.C., 1992. *Chimpanzee Material Culture: Implication for Human Evolution*. Cambridge: Cambridge University Press.

McGrew, W.C., 1993. Brains, hands, and minds: puzzling incongruities in ape tool use, in *The Use of Tools by Human and Non-Human Primates*, eds. A. Berthelet &

A. Chavaillon. Oxford: Clarendon Press, 143–67.

McGrew, W.C., R.M. Ham, L.T.J. White, C.E.G. Tutin & M. Fernandez, 1997. Why don't chimpanzees in Gabon crack nuts? *International Journal of Primatology* 18, 353–74.

Meijer, O.G. & K. Roth (eds.), 1988. *Complex Movement Behaviour: the Motor Action Controversy*, vol. 50. Amsterdam: Elsevier Science Publisher (North Holland).

Miller, G.A., E. Galanter & K. Pribram, 1960. *Plans and Structure of Behavior*. New York (NY): Holt, Rinehart & Winston.

Myowa-Yamakoshi, M. & T. Matsuzawa, 2000. Imitation of intentional manipulatory actions in chimpanzees. *Journal of Comparative Psychology* 114, 381–91.

Newell, K.M., 1986. Constraints on the development of coordination, in *Motor Skills Acquisition*, eds. M.G. Wade & H.T.A. Withing. Dortrech: Martinus Nijhoff, 341–60.

Newell, K.M., 1996. Change in movement and skill: learning, retention and transfer, in *Dexterity and its Development*, eds. M.L. Latosh & M.T. Turvey. Mahwah (NJ): Lawrence Erlbaum Associates, 393–429.

Parker, S.T. & C. Milbrath, 1993. Higher intelligence, propositional language, and culture as adaptation for planning, in *Tools, Language and Cognition in Human Evolution*, eds. K.R. Gibson & T. Ingold. Cambridge: Cambridge University Press, 314–33.

Pelegrin, J., 1993. A framework for analysing prehistoric stone tools manufacture and a tentative application to some early lithic industries, in *The Use of Tools by Human and Non-human Primates*, eds. A. Berthelet & J. Chavaillon. Oxford: Clarendon Press, 302–14.

Reed, E.S., 1988. Applying the theory of action system to the dtudy of motor skills, in *Complex Movement Behaviour: the Motor-action Controversy*, eds. O.G. Meijer & K. Roth. (Vol. 50.) Amsterdam: Elsevier Science Publisher (North Holland), 45–86.

Roby-Brami, A., G. Hoffman, I. Laffont, M. Combeaud & S. Hanneton, 2005. Redondance du membre supérieur et compensation des déficiences motrices, in *Vision espace et cognition, fonctionnement normal et pathologique*, eds. Y. Coello & C. Moroni. Lille: Presse du Septentrion, 143–60.

Roche, H. & P.-J. Texier, 1996. Evaluation of technical competence of *Homo erectus* in east Africa during the Middle Pleistocene, in *1893–1993*, vol. 1: *Palaeoanthropology: Evolution and Ecology of* Homo erectus, eds. J.R.F. Bower & S. Sartono. Leiden: Pithecanthropus Centennial Foundation, 153–67.

Roche, H., A. Delagnes, J.-P. Brugal, C. Feibel, M. Kibunja, V. Mourre & P.J. Texier, 1999. Early hominid stone tool production and technical skill 2.34 Myr ago in West Turkana, Kenya. *Nature* 399, 57–60.

Roux, V., 2003. A dynamic systems framework for studying technological change: application to the emergence of the potter's wheel in the southern Levant. *Journal of Archaeological Method and Theory* 10(1), 1–30.

Russon, A.E., 1999. Orangutans' imitation of tool use: a cognitive interpretation, in *Mentalities of Gorillas and Orangutans*, eds. S.T. Parker, R.W. Mitchell & H.L. Miles. Cambridge: Cambridge University Press, 119–45.

Savage-Rumbaugh, S.R. & R. Lewin, 1994. *Kanzi: the Ape at the Brink of the Human Mind*. New York (NY): Wiley.

Schick, K.D., N. Toth & G. Garufi, 1999. Continuing investigations into the stone tool-making and tool-using capabilities of a Bonobo (*Pan paniscus*). *Journal of Archaeological Science* 26, 821–32.

Schlanger, N., 1996. Understanding Levallois: lithic technology and cognitive archaeology. *Cambridge Archaeological Journal* 6(2), 231–54.

Shaw, R.E. & J.B. Wagman, 2001. Explanatory burdens and natural law: invoking a field description of perception-action. Commentary on Hommel *et al.*: Theory of event coding. *Behavioral and Brain Sciences* 24, 905–6.

Stoffregen, T.A., 2000. Affordances and events. *Ecological Psychology* 12(1), 1–28.

Sugiyama, Y. & J. Koman, 1979. Tool-using and making behaviour in wild chimpanzees at Bossou, Guinea. *Primates* 20(4), 513–24.

Tixier, J., 1967. Procédés d'analyse et questions de terminologie concernant l'étude des ensembles industriels du Paléolithique récent et de l'Epipaléolithique dans l'Afrique du Nord-Ouest, in *Back-ground to Evolution in Africa*, eds. W.W. Bishop & J. Desmond-Clark. (Proceedings of a symposium held at Burg Wartenstein Austria, July–August 1965.) Chicago (IL): University of Chicago Press, 771–820.

Tomasello, M., 1999. *The Cultural Origins of Human Cognition*. Cambridge (MA): Harvard University Press.

Toth, N., 1993. Early stone industries and inferences regarding language and cognition, in *Tools, Language and Cognition in Human Evolution*, eds. K.R. Gibson & T. Ingold. Cambridge: Cambridge University Press, 346–62.

Toth, N., K.D. Schick, E.S. Savage-Rumbaugh, R.A. Sevcik & D.M. Rumbaugh, 1993. Pan the tool-maker: investigations into the stone tool-making and tool-using capabilities of a Bonobo (*Pan paniscus*). *Journal of Archaeological Science* 20, 81–91.

Turvey, M.T., H.L. Fich & B. Tuller, 1982. The Bernstein perspective: the problem of degrees of freedom and context-conditioned variability, in *Human Motor Behavior: an introduction,* ed. J.A. Kelso. Hillsdale (NJ): Lawrence Erlbaum Associates, 239–52.

van der Leeuw, S.E. & R. Torrence (eds.), 1989. *What's New? A Closer Look at the Process of Innovation*. (One World Archaeology.) London: Unwin Hyman.

van Schaik, C.P. & G.R. Pradhan, 2003. A model for tool-use traditions in primates: implications for the coevolution of culture and cognition. *Journal of Human Evolution* 44, 645–64.

van Schaik, C.P., R.O. Deaner & M.Y. Merrill, 1999. The conditions for tool use in primates: implications for the evolution of material culture. *Journal of Human Evolution* 36, 719–41.

Warren, W.H., 1990. The perception-action coupling, in *Sensory Motor Organisations and Development in Infancy and Early Childhood*, eds. H. Bloch & B.I. Bertenthal. Dordrech: Kluwer Academic Publishers, 23–38.

Westergaard, G.C. & D.M. Fragaszy, 1987. The manufacture and use of tools by capuchins monkeys (*Cebus apella*). *Journal of Comparative Psychology* 101, 159–68.

Whiten, A., J. Goodall, W.C. McGrew, T. Nishida, V. Reynolds, Y. Sugiyama, C.E.G. Tutin, R.W. Wrangham & C. Boesch, 1999. Cultures in chimpanzees. *Nature* 399, 682–5.

Wright, R., 1972. Imitative learning of flaked tool technology: the case of an orangutan. *Mankind* 8, 296–306.

Wynn, T., 1985. Piaget, stone tools and the evolution of human intelligence. *World Archaeology* 17, 31–43.

Wynn, T., 1991. Archaeological evidence for modern intelligence, in *The Origins of Human Behaviour*, ed. R.A. Foley. London: Unwin Hyman, 52–66.

Wynn, T., 2002a. Archaeology and cognitive evolution. *Behavioural & Brain Sciences* 25(3), 389–402.

Wynn, T., 2002b. Comments on 'Skill and cognition in stone tool production' by D. Stout. *Current Anthropology* 43(5), 718.

Wynn, T. & W.C. McGrew, 1989. An ape's view of the Oldowan. *Man* 24, 383–98.

Part I

Stone Knapping:
Characterizing a Tool-related Task

Section A

Stone Knapping: a Technical Characterization

Chapter 2

Remarks about Archaeological Techniques and Methods of Knapping: Elements of a Cognitive Approach to Stone Knapping

Jacques Pelegrin

The preservation of hard stone and the regularity of the conchoidal fracture technique allows for a highly-detailed analysis of stone-knapping techniques and methods throughout prehistory. Though frequently disputed, the earliest stone knapping produced by conchoidal fracture should not be conflated with the cracking of nuts by some chimpanzees, nor the simple 'splitting' technique used by Kanzi, who clearly failed to produce true flakes. This failure may suggest that the control of conchoidal fracture is more a matter of 'understanding' rules than of motor skill. Moreover, the very early flake production of Lokalelei IIc (Roche this volume) shows that core reduction was sometimes interrupted in order to evaluate a problem and determine an adequate solution. Several hundreds of thousands of years ago, by the time of Homo erectus, *the morphological redundancy of the handaxe demonstrates that it was the result of a mental template. Somewhat later, typical Levallois flake production provides evidence of a goal-structured process, which again implies mental representations and also an evaluation of technical solutions which had to compromise between what was feasible and what was desirable. This indicates the existence of propositional reasoning, which is the basis of modern technical intelligence.*

Over the last 40 years, Palaeolithic archaeologists have developed a methodological basis for the technological study and understanding of prehistoric lithic production, including the tentative analysis of the cognitive abilities they indicate (Leroi-Gourhan 1993; Bordes 1971; see also Alimen & Goustard 1962; Wynn 1979; 1985; 1988; 1991; Roche 1980; 1989; Roche & Texier 1996; Goren-Inbar 1988; Pelegrin 1990; 1991a; Toth 1993).

The methodological basis of lithic analysis

Thanks to the excellent preservation of hard stone and to the legibility of flaking stigmata, some 20 years ago research on 'lithic technology' was able to codify its concepts and terms (Tixier 1978; Inizan *et al.* 1999).

Stone records unalterable traces of the physical actions applied to it. Any percussive event, even though no flake was detached, leaves a visible crack

or crush mark. Fractures leave two kinds of marks: 1) on the core from which the flake is detached, that is the flake-scar or negative; and 2) on the ventral surface of the flake itself. Thus both flakes and flake-scars indicate directional orientation: both the point of origin and the direction of percussion can be determined without ambiguity. It is also possible to determine the sequential order of production of two adjacent flakes whose scars overlap.

The combination of such observations concerning the origin, direction and order of different percussive scars visible on a core, flake, preform or stone tool can thus reveal with exactitude a whole sequence of knapping actions (which can be illustrated schematically by a 'diacritic scheme'). Assembling schemes from different knapping sequences, which is accomplished by actual or mental refitting by a lithic technologist, permits an objective reconstruction of

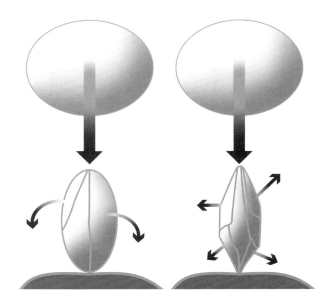

Figure 2.1. *Split-breaking technique.*

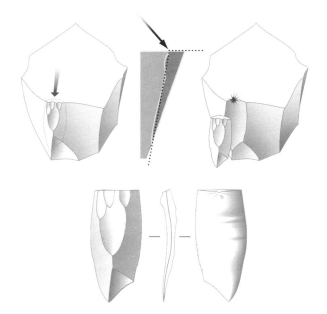

Figure 2.3. *Conchoidal fracture resulting from a Hertzian cone produced near a 70–80° edge angle with a 40–50° incidence of percussion (standard parameters).*

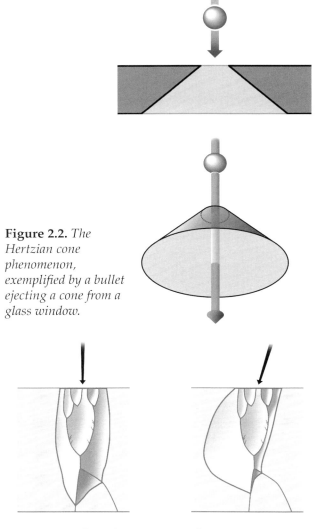

Figure 2.2. *The Hertzian cone phenomenon, exemplified by a bullet ejecting a cone from a glass window.*

Figure 2.4. *Effect of the direction of percussion; skewing the flake.*

the entire knapping process. (Tixier *et al.* 1980; Pigeot 1987; Karlin 1991; Ploux *et al.* 1991; Pelegrin 1995a). This is called 'lithic reading'.[1]

Thanks to his practical expertise and understanding of 'lithic reading', Tixier made a very relevant distinction within the knapping process: between technique and method (Tixier 1967).

'Technique' refers to the physical mode of execution of flake detachment(s) (or 'removals'); e.g. per-

cussion with or without an anvil, the shape and raw material of the tool(s) employed, how the piece being worked is held and other aspects of body position.

'Method' refers to the spatial and temporal organization of different flaking actions (i.e. 'the reduction process'). Within a given archaeological assemblage, when the same spatial and temporal organization of a reduction process is repeatedly used on multiple cores or flakes, a knapping method is thus identified, corresponding to a systematized, if not a reasoned, behaviour or action.

Such a distinction between technique and method is also relevant at a methodological level. Techniques can only be identified by analogy with experimental data; that is, through modern knapping studies. On the other hand, methods can be identified only by a precise 'lithic reading' of an entire archaeological assemblage. In this regard, knapping experiments can aid the 'reading' (for instance, in understanding technical variants), but such experiments cannot serve as the referent for reconstructing a prehistoric knapping method.

Remarks about techniques: split breaking and conchoidal fracture

It is essential here to differentiate two mechanisms of fracture: split breaking and conchoidal fracture.

A forceful stroke can be enough, without any other consideration, to break a hard or semi-hard stone. The most favourable condition in this regard involves placing the stone to be fractured lengthwise on a large piece of hard material — such as an anvil — and striking the top with something sufficiently hard and heavy such that the stone is squeezed until it splits. Experience shows that a flat pebble with a round edge can be split in two halves, while stones with irregular shapes or edges will break in unexpected ways: this technique of breaking cannot be controlled (Fig. 2.1). On the other hand, a stone can be thrown violently on an anvil (although it is better for the throwing hand to release the piece before impact), in which case a so-called splinter may be detached (the proximal edge of a splinter is crushed more than the edge of a true platform, and it shows no clear bulb of percussion).

Conversely, a conchoidal fracture is the result of a very different and much more specific knapping technique. Although it is not yet well explained by physicists, a conchoidal fracture refers to the phenomenon producing a Hertzian cone. Visualized at its simplest, when a bullet hits a glass window, a cone-like flake is ejected or detached, showing that the fracture diverges obliquely out from the point of contact and through the material at a constant angle, depending on the raw material (Fig. 2.2).

The same conchoidal fracture can be used to detach a flake from the side of a core, when the percussive stroke is: 1) placed near an edge — but not on the edge; and 2) strikes the core at no less than a 90° angle. In this scenario, edge effects are added to the cone-producing phenomenon. Specifically, the ventral face of the flake just below the initial Hertzian cone — or bulb ('*conche*' in Greek) — will retain a slightly convex transverse cross-section (Fig. 2.3). Given the proper configuration of two core surfaces (a potential platform intersecting at an acute angle with a second surface from which the flake will detach), the length, width and thickness of a flake detached by conchoidal fracturing are strictly determined by the parameters of percussion (direction, incidence, location of the point of contact) (Figs. 2.4, 2.5 & 2.6). This determination opens up several possibilities: not only the rote anticipation of the flake to be detached with adequate percussion, but also the controlled adaptation of the percussive stroke to various configurations of the core (Fig. 2.7), as well as the various intentions of the knapper (detaching a shorter or longer, thinner or thicker flake).

I thus suggest the following:
1. conchoidal fracture implies much more percussive precision than does the split breaking of stone pebbles or nuts. In split breaking, the pebble or nut is hit vertically by the wide flat surface of the hammer, which permits significant precisional latitude. In conchoidal fracture on a flat platform, the convex end of the hammer must strike adequately back from the edge of the platform, and it is this degree of striking precision and incidence which determines the geometric thickness (and thus width) of the detached flake (Figs. 2.5, 2.6 & 2.7).
2. conchoidal fracture implies true bi-manual dexterity; while the left hand orients the core within the three dimensions of space so as to control the direction and incidence of percussion delivered by the right arm, the left arm produces an antagonist muscular contraction exactly synchronic with impact. For split breaking, the left hand just needs to hold the nut or pebble on the anvil.

Given these observations, what should we make of Kanzi's stone tool-making activities? Kanzi is a strong male Bonobo to whom Nick Toth demonstrated a technique for detaching a flake from a hand-held stone (core). After long trials, Kanzi could at best exhibit an axial percussion technique that could only, after many repeated strokes, detach small splinters (including a few conchoidal-looking flakes; split-breaking techniques will accidentally produce, at a low rate, conchoidal-looking 'flakes' which are similar to those created when pebbles fall off a cliff or are tossed about by waves crashing on the shore). On his own, Kanzi then switched to a smashing or throwing-on-anvil technique (Toth *et al.* 1993; Schick *et al.* 1999), which still produced mostly splinters. It is thus very clear that Kanzi does not produce anything other or better than a variation on the 'nut-splitting' technique, and he thus remains very far from controlling conchoidal fracture.

Some early hominins split rounded pebbles, but only when small quartz pebbles were the only available raw material: with such blanks, this is the only knapping technique possible. But the earliest known lithic industries provide clear evidence of the use of conchoidal fracture (see Roche 1980, and in this volume).

Let us now consider the practical aspects of these earliest knapping techniques.

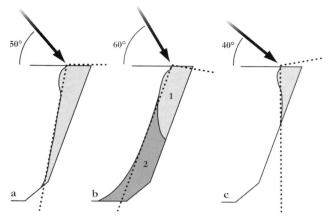

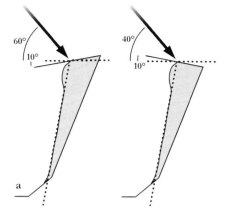

Figure 2.5. *Effect of the incidence of percussion (given (1) a standard edge angle situated between a flat platform and the flaking surface, and (2) a standard depth of impact): a) proper incidence produces a proper flake; b1) excessive incidence produces a short hinged flake, if the force of percussion is the same as in 5a; b2) excessive incidence together with a strong percussive stroke produces an overpass flake (usually something to avoid, except in cases where it helps intentionally modify the core); c) insufficient incidence produces a short feathering flake.*

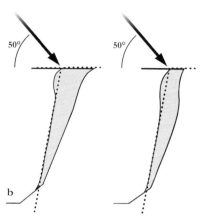

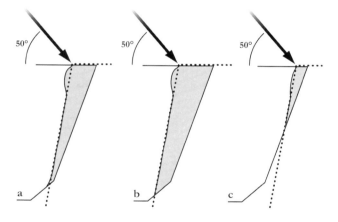

Figure 2.6. *Effect of the depth of impact, given a standard edge angle. Note that for a given transversally convex flaking surface, the width of the flake correlates with its thickness: a) effect of a proper depth of impact; b) effect of an increased depth of impact (presupposing that the impact force also increases); c) effect of a reduced depth of impact.*

Figure 2.7. *Adaptation of percussion incidence to a variable edge angle (a), and adaptation of the depth of impact to variable edge morphology (b). Note that in both cases the knapper, once s/he is in proper striking position, only sees the platform surface tilted slightly towards the ground: s/he does not see the actual edge angle nor the overhang of the edge. The knapper thus has to pre-program such adaptations of percussion after having inspected the core and appreciated the edge angle and its morphology.*

To detach a few flakes from a flat pebble using direct stone percussion, at the least one should:
- select an area of the edge that is not too thick;
- orient the pebble to the direction of the in-coming percussive stroke;
- adjust the point of percussion relative to the pebble's edge, to making it neither too far nor too close; and
- turn or re-orient the pebble a few centimetres before the next flake removal.

To detach a series of flakes from a large flat surface using direct stone percussion, at the least one should:
- select a likely platform area on a side of that flat surface with an edge angle of about 75±5°;
- orient the blank so that the large flat surface — that which becomes the flaking face — is tilted toward the ground;
- adjust the point of percussion, locating it about 1 centimetre in from the very edge;

- strike obliquely, at an angle of about 50° (depending on the edge angle) relative to the flaking surface (which is now oriented toward the ground);
- shift the blank laterally for the next flake removal, but only after evaluating the current situation (for instance, if the last flake went rather wide or hinged, the next has to start further away from the edge).

On this basis, I do not accept the assumption proposed by others who argue that the earliest stone tools are equivalent to the stone 'flake' debris of chimpanzee nut-crackers (e.g. Wynn & McGrew 1989; McGrew 1993, 165).

Methods of knapping

Once again, we can recognize methods of knapping by the 'technological reading' of an archaeological assemblage, that is by considering the order and direction of negatives (flake scars) observable on extant flakes, cores and shaped tools. Indeed, it is the consistency underlying the conchoidal fracture technique that allows the development of true knapping methods: if one flake detachment can be thus controlled, it becomes possible to control a series of flake removals and organize them in a systematic (repetitious or patterned) manner.

Roughly speaking, one can distinguish two families of knapping methods in the archaeological record: so-called 'simple methods', in which the flakes are arranged systematically and repeated according to a simple rule or 'formula'; and 'elaborated methods', in which the knapping process achieves a morphological goal (most likely through a number of intermediate goals).

Simple methods seem to be reducible to the knapper repeating elementary ('by rote') flake removal techniques following a simple formula (which I originally called an 'algorithm': cf. in Forestier 1992; Pelegrin 1995b; 2004), for instance:

- adjacent flakes are removed along or around the edge of a large flat surface which acts as a platform;
- alternating flakes are removed along the edge of a relatively flat blank (Fig. 2.8).

In such cases, archaeological assemblages and contemporary experiments show that as the knapper proceeds there is no need to monitor the shape of the core, even though the exhausted core will have a diagnostic shape (that is, adjacent flake removals leave behind a unipolar-faced, or sub-conical, core, while alternating flake removals produce a 'discoidal' core).

The earliest-known flaked pebbles and cores were once analyzed as having been produced by

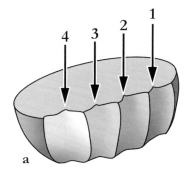

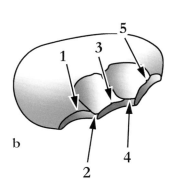

Figure 2.8. *Two examples of simple core reduction methods based on an 'algorithmic' formula: a) sequence of adjacent flakes along or around the edge of a large flat surface serving as the platform; b) alternating flake removals along the edge of a relatively flat blank.*

such stereotypical formulas (Bordes 1971; Roche 1980). But the Lokalelei 2c refittings accomplished by Roche & Delagnes, which conjoined several series of sub-parallel flakes, provide the first strong evidence that the hominins who produced them (*Homo habilis*?) were monitoring the core as they worked (Roche *et al.* 1999; Roche this volume). Indeed, evidence shows that the platform of several cores from Lokalelei 2c was repaired by removing a small flake in the course of actual flake production. I see this as an important cognitive indicator: not only could the knapper ascertain that there was something wrong with the existing platform, but s/he also occasionally interrupted the regular knapping process to correct the platform by striking off an appropriate flake — but one which was obviously not of the same order as regular flake products. Thus, the knapper demonstrated the ability: 1) to evaluate on an ongoing basis both the orientation and regularity of the platform; and 2) to modify it as needed, instead of simply stopping when the situation (core) was no longer adequate. In other words, the knapper was capable of a degree of *decision making* that could optimize the actual condition of the core (Goren-Inbar 1988). Moreover, there is no haphazard 'hammering' on any of the Lokalelei 2c cores.

True elaborated methods appear in the archaeological record several hundreds of thousands of years ago. With elaborated methods, the knapping process involves more than one sequence, and is marked

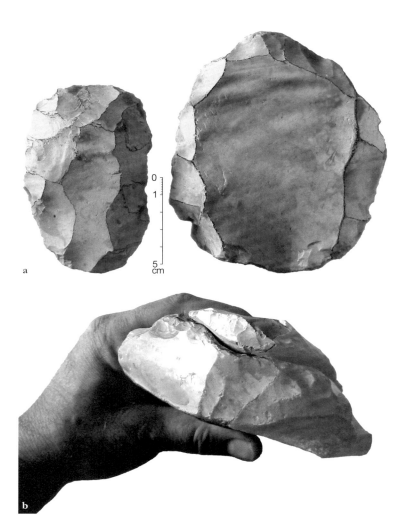

& Roche 1995; Roche this volume). Hundreds of bifaces recovered from this one site bear a strikingly identical shape, with little homothetic (or harmonic) variation. Such morphological stability demonstrates that the knappers had in mind a 'picture', a mental template, of a desired object with an 'elongated almond' shape, and this goal was accomplished despite the dozens of highly-contingent shaping flakes required to produce each biface to the same desired form.

2. Somewhat later in Europe, we find another remarkable family of elaborated knapping methods used to produce standardized products: the Levallois method of 'predetermined flake production' (identified as such in the early work of Commont (1913, 266); see also Boëda 1994; Boëda *et al.* 1990) (Fig. 2.9). In this method, the core is first shaped by a very well adapted — that is, a variable — series of shaping flakes, such that the core's upper surface is made regularly convex (Fig. 2.10a; note that the position and orientation of this 'upper surface' are established at the very beginning of the knapping process: this convex surface does not appear by chance during Levallois knapping). When this convex (upper) surface is ready, the knapper then shapes the predetermined percussion area of the platform (Fig. 2.10b,c) so that it is precisely oriented and protrudes as desired (Pelegrin, in Boëda & Pelegrin 1979–80, fig. 5). The final percussive stroke removes a large pre-shaped flake, which intersects with the convex surface of the upper face (Fig. 2.10d). Consequently, the morphology of this flake is precisely predetermined. In some cases, the core is re-shaped to produce one more similarly predetermined product. In other cases, where the production phase includes knapping a series of overlapping flakes, these are also intentionally produced to a desired form and also carefully organized in order to control the modification of the core (Boëda 1994; 1995).

Figure 2.9. *a) A Levallois core (right) and a Levallois flake (left) from the Ault site (a Levallois workshop in the north of France which has provided hundreds of similar Levallois cores: Perpère 1999). The flake was probably left in the workshop because of its rather hinged distal edge. It does not come from the core illustrated (right) but could almost be a refit. b) The conjunction of the flake on the core shows the specific* 'chapeau de gendarme' *facetting preparation of the platform, as illustrated in Figure 2.10.*

either by some change in an intermediate goal (such as pre-shaping, actual flake production, reshaping, or platform preparation using other knapping tools), or by some change of technique (including abrading and grinding). The results of elaborated knapping procedures include standardized products, the formal features of which are completely independent of the initial morphology of the raw material.

Two types of archaeological examples of elaborated methods can be distinguished:

1. The shaping of regular and symmetrical bifaces, such as those from Ysenia, an Acheulean site in Kenya dated to about 700,000 years ago (Texier

Such elaborated adaptations of successive flake removal to effect a pre-planned objective testifies to the

Figure 2.10. *Schematic of the Levallois method, with the classic (but not exclusive) platform preparation known as 'en chapeau de gendarme' (from Pelegrin, in Boëda & Pelegrin 1979–1980): a) final shaping of the properly-oriented flaking surface, as seen from what will be the future platform of the Levallois flake; b) first step in platform preparation; two medium size flakes are very precisely detached so that a triangular 'bump' (boss, hump) appears in relief; c) second step in platform preparation; tiny bladelet-flakes are detached, by very careful flaking or abrasion, so that the triangular bump becomes regularly facetted and rounded. Note that if the bump is asymmetrical or off-centre (too high or too low), the Levallois flake will detach side-ways ('skewing') or end up either too thin or too thick; d) with a right-handed knapper, the right arm tends to move in a constant direction. But it is the precise inclination of the core held in the left hand which determines the incidence of percussion. The 'trick' is that, on a correctly-prepared platform properly inclined to produce the correct incidence, the hammerstone will necessarily hit the convex base of the facetted bump and, at this very point inaugurate a fracture plan (thereby determining both the thickness and width of the flake, given the transversally convex nature of the prepared flaking surface). If the appropriately estimated force is delivered properly (that is, if the speed of movement is appropriate to the mass of the selected hammerstone), then the fracture plan will run toward the distal end of the core and produce a regular flake with a sharp distal end. An insufficient amount of force will foreshorten the flake, while an excessive amount of force will lead it to overpass its mark (that is, reach but also remove the distal end of the core).*

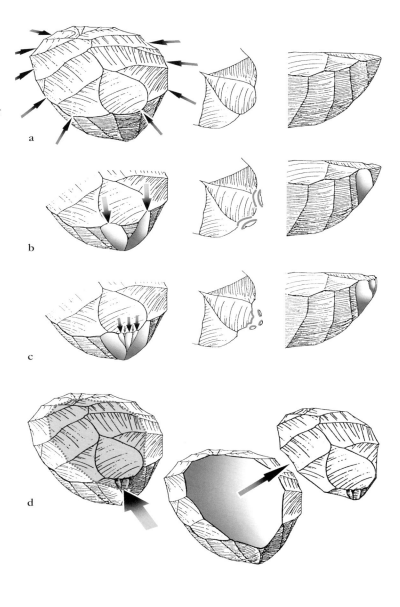

existence a specific cognitive skill capable of mentally constructing and selecting short- and long-term sequences of flake removals to meet the desired goal.

I argue strongly that such elaborated knapping procedures cannot be reduced to repeated elementary gestures or stereotypical (by rote) sequences such as in the simple 'algorithms' mentioned above. Elaborated methods do not involve simply detaching flakes by taking advantage of naturally-favourable configurations of the core being worked. An elaborated knapping method depends upon specifying and then working toward predetermined morphological objectives, and these undoubtedly testify to the existence of operative mental templates. If this were not the case it would

mean that, from site to site, Acheulean and Levallois knappers were carrying around and working from copies.

It is also important to underscore that this trend, from simple formula-based knapping methods to elaborated lithic products created by a variable set of predetermining (shaping) methods, corresponds to a profound evolution in the knapping process.

If simple methods can cope with standard percussion gestures applied to favourable geometric configurations, then elaborated methods of flake or blade production are based on accomplishing successive geometric goals (concerning, for example, overall shape or discrete details regarding angles, bevels, platform zones, etc.). In this second instance, most flake detachments are not intended as products in themselves, but are carefully adapted via a clear understanding of their effect on the core or on the desired morphology of the preform flake (product). When intimately combined in an elaborated core-reduction process, there is a clear hierarchy in the production of predetermin*ed* flakes — intended as products — and predetermin*ing* (or shaping) flakes within that same *chaîne opératoire*. I see this as evidence of a wholly new — and a decidedly 'modern' — cognitive dimension in stone knapping.

To go further, such a goal-structured process presupposes a two-fold appreciation of 'what should be done next' — in addition to what is *feasible*, we now see a concern with what is *desirable* — and desirability comes to dominate the knapping process. Production of the next flake not only depends on the condition of the core at any given moment, but also must be produced according to a geometric objective. This two-fold appreciation of feasibility and desirability is dialectic: what is desirable can frequently diverge from what is most practical (feasible).

At the same time, the skill involved in elaborated and predetermined knapping methods can be defined to include not only motor skills (those involved in pre-programming and executing each and every flake removal). Skill here also includes the ability to plan out a series of variable shaping flakes, each of which is itself prefigured to effect a desired end (that is, to effect a preconceived geometric feature in the most dependable and effective way). At the mature level of experienced flint knapping, such pre-planning and anticipation is so rapid as to be practically invisible to the naive observer. For example, a recent survey of 13 modern medium- to highly-experienced flint knappers demonstrates that they all proceed with predetermined mental solutions to anticipated situations (Pelegrin in prep.). Most interestingly, except for the least experienced, all the informants admitted to occasionally or even frequently using what can be called 'reverse reasoning'. Reverse reasoning starts with a desired goal in mind which is not immediately attainable (for example, removing a bump from one face of a working core or repairing an accident), then imagining — backwards — the series of a non-redundant flakes which must be struck in order to achieve that goal.[2] Moreover, but for the less experienced of them, all the knappers admit to recourse occasionally or frequently to 'backwards or reverse reasoning': starting from an objective (for example removing a hump in the middle of a face or repairing an accident) that is not immediately attainable, by imagining a solution of several non-monotonous flakes in a reverse construction so as

to fulfill the objective. I propose calling this discrete skill, 'ideational', or 'constructive' know-how (after terminology used in neuropsychology) — and define it as the detailed pre-planning of a short series of anticipatory actions (cf. 'hierarchical mental construction skills' in Gibson 1993, 135, and 'type 3B planning' in Parker & Milbrath 1993, 318).

The structure of anticipatory reasoning, which takes into account both the feasibility of a proposed action and the desirability of the anticipated result, is known as propositional thinking — *if I do this, then I will get this; if I do that, then I will get that.*

Moreover, since the duration of elaborated knapping procedures extends from several minutes to as much as a half hour, the knapper must maintain continuous attention and vigilance. Modern knappers also admit to facing difficulties in developing the skills required of elaborated knapping methods, which helps account for the relatively long period of learning required.

Conclusion

The earliest evidence of stone-tool production, at 2.6 million years, clearly shows that the knappers employed the conchoidal fracture technique, and implies truly dynamic bi-manual dexterity and precision strokes. This is very different from what chimps do when they crack nuts, and what a Bonobo like Kanzi does when he 'hammers' or throws a stone on an anvil to break or split it.[3]

As a method, it is possible that these earliest knapping procedures were based on simple formulas involved in arranging a few highly-repetitious flakes on (generally) pre-selected blanks.

By 2.3 million years, however, evidence of platform preparation or repair suggests that basic knapping parameters were not only spontaneous, but that the knapper was capable of judging and improving the platform (without smashing it first) in order to render it more suitable for detaching the next flake or series of flakes.[4]

For palaeohominins such as *Homo erectus*, their elaborated knapping methods provide evidence that hundreds of thousands of years ago they possessed not only accurate motor skills but that mental templates framed the entire knapping process. Technical actions were thus subordinate to, and structured by, geometric intentions.

Indeed, their actions were the result of a compromise: between the constraints of the current state of the core (*viz.* what was technically possible), and the intended (desired) shape of the core (*viz.* what was appropriate to achieve the next intermediate goal or form). The mental capacity to evoke 'solutions' and select the one that is both appropriate and realistic is in French known as 'savoir-faire idéatoire', and can be translated as 'constructive know-how'. Whether conscious or semi-conscious, the psychological operations involved constitute propositional reasoning, and make such processes 'deliberate'.[5]

On the other hand, such goal-oriented methods combined with flexibility and the ability to anticipate successive actions and situations, strongly suggest that the properties of flakeable stone were not only finely perceived (in the sense of the ecological paradigm), but also interpreted, understood and mastered. Through the likelihood of intentional experimentation, the knapper could thus abstract a set of rules from his or her understanding of flakeable stone, then apply them to effect a desired goal. At the very least, the knappers who then invented and adapted alternative techniques to basic hard stone percussion (e.g. direct organic percussion during the Acheulean, soft stone percussion during the late Mousterian, pressure flaking during the Upper Palaeolithic) must have built up such understandings on the basis of their own antecedent experiences.

As I see it, such goal-structured methods testify to a modern form of intelligence; perhaps not in terms of theoretical abstractions, but certainly within the domain of technical ability.

Notes

1. This reading of knapped stone provides information similar to transcriptions of a sequence of chess moves(s), transcriptions which allow for an analysis of the participants' strategy. Such analysis requires specific methodological competence. It would be very difficult for a non-chess player to analyze a game's transcription and properly evaluate the psychological abilities of the players. One can therefore appreciate the value of practical flint-knapping experience (that is, replicative experience) and of conducting comparative lithic research prior to offering 'interpretations'. Coupled with the ability to recognize the physical properties and constraints of the raw material and techniques employed, that is in understanding the 'rules of the game', practical experience is necessary to distinguish within any knapping sequence the intentional and contingent factors involved, to understand what is easy and what is difficult (and why), etc. (Tixier et al. 1980; Pelegrin 1991b).

2. We use reverse reasoning all the time. An easy example is when you want to reach the airport at a particular time in the morning. So you begin to compute when you should wake up by starting with your goal — your flight leaves at 6 am. Reasoning in reverse, you subtract an hour because you know you need to be at the airport by 5 am. You also need 20 minutes to find a parking space

and reach the terminal (that makes it 4:40 am). It takes an hour to drive to the airport (that makes it 3:40 am, but let's err on the side of caution and make it 3:30 am). Thus, if you know you need only 30 minutes to shower and brush your teeth (you packed the night before), that means you should set the alarm for 3 am. A more complicated example of reverse reasoning, and perhaps closer to what the knapper considers to reach his goal, would be deciding between taking a train (subway) to the airport or driving — the car is easier though parking is expensive while the train is more secure though you do have to get up earlier . . . then again, you also need to factor in what will be the most convenient method if your return flight gets you back to town in the middle of the night . . .

3. In opposition to the ecological paradigm (e.g. Bril et al. this volume; Roux & David this volume), a first-order question is: If Kanzi could not clearly 'integrate' the most basic conditions (prerequisites) of conchoidal fracture, is it because chimpanzees lack skill or is it because the most basic knapping skill implies some kind of 'understanding'?

4. Even if the ecological paradigm possibly accounts for producing standardized flake through a simple integration of the most basic properties (or conditions) of flakeable stone (which is the first-order question, ff. 2), then a second-order question is: How do we explain the acquisition of an ability which allows the knapper: 1) not only to detach the most obviously-possible flake (given the core's current condition) or simply discard the core when it cannot be worked anymore; but also 2) to decide if it is possible to solve some problem with the core and figure out an effective technique for doing so.

5. A third-order multi-component question for the ecological paradigm, is: How does the 'integration of basic properties' or 'affordances' account for such clear evidence of operative mental templates?; How does it account for the hierarchy existing between predetermining (shaping) flakes and predetermined flake products?; How does it account for the dialectic evaluation of alternative solutions, based on their feasibility and their appropriateness for a goal-structured process?

References

Alimen, M.-H. & M. Goustard, 1962. Le développement de l'intelligence et les structures paléobiopsychologiques. Bulletin de la Société Préhistorique Française 59(5–6), 386–406.

Boëda, E., 1994. Le concept Levallois: variabilité des méthodes. (Monographie du CRA 9.) Paris: CNRS Editions.

Boëda, E., 1995. Levallois: a volumetric construction, methods, a technique, in The Definition and Interpretation of Levallois Technology, eds. H.L. Dibble & O. Bar-Yosef. (Monographs in World Archaeology 23.) Madison (WI): Prehistory Press, 41–68.

Boëda, E. & J. Pelegrin, 1979–80. Approche technologique du nucléus Levallois à éclat. Études Préhistoriques 15 (published in 1983), 41–8.

Boëda, E., J.-M. Geneste & L. Meignen, 1990. Identification de chaînes opératoires du Paléolithique ancien et moyen. *Paléo* 2, 43–88.

Bordes, F., 1971. Physical evolution and technological evolution in man: a parallelism. *World Archaeology* 3(1), 1–5.

Forestier, H., 1992. *Approche technologique de quelques séries dites clactoniennes du nord-ouest de la France et du sud-est de l'Angleterre.* Nanterre: Mémoire de Maîtrise de l'Université de Paris X.

Commont, V., 1913. Les hommes contemporains du renne dans la vallée de la Somme. *Mémoires de la Société des Antiquaires de Picardie* 37, 207–646.

Gibson, K.R., 1993. Part II, Introduction. Generative interplay between technical capacities, social relations, imitation and cognition, in *Tools, Language and Cognition in Human Evolution*, eds. K.R. Gibson & T. Ingold. Cambridge: Cambridge University Press, 131–7.

Goren-Inbar, N., 1988. Notes on 'decision making' by lower and middle Palaeolithic hominids. *Paléorient* 14(2), 99–108.

Inizan, M.-L., M. Reduron-Ballinger, H. Roche & J. Tixier, 1999. *Technology and Terminology of Knapped Stone.* (Préhistoire de la Pierre Taillée 5, multilingual vocabulary.) Nanterre: CREP.

Karlin, C., 1991. Connaissances et savoir-faire: comment analyser un processus technique en Préhistoire: introduction, in *Technología y cadenas operativas líticas. Reunion internacional 15–18 Enero 1991*, eds. R. Mora, X. Terradas, A. Parpal & C. Plana. (Treballs d'Arqueologia I.) Bellaterra: U.A.B., 99–124.

Leroi-Gourhan, A., 1993. *Gesture and Speech.* Cambridge (MA) & London: The MIT Press.

McGrew, W.C., 1993. The intelligent use of tools: twenty propositions, in *Tools, Language and Cognition in Human Evolution*, eds. K.R. Gibson & T. Ingold. Cambridge: Cambridge University Press, 151–70.

Parker, S.T. & C. Milbrath, 1993. Higher intelligence, propositional language, and culture as adaptations for planning, in *Tools, Language and Cognition in Human Evolution*, eds. K.R. Gibson & T. Ingold. Cambridge: Cambridge University Press, 314–33.

Pelegrin, J., 1990. Prehistoric lithic technology: some aspects of research. *Archaeological Review from Cambridge* 9(1), 116–25.

Pelegrin, J., 1991a. Les savoir-faire: une très longue histoire. *Terrain, Carnets du Patrimoine Ethnologique* 16, 106–13.

Pelegrin, J., 1991b. Aspects de démarche expérimentale en technologie lithique, in *25 ans d'études technologiques en Préhistoire: bilan et perspectives*, ed. coll. Actes des XIèmes rencontres internationales d'Archéologie et d'Histoire d'Antibes. Juan-les-Pins: APDCA, 57–63.

Pelegrin, J., 1993. A framework for analysing prehistoric stone tools manufacture and a tentative application to some early lithic industries, in *The Use of Tools by Human and Non-human Pprimates: a Symposium of the Fyssen Foundation*, eds. A. Berthelet & J. Chavaillon. Oxford: Clarendon Press, 302–14.

Pelegrin, J., 1995a. *Technologie lithique: le Châtelperronien de Roc-de-Combe (Lot) et de La Côte (Dordogne).* (Cahiers du Quaternaire 20.) Paris: CNRS Editions.

Pelegrin, J., 1995b. Sur le milieu intérieur d'André Leroi-Gourhan: éléments pour l'analyse de la taille des outils de pierre et autres réflexions. Paper presented at the conference *Geste technique, Parole, Mémoire: actualité scientifique et philosophique de Leroi-Gourhan: Meudon, 17–19 mai 1995*; to be edited in 2004 by F. Audouze.

Pelegrin, J. 1995b (2004). Le milieu intérieur d'André Leroi-Gourhan et l'analyse de la taille de la pierre au Paléolithique. Paper presented at the Leroi-Gourhan colloquium held in Meudon, May 1995, in *Autour de l'homme: contexte et actualité d'André Leroi-Gourhan*, eds. F. Audouze & N. Schlanger. Antibes: Editions APDCA, 149–62.

Pelegrin, J., in prep. *Enquête sur le savoir-faire engagé dans la taille des roches dures.*

Perpère, M., 1999. Le débitage Levallois d'Ault (Somme, France). *L'Anthropologie* 103(3), 343–76.

Pigeot, N., 1987. *Magdaléniens d'Etiolles: économie du débitage et organisation sociale (l'unité d'habitation U 5).* (XXVe supplément à *Gallia-Préhistoire.*) Paris: CNRS.

Ploux, S., C. Karlin & P. Bodu, 1991. D'une chaîne l'autre: normes et variations dans le débitage laminaire magdalénien. *Techniques et Culture* 17–18, 87–114.

Roche, H., 1980. *Premiers outils taillés d'Afrique.* Paris: Société d'ethnographie.

Roche, H., 1989. Technological evolution in early hominids. *OSSA* 14, 91–8.

Roche, H. & P.-J. Texier, 1996. Evaluation of technical competence of *Homo erectus* in East Africa during the Middle Pleistocene, in *Proceedings of the Pithecanthropus Centennial, 1893–1993*, vol. I: *Palaeoanthropology: Evolution and Ecology of* Homo erectus, eds. J.R.F. Bower & S. Sartono. Leiden: Pithecanthropus Centennial Foundation, 153–67.

Roche, H., A. Delagnes, J.-P. Brugal, C. Feibel, M. Kibunja, V. Mourre & P.-J. Texier, 1999. Early hominid stone tool production and technical skill 2.34 Myr ago in West Turkana, Kenya. *Nature* 399, 57–60.

Schick, K.D., N. Toth & G. Garufi, 1999. Continuing investigations into the stone tool-making and tool-using capabilities of a Bonobo (*Pan paniscus*). *Journal of Archaeological Science* 26, 821–32.

Texier, P.-J. & H. Roche, 1995. The impact of predetermination on the development of some acheulean chaînes opératoires, in *Evolucion humana en Europa y los yacimientos de la Sierra de Atapuerca*, vol. 2. Junta de Castilla y Leon: Actas, 403–20.

Tixier, J., 1967. Procédés d'analyse et questions de terminologie concernant l'étude des ensembles industriels du Paléolithique récent et de l'Epipaléolithique dans l'Afrique du Nord-Ouest, in *Background to Evolution in Africa: Proceedings of a Symposium held at Burg Wartenstein Austria, July–August 1965*, eds. W.W. Bishop & J. Desmond-Clark. Chicago (IL): University of Chicago Press, 771–820.

Tixier, J., 1978. Notice sur les travaux scientifiques. Unpublished Thèse de Doctorat d'Etat, Université de Paris X-Nanterre.

Tixier, J., M.-L. Inizan & H. Roche, 1980. *Préhistoire de la pierre taillée: I Terminologie et technologie*. Valbonne: CREP. [Extended English edition see Inizan *et al.* 1999.]

Toth, N., 1993. Early stone industries and inferences regarding language and cognition, in *Tools, Language and Cognition in Human Evolution*, eds. K.R. Gibson & T. Ingold. Cambridge: Cambridge University Press, 346–62.

Toth, N., K.D. Schick, E.S. Savage-Rumbaugh, R.A. Sevcik & D.M. Rumbaugh, 1993. Pan the tool-maker: investigations into the stone tool-making and tool-using capabilities of a Bonobo (*Pan paniscus*). *Journal of Archaeological Science* 20, 81–91.

Wynn, T., 1979. The intelligence of the later Acheulean hominid. *Man* 14(3), 371–91.

Wynn, T., 1985. Piaget, stone tools and the evolution of human intelligence. *World Archaeology* 17, 31–43.

Wynn, T., 1988. Tools and the evolution of human intelligence, in *Machiavellian Intelligence*, eds. R.W. Byrne & A. Whiten. Oxford: Clarendon Press, 271–84.

Wynn, T., 1991. Archaeological evidence for modern intelligence, in *The Origins of Human Behaviour*, ed. R.A. Foley. London: Unwin Hyman, 52–66.

Wynn, T. & W.C. McGrew, 1989. An ape's eye view of the Oldowan. *Man* 24, 383–98.

Chapter 3

From Simple Flaking to Shaping:
Stone-knapping Evolution among Early Hominins

Hélène Roche

The first earliest-known evidence of stone knapping occurs in East Africa during the late Pliocene, c. 2.6 Myr. Rather than attempting a rapid overview of over two million years of lithic technology, this paper focuses on archaeological examples from the Late Pliocene (c. 2.3 Myr), the Early Pleistocene (c. 1.7 Myr) and the Middle Pleistocene (c. 0.7 Myr), which illustrate significant steps in the evolution of stone knapping. Lithic production is characterized in each case by studying two main knapping actions: flaking and shaping. A greater degree of planning and more accurate technical abilities are shown to have led to the large-scale production of cutting flakes as early as 2.3 Myr. A further 1.5 million years elapsed, however, before artefacts of standardized shape began to be mass-produced. These artefacts were totally free from the original morphology of the raw material employed, and were the outcome of chains of technical actions that clearly depended on forward planning.

The tendency to pick up unmodified natural objects and use them, however slightly, as 'tools', is shared by a number of animal species, including human and non-human primates, as is the ability to alter, prior to use, a naturally-occurring soft and/or plastic material. The ability, however, to modify intentionally a naturally-occurring hard and rigid, i.e. brittle material, is the prerogative of human primates and their direct ancestors (although, natural elements made of hard stone, altered through repeated used, may happen to be modified). A case in point are the stone anvils and hammers used by Tai forest chimpanzees to crack the extremely tough local Panda oleosa nuts (Boesch et al. 1994). Anvils may be hollowed out by depressions, or even break into several pieces; fragments may accidentally detach from the stone hammers, which sometimes also break. In no way, however, do the products thus obtained mimic the earliest lithic assemblages currently known. These arise from the intentional fracturing of a homogeneous, isotropic, hard and rigid material, according to the very specific mechanism of conchoidal fracture[1] (Pelegrin this volume; Pelegrin & Texier 2004), which causes absolutely characteristic scars to appear on the products. Owing to their particular morphology, due to this fracture pattern, the products thus detached are endowed with an additional property, which does not (or only very seldom) occur naturally: they have razor-sharp edges. It has been suggested plausibly (Marchant & McGrew this volume) that the repeated observation of accidental fracturing of brittle materials combined with the discovery that some of the fragments accidentally fractured according to the conchoidal fracture pattern[2] had sharp cutting edges, may have resulted, through trial and error, in the intentional fracturing of stones along a similar principle.[3] Owing to its necessarily random and diffuse character, however, this phase of hominin technological development will always be speculative. The prerequisite for identifying a production as intentional is the presence, in a reliable context, of a minimum number of objects displaying the diagnostic scars of hard rock knapping: this is precisely the situation we see in the oldest currently known archaeological sites. In this connection, a knapper's individual performance and the level of skill reached by a group constitute a riddle that can only be solved by technological analysis.

The aim of this paper is to present the archaeological facts by which early stone knapping may be characterized. Why the early period rather than the

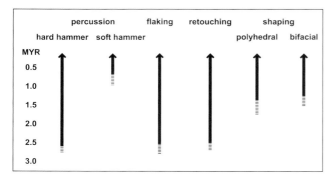

Figure 3.1. *Mode of fracturing and basic specific knapping actions through time.*

inception of stone knapping? Because, as emphasized above, the first archaeological evidence available does not correspond to the very beginning of stone knapping. On the contrary, the first lithic archaeological traces correspond to already-controlled stone knapping. What is meant by 'controlled stone knapping' is the mastery of the elementary gestures necessary for detaching from a chunk of raw material (the core) some fragments of this raw material (the flakes) displaying the diagnostic elements by which conchoidal fracture is characterized, mainly: striking platform, debitage surface, etc. for the cores; bulb of percussion, butt (i.e. the part removed from the striking platform of the core), a lower (ventral) fracture face opposed to an upper (dorsal) face, a sharp peripheral cutting edge etc. for the flakes. Even (and notably) in the case of the earliest acknowledged traces of stone knapping, these diagnostic elements are present and indicate that such controlled stone knapping is fundamentally different from the other technical gestures with which it is usually compared (cracking nuts for instance) or indeed sometimes identified. The distinction is not only based on the products thereby obtained, but also on one of the most remarkable aspects of stone-tool manufacture, that pertains to the way hominins interact with their environment. As previously mentioned, sharp cutting edges do not occur in nature. To knap a stone obviously amounts to transforming it, and to endlessly re-produce a cutting (or scrapping) edge,[4] which will, in turn, be used to act on other materials. Besides, in the animal world, there is always a direct relationship between the 'tool' used and the food intended for consumption, the nest that needs to be built, etc. In the recurrent nut-cracking example, the hammer is used for cracking the hard shell of the nut that is going to be eaten immediately. In the case of stone knapping, even for the most basic *chaîne opératoire*, the hammerstone is an intermediary tool, which enables the knapper to fracture the raw material whose fragments will themselves in turn become tools.

In more complex *chaîne opératoire*, these stone tools can be used to manufacture other tools in other type of materials (wood, bone, etc.). This fundamental notion is generally overlooked by ethno-primatologists (McGrew 1992; Boesch & Boesch-Achermann 2000), and yet it is an essential prerequisite of a vast array of technical behaviours and most certainly of stone knapping — the earliest acknowledged technical behaviour.

Methodological and contextual background

Before we discuss a number of archaeological examples which illustrate significant steps within the evolution of stone knapping, we will begin with a brief explanation of the basics of this technique (further developed by Pelegrin, this volume). They involve:[5]

- two modes of fracturing the raw material: percussion and pressure;
- three main specific knapping actions: flaking (from simple flaking to more elaborate debitage), shaping and retouching;
- dozens of techniques,[6] such as direct percussion with a hard stone hammer, indirect percussion with a punch, pressure with a pectoral crutch, microburin-blow technique, thermal treatment to improve the flaking qualities of some siliceous rocks, etc.;
- dozens of methods[7] invented throughout prehistoric times, such as Kombewa methods of debitage, Levallois methods of debitage, bifacial shaping methods, pressure debitage of blades), etc.

Percussion, with its many variants, was for the greater part of prehistory the only mode by which raw material was intentionally fractured, and it remains the most important. For the whole time period considered in this paper (Late Pliocene to Middle Pleistocene), it is indeed the only mode used (Fig. 3.1).

The action of *flaking* has one goal: to obtain multiple products that can be directly used as a tool without any modification or subsequently shaped or retouched. *Simple flaking* is self-defining insofar as it consists in the repetition of blows intended to detach a few flakes from a chunk of raw material. More *organized debitage* must correspond to stable and relatively effective (in terms of production) technical principles, which are repeatedly applied to a significant number of cores. Opposed to flaking in its conception, *shaping* refers to a knapping operation carried out for the purpose of manufacturing one single artefact by sculpting the raw material in accordance with the desired form. Lastly, *retouching* corresponds to the intentional modification of a blank by means of specific removals, for the purpose of obtaining a tool.

In terms of chrono-technical and cultural entities (Fig. 3.1), simple expedient flaking, more organized debitage, and occasional retouching are the three technical activities by which Pre-Oldowan was characterized between 2.6 and 1.9 Myr (that is to say for a time period of *c.* 0.7 Myr). It is at this stage, during the Oldowan, that polyhedral and spheroidal shaping appears. From 1.7/1.6 Myr onwards, more complex knapping activities come into being, concurrently with a diversification of techniques and methods and the inception of bifacial shaping, which represents the emblematic technical activity of the Acheulean.

Lastly, for the Late Pliocene and the Early Pleistocene (i.e. from *c.* 2.6 Myr to *c.* 0.9 Myr) two **techniques** are testified to: direct percussion with a hard stone hammer and direct percussion on a stone anvil. It is during the Middle Pleistocene (from *c.* 0.9 Myr onwards) that a new technique was brought into play: direct percussion with a 'soft' hammer, that is to say a hammer made from vegetable or animal wood, and indeed softer than hard rock (Fig. 3.1).

Knapping activities developed following a wide range of *chaînes opératoires*. Equally used as a concept and an analytical tool (Julien 1992) a *chaîne opératoire* is, and makes possible, the reconstruction of successive stages of manufacture (raw material procurement, flaking, shaping, retouching) of a type of artefact, from conception of the project to discard of the artefact, while at the same time identifying the technique(s) and method(s) followed. The study of a lithic assemblage, which is made of each and every piece retrieved from a single archaeological site and considered as a whole, has to be conducted in combination with experimental work if this proves necessary, and with refitting and microwear studies when these can be carried out. Refitting — which involves matching complementary pieces belonging to the same block of raw material (a core and its debitage products for instance) in order to reconstitute it — is extremely informative as to how the different sequences of core reduction have been carried out. Refitting implies relative integrity of the assemblage and thus good preservation of the archaeological site, which is not always the case for very old sites. Microwear studies, which aim to explain how a tool was used, have not yielded many results for the earlier periods of prehistory, largely because the materials used (coarse-grained rocks) imperfectly retain the traces left on them by the substance worked (wood, bone, meat, etc.), rather than owing to the antiquity of the artefacts.

It goes without saying that upstream from any knapping activities, there are one brain, two hands and, of course, specific needs. But knapping stones also implies a number of constraints: those intrinsic to the material worked, and those pertaining to the technical traditions of a group. As far as the second point is concerned, however, and considering the period addressed, it is more apposite to speak in terms of indisputable but basic skills, which may well have constrained technological innovation among small and territorially-isolated groups of hominins.

Late Pliocene archaeological sites are restricted to one time period, ranging from 2.6 Myr to 2.2 Myr, and to a very few areas in East Africa:

- along the Awash Valley in Ethiopia: Gona (Roche & Tiercelin 1977; 1980; Semaw *et al.* 1997; 2003), Hadar (Kimbel *et al.* 1996), and Bouri (de Heinzelin *et al.* 1999);
- within the Turkana basin, in Ethiopia and Kenya: Omo (Chavaillon 1976; Merrick & Merrick 1976), and West Turkana (Kibunjia *et al.* 1992; Roche *et al.* 2003);
- in Kanjera South in Western Kenya (Plummer *et al.* 1999).

It is only during the Early Pleistocene, from 2 Myr onwards, that the number of archaeological sites expanded, first in Africa and then 'out of Africa'. For the same Late Pliocene time period, and until all the other hominins were superseded by those belonging to the genus *Homo* (*ergaster/erectus*), the family picture is varied, not to say muddled, at least in East Africa where no less than five species grouped into two genus (*Australopithecus* and *Homo*) are present: *Australopithecus aethiopicus* and *A. boisei* (Lake Turkana basin), *Australopithecus garhi* (Middle Awash), *Homo rudolfensis* (Lake Turkana basin and Hadar) and another form of *Homo* sp. indet., or Early *Homo* (Omo, West Turkana).

Flaking

It cannot be denied that Late Pliocene lithic assemblages give off a general impression of overall simplicity. However, when each and every one of them is assessed by means of an in-depth technological analysis (see for instance the re-assessment of the Omo material, de la Torre in press), a more diverse and complex picture will no doubt emerge. On the basis of the first lithic artefacts aged 2.6 Myr discovered at Gona (Roche & Tiercelin 1977; 1980), and then from the artefacts of Lokalalei 1 at 2.3 Myr[8] (Kibunjia *et al.* 1992; Kibunjia 1994), I thought for a long time that they reflected not only quite simple and unvaried knapping sequences, but also a certain clumsiness, and poor manual dexterity (for instance, blows delivered with a strength ill-matched to the resistance of the raw material knapped, or inaccurately aimed). Although such simplicity and clumsiness resulted in

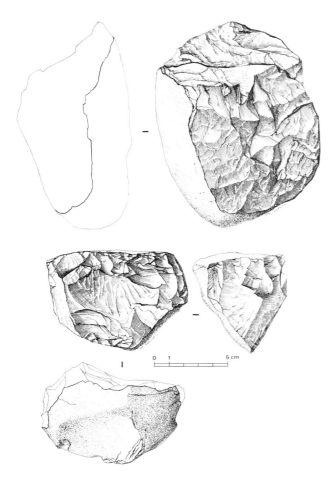

Figure 3.2. *Cores from Lokalalei 1 (West Turkana, Kenya, 2.34 Myr) showing many accidental breaks which occurred during knapping.*

the low production of flakes and a high proportion of accidental breaks observable on the cores as well as on the flakes (Fig. 3.2), it did not obscure the already controlled character of the technique employed (cf. *supra*), here direct percussion with a stone hammer. This assertion, however, has been fully contradicted by the data recovered from the 2.3 Myr site of Lokalalei 2C excavated in the Nachukui Formation, on the west side of Lake Turkana, in northern Kenya (Roche *et al.* 1999). Based on an in-depth technological analysis of the site (Delagnes & Roche in press), the points discussed below are those which have contributed most to the workshop and meet the focus of the present volume.

The Lokalalei 2C data

The Late Pliocene lithic assemblage of Lokalalei 2C yielded more then 2600 artefacts, which include whole and broken flakes, whole and broken cores, worked cobbles, hammerstones and unworked cobbles and pebbles. Owing to the spatially-restricted character of

this small site (exhaustively excavated over a total of 17 m²), and to the excellent preservation of the material, it was possible to reconstitute some of the cobbles knapped on site by fitting the discarded pieces back together. The 59 refitting groups account for over 10 per cent of the entire lithic assemblage. Several refitting groups are very substantial (between 10 to 39 refitted pieces, including the cores), thus allowing a step-by-step reconstitution of the work of the knapper(s). As a result, the degree of accuracy of the technological analysis is remarkable, and so far quite unique for such an ancient industry (Roche *et al.* 1999).

The Lokalalei 2C lithic assemblage (Delagnes & Roche in press) is made of two different sets. The most important set by far is characterized by an organized debitage of flakes, and is combined with a smaller set of cores and flakes corresponding to a simple blow-after-blow flaking. This simple expedient flaking, however, already requires the previously-described control of elementary percussion gestures. It is a very (if not the most) common way of intentionally splitting up the raw material to obtain sharp-edged objects during Late Pliocene times. It is the one evidenced in the nearby contemporaneous site of Lokalalei 1. This poorly-productive flaking process strongly contrasts, at Lokalalei 2C, with the more organized debitage from which a very high productivity ensues. For the 13 most important refitting groups, the average is 18 flakes per core, with a minimum number of 9 flakes. In one case, it could be shown that over 30 flakes were knapped from 2 fragments belonging to the same cobble (Fig. 3.3); in another, 50 flakes were knapped from the same whole cobble; in a third example, concerning 3 independently-knapped fragments[9] originating from the same cobble, production amounts to over 73 flakes for this cobble. So far, there is no example of such a high number of flakes being produced from a single chunk of raw material in the entire Late Pliocene, or even Early Pleistocene, record.[10]

Technologically speaking, the organized debitage of Lokalalei 2C is conducted on blanks that display natural peripheral striking platforms with immediately-serviceable flaking angles (<90°, ideal values ranging between 80° and 60°). These slightly acute flaking angles result from the asymmetric morphology of the blanks (angular cobbles, cobble fragments, flakes), which have a large flat face, the future flaking surface, opposed to a markedly convex and/or irregular one (Fig. 3.4). Debitage consists in achieving a series of sub-parallel and sometimes quite invasive removals, which lower the debitage surface while keeping it reasonably flat, ensuring that the initial suitable morphological attributes are maintained throughout reduction (Figs. 3.3 & 3.4).

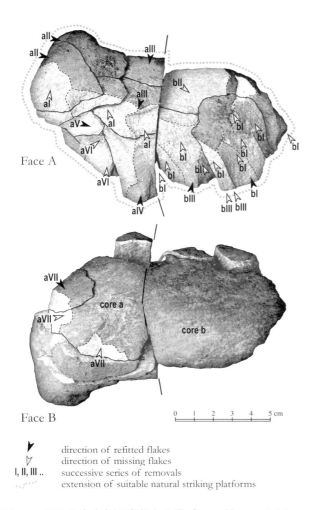

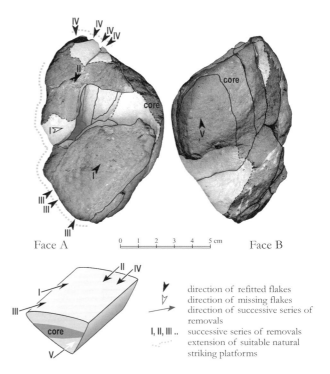

Figure 3.4. *Lokalalei 2C (West Turkana, Kenya, 2.34 Myr). Refitting set no. 9, a good example of the chosen cobble morphology (from Delagnes & Roche in press).*

Figure 3.3. *Lokalalei 2C (West Turkana, Kenya, 2.34 Myr). Refitting set no. 35. A minimum of 32 flakes have been removed from the core, 13 of which are refitted (from Delagnes & Roche in press).*

The analysis of the organized debitage thus led to the first conclusion that the Lokalalei knappers understood the striking platform constraints, which can be confirmed by the several other observations:

- blanks with suitable morphological attributes are selected from the mineral environment, or a cobble may be fractured in order to obtain the required morphology;
- then, throughout debitage, flaking is restricted to those portions of striking platforms which were serviceable;
- failed attempts on rounded or obtuse zones never occur. Better still, in several cases where some defect was liable to impede the progress of debitage, the striking platform has been rectified;
- another important aspect is the maintenance of the initial suitable morphology, by which a maximum

reduction of the core, resulting in a high productivity, is ensured. In order to keep the flaking surface flat, a short series of sub-parallel or converging removals travelling across part of the flaked surface were alternately struck from the different edges of the core, the latter being rotated between each series. In a similar way, repairing the consequences of minor knapping accidents for the purpose of flaking surface maintenance is also a recorded practise.

These observations lead to the next conclusion, which concerns the Lokalalei 2C knappers' high level of manual dexterity. This dexterity is mainly evidenced by a set of 18 hammerstones recovered from the site (Fig. 3.5). Although displaying a wide range of morphologies, these bear well-circumscribed impact zones (sometimes two or three on the same hammerstone) testifying to their repeated use according to a recurrent and perfectly well-controlled mode of prehension.[11] Moreover, the cores do not show any traces of impact damage from failed blows, delivered either way, behind the striking platform or at a tangent — which is exactly what is observable on the cores tentatively struck by Kanzi for instance (Toth *et al.* 1993; Schick *et al.* 1999; and pers. obs.). The high degree of control over the percussion gestures therefore complements

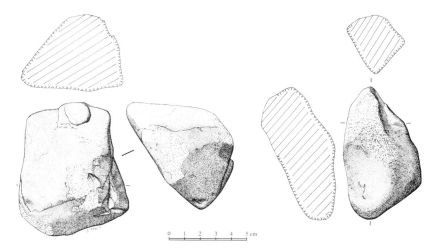

Figure 3.5. *Two hammerstones of Lokalalei 2C site (West Turkana, Kenya, 2.34 Myr).*

the ability to *anticipate* the repairing function of a removal (rectifying the striking platform, correcting a knapping accident) and the expected outcome of a series of removals (keeping the flaked surface flat). Lastly, consistency in the morpho-dimensional attributes of the pieces brought to the site also points to anticipation in the management of raw material transport: whereas small to medium-sized cobbles were brought to the site in one piece, larger cobbles were broken up prior to transport (possibly where the raw material was collected: Harmand in prep.) with the aim of obtaining, once again, a morphology suitable for the conducting of organized debitage.

The analysis of the organized debitage thus lead to the general conclusion that it goes beyond the simple stereotyped repetition of elementary knapping gestures that characterize other assemblages, and already evinces a certain degree of planning. In other words, the Lokalalei 2C knappers show a higher level of technological skill than documented so far for sites of the same period. The paucity of the archaeological documentation[12], however, and favourable circumstances for technological observations[13] should not be overlooked. Less scanty data and further descriptions backed by in-depth analyses will no doubt help bridge the technological gap that currently seems to exist between the Lokalalei 2C knappers and their sub-contemporaneous (*c.* 2.3 Myr) or even slightly younger (up to 1.9 Myr) counterparts, and will arguably lead to a finer analysis of the already identified intra-site and inter-site factors of variability (Delagnes & Roche in press).

There is, however, some evidence that shows the stone-knapping limitations of Lokalalei 2C hominins. While able to select and adequately take advantage

of suitable morphological attributes, they were also in a way dependent on these attributes. They were not capable of creating serviceable striking platforms when these did not occur naturally, nor of repairing the consequences of a major knapping accident when they drastically modified the morphology of the flaking surface. Their skills reached no further than the maintenance of suitable morphologies, and it is only with the next stage of technological development within the Early Pleistocene, *c.* 1.9/1.8 Myr, that prehistoric knappers display new abilities. Not only are they no longer dependant on the morphological attributes of raw materials, but by freeing themselves from these constraints they also became capable of creating new topographies. Through shaping operations in particular, the manufacture of normalized products would become possible, thanks to new techniques and methods.

Shaping

As mentioned in the introduction, flaking and shaping differ in their conception. The first one aims to produce in a repetitive manner a number of sharp-edged objects, the flakes, which are the intended products, while the core is the waste. The second one aims to manufacture one single object with a definite morphology, which is the intended object, the flakes being the waste. Also important is the fact that shaping could not have been achieved without a geometric mental template, whether the desired form applied to bifacial, polyhedral or trihedral pieces. The evolution of shaping shows how the mental template will become more precise, how the volumetric construction of the intended tool develops around the notion of symmetry and lastly, how this construction is eased by the introduction within the *chaîne opératoire* of the notion of predetermination.

Shaping generally involves two successive phases, roughing-out and finishing. It can bring into play a number of different techniques and sometimes results in series of highly-standardized products.

Polyhedral and spheroidal shaping
Polyhedrons and spheroids are similar in their concept (Texier & Roche 1995a; Roche & Texier 1995): the aim is to achieve a particular volume, more or less regularly distributed around a theoretical central point

(Fig. 3.6a). While in the case of polyhedrons this is a point of equilibrium, it can become a genuine point of symmetry in the case of spheroids, and even more so for bolas, which belong to the same *chaîne opératoire* but only come into being later during the Acheulean (Fig. 3.7). Such objects are facetted through shaping operations, and tend towards the shape of a sphere. What is required to achieve a spherical shape by direct percussion with a stone hammer, is a rational ordering of removals that takes into account angle criteria diametrically opposed to those required by flaking. As previously mentioned for Lokalalei (but this is a general law for flaking), the flaking surface and the striking platform should — for purely mechanical reasons — ideally form an angle lower than 90°. But to shape a polyhedral volume and to come as close as possible to a spherical shape, it is necessary to obtain and maintain much higher angle values. This can be attained by carrying out consecutive rather than contiguous removals, the negative of flake no. 1 being used as a striking platform for flake no. 2 and removals following either similar or perpendicular directions. Small short flakes can also be detached, the purpose of which is to open the angle formed by two removal negatives (Fig. 3.6b).[14] This type of shaping therefore contrasts with flaking both in the 'method' used and the final purpose, which is to give a particular shape to a chunk of raw material, rather than to detach the largest possible number of useable flakes. It follows that the flakes resulting from such knapping operations can be looked upon primarily as knapping waste, even though they may also be used for certain tasks.

Bifacial shaping
One of the best-known shaped objects is the handaxe, and ever since it first occurred this object has never disappeared from the archaeological landscape.

A handaxe is a bifacial object with two convex faces and a pointed extremity (tip) opposed to a rounded convex one (butt). It is shaped following two planes (Fig. 3.8): a bilateral equilibrium plane and a bifacial equilibrium plane (Roche & Texier 1995). In some cases, these equilibrium planes can tend towards genuine planes of symmetry. To obtain the intended planform, the knapper must have the capacity to assess and deal with successive unstabilized morphologies until the geometrical references of the handaxe are set up. In other words, he must have the capacity to assess and deal with inadequate morphologies, an ability which is far more skilled than simply exploiting adequate morphology.

However, although the first handaxes that appear in the archaeological record between 1.7 and 1.6 Myr

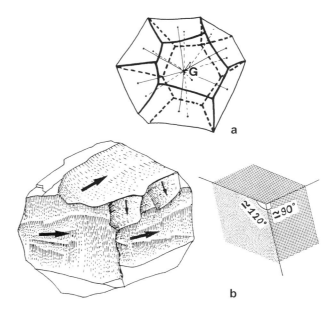

Figure 3.6. *Polyhedral shaping: a) theoretical central point of gravity (from Inizan et al. 1999); b) flaking angles and examples of removals organization (from Texier & Roche 1995a).*

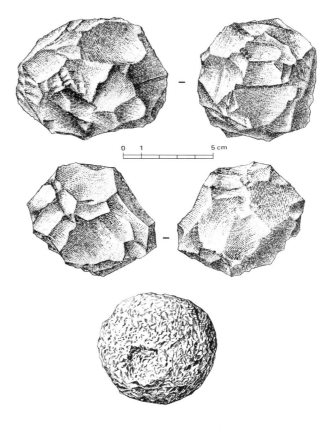

Figure 3.7. *Polyhedron, spheroid and bola of the Acheulean site of Isenya (c. 0.7 Myr).*

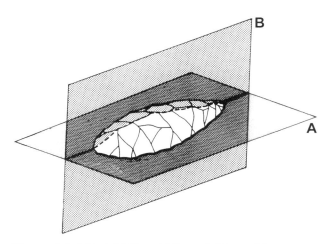

Figure 3.8. *Bifacial (A) and bilateral (B) equilibrium planes of a handaxe (from Inizan* et al. *1999).*

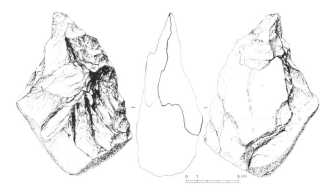

Figure 3.9. *Crude handaxe of the site of Kokiselei 4 (West Turkana, Kenya c. 1.7 Myr).*

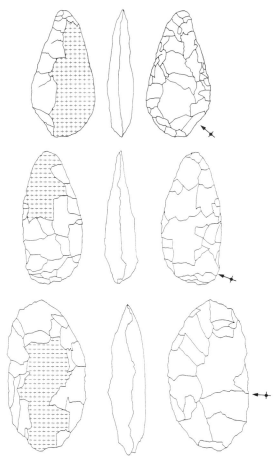

Figure 3.10. *Schematic drawings of handaxes from Isenya (Kenya, c. 0.7 Myr). The fill pattern indicates the remaining part of the lower face of the flake used as blank, and the dotted arrow the direction of percussion of this flake (from Texier & Roche 1995b).*

correspond to the handaxe mental construct as described above (a pointed tip opposed to a convex butt), the operational procedures were not yet mastered, in the sense that the handaxes were unbalanced and crudely made. A typical example is shown in Figure 3.9, which is a handaxe from the Early Acheulean site of Kokiselei 4, Kenya.[15] The site has yielded relatively massive lithic artefacts, comprising large cores, flakes, crude handaxes and trihedrals (Roche *et al.* 2003). This particular specimen is manufactured from a bulky and angular phonolite cobble. One end is directly shaped into a point by means of invasive bifacial removals along one edge and short unifacial removals along the other edge. This rather crudely made tip is opposed to a massive butt, which has remained cortical. The only technique used is direct percussion with a stone hammer, and the shaping operations are minimal. Nevertheless, the term of shaping is warranted as this specific action is repeated on a large number of specimens which all tend towards the same morphology.

Several hundreds of thousands of years will have to go by, however, before perfectly-balanced handaxes appear, reflecting more complex chains of actions. To illustrate this, reference is made to the large series of handaxes excavated from the Acheulean site of Isenya. The site is dated close to 0.7 Myr, that is to say 1 Myr after the appearance of the first handaxes in East Africa in sites like Kokiselei 4 (Roche *et al.* 2003) or Olduvai (Leakey 1971).

Although the methods brought into play may vary considerably, the process of bifacial shaping can be divided into two main phases: roughing out and finishing. Any blank, be it a cobble, a nodule, a flat tablet, a flake or a fragment, can be shaped into a handaxe. The more the morphology of the original blank departs from the intended final shape, the longer the shaping-out phase is likely to be. Conversely, only a limited number of roughing-out flakes is necessary

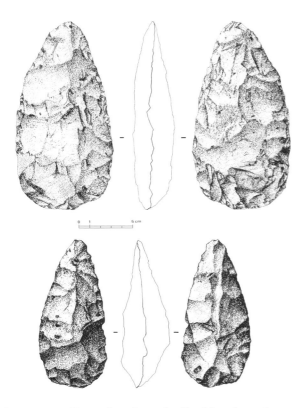

Figure 3.11. *Examples of standardized handaxes from Isenya (Kenya, c. 0.7 Myr). The raw material is a phonolite which outcrops very close to the site.*

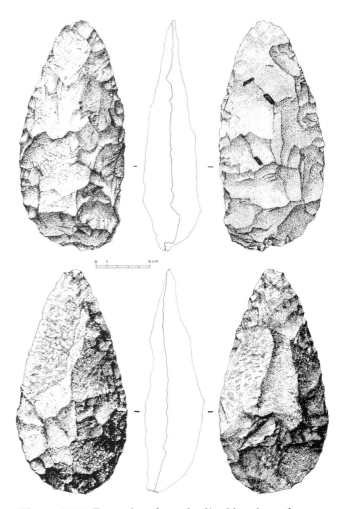

Figure 3.12. *Examples of standardized handaxes from Isenya (Kenya, c. 0.7 Myr). The raw material is a phonolite which outcrops very close to the site.*

in the case of handaxes manufactured from flat cobbles, tablets and, of course, flakes. In other words, the greater the technological effort expended in obtaining the blank (by detaching a large flake from a cobble, for instance), the smaller becomes the need to invest in the shaping out phase.

At this stage, it is apposite to introduce the notion of predetermination (Texier & Roche 1995b), also as a prerequisite to a discussion of the cleaver, another characteristic tool of the Acheulean and one from which this notion cannot be dissociated. In this Acheulean context, and for both handaxe and cleaver, predetermination refers to a particular conception of debitage, which is implemented through a series of technical actions carried out beforehand and at the very moment of the acquisition of a blank. The preparation of the core is essentially aimed at controlling one or several parameters enabling the knapper to obtain one, several, or all the morpho-technical attributes of the intended object. At the site of Isenya, it was shown that at a large majority of handaxes (over 800 pieces) were made from flakes obtained through various methods, but in several of them the concept of predetermination was identified. Indeed, the large

systematic remnants of a lower face of a flake observed on many handaxes indicate that the blank is a flake, but also suggest that the very convex lower face was obtained on purpose (Figs. 3.10–3.12). This convexity obtained by debitage process is very similar to a convexity habitually obtained by shaping (Texier & Roche 1995b). It could, moreover, be specified through further observations that these partially-shaped handaxes were made from short and wide *déjeté* flakes with a very convex lower face. These bifacial pieces possess the same morphological attributes as the handaxes manufactured by painstaking shaping and are quite as well balanced, but a substantial economy in gestures and raw material has been achieved through predetermination.

A cleaver is by definition a tool made from a flake (Tixier 1956), which depends upon the appearance of the concept of predetermination. Opposed to a more

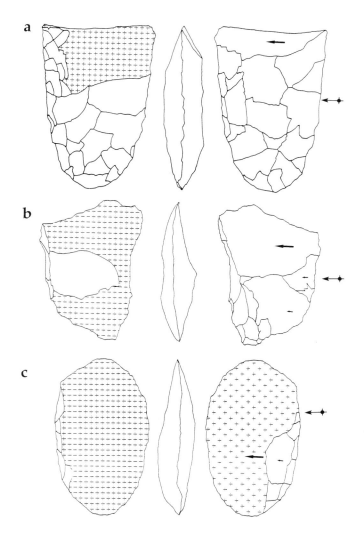

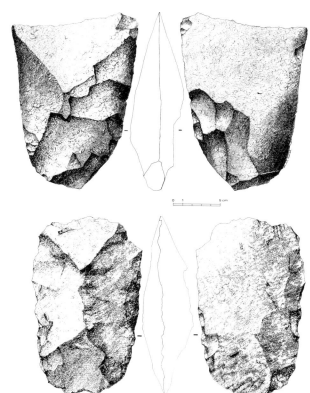

a

b

c

Figure 3.13. *Schematic drawings of cleavers from Isenya (Kenya, c. 0.7 Myr): a) ordinary blank; b) 'one-blow' cleaver (almost no finishing retouches); and c) cleaver on Kombewa flake (id.). The fill pattern indicates the remaining part of the lower face of the flake used as blank, the dotted arrow the direction of percussion of the flake and bold simple arrow the direction of the predeterminant flakes (from Texier & Roche 1995b).*

Figure 3.14. *Cleavers from Isenya (Kenya, c. 0.7 Myr).*

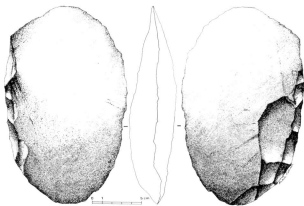

Figure 3.15. *Cleavers from Isenya (Kenya, c. 0.7 Myr).*

or less convex extremity, its terminal bevelled cutting edge (the cleaver bit) results from the intersection of two unretouched planes, that is to say the lower face of the flake blank (or cleaver-flake), and the negative of one (sometimes two) flake(s) predetermined on the core prior to the detachment of the cleaver-flake. At Isenya, a vast majority of the cleavers (over 1300 pieces) results from a unipolar exploitation of the cores, so that the debitage axis of the predetermining flake and that of the original flake blank follow identical or slightly converging directions (Fig. 3.13). Three

per cent of these cleavers, however, are supported by Kombewa[16] flakes, testifying thereby to an even higher degree of predetermination

the intersection of the lower convex face of the cleaver-flake with the regular convex debitage surface (former lower face) of the core flake nearly always generates an ideally convex cleaver edge (Texier & Roche 1995b).

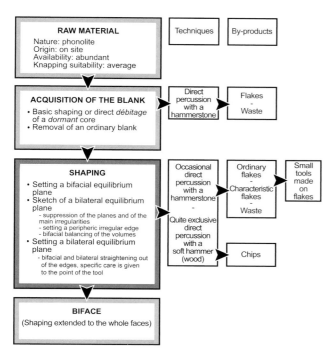

Figure 3.16. *Isenya (Kenya, c. 0.7 Myr), operational scheme for handaxe made on ordinary flaked blank (from Texier & Roche 1995b).*

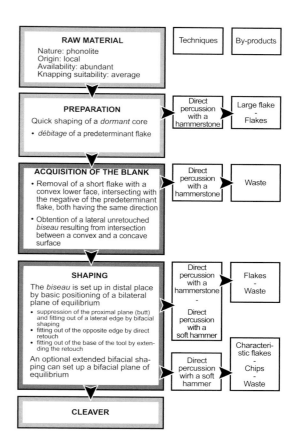

Figure 3.18. *Isenya (Kenya, c. 0.7 Myr), operational scheme for cleaver made on predetermined flaked blank (from Texier & Roche 1995b).*

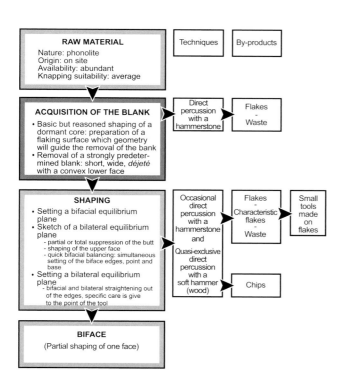

Figure 3.17. *Isenya (Kenya, c. 0.7 Myr), operational scheme for handaxe made on predetermined flaked blank (from Texier & Roche 1995b).*

It also generates two convex faces, which do not require any further roughing out to be perfectly balanced, with the possible exception of a few removals intended to suppress or thin the butt-bulb part of the cleaver-flake (Figs. 3.13–3.15).

As for finishing, this is an optional operation. Quite often — and mainly where cleavers are concerned — it does not further modify the overall intended shape. Its main purpose is to perfect the symmetry — or the balance — of the piece and even more so to trim the edges so that they are well delineated. At Isenya, this operation was generally conducted with a soft hammer, most probably of vegetable origin, whereas detaching the large flake blanks could only have been achieved with a stone hammer, also required for the initial removals of the roughing-out phase.[17] Thus, at least two, and perhaps three, different knapping tools are successively used in the course of the manufacture of handaxes and cleavers: a more bulky stone hammer for the initial debitage of the flake

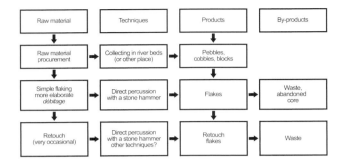

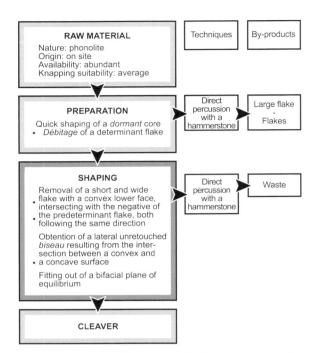

Figure 3.19. *Isenya (Kenya, c. 0.7 Myr), operational scheme for handaxe made on predetermined flaked blank, with almost no shaping and no retouch (from Texier & Roche 1995b).*

blanks than for the subsequent roughing-out phases, a soft hammer for the finishing phases.

Conclusion

The site of Isenya formed 2 Myr after the earliest acknowledged traces of stone knapping resulting from the technical actions of either *Australopithecus* or/and Early *Homo*, and 1 Myr after the inception of the Acheulean resulting from the technical action of *Homo erectus*. This site — one example among many such other Middle Pleistocene occurrences — has been used here to illustrate the potential complexity of bifacial shaping, and to show that this complexity does not necessarily require — although it sometimes does — lengthier *chaînes opératoires* (Roche & Texier 1991). On the contrary, a high degree of predetermination in the acquisition of a blank the shape of which comes as close as possible to that of the completed object may lead to a substantial economy in gestures. Whatever the method used, however, the end products — handaxes or cleavers — display remarkably consistent morphological attributes, with variations pertaining exclusively or mainly to size. The characteristics of some of the Isenya shaping *chaînes opératoires* are summarized in Figures 3.16 to 3.19. A comparison between these diagrams and the diagram summarizing

Figure 3.20. *Lokalalei 2C (West Turkana, Kenya, 2.34 Myr). Operational scheme for simple flaking and more elaborate debitage.*

the flaking *chaîne opératoire* at Lokalalei 2C (Fig. 3.20) highlights the conceptual and operational distances separating these different operations. Whatever the distance, however, these technical operations are backed in each and every case by a pre-existing project and a psychomotor skill. As previously discussed, shaping, and more essentially bifacial shaping, corresponds to a concept that is in contrast to the concept of debitage, and certainly also meets other new technical needs. With the development of shaping processes during the Early Pleistocene — which also corresponds to the development of the genus *homo* — the range of the psychomotor abilities brought into play expands, knapping principles stabilize and are converted into methods as they become more elaborate, more complex and perceptible on a long-time basis, and technical innovations increase in number.

But before this and for a very long period of time, the aim of hominin stone knappers has arguably been to produce objects endowed with cutting properties, i.e. flakes with razor-sharp edges. This aim is achieved through a single specific type of action brought to bear on the raw material, the action of flaking.

Notes

1. A very characteristic and predictable fracture pattern (smooth, curved and shell-shaped) produced by the properties of such a material. In fracture mechanics, a conchoidal fracture is characteristic of the fractures that develop in brittle materials (very strong in compression and very weak in tension).

2. Identical effects resulting from identical causes, it occasionally happens that a natural and/or accidental shock between two such elements occurs according to the essential prerequisites of conchoidal fracture, in particular where the angle of incidence is concerned. This will result in the detachment of a naturally (or accidentally) produced flake, which displays the same characteristics as a flake that is intentionally detached

3. This implies, however, that such cutting properties met very important needs.

4. Cutting or scraping requires a sharp edge. Hammering, or pounding, do not necessitate peculiar morphological properties, only hardness, and can be performed with any solid implement, including natural stones.

5. All the definitions given in this section are from Inizan *et al.* 2000.

6. A technique is the practical manner of accomplishing a particular task.

7. A method is an orderly sequence of actions carried out according to one or more techniques and guided by a rational plan.

8. Lokalaei 1 is the first Pliocene site to have been excavated within the Nachukui Formation in the Turkana Basin. The lithic material it contains is composed of unworked cobbles, flakes and crude cores, which correspond to simple flaking conducted with poor skill.

9. First the original core, and then a large flake detached from this core and broken in half in the process (a relatively common knapping accident), both parts being recycled as cores.

10. It should, however, be stressed that this productivity could never have been demonstrated without the refittings and their painstaking analysis.

11. Hammerstones used with lesser control will display multiple and randomly-distributed impact zones.

12. Relating to under a dozen sites with a fully reliable chrono-stratigraphic context of occurrence.

13. Our analytical approach relies very heavily on the Lokalalei 2C refittings, however the number of very old sites offering similar refitting possibilities is undoubtedly — and unfortunately — very small.

14. During a subsequent stage of the *chaîne opératoire* and when seeking to achieve sub-spheroids or spheroids, this angle is even further opened by the crushing of the ridges formed by the intersecting removal negatives.

15. Kokiselei 4 is one of the oldest (if not the oldest) East African Acheulean sites.

16. Kombewa method: a method for obtaining a circular, semi-circular or elliptical flake. The shape is predetermined by the convexity of the lower face of another flake, previously knapped to serve as a core. An unretouched Kombewa flake thus possesses two lower faces. (Inizan *et al.* 1999).

17. The nature of the hammers used can be quite reliably inferred from some of the scars displayed by the flakes — particularly on their butts.

Acknowledgements

We thank the Government of Kenya (Office of the President) and the Board of Governors of the National Museums of Kenya to allow the work at Isenya and in West Turkana. This work was funded by the French Ministry of Foreign Affairs (*Sous – Direction de la Recherche*) and by the CNRS.

References

Boesch, C. & H. Boesch-Achermann, 2000. *The Chimpanzees of the Tai Forest: Behavioural Ecology and Evolution*. Oxford: Oxford University Press.

Boesch, C., P. Marchesi, N. Marchesi, B. Fruth & F. Joulian, 1994. Is nut cracking in wild chimpanzees a cultural behaviour. *Journal of Human Evolution* 26, 325–38.

Chavaillon, J., 1976. Evidence for the technical practices of early pleistocene hominids, Shingure Formation, Lower Omo Valley, Ethiopia, in *Earliest Man and Environment in the Lake Rudolf Basin: Stratigraphy, Paleoecology, and Evolution*, eds. Y. Coppens, F.C. Howell, L. Isaac & E.F. Leakey. Chicago (IL): University of Chicago Press, 565–73.

de Heinzelin J., J. Desmond Clark, T. White, W. Hart, P. Renne, G. Woldegabriel, Y. Beyene & E. Vrba, 1999. Environment and behaviour of 2.5-million-year-old Bouri hominids. *Science* 284, 625–9.

de la Torre, I., in press. Omo revisited: evaluating the technological skill of Pliocene hominids. *Current Anthropology*.

Delagnes, A. & H. Roche, in press. Late hominids knapping skills: the case of Lokalalei 2C, West Turkana, Kenya. *Journal of Human Evolution*.

Harmand, S., in prep. Matières premières et comportements économiques dans les gisements plio-pléistocènes de l'Ouest Turkana, Kenya. Unpublished Doctoral thesis, Université de Paris X-Nanterre.

Inizan, M.-L., M. Reduron-Ballinger, H. Roche & J. Tixier, 1999. *Technology and Terminology of Knapped Stone.* (Préhistoire de la Pierre taillée 5.) Nanterre: CREP.

Julien, M., 1992. Du fossile directeur à la chaîne opératoire: evolution de l'interprétation des ensembles lihiques et osseux en France, in *La préhistoire dans le monde.* (Nouvelle Clio.) Paris: P.U.F., 163–93.

Kibunjia, M., 1994. Pliocene archaeological occurences in the Lake Turkana basin. *Journal of Human Evolution* 27, 159–71.

Kibunjia, M., H. Roche, F.H. Brown & R.E.F. Leakey, 1992. Pliocene and Pleistocene archaeological sites west of Lake Turkana, Kenya. *Journal of Human Evolution* 23, 431–8.

Kimbel, W.H., R.C. Walter, D.C. Johanson, K.E. Reed, J.L. Aronson, Z. Assefa, C.W. Marean, G.G. Eck, R. Bobe-Quinteros, E. Hovers, Y. Rak, C. Vondra, T. Yemane, D. York, Y. Chen, N.M. Evensen & P.E. Smith, 1996. Late Pliocene *Homo* and Oldowan tools from the Hadar formation (Kada Hadar Member), Ethiopia. *Journal of Human Evolution* 31, 549–61.

Leakey, M., 1971. *Olduvai Gorge*, vol. 3. Cambridge: Cambridge University Press.

McGrew, W.C., 1992. *Chimpanzee Material Culture: Implications for Human Evolution*. Cambridge: Cambridge University Press.

Merrick, H.V. & J.P.S. Merrick, 1976. Archaeological occurrences of earlier pleistocene age from the Shungura Formation, in *Earliest Man and Environment in the Lake Rudolf Basin: Stratigraphy, Paleoecology, and Evolution*, eds. Y. Coppens, F.C. Howell, L. Isaac & E.F. Leakey.

Chicago (IL): University of Chicago Press, 574–84.

Pelegrin, J. & P.-J. Texier, 2004. Les techniques de taille de la pierre préhistoriques. *Dossier de l'Archéologie* 290, 26–35.

Plummer, T., L. Bishop, P. Ditchfield & J. Hicks, 1999. Research on Late Pliocene Oldowan sites at Kanjera South, Kenya. *Journal of Human Evolution* 36, 151–70.

Roche, H. & P.-J. Texier, 1991. La notion de complexité dans un ensemble lithique. Application aux séries acheuléennes d'Isenya (Kenya), in *25 d'Etudes Technologiques en Préhistoire, XI ème Rencontres Internationales d'Archéologie et d'Histoire d'Antibes*. Juan-les- Pins: Editions APDCA, 99–108.

Roche, H. & P.-J. Texier, 1995. Evaluation of technical competence of *Homo erectus* in East Africa during Middle Pleistocene, in *Pithecanthropus Centennial 1893–1993: Human Evolution in its Ecological Context*, vol. 1: *Paleoanthropology: Evolution and Ecology of* Homo erectus. Leiden, Pays-Bas: Royal Netherlands Academy of Arts and Sciences, 153–67.

Roche, H. & J.-J. Tiercelin, 1977. Découverte d'une industrie lithique ancienne *in situ* dans la formation de Hadar, Afar central, Ethiopie. *Comptes rendus de l'Académie des sciences Paris* Série D, 1871–4.

Roche, H. & J.-J. Tiercelin, 1980. Industries lithiques de la formation plio-pléistocene d'Hadar Ethiopie (campagne 1976), in *Proceedings, VIIth Panafrican Congress of Prehistory and Quaternary Studies*, eds. R.E.F. Leakey & B.A. Ogot. Nairobi: TILLMIAP, 194–9.

Roche, H., A. Delagnes, J.-P. Brugal, C.S. Feibel, M. Kibunja, V. Mourre & P.-J. Texier, 1999. Early hominid stone tool production and technical skill 2.34 Myr ago, in West Turkana, Kenya. *Nature* 399, 57–60.

Roche, H., J.-P. Brugal, A. Delagnes, C.S. Feibel, S. Harmand, M. Kibunjia, S. Prat & P.-J. Texier, 2003. Les sites archéologiques plio-pléistocènes de la Formation de Nachukui, Ouest Turkana, Kenya: bilan synthétique 1997–2001. *Palévolution* 2, 663–73.

Schick, K.D., N. Toth, G. Garufi, E.S. Savage-Rumbaugh, D. Rumbaugh & R. Sevcik, 1999. Continuing investigations into the stone tool-making and tool-using capabilities of a bonobo. *Journal of Archaeological Science* 26, 821–32.

Semaw, S., P. Renne, J.W.K. Harris, C. Feibel, R.L. Bernor, N. Fesseha & K. Mowbray, 1997. 2.5-million-year-old stone tools from Gona, Ethiopia. *Nature* 385, 333–6.

Semaw, S., M.J. Rogers, J. Quade, P.R. Renne, R.F. Butler, M. Dominguez-Rodrigo, D. Stout, W.S. Hart, T. Pickering & S.W. Simpson, 2003. 2.6-million-year-old stone tools and associated bones from OGS-6 and OGS-7, Gona, Afar, Ethiopia. *Journal of Human Evolution* 5, 169–77.

Texier, P.-J. & H. Roche, 1995a. Polyèdre, sphéroide et bola: des segments plus ou moins longs d'une même chaîne opératoire. *Cahier Noir* 7, 31–40.

Texier P.-J. & H. Roche, 1995b. The impact of predetermination on the development of some acheulean *chaînes opératoires*, in *Evolución humana en Europa y los yacimientos de la Sierra Atapuerca*, ed. J. Bermudez de Castro. Junta de Castilla y León, 403–20.

Tixier, J., 1956. Le hachereau dans l'Acheuléen nord-africain. Notes typologiques, in *Congrès Préhistorique de France*, XV. Poitiers, 914–23.

Toth, N., K. Schick, E.S. Savage-Rumbaugh, R.A. Sevcik & D.M. Rumbaugh, 1993. Pan the tool-maker: investigations into the stone tool-making and tool-using capabilities of a bonobo (*Pan paniscus*). *Journal of Archaeological Science* 20, 81–91.

Section B

Stone Knapping:
Characterizing the Skills Involved

Skills Involved in Stone Knapping

Chapter 4

Stone Knapping:
Khambhat (India), a Unique Opportunity?

Blandine Bril, Valentine Roux & Gilles Dietrich

Cambay is one of the very rare places in the world where the stone-knapping technique still responds to the principles of the conchoidal fracture. The technique practised is an indirect percussion by counter-blow and is used for making stone beads. This technique is a recent one in the history of techniques. It can provide, however, an appropriate reference situation to study the skills involved in stone knapping. In effect, given that for all stone-knapping techniques, the stable parameters of conchoidal fracture must be controlled, we can assume then that similar skills are involved. In order to characterize the skills involved in stone knapping in Cambay, a program of field experimentation was developed. At Cambay, the knappers are distinguished according to different levels of competence. In psychology, studies of apprenticeship are often based on transfer tasks. We tested the following hypothesis: the degree of success attained in modified situations reflects the capacities of adjustment, flexibility and planning of the artisan. A highly-skilled artisan should be capable of transferring his planning and motor skills to new situations. In addition, we would expect the differences that characterize distinct expertise levels to be amplified in the context of transfer tasks. Modifications were introduced into the knapping activity of the artisan, varying the nature of the raw material to be worked (glass versus stone) and the objective to be attained (bead dimensions and shapes). We worked with 12 artisans distributed equally among two levels of expertise: a high-level, and a low-level. The participants were instructed to produce superior-quality beads. The ensemble of fabrication processes of each bead was recorded with a video camera and an accelerometer attached to the head of the knapper's hammer in order to analyze the succession of actions realized, as well as the characteristics of the elementary movements and their sequencing.

Our results emphasize the critical role of the elementary movement and as such raise the question of the complexity of the elementary gestures produced by first hominins when knapping stone and their specificity as compared to the technological gestures produced by non-human primates. We make here the hypothesis that the knapping gestures reveal cognitivo-motor skills proper to hominins.

Our understanding of stone-knapping skills depends on the possibility of working with people who have the ability to knap stone, producing flakes characterized by a conchoidal fracture (see J. Pelegrin

this volume). The main characteristic of stone knapping is that flaking must obey the conchoidal fracture. A simple fracture of the cobble would make the whole process of knapping totally out of control (Pelegrin this volume). Consequently split breaking cannot lead to a controlled shape.

This chapter relates an experimental field study on stone knapping with Indian craftsmen (Khambhat, Gujarat). The aim of this study was to find out what distinguishes expert knappers from less expert ones (Bril *et al.* 2000; Roux *et al.* 1995). The rationale of the study was the following: if we assume that the con-

Figure 4.1. *Stone knapping in Khambhat: a) a craftsman knapping a stone bead, using a buffalo hammer and an iron bar as anvil; b) counter-blow technique; c) two successive flake removals.*

choidal fracture by itself imposes the characteristics of the action, then we can assume that regardless of the technique used to produce such a fracture, the necessary skills involved have much in common. Furthermore, the study of different levels of expertise should help understand what kinds of abilities are involved and consequently what kind of abilities have to be developed during the learning process.

Now, if we accept this groundwork, we may hypothesize that an analysis of any present-day technique that produces flakes (detached by means of a conchoidal fracture) will shed light on our understanding of the necessary capacities involved in stone knapping regardless of the historical period concerned, and regardless of the technique involved.

Apart from modern experimental knappers reproducing prehistoric techniques, only a handful of people around the world still knap stone as a common task (see Stout this volume). Khambhat is one of the very rare places in the world were the stone-knapping technique still follows the principles of the conchoidal fracture. However, although the technique used in Khambhat uses indirect percussion which differs from the direct percussion that characterized ancient prehistoric lithic technologies (Pelegrin this volume) or the last human stone tool-

maker technique in New Guinea (Stout 2002; and this volume), the task at hand is analogous, i.e. making a final product having a specific shape well-defined in advance.

In this chapter, following a description of the technique and methods of knapping stone used in Khambhat, we shall discuss the theoretical framework referred to in our analysis of expertise in stone knapping, and then present a field experiment designed to work on the question of the 'nature' of the skills involved depending on the level of expertise.

Stone knapping: why is Khambhat a unique opportunity?

Nowadays, knapping stone as a regular craft activity is exceptional. In Khambhat, more commonly known as Cambay (name given before India's independence), craftsmen still manufacture carnelian and agate beads using a technique that meets the conchoidal fracture constraints. The production of beads is in the hands of workshops which produce either superior-quality objects or objects of a lower quality. We saw this organization of production as a unique opportunity to carry out a study of stone-knapping skills. Before moving into the study, we shall describe the *technique*

Ellipsoid bead

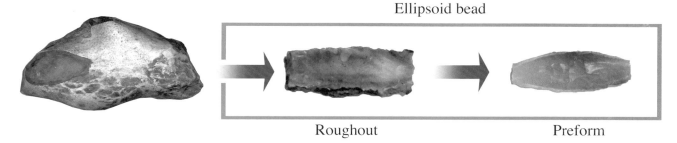

Roughout   Preform

Figure 4.2. *The two stages of bead fabrication, from cobble to roughout, and from roughout to preform. The second stage only is discussed in this chapter.*

used to detach a flake, and the *method* employed to produce beads of different shapes.

The **technique**: *an 'indirect percussion by rebound'*

The knapping *technique* in use in Khambhat employs an original principle. It has been described as an 'indirect percussion by counter-blows' (Pelegrin 1993; 2000). The knapper, sitting on a rug on the ground, uses two tools jointly (Fig. 4.1):

- a sharp-pointed iron bar about fifty centimetres long and two centimetres thick, stuck obliquely into the ground in front of the knapper;
- a buffalo-horn hammer mounted on a thin wooden stick.

To detach a flake, the knapper holds the piece of stone to be knapped between his fingers and applies the edge of the piece against the pointed tip of the iron bar. The hammer held in the other hand strikes the piece to detach a flake from the point of contact with the iron bar. This technique makes it possible to detach flakes of various shapes, sizes, and thickness. The craftsman uses hammers of different sizes and weights depending on the size of the core and of the flake to be detached. The weight of the head of the hammer varies approximately from 15 to 50 grams. The head of the hammer gets worn quite rapidly and is replaced after a few dozen hours of use. The stick, which is quite flexible, weighs between 7 and 10 grams. The upper point of the iron bar is sharpened from time to time.

The method of knapping

The *method* of knapping is an orderly set of functional operations that must be undertaken to obtain the desired shape, starting from the raw material (see Fig. 4.2). Bead knapping is a two-staged process. First, in an initial reduction phase, a roughout blank is produced (see Roux & David this volume). The roughout displays its basic geometric characteristics which are determined by the intended final shape — i.e. the

roughout for a spherical bead is a cube; for a cylindrical or ellipsoidal bead a parallelepiped roughout is knapped. The second phase changes the roughout to a preform, which is then ground, drilled, polished and buffed (for more details see Roux 2000).

For example, to knap a ellipsoid preform, you need to start with a roughout whose shape is a parallelepiped with four crests; and the following operations must be performed (Fig. 4.3):

- *calibration of the crests*, final shaping of the roughout and regularization of the crests through transversal removals in order to achieve successful fluting;
- *end preparation*, preparation of micro-platforms prior to crest fluting or axial removal;
- *crest fluting*, axial removals of the crest from the end;
- *axial removals* from the end, bladelet-like;
- *reduction of the residual crest* through very short transversal flakes;
- *end finishing* by shorter axial removals.

Each operation, or sub-goal, is achieved by chaining a succession of flake removals, which characteristics are dictated by the operation.

Figure 4.3 describes the succession of operations required to produce a truncated ellipsoid preform. It shows the succession of steps required as a previous condition for the next step, i.e. for example, end preparation is a prerequisite for fluting — i.e. preparing the micro-platform to achieve successful fluting. Once the prerequisite is met, the sequence of operations may be unfolded in various ways that we call strategies. The calibration of the crest may either be performed successively from the first crest to the fourth, with end preparation performed next, and so on; or after the first crest calibration, the craftsman may decide to prepare a micro-platform to perform the fluting of that crest, and then resume calibration of the second crest, and so on. Figure 4.4 summarizes the four main theoretical strategies that can be chosen to produce an ellipsoid preform from a parallelepipedic roughout.

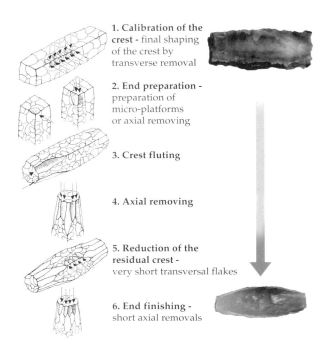

1. **Calibration of the crest** - final shaping of the crest by transverse removal

2. **End preparation** - preparation of micro-platforms or axial removing

3. **Crest fluting**

4. **Axial removing**

5. **Reduction of the residual crest** - very short transversal flakes

6. **End finishing** - short axial removals

Figure 4.3. *The different sub-goals necessary to transform a parallelepipedal roughout into a ellipsoidal preform.*

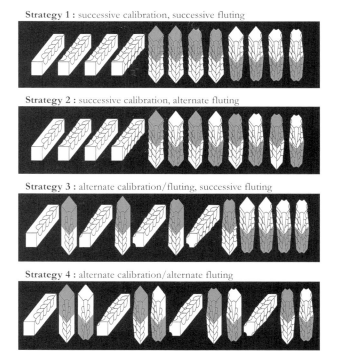

Strategy 1 : successive calibration, successive fluting

Strategy 2 : successive calibration, alternate fluting

Strategy 3 : alternate calibration/fluting, successive fluting

Strategy 4 : alternate calibration/alternate fluting

Figure 4.4. *The four theoretical strategies summarizing the different paths from calibration of the crests to the fluting of the four crests.*

Knapping a bead: from goal to movements to end product

How does the wish to knap a specific shape from a piece of raw material give rise to a sequence of movements, resulting in a piece of stone of a specific shape? In other words, what is the process that causes the desired goal-oriented action — knapping a specific shape — to be used? And what are the mechanisms called upon to give rise to this process?

Reaching this aim obviously requires some knowledge of the task at hand. Once again, what does this mean? Or how can we bridge the gap between the idea 'I want to make a small regular spherical bead or a long ellipsoidal one' and the behaviour that will allow the production of such a bead? What are the prerequisites to succeed, that is what 'knowledge', 'skill' and 'dexterity' must have been acquired to be able to perform such a task?

How is the goal of the action, here a piece of stone of the desired shape 'the knapper has in mind' (Pelegrin this volume) determined by its 'geometric objective', reached through a sequence of movements? What brings the 'template' — the 'image' — into existence?

The first issue here is to define a complex motor skill that clearly differentiates an action from the movements that allow this action to be carried out. An action may be referred to along two dimensions: the goal, referring to the intentional aspect of the action, and the means, that is the operational aspect of it, in other words, the way the goal is reached (Connoly & Dalgleish 1989):

1. In stone knapping, the goal is the production of a stone of a certain shape. It may be either a chopper with a cutting edge as for the Oldowan choppers, or a whole shaped object such as the tools described in this volume by Roche and Pelegrin, or the beads of various qualities knapped by the craftsmen in Khambhat.

2. The means correspond to a succession of operations performed to reach the goal. This process corresponds to the 'actualization' of the method. Each craftsman may have his own way of working out the succession of operations necessary to reach the desired shape: this process is designated by the *course of action*. The method, and consequently the sequence of operations, vary according to the shape to be produced (Roux & Pelegrin 1989; Pelegrin 2000). The sequence of actions performed by the craftsman, that is the *course of action*, corresponds to the 'actualization' of one of the basic strategies used in Khambhat to obtain beads of different qualities and shapes. According to our terminology, the course of action is composed of a

sequence of sub-goals. A sub-goal corresponds to the actualization of an operation, that is when and how a craftsman carries out an operation. Such a definition helps differentiate planning 'What to do' *vs* planning 'How to do it'. Here again difficulties arise. The process of performing an action, once the goal is set, is not easy to describe. An operational way to split up a complex sequence of actions is to refer to the three levels put forward by Richard (1990) among others.

1. The first level concerns the overall organization of the task: the way the method is actualized in a succession of functional actions in order to complete the task. It is referred to as the *course of action*. In other words, the course of action corresponds to the way each craftsman carries out the different operations to produce the intended shape, that is a chaining of sub-goals.

2. The intermediate level expresses the way the operations are actualized, that is how the sub-goals are carried out. Most of the time — but not always — carrying out a sub-goal requires performing a succession of elementary actions — the third level. For example, as we have described, calibration is an operation that may require dozens of flake removals. On the other hand, fluting may be achieved with a single strike. In addition, calibration may be performed in different ways: either by a succession of adjacent strikes along one edge, going one way, and then back along the crest but from the other side, or carried out by a succession of alternate flaking along the crest (Fig. 4.5).

3. The last level, the elementary action, concerns any goal-oriented action that cannot — functionally — be split into parts. In the case of knapping it refers to the removal of one flake typified by the conchoidal fracture. This level corresponds to the *actualization* of the technique, that is the way a craftsman performs the movement that allows the action to come into existence. The characteristics of the flake can be manifold and are determined by the operation to be carried out. In the case of calibration for example, the flake is very thin and more or less disc-shaped. On the other hand, fluting corresponds to a thick, long flake, and axial removal to a long, bladelet-like flake. End finishing is characterized by small, thin flakes. All of these respond to the same technique. Performing any of these strikes, however, requires adapting the movement in such a way as to successfully produce the proper removal. Indeed it is not the movement itself that must be examined but what the movement allows for, that is the exact relative position and force ratio of the stone, the hammer

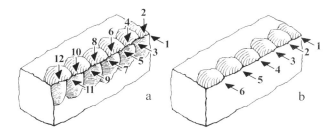

Figure 4.5. *Two ways of actualization of the calibration operation: a) succession of alternate flakings along the crest; b) succession of adjacent flakings along the crest.*

and the anvil. As we can see, to be effective the actualization of the technique necessitates a very high degree of flexibility.

The interesting point here is the following: when planning is alluded to, to which level does it refer: the planning of a succession of sub-goals, the planning of the succession of strikes necessary to carry out a sub-goal or the planning of the striking movement? To answer this question, we need to clearly differentiate the level referred to. The different action planning theories usually refer to a level of action, rarely to all three levels simultaneously. Yet, if one wants to understand what a skilled behaviour refers to, what expertise means, a theory linking together the three levels of action as defined here must be used.

As discussed in the introductory chapter the first theoretical approach, often referred to as the 'motor-system approach', emphasizes an information-processing perspective, the existence of a kind of 'central representation', 'internal models' and 'motor commands'. The second theoretical approach, referred to as the 'action-system approach' stresses the reciprocal role of the organism and the environment acting as a set of constraints from which behaviour emerges. Three types of constraints may be considered (Newell 1986; 1996): the organism, the task and the environment (see Fig. 4.6). Any change in one of these three sub-system may produce a different outcome. This is particularly explicit in the case of tool use. Depending on the type of hammer (element of the environment) used for example, the constraints on the hammering movements will be different due to the weight of the head of the hammer and/or the length of the handle. As a consequence the outcome will be different.

A skilled action combines precision, flexibility, adaptation, smoothness, regularity, optimization and swiftness (Bernstein 1996; Ericsson & Lehmann 1996). In other words, an expert is able to carry out an action in any situation and under all conditions. The level of expertise refers to the degree attained by each of the qualities of action listed here.

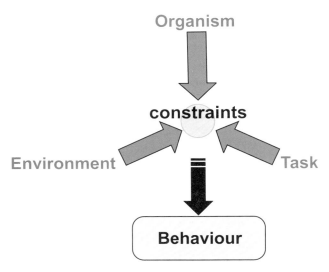

Figure 4.6. *The three main types of constraints that set up the work space (adapted from Newell 1986).*

How can we characterize the abilities of a high-level expert compared to a low-level expert? What specific capacity or aptitude or ability does the expert possess that the less expert does not have? Does the expert have a better 'mental representation' of the action of the goal to be reached? Or does the expert have an extensive capacity to detect the appropriate information resulting from the ongoing course of action coupled with the ability to incorporate these into his action?

To investigate such questions it is necessary first to more clearly outline the different components such a task entails. These questions about expertise were at the origin of the field experiment reported in this chapter.

A field experiment

The experiment described in this chapter was designed to uncover the features that might distinguish high-level experts from lower-level experts. Our aim was to tentatively disentangle the different dimensions of expertise, i.e. the underlying abilities, controlled factors, skills and knowledge involved.

Experimental setting
The motivation of the experiment was twofold. First, the craftsmen should be in a situation as close as possible to their everyday activity. Second, the data obtained should allow for analysis of parameters usually studied in laboratory experimental situations. To satisfy these criteria we considered an experimental paradigm based on the capacity of transfer and generalization. We assumed that the higher the dexterity of

the craftsmen, the higher their capacity of transferring to new situations.

The experiment was based introducing new situations to the craftsmen. They had to transfer their knowledge to a new raw material and to knapping shapes that were unknown or at least unusual to them.

The new raw material chosen was glass. Three reasons justify this choice:
1. As far as knapping is concerned, the mechanical properties of glass are the same as chalcedony (conchoidal fracture).
2. Glass is not as hard as chalcedony, presenting a basic difference with the raw material commonly knapped.
3. Glass also provides a homogeneous raw material and the possibility to start from a roughout of exactly the same size and weight for all the craftsmen; consequently glass as a raw material allows for a more reliable interpretation of the results obtained.

The main hypothesis was the following: the participants' ability to transfer their knapping knowledge to the new raw material and new shapes indicate their level of dexterity.

Participants
The choice of participants of different levels of expertise derived from the existence in Khambhat of workshops specialized in the production of objects of different quality. Indeed, the bead-manufacturing workshops are divided into two categories: those specialized in high-quality beads, and those specialized in low-quality beads. The craftsmen who produce high-quality beads are able to knap all kind of beads of various shapes and sizes. The duration of their apprenticeship period is about ten years. The craftsmen who produce low-quality beads knap beads with irregular shapes and of small size — less than three centimetres. Their apprenticeship lasts approximately three years. It was, therefore, reasonable to map the two levels of expertise with the two types of workshops.

The experiment was carried out with six craftsmen accustomed to knapping high-quality beads — referred to as group 1, and six craftsmen knapping low-quality beads — referred to as group 2. It is important however to note that craftsmen from both groups are experts, though with different levels of expertise.

Methods and recordings
The choice of the data recorded depends on quite a few parameters. As mentioned earlier in the chapter, we consider that a field experiment must provide data similar to those recorded in the lab. It also depends, however, on the type of technical devices available

and, naturally for a field experimentation, which are easily transported. It is not necessary here to list the differences between a university lab in Europe or elsewhere and a workshop in a small Indian town.

The technical devices used in this experiment had to allow us to analyze the course of action and the elementary action (Fig. 4.7). The course of action was recorded using a video camera with a sampling rate of 50 frames per second. The camera was located in the axis of the movement, and recordings of the whole knapping activity were carried out.

The elementary action was recorded using a uniaxial accelerometer affixed to the not-used end of the hammer head. The choice of the accelerometer as a means of recording was dictated by several considerations. What is important in knapping is not the movement in itself, but the fracture that is produced due, at least in part, to the hammer's movement (displacement, velocity, force of impact). The forces produced being proportional to the acceleration, the hammer acceleration was considered a good parameter characterizing the elementary action. In addition, the small dimension of an accelerometer makes it easy to transport. The accelerometer which was designed especially for this experiment, had the following characteristics: range, ± 250 g; natural frequency, 3000 Hz; accuracy, ± 0.2 m/s^2. It was connected to a portable Toshiba 600 computer via an ADC (analogue-to-digital converter, sampling frequency, 200 Hz; 12-bit resolution). It gives the acceleration of the hammer along the progression axis, i.e. according to the hammer's reference axis. The recording programs were developed by the third author.

Protocol
As noted earlier in the chapter, this experiment concerns the second step of knapping a bead, i.e. going from a roughout to a preform (Fig. 4.2). Each craftsman had to knap 10 preforms of four different shapes, using the two raw materials, chalcedony and glass, for a total of 80 preforms (Fig. 4.8). The stone roughouts were prepared in advance. They were made of chalcedony, the raw material commonly knapped in Khambhat. They had been made by the same craftsman in order to obtain, as best as possible, the same dimensions for all the roughouts. The glass roughouts were orange, a colour close to chalcedony. They have been manufactured by a French corporation, Saint Gobain.

The following four shape preforms were to be knapped: two slightly bitruncated ellipse-shaped preforms of two different lengths, one spherical-shaped preform, and one bitruncated ellipse-shaped preform with a quadrangular section.[1]

The experiment was held in a workshop which

Figure 4.7. *Experimental setting, data recordings: 1) a video camera is situated in the axis of the movement; 2) an uniaxial accelerometer is attached to the head of the hammer, and data are recorded via a portable computer.*

was quite calm as only one craftsman producing high-quality beads was working there. Each craftsman came to the workshop for a whole day, as the experiment lasted around six to seven hours.[2] After a trial in order to get used to the new raw material and the experimental situation, each participant was asked to knap the different preforms in the same order, first the glass preforms, then the stone ones. The first two preforms of each type were eliminated from the study as we considered that they might reflect the need to familiarize oneself with the task.

Data reduction
The analysis is based on three types of record: the preforms produced, the video records and the time series of the hammer acceleration.

Analysis of the preforms produced: The preforms that we brought back to our laboratory in Paris, have been analyzed one by one. All the preforms have been filmed with a video camera, from eight different angles in order to systematically analyze their contour. For this purpose, each view was digitized. A pattern-recognition program, developed by the third author, automatically analyzes each contour. The different parameters chosen are based on three criteria: techno-economic (i.e. refers to the economy of raw material as it is economically important not to

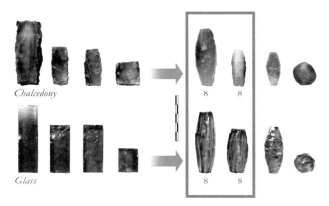

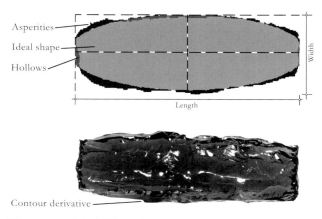

Chalcedony

Glass

Figure 4.8. *The different roughouts to be knapped into preforms.*

Asperities
Ideal shape
Hollows

Width

Length

Contour derivative

Figure 4.9. *Modelling of a stone: comparing the bead produced to the ideal shape. The different shaded areas correspond to a) a lack of material, b) to a surplus of material, and c) to the good shape.*

waste raw material), morphological (i.e. indexes the geometry of the knapped pieces, sphericity and symmetry), and technological (i.e. indexes the regularity of the shape, bumps and holes).

The general idea underlying the computation of most of the parameters, was to compare the knapped product to an 'ideal' shape.[3] These parameters index (a) the overall shape of the preform produced, (b) the symmetries along the longitudinal and transversal axis of the preform, and (c) the contour of the preform in terms of regularity or smoothness (for more details see Bril *et al.* 2000).

The behaviour of the craftsman knapping a preform: The three levels of action described earlier have been investigated:

a. The course of action (level 1)
We systematically analyzed the different paths taken by the craftsman as far as sub-goals are concerned — the

course of action — that is, the organization of the sequences of sub-goals to reach the goal. The analysis was performed using Kronos software initially designed for ergonomics studies (Alain Kerguelen CNAM).

The succession of sub-goals was noted, as was their duration. From this coding procedure, two different types of parameters were analyzed for each condition:
1. the number of different 'strategies', or more precisely 'sub-strategies', including non-coherent ones;
2. temporal parameters such as total duration of the task, or total duration of sub-goals corresponding to one operation.

b. The sub-goal: chaining of elementary movements (level 2)
Level 2 of the action was considered from the point of view of the characteristics of the chaining of elementary actions (i.e. chaining of strikes). The dynamics of the succession of elementary actions was analyzed, from the accelerometer time series, using two types of analysis:
1. *Power spectral density analysis of the accelerometer signal* (Fourier analysis), provides information on the timing of the actions and on the preferred striking frequency.
2. *Harmonic modelling*. Harmonic analysis is a tool for observing the structure of the dynamics of a movement with a limited number of parameters (Fourier coefficients). The procedure consists in 'constructing' a harmonic model of the signal by gradually increasing the number of coefficients (number of harmonics). At each step, a higher-order harmonic is added until the best fit is found between the model and the signal being studied. The output is a curve representing the distance (in fact, the standard deviation) between the signal and the model, depending on the number of harmonics. Here, we took a given number of harmonics (300) and computed the distance between the harmonic model and the signal. Since the acceleration of the hammer is proportional to the forces exerted, small distances between the source signal and the model correspond to more harmonic behaviour, and consequently less energy expenditure (Cordier *et al.* 1996).

We restricted the analysis of sub-goals to one subpart of the total sequence of sub-goals, starting with the first end-preparation and ending 50 seconds later. In most cases, this included at least the four first flutings, and usually more. Many different equivalent paths are possible here, all leading to the fluting of the four crests.

c. The elementary action (level 3)

In analyzing the elementary movement, we focused on the fluting movement, whose weight is critical as far as the shaping of a ellipsoidal preform is concerned. We chose to analyze the first fluting of each crest, for a fair comparison, since all crests are of approximately the same length at that point of the preform knapping process.

The coding of the course of action (KRONOS) was used to locate the exact timing of flutings. Once the instant of the fluting was determined, it was possible to calculate the variation of acceleration produced for each individual fluting strike (Fig. 4.10). From the acceleration curve we computed the variation in acceleration during the movement, from the positive peak prior to the impact of the hammer on the stone up to the time of impact.

Results

Our results concern the knapping of large and small ellipsoid preforms, except for the power spectral analysis and the harmonic analysis, which were performed on large ellipsoidal preforms (stone and glass) and spherical preforms (stone and glass). This was dictated by the fact that the small ellipsoidal stone preforms were much smaller than the glass ellipsoidal preforms, making a comparison between glass and stone difficult. Spherical preforms were knapped from stone and glass roughouts having the same dimensions, consequently any comparison is legitimate.

The product of the knapping process: the preforms

A look at the pieces produced by the craftsmen of both groups makes it easy to tell the difference. For the purpose of objectivity, however, we decided to quantify this qualitative but reliable perception of the differences. This task proved to be extremely difficult and complex. The eye considers and integrates a large number of different indices that are often difficult to isolate.

Figure 4.11 shows an example of the pieces knapped by one craftsman from group 1 and one craftsman from group 2. The production reveals a clear disparity of dexterity. The top row of both stone and glass products are more equal in shape and dimension suggesting a higher level of skill. Furthermore, the glass pieces from the craftsman of group 2 are far from a truncated ellipsoid with a circular section. The parallelepipedal roughout has barely been knapped. As hypothesized, the use of glass as a new material increases the differences between the two groups of craftsmen.

Parameters taken from the three criteria defined earlier significantly distinguish the production of the two groups. The results concerning the parameters

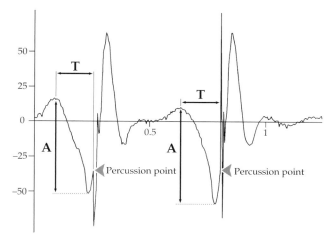

Figure 4.10. *Graph of the acceleration of the hammer (from the accelerometer) for two consecutive fluting movements. (A: maximal amplitude of the acceleration of the hammer).*

that better distinguish the two groups are given here: sphericity (morphological criteria), bump (i.e. the excess of raw material compared to the ideal shape), and the derivative of the contour of the preform (technological criteria). Sphericity is significantly higher for group 1 when compared with group 2. In addition, while in group 1, the sphericity values are approximately the same for both stone and glass products, this is not true for group 2. The production of the craftsmen of this group is significantly less spherical for glass preforms (see Fig. 4.12a). The analysis of the bump parameter is very instructive. It highlights the difference between the production of group 1 and group 2, highlighting the difficulties for the craftsmen of group 2 in transferring their knapping skill to the new raw material, glass (Fig. 4.12b). Stone production does not differentiate the two groups. While for group 1, however, the bump values are 48 per cent higher for glass than for stone, the difference rise to 128 per cent for group 2. Similar figures appear for the small preforms. While there were major differences between the craftsmen in both groups, this result clearly suggests a lower transfer ability for the craftsmen of group 2.

The last parameter reported here evokes once again a clear difference in skill between the two groups. The smoothness of the contour of the produced preform to the contour of the ideal preform, shows that, in all cases, the craftsmen of group 1 are better than the craftsmen of group 2. When the production of both stone and glass are compared, the values show that when glass is concerned smoothness deteriorates significantly more in group 2 than in group 1 (Fig. 4.12c).

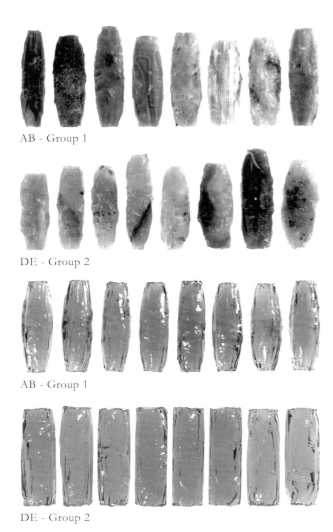

AB - Group 1

DE - Group 2

AB - Group 1

DE - Group 2

Figure 4.11. *Examples of the production of a craftsman of group 1 and a craftsman of group 2: a) stone preforms knapped by AB (craftsman of group 1) (top row) and by DE (craftsman of group 2) bottom row; b) glass preforms knapped by AB (craftsman of group 1) (top row) and by DE (craftsman of group 2) bottom row.*

The action plan
The course of action corresponding to each preform produced has been systematically coded and analyzed using the KRONOS software (Fig. 4.13). This analysis provides information on how the method was adjusted to produce an ellipsoidal preform. Two main aspects of the course of action were analyzed. The first concerns the strategies or sub-strategies used by the craftsmen, that is how the sub-goals are sequenced to make a preform. The second deals with the temporal structure of the course of action.

The overall strategy: adjusting the method: A comparison of the course of action displayed by each knapper for

each preform shows two important aspects of the craftsmen's plan of action.
1. The craftsmen of group 2 rarely perform calibration or regularization of the crest for successful fluting. Only two of them (SU and DE), sometimes perform calibration; it is interesting to note that shortly before the experiment, SU had spent a few months at a higher-quality workshop.
2. Apart from calibration, all the craftsmen's courses of action, from both group 1 and group 2, match two of the four basic strategies. Of the four theoretically possible strategies (see Fig. 4.4) the first two are used most of the time. The third one was applied systematically by one craftsman from group 1 only, and occasionally by two others. The fourth has never been observed. It must be noted, however, that what has been described as one strategy is not rigid and that sub-strategies, i.e. variations on a strategy, have been often observed.

There is major variability both within and among participants (Fig. 4.13). The number of sub-goal paths performed by each craftsman corresponding to different sub-strategies, is shown in Table 4.1. On average, the number of different sub-strategies used is slightly lower for group 2 than for group 1. In the same way, the number of sub-strategies used to produce glass preforms is lower than those used to produce stone preforms. A few craftsmen systematically follow the same path, i.e. use only one strategy (IN, HA from group 1 for large ellipsoidal stone preforms, SU for group 2), but other craftsmen may display as much as five to seven different paths while making eight preforms in sequence (HU from group 1 for stone large ellipsoidal preforms, or NA from group 2).

The glass condition seemed to reduce the average number of paths in both groups, although not significantly. This is coherent as the stone is not homogeneous, unlike glass. It is therefore understandable that a less homogeneous raw material leads to a necessary adaptation to the contingency of the raw material. However the high variability exhibited by some craftsmen from both groups is difficult to explain. Why IN from group 1 and SU from group 2 exhibit only one sub-strategy while HU from group 1 and NA from group 2 exhibit more than five sub-strategies, is still not clear. IN is recognized as the best craftsman in Khambhat, but HU also produced high-quality beads.

The temporal structure of the course of action: The duration of the entire knapping process is far greater in group 1 than in group 2 (Table 4.2), which confirms the previous study by Roux & Pelegrin (1989). This difference reflects the absence of calibration for craftsmen in group 2. But when considering the duration

A

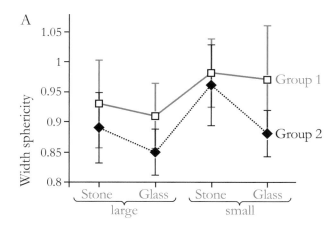

B

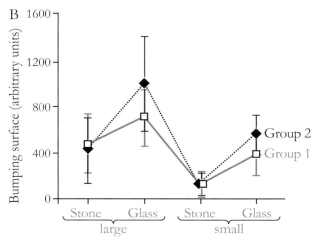

C

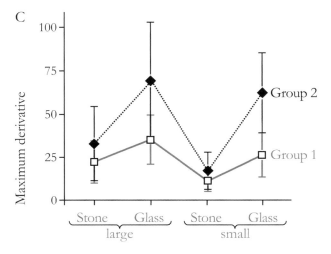

Figure 4.12. *Values of parameters indexing morphological and technological criteria of a good product: a) spericity; b) bumping; c) contour smoothness.*

of partial knapping, that is, not including calibration and finishing, group 1 and group 2 spend approximately the same time on each preform. On average,

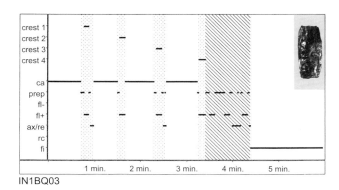

IN1BQ03

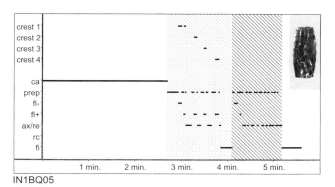

IN1BQ05

Figure 4.13. *KRONOS diagram representing the course of actions corresponding to the knapping process of an ellipsoid preform.*

for both group 1 and 2, the time spent knapping glass preforms was higher than the time spent on stone preforms (see Table 4.2). The partial number of sub-goals, however, is higher for craftsmen of group 1 compared with group 2. This could mean that the craftsmen of group 2 skip some operations (i.e. end preparation), a behaviour which is less frequently observed in craftsmen of group 1.

When the relative number of sub-goals is computed, that is the ratio of the number of sub-goals to the total duration of the knapping process, it is higher for the craftsmen of group 1 when glass is considered. The opposite is true when stone is considered: the relative number of sub-goals is higher for the craftsmen of group 2. In other words, the duration of a sub-goal (inverse of frequency) is longer for the craftsmen of group 2 working on glass preforms than for the craftsmen of group 1; the opposite being true for stone preforms where the craftsmen of group 1 spend more time on each sub-goal while knapping a stone preform. The shorter time spent on each operation by the craftsmen of group 1 when knapping glass suggests that they take advantage of the homogeneity of the glass raw material, while the craftsmen from group 2 have more difficulty adapting to the new raw material.

In spite of the significant differences between the two groups of craftsmen described in this section, major variability appears between the craftsmen within each group. The total duration of the process of knapping a large preform of glass may vary between 299 seconds and 533 seconds in group 1, and between 92 seconds and 347 seconds in group 2. The same extreme variations are observed for the partial number of operations a craftsman performs, varying from 19 to 43 in group 1, and from 8 to 36 in group 2.

Table 4.1. *Number of different sub-strategies displayed by craftsmen of both groups depending on the raw material and the shape of the roughout to be knapped.*

		STONE		GLASS	
		LARGE	SMALL	LARGE	SMALL
GROUP 1	RA	3	3	2	4
	HU	7	5	4	5
	HA	1	5	1	3
	IN	1	2	1	1
	AB	2	3	1	1
	RN	3	5	5	2
GROUP 2	DE	2	2	2	2
	SU	1	1	1	1
	SA	2	2	1	1
	NA	5	5	3	2
	AS	1	–	1	1
	HK	3	6	3	2

Table 4.2. *Temporal characteristics of the knapping process: total duration, partial duration (total duration – calibration and finition), relative frequency of operations.*

	Total duration	Partial duration	Relative frequency of operations
Large Stone			
Group 1 ($n = 48$)	330.88 (93.34)	179.12 (89.87)	0.17 (0.05)
Group 2 ($n = 48$)	159.04 (58.71)	117.72 (44.61)	0.21 (0.05)
Large Glass			
Group 1 ($n = 48$)	382.02 (110.64)	140.88 (65.23)	0.23 (0.15)
Group 2 ($n = 48$)	210.71 (95.73)	129.60 (69.02)	0.16 (0.10)
Small Stone			
Group 1 ($n = 48$)	180.25 (63.17)	79.79 (31.51)	0.26 (0.06)
Group 2 ($n = 48$)	99.57 (47.07)	67.03 (28.19)	0.28 (0.09)
Small Glass			
Group 1 ($n = 48$)	294.4 (43.51)	114.68 (42.73)	0.27 (0.06)
Group 2 ($n = 48$)	196.77 (92.39)	99.90 (31.52)	0.21 (0.05)

The dynamics of elementary movements
Power spectral density analysis (large ellipsoidal preforms): The range of frequencies is between 1 and 5 Hz; Figure 4.14 gives the average power spectral density curve for the eight preforms for stone and glass large preforms. The curves are not different in the two situations for all participants (group 1 and group 2).

For all participants, the power spectral density curves present one peak at 3.5–3.7 Hz, regardless of the raw material — glass or stone.

The power spectral density curves show specific characteristics for each group. All the craftsmen from group 1 have a non-symmetrical pattern, in the low frequencies. On the other hand, most of the participants of group 2 present symmetrical curves. SU's curves, however, are more like the curves of group 1 than group 2. The interesting point here is that SU had spent some time working in a workshop producing superior-quality beads.

Harmonic analysis: Figure 4.15 shows an example of the original signal and of the model using the first 300 harmonics. Figure 4.16 summarizes the harmonic analysis. For both group 1 and group 2, it gives the average distance between the accelerometer signal and the reconstructed signal based on the harmonic model. This graph clearly shows that the craftsmen from group 2 have higher values than the craftsmen from group 1, regardless of the condition, suggesting a more harmonic behaviour for subjects from group 1.

Compared with the stone condition, the values are always lower in the glass condition for the craftsmen of group 2. This is true, however, for the craftsmen of group 1 for spherical roughouts but not for the large ellipsoidal ones where there is no difference between conditions (stone and glass). This suggests that the raw material affects the harmonization of the behaviour, except for the large roughout in group 1.

The interpretation is not obvious. The smaller values for glass may be interpreted differently for group 1 and group 2. If we take into account the product (the roughout characteristics) it has been shown that group 2 craftsmen hardly modified the roughouts, although the preform is far from an ellipsoid shape. It could be that the sequence of actions was more stereotyped and less flexible resulting in a less energy-consum-

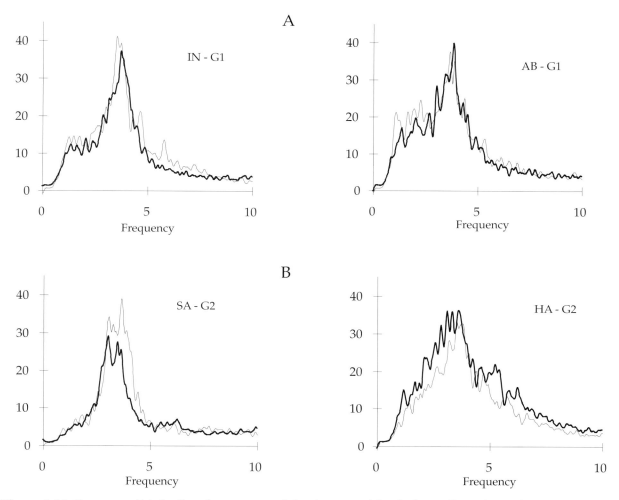

Figure 4.14. *Frequency distributions (power spectral density curves) for the large ellipsoidal preforms for craftsmen of group 1 (A) and group 2 (B) (average for 8 beads). Thin lines correspond to stone preforms, thick lines correspond to glass preforms.*

ing situation. On the other hand, for the craftsmen of group 1, since knapping a spherical roughout from glass is easier, the sequence results in a more harmonic behaviour, while in the case of large ellipsoidal preforms which are harder to knap, and the final preform being of good quality, the raw material does not affect the global process.

The elementary action
The analysis of the elementary action concerns the fluting sub-goal. As mentioned earlier, this choice was dictated by the difficulty in comparing actions in exactly the same condition — i.e. same state of the roughout. The first flutings — one for each crest — may be considered as a situation which is approximately the same for all the roughouts, since the crest has more or less the same length at this point of the knapping process, and

the goal is to strike a long, thick flake along the crest.

The fluting operation is interesting for another reason as well. It is quite easy to identify failure or success while performing a fluting operation, as the movement performed is quite characteristic, and the flake produced is quite large.

A first difference between the two groups is the number of failures while performing this operation. On average, the number of fluting failures is higher for the craftsmen of group 2, for both stone and glass roughouts, and is about twice as high in group 2: 1.7 failures on average compared with 0.5 for large glass ellipsoidal preforms for craftsmen of group 2 and group 1 respectively, and 2.4 failures on average compared with 0.9 for large stone ellipsoidal preforms. Here again, major variability characterizes both groups, but is larger in group 2 than in group 1.

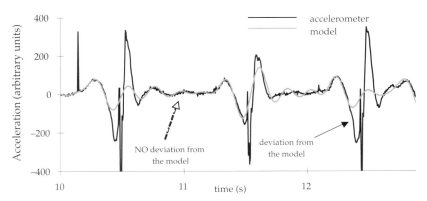

Figure 4.15. *Harmonic model. (The accelerometer curve is black and the model computation curve is grey.)*

Amplitude of acceleration: The values for the variation in the acceleration of the head of the hammer during the movement prior to the hammer strike on the roughout differentiate the two groups of participants in all conditions (see Fig. 4.15 & Table 4.3). It must be emphasized, however, that all the craftsmen are experts, in some ways.

Adaptation to the raw material: As far as the transfer to the new raw material is concerned, the acceleration is higher when fluting stone than when fluting glass (see Table 4.3 & Fig. 4.15). This is true in all cases. It means that all the craftsmen, regardless of their level of expertise, do make a distinction between the two raw materials: glass is not as hard as stone. For large ellipsoidal stone preforms, the average acceleration is 67.59 m/s² for group 1, compared with 51.41 m/s² for the glass preform; for the craftsmen of group 2 these values are respectively 63.10 m/s² for stone and 42.97 m/s² for glass. In addition, when looking at the variations between the craftsmen of the same group, it is interesting to note that there is less variation in the values of the acceleration displayed by the craftsmen of group 1 compared with those of group 2: that is, in group 1 the difference between the highest average value and the lowest is 19.6 m/s² (from 58.1 to 77.85 m/s²) while it is 54.1 m/s² for group 2 (from 41.3 to 95.5 m/s²). This phenomenon is present for glass as well, but to a lesser degree: 36.4 m/s² for group 1 and 43.4 m/s² for group 2.

Adaptation to the length of the crest[4]: In the case of large and small stone roughouts where the difference between the length of the crest is 3.5 cm (the length of the crest is 7 cm for large preforms and 3.5 cm for the small ones), the craftsmen from both group 1 and group 2 produce statistically higher acceleration when removing the longer crests (Table 4.3). In the case of glass, however, where the difference in length between

the crests is only 2 cm (7 cm for the large ones and 5 cm for the small ones), all the craftsmen from group 1 show statistically significantly ($p < 0.001$) greater acceleration for the longer crest lengths, while in group 2, four craftsmen show no difference at all, and two craftsmen show only small differences ($p < 0.05$).

Table 4.3 gives the average values of acceleration for each of the craftsmen comparing the acceleration produced during fluting for large and small stone and glass preforms. These results express greater homogeneity in group 1 than in group 2. This highest homogeneity may be summarized along two main lines:
1. smaller inter-individual variability in group 1;
2. more stable difference in the values of acceleration displayed for large and small roughouts.

The low inter-individual variability in the craftsmen from group 1 suggests that a high level of expertise corresponds to a quite stable action solution from one individual to the next. A high level of mastery of action may allow for less latitude for inter-individual variations. In contrast, the individual solution of group 2 appears to be more diversified and results in a finished product of lower quality.

The coefficients of variation (standard deviation divided by mean) have been computed for acceleration in all situations for each craftsman of group 1 and group 2. Contrary to the commonly accepted idea that experts behave in a more consistent and nearly automatic manner, intra-individual variability, indexed by the coefficient of variation, is slightly greater for group 1 than for group 2.

A final aspect of the elementary action should be addressed here even though it has not been subjected to systematic quantification. As described earlier, the elementary action is bimanual, where each hand is specialized: for a right-hander, the roughout is held in the left hand, i.e. the postural hand, and the hammer in the right. The hand holding the stone can be more or less stable, that is more or less disturbed when the hammer hits the roughout. Based on the videos, we can say that globally, the postural hand of the craftsmen from group 2 is less stable than of those from group 1. At the moment of impact, the head of the hammer is either stopped, or its trajectory continues after the moment of the impact on the stone. The first strategy is usually displayed by the craftsmen of group 1, the second by the craftsmen of group 2. Here again, we can hypothesize that the craftsmen from group 1

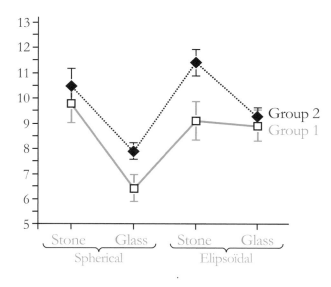

Figure 4.16. *Harmonic model: mean values of the deviation from accelerometer and harmonic model (in %) for each group and condition.*

Table 4.3. *Mean values of acceleration of the hammer for each craftsman of both groups (m/s²) (* = statistically significant at* p <.05; *** = statistically significant at* p <.01; *ns = non-significant).*

		STONE		GLASS	
		LARGE	SMALL	LARGE	SMALL
GROUP 1	RA	58.2	34.8	27.5	24.4 *
	HU	75.4	44.5	63.9	44.9 **
	HA	77.8	67.4	47.8	40.4 **
	IN	66.4	49.3	57.8	46.1 **
	AB	68.4	52.6	57.1	52.6 **
	RN	61.4	42.4	53.7	45.4 **
GROUP 2	DE	95.5	74.5	69	65.6 ns
	SU	72.2	45.7	48.8	44.2 *
	SA	54.8	48.7	40.8	41 ns
	NA	41.4	35.5	25.6	23.8 ns
	AS	55.2	40.7	37.7	39.3 ns
	HK	59.2	47.1	40.9	33.3 *

better anticipate the disruption caused by the shock of striking the stone. In addition, they are able to control the hammer movement in such a way that the impact is almost totally absorbed by the stone, resulting in higher strike efficiency.

Discussion: What is expertise?

This experimental study was based on the hypothesis that, compared with less-expert craftsmen, expert craftsmen would be better able to transfer their knapping skill to a new situation. This should be true in particular with a new raw material, provided that the new raw material responds to the same mechanical principles as chalcedony, that is those associated with the conchoidal fracture. In addition, as a raw material, glass had the immense advantage of being homogeneous. Thus, as the aim of this experiment was to try to characterize the nature of expertise, a homogeneous raw material lets us discuss the differences in behaviour among craftsmen with respect to their production in terms of differences in skill. It was quite improbable that these differences would be due to the raw material as might be the case for stone, as stone is not a homogeneous raw material.

One of the innovative aspects was that this study was designed to enable simultaneous analysis of the action — the knapping process from roughout to preform — as well as the product of this process — the preform. In addition, three levels of action were investigated, based on recording methods adapted to the level of action referred to — i.e. video for the course

of action, and accelerometer for the elementary action. In this discussion, we shall highlight the differences in the behaviour between the two groups of craftsmen who participated in the study, and relate them to the characteristics of the end-product, the preforms.

The characteristics of expert production and behaviour
The roughout produced by the craftsmen of both groups corroborate what everyone in Khambhat knows: during the experiment, the craftsmen producing high-quality beads (participants of group 1) for a living knapped more regular, spherical, better-shaped preforms with smooth contours. On the contrary, and as expected, the craftsmen producing low-quality beads for a living, produced less regular, less spherical, less well-shaped, and more bumpy preforms compared with the participants of group 1. The participants of both groups adapted very differently to the new raw material, i.e. glass. The craftsmen from group 1 were able to adapt quite well to the new raw material. Confirming our hypothesis, knapping glass produced a zooming effect on the difficulty of the task. This was particularly true for the craftsmen of group 2. When comparing the sphericity of the preforms produced by the craftsmen of group 2, the mean value obtained is much lower for glass than for stone. For the craftsmen of group 1, these values are very similar for stone and glass, reflecting near perfect adaptation to the new raw material. Similar facts can be reported from other characteristics of the preforms as well. The contour of the preforms produced by group 2 was much less smooth. In other words, the

production of group 2 is more irregular. In the same way, bumps are larger for group 2, and the final shape of the preform is quite far from the ideal shape. In this group, the glass roughouts were barely transformed and it is easy to see the original parallelepipedic shape in the knapped preform.

Clearly, the difference in the production from both groups is substantial and can be attributed to differences in the competence of the craftsmen. We suggest here that an analysis of all three levels of action referred to in this study is necessary to understanding expertise.

Is the course of action a good indicator of planning capacity?

As discussed earlier, some theoretical approaches to action stress the role of representations that are considered to be at the origin of skilled behaviour. In line with this perspective, the course of action reflects the person's ability to plan.

The course of action proved to be quite similar in both groups except for the absence of the calibration operation for most of the craftsmen from group 2. Why did they omit this operation, even though it is important for good fluting? It could be that it was not worth spending time on a time-consuming operation for low-quality beads. Or could it be that the craftsmen did not know about this operation, or that they were not able to perform it? An experiment conducted more recently (see L. Biryukova *et al.* this volume) suggests that all the craftsmen know what calibration is, but it is not clear whether they have good knowledge of why it may be important to obtain a more perfect ellipsoidal preform. However, even when done by craftsmen from group 2, calibration turned out to be quite crude and did not meet its purpose, i.e. to prepare the shape of the crest to allow efficient fluting. As will be discussed in the section on elementary action, the hypothesis here is that the control of the elementary action of the craftsmen from group 2 is not sufficiently fine to produce very thin flakes. Consequently, since they do not really understand the purpose of calibration, they skip it.

The analysis of the course of action clearly suggests that all the craftsmen know about the method. Very few incoherent paths of sub-goals were noticed. However, the method used to knap a preform from a parallelepipedic roughout is quite simple, and it is not surprising that all the craftsmen were able to apply the method in a coherent path of sub-goals. More surprising is the very significant variability found among the craftsmen in both group 1 and group 2. Some of the craftsmen, in both groups displayed only one path of sub-goals, corresponding to one strategy. On the other hand, other craftsmen from group 1 as well as group 2, while knapping eight preforms of a similar shape, displayed up to five or seven different paths corresponding to one or even two strategies. This idiosyncratic behaviour is difficult to explain, but suggests that the quality of the end-product does not depend on the way the method is applied. This dramatic diversity in the application of the method suggests that there is no advance planning of the sequence of sub-goals to be carry out, otherwise why would some of the craftsmen follow a different path for almost every roughout? While the sequence of sub-goals is undoubtedly controlled, the knowledge of the method, i.e. the main steps, or sub-goals to reach the desired shape is necessarily associated with the knowledge of what constitutes the prerequisite for the next sub-goal to be performed. Along this line, what is referred to as planning is a 'resource' as Agre & Chapman (1990) put it. Along this line, the course of action is the expression of a continuous dynamic between the organism — the craftsman — and the environment. The question is then, what is this dynamic composed of?

The critical role of elementary action

An elementary action has been defined as the smallest unit of a functional action. It corresponds to a functional strike, i.e. the removal of one flake through the action of the hammer. In other words, the removal of one flake corresponds to the *actualization* of the technique. This study focused on the elementary action and not on the movement. The rationale of this choice was that it is necessary first to understand what functional aim the movement fulfils. Only then can the analysis of the movement of the striking arm make sense. Here, the functional goal — removing a flake — is achieved by the movement of the hammer. The trajectory, velocity and force displayed by the hammer index the performance of a stroke, and hence of the craftsmen's level of expertise.

The analysis of the hammer acceleration during fluting made obvious the necessary adaptation of the hammer movement to succeed in flaking. The smaller acceleration displayed by all the craftsmen when knapping the glass roughout, compared with stone, makes it clear that adapting to the characteristics of the task is one of the main requirements for successful flaking. In addition, the acceleration of the hammer must be tuned to the dimensions of the flake to be removed. The analysis of flutings of crests of different dimensions revealed that all the craftsmen are more or less able to adapt to the length of the crest. However, and this is one of the main results of our study, the craftsmen from group 1 demonstrate a finer tuning to the characteristics of the flake to be taken off than the craftsmen from group 2. When knapping glass roughouts, all the craftsmen from group 1 produced an acceleration of the hammer which was smaller when knapping a crest of 5 cm compared with one of 7 cm. The craftsmen from group 2 were not able to perform this fine tuning.

The results on the dynamics of the sequencing of elementary movements are interpreted as corroborating this interpretation. The frequency distributions displayed different features for the craftsmen of group 1 and group 2. The non-symmetrical distribution of group 1 was attributed to a different timing pattern for fluting and end preparation, the low frequency corresponding to fluting and axial removal, and the higher frequency reflecting end preparation. On the other hand, the symmetrical distribution displayed by the craftsmen of group 2 was interpreted as reflecting non-differentiated timing for the different operation. In addition, the major variation in the range of frequencies, either quite small or quite large, was interpreted as rigidity, or uncontrolled variability.

A common feature of these distributions, however, concerns the peak of frequency, which is approximately the same for all the distributions. This property is attributed to the natural physical properties of the hammer. Like a pendulum whose frequency depends on its mass and length we suggest that the frequency of the hammer might reflect a similar phenomenon. A recent experiment with craftsmen of different levels of expertise corroborates this hypothesis (Bril *et al.* 2001). In a similar experiment to the one reported in this chapter, the craftsmen were asked to work with a heavier hammer or one with a shorter handle. Depending on the characteristics of the hammer, the peaks of frequencies were different — higher with a shorter handle, lower with a heavier hammer. So, we can hypothesize that the value of the peak of frequency depends on the hammer's characteristics, while the profile of the distribution reflects the craftsman's adaptation to the specificity of the successive flakings corresponding to the different operations. A non-symmetrical profile in the low frequencies is interpreted as a voluntary modulation of the natural properties of the hammer, corresponding most probably to flutings and axial removals. On the other hand, a symmetrical profile around this peak value would reflect the absence of voluntary mastery of the natural properties of the hammer.

Here again, the adaptation revealed by the frequency profile is a salient feature of the craftsmen of group 1, and reflects the outstanding capacity of the craftsmen producing high-quality beads to adapt their striking action to the very precise characteristics of the flake to be removed depending on the operation performed.

The perception/action coupling

One characteristic of the group 1 elementary action is recurrent: the ability to very precisely adapt to the properties of the task at hand. The adaptation referred to here bears on the hardness of the stone, on the dimension of the flake to be removed, and on the tool, i.e. the properties of three elements constituting the system at hand. In other words, adaptation pertains to the level of the elementary action, i.e. to the technique.

In any case, adaptation to the specificity of the task cannot be achieved without the ability to perceive the necessary information that will allow the craftsman to tune the action in order to reach a very precise outcome. Adaptation and flexibility have often been addressed as the critical dimensions of expertise. The expert is one who, when confronted with the constraints of the task (the raw material, the hammer, the physical characteristics of the conchoidal fracture, the length of the roughout, the expected shape of the final product), is able to actualize the method through a constant dynamic fit between the state of the roughout and the next step, in other words, to remove the exact flake.

The common value of the peak of frequency for all the craftsmen has been interpreted as emerging from the linking of the three components — hammer, body, and raw material. We suggest that expertise consists not only in tuning as well as possible the properties of the system, but the expert is one who is able to *force* the system in one direction or another to adjust to the local features of the situation.

Such a perspective suggests that the core of expertise lies in the very precise control of the elementary action, i.e. on the bimanual activity that underlies the elementary action. Going one step further, we suggest that this fine control constitutes an (or even *the most*) important dimension of the possibility of carrying out the method. The ability to perceive the real meaning of what the sequences of operation relative to a method are about could well be limited by the ability to control the elementary action. Cognitivist theories have emphasized the role of planning the sequence of actions, the role of a mental representation of the desired goal to be reached. These theories focus on the prescription for action: they attribute a large portion of the behaviour to an intelligent executive device, regardless of the nature of the device. These theories focus very little on the execution phase of the action, which is often taken for granted. An analysis of the entire process of performing a complex goal-oriented action highlights the need to understand how the three levels of action interweave simultaneously.

We argue here that an adequate account of the knapper behaviour while knapping a roughout re-

69

quires that we understand how the constraints of the system — task, raw material, organism, tool — work together. The necessary knowledge of the method to produce a roughout of a specific shape may be referred to as a 'mental representation' or a template. However, ascribing the observed course of actions to a kind of prescription defining a plan established in advance, makes it very difficult to explain the very important variations observed either within a group of craftsmen of approximately the same level of expertise, or perhaps more importantly within the behaviour of a given craftsman, whatever his level of expertise. We share the conviction that the most rewarding way of approaching an understanding of complex behaviour is to be found in a functional approach. This means focusing on the relationship between the environmental constraints and the behaviour produced. This approach does not deny the existence of a 'representation' regardless of the name given, but it does not consider a close causality between representation and the behaviour that may be observed. It emphasizes an understanding of the course of action based on an analysis of the dual complementarity between the organism and the environment.

Conclusion: a masterful technique for an efficient method?

The results of this experiment have highlighted the fact that a craftsman may have practised a method for years and still produce mediocre roughouts. This produces evidence that knowing the method, i.e. the operations needed to knap a preform of a specific shape, does not constitute the hallmark of expertise. It suggests that a prerequisite to expertise is to be found in the ability to finely tune the goal of the elementary action, that is to be able to produce a flake with the right characteristics at the right time in the sequence of flake removals. This may be fulfilled only through the movement of the hammer direction, amplitude, velocity, force (Biryukova *et al.* this volume) and the positioning of the stone. To produce the right values for these different parameters that define the production of a flake along the conchoidal fracture, the movement must be very well controlled. In other words, the knowledge of the method is of no use if the technique is not very finely controlled.

What we argue here is that a high level of expertise depends on the ability of the knapper to control the elementary movement. This leads to the hypothesis that a very fine tuning of the elementary movement determines the ability to plan the whole sequence of strikes. We simply need to consider someone who has a very good knowledge of the method

but no experience in the elementary movement. We bet that s/he won't be able to produce anything at all. In other words, the ability to 'plan well' the sequence of sub-goals depends on the level of mastery of the elementary movement.

It will appear a truism to emphasize the fact that experts are better able to adapt their action, that is to utilize information on the state of the roughout in such a way as to adapt the next action to achieve a better functional fit than do less expert craftsmen.

The detection of information necessary to guide the entire knapping process depends on the level of expertise in the 'technique'. A high-level expert will be able to constrain mutuality relations between himself and his environment (i.e. the stone at different points in the knapping process) in such a way as to perceive the affordances (Gibson 1977; 1986; Stoffregen 2000), that is the properties of the system (stone/hammer/organism) that lead to the characteristics of the next flake, and consequently the next strike. In other words, the high-level expert knows better what to look for and how to turn the information perceived into action and movement: this capacity is directly associated to a high degree of control of the technique.

However, a basic question remains: what are the properties of the 'template' the knapper relies on to guide the sequence of flake removals. What has to be worked out is how the specific removal fits, and relates to the knapper's global goal.

Acknowledgements

We warmly thank the craftsmen who accepted an unusual working situation and the Akikwala family who put their workshop at our disposal. This research was funded by the French Ministère délégué à la recherche et aux nouvelles Technologie (Science de la cognition, ACI Cognitique L103, ACI TTT P7802 n° 02 2 0440, and the French Institute of Pondicherry). Drawings have been made by Gérard Monthel (CNRS, UMR 7055).

Notes

1. Description of the four different shapes to be knapped in the two raw materials:
   1. two ellipsoidal beads of different length (from roughout of 7 cm × 2 cm × 2 cm for both stone and glass; and 5 cm × 2 cm × 2 cm for glass and 3.5 cm × 2 cm × 2 cm for stone);
   2. one spherical bead from a cubic roughout of 2.5 cm per side for both stone and glass;
   3. one curved-prismatic-four-sided bead from roughout of 5 cm × 2 cm × 2 cm for glass and 3.5 cm × 2 cm × 2 cm for stone.

   The smaller size of carnelian roughout was unfortunately due to the hazard of field work. When we arrived

in 1993, Khambhat was under curfew and there was a shortage of raw materials.

2. All the craftsmen participating in the study were paid the same amount of money, slightly more than what an expert earns in one day.

3. The ideal shape was calculated taking into account the preform produced. At first we had planned to compute the 'ideal' shape from the roughout. This did not take into account, however, the possibility of the raw material not being available. We then chose to determine the 'ideal' shape from the preforms produced.

4. See note 1.

References

Agre, P.E. & D. Chapman, 1990. What are plans for?, in *Designing Autonomous Agents*, ed. P. Maes. Cambridge: Elsevier, 17–34.

Bernstein, N., 1996. Dexterity, in *Dexterity and its Development*, eds. M. Latash & M. Turvey. Hillsdale (NJ): Erlbaum Associates, 1–235.

Bril, B., V. Roux & G. Dietrich, 2000. Habiletés impliquées dans la taille des perles en calcédoine. Caractéristiques motrices et cognitives d'une action située complexe, in *Cornaline de l'Inde: Des pratiques techniques de Cambay aux techno-systèmes de l'Indus,* ed. V. Roux. Paris: Editions de la MSH, 207–332. www.epistemes.net/arkeotek/p_cornaline.htm.

Bril, B., G. Dietrich, L. Byriukova, A. Roby-Brami & V. Roux, 2001. Hammering, Adaptation to Tool Properties and Raw Material. Poster presented at the International Workshop 'Knapping Stone, a Uniquely Hominid Behavior?'. Abbaye des Premontrés, Pont-à-Mousson (France), 21–24 November.

Connoly, K.J. & M. Dalgleish, 1989. The emergence of tool using skill in infancy. *Developmental Psychology* 6, 894–912.

Cordier, P., G. Dietrich & J. Pailhous, 1996. Harmonic analysis of a complex motor behavior. *Human Movement Science* 15, 789–807.

Ericsson, K.A. & A.C. Lehmann, 1996. Expert and exceptional performance: evidence on maximal adaptations on task constraints. *Annual Review of Psychology* 47, 273–305.

Gibson, J.J., 1977. The theory of affordance, in *Perceiving, Acting, and Knowing,* eds. R.E. Shaw & J. Bransford. Hillsdale (NJ): Lawrence Erlbaum Associates, 67–82.

Gibson, J.J., 1986. *The Ecological Approach to Visual Perception.* Hillsdale (NJ): Lawrence Erlbaum Associates. [First published in 1979.]

Meijer, O.G. & K. Roth (eds.), 1988. *Complex Movement Behaviour: the Motor-action Controversy.* Amsterdam: Elsevier North Holland.

Newell, K., 1986. Constraints on the development of coordination, in *Motor Skills Acquisition*, eds. M.G. Wade & H.T.A. Withing. Dortrech: Martinus Nijhoff, 341–60.

Newell, K., 1996. Changes in movement skill: learning, retention and transfer, in *Dexterity and its Development*, eds. M. Latash & M. Turvey. Hillsdale (NJ): Erlbaum Associates, 431–51.

Pelegrin, J., 1993. A framework for analyzing stone tools manufacture, and a tentative application to some early lithic industries, in *The Use of Tools by Human and Non-human Primates*, eds. A. Berthelet & J. Chavaillon. Oxford: Oxford University Press, 302–14.

Pelegrin, J., 2000. Technique et méthodes de taille pratiquées à Cambay, in *Cornaline de l'Inde: Des pratiques techniques de Cambay aux techno-systèmes de l'Indus,* ed. V. Roux. Paris: Editions de la MSH, 207–329.

Richard, J.F., 1990. *Les activités mentales: comprendre, raisonner, trouver des solutions.* Paris: Armand Colin.

Reed, E., 1988. Applying the theory of action systems to the study of motor skills, in *Complex Movement Behaviour: the Motor-action Controversy*, eds. O.G. Meijer & K. Roth. Amsterdam: Elsevier North Holland, 45–86.

Roux, V. (ed.), 2000. *Cornaline de l'Inde: Des pratiques techniques de Cambay aux techno-systèmes de l'Indus.* Paris: Editions de la MSH.

Roux, V. & J. Pelegrin, 1989. Taille des perles et spécialisation artisanale: enquête ethnoarchéologique dans le Gujarat. *Techniques et culture* 14, 23–49.

Roux V., B. Bril & G. Dietrich, 1995. Skills and learning difficulties involved in stone knapping: the case of stone bead knapping in Khambhat, India. *World Archaeology* 27(1), 63–87.

Stoffregen, T.A., 2000. Affordances and events. *Ecological Psychology* 12(1), 1–28.

Stout, D., 2002. Skill and cognition in stone tool production: an ethnographic case study from Irian Jaya. *Current Anthropology* 43, 693–722.

Chapter 5

The Organization of Arm Kinematic Synergies: the Case of Stone-bead Knapping in Khambhat

Elena V. Biryukova, Blandine Bril, Gilles Dietrich,
Agnès Roby-Brami, Mikhail A. Kulikov, Petr E. Molchanov

This paper focuses on an experiment which was carried out with craftsmen from Khambhat who had also participated in the study reported in Chapter 4 of this volume. Craftsmen of four levels of expertise were involved: high-level experts, low-level experts, high-level learners, and low-level learners. The elementary movement corresponding to one flake removal during stone-bead knapping was analyzed from the point of view of the arm inter-joint co-ordinations. In any skill such as stone knapping, dexterous and adaptive behaviour is characterized by stable coordinative changes in the joint angles. In any arm movement, seven mechanically-independent rotations in the arm joints (three in the shoulder, two in the elbow and, two in the wrist) are organized in the so-called kinematic synergies. Our basic hypothesis is that the peculiarities of the kinematic synergies reflect the peculiarities of motor-control strategy on the different level of mastery of skill. The comparative analysis of kinematic synergies in high-level and low-level experts and in high-level and low-level learners leads to the following conclusions. The high level of mastery of skill is characterized by stereotyped kinematic pattern of both joint trajectories and hammer trajectory. At the same time, the flexible behaviour of high-level experts manifests in: 1) rich kinematic content of the synergies, i.e. large number of degrees of freedom, involved in the motion; and 2) at the highest level of expertise, the large repertory of motor synergies facilitates the successful completion of the task. These distinguishing features of elementary movement kinematics are in line with theoretical basis of motor learning and adaptation (Bernstein 1967) as well as with the results of frequency analysis of hammer acceleration reported in previous papers (Roux et al. 1995; Bril et al. 2000).

The research reported here is grounded on the belief that the conchoidal fracture responds to similar necessities regardless of the technique used to produce it. Consequently, it is assumed that the skills required to master flake removal will have a great deal in common regardless of the technique used to detach a flake, provided that it responds to the conchoidal fracture. A restriction, however, is that the technique referred to entails the use of a hammer. Using a hammer generally implies bimanual activity. The arm holding the hammer is designated as the striking arm, while the arm holding the item to be knocked is called the postural arm.

In this paper, we concentrate on the movement of the striking arm. We consider the elementary functional movement, i.e. the movement ending, when successful, in the detachment of a flake. From a functional point of view it cannot be split into parts. This movement is naturally considered as 'elementary' from the point of view of the general strategy of stone-knapping (Chapter 4 this volume). Results from a previous experiment (Bril *et al.* 2000) showed

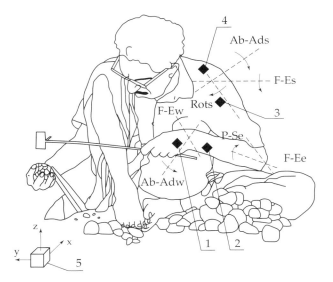

Figure 5.1. *The locations of STS sensors: 1) on the hand; 2) on the forearm; 3) on the arm; 4) on the acromion. The stationary system XYZ (5) is located on the ground. The axes of independent rotations in the joints are given: abduction–adduction (Ab-Adw) and flexion–extension in the wrist (F-Ew), pronation–supination (P-Se) and flexion–extension (F-Ee) in the elbow and, abduction– adduction (Ab-Ads), flexion–extension (F-Es) and rotation (Rots) in the shoulder. (Adopted from Roux 2000 and modified).*

the importance of the elementary movement in the knapping skill. More specifically, when considering the functional outcome of the striking arm movement, that is the movement of the hammer, high-level experts adapted the acceleration of the hammer in a more finely-tuned manner than low-level experts. Subsequently, if this tuning capacity were recognized as one dimension of a high level of expertise, it is then necessary to understand how it is produced. On this basis, a subsequent experiment was undertaken aimed at qualifying kinematic arm synergies in craftsmen of different levels of expertise.

Before looking at the complex biomechanical system of the arm producing the movement, let us rapidly review the essential characteristics of a stroke associated with stone knapping. The core orientation and the hammer trajectory must create a precise angle (see Chapter 2 this volume), the percussion point has to be very exact, the hammer must deploy accurate velocity (see Chapter 8 this volume), and the postural hand must hold the core with good stability (see Chapter 16 this volume).

The question is then: how is such a stroke produced by the hammer-arm moving system? In this chapter, we propose an analysis of such a moving sys-

tem, in the case of large ellipsoidal beads being shaped by stone knappers having different levels of expertise (see Chapter 4 this volume, for a detailed description of the technique and method used in Khambhat).

The human arm represents a complex biomechanical system. Its anatomy allows seven independent rotations in three arm joints: i) in the wrist, abduction–adduction and flexion–extension of the hand relative to the forearm; ii) in the elbow, pronation–supination and flexion–extension of the forearm relative to the arm; and iii) in the shoulder, abduction–adduction, flexion–extension and rotation of the arm relative to the body (Figs. 5.1 & 5.5b). These different rotations are independent from a mechanical point of view, and, therefore, referred to as the kinematic degrees of freedom (DoF) of the upper limb. Any movement of the arm is a combination of these seven rotations. Consequently, the only way to produce the right trajectory of the hammer is to perform multiple rotations in the arm joints (Figs. 5.1 & 5.5b) in a co-ordinated manner. From the point of view of central nervous system control, this is a quite complex task. The human arm is kinematically redundant, which means that, owing to the different combinations of rotations in the joints, there is theoretically an almost unlimited number of ways the same movement of the hammer can be performed.

Any rotation is put in motion using different groups of muscles. Nervous control of the muscles provides the stable inter-joint co-ordination which allows an adaptive and dextrous skill like stone-bead knapping. Before trying to understand the nature of the control performed by the nervous system, however, we need to understand what is controlled, here the specific pattern of joint rotations of striking movements. The co-ordinated changes in the joint angles during movement execution are called kinematic synergies. The notion of *motor synergy* is commonly used in motor-control literature to describe the co-ordination between different kinds of motor parameters, e.g. joint angles (Levin 1996), joint torques (Gottlieb *et al.* 1996), muscle forces (Gelfand *et al.* 1971) and parameters of central nervous system control (Feldman & Levin 1995). We focus our analysis on the kinematic synergies believing that the movement kinematics reflect the peculiarities of central nervous system control. This idea, dating back to Sechenov (1866) and Marey (1868), were later developed by Bernstein, who wrote:

> … if the centre transmits a regular and efficient chain of effector impulses to the periphery, it will appear at the periphery in the form of equally regular and efficient movements; if the chain of the central effector impulses is irregular and inefficiently organized,

a

b

Figure 5.2. *a) The result of fluting stroke, the arrow shows the direction of the fluting (adapted from Roux 2000). b) An example of a final glass preform and of two flakes detached by the fluting strokes.*

its peripheral projection will also be an irregular and badly organized movement ... Both of them will be accurately reflected at the motor periphery in exactly the same way as a grand piano reflects with equal accuracy the playing of a good or a bad pianist (Bernstein 1940).

If so, a comparative analysis of kinematic synergies will distinguish between the peculiarities of the nervous control at the different levels of mastery of skill. The analysis presented here consists in the description of the kinematic synergies of the elementary striking movement.

As emphasized earlier, the effectiveness of the stroke detaching the correct flake depends on quite a few factors. Among them, two are especially decisive: the stroke direction relative to the stone and stroke power. Therefore, two parameters are used to evaluate stroke efficiency: variation in the stroke direction and the kinetic energy transmitted to the stone at the time of the stroke. Results on stroke efficiency at different levels of expertise are discussed in relation to the characteristics of kinematic synergies.

Of the elementary movements corresponding to different sub-goals of the basis strategy (Chapter 4 this volume) fluting is obviously the most important stroke that leads to the final ellipsoidal shape of the stone (Fig. 5.2a). This stroke should be at the same time: i) powerful, in order to detach a big flake; and ii) precise, in order to detach a flake of a specific pyramidal shape (Fig. 5.2b). Preliminary results on kinematic synergies of crest flutings are presented in this paper.

Method

The data discussed here are part of a larger set of data, from a field experiment held on December 1998 in the same workshop in Khambat as the experiment

reported in Chapter 4 (this volume). The experimental setting was modified in order to understand the dynamics of the hammer-arm system, and to test the craftsmen's capacity to adapt to the properties of the tool depending on their level of expertise. Indeed, one of the main results of a first experiment was that the greater the expertise, the greater the capacity to adapt the hammer movement to the constraints of the task (hammer-arm properties, raw material characteristics) in order to detach the exact planned flake. In addition, our aim was to work not only on the functional result of the craftsmen's movement, i.e. the hammer movement, but also on co-ordination at the arm joints. Consequently, the recording techniques were expanded, and the number of craftsmen participating in the experiment increased.

Participants
Twenty-two artisans took part in the experiments. They were subdivided into four groups following their socially-recognized level of competence: 1) high-level experts (six subjects); 2) low-level experts (six subjects); 3) high-level learners (five subjects); and 4) low-level learners (five subjects). In this paper we analyze the movements of two high-level experts, Abdul-Latif and Inayat, one low-level expert, Prabhin, one high-level learner, Anwar, and one low-level learner, Kausaik.

Movement recordings
1. *Video cameras*
Two video cameras were positioned in front of, and beside, the craftsmen. The entire session was recorded for each craftsman.

2. *Accelerometer*
A uniaxial accelerometer with the following characteristics: range ±250 g, natural frequency 240 Hz,

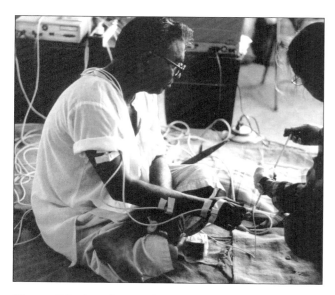

Figure 5.3. *A craftsman during the experimental session.*

accuracy ±0.2 m/s², was used to assess the movement of the hammer. It was attached to the curved end of the hammer head that is not used. It gives the acceleration of the hammer along the progression axis according to the hammer's reference axis.

3. Spatial Tracking System
We used the Spatial Tracking System (STS) to record the arm segment movements. This system uses the electromagnetic field to determine the 3-D positions and orientations of the sensors relative to the stationary system (denoted by 5 in the Fig. 5.1). Three Euler angles of rotation of sensor reference frames relative to the stationary system are used to determine the sensor orientations: azimuth Ψ_{az}, elevation Ψ_{el} and rotation Ψ_{ro}.

Four sensors operating at an update rate of 30 Hz were used. The static accuracy of the STS system was 0.08 cm RMS for the sensor positions and 0.15° RMS for the sensor orientations. Calibration measurements showed that the system was accurate within 0.7 m of the stationary system origin.

The locations of the sensors for the movement recordings were chosen to minimize their displacement relative to the arm segments. They were placed: 1) on the dorsal surface of the hand; 2) on the dorsal surface of the forearm, approximately 10 cm from the wrist joint; 3) on the dorsal surface of the upper arm, approximately 15 cm above the trochlea humeri; and 4) at the highest point of the acromion (Fig. 5.1). The sensors were attached to the skin with adhesive tape. All sensors were within a 0.7 m sphere of the stationary system origin during movement recordings.

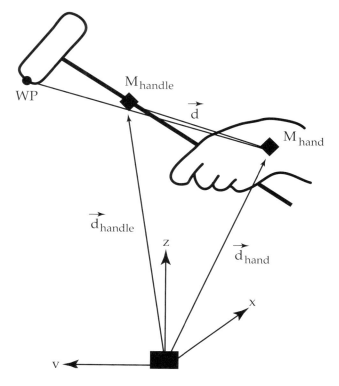

Figure 5.4. *The positions of the STS sensors during the 'model' series: M_{hand} is the sensor located on the hand, M_{handle} is the sensor located on the hammer handle. $\vec{d}_{hand}$ and $\vec{d}_{handle}$ are the positions of these sensors in the stationary system XYZ measured by the STS. $\vec{d} = \vec{d}_{hand} - \vec{d}_{handle}$ is the vector used for validation of rigid body assumption for the system 'hand + hammer'.*

The data from the accelerometer and the Spatial Tracking System were synchronized during movement recording. The recording software was developed by Gilles Dietrich.

Experimental sessions
Protocol
Each participant had to knap an ellipsoidal preform from parallelepipedal roughout (see Chapter 4 this volume). Two raw materials were proposed, stone and glass. A session consisted in knapping series of 10 preforms for three tool conditions (normal hammer, weighted hammer, shorter handle hammer: Bril *et al.* 2001), for the two raw materials, stone and glass. That is each craftsman had to knap 60 preforms. The roughouts were 6 cm × 2.5 cm × 2.5 cm. In this chapter the 'normal' condition only has been analyzed.

In addition, a 'model' series, and a 'passive rotations' series have been recorded. Each condition is described in more details in the subsequent paragraphs.

Table 5.1. *Validation of rigid body assumption for the system 'hand + hammer' (Fig. 5.4).*

Craftsman	$|\vec{d}|$ (cm)	Euler angles of the orientation of handle sensor relative to hand sensor (deg)			Working point coordinates in the reference frame of hand sensor (cm)		
		Ψ_{az}	Ψ_{el}	Ψ_{ro}	WP_X	WP_Y	WP_Z
Abdul-Latif	16.6±0.6	20±4	27±4	107±8	25.4±1.2	2.1±1.7	15.7±1.3
Inayat	12.9±0.3	46±2	43±3	86±3	16.4±0.7	8.2±0.8	30.7±0.6
Prabhin	18.5±0.1	41±2	25±3	101±5	23.4±0.8	14.0±0.9	−0.6±1.3
Anwar	20.0±0.2	29±1	37±3	93±4	21.8±1.0	0.3±0.8	23.8±1.1
Kausaik	15.1±0.1	20±1	16±3	106±2	28.6±0.7	7.0±0.5	7.4±1.1

1. Normal conditions series

The movement of the striking arm was recorded during these series. The participants performed their usual task in the natural conditions of the workshop. The four sensors of the Spatial Tracking System used for movement recording were attached with adhesive tape to the hand, the forearm, the arm and the scapula of the participants (Fig. 5.3).

The data acquired during the knapping of one stone preform for each of the five craftsmen listed above were used in the subsequent analysis.

2. Model series

To calculate the 3-D coordinates of the head of the hammer (knapping working point) from Spatial Tracking System data, we have to know the working point coordinates in the reference frame of the hand's sensor (Fig. 5.4). To calculate these coordinates, we placed an additional sensor on the hammer handle and recorded the series of one stone knapping.

3. Passive rotation series

The positions and orientations of the axes of rotation in the joints are individual parameters necessary to calculate the joint angles (Biryukova *et al.* 2000). To determine them, the passive rotations around the corresponding axes were recorded in all subjects immediately following each experimental session, with the sensors in place. The participants were asked to relax their arm and to allow the experimenter to execute sequences of five to eight rotations corresponding to all seven arm DoF (Fig. 5.5b). All movements started from a neutral position at the joint. The rotation amplitudes were 0.7–0.8 of maximal physiological range. Special care was taken to ensure that only one of the above rotations was performed at a time.

Data analysis

1. Calculating the hammer trajectory

First, we calculated the relative positions and orientations of the hand's sensor and the handle's sensor and concluded that they vary little during the movement

(Table 5.1). Thus, we considered the hand + hammer system to be rigid and calculated the working point coordinates in the reference frames of the hand's sensor (vector directed from the sensor M_{hand} to the working point WP in the Fig. 5.4). Then, assuming that this vector always remains the same, we calculated the working point trajectories during the experimental sessions.

We then calculated two parameters: i) the working point amplitude; and ii) the direction of the stroke (tangential to the working point trajectory at the moment of knapping). These parameters were used to determine the variability of the working point trajectory.

2. Calculating the joint angles

The method of arm joint angles calculation using Spatial Tracking System recordings has been described previously (Biryukova *et al.* 2000). It is based on the model of the human arm consisting of rigid bodies connected by joints of invariant geometry. First, the geometry of the joints, i.e. the positions and orientations of the axes of rotation in the joints are calculated individually for each craftsman from the data of 'passive rotations' series. Second, the time courses of angle variation during the movement are calculated under the so-called rigid body assumption that implies an invariant shape of the segments and an invariant geometry of the joints (Prokopenko *et al.* 2001). As a result, the kinematics of the elementary movement has been determined in the form of time courses of rotation angles corresponding to seven DoF of the arm: abduction–adduction (Ab-Adw) and flexion–extension in the wrist (F-Ew), pronation–supination (P-Se) and flexion–extension (F-Ee) in the elbow and, abduction–adduction (Ab-Ads), flexion–extension (F-Es) and rotation (Rots) in the shoulder (Fig. 5.5).

3. Statistical analysis

Averaging: The angular trajectories were averaged for all flutings performed during the knapping of one glass preform. The mean squared deviations were

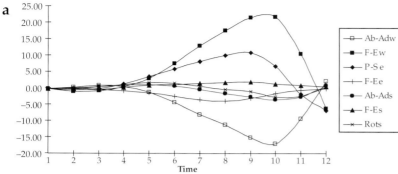

a

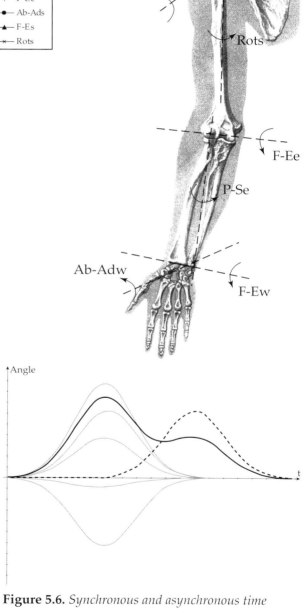

b

Figure 5.5. *a) Time courses of the arm joint angles calculated from STS recordings for one fluting: Ab-Adw = the abduction–adduction in the wrist; F-Ew = the flexion–extension in the wrist; P-Se = the pronation–supination in the elbow; F-Ee = the flexion–extension in the elbow; Ab-Ads = the abduction–adduction in the shoulder; F-Es = flexion–extension in the shoulder; Rots = the rotation in the shoulder. The time interval between two dots is 33 ms, corresponding to the STS operating sampling frequency. b) The independent rotations in the arm joints shown on an anatomical figure. (Adapted from Sinelnikov 1967.)*

calculated for each time point of the movement. The average of the mean squared deviations was used to assess the variability of angular trajectory.

Method of principal components: The common variance of joint angles can be described by a number of independent movements, called principal components, smaller than the number of joint angles. The first principal component describes the most of the common variance of joint angles; the second describes the most of the remaining variance and so forth. The first principal component is equal to 100 per cent if all seven joint angles of the arm have time profiles that are exactly synchronous. The more asynchronous the time courses are, the smaller the first principal component (Fig. 5.6). Therefore, we have taken its value as the assessment of a degree of coordination between the joint angles.

Each component is a linear combination of the joint angles. The coefficients (loading factors) of the principal component define the degree of its relation with the corresponding angle.

We have taken the coefficients of the first principal component to be assessments of the relative contributions of the joint angles to the movement. We consider a degree of coordination between the joint angles and their relative contributions in the movement to be a description of kinematic synergy.

Figure 5.6. *Synchronous and asynchronous time profiles of joint angles. The angles denoted by grey lines contribute in the first principal component. The angle denoted by dashed line contributes in the second one. The angle denoted by the bold line contributes to both principal components.*

Other statistical method: One-way analysis of variance (one-way ANOVA) and the least significant difference (LSD) test with standard significance of $p < 0.05$

Table 5.2. *The number of flutings performed by the craftsmen.*

Group	Craftsman	Glass	Stone
High-level expert	Abdul-Latif	6	9
High-level expert	Inayat (P-S pattern)	8	7
	Inayat (F-Ew pattern)	8	7
Low-level expert	Prabhin	11	17
High-level learner	Anwar	13	9
Low-level learner	Kausaik	19	26

a

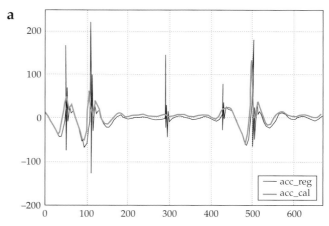

b

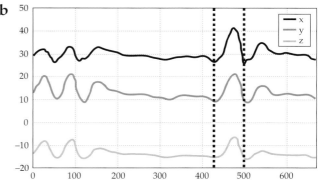

Figure 5.7. *a) Acceleration of the working point of the hammer i) measured by the accelerometer and ii) calculated as the second derivative of the working point trajectory; b) 3D coordinates X,Y,Z of the working point trajectory. Dashed vertical lines denote one fluting movement.*

were used to find statistically-significant differences in kinematic synergies.

Procedure of data reduction: First, using video recordings, we identified the elementary striking movements corresponding to crest flutings. Table 5.2 gives the number of flutings analyzed for each craftsman, depending on the raw material (glass and stone).

Second, we extracted the parts of the Spatial Tracking System recordings corresponding to the flutings (Fig. 5.7b). Then, we calculated the joint angles and the working point trajectories. Working point acceleration, calculated numerically as the second derivative of the working point trajectory (Fig. 5.7a, grey line), was then compared with the recorded acceleration of the hammer (Fig. 5.7a, black line) to check data consistency. Finally, we analyzed the kinematic synergies with the methods described above.

Results

In the following analysis, specific attention is paid to the mode of variation of the various parameters calculated depending on the level of expertise. It is important to emphasize that the degree of variability is a relative issue. Indeed, most definitions of skill incorporate either directly or indirectly reduced variability as an inherent feature. For example, Guthrie (1935) (cited by Newell *et al.* 1993) suggested that the production of some predetermined outcome with *maximal certainty* is an integral part of skilled performance. Thus, reduced variability is considered to reflect higher levels of skill. However, skilled performers may minimize the discrete movement parameter selected as the task criterion, but have higher joint motion variability than their less-skilled counterparts (Arutyunyan *et al.* 1968; 1969). This joint motion variability can be considered as the index of adaptability to changes in task conditions as well as in internal parameters (trauma, fatigue). Consequently, the comparative analysis of kinematic synergies will focus specifically on the nature of parameter variability.

First, we analyzed the arm movements during the knapping of a glass preform in order to obtain the same initial conditions for the craftsmen of different groups. Then, we compared the differences in the kinematic patterns of stone-bead knapping and glass-bead knapping.

Working point trajectories
1. Amplitude
The working point trajectories of all flutings performed during the knapping of one glass preform by the craftsmen of different groups differ by their amplitudes (Fig. 5.8a). The two high-level experts perform the most amplified flutings. Among them, Inayat, considered to be the most qualified high-level expert in Khambhat, performs the most amplified movements.

The greater the amplitude, the greater the potential energy (equal to *mh*, where *m* is the mass of the hammer and *h* is its altitude) acquired by the

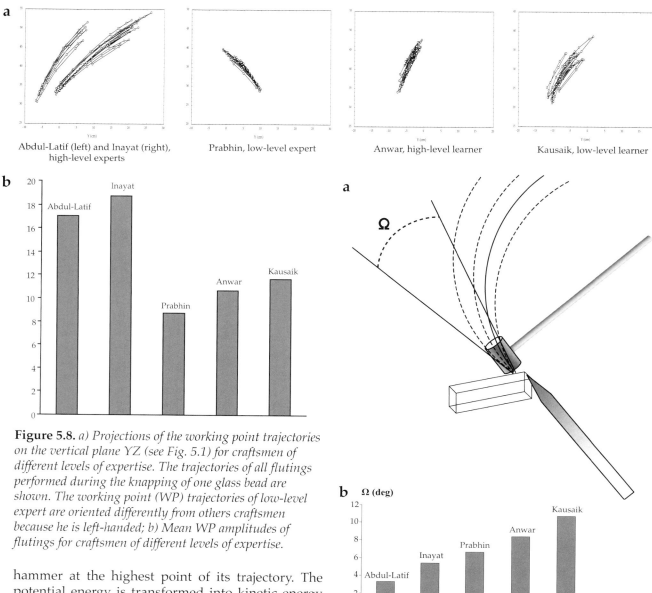

Figure 5.8. *a) Projections of the working point trajectories on the vertical plane YZ (see Fig. 5.1) for craftsmen of different levels of expertise. The trajectories of all flutings performed during the knapping of one glass bead are shown. The working point (WP) trajectories of low-level expert are oriented differently from others craftsmen because he is left-handed; b) Mean WP amplitudes of flutings for craftsmen of different levels of expertise.*

Figure 5.9. *a) Relative position of the anvil, the bead and the hammer during stone knapping. Fluting trajectories and the cone of fluting directions are shown. Ω is maximal angles between fluting directions. b) Maximal angle between fluting directions Ω for craftsmen of different levels of expertise.*

hammer at the highest point of its trajectory. The potential energy is transformed into kinetic energy (equal to $mV^2/2$, where m is the mass of the hammer and V is its final velocity) transmitted from the hammer to the stone at the time of impact. Kinetic energy characterizes the stroke power. Therefore, the more amplified the flutings performed by the high-level experts, the more powerful they are, if no additional effort is applied.

The working point trajectories of the low-level expert and high-level learner are quite stable. On the other hand, the high-level experts and the low-level learners perform more variable trajectories (Fig. 5.8a).

2. Direction of the flutings

The mutual orientations of the anvil axis, the roughout axis and the fluting direction (Fig. 5.9a) are crucial for

successful detachment of the flake. Bimanual coordination is essential for the good reciprocal adaptation of the direction of the stroke and the orientation of the roughout. The direction of the hammer trajectory in three-dimensional space depends on the craftsman's posture and is obviously specific to each craftsman

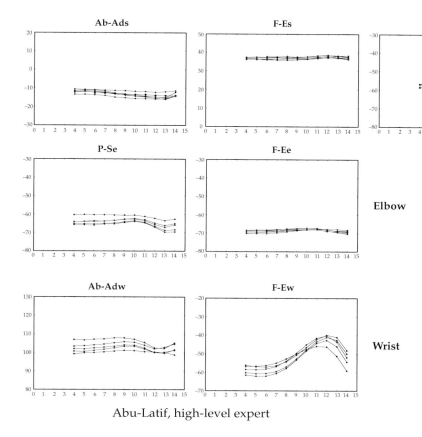

Abu-Latif, high-level expert

Figure 5.10. *Time courses of joint angles for different flutings performed during the knapping of one glass preform by the high-level expert, Abdul. The figures in the top line correspond to the rotations in the shoulder joint: abduction–adduction (Ab-Ads), flexion–extension (F-Es) and rotation (Rots). The figures in the middle line correspond to the rotations in the elbow joint: pronation–supination (P-Se) and flexion–extension (F-Ee). The figures in the bottom line correspond to the rotations in the wrist joint: abduction–adduction (Ab-Adw) and flexion–extension (F-Ew). The distance between time points is 33 ms corresponding to the STS operating rate.*

(Fig. 5.8a). However, the stability of this direction can be considered as a characteristic of the craftsman's functional outcome. Maximal span of the cone of fluting directions (marked by Ω in Fig. 5.9a) is taken as a measure of this stability. This maximal span, or in other words, the highest variability of fluting directions is demonstrated by the low-level learner, and the lowest variability by both high-level experts and the high-level learner (Fig. 9b).

Kinematic pattern
The kinematic pattern of fluting is determined by the time courses of the seven joint angles of the arm, as shown in Figure 5.10 (the high-level expert, Abdul-Latif), Figure 5.11 (the low-level expert, Prabhin), Figure 5.12 (the high-level learner, Anwar) and Figure 5.13 (low-level learner, Kausaik). Each figure contains seven small graphs corresponding to arm DoFs and showing the time courses of each joint angle for all flutings performed during the knapping of one glass preform. The initial point of the curves corresponds to the beginning of hammer elevation and the final point corresponds to the stroke. Three patterns of curve profiles appear:
i) with small variations both in the profile itself and in the starting point (superimposed curves, as in Fig. 5.10);

ii) with small variations in the profile, but large variations in the starting point (parallel translated curves, as in Fig. 5.12);
iii) with large variations both in the profile and in the starting point (as in Figs. 5.11 & 5.13).

The high-level expert has the most stereotyped profiles of the first type (Fig. 5.10). In the low-level expert there are almost no changes in the joint angles, except in the flexion of the wrist (Fig. 5.11). The physiological 'sense' of small variability of the majority of the joints lies, therefore, in their fixation. In contrast, the physiological 'sense' of the small variability in the angular trajectories of the high-level expert is the high stereotypy of angular displacements. The variability of the flexion in the wrist in the low-level expert is of the third type (Fig. 5.11). The high-level learner demonstrates variability of the second type (Fig. 5.12) and, the low-level learner variability of the third type (Fig. 5.13).

To emphasize the differences between levels of expertise, the amplitudes of averaged angular trajectories and the variability of angular trajectories were compared for i) the high-level expert and the low-level expert (Fig. 5.14); ii) for the high-level expert and the high-level learner (Fig. 5.15); and iii) for the low-level expert and the low-level learner (Fig. 5.16). The amplitudes of all joint angles, except for flexion

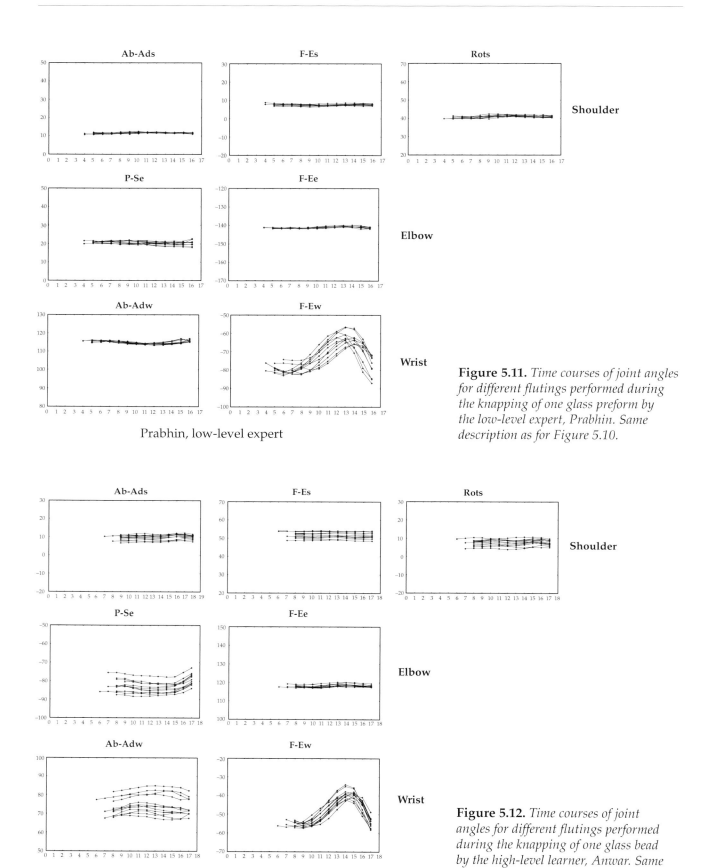

Figure 5.11. *Time courses of joint angles for different flutings performed during the knapping of one glass preform by the low-level expert, Prabhin. Same description as for Figure 5.10.*

Figure 5.12. *Time courses of joint angles for different flutings performed during the knapping of one glass bead by the high-level learner, Anwar. Same description as for Figure 5.10.*

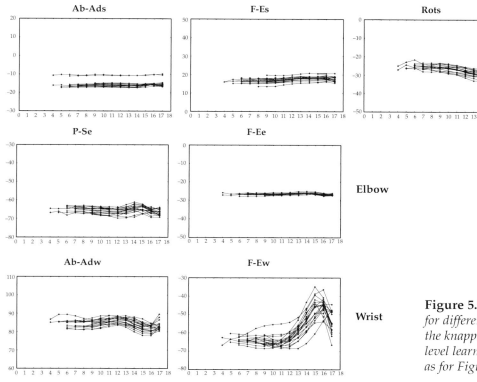

Kausaik, low-level learner

Figure 5.13. *Time courses of joint angles for different flutings performed during the knapping of one glass bead by the low-level learner, Kausaik. Same description as for Figure 5.10.*

in the wrist, were greater in high-level expert than in low-level expert (Fig. 5.14a). The variability was smaller in the low-level than in the high-level expert (Fig. 5.14b). However, in the low-level expert, joint angle variability was comparable with the joint angle values, while in the high-level expert the variability was much smaller than the joint angles themselves (Fig. 5.14). So, the angular trajectories of the high-level expert can be considered as less variable than those of the low-level expert. Similarly, the high-level expert had greater angular amplitudes (Fig. 5.15a) and less angular variability (Fig. 5.15b) than the high-level learner. The angular trajectories of the low-level expert were less amplified than those of the low-level learner (Fig. 5.16a), but still less variable (Fig. 5.16b).

These results suggest that more experienced craftsmen perform more amplified movements than less experienced craftsmen. As a result, their working point trajectories are also more amplified (Fig. 5.8b). It

Figure 5.14. *a) Angular amplitudes of arm joint angles averaged over all fluting performed during the knapping of one glass preform. b) Angular variability of arm joint angles averaged over all fluting performed during the knapping of one glass preform, and then averaged over all time points. Comparison of the high-level expert and the low-level expert.*

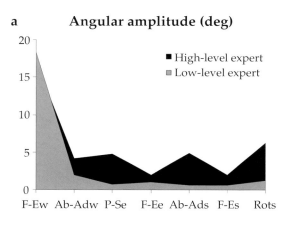

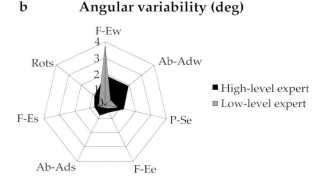

a **Angular amplitude (deg)**

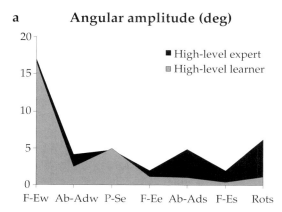

a **Angular amplitude (deg)**

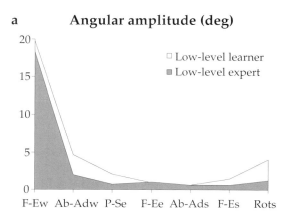

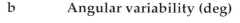

b **Angular variability (deg)**

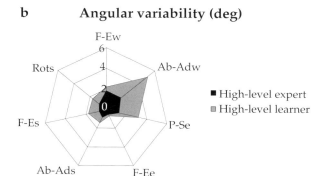

b **Angular variability (deg)**

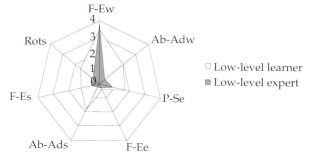

Figure 5.15. *a) Angular amplitudes of arm joint angles averaged over all fluting performed during the knapping of one glass bead. b) Angular variability of arm joint angles averaged over all fluting performed during the knapping of one glass preform, and then averaged over all time points. Comparison of the high-level expert and the high-level learner.*

Figure 5.16. *a) Angular amplitudes of arm joint angles averaged over all fluting performed during the knapping of one glass bead. b) Angular variability of arm joint angles averaged over all fluting performed during the knapping of one glass preform, and then averaged over all time points. Comparison of the low-level expert and the low-level learner.*

is interesting that the large amplitude of the working point is provided by an increase in the amplitude in *all* joint angles, not in the selected ones (Figs. 5.14a & 5.15a). This means that during execution of the stroke all arm DoFs are unified in a kind of kinematic synergy. Skill perfection should be related with the perfection of kinematic synergies which become functionally appropriate (more amplified in the case of fluting execution) (Figs. 5.14a & 5.15a) and more stereotyped (Fig. 5.15b). As a result, the functional outcome is quite stable, as manifested in the low variability of fluting directions (Fig. 5.9b). In less-experienced craftsmen the synergies are at the beginning of their formation. Therefore, angular variability is high (Fig. 5.16b), leading to high variability of fluting directions (Fig. 5.9b). Although even the flutings of low-level learners are powerful due to their large amplitude (Figs. 5.8b & 5.16a), the functional outcome can be bad, because of the unsuitable direction of the stroke.

Synergies of the fluting movements

Two parameters were used to describe the kinematic synergies of the flutings: the coordination between the joint angles and the relative contributions of the joint angles to the movement. The flutings in all groups of craftsmen were found to be highly coordinated: the correlation between the joint angles varied from 83 per cent to 98 per cent. Unexpectedly, the correlation was highest (98 per cent) in the low-level expert and lowest (83 per cent) in one of two high-level experts, Inayat, the most qualified high-level expert of Khambhat. This can be explained by looking at the contributions of the joint angles to the movement (Fig. 5.17).

Let us begin the analysis of the contents of kinematic synergies with distal joints and finish with proximal ones. Flexion in the wrist (F-Ew) contributes the most in the craftsmen of all the groups; abduction in the wrist (Ab-Adw) is manifested in the low-level expert (Fig. 5.17b) and the low-level learner (Fig.

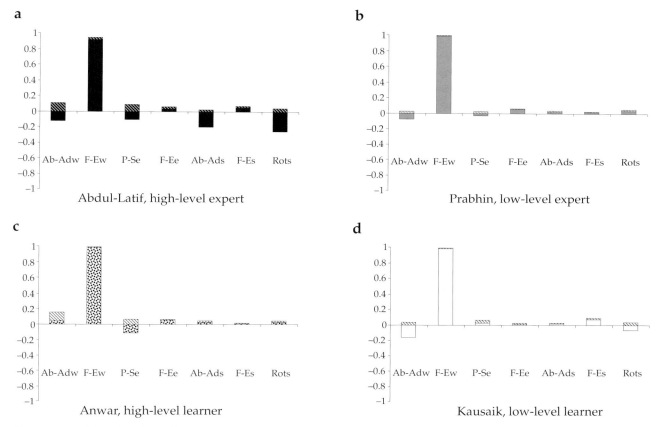

Figure 5.17. *Contributions of arm joint angles in the first principal component for craftsmen of different levels of expertise. Mean standard deviations calculated for all fluting performed during the knapping of one glass preform are shown by shaded areas. A degree of coordination between joint angles assessed by the value of the first principal component PC_1 is indicated.*

5.17d). Pronation of the forearm (P-Se) occurs in the high-level learner (Fig. 5.17c), and none of the other craftsmen do not uses rotations in the elbow. Only the high-level expert (Fig. 5.17a) uses rotation in the shoulder significantly (Rots); the low-level learner shows little rotation and a non-functional extension (Fig. 5.17d). The kinematic synergy of the high-level expert is characterized, therefore, by the correct contribution of the proximal joints at the same time as the distal joints. The high inter-joint correlation in the low-level expert is due to the fixation of all joint angles except for flexion in the wrist. The lower (but still high) inter-joint correlation in the other craftsmen reflects the co-ordination between several joint angles: the wrist and the shoulder angles (in the high-level expert: Fig. 5.17a) and between the wrist and the elbow angles (in the high-level learner: Fig. 5.17c).

The lowest inter-joint correlation in the more qualified high-level expert, Inayat, is probably due to even more joint angles involved in movement execution. Of the sixteen flutings performed by Inayat, eight were performed using chiefly pronation in the elbow

(Fig. 5.18a) and another eight using primarily flexion in the wrist (Fig. 5.18b). In both cases, the shoulder angles were actively involved in the movement. In this way, Inayat not only uses all arm DoFs, but also varies their contributions during the knapping of a single glass preform. Another peculiarity of Inayat's flutings is their inter-trial variability: the mean squared deviations of joint angles contributions calculated over all flutings are greater in Inayat than in the other craftsmen (compare Figs. 5.17 & 5.18).

The differences in kinematic patterns of stone-bead knapping and glass-bead knapping
We compared the kinematic patterns of stone flutings and glass flutings for craftsmen of different groups. The statistical significance of the differences between joint contributions for stone flutings and glass flutings is presented in Table 5.3, where the asterisks denote statistically significant differences ($p < 0.05$). The low-level expert, Prabhin, shows the minimal dependence of the kinematic pattern on raw material (only in abduction in the wrist).

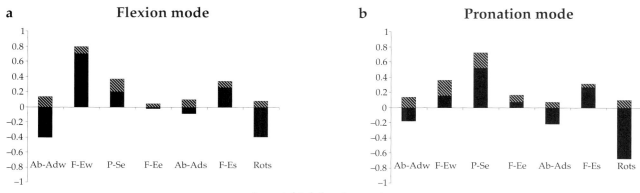

a **Flexion mode**

b **Pronation mode**

Inayat, high-level expert

Figure 5.18. *Contributions of arm joint angles in the first principal component for the high-level expert, Inayat. Mean standard deviations calculated for all fluting performed during the knapping of one glass bead are shown by shaded areas. a) 'Flexion mode', is characterized by flexion in the wrist that contributes the most to the movement; b) 'Pronation mode' is characterized by pronation in the elbow (and rotation in the shoulder) that contributes the most to the movement.*

Table 5.3. *Statistical significance of the differences between joint contributions during fluting glass roughouts and stone flutings. The asterisks denote statistically-significant differences (p <0.05).*

	Inayat	Abdul-Latif	Prabhin	Anwar	Kausaik
Ab-Adw			*		*
F-Ew	*	*			*
P-Se	*				*
F-Ee					
Ab-Ads	*	*		*	*
F-Es	*				
Rots	*	*		*	*

Despite statistically-significant differences, the joint contributions, averaged over all performed flutings, are approximately the same in the low-level expert (Fig. 5.19d), high-level learner (Fig. 5.19e) and low-level learner (Fig. 5.19f). In contrast, in the high-level experts the differences between the averaged joint contributions for glass and stone were quite large (Fig. 5.19a,b,c).

Discussion

Joint angles as a relevant parameter of motor control
Despite the prominence of joint angles in theoretical discussions of perceiving limb positions and controlling limb trajectories (e.g. Hollerbach 1990), their status as the relevant perceptual and control variable is questionable (Soechting & Ross 1984). For example, in perceiving and controlling limb directions at the level of muscular-articular links, the configuration of the arm is not in terms of joint angles but of relative directions of segmental inertial ellipsoids (Turvey 1998).

However, in the hierarchical planning of the movement, its kinematics define the solution space, and control strategies are selected to reduce the number of possible motor patterns (Young & Marteniuk 1998). If this is true, the CNS should contain a parallel kinematic and dynamic representation (Kalaska 1991; Scott & Kalaska 1995; 1997).

Using a comparative analysis of kinematic synergies, we found the peculiarities specific to different levels of mastery of skill. The synergies of only one craftsman from each group (except for two high-level experts) were analyzed. Our results are therefore preliminary ones. However, they let us put forward a hypothesis on the organization of skilled movement consistent with the theoretical and experimental data of movement physiology and biomechanics.

What kinematic peculiarities are specific for high level of mastery of skill?
The high level of mastery of skill is characterized by:
i)   great amplitude of hammer trajectory (Fig. 5.8);
ii) stereotyped direction of the stroke (Fig. 5.9b);
iii) stereotyped joint trajectories (Figs. 5.10, 5.14 & 5.15);
iv) a large number of degrees of freedom involved in the motion (Figs. 5.17a & 5.19);
v) pronounced adaptability of the kinematic pattern to the raw material (Fig. 5.19a,b,c).
The first two points concern the functional output of the stroke. We can suggest that the high-level experts adjust the amplitude of the stroke in such a way that the kinetic energy transmitted from the hammer to the stone corresponds exactly to the power required to detach a 'correct' flake. The stability of stroke direction suggests that the postural arm assures the fine preset of the stone allowing the striking arm to

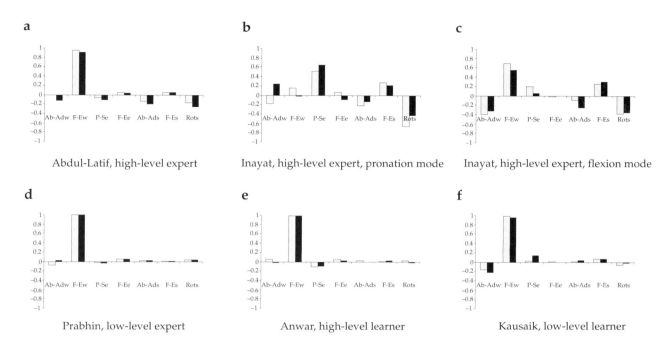

Figure 5.19. *Comparison of kinematic patterns (contributions of arm joint angles in the first principal component) between flutings of stone roughout and glass roughout. The contributions are averaged over all performed flutings. a) The high-level expert, Abdul-Latif; b) the high-level expert, Inayat, 'pronation mode' of the movement; c) the high-level expert, Inayat, 'flexion mode' of the movement; d) the low-level expert, Prabhin; e) the high-level learner, Anwar; f) the low-level learner, Kausaik.*

perform a kind of 'standard' stroke keeping the stable angle between the stroke direction and the orientation of the anvil. This suggestion might be correct for all groups of craftsmen, not only for high-level experts. Although the cone of stroke directions is three times larger in the low-level learner than in the high-level expert (Fig. 5.9b), it remains quite small: just 10°.

The stability of functional output is assured by the stability of joint trajectories. It provides evidence for stable and reliable co-ordination between all arm joints, because in high-level experts, all arm DoFs are involved in the movement. The wrist, elbow and shoulder are controlled by completely different groups of muscles. Stable co-ordination between the joints is, therefore, a complex problem of central nervous system control. How is this problem solved at the high level of expertise? There is simple functional evidence for using the shoulder joint: owing to leverage, even small rotations in this joint contribute significantly to the displacement of the hammer. Apparently, this reason is not the decisive one. The amplitude of the hammer is small with respect to the length of the arm and can be successfully achieved by the rotations in the wrist, which is the case in most of the craftsmen.

The more important reason is the flexibility of movement with many DoFs. The human arm is redundant from a mechanical point of view: seven

independent rotations in the arm joints are available to perform hammer trajectory, or, in other words, to guarantee three independent coordinates of the hammer working point. In general, there is an infinite number of motor solutions, i.e. the infinite number of different combinations of rotations in the joints which give the same hammer trajectories. The ability to use different strategies to solve the excess DoF problem is an inherent property of the central nervous system: so-called motor equivalence (Abbs & Cole 1987). The difficulties in controlling all DoF simultaneously are commonly referred to as the 'redundancy problem' or the 'Bernstein problem'. On the other hand, the freedom of choice between different motor solutions ensures motor flexibility. In this sense, 'abundance' might be a more suitable term than 'redundancy': numerous DoFs should not be viewed as a source of control problems for the nervous system but as a useful apparatus that requires proper organization (Gelfand & Latash 1998). Obviously, motor flexibility is closely related to the adaptation of the movement to external (raw material, possible environmental changes) and internal (trauma, fatigue) perturbations.

One of the high-level experts, Abdul-Latif, uses the synergy which includes the wrist and the shoulder DoF (Fig. 5.17a). The flexibility of the synergy is revealed in the variation of the relative contributions of the joint angles depending on the raw material (glass or stone) (Fig. 5.19a). The other high-level expert, Inayat, the most experienced of the high-level experts of Khambhat, uses not only all arm joints (the wrist, the elbow and the shoulder) but also their different combinations which can be subdivided into two synergies (Fig. 5.18). One might suggest that at the highest level of expertise the large repertory of motor synergies allowing successful task completion can be used. The ability to use different motor synergies from this repertory is manifested in the process of adaptation to the raw material: in the high-level experts the relative contributions of joint angles vary significantly (Fig. 5.19a,b,c).

In contrast, the low-level expert and the learners use only flexion–extension in the wrist fixing the elbow and the shoulder joints (Fig. 5.17b,c,d). This strategy can be successful, at least for low-level experts who produce stones of acceptable quality. However, it would be difficult for these groups of craftsmen to adapt to changes in movement conditions, because of the lack of available DoFs. As a consequence, when passing from glass to stone, these craftsmen do not change their motor synergy (Fig. 5.19d,e,f). One might say that the difference between high and low levels of mastery of skill is revealed in the flexible versus fixed nature of motor synergies.

What can we suggest about stone-knapping central control and learning?

Bernstein defines synergy as a higher-level organizing principle of movement rather that muscle groupings, emphasizing the importance of having a common functional goal for a large group of muscles. For example, he describes locomotion as

> an extremely widespread synergy incorporating the whole musculature and the entire moving skeleton and bringing into play a large number of areas and conduction pathways of the central control system (Bernstein 1967).

A solution to this motor-control problem can be presented in the form of a hierarchical control diagram. In planning a movement, a high-level strategy is selected by the nervous system. Strategies are formulated in terms of mechanical parameters. A strategy is then implemented by selecting a spatial and temporal patterning of muscle activities which can be called **flexible synergies**. Although muscle groupings are not fixed, they are determined by simple rules of combination. Therefore, control is simplified while at the same time allowing flexibility in movement possibilities (Macpherson 1991).

In this context, the simplification of movement control implies the cooperation of loosely-defined descending commands with on-line corrective regulation from peripheral systems. This might more easily explain the variability as well as the adaptability of the motor system. The external behaviour of flexible synergy, the kinematic pattern, will be defined by movement purpose and by current external conditions.

The process of learning new skilled movements can be roughly subdivided into the following stages (Bernstein 1967). In the beginning, the excessive number of DoFs makes it difficult to perform the movement precisely. At this stage, the learner tries to decrease the number of DoFs by freezing some joints. In the subsequent stages of improving the skill, he has to involve additional rotations in the joints in the movement in order to obtain more freedom for successful task completion. Little by little the DoFs become co-ordinated, forming what is called synergy. At the highest level of motor skill, the expert has at his disposal a large number of synergies and, switching from one to another, can easily adapt his movement to changes in the environment and in task parameters.

The high inter-joint co-ordination found in the craftsmen leads us to believe that the control of elementary movement can be fairly simple despite the large number of DoF involved in the task. Fluting movement is a fast movement with a period of about 300 ms. One might suggest that its central control is of a feedforward nature: it consists in the signal to the beginning of the movement and does not intervene during movement execution. Our previous experience in motor-control modelling (Biryukova et al. 1999) suggests that this type of control consists in the preset of visco-elastic parameters of the arm joints and the signal for movement initiation. One could imagine the arm as a multidimensional spring which moves toward its position of equilibrium. How can the accuracy of percussion be achieved under this type of control? We suggest that the accuracy of percussion is achieved by the appropriate positioning of the stone by the postural arm that plays the main role in the task.

Acknowledgements

The authors are grateful to Valentine Roux for organizing the experiments in Khambhat and for her support of our approach to data analysis. We warmly thank the craftsmen who accepted an unusual working situation. We are deeply indebted to Vadim Roschin and Olga Pavlova for fruitful discussions and, to Eva David for her painstaking work in knapping time-keeping.

This research was funded by the French Ministère délégué à la recherche et aux nouvelles Technologies (ACI Cognitique L103, ACI TTT P7802 n° 02 2 0440) and by the Russian Foundation for Basic Research (projects 4-4-48989a and 2-4-48410a).

References

Abbs, J.H. & K.J. Cole, 1987. Neural mechanisms of motor equivalence and goal achievement, in *Higher Brain Functions: Recent Exploration of the Brain's Emergent Properties*, ed. S.P. Wise. New York (NY): Wiley, 15–43.

Arutyunyan, R.H., V.S. Gurfinkel & M.L. Mirskii, 1968. Investigation of aiming at a target. *Biophysics* 13, 536–8.

Arutyunyan, R.H., V.S. Gurfinkel & M.L. Mirskii, 1969. Organization of movements on execution by man of an exact postural task. *Biophysics* 14, 1162–7.

Бернштейн, Н.А., 1940. Биодинамика локомоции, В сб Изучение биодинамики ходьбы, бега и прыжка. Москва: Физкультура и Спорт, 9–47. (Bernstein N.A., 1940. Biodynamics of locomotion, in *Studies of the Biodynamics of Walking, Running and Jumping*. Moscow: Fizkultura i Sport, 9-47. [In Russian.]

Bernstein, N.A., 1967. *The Coordination and Regulation of Movements*. Oxford: Pergamon Press.

Biryukova, E.V., V.Y. Roschin, A.A. Frolov, M.E. Ioffe, J. Massion & M. Dufosse, 1999. Forearm postural control during unloading: anticipatory changes in elbow stiffness. *Experimental Brain Research* 124(1), 107–17.

Biryukova, E.V., A. Roby-Brami, A.A. Frolov & M. Mokhtari, 2000. Kinematics of human arm reconstructed from spatial tracking system recordings. *Journal of Biomechanics* 33(8), 985–95.

Bril, B., V. Roux & G. Dietrich, 2000. Habiletés impliquées dans la taille des perles en calcédoine: caracteristiques motrices et cognitives d'une action complexe, in *Cornaline de l'Inde: des pratiques techniques de Cambay aux technosystèmes de l'Indus*, ed. V. Roux. Paris: Edition de MSH, 211–303. [English CD-Rom.] www.epistemes.net/arkcotek/p_cornaline.htm.

Bril, B., G. Dietrich, L. Byriukova, A. Roby-Brami & V. Roux, 2001. Hammering, adaptation to tool properties and raw material. Poster presented at the International workshop 'Knapping stone, a uniquely hominid behavior?'. Abbaye des Premontrés, Pont-à-Mousson (France), 21–24 November.

Feldman, A.G. & M.F. Levin, 1995. The origin and use of positional frames of reference in motor control. *Behavioral and Brain Sciences* 18, 723–806.

Gelfand, I.M. & M. Latash, 1998. On the problem of adequate language in biology, in *Progress in Motor Control*, vol. 2, ed. M.L. Latash. Champaign (IL): Human Kinetics, 209–27.

Gelfand, I.M., V.S. Gurfinkel, M.L. Tsetlin & M.L. Shik, 1971. Some problems in the analysis of movements, in *Models of the Structural-functional Organization of Certain Biological Systems*, eds. I.M. Gelfand, V.S. Gurfinkel, S.V. Fomin & M.L. Tsetlin. Cambridge (MA): MIT Press, 329–45.

Gottlieb, G.L., Q. Song, D.-A. Hong & D.M. Corcos, 1996. Coordinating two degrees of freedom during human arm movement: load and speed invariance of relative joint torques. *Journal of Neuroscience* 76, 3196–206.

Guthrie, E.R., 1935. *The Psychology of Learning*. New York (NY): Harper.

Hollerbach, J.M., 1990. Planning of arm movements, in *Visual Cognition and Action: an Invitation to Cognitive Science*, eds. D.N. Osherson, S.M. Kosslyn & J.M. Hollerbach. Cambridge (MA): MIT Press, 183–211.

Kalaska, J.F., 1991. What parameters of reaching are encoded by discharges of cortical cells?, in *Motor Control: Concepts and Issues*, eds. D.R. Humphrey & H.-J. Freund. New York (NY): Wiley, 307–30.

Levin, M.F., 1996. Interjoint coordination during pointing movements is disrupted in spastic hemiparesis. *Brain* 119, 281–93.

Macpherson, J.M., 1991. How flexible are muscle synergies? in *Motor Control: Concepts and Issues*, eds. D.R. Humphrey & H.-J. Freund. Chichester: John Wiley & Sons Ltd, 33–47.

Marey, E.-J., 1868. *Du mouvement dans les fonctions de la vie, leçons faites au Collège de France*. Paris: Germer Baillière, V–VII.

Newell, K.M., R.E.A. van Emmerik & R.L. Sprague, 1993. Stereotypy and variability, in *Variability and Motor Control*, eds. K.M. Newell & D.M. Corcos. Champaign (IL): Human Kinetics, 475–96.

Prokopenko, R.A., A.A. Frolov, E.V. Biryukova & A. Roby-Brami, 2001. Assessment of the accuracy of a human arm model with seven degrees of freedom. *Journal of Biomechanics* 34(2), 177–85.

Roux, V., 2000. *Cornaline de l'Inde: des pratiques techniques de Cambay aux technosystèmes de l'Indus*. Paris: Edition de MSH, 211–303. [English CD-Rom.] www.epistemes.net/arkcotek/p_cornaline.htm.

Roux, V., B. Bril & G. Dietrich, 1995. Skills and learning difficulties involved in stone knapping: the case of stone-bead knapping in Khambhat, India. *World Archaeology* 27(1), 63–87.

Scott, S.H. & J.F. Kalaska, 1995. Changes in motor cortex activity during reaching: movements with similar hand paths but different arm postures. *Journal of Neurophysiology* 73, 2563–7.

Scott, S.H. & J.F. Kalaska, 1997. Reaching movements with similar paths but different arm orientations, part I: Activity of individual cells in motor cortex. *Journal of Neurophysiology* 77, 826–52.

Сеченов, И.М., 1866. Рефлексы головного мозга. СПб. (Sechenov, I.M., 1866. *The Reflex of the Brain*. St Petersburg.) [In Russian.]

Синельников, Р.Д., 1967. Атлас анатомии человека. Москва: Медицина. (Sinelnikov, R.D., 1967. *Atlas of the Human Anatomy*, vol. 1. Moscow: Meditsina.) [In Russian.]

Soechting, J.F. & B. Ross, 1984. Psychophysical determination of coordinate representation of human arm orientation. *Neuroscience* 13, 595–604.

Turvey, M.T., 1998. Dynamics of effortful touch and interlimb coordination. *Journal of Biomechanics* 31(10), 873–82.

Young, R.P. & R.G. Marteniuk, 1998. Stereotypic muscletorque patterns are systematically adopted during acquisition of a multi-articular kicking task. *Journal of Biomechanics* 31, 809–16.

Chapter 6

Planning Abilities as a Dynamic Perceptual-motor Skill: an Actualist Study of Different Levels of Expertise Involved in Stone Knapping

Valentine Roux & Eva David

In order to get a better understanding of the role of planning abilities in stone knapping as well as on the dynamic of their emergence, an actualist study has been conducted in India where stone beads are still knapped according to a traditional technique. The course of action aimed at transforming pebbles into parallelepipedals is studied for subjects with different levels of expertise. Patterning of planning is investigated through the following points: the ordering of the operations, the variability at both the intra- and inter-subject levels and the temporal structure of the sequences. Results show that the knapping expertise results from a dynamic involving interaction between the elementary movements, perceptual information and planning. The elementary movements are tuned according to the goal of the knapper, here the quality of the beads. Perception of the stone characteristics and adjustment of the subgoals to the final goal depend on this regulation. The same way, data on apprenticeship suggest that planning should be construed as a perceptual-motor skill emerging from action and perception. This result has direct implications for studying evolution of lithic industries. In particular, it appears that technical actions as expressed by lithic industries should be considered as complex phenomena whose actualization is not reducible to a sole prime mover alleged to be the development of planning abilities.

Prehistoric stone tools are commonly looked upon as the evidence from which inferences about our ancestors' cognitive abilities can be drawn. According to a very broad evolutionary scheme, Oldowan technology supposedly reflects the mental capacities of extant apes, whereas the later Acheulean industries betoken the ability to elaborate mental schemes, the complexity of which increases with Middle Palaeolithic technologies (e.g. Ambrose 2001; Pelegrin 1993; Wynn 2002). Mental schemes are thought to be crucial to the execution of complex efficient knapping sequences. Not only are they supposed to exist prior to the manufacture of the tool, but also to guide the course of action. As stated by Keller (2002, 117): 'Monitoring the progress of each piece requires constant comparison of mental images of the goal form, as well as appropriate intermediate shapes, with the actual state of the work piece'.

The evolution of lithic industries is supposedly bound to the evolution of this capacity to elaborate mental schemes. It is therefore argued that since lithic industries reflect our ancestors' planning and decision-making abilities, they can be used to directly assess the latter's mental capacities or 'intelligence'.

In a previous experiment with Indian stone-bead knappers, the question of the role of planning capacities for stone knapping has been raised through the analysis of the course of action followed by craftsmen to obtain truncated ellipsoid beads (see Bril *et al.* this volume). Courses of action are the observable succession of sub-goals performed in order to actualize knapping methods in particular contexts, that is on stones whose properties are not standard. Knapping methods are here defined as an orderly set of functional operations aimed to transform a pebble into a bead.

They are highlighted from the comparative analysis of the courses of action. They are distinct from the technique defined as the physical modalities according to which the raw material is transformed (Tixier 1967). In this previous experiment, the comparative analysis of the courses of action concentrated on the transition from parallelepiped roughout to ellipsoid preform. The hypothesis was that different qualities of finished products would be obtained through different courses of action, expressing therefore a variability in planning capacities that would enable us to approach the role of these capacities in the effectuation of the knapping task. The results obtained showed, on the one hand, that the courses of action were not determinant of the quality of the product — similar courses of action could be followed and nevertheless produce different results: high-quality pieces in one case, low-quality pieces in another; and on the other hand, that the knowledge of the method was determinant for the general organization of the sequences, but not sufficient for transforming a parallelepipedal roughout into a sub-ellipsoidal preform. This was extremely obvious in the case of glass preforms, for which constraints intrinsic to the material worked cannot have been relevant (glass has the advantage of being homogeneous and not as hard as stone). Craftsmen knew the methods to follow as shown before on stone pieces, and nevertheless were unable to transform glass roughouts. We concluded that the course of action does not characterize the knappers' competencies. Expertise is to be found at the level of the elementary gestures and its succession, that is at the technique level (Bril *et al.*; 2000). As put by Bril and colleagues (this volume), making use of a technique implies the functional utilization of postures and movements in interaction with the environment (Reed & Bril 1996). Thus, making use of the 'Cambay technique' — indirect percussion by counterblows — implies the functional utilization of the postural hand and the arm in interaction with the stone, the rod and the hammer (see Bril *et al.* this volume). This interactive functional utilization corresponds to the tool + target system (Smitsman *et al.* this volume). Our previous experimental results stress the importance of this system, of the mastery of the functional movements over the course of action for the efficient knapping of stone beads.

These results, however, do not explain how a succession of actions unfolds, how decisions are made, how courses of action adapt to the goal to be achieved, what the relationship is between the mastery of the functional movements and the course of action. If the plan is a 'resource' on which the subject draws to construct his action (Agre & Chapman 1990), how is this action constructed? The ecological approach proposes to consider planning as emerging from action. As stated by Ingold (2001, 29):

> Planning is a skilled, environmentally situated practice which, like rehearsal, prepares one for the actions that follow without actually specifying it in all its concrete detail.

The hypothesis on the strong relationship between motor and cognitive abilities has been emphasized in different activities. Lenay *et al.* (2002), for example, have shown how blind people construct mental representations of space through action, Salembier (1996) has illustrated how the decisions taken by air-traffic controllers arise from shuffling strips on multi information board, Cordier *et al.* (1996) has characterized different levels of expertise in rock climbing in terms of energy reduction — planning decisions emerging from a dynamic between the whole body and the rock and not from pre-existing mental images — and Suchman (1986) has studied the route taken by canoe racers and explained their decisions in the same dynamic terms.

In order to understand the relationships between motor and cognitive abilities, between the mastery of the functional movements and the course of action, we developed a new experiment. Indeed, in the previous experiment, courses of action were studied for the creation of preforms from roughouts, a technique which is fairly standardized and therefore which does not let us understand how craftsmen adjust their sub-goals to the specifics of the situation. The new experiment focuses on the initial reduction stage, from the pebble to the roughout. This knapping stage is supposed to be more informative as far as planning is concerned because shapes of pebbles and raw material are not standardized. In order to obtain roughouts, courses of action supposedly will have to take into account the variable properties of pebbles. We should be then in a better position to assess how craftsmen adjust courses of action to their goals.

Moreover, the new experiment includes not only experts and lesser experts, but also apprentices. Courses of action followed by apprentices attached to experts and lesser experts should give us information of what is learnt depending on the goal aimed at and how the methods, supposedly known by all the apprentices, are turned to courses of action.

The report of the experimentation is preceded by a brief presentation of the ethnographic data related to apprenticeship. These data describe empirically what is learnt from one stage to the next and what are the difficulties met by the apprentices in the course of their apprenticeship. Empirical data raise the question of the capacities developed through the different stages of apprenticeship, a question to be answered thereafter on the basis of our experimental results.

Stone-knapping apprenticeship in Khambhat

Knapping apprenticeship takes place mainly within workshops, and these are specialized according to the finished products they turn out: high-quality beads of all dimensions, and low-quality beads of standard dimensions (2.5 cm) (Roux 2000; Roux & Pelegrin 1989). Children start learning to knap when they are about 10 or 12 years old. The duration of the apprenticeship is estimated at approximately 7 years for high-quality beads, and 3 years for low-quality ones. In the high-quality bead workshops, teaching is done by a master who gives apprentices oral instructions and/or shows them the hand positions they need to master in order to progressively tackle the technical difficulties they encounter. The oral instructions and/or demonstration of knapping gestures pertain to the way the stone should be held, to the suitability of striking angles for the initial blows, to the preparation of the striking platforms for the removal of the right kind of flake, to the strength with which blows should be delivered, and lastly to the final shape that is to be achieved. In the low-quality bead workshops, teaching is minimal. The ones in charge of the workshop make a few observations about how to hold the stone and strike the pebble as well as some comments about the quality of the production.

In both types of workshops, the succession of the learning stages is the same. These learning stages are organized according to the sizes and shapes of beads, and to the knapping stage (preform and roughout). Whatever the shapes and sizes of the beads, preforms are systematically learnt before roughouts. Experienced craftsmen make the roughouts subsequently transformed into preforms by apprentices. It is only when knapping of preform and roughout of a given bead is mastered that apprentices learn how to make preforms of new shapes and sizes. As for bead sizes, apprentices start with small beads, and progressively move up to bigger ones. The knapping of either large spherical pieces or very long cylindrical beads (over 8 cm long) represents the last stage of apprenticeship in the manufacture of high-quality beads. Concerning the shapes of the beads, triangular cross-section pieces are learnt before quadrangular ones: knapping is far easier when the edges form 60° dihedral angles rather than 90° ones, this latter angle representing the classic limit of detachment by conchoidal fracture (Roux & Pelegrin 1989). Moving up from preforms to roughouts, from small pieces to bigger pieces, from triangular to quadrangular cross-section pieces requires not only to be successful regularly but also to be rapid. It can take more than a few months.

Indeed the duration of apprenticeship is not only explainable in terms of knowing how to produce the

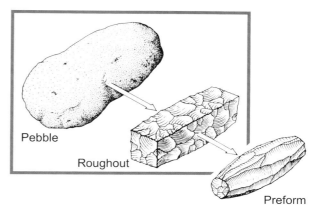

Figure 6.1. *The knapping process for making stone beads.*

appropriate course of action. For example, the courses of action for making small and large beads of the same shape can be identical (Bril *et al.* 2000). Still, it will take a few years for high-quality bead knappers to master the knapping of large-size beads and therefore to move up from one stage of apprenticeship to the next. Similarly, knappers who have specialized in low-quality beads and who have practised for more than ten years will need an extra three years to learn how to make high-quality beads even though they are experts for achieving the goal they have learned (low-quality beads) and even though the knapping sequences for making low- or high-quality beads can be similar (Bril *et al.* 2000). In fact, this situation seldom occurs because high-quality bead knappers are generally not inclined to train low-quality bead knappers: during these three years, they will have to feed adults who do not bring in any money. Hence the following questions: if the knapping sequences do not differ for beads of various qualities and/or sizes, what is it that is learnt throughout the different stages of apprenticeship pertaining to the size or the quality of the beads? Is this mainly a question of the mastery of the elementary movements? What role is planning supposed to play in successful bead making?

An experiment[1] for studying the planning abilities involved in stone-bead knapping

The experiment here presented focuses on the passage from chalcedony pebbles to roughouts (Fig. 6.1). The subjects included experienced and less-experienced knappers, who have been trained by high- and low-level experts respectively, and accordingly practise in high- and low-quality bead workshops. The less-experienced knappers are young craftsmen who have all had a few years' practice, but, for different reasons,[2] only make small beads (they have never knapped beads longer than 1.5 cm).

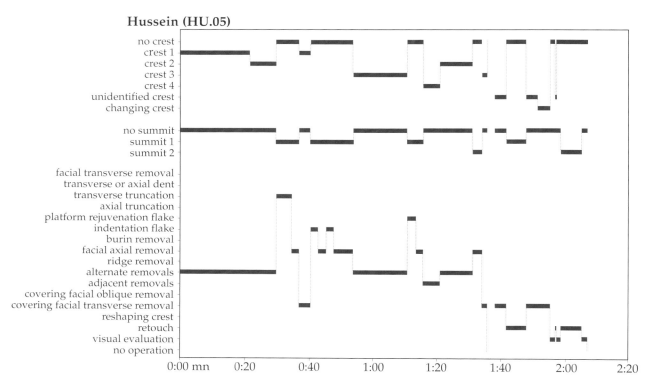

Figure 6.2. *Temporal transcription of succession of actions into sequences in the form of a diagram.*

Subjects

We worked with 22 artisans distributed across 4 levels of expertise:

- High-level experts, called group 1, averaging 48 years old[3];
- Low-level experts, called group 2, averaging 33 years old[4];
- High-level learners, called group 3, averaging 20 years old;
- Low-level learners, called group 4, averaging 18 years old.

Protocol

Each artisan was asked to choose a selection of pebbles from those provided by the workshop where the experiment took place. They were approximately the same size, about 6 cm long and 3 cm wide. However, since it was difficult to obtain such big nodules, the size range was actually quite large. Each pebble was drawn and described before being handed to the knapper. Each artisan were asked to knap a total of 16 roughouts: 8 with a parallelepipedal cross-section, and 8 with a triangular cross-section. Artisans were instructed to produce high quality roughouts, at their own personal rate.

Methods of data recording

The entire manufacturing process of each bead was recorded with a video camera.

Methods of analysis

Using the video tapes, the first step of analysis has consisted in defining all the different types of removals and in classifying them according to their function in the reduction process. The sequences of action were then described and coded in terms of the succession of typical removals and their temporal distribution, owing to a computer software used in ergonomics.[5] This software carries out a temporal analysis of the succession of actions, which are transcribed into sequences in the form of diagrams (Fig. 6.2). The sequences of action could be interpreted in terms of course of actions, that is in terms of succession of sub goals performed in order to actualise the functional operations which organize knapping methods, since each observable removal could be identified from a functional point of view.

Each course of action is here noted after the name of the craftsmen (the 2 first letters) and the number of the knapping sequence achieved (ex. *HA3* (*name of craftsman*, number of the knapping sequence analyzed)).

To ensure that relevant results were obtained and because methods can vary according to the shape of the pebble, comparisons were restricted to courses of action related to a similar initial pebble morphology and resulting in a parallelepiped with a quadrangular cross-section. Pebbles were classified into nine

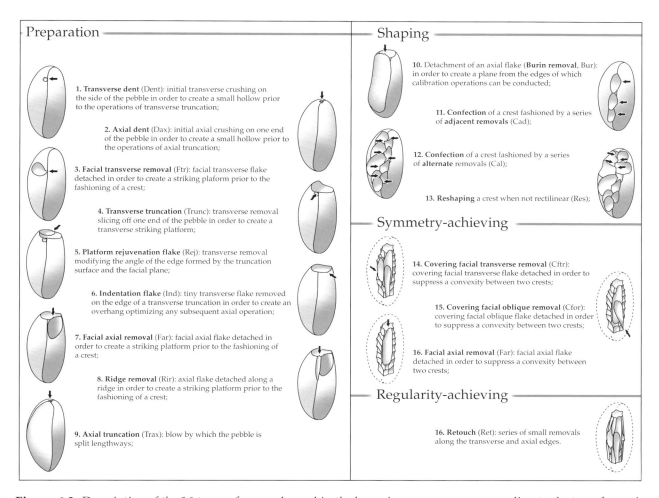

Figure 6.3. *Description of the 16 types of removals used in the knapping sequence corresponding to the transformation of a plano-convex pebble into a parallelepipedal roughout.*

morphological types. The present paper focuses on the analysis of the knapping sequences applied to plano-convex pebbles. The number of subjects participating in the experiment and the number of analyzed sequences are given in Table 6.1. Let us outline that the results here presented are based on a total of 30 courses of action. This low number allows trends to be highlighted, but the generalization of these trends. In this regard, our results are preliminary.

Results

1. The knapping methods

Generally speaking, making a quadrangular roughout from an elongated pebble with a plano-convex cross-section consists in removing both opposite ends of the pebble, and in shaping four planes intersecting at an angle approaching 90°. The beginning of the course of action generally takes advantage of the longest plane displayed by the pebble.

More precisely, the reduction process is organized according to four main successive functional operations: preparation operations, shaping operations, symmetry-achieving operations and regularity-achieving operations. These operations are necessary to transform pebbles into roughouts, here quadrangular cross-section pieces. They are interdependent in the sense that preparation operations are a prerequisite for the shaping operations and that symmetry-achieving and regularity-achieving operations come after.

Each functional operation is achieved by typical removals. These typical removals correspond to a single or a series of percussion removal(s). Sixteen typical removals have been identified (Fig. 6.3):

- Removals associated with preparation operations (whatever the chronological place of the removal in the sequence): transverse or axial truncations (TRUNC, TRAX) initiated by transverse crushing (DENT or DAX), in order to create transverse strik-

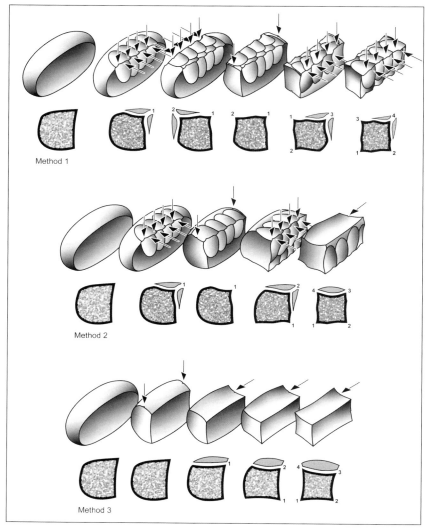

Method 1

Method 2

Method 3

Figure 6.4. *The three identified knapping methods brought into play for obtaining parallelepipedal roughouts from plano-convex pebbles.*

ing operations. These operations consist mainly in regularizing the edges of the parallelepipeds by retouch (RET).

These main functional operations are organized according to three main methods which can be employed following different strategies (see boxed article and Fig. 6.4):

Method 1: the quadrangular cross-section is obtained solely through the fashioning of crests. Two strategies have been observed depending on the number of fashioned crests (two or four).

Method 2: the quadrangular cross-section is obtained by associating the fashioning of crests with thick burin removals. Two strategies have been observed depending on the number of fashioned crests (one or two).

Method 3: the quadrangular cross-section is obtained solely through thick burin removals. The edges created when transforming the volume may be modified or left unmodified.

The methods used by each subject for knapping plano-convex pebbles are indicated in Table 6.1. In the first place, Table 6.1 shows that each group produces courses of action that can be clearly identified as belonging to one of the three methods. This knowledge of the knapping methods is expressed by the use of the main types of shaping removals required for transforming a pebble into a parallelepiped (TRUNC, CAL, CAD, BUR) and by their patterning according to the main steps that characterize a given method. In particular, it appears that groups 3 and 4 knew the methods to follow for transforming a pebble into a parallelepiped even though they had never made such pieces before, i.e. pieces of that length.

In the second place, it appears that there is a correlation between the level of expertise and the method followed, explainable in terms of goals pursued by the craftsmen. Method 1 is found mainly within groups 1 and 3, and method 3 only within group 2. Method 2 is most commonly practised within groups 2 and 4. This method is said to be faster than method 1 and to be

ing platforms, usually on both ends of the pebble.

• Removals associated with shaping operations. Shaping four faces is obtained: either by creating crests; each crest is fashioned by a series of transverse removals (CAL or CAD) initiated by a preliminary axial or transverse facial removal (FAR, FTR), or a ridge removal (RIR); or by creating planes by means of burin removals struck from one or both ends of the pebble (BUR). The two practices can occur in combination.

• Removals associated with symmetry-achieving operations. These operations comprise: reshaping the crests when these are not parallel (RES), achieving symmetry by suppressing the convexity between two crests (FAR or CFTR or CFOR), and rejuvenating the end platforms (REJ or IND).

• Removals associated with regularity-achiev-

Knapping methods brought into play for obtaining a parallelepipedal roughout from plano-convex pebbles

Method 1

In this method, the pebble is transformed by fashioning crests through alternate or adjacent removals. The two ends can be truncated at different points of the sequence, either during or just after the shaping of the crests.

Strategy a) The four crests are fashioned successively. This method has the advantage of better preserving the original size of the pebble.

Strategy b) Two diagonally-opposing crests are fashioned by series of alternate removals, while the two other edges are automatically created by these converging removal negatives. This method's drawback is that the knapper cannot perfectly control the shape of the transverse cross-section.

Method 2

In this method, the pebble is transformed by combining the fashioning of crests with burin removals. One end of the pebble is truncated before the burin removal occurs, while the other is dealt with during the fashioning of the crests.

Strategy a) Two adjacent crests are fashioned by series of removals. A burin removal creates the two other edges, which are then transformed into crests by removals. The burin removal takes place before or after the fashioning of the first crest.

Strategy b) Only one crest is fashioned by a series of removals. This crest creates at least one face. The opposite face is sliced off by a thick burin removal in order to create a parallel plane with two longitudinal edges. These are subsequently modified by a series of removals in order to obtain rectilinear crests.

Method 3

In this method, there is no fashioning of genuine crests. The quadrangular cross-section is obtained by a minimum of 3 burin removals. Their edges may be left unmodified. Truncating the ends of the pebble occurs in the course of the burin removals. This method implies numerous rejuvenations of both extremities depending on the quality (length and depth) of the burin removals. It follows that this method has the disadvantage of considerably reducing the length of the pebble.

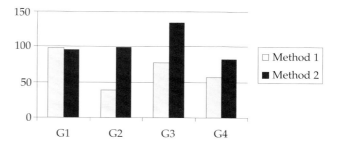

Figure 6.5. *Comparison of time manufacturing (in seconds) between methods 1 and 2 (17 craftsmen, 30 knapping sequences).*

Table 6.1. *Subjects, sequences and methods recorded for the reducing of plano-convex pebbles into parallelepiped roughouts. Knapping strategies are indicated by letters a and b (see p. 97).*

	number of sequences	Method 1 (a,b)	Method 2 (a,b)	Method 3
Group 1				
HA	3	3(a)	-	-
HU	1	1(a)	-	-
RA	1	-	1(a)	-
AB	1	1(b)	-	-
YU	1	1(b)	-	-
Total	*7*	*6*	*1*	*-*
Group 2				
PR	3	-	3(b?)	-
MR	1	-	1(b)	-
DK	1	1(b)	-	-
NA	1	-	1(b)	-
RJ	1	-	-	1
Total	*7*	*1*	*5*	*1*
Group 3				
MO	1	-	1(a)	-
AN	2	1(b)	1(a)	-
JA	4	3(a), 1(b)	-	-
MU	3		2(a),1(b)	-
Total	*10*	*5*	*5*	*-*
Group 4				
KU	2	-	1(a), 1(b)	-
KM	1	-	1(b)	-
SA	3	1(a)	2(a)	-
Total	*6*	*1*	*5*	*-*
Total	**30**	**11**	**19**	**1**

commonly followed in low-quality bead workshops where productivity rather than quality is sought. When comparing time manufacturing between the two methods (Fig. 6.5), however, it appears that method 2 is in fact not as quick as method 1. The point is that method 1 necessitates the control of invasive flakes which, as shown by our previous experiment, is not really mastered by group 2 craftsmen (Bril *et al.*

2000). The fact that group 3 craftsmen practise either method suggests that some of them do not yet control what characterizes partially group 1 expertise. Method 3 is practised by only one craftsman. As previously mentioned, it has the disadvantage of considerably reducing the size of the pebble.

In the third place, it should be noted that the different methods are achieved by means of removals that are all known to the subjects of the four groups. There are but two exceptions, concerning removals of the RIR and CFOR type. RIR is not used by groups 1 and 4 (and only by a single group 2 craftsman, and two group 3 craftsmen). CFOR is not used by group 4 only.

Finally, one sees that, among the craftsmen who knap more than one bead (7 of them), two of them use both methods 1 and 2. They are craftsmen from group 3 and 4 (*AN*, group 3, *SAN*, group 4).

2. The dynamics of planning: the courses of action

The courses of action are the actualization of the methods and describe how craftsmen transform pebbles into roughouts. In order to assess how far these courses of action represent 'mental schemes' that would pre-exist to action, we propose to examine how the courses of action vary from one group to the other, from one craftsman to the other and at the individual level. We suppose that a description of this variability will give us clues about the way craftsmen use knapping methods, and what is acquired when upgrading from one level of expertise to another, on the role of planning in the success of the task.

Variability of the courses of action is described according to the following parameters : the ordering of the operations and the types of removals, the temporal structure of the course of action and the variability at the intra- and inter-subject levels.

Ordering of operations and types of removals

There is a 'logic' underlying the ordering of the operations, which accounts for their sequencing according to a certain order. Thus, symmetry-achieving operations come after the fashioning of the crests and before regularity-achieving operations. This 'logic' applies also for the ordering of typical removals. Thus preliminary facial removals (DENT, FAR, FTR) precede shaping removals since they are used in order to initiate them when necessary.

When examining the courses of action followed by the different craftsmen, the subsequent observations can be made:

a) most often, it is impossible to infer a level of expertise from the courses of action themselves: whatever the level of expertise, the order followed by the subject may show remarkable consistency. Thus, subjects belonging to groups 3 and 4 present courses of action which do not evince any planning mistakes (Table 6.2). The achieved courses of action are very much comparable with the courses of action produced by craftsmen of group 1 (here *HA3*, Table 6.2). Variability is found in the placement of truncating and fashioning removals: truncating of the ends of the pebble occurs during or after the fashioning of the crests; fashioning of the crests, accordingly, may be preceded by preliminary facial removals and followed by reshaping, symmetry-achieving and regularity-achieving operations. The point is that these consistent and comparable courses of action produce roughouts of very different qualities.

b) some courses of action may present some mistakes assessed as such given the characteristics of the pebble, the effects of the blows on the pebble and the range of possibilities offered by the state of the piece after each removal. They are expressed:

- either by a significant repetition of the same typical removal, indicating that the operation failed and that the subject tried again and again (ex. *MU5*, group 3, Table 6.5).
- or, by switching the order of removals, e.g. regularizing a particular crest before all the crests have been fashioned (ex. *SA4*, group 4, Table 6.6).

Such mistakes do not occur in group 1 of the analyzed corpus. Group 1 subjects, however, may also sometimes fail to detach flakes. When this happens, and contrary to the less-experienced knappers, instead of repeatedly attempting the same typical removal, they will perform one or several other removals that will ensure the success of the previously failed removal (ex. *HA3*, after several failed FAR, execution of a REJ, Table 6.3).

The temporal structure of the courses of action

The temporal structure of a knapping sequence is expressed in terms of number of typical removals and duration per typical removals. Several parameters describe this temporal structure: the course of action duration, the relative number of typical removals (number of typical removals divided by the course of action duration), as well as the duration of each typical removal and of the main knapping operations: preparation (DENT, FAR, FTR), shaping (CAL, CAD, BUR), symmetry-achieving (RES, CFTR, CFOR, FAR) and regularity-achieving (RET).

For comparative purposes, only courses of action related to method 2 are considered. Given the small number of courses of action per group (one for group 1, and five for groups 2, 3 and 4), let us recall that results are presented in terms of trends only.

The analysis of temporal data shows that the course of action duration differs mainly between groups 1 and 2, and groups 3 and 4: groups 1 and 2 produce courses of action of comparable duration, whereas group 3 produces the longest ones and group 4 produces the shortest ones (Fig. 6.6).

At the same time, the relative number of typical removals (Fig. 6.6) is comparable for groups 1 and 3 (0.20 & 0.19), and for groups 2 and 4 (0.24 & 0.25) respectively; group 3 presenting courses of action with the highest (23) and group 4 the lowest (20) number of typical removals (21 for group 1, and 22 for group 2). Here, the relative number of typical removals indicates that, respectively, groups 1 and 3, and groups 2 and 4 spend comparable time upon the removals. Groups 1 and 3 spend more time than groups 2 and 4. This difference in time upon the typical removals correlates with the difference of care granted to the different qualities of beads.

The percentage of time each group spends on the different knapping operations, points to a similar picture. It appears that group 4 spends proportionately much more time on preparation and shaping operations than the other groups (Fig. 6.7). Group 2 comes second. Groups 1 and 3 show similar relative shaping durations. The large amount of time spent by group 4 on preparation and shaping operations can be here correlated with the significant number of ineffective blows delivered by this group. As far as symmetry-achieving operations are concerned, groups 1 and 4 present the lowest percentages. In the case of group 1, this may be correlated with the quality of the shaping removals achieved in order to obtain a parallelepiped. In the case of group 4, this may be correlated with a weaker concern for the quality of the piece, as expressed by the low percentage of duration of regularity-achieving operations. On the contrary, group 1 spends a considerable time on regularizing the pieces, because producing good-quality roughouts is a major concern. This concern is shared by group 3, which evinces a higher percentage regularity-achieving operations than group 2.

Intra- and inter-subject variability: how new situations are negotiated

Intra-subject, or within-subject, variability describes the variability between courses of action produced by a single craftsman. Inter-subject, or between-subject, variability describes the variability between courses of action produced by different craftsmen belonging to the same level of expertise. Variability should allow more precise examination of the process leading to which courses of action get modified.

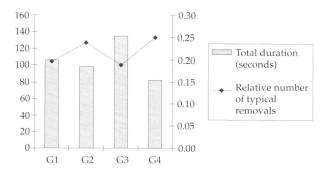

Figure 6.6. *Sequence duration and relative number of typical removals related to method 2 (number of typical removals divided by the sequence duration) distributed per group (15 knapping sequences).*

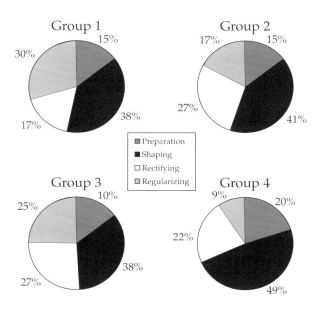

Figure 6.7. *Temporal structure followed by the four groups of craftsmen for obtaining roughouts according to method 2.*

Intra-subject variability: Considering that pebbles are not standardized in terms of either shape or raw material, intra-subject variability reflects the way the craftsman adapts his course of action to unexpected situations (bumps, cracks). The corpus is made up of courses of action derived from one or two subjects per group, i.e. the subjects displaying at least three sequences related to the transformation of plano-convex pebbles. Some trends are suggested by the analysis of these sequences.

Concerning group 1, represented by *HA*, intra-subject variability is characterized by the insertion of specific shaping removals between the main ones, whose ordering is, however, recurrent from one sequence to another (Table 6.3). Thus, sequence HA5 presents additional shaping removals compared to sequence HA3:

a) a burin removal, which occurs during the fashioning of the first crest; this operation was required by the specific shape of the pebble, which needed to be reduced to a plano-convex shape;

b) a truncation removal between the fashioning of crests 3 and 4; this operation was made necessary by a knapping accident, which broke the stone into two parts. In sequence HA3, the occurrence of a rejuvenation operation before the symmetry-achieving operations is due to previously-failed facial removals.

Concerning group 2, represented by PR, because shaping removals were only weakly controlled, a significant number of symmetry-achieving removals (CFTR, FAR) are inserted between the main operations, whose ordering is, however, recurrent from one sequence to another (Table 6.4). Thus, a comparison between courses of action PR1 and PR6 shows that some types of removals, represented in the latter, are absent from the former: CFTR, for instance, which occurs after the first burin removal, and the purpose of which is to correct the plane created by the burin removal. In sequence PR2, the numerous FAR are used in order to achieve symmetry and not only in preparation operation.

Within group 3, there are two cases (Table 6.5):

- One craftsman exhibits a low variability (JA). In the three sequences he produced, JA first fashions 2 or 3 crests, which may or not be preceded by preparation removals (FAR in JA3, FTR in JA7). Truncating the ends of the pebble mainly occurs by the end of the sequence after symmetry-achieving (RES, CFTR) and/or regularity-achieving (RET) operations.

- A second craftsman exhibits a high variability (MU). In the three sequences MU produced, the high variability is due to several failed operations and therefore to the repeated attempts at achieving a single operation: for instance the removal of a burin flake (repeated up to 5 times in MU5), or the slicing off the extremities (repeated up to 4 times in MU2).

It should be mentioned that MU is only 16 years old, and that it is only a year ago that he started to learn daily how to make roughouts of different types. As for JA, he is 19 years old and has been working for a few years in a high-quality workshop, making small items.

Concerning group 4, represented by SA, variability only bears on the beginning of the course of action (Table 6.6). In one case (SA4), the first removals

consist of calibrating the roughout, whereas in the second case, they consist of truncating the end of the pebble and subsequently achieving a burin removal. In the first case, the subject had a faulty perception of the general shape of the pebble and changed sub-goals in the course of knapping as expressed by a long preliminary CAD and CAL and a postponed truncation when compared to sequence SA5.

Inter-subject variability: Inter-subject variability is examined for courses of action relating to a similar method, method 1 for group 1 (6 knapping sequences) and method 2 for the other groups (15 knapping sequences).

Group 1 (method 1, HA3, AB8, YU7, HU; Table 6.7). Depending on the initial shape of the pebble, group 1 craftsmen fashion 2 to 4 crests. Truncating the extremities may be done during or after fashioning the crests. Inter-subject variability is reflected by the types of removals used for finishing the pieces: thus HA uses CFOR in order to achieve symmetry unlike, for example, YU, who prefers FAR and CFTR. Inter-subject variability relating to the regularity-achieving operation overlaps with intra-subject variability. Indeed, as we can see for example in Table 6.3, this operation can present strong variability from one course of action to the other even though when produced by the same craftsman. It would be difficult to distinguish between this intra-variability and the one we can observe from one craftsman to the other.

Group 2 (method 2, PR1, MR6, NA6; Table 6.8). In this group, it is not possible to distinguish between craftsmen on the basis of courses of action. Inter-subject variability is low, as shown by the three courses of action here taken into consideration: these follow very closely the order of the removals defined by the method itself. For this group, inter-subject variability also seems to overlap with intra-subject variability.

Group 3 (method 2, MO5, AN6, MU2; Table 6.9). Unlike group 2, group 3 evinces strong inter-subject variability. This variability may be explained in terms of age and training duration: subjects are 16 to 25 years old, and although they all started to knap when they were about 10, some of them interrupted their training for a few years in order to go to school. In fact, this group is the most heterogeneous group in terms of level of expertise.

Group 4 (method 2, KU1, KM6, SA5; Table 6.10). Subjects are 17 to 20 years old. They all started to knap when they were about 10. The courses of action produced are, in all cases, quite oversimplified, in the sense that they consist mainly of shaping operations. Symmetry- and regularity-achieving operations are practically absent. Variability bears only on the order of the main shaping removals.

Discussion

Let us first recall that groups 1 and 2 can both be considered to be experts: in both groups, knappers have been practising their craft 8 hours a day for 20 up to 40 years (Roux *et al.* 1995; Bril *et al.* 2000). These two groups of experts make stone beads whose morphological types change over time in response to commercial demand (Roux 2000). It is the quality of the beads they produce that distinguishes one group from the other. Group 1 makes high-quality beads, i.e. finely-retouched symmetrical beads, while group 2 makes low-quality beads. The quality of a bead represents a specific goal for which different levels of expertise are developed. The expertise developed by the craftsmen of group 2 is not sufficient for making high-quality beads, as shown by the quality of the roughouts and the preforms obtained during the different experiments we performed (in 1988: Roux 1993–94; in 1993: Roux *et al.* 1995; Bril *et al.* 2000; and in 1998). This quality, assessed in terms of symmetry, dimensions, depressions and bumps, systematically distinguishes group 1 from group 2, as group 3 from group 4, even though these groups are instructed to produce high-quality beads (Fig. 6.8).

Methods and courses of action: not sufficient for achieving a successful task

One of the conclusions of our previous experiment during which the subjects had to knap glass roughouts, i.e. standardized pieces, was that the knowledge of the methods and courses of action was not sufficient for manufacturing high-quality beads (Roux *et al.* 1995; Bril *et al.* 2000). Because the pieces were standardized, and therefore the situation quite constrained, we were uncertain of the generalizability of our findings. The results related to the knapping of chalcedony pebbles and their fashioning into roughouts tend to confirm these previous conclusions.

Knapping methods: guidelines for acting

Whatever the level of expertise, all the craftsmen know about the methods to follow for transforming pebbles into roughouts. These methods vary depending on the desired quality of beads, method 1 for high-quality beads, method 2 for low-quality beads. Craftsmen clearly choose one or the other method when making a bead. Among groups 3 and 4, two craftsmen have used successively the two different knapping methods. This suggests that craftsmen are very much aware about the different methods at use in Khambhat. When becoming experts, they go usually for one or the other.

The method can be considered as a guideline along which the course of action unfolds. This guideline is apparently known even without practising. Group 3 and 4 had never knapped pebbles of that length. Still, they knew the main steps to follow for making the roughouts. The same way, during the 1998 experiment, one subject made ovoid beads for the first time in his life. Difficulties were not met at the method level, but very much so at the removal level. The method was known as shown by the main sub-goals achieved by the knapper, but it could not be actualized according to a proper course of action as shown by the finished product which was very awkward. As a matter of fact, Khambhat apprentices quickly come to know the different methods they need to master through seeing them used in the workshops where they mingle with professionals who are expert at fashioning all the different types of beads. The methods themselves are not taught properly speaking. The methods appear as mental schemes that pre-exist to action but that are not sufficient for the craftsman to act efficiently.

Courses of action: actualizing the methods

Concerning the course of action, all the craftsmen of the different groups of expertise can produce coherent courses of action from which it would be difficult to infer a level of expertise. It means that a sole proper course of action is not sufficient for making high-quality beads. A same course of action can produce a high- or low-quality roughout. Courses of action are the actualization of methods through sub-goals which organize differently the courses of action from one piece to the other, taking into account the particularities of situations that are not constrained (different shape, size and properties of stones). We could expect therefore that the more expert craftsmen would produce 'original' courses of action in terms of particular succession of sub-goals for a successful task. These 'original' courses of action would be 'ideal' ones. In fact, experts do not produce specific courses of action as such compared with the ones produced by less expert craftsmen.

Correlation between courses of action and level of expertise is more to be found at the error level. According to the level of expertise of the craftsman, a failed removal will be dealt with differently: for example, after a failed removal, an expert produces a rejuvenation operation, whereas an apprentice keeps repeating the same operation. The former will thus modify positively the situation contrarily to the latter. This difference in behaviour suggests a difference in the mastery of the subgoals aimed at transforming the pebbles. Indeed, it is not in the knowledge itself of the sub-goals: we have seen that they are all known by the different craftsmen. The difference is more to be found at the level of the execution of the sub-goals whose mastery enables the craftsman to control the modification of the stone. When not mastering this execution, craftsmen are not in a position to opt for the sub-goal which would enable them to correct the situation.

The same applies to errors in the ordering of the sub-goals which are mainly due to an incorrect assessment of the way each sub-goal modifies the stone: for example, when group 3 or 4 craftsmen regularize a crest before the fashioning of all four of them, they do not realize that this will prevent them from fashioning each crest properly.

In brief, mastery of the courses of action depends very much on the way craftsmen master the execution of sub-goals. As we shall see below, learning how to master sub-goals structures the whole process of apprenticeship.

Technique: learning how to achieve a successful task
In the course of apprenticeship, teaching never bears on the methods or the courses of action, but on the subgoals, that is on the technique itself.

As a matter of fact, it takes time for apprentices to move up from one stage to another, but this is only because, unlike the knapping methods or courses of action, the different types of removals necessary for making the beads in demand at Khambhat are difficult to master. Acquiring this skill can only be achieved by practising blows over and over again. In the high-quality bead workshops, this rehearsal is practised for a year or two before the knappers move up to the next stage. The removals necessary for making roughouts are always learnt after the ones for making preforms, probably because they require greater motor control.

Similar observations on apprenticeship have been made in other actualist contexts, where the difficulties met by the novices are reported to be found at the removal level rather than at the method level. Thus, in Indonesian Irian Jaya, Stout (2002, 706–9; this volume) observes that the difficulties met by the Langda apprentices consist mainly in the inability to effect a particular type of flake removal on the 'dorsal' ridge of the adze. This particular type of removal is an alternate invasive one, and can be compared to the alternate removal used by the Indian knappers for fashioning the crests. In Khambhat, the alternate removal is perfectly mastered by group 1 and used extensively in method 1. This method has the advantage of better preserving the original size of the pebble and is favoured by groups 1 and 3. Group 4 subjects find it very difficult to make this type of removal, they never use method 1 and as a substitute they adopt adjacent removals for fashioning crests. For her part, Winton (this volume) examines the difficulties faced by modern-day inexperienced knappers. She observes that the most difficult

task to master in handaxe manufacture is the initial 'roughing out' phase, for which large flakes have to be detached. This conclusion tallies with the observations made by Schick (1994) according to which the striking of invasive flakes for thinning handaxes was a major difficulty faced by novice knappers. As in Khambhat, this difficulty arises at the roughout stage, characterized by removals the geometric characteristics of which are of critical importance for fashioning the volume of the piece as well as for preparing the suitable flaking angles for subsequent operations (preform stage).

Moreover, it should be noted that during the apprenticeship process in both ethnographic cases (India and Irian Jaya), the verbal instructions only bear on the actions, and never on planning. Thus Stout reports that 'an apprentice may be reminded to work edges bifacially and to strike at high points rather than concave flake scars so that the flakes removed will tend to follow ridges on the core' (Stout 2002, 703). When it comes to describing reduction strategies, either the description bears on the method (which can be acquired without practising) or on specific operations for which the craftsman has used a specific strategy because he fully controls the elementary movements and can therefore choose between different types of removals to solve a particular technical problem.

Apprentices are thus taught mainly at the removal level. As for the courses of action, they acquire them as they go along. Learning how to plan courses of action is done in interaction with the mastery of the elementary movements. By learning how to control the flaking technique, the knapper perceives the properties of each sub-goal, their consequence in terms of modification of the stone, and therefore the subgoals suitable for achieving the desired end-product. This is why no verbal instructions bear on the courses of action themselves which emerge from the mastery of the elementary movement, from oft-repeated actions. In this perspective, planning can be construed as a perceptual-motor skill emerging from action and perception (Gibson 1977; 1979) as we shall see below.

Mastery of the technique and courses of action
The hypothesis according to which courses of action emerge from the mastery of the technique rests not only on the fact that a proper course of action is not sufficient for achieving a good product, and the mastery of the execution of the sub-goals depends on their ordering, but also on the way the courses of action vary depending on the level of expertise.

Craftsmen of different levels of expertise can produce similar courses of action, yet the courses of action can vary differently within each group of craftsmen.

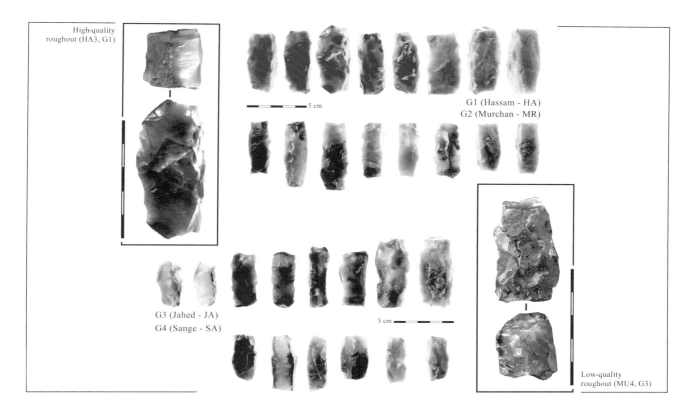

Figure 6.8. *Roughouts produced by one representative craftsman from each group.*

In particular, intra- and inter-subject variability tends to be lower within groups 2 and 4. Contrary to group 1, group 2 makes fewer personal choices than group 1, whose craftsmen show individual preferences for specific types of removals. It follows that knapping courses of action are less diversified, reflecting a less flexible behaviour in relation to the possibilities offered by the different types of removals. Group 4 subjects, taught by group 2, display courses of action that are even less diversified, as expressed, in particular, by the lowest number of operations per sequence. This low number is also to be found among the youngest subjects of group 3. Now, group 2, and to a certain extent group 4, produces at group level a range of typical removals comparable to that produced by group 1. The low diversity of courses of action carried out by groups 2 and 4 expresses a limited use of the available sub-goals. This limited use suggests a rigid behaviour by contrast with a more flexible behaviour found within groups 1 and 3.

Given the fact that mastery of the sub-goals is the premise for efficient courses of action, flexibility *versus* rigidity of courses of action, in relationship with degree of expertise, suggests that the degree of mastery of the sub-goals depends on the way methods are actualized. Mastery of the technique is developed according to the goal followed by the Khambhat stone knappers, that is low- or high-quality beads. Depending on this mastery, the courses of action appear to be more or less flexible as opposed to rigid.

In other words, the level of expertise in stone knapping depends on the level of control of the elementary movements and on the consequent interactions in terms of feedback between movements and planning. Depending on way the conchoidal fracture is mastered, the knapping courses of action present an either flexible or rigid ordering of subgoals. A rigid ordering of subgoals, found in groups 2 and 4, is considered here as reflecting the fact that the properties of the elementary movements are not as fully exploited as in the other groups, thus providing fewer opportunities for idiosyncrasies or exploration. What is a constraint for groups 2 and 4 has been transformed into resources by groups 1 and 3.

Mastery of the technique and perception of the task
Differences in the mastery of the technique, which depends on the goal followed, means not only different behaviour in planning, but also different perception of the task. Perception of the task can be approached through the temporal structure of the courses of action as well as through verbal data.

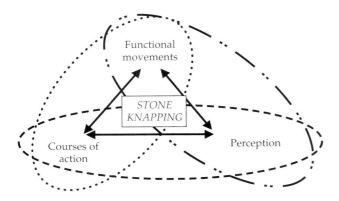

Figure 6.9. *The dynamic of the knapping task.*

The temporal structure of the courses of action

As for the temporal structure of the courses of action followed by the different groups, it underlines the interaction between the mastery of the technique, the perception of the task and the courses of action. In particular, unlike groups 1 and 3, groups 2 and 4 spend little time on the regularity-achieving operations. These are important for obtaining high-quality roughouts and are conducted by detaching thin small flakes. Groups 2 and 4 do not pay much attention to this operation, since they are satisfied with low-quality finished products, which they consider to be the type of product they have learnt (or are learning) to turn out and are therefore expected to achieve. Because they do not perceive what a high-quality product implies in terms of knapping removals, group 4 subjects do not practise so as to be in a position to control the flake removals the way group 3 does. This lessened perception of the situation results in an oversimplification of the courses of action.

Verbal data

Verbal data consist here of the records of the interviews with the 22 subjects, bearing on knapping experiments with various hammers. The weights and lengths of the hammer handles had been modified in order to test the hypothesis according to which the craftsmen used the rhythm of the hammer. After knapping, they were asked about the difficulties they had met while using the hammers. Group 1 subjects were very reluctant to use the modified hammers, considering that they would not be able to knap correctly. They argued that when the hammer was too heavy or too light, they had problems of balance and therefore had some difficulty in removing flakes. When the handle was too short, more strength had to be applied in order to detach flakes. When the handle was too long, problems of vibration and balance arose. Group 2 was not affected by the weight of the hammer. The subjects had trouble

only with the short handle hammers, as these made it more difficult for them to detach flakes and therefore slowed their work down. Group 3 subjects were also disturbed by the length of the handle, arguing, like group 1, that they had to deliver stronger blows in order to detach flakes. Group 4 subjects said that they could not perceive the slightest difference and that they could go on knapping quite happily. Eventually, all four groups knapped roughouts with the modified hammers. According to their perception of the properties of the hammers, they found this a more or less difficult task, i.e. they found it more or less difficult to adapt their blows to these properties in order to obtain the desired removals. Because group 4 subjects did not perceive the alterations, they had no difficulty in knapping the roughouts. It is assumed that they did not modulate their blows accordingly, something that is also suggested by the preliminary results given by the accelerometer (Bril pers. comm.).

Stone knapping: interactions between functional movements, perceptual information and planning

The results of our experiment suggest that knapping expertise results from a dynamic involving interaction between functional movements, perceptual information and planning (Fig. 6.9). As we saw, action is achieved through movements whose mastery depends on the level of expertise. Perception of the stone and adjustment of the sub-goals to the final goal depend on this mastery. In Khambhat, groups 1 and 2 master differently the elementary movements in response to the different goals followed (high- and low-quality beads). The result is a dynamic determining different outcomes when assessed in terms of end-product quality, even though the succession of sub-goals follows the general schema for obtaining a parallelepiped (the knapping method), and even though the ordering of sub-goals can be similarly patterned. In other words, what explains why a similar ordering of subgoals may correspond to different outcomes is the way that the dynamic adjusts to the complex interaction between elementary movements, perceptual information and planning.

Mastery of the elementary movements is acquired as apprenticeship progresses. Once acquired, the craftsmen are experts and can achieve one goal, but not necessarily all the goals that can be accomplished with the same technique. Hence the difficulties experienced by a group 2 craftsman when he wants to become a group 1 expert: he masters elementary movements that enable him to make only low-quality beads, and he must modify them in order to turn out high-quality ones. This modification which is mainly a different tuning of the elementary movements, requires the rehearsal of blows many thousands of time. From this modification will follow a modification in the dynamic at play in stone knapping, that is in the interactions between perception, sub-goals and planning. In the same way, groups 3 and 4 are distinguished from each other on the basis of the dynamic they are learning in connection with different goals.

In this volume, A. Smitsman *et al.* elaborate on the way planning is dynamically regulated. In stone knapping, planning develops by integrating the relative parameters of the elementary movements as well as information pertaining to different spheres (perception, memory, intention, success, failure, etc.). As underlined by Stout in this volume, cognitive approaches to stone tools and cognition (e.g. Gowlett 1992; Karlin & Julien 1994; Pelegrin 1993; Wynn 2002) generally focus on abstract planning rather than on the perceptual-motor skill required for effectively detaching flakes. In the present case, abstract planning is powerless to explain the complexity of the data. In particular, it fails to explain why similar courses of action can lead to different end-products, why although acquiring the main knapping methods requires no practice it takes so long to learn how to make different types and qualities of beads, why it takes two years for a low-quality bead knapper to make high-quality beads. The concept of abstract planning reduces planning abilities to mental problem-solving abilities. Problem-solving abilities represent only one aspect of planning abilities, and the latter cannot be disconnected from action and perception.

Conclusions

The Khambhat data give the possibility to assess, in terms of skills, what differentiates knappers with varying levels of expertise from one another, and what young craftsmen learn over the different stages of apprenticeship depending on the quality of the required end product. Expertise lies in the regulation of the elementary movements. This regulation is crucial to the dynamic at play for achieving different goals, here different qualities of beads. As far as planning is concerned, whereas the method can be learnt without practising, the ordering of the sub-goals and its acquisition comes about in the course of action.

This result has direct implications for the study of the evolution of lithic industries. According to cognitive approaches, the evolution of lithic industries reflects an evolution towards an advanced level of operational and conceptual faculties. This advanced level, which is considered a necessary pre-requisite for the evolution of lithic industries, is expressed through the lengthy chaining of operations characterized by pre-determining and pre-determined flakes. With

regard to the complexity of planning, the Acheulian handaxe maker, contrary to the Oldowan tool maker, is looked upon as possessing a genuine operational intelligence comparable to that of modern man.

Now, if planning is regarded as integral to technical actions, and because lithic industries reveal technical actions, then the evolution of lithic industries may be construed not as the consequence of the sole evolution of hominins' mental capacities, but as a complex phenomenon, characterized by interactions among numerous non hierarchically-ordered components, which operate in and across the technological, environmental and social domains (Roux 2003). More precisely, the components at work in technological change are task-related: the technique and the body and their properties; environmental: the environment in relation with the technical task; and, lastly, intention related: the subject's intention(s), which are rooted in the group's socio-cultural representations (Lemonnier 1993) and which may be approached through the function of the finished product. Technological change, and the related lithic industries, may be seen as emerging from interactions among the properties of these different components, each component being likely to evolve as a result of these interactions. At the task level, it is suggested that the evolution of the courses of action, as expressed in prehistoric technical knapping actions, results from a co-evolution of the body/brain and the technique. The evolution of the body/brain is not to be looked upon as a prerequisite for the evolution of the courses of action, but as resulting from a complex process on which the technical practise itself may have had an impact (see also Corbetta, Steele in this volume), all the more since planning comes about in the course of action. As for techniques, considering that they have a potential for internal change that requires no social motivation (Simondon 1958; Creswell 1996), their pattern of evolution depends also on the possibilities offered by the technique itself. In other words, as the hominins were developing the requisite biological properties to master the tool + target system, they were exploring the percussion technique and inventing, in the dynamic of action, new ways of making tools. Actualization of invention emerge from a changing demand in interactions with the environment (in the broad sense of the word) and given socio-economic context of tool production. Understanding technological change, i.e. change in technical actions, implies in the future a fine analysis of the constraints related to the properties of the different components at work. Only at this cost will it be possible to analyze technical actions as complex phenomena whose actualization is not reducible to a sole prime mover alleged to be the development of planning abilities.

Acknowledgements

The experimentation which took place in Khambhat in 1998 has been funded thanks to the GDR 1546 ('Evaluation des habiletés techniques chez les hominidés. Habiletés impliquées dans l'action chez les *Homo sapiens sapiens* et chez les primates' CNRS, France). The analysis of the video films has been achieved by E. David within the framework of the ACI cognitique (L103) and Terrain, Techniques et Théories (P7802, n°02 2 0440) financed by the French Ministry délégué à la recherche et aux nouvelles technologies. Conception of the drawings are by E. David. Realization has been achieved by Gérard Monthel (UMR 7055, CNRS).

Notes

1. This experiment was conducted in December 1998 in collaboration with B. Bril, E. Biryukova, G. Dietrich, A. Roby-Brami.
2. One of the main reasons is that, at that time, the demand was mainly for small beads.
3. All of them had participated in the first experiment.
4. Three of them had participated in the first experiment.
5. This software called KRONOS has been developed by A. Kergelen.

References

Agre, P.E. & D. Chapman, 1990. What are plans for?, in *Designing Autonomous Agents*, ed. P. Maes. Cambridge: Elsevier, 17–34.

Ambrose, S., 2001. Paleolithic technology and human evolution. *Science* 291, 1748–53.

Bril, B., V. Roux & G. Dietrich, 2000. Habiletés impliquées dans la taille des perles en calcédoine. Caractéristiques motrices et cognitives d'une action située complexe, in *Cornaline de l'Inde. Des pratiques techniques de Cambay aux techno-systèmes de l'Indus*, ed. V. Roux. Paris: Editions de la MSH, 207–332. [English CD-rom.] (www.epistemes.net/arkeotek/p_cornaline-eng.htm)

Cordier, P., G. Dietrich & J. Pailhous, 1996. Harmonic analyses of a complex motor behaviour. *Human Movement Sciences* 15, 789–807.

Creswell, R., 1996. *Prométhée ou Pandore? Propos de technologie culturelle*. Paris: Kimé.

Gibson, J.J., 1977. The theory of affordances, in *Perceiving, Acting and Knowing*, eds. R.E. Shaw & J. Bransford. Hillsdale (NJ): Lawrence Erlbaum Associates, 67–82.

Gibson, J.J., 1979. *The Ecological Approach to Perception*. 2nd edition 1986. London: Lawrence Erlbaum.

Gowlett, J.A.J., 1992. Early human mental abilities, in *The Cambridge Encyclopedia of Human Evolution*, eds. S. Bunney & S. Jones. Cambridge: Cambridge University Press, 341–5.

Ingold, T., 2001. Beyond art and technology: the anthropology of skill, in *Anthropological Perspectives on Technology*, ed. M.B. Schiffer. Albuquerque (NM): University of New Mexico Press, 17–32.

Karlin, C. & M. Julien, 1994. Prehistoric technology: a cognitive science?, in *The Ancient Mind: Elements of a Cognitive Archaeology*, eds. C. Renfrew & E.B.W. Zubrow. Cambridge: Cambridge University Press, 152–64.

Keller, C.M., 2002. Comments to 'Skill and cognition in stone tool production' by D. Stout. *Current Anthropology* 43(5), 717.

Lemonnier, P. (ed.), 1993. *Technological Choices: Transformation in Material Cultures since the Neolithic*. London & New York (NY): Routledge.

Lenay, C., J. Stewart & O. Gapenne, 2002. Espace d'action technique et geste perceptif, in *Le geste technique. Réflexion méthodologiques et anthropologiques*, eds. B. Bril & V. Roux. (Technologies/Idéologies/pratiques.) Ramonville Saint-Agne: éditions érès, 215–30.

Pelegrin, J., 1993. A framework for analysing prehistoric stone tools manufacture, and a tentative application to some early lithic industries, in *The Use of Tools by Human, and Non Human Primates*, eds. A. Berthelet & J. Chavaillon. Oxford: Oxford University Press, 302–14.

Reed, E.S. & B. Bril, 1996. The primacy of action in development. A commentary of N. Bernstein, in *Dexterity and its Development*, eds. M. Latash & M. Turvey. Mahwah: LEA, 431–51.

Roux, V., 1993–94. Analyse techno-psychologique des perles en roches dures. *Bulletin du Centre Genevois d'Anthropologie* 4, 51–70.

Roux, V. (ed.), 2000. *Cornaline de l'Inde. Des pratiques techniques de Cambay aux techno-systèmes de l'Indus*. Paris: Editions de la MSH. [English CD-rom.] (www.epistemes.net/arkeotek/p_cornaline-eng.htm)

Roux, V., 2003. A dynamic systems framework for studying technological change: application to the emergence of the potter's wheel in the southern Levant. *Journal of Archaeological Method and Theory* 10(1), 1–30.

Roux, V. & J. Pelegrin, 1989. Taille des perles et spécialisation artisanale: enquête ethnoarchéologique dans le Gujarat. *Techniques et culture* 14, 23–49.

Roux V., B. Bril & G. Dietrich, 1995. Skills and learning difficulties involved in stone knapping: the case of stone bead knapping in Khambhat, India. *World Archaeology* 27(1), 63–87.

Salembier, P., 1996. Cognition(s): située, distribuée, socialement partagée. *Bulletin du LCPE* 1, 1–14. (Ecole normale supérieure, Paris.)

Schick, K., 1994. The Movius line reconsidered: perspectives on the earlier Paleolithic of eastern Asia, in *Integrative Paths to the Past: Paleoanthropological Advances in Honor of F. Clark Howell*, eds. R.S. Corrucini & R.L. Ciochon. Englewood Cliffs (NJ): Prentice-Hall, 569–96.

Simondon, G., 1958. *Du mode d'existence des objets techniques*. Paris: Aubier.

Stout, D., 2002. Skill and cognition in stone tool production: an ethnographic case study from Irian Jaya. *Current Anthropology* 43(5), 693–722.

Suchman, L.A., 1986. *What is a Plan?* ISL Technical Note 20708.

Tixier, J., 1967. Procédés d'analyse et questions de terminologie concernant l'étude des ensembles industriels du paléolithique récent et de l'Epipaléolithique dans l'Afrique du Nord-Ouest, in *Background to Evolution in*

Africa: Proceedings of a Symposium held at Burg Warstentein Austria, July–August 1965. Chicago (IL): University of Chicago Press, 771–820.

Wynn, T., 2002. Archaeology and cognitive evolution. *Behavioural and Brain Sciences* 25(3), 389–402.

Table 6.2. *Comparison of the organization of the sequences related to method 1 and followed by subjects from different levels of expertise. The number after CAL and CAD indicates the knapped crest. The number after TRUNC indicates the knapped summit.*

HA3 (group 1)	JA3 (group 3)	SA6 (group 4)
CAL1	DAX	CAD1 & 3
DENT/FAR	CAD1	**TRUNC1**
CAL2 & 3	DENT/**TRUNC1**/FAR	CAD2
FTR/**TRUNC1**/FAR	CAL2 & 3	**TRUNC2**
CFTR	CFTR	REJ
TRUNC2/FAR	RET	CFTR
REJ	**TRUNC2**	RET
CFOR/RET	CFOR	CFTR
CFOR/RET	RET	RET
CFOR/RET/CFOR		
RET/CFTR		
RET		

Table 6.4. *Comparison of the ordering of technical operations between sequences following method 2 and achieved by one subject from group 2 (PR). The number after CAL and CAD indicates the knapped crest.*

PR1	PR6	PR2
CAL1	CAL1	DENT
DENT/TRUNC	TRUNC	BUR
BUR	BUR	FAR
DENT/TRUNC/FAR	CFTR	TRUNC/FAR
CFTR/FAR	DENT/TRUNC	CAD1
CAD3 & 4	BUR	FAR
RIR/FAR	FAR	CFTR1
CFTR2 & 1	CAD3	TRUNC
CFTR/RET	CFTR	FTR/TRUNC
	RIR/FAR	FAR
	RET	CAD3
	CFTR/RET	RET
		FAR
		RET/CFTR
		IND/FAR
		RET/CFTR

Table 6.3. *Comparison of the ordering of technical operations between two sequences following method 1 and achieved by one subject from group 1 (HA). The operations marked in bold indicate the 'specific' ones, that is the intra-individual variability. The number after CAL and CAD indicates the knapped crest.*

HA3	HA5
CAL1	CAL1
	BUR
	CAL1 & 2
DENT/FAR	FTR
CAL2 & 3	CAL3
	TRUNC
	CAL4
FTR/TRUNC/FAR	TRUNC/FAR
CFTR	CFTR
TRUNC/FAR	TRUNC/FAR
REJ	
CFOR/RET	RES
CFOR/RET	CFTR/RET
CFOR/RET/CFOR	IND
RET/CFTR	RET/CFTR
RET	

Table 6.5. *Comparison of the ordering of technical operations between sequences following a) method 1 and achieved by one subject from group 3 (JA); b) method 2 and achieved by one subject from group 3 (MU). The number after CAL and CAD indicates the knapped crest.*

JA1	JA3	JA7	MU2	MU3	MU5
TRUNC	DAX	CAL1	CAL1	TRUNC	TRUNC
DAX	CAD1	FTR	BUR	CAD1	FAR
CAD1	DENT/TRUNC1/FAR	CAL2	TRUNC	TRUNC	BUR
CAL4 & 3	CAL2 & 3	RES	IND	REP1	CAD1
FAR	CFTR	TRUNC1	CAL1	CAD3	REJ
CFTR	RET	TRUNC2	BUR	BUR	REP1
TRUNC	TRUNC2	RET	CAL4	CAL3	BUR
FAR	CFOR		TRUNC	DENT/DAX	CFTR
CFTR	RET		FAR	CAL3	RET
RET			REP1	BUR	TRUNC
			TRUNC	FAR	BUR
			FAR	CFTR	CFTR
			CAL3	BUR	BUR
			REP4	CFTR	RET
			CFTR	RET	BUR
			RET	CFTR	RET
			TRUNC		
			RIR		
			TRUNC		
			FAR		
			IND		

Table 6.6. *Comparison of the order of the technical operations between two sequences belonging to method 2 and achieved by one subject from group 4 (SA). The number after CAL and CAD indicates the knapped crest.*

SA4	SA5
CAD1	TRUNC/FAR
CAL1	BUR
TRUNC/FAR	TRUNC/FAR
RET1	CAD1 & 3
CAD2	BUR
TRUNC	RET
CFTR1	
BUR	
CFTR1 & 2	
FAR	
RET	

Table 6.7. *Comparison of four knapping sequences related to method 1 and achieved by four subjects from group 1. The number after CAL and CAD indicates the knapped crest.*

HA3	AB8	YU7	HU5
CAL1	CAD1	CAL1	CAL1
DENT/FAR	CAL3	TRUNC/FAR	TRUNC/FAR
CAL2 & 3	CAD2	CAL3	CFTR
FTR/TRUNC1/FAR	TRUNC/FAR	FTR/TRUNC/FAR	IND/FAR/IND/FAR
CFTR	CFOR	CAL3	CAL3
TRUNC2/FAR	DENT/TRUNC/FAR	FAR/CFTR	REJ
REJ	RET	FAR /CFTR	FAR
CFOR/RET	IND		CAD4
CFOR/RET	RET/CFTR		CAL2
CFOR/RET/CFOR	RET/FAR		FAR/CFTR
RET/CFTR	RET		RET/CFTR
RET			RET

Table 6.8. *Comparison of three knapping sequences related to strategy 2 and achieved by three subjects from group 2. The number after CAL and CAD indicates the knapped crest. The number after TRUNC indicates the knapped summit.*

PR1	MR6	NA6
CAL1	CAL1	CAL1
DENT/**TRUNC1**	**TRUNC1**	**TRUNC1**/FAR
BUR	BUR	REJ
DENT/**TRUNC2**/FAR	**TRUNC2**	BUR
CFTR/FAR	CAL3	CAL3
CAD3 & 4	CFTR	DENT/**TRUNC2**
RIR/FAR	REJ	CAL4
CFTR1 & 2	RIR	REJ/FAR
CFTR/RET	RET	RET

Table 6.9. *Comparison of three knapping sequences following method 2 and achieved by three subjects from group 3. The number after CAL and CAD indicates the knapped crest. The number after TRUNC indicates the knapped summit.*

MO5	AN6	MU2
CAL1	CAL1	CAL1
TRUNC1/FAR	CAD2	BUR
CAD2	**TRUNC1**	TRUNC
DENT/FAR	BUR	IND
TRUNC2	**TRUNC2**	CAL1
BUR		BUR
CAL3		CAL4
FAR		**TRUNC**
IND		FAR
RET		REP1
		TRUNC
		FAR
		CAL3
		REP4
		CFTR
		RET
		TRUNC
		RIR
		TRUNC
		FAR
		IND

Table 6.10. *Comparison of three knapping sequences following method 2 and achieved by three subjects from group 4. The number after CAL and CAD indicates the knapped crest.*

KU1	KM6	SA5
CAD1	TRUNC	TRUNC/FAR
TRUNC	CAD1	BUR
BUR	BUR	TRUNC/FAR
CAD3	TRUNC	CAD1 & 3
TRUNC	BUR	BUR
BUR	CFTR	RET
CAD3		
CAD		

Chapter 7

An Investigation of Knapping-skill Development in the Manufacture of Palaeolithic Handaxes

Vicky Winton

This paper examines the evidence for knapping skill as exhibited by handaxes made during modern-day experiments and discusses handaxe-making procedure in terms of the difficulties faced by inexperienced knappers. The aim of this research is to understand better handaxe morphological variability and hominin behaviour, with particular reference to Palaeolithic northwest Europe.

Handaxes are bifacially-worked stone tools. Although it is actually not known why they were made, there is every indication that they were designed to be held in the hand and used in tasks such as butchery (Keeley 1980; 1993; Mitchell 1996; 1998) or the processing of vegetable matter (Dominguez-Rodrigo *et al.* 2001). The earliest-known examples of handaxes are found in East Africa and date to around 1.6 million years ago (Asfaw *et al.* 1992). In northern Europe, handaxes of varied size and shape were being made by archaic humans from at least 500,000 years ago (Roberts *et al.* 1995, 166–75; Wymer 2001, 178) until as late as 40,000 years ago (White & Jacobi 2002, 128).

Repeated forms of 'handaxe' can be recognized in the northwest European Palaeolithic artefact assemblages (Bordes 1961; Roe 1968). It was once thought that handaxe morphology changed through time as a consequence of technological evolution, such that early forms of handaxe were less sophisticated than their later counterparts. This scheme has since been invalidated by the discovery of refined handaxes, that is symmetrical tools with sharp, regular edges, at some of the earliest sites in northwest Europe such as Boxgrove, West Sussex or Warren Hill, Suffolk (Roberts & Parfitt 1999; Wymer 1999, 139). The differences in handaxe size and shape cannot, therefore, be explained simply on the basis of technological evolution or improved dexterity through physical evolution during the Lower and Middle Palaeolithic periods. Many alternative theories to explain variability in handaxe morphology have been constructed (e.g. Wynn & Tierson 1990; Ashton & McNabb 1994; Gowlett & Crompton 1994; Jones 1994; White 1998; McPherron 1996; 2000; Boëda 1991). However, since the variability in the morphology of handaxes from Palaeolithic northwest Europe cannot be understood simply as an increase in technical skills, it is surprising that the actual role of skill as a factor affecting handaxe morphological variability has scarcely been considered.

The reasons for undertaking an investigation of knapping-skill development are twofold. In the first instance, the visible effects of differential levels of skill upon handaxe morphological variability have not been explicitly defined. Meanwhile, ethnoarchaeological studies have demonstrated that modern-day apprentice knappers are unable to manufacture the same quality of artefacts as their more skilled counterparts and that characteristic knapping errors can be identified in the morphology of objects made by less skilled knappers e.g. in the production of carnelian stone beads in India (Roux *et al.* 1995) and the making of stone adzes in Indonesian Irian Jaya (Stout 2002). A better understanding of the ways in which knapping skill affects the size and shape of handaxes is necessary as other models of explanation for handaxe morphological variability (raw material constraint, use efficiency and tool maintenance arguments) are not comprehensive. Indeed, it could reasonably be argued that any explanation of handaxe morphological variability that does not include specific reference to skill is flawed, since knapping skill must have been as ubiquitous a variable in the production of handaxes as the properties of raw materials or functional requirements.

Secondly, the commonly-practised manufacture of handaxes during the very long period of time we refer to as the Lower and Middle Palaeolithic would seem to bear testimony to levels of skill which must have been learnt and developed by each individual archaic human who made such tools. During a butchery experiment Winton (2004) noted that, as expected, handaxes made by modern knappers with little practised knapping skills made poor tools as the irregular morphology of these implements made them awkward to grip. It was also not possible to apply even cutting strokes because the edges of the tools were of inconsistent angles. It is significant to note the inefficiency of poorly made handaxes as tools since this suggests that archaic humans would have experienced the learning process as a bridge between being an incompetent infant, for instance, and a capable adult. It is important to our understanding of archaic humans to know how Palaeolithic people became skilled practitioners of routine tasks, of which the making (and using) of handaxes is a good example.

Hominins, handaxes and *chaînes opératoires*

The first step in investigating Palaeolithic handaxe-making skill development is to establish an understanding of the tasks involved in the manufacturing process. Newcomer (1971) gives a generic model of handaxe manufacture based on his own experience as a flint-knapper. In instances in which handaxes are made from quite flat nodules of good-quality flint, such as may often have been available to Palaeolithic knappers in northwest Europe,[1] he proposes a three-stage knapping process. The knapping sequence begins with the rough shaping ('roughing-out') of the handaxe in which hard stone hammers are used to detach between 10 and 20 relatively large flakes. The objective of 'roughing-out' is to remove quickly large amounts of raw material in order to produce a unit of stone suitable for further reduction and shaping into a handaxe. Subsequently, large or medium-sized 'soft' hammers (e.g. batons of deer antler or bone) are used to detach between 10 and 20 long 'thinning and shaping' flakes which remove the remaining irregularities from the surface of the nascent handaxe and reduce its thickness (in profile view) without greatly diminishing the width (in plan view). The third and final stage of knapping requires that between 15 and 30 small flakes are detached in order to perfect the straightness and final form of the handaxe's edges. The second and third stages of handaxe manufacture are dependent upon an ability to detach thin flakes, in particular, those with narrow striking platforms (i.e. the area of flint about the point of impact which is ap-

proximately perpendicular to the ventral and dorsal surfaces of a flake) since thick striking platforms will result in the reduction of handaxe width relative to handaxe thickness.

In terms of the difficulties faced by present-day humans in the development of skills required to make handaxes, Schick (1994, 584) provides a most useful guide:

> Common problems encountered by beginning knappers include removing too much width before the piece is adequately thinned (producing thick, narrow, even quaduhedral [sic.] products), failure to maintain a good plane (e.g. producing bowed or extremely sinuous bifaces or just a lot of flake waste and an amorphous core), poor control over the outline shape (producing very asymmetrical products or whittling the biface down through a series of overcorrections), failure to extend the bifacial edge through more obtuse areas of the blank, removing the tip end through uncontrolled flaking, or breaking the biface in half with too strong a blow after it has been substantially thinned.

These observations suggest that modern-day novice knappers struggle with each of the stages of handaxe-making identified by Newcomer (1971), from initial hard-hammer flaking (in which a bifacial, rather than quadrihedral shape is defined) through to the final stages in which vulnerable tips and well-thinned tools can be broken during poorly-controlled soft-hammer percussion. Further to Newcomer's (1971) three phase model of handaxe manufacture, Schick (1994, 584–5) suggests the following as key procedures to be mastered in the successful production of handaxes:

- raw material selection, or the preparation of flake blanks (which requires a level of expertise, see footnote above);
- choice and definition of the major plane of the handaxe and its two faces;
- detachment of thinning flakes (often with carefully-prepared striking platforms);
- development and maintenance of symmetry in cross-section and plan view;
- final shaping of the tip and/or cutting edge.

In order to test the validity of Newcomer (1971) and Schick's (1994) suggestions with regard to the particular knapping skills required to make handaxes, and to attempt some further qualification of the effects of poor knapping skill upon handaxe morphological variability, a study was devised — the results of which are now discussed.

Methodology

For the purposes of this investigation a sample of forty-nine handaxes was gathered for analysis; these were made by five individuals, namely Mr Phil

Harding and Professor Nick Barton (both skilled knappers) and Mr R.J. MacRae, Mr Martin Green and Mr Geoff Halliwell (relatively less-skilled knappers). Constraints upon time and money prevented a large-scale, controlled experiment in which raw material properties and environment were standardized and the entire trajectory of knapping skill development was represented, from the earliest attempts at flake removal, through to the consistent manufacture of well-made handaxes. Such a study would be of great value however, and it is intended that future research will incorporate greater experimental controls and in so doing provide additional detailed information about Palaeolithic handaxe manufacture and the requisite knapping skill development.

The less-practised knappers were not given particular designs of handaxe to replicate and a number of morphological types are represented. The collection of handaxes made by the two skilled knappers comprised a ficron, several ovates, a large limande, a very small ovate handaxe, and a number of pointed, plano-convex forms. The inclusion of these varied morphologies facilitated an investigation of whether or not handaxe size and particular shape led skilled knappers to produce features otherwise associated with the handiwork of less-skilled individuals. The effects of tool re-sharpening did not contribute to the morphological variability of handaxes discussed here.

Results

Evidence of failures to master the stages of handaxe manufacture as defined by Newcomer (1971) and Schick (1994) can be recognized in all the handaxes produced by the less-practised knappers. The most significant factor, regardless of the outline shape as viewed in plan, is the tendency for inexperienced knappers to make small tools and more specifically handaxes that are also relatively thick when compared to those made by the skilled knappers. There was a strong proportional relationship between length and thickness of handaxes made by the two skilled knappers (correlation coefficient = 0.93) whilst the handaxes made by Halliwell, Green and MacRae lacked a strongly consistent relationship of length to thickness (correlation coefficients = 0.35, 0.37 and 0.71 respectively). The apparently better correlation of length and thickness of tools made by MacRae can be explained as a feature of raw material selection and choice of knapping strategy. In seven out of twelve cases, MacRae made his handaxes upon thin naturally-shattered fragments of flint or flakes, rather than reducing whole nodules. The greater consistency in tool proportions therefore relates to a good

consistency in the proportions of raw material units selected for use.

In contrast to all the novice knappers, the skilled individuals were able to impose approximately constant proportions of length and thickness upon handaxes made from both very small and very large units of raw material. The handaxes they made ranged in length from 67 mm to 235 mm, compared with a range in length from 72 mm to 182 mm for the less-skilled knappers. Interestingly, only Green amongst the less-practised knappers made handaxes in excess of 125 mm long, though the fact that these handaxes bore areas of natural, unmodified surface on both faces implies that Green's ability to manufacture large tools was due to the selection of relatively long and thin nodules of raw material coupled with limited reduction rather than a mastery of knapping skills.

It appears that by selecting appropriately-shaped raw material, both MacRae and Green were able to by-pass much of the major 'roughing-out' and shaping of stages 1 and 2 in Newcomer's (1971) model of handaxe manufacture and in effect produced handaxes by a single knapping strategy somewhat equivalent to Newcomer's stage 3.

Irregularities in the profile and end-on views of handaxes made by the less-skilled knappers exhibited further signs of an inability to control the early and middle stages of the handaxe-making process. Specifically, partial twists in the edges of tools demonstrate that the knapper failed to define the plane of the tool during the early stage of knapping, or maintain the bilateral plane during subsequent shaping. In fact, the presence of large areas of cortex and marked asymmetry of the volume of the tool on either side of the edge suggest that indeed, it was a failure to effect competent hard-hammer flaking during the earliest phase of knapping that created the irregularities in handaxe profile and end-view observed and not incompetent shaping and thinning after a successful first phase of reduction. Moreover, areas of pronounced asymmetry, often bearing unmodified cortex, are frequently adjacent to flake scars with abrupt distal terminations (hinge fractures). The co-occurrence of pronounced asymmetries and hinge flake scars is a clear sign of failure on the part of the knapper to remove accurately the desired flake from a viable striking platform. Skilled knappers sometimes make errors of this sort, though in both of the two examples found on handaxes made by the skilled knappers, the asymmetries are associated with hinge flake scars that were deep and wide enough to have detached the protuberance. In instances of association between hinge flake scars and asymmetry in tools made by the less-practised knappers, the hinge flake scars were of insufficient depth or breadth to have detached the protrusion they appear to have been aimed at removing. Once again, the fact that the less-skilled knappers attempt to remove marked asymmetries at a late stage in the handaxe-shaping process indicates failure to successfully accomplish stages 1 and 2 of Newcomer's (1971) model of handaxe manufacture and a lack of understanding as to what can realistically be achieved at a late stage in handaxe shaping.

Deliberate asymmetry imposed by skilled knappers as in the case of plano-convex handaxes was quite distinct from asymmetry resulting from incompetent knapping efforts, since skilfully-made plano-convex handaxes had a regular angle along the long edges of the tool and strongly-defined bilateral symmetry in cross-section. The relationship between regular edge angle and symmetry is crucial to the shaping of useful tools since the production of regular edges that can be applied in even and effective cutting strokes is directly related to the achievement of volumetric symmetry (including the bilateral symmetry of well-made plano-convex handaxes). Moreover, volumetric symmetry allows a balanced grip during use and is therefore desirable in its own right.

Failure to 'extend the bifacial edge through more obtuse areas of the blank' (Schick 1994, 584) was a recognizable feature on many of the handaxes made by less practised knappers studied here. Numerous small hinge scars adjacent to or comprising obtuse sections of tool edge on handaxes made by the less-skilled knappers indicate repeated attempts to correct such errors which only stop when all possible angles for further flake removals have been exhausted. On two of the handaxes made by the skilled knappers, quite substantial obtuse sections of possible working edge remain, but these are not associated with numerous hinge flake scars. Rather, the edge seems to have been left without the finest of shaping since the knapper was not intending to use the tool. In another example, obtuse edge angles are found across the butt of a pointed tool but this does not affect the potential of the cutting edges and should not be considered a sign of knapping incompetence.

In this study, plan view outline symmetry was not found to be noticeably more prevalent in the handiwork of skilled knappers than less-practised individuals. The differences lie in how plan-view outline symmetry is achieved. In the handaxes made by the skilled knappers, symmetry is achieved in association with cross-section and profile regularity and edge-angle consistency, which all attests to a long process of well-controlled shape formation and maintenance. In contrast, the less-skilled knappers tended to impose outline symmetry as a cosmetic, aesthetic

measure upon otherwise irregularly-shaped tools. In these instances the imposition of outline symmetry is of no actual, functional benefit, since the irregularities of volume in profile and end-view and inconsistency of edge angle far outweigh the value of outline symmetry from a functional standpoint.

To summarize the results, it was found that, regardless of the overall shape of the handaxes (pointed or ovate, for instance) the two more practised knappers obtained regular and evenly-shaped tools which attest to knowledgeable control of hard hammer flaking in the roughing-out stage of manufacture and consistently competent use of a soft hammer in thinning and shaping. In contrast, on the handaxes made by the three knappers who had devoted a great deal less time to the development of their knapping skills, the following features were commonly observed:

- short and relatively thick morphology, unless made on units of naturally-thin raw material;
- pronounced asymmetry in profile and cross-section;
- irregular surfaces, though not necessarily associated with plan-view outline asymmetry;
- cortex retention on surfaces associated with areas of pronounced asymmetry or adjacent flake scars with hinge distal ends indicating failed attempts to remove cortex or surface irregularity;
- obtuse sections on the bifacial edge of the middle and upper parts of the tool associated with numerous, small hinge flake scars (i.e. affecting the potential working edges of the tool, not including the butt area);
- evidence that the reduction sequence did not comprise three distinct phases of knapping, but rather one undifferentiated unit of removals more akin to the final stage of Newcomer's model of handaxe manufacture i.e. flake removals that primarily effected edge trimming and shaping in plan-view upon inadequately roughed-out and poorly-thinned tool forms.

Discussion

This brief discussion is centred on three main points: 1) how successful the knappers were in achieving the desired tool size and shape; 2) the difficulty of the handaxe-making process in terms of its composite tasks; and 3) the wider context in which Palaeolithic knappers made and used handaxes is considered, with archaeological examples.

In this study the less-skilled knappers produced relatively short and proportionally thick handaxes compared to those made by skilled knappers. A comparative trend for apprentice knappers to produce smaller (and less regularly-shaped) tools than do the skilled craftsmen has been noted among the adze-makers of Langda village in Indonesian Irian Jaya (Stout 2002, 706–9). This, he suggests, is largely due to the apprentices' inability to effect a particular type of flake removal on the 'dorsal ridge' of the adze. In the case of the handaxes studied here, the shorter, thicker tool proportions appear to be due to difficulties encountered during the early and middle stages of the reduction sequence. In particular, the less-skilled knappers showed an inability to detach the large flakes during 'roughing-out' which are necessary not only to define both faces of the tool (Schick 1994, 585) but also to prepare suitable flaking angles at the edge of the rough-out for exploitation during the second 'thinning and shaping' phase of knapping. The relative thickness of the tools attests to an inability to effect thinning removals in stage 2 of Newcomer's (1971) model of handaxe reduction. Failure to prepare a suitable handaxe rough-out during the first stage of knapping predetermines the outcome of later attempts to thin and shape the tool and to this extent the first phase of flaking is the most crucial.

The handaxes made by less-skilled knappers Green and MacRae included well-proportioned examples as a result of using suitably proportioned raw material and only partially modifying this during the reduction sequence. This shows that the shape of raw material is an extremely influential factor in determining the dimensions of handaxes made by novice knappers. Future experiments are needed to investigate further this relationship between raw material properties, knapping skill and handaxe morphology. Further support for this approach is to be found (in a different context) in the work of Bril *et al.* (2000) who noted that the properties of raw material had a strong influence on the morphology of products made by apprentice carnelian bead makers at Khambat.

The results of this study also indicate that regardless of the plan-view outline shape sought by less-skilled knappers (e.g. whether pointed or ovate) poor control and lack of understanding of the handaxe-making process as a whole, lead to characteristic knapping failures. In fact, plan-view outline shape can often be imposed at a late stage in the knapping sequence and as a purely cosmetic feature. It is the achievement of overall regularity of surfaces and the bifacial cutting edge plus surface and edge regularity that turns a bifacially-knapped stone into a useful handaxe. It would seem therefore that regardless of tool shape, knappers (as humans) share a generic and practically understood concept of tool regularity (often expressed as symmetry) and proportion. This suggests that throughout the Lower and Middle Palaeolithic the same types of knapping error relating to novice

handiwork, whether the novice was attempting to make, say, pointed or ovate-shaped handaxes are to be expected. However, as Ingold (2000, 21) reminds us, we learn how to do things by having things 'shown' to us by a skilled individual and by personal experience. Thus, the finer details of tool-shaping; the things that made handaxes into tools adapted to particular modes of use in particular circumstances, may be better recreated in modern experiments if each time a knapper made a tool it was then necessary to use it! During the utilization of the tool the knapper's attention would be drawn to any particular morphological features of a handaxe that were not effective. This particular learning process was not a part of the study reported here.

Particular types of removal, as identified by Newcomer (1971) do indeed present discrete types of problem for learner knappers, namely, hard-hammer 'roughing-out', soft-hammer thinning and shaping, and soft-hammer bifacial edge preparation. Knapping skills, in terms of 'knowledge' and 'know-how' (Pelegrin 1990; 1993), are important concepts since they draw a distinction between awareness of knapping methods and aims of certain strategies and the combination of mental and physical coordination required in the successful achievement of a desired product. This study indicates that the most difficult task to master in handaxe manufacture, as a test of knapping 'knowledge' if not 'know-how', is the initial 'roughing-out' phase. This is perhaps because each new piece of unmodified raw material has unique properties (geometrically and constitutionally) that provide an unprecedented challenge for the knapper. In addition, the initial phase ends not with the production of a recognized tool form but at an intermediate stage from which it is judged that thinning and further shaping can proceed. Later stages of handaxe manufacture are perhaps, therefore, more standardized, since the morphology of the 'rough-out' more closely resembles the end product than did the unmodified unit of raw material and the sequence of required flake removals may now be more easily perceived. Certainly, the thinning and shaping of handaxes using soft hammer percussion is a difficult skill over which to gain control. At this stage, however, the objectives should be more precisely defined, given that the first stage of knapping was accomplished successfully! The final stage of edge shaping may be the easiest for learner knappers to accomplish (excluding specialist touches such as the 'tranchet' edge finish in which a long, thin flake is very skilfully prepared and struck along a side of the tool to provide an extremely sharp cutting edge). The tendency of the novice knappers to attempt radical re-shaping or thinning tasks during the last phase of knapping, however, demonstrates a lack of understanding of what can and cannot be achieved with certain types of removal.

Of course, not all handaxe reduction sequences follow the 3-stage model proposed by Newcomer (1971). As we have seen, it is perfectly possible to produce handaxe rough-outs by striking large flake blanks instead of shaping the rough-out from progressive flake removals and indeed, this is the most common mode of production in certain geographical regions. The striking of large flake blanks may have its own difficulties for learner knappers and this method of 'roughing-out' deserves an independent experimental study in terms of skill acquisition. A similar two-stage knapping strategy might be adopted where the unmodified form of the utilized raw material already naturally approaches the desired morphology of the sought handaxe and where suitable natural striking platforms exist to allow reduction. Indeed, Austin (1994, 125) maintains that Newcomer's three stage model of handaxe reduction is not attested in the knapping debris refitted at the site of Boxgrove where thinning (stage 2) and finishing (stage 3) are indistinguishable. This is somewhat different to the results of less-skilled knapping observed here, where it is stage 1 in Newcomer's model that appears to be conspicuously reduced or absent.

A key factor identified in this study was that novice knappers were unable to effect consistent proportions in the handaxes they produced. Therefore, one would expect handaxe assemblages made exclusively by skilled knappers to exhibit a strong proportional relationship between length and thickness. Alternatively, assemblages comprising tools made by mixed ability knappers would not have standardized length to thickness ratios, demonstrating the presence of knappers unable to control the proportions of tools made. In order to demonstrate the application of ideas discussed in this paper, two assemblages of actual Palaeolithic handaxes were chosen for a study of proportional dimensions. The first was an assemblage of 19 handaxes from the site of Dickett's Field (a site in Hampshire, formerly known as 'Holybourne': see Roe 1968). At this site, raw material suitable for the manufacture of handaxes was locally available. The tools comprise a range of sizes and shapes including plano-convex tools, ovates and more limande-shaped artefacts, though Roe (1968) found ovate shapes to be prevalent. The measurements from 49 handaxes from a second site called Wolvercote (Oxfordshire) provide a further example (Tyldesley 1986). This site is thought to be located at some 20 km distance from the source of raw material utilized. The Wolvercote assemblage is dominated by pointed handaxes (Roe 1968) and

include a number of pointed, plano-convex morphology. Again, a range of handaxe sizes is represented in the Wolvercote assemblage.

The proportional relationship between length and thickness amongst the Dickett's Field handaxes is consistent and has a correlation coefficient of 0.92. The Wolvercote assemblage exhibits only weakly-defined proportional relationship between length and thickness of handaxes with a correlation coefficient value of 0.52. This could, on the basis of the study presented here, be interpreted as evidence that the Dickett's Field assemblage was manufactured by skilled knappers who were consistently able to impose particular proportions upon the raw material used whilst the Wolvercote assemblage included handaxes made by less-skilled knappers who were unable to replicate particular proportions on different tools. Interestingly, the handaxe length and width measurements have a very different relationship. The Dickett's Field handaxes are much less inclined to have the same proportions of length to width than are the bifaces in the Wolvercote assemblage, with correlation coefficient values of 0.75 and 0.90 respectively. At Dickett's Field, as amongst the handaxes made by skilled modern knappers studied here, the handaxes were of different morphologies which may explain the relatively low coherency of relationship between length and width. In contrast, the Wolvercote assemblage may contain handaxes which represent a number of less-skilled knappers who had been unable to produce reliably well-thinned handaxes, but were at least able to effect a reasonable degree of control over the plan-view outline of their tools, just as less-skilled knappers in the study presented here were able to produce handaxes with plan-view outline symmetry. This interpretation potentially contradicts Schick's (1994, 584) observation that learner knappers tend to reduce the width of a handaxe excessively before the piece is adequately thinned and therefore have poor control over plan-view outline symmetry. I would suggest, however, that novice knappers are much more able to control handaxe plan-view outline and, as a result, specific length to width ratios, than they are able to control profile outline proportions (e.g. length to thickness) since the latter are dependent upon the successful removal of invasive flakes. A study of the other knapping errors identified above (e.g. hinge flake scars and edge and profile irregularities) is now required to gain a better understanding of the knapping-skill related morphological variability observed amongst the handaxes from Dickett's Field and Wolvercote.

Doubtless, an entirely skill-based explanation of the total variability in handaxe morphology amongst these two assemblages will prove to be too simplistic, since raw material properties and availability and the effects of any tool re-sharpening also need to be considered.[2] However, this example does demonstrate how a consideration of knapping-skill level contributes new insights into Lower and Middle Palaeolithic stone artefact assemblages and the real human individuals who made them.

Conclusion

As a result of the study presented here, it was possible to verify much of what Newcomer (1971) and Schick (1994) suggested about the stages of handaxe manufacture and problems facing novice knappers in their attempts to make well proportioned, useful handaxes. In addition, a number of further characteristics of relatively low levels of knapping skill were identified. The relationship of handaxe length and thickness appears to be the most easily measured and significant skill-related feature. When the relationships of handaxe length and thickness in the archaeological assemblages were analyzed, it was found that these were patterned in ways that could be explained in terms of the degree of variability in skill of the knappers, though other factors are likely to figure in a full explanation.

Further research, incorporating the ideas set out here is certainly required. Clearly, knapping skill, as an important theme in our understanding of early human behaviour and as one of the key variables in understanding handaxe morphological variability, deserves a great deal more consideration than it has traditionally received.

Acknowledgements

Many thanks to Phil Harding, Nick Barton, Geoff Halliwell, Martin Green and The Pitt Rivers Museum for allowing access to the handaxes used in this study and for help with my research. I would like to express a particular debt of gratitude to my doctoral project academic supervisors Dr Julie Scott-Jackson (PADMAC Unit, University of Oxford) and Professor Derek Roe (Donald Baden-Powell Quaternary Research Centre, University of Oxford). Thanks to the organizers and participants of the 2001 'Knapping Stone: a Uniquely Hominid Behaviour?' workshop for their inspiration, critique and encouragement.

Notes

1. Contrast this with the situation in East and Southern Africa, for example (see Gamble & Marshall 2001; Jones 1994; Isaac 1977). Here raw material tends to be coarse-grained, igneous rock which is both relatively intractable and occurs in large units. When using this stone resource for handaxe manufacture, the initial 'roughing-out' may be replaced by the shaping and removal of a large flake blank which may be further shaped to create the final form of the tool.

2. Mitchell (1998) suggests that Lower Palaeolithic handaxes at the site of Boxgrove, West Sussex, were used expediently and were not resharpened, whilst others maintain handaxe re-sharpening regimes may on some occasions be a strong determinant in handaxe morphology (Soressi & Hays 2003; Ashton 2001; Boëda 1991; McPherron 1996; 2000).

References

Asfaw, B., Y. Beyene, G. Suwa, R.C. Walter, T.D. White, G. Woldegabrie & T. Yemane, 1992. The earliest Acheulian from Konso-Gardula. *Nature* 360, 732–5.

Ashton, N., 2001. One step beyond: flint shortage above the Goring Gap: the example of Wolvercote, in *A Very Remote Period Indeed: Papers on the Palaeolithic Presented to Derek Roe*, eds. S. Milliken & J. Cook. Oxford: Oxbow Books, 199–206.

Ashton, N. & J. McNabb, 1994. Bifaces in perspective, in *Stories in Stone*, eds. N. Ashton & A. David. London: The Lithics Study Society, 182–91.

Austin, L., 1994. The life and death of a Boxgrove biface, in *Stories in Stone*, eds. N. Ashton & A. David. London: The Lithics Studies Society, 119–26.

Boëda, E., 1991. Approche de la variabilité des systèmes de production lithique des industries du Paléolithique Inférieur et Moyen: chronique d'une variabilité attendue. *Techniques et Culture* 17–18, 37–79.

Bordes, F., 1961. *Typologie du Paléolithique ancien et moyen*. Bordeaux: Institut de Préhistoire de l'Université de Bordeaux.

Bril, B., V. Roux & G. Dietrich, 2000. Habiletés impliquées dans la taille des perles en calcédoine. Caractéristiques motrices et cognitives d'une action située complexe, in *Cornaline de l'Inde: des pratiques techniques de Cambay aux techno-systèmes de l'Indus*, ed. V. Roux. Paris: éditions de la MSH, 207–332. [English cd-rom.]

Dominguez-Rodrigo, M., J. Serrallonga, J. Juan-Tresserras, L. Alcala & L. Luque, 2001. Woodworking activities by early humans: a plant residue analysis on Acheulian stone tools from Peninj (Tanzania). *Journal of Human Evolution* 40, 289–99.

Gamble, C. & G. Marshall, 2001. The shape of handaxes, the structure of the Acheulian world, in *A Very Remote Period Indeed: Papers on the Palaeolithic Presented to Derek Roe*, eds. S. Milliken & J. Cook. Oxford: Oxbow Books, 19–27.

Gowlett, J.A.J. & R.H. Crompton, 1994. Kariandusi: Acheulian morphology and the question of allometry. *The African Archaeological Review* 12, 3–42.

Ingold, T., 2000. *The Perception of the Environment: Essays in Livelihood, Dwelling and Skill*. London: Routledge.

Isaac, G.L., 1977. *Olorgesailie: Archaeological Studies of a Middle Pleistocene Lake Basin in Kenya*. Chicago (IL): University of Chicago Press.

Jones, P.R., 1994. Results of experimental work in relation

to the stone industries of Olduvai Gorge, in *Olduvai Gorge*, vol. 5: *Excavations in Beds III, IV and the Masek Beds, 1968–1971*, eds. M.D. Leakey & D.A. Roe. Cambridge: Cambridge University Press, 254–98.

Keeley, L.H., 1980. *Experimental Determination of Stone Tool Uses: a Microwear Analysis*. London: The University of Chicago Press.

Keeley, L.H., 1993. Microwear analysis of lithics, in *The Lower Palaeolithic Site at Hoxne, England*, eds. R. Singer, B.G. Gladfelter & J.J. Wymer. London: The University of Chicago Press, 129–38.

McPherron, S.P., 1996. A reexamination of the British biface data. *Lithics* 16, 47–63.

McPherron, S.P., 2000. Handaxes as a measure of the mental capabilities of early hominids. *Journal of Archaeological Science* 27, 655–63.

Mitchell, J.C., 1996. Studying biface utilization at Boxgrove: Roe deer butchery with replica handaxes. *Lithics* 16, 64–9.

Mitchell, J.C., 1998. A Use-wear Analysis of Selected British Lower Palaeolithic Handaxes with Special Reference to the Site of Boxgrove (West Sussex): a Study Incorporating Optical Microscopy, Computer-aided Image Analysis and Experimental Archaeology. Unpublished DPhil, University of Oxford, Oxford.

Newcomer, M.H., 1971. Some quantitative experiments in handaxe manufacture. *World Archaeology* 3(1), 85–94.

Pelegrin, J., 1990. Prehistoric lithic technology: some aspects of research. *Archaeological Review from Cambridge* 9, 116–25.

Pelegrin, J., 1993. A framework for analysing prehistoric stone tools manufacture and a tentative application to some early lithic industries, in *The Use of Tools by Human and Non-human Primates: a Symposium of the Fyssen Foundation*, eds. A. Berthelet & J. Chavaillon. Oxford: Clarendon Press, 302–14.

Roberts, M.B. & S.A. Parfitt (eds.), 1999. *Boxgrove: a Middle Pleistocene Hominid Site at Eartham Quarry, Boxgrove, West Sussex*. London: English Heritage.

Roberts, M.B., C.S. Gamble & D.R. Bridgland, 1995. The earliest occupation of Europe: the British Isles, in *The Earliest Occupation Of Europe: Proceedings of the European Science Foundation Workshop at Tautavel (France)*, eds. W. Roebroeks & T. van Kolfschoten. Leiden: University of Leiden, 165–91.

Roe, D.A., 1968. British Lower and Middle Palaeolithic handaxe groups. *Proceedings of the Prehistoric Society* 34, 1–82.

Roux, V., B. Bril & G. Dietrich, 1995. Skills and learning difficulties involved in stone knapping: the case of stone-bead knapping in Khambhat, India. *World Archaeology* 27, 63–87.

Schick, K.D., 1994. The Movius line reconsidered: perspectives on the earlier Palaeolithic of Eastern Asia, in *Integrative Paths to the Past: Paleoanthropological Advances in Honor of F. Clark Howell*, eds. R.S. Corruccini & R.L. Ciochon. Englewood Cliffs (NJ): Prentice-Hall, 569–95.

Soressi, M. & M.A. Hays, 2003. Manufacture, transport, and use of Mousterian bifaces: a case study from the Périgord (France), in *Multiple Approaches to the Study of Bifacial Technologies*, eds. M Soressi & H.L. Dibble. Philadelphia (PA): University of Pennsylvania Museum of Archaeology and Anthropology, 125–47.

Stout, D., 2002. Skill and cognition in stone tool production: an ethnographic case study from Irian Jaya. *Current Anthropology* 43, 693–722.

Tyldesley, J.A., 1986. *The Wolvercote Channel Handaxe Assemblage: a Comparative Study*. (British Archaeological Reports 153.) Oxford: BAR.

White, M.J., 1998. On the significance of Acheulian biface variability in southern Britain. *Proceedings of the Prehistoric Society* 64, 15–43.

White, M.J. & R.M. Jacobi, 2002. Two sides to every story: bout coupé handaxes revisited. *Oxford Journal of Archaeology* 21, 109–33.

Winton, V.S., 2004. A Study of Palaeolithic Artefacts from Selected Sites on Deposits Mapped as Clay-with-flints of Southern England, with particular reference to Handaxe Manufacture. Unpublished Doctoral thesis, University of Oxford, Oxford.

Wymer, J., 1999. *The Lower Palaeolithic Occupation of Britain*. Salisbury: Trust for Wessex Archaeology in association with English Heritage.

Wymer, J.J., 2001. Palaeoliths in a lost pre-Anglian landscape, in *A Very Remote Period Indeed: Papers on the Palaeolithic Presented to Derek Roe*, eds. S. Milliken & J. Cook. Oxford: Oxbow Books, 174–9.

Wynn, T. & F. Tierson, 1990. Regional comparison of the shapes of later Acheulian handaxes. *American Anthropologist* 92, 73–84.

Further Considerations on the Skills Involved in Tool Use

Chapter 8

The Biomechanics of the Complex Coordinated Stroke

Galina P. Ivanova

The present chapter focuses on the biomechanical analysis of the complex coordinated stroke. To be successful, a stroke necessitates the consecutive involvement of all moving segments in order to provide the desired final velocity of the working point. The working point of a tennis stroke is the racket, the working point of the volleyball stroke is the hand, and for the football stroke (or kick) it is the foot. The working point when wielding a hammer is the hammer's head. This chapter considers mechanisms of optimal impulse transmission from body segment to body segment (which is what enables successful strokes), inter-segment and inter-muscle coordination, as well as modification of the stroke's motor structure over the course of the learning process.

From a mechanical point of view, the human body performing a tennis, football or volleyball stroke, the arm knapping a stone, as well as the primate arm cracking nuts, represents a complex mechanical system. Each movement involves a primary organ under the control of the central nervous system. Although belonging to very different action systems, the organization of various motor strokes have many features in common. To produce an effective stroke the working point, be it the hand, foot, racket or hammer, must reach the desired final velocity. Such a stroke is achieved by impulse transmission (impulse is calculated as the product of segment mass by segment velocity) from proximal to distal body segments. The greater the number of segments involved in the movement, the finer the regulation of velocity. Specifically, involving multiple body segments produces the very large velocity values necessary for sport-related strokes. The control of inter-segment coordination by the central nervous system is complicated, both crucially and dynamically, by the mutual influence of different body segments during their successive involvement in the movement (Bernstein 1990; Donskoi 1995). The main difficulty here stems from the reactive forces of joints, which are caused by the movement itself and which, in turn, can disturb the intended movement. A long period of motor learning is therefore necessary in order to acquire the sensory corrections allowing one to take into account these dynamic disturbances

and still produce the desired final velocity (see, for example, Thelen *et al.* 1996). After a long period of training, this biomechanical system, characterized by flexibility in coping with such reactive forces, becomes highly integrated and effective.

Fine control of a multi-segment biomechanical system by the central nervous system is manifested in several features common to different kinds of strokes. First, the segments involved in the movement are highly coordinated due to specific muscular synergies. Second, there is a waveform kind of impulse transmission, which travels from proximal to distal segments. Such impulse transmission is optimal if there is no dynamic imbalance between the segments involved. To meet this requirement, the projection of working-point acceleration in the stroke direction, as well as of acceleration at the centre of the mass of each segment, must be zero at the moment of the stroke. Thus, both working-point velocity and each segment's centre of mass velocity must be at their maximum.

The optimal stroke is not only effective but also reliable. For example, in a tennis stroke reliability results from a fine regulation of joint stiffness (of muscle-antagonists coactivation), which provides stable energy transmission from body segments to the racket. Such fine regulation of reciprocal activities involving muscle-antagonists is also crucial to producing the right amount of force during the contact phase of the stroke. Because the length of this contact phase is very

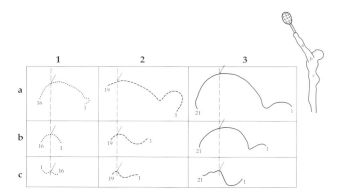

Figure 8.1. *Joint trajectories during a tennis stroke in players with different skill levels: low (1); middle (2); and high (3). Presented are trajectories of the centres of the wrist joint (a); shoulder joint (b); and the centre of mass of the body (c). Shown are frame numbers shot at 24 frames per second. The moment of the stroke is marked by arrows.*

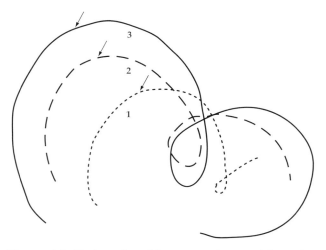

Figure 8.2. *Trajectories of the centre of mass of the racket in novice (1); middle (2); and highly-skilled (3) players. The moment of the stroke is marked by arrows.*

short, effective muscle-antagonist activities need to be anticipated. This kind of muscular preparedness is the third important characteristic common to most effective strokes.

Based on experimental data derived from the study of the tennis stroke, as well as volleyball and football strokes (or kicks), this chapter illustrates the problems of multi-body system control, as described above. To be successful in their tasks, I hypothesize that the tennis player performing a serve, the craftsman knapping stone, as well as the chimpanzee cracking nuts all have to solve similar biomechanical problems.

The data reported here summarize my previously-published research (Lukirskaia 1965; 1967;

Ivanova 1972; 1991). It is important to note that the recording devices employed were those typically used in experimental studies of biomechanical movement: 1) high-speed film enabled calculations of the kinematics (the spatio-temporal characteristics) of movements of different body segments; 2) 3-dimensional accelerometers recorded accelerations of body segments; and 3) force-plates recorded reactive forces during a stroke. The transmission of velocity from body segments to ball or racket is performed mainly on a saggital plane. After the point of contact, the ball flies in this same plane. Consequently, the analysis reported here is based exclusively on saggital plane values of mass trajectories of different segment centres. All observations were made under natural conditions; that is, this study assumes that the movements analyzed were not disturbed by the recording system itself. Finally, all strokes analyzed were based on statistically-significant samples.

The spatio-temporal structure of the stroke

The goal of the stroke is to achieve the necessary speed desired for the striking segment of the body. In his cyclogrammometry studies of the hammer stroke, Bernstein (1923; 1926) described the mechanics of speed generation of this striking segment. Two main principles were identified: 1) the stroke is effective only if the direction of hand velocity coincides with the direction of the future movement of the hammer; 2) in order to generate a high speed and transmit that impulse to the hammer, it is necessary to decelerate appropriately the upper arm, forearm and hand. The first condition allows one to avoid unnecessary loss of energy from rebound; the second condition prevents dynamic disturbances to the overall stroke system. These principles also hold true for the tennis stroke.

In tennis, in order to achieve the desired velocity of the racket the complex motor task of coordinating body joint rotations has to be solved. A tennis player needs 10–13 years to learn the stable and reliable coordination of joint rotations. During any stroke, the human body can be considered an open kinematic chain. The chain of a skilled stroke performance begins with the support segment, which initiates a force pushing away from that support. For example, when kicking a football the support leg moves first, while both legs move together to begin a tennis or volleyball serve. In all cases, the torso and arm are then integrated into the overall movement. Movement amplitude of all segments increases during learning (Fig. 8.1). Consequently, the amplitude of the racket will also increase (Fig. 8.2). Increase in the length of the

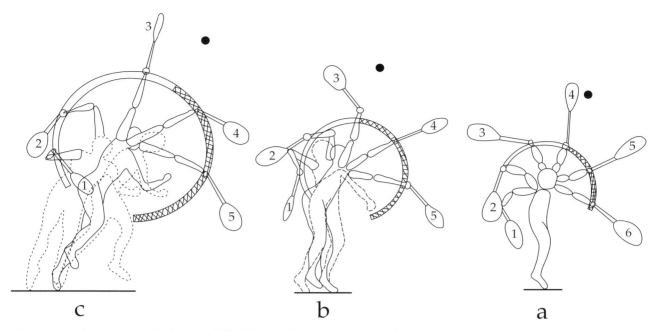

Figure 8.3. *Movements of variously-skilled players during a tennis stroke: a) a child playing tennis after three months of learning; b) a teenager playing tennis after two years of practice; c) a highly skilled player. Shaded areas indicate movement after the stroke.*

racket's trajectory has a clear functional foundation: the longer the trajectory, the greater velocity and thus the stronger the stroke.

Figure 8.3 illustrates the transformation of the spatio-temporal structure of a tennis player's stroke during learning. Beginners (Fig. 8.3a) use mainly the shoulder, elbow, and wrist joint. As the stroke improves (Fig. 8.3b), the torso comes into play, specifically as the hip joint rotates. Highly-skilled tennis players (Fig. 8.3c) use the entire kinematic chain of their body, including knee and ankle joints. The lengthening of the racket's trajectory and the greater velocity of the stroke is, therefore, mainly due to the added movements of these more distal segments (torso, knee and ankle). This same observation is true for a volleyball stroke: to increase the length of the hand trajectory when serving, highly-skilled volleyball players start with a forward and upward jump which they perform well behind the back line of the court.

The sequence in which different muscles become involved in a tennis stroke is clearly evident in the timing of each muscle's electrical activity (Fig. 8.4). Movement is initiated 'from bottom to top', i.e. beginning with the legs. Shoulder muscle (m. trapezius) activity then provides the stiffness and reliability necessary for the successful functioning of arm muscles. Finally, during the last third of the movement, the stroke of the racket toward the ball is provided by the short and strong activity of arm muscles.

Generation of working-point velocity: impulse transmission

As mentioned above, to perform an effective tennis stroke two motor tasks must be solved: 1) generating maximum racket speed just before contact with the ball; and 2) accurately directing the ball toward a desired point in the opponent's court. From a biomechanical point of view, these components of the task are contradictory and the price of the error is great: during the serve, a directional error of 1° leads to the error of 2 m in terms of where the ball lands (Golenko 1973). For highly-skilled tennis players, the racket's horizontal velocity at the moment of contact (with the ball) is about 160 km/h, while ball velocity just after contact is about 220 km/h. What, then, are the mechanisms providing such high velocities in a desired direction?

We have seen that velocity generation originates in the feet and legs. Velocity then picks up momentum in the pelvis. For example, during a tennis serve pelvic velocity is about 2 m/s. In football and volleyball, where a running jump is allowed, this velocity can increase twofold. At this point, the active displacement of the shoulder relative to the pelvis occurs. The resulting velocity of the shoulder reaches 4 m/s during a tennis serve, and 6 m/s during a volleyball serve. When the torso subsequently achieves maximum velocity, upper arm velocity quickly increases.

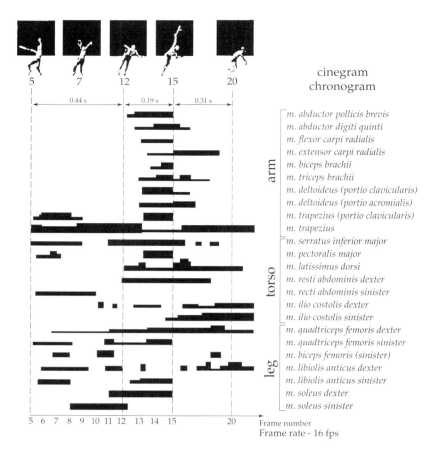

Figure 8.4. *Scheme of electrical activities of muscles during a tennis serve.*

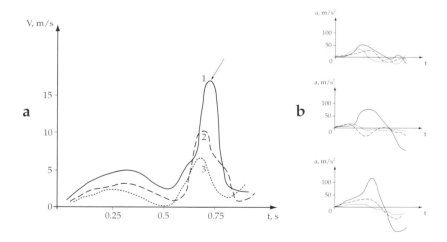

Figure 8.5. *a) Time courses of racket (1); hand (2); and forearm (3) velocities during a tennis stroke. The moment of the stroke is marked by the arrow. b) Time courses of corresponding accelerations for beginners after (from top to bottom) one month, two months, and three months of learning.*

Maximum velocity of the upper arm is then transmitted to the forearm, again increasing velocity. In turn,

at the height of forearm velocity, hand velocity increases. Finally, as hand velocity decelerates racket velocity increases sharply. Thus there is a kind of waveform transmission of velocity from proximal to distal segments of the body (Fig. 8.5 illustrates this transmission of velocity from forearm to racket, for a tennis stroke). In 1926, Bernstein described this waveform velocity profile for a hammer stroke. An analogous waveform velocity profile, or structure, which mimics a similar sequence of segment involvement, has been reported for a football kick (Tchkhaidze 1970) and a volleyball stroke (Fetisova 1978).

The mechanical model of the arm consisting of three bodies (specifically the arm, the forearm and the hand) related by the springs of different stiffness and lengths (Tutevitch 1969) was used to understand the mechanics underlying the successive involvement of body segments for the sort of stroke just described. The successive involvement of body segments is what transmits a quantity of movement, or impulse (calculated as the product of the mass of the segment by the velocity of its centre of mass), from heavy/proximal segments to lighter/distal segments. When a proximal segment decelerates, its quantity of movement (impulse) is transmitted to the next distal segment. The smaller the mass of this distal segment, the shorter the deceleration phase of the proximal segment and also the greater the velocity of the distal one. From a mechanical point of view, the successive involvement of body segments is optimized for high velocity. These relationships were confirmed experimentally, by comparing a stroke executed with a 'rigid arm' and fixed joints to a stroke executed with a 'whip-like arm' and rotating joints (Dorokhov 1983). The hand velocity generated by the 'whip-like arm' action was substantially greater than that generated by the 'rigid arm'.

Figure 8.6a presents the different impulse values of body segments making up a highly-skilled tennis

a

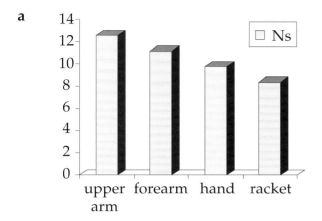

b

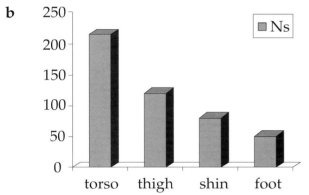

Figure 8.6. *Quantities of movement (impulses) of body segments (in Ns) at the time of impact: (a) for a tennis stroke;(b) for a football stroke.*

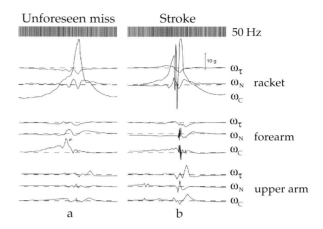

Figure 8.7. *Acceleration of the racket, forearm and upper arm experiencing an unanticipated mis-stroke (a); and a real stroke (b). ω_τ is tangential acceleration; ω_N is acceleration in the direction of the stroke; ω_c is acceleration of the centre of the mass.*

stroke, while Figure 8.6b presents similar findings for a football stroke (or kick). In a football kick, the impulse of the foot is only 23 per cent of the impulse of the torso. In other words, only about 60 per cent of the impulse is transmitted from proximal to distal segments. In comparison, up to 85 per cent of the impulse of tennis stroke is transmitted from proximal to distal segments.

To understand the mechanics of impulse transmission, the values of different segment accelerations on the direction of the stroke were recorded. In terms of tennis players with different levels of skill, Table 8.1 presents the maximum values of segment acceleration (a_{max}) and the temporal interval between the time of maximum acceleration and the moment of stroke (τ).

It follows from Table 8.1 that maximum acceleration of the racket is greatest and closest to the stroke in highly-skilled players. At the moment the racket makes contact with the ball, the value of racket velocity on the direction of the stroke is at its maximum and, therefore, acceleration

is zero. From a mechanical point of view, the fact that the value of acceleration in the direction of the stroke is zero is very important: in this instance there is no dynamic imbalance between segments during impulse transmission from proximal to distal segment. As a result, highly skilled players can quickly solve the problem of optimal impulse transmission. As seen in Figure 8.7b, relative to the direction of the stroke, the acceleration values of racket, forearm and upper arm are all zero ($\omega_N = 0$).

The acceleration pattern is even clearer in the case of unforeseen mis-strokes, because after-stroke vibration does not disturb the acceleration pattern (Fig. 8.7a). Mis-stroke errors were modelled experimentally: i.e., the ball was unpredictably removed a short time before a stroke was completed but beyond the point when any correction was possible. The pattern of acceleration characterizes the effort of stroke preparation (marked by the arrow in Fig. 8.7a). In the case of unforeseen mis-strokes, acceleration in the direction of the stroke is greater than in the case of the stroke. This observation means in order to produce forces great enough to prevent rebound after a (mis-)stroke

Table 8.1. *Maximum values of acceleration (a_{max}) and the interval between maximum acceleration and stroke (τ) for tennis players of different skill levels.*

Level of skill	Racket		Hand		Forearm		Shoulder	
	a_{max} (m/s²)	τ (ms)	a_{max} (m/s²)	τ (ms)	a_{max} (m/s²)	τ (ms)	a_{max} (m/s²)	τ (ms)
High	575	25	277	33	92	66	41	83
Middle	340	37	150	55	140	77	30	10
Low	132	55	46	0	18	55	7.6	16

Table 8.2. *Stiffness coefficients for the elbow joint a the moment of a stroke. Stroke impulse ranges from 2.2–3.4 Ns.*

Sport	Type of stroke and number of strokes	Level of skill	K_{st} (N/m)	K_w
Volleyball	Serve N = 37	High	146,000	0.74
	N = 18	Low	37,00	0.22
Tennis	Serve N = 15	High	122,000	0.61
	N = 9	Low	12,000	0.26

Table 8.3. *Coefficients of correlations between the velocity of a volleyball (below 15 m/sec) after a stroke and the parameters of the striking movement.*

Level of skill	$\omega_{forearm, before}$	$\omega_{forearm, after}$	a_{hand}	$a_{forearm}$	K_{st}
high	0.922	0.854	0.921	0.958	0.092
low	0.786	0.375	0.300	−0.351	−0.527

the additional effort of wrist and elbow muscles is prepared in advance.

The effort structure of the stroke

The following experiment was designed to investigate how a stroke's effort structure is organized. A tennis player was asked to keep the racket motionless when a ball (shot from a tennis cannon) struck it. The time necessary to prepare racket resistance was regulated by the player's distance from the tennis cannon and the starting speed of the ball. In this experiment, the loading of the hand at the moment of contact was accepted to be equal to 300 N (Knudsonn & White 1989). A fast speed (of ball delivery) was utilized so that the anticipatory activity of the muscles (needed to immobilize the racket) would nonetheless be insufficient to keep it still. The task could be accomplished successfully only by applying fast force impulse in the hand and fingers at the moment of contact.

The mechanical energy spreading kinematically from the support leg to the racket and, in the opposite direction, from the racket (just after the stroke) back into the body, depends on the stiffness of the body joints involved. Two coefficients assess joint stiffness: so-called 'static stiffness' K_{st}, and so-called 'rotational stiffness' K_ω. The first coefficient is the ratio of perturbation impulse to the response displacement of the segment involved; the second coefficient is the ratio of angular velocity in the joint both before and after the stroke. During the stroke, force impulse is assumed to be constant.

Table 8.2 presents the coefficients K_{st} and K_ω for the elbow joint at the time of the contact for differ-

ent skill levels in both volleyball and tennis (Pershin 1987). Compared to a beginner, elbow stiffness is approximately four times greater in someone with a high level of skill. For the wrist joint, this difference is even more pronounced: at the moment of contact wrist stiffness in a highly-skilled player is seven times greater than it is in a beginner. In sum, the stroke of highly-skilled player is stronger because of a lower dissipation of energy.

The stroke of a highly-skilled player is not only strong and effective; it is also reliable. This means that under different conditions there is a high degree of stability in the kinematic transmission of potential energy as each body segment is integrated into the stroke. Table 8.3 reports the results of studying the correlation of ball velocity with different elements of a striking movement.

At a high level of skill, there is a strong correlation of ball velocity and the angular velocity of the hand and forearm, both before and after a stroke. Ball velocity also strongly correlates with the linear acceleration of the hand and forearm. Novice tennis players show a much weaker correlation between these elements. At the same time, skilled players show no correlation between ball velocity and joint stiffness (characterized by the coefficient K_{st}). These data allow for the following hypothesis: level of skill is characterized by the fine regulation of joint stiffness, which provides a stable relationship between movement elements before and after a stroke. Therefore, joint stiffness can be considered the parameter that defines motor regulation. After a long period of training this biomechanical system, which is characterized by a significant degree of flexibility, becomes a highly-integrated system. From my point of view, such flexibility in an integrated biomechanical system indicates *optimization of stroke exactness control.*

Regulation of reciprocal activity in muscle-antagonists

Let us now consider a quantitative description of the contact phase during which the racket meets the ball (Fig. 8.8). There are two clear and distinct phases comprising this 'moment' of contact: a phase during which the velocity of both ball and racket are altered, and a phase during which they are restored. During the alteration phase (approximately 7 m/s long), the velocity of the racket decreases from 25 m/s to 12 m/s. At the moment of impact, the ball has zero velocity. Then, when making contact with and altering (momentarily) the condition of the racket strings, the ball achieves a velocity of 12 m/s. During the second (or restoration) phase, the strings and racket return

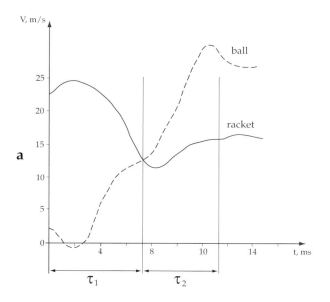

Figure 8.8. *Velocities of the racket and centre of the mass of a ball during the contact phase.* τ_1 *is the period of deformation;* τ_2 *is the period of restoration.*

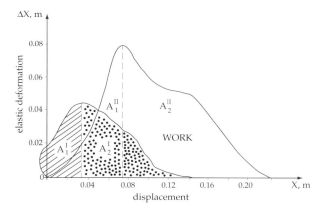

Figure 8.9. *Deformation of the ball as a function of ball displacement. A is the mechanical work; Index 1 corresponds to the phase of alteration; Index 2 corresponds to the phase of restoration; Index I corresponds to a high ball stiffness; Index II corresponds to a low ball stiffness. The higher the ball stiffness is, the stronger the stroke. Indeed, low ball stiffness causes significant ball deformation and, consequently, increases the work involved (that is, it results in a useless expenditure of energy).*

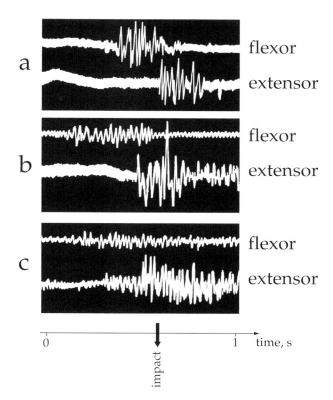

Figure 8.10. *Different types of muscle activity for wrist flexors and extensors during a tennis serve: short and strong reciprocal activity (a); strong and short simultaneous activity (b); and weak and long simultaneous activity (c).*

to their initial condition while the velocity of the ball increases to 30 m/s. Throughout, the racket continues to move at 16 m/s (Fig. 8.8).

Before contact, total kinetic energy (equal to $mV^2/2$, where m is the mass of the ball and V is ball velocity) equals 219 Nm, while after contact it decreases to 144 Nm. The coefficient of energy restoration is, therefore, 0.65. This value is larger than that which can be provided by the elasticity of strings (Groppel *et al.* 1987). This means that during the simultaneous displacement of racket strings and ball (which can range from 10 cm to 30 cm), the forces produced by arm muscles continue to act, thereby adding still more energy to the stroke. Let us assume that this alteration of ball velocity is proportional to (1) the force of the stroke as well as (2) the force produced during the simultaneous alteration of the racket strings and ball (in tennis), the hand and ball (in volleyball), the foot and ball (in football). Experiments have shown that the mechanical work of the deformation force (which is equal to the product of the force by the displacement) is less than the work of restoration forces (Fig. 8.9). What this means is that during the contact phase additional energy (and thus forces) are generated. Regulating energy flow during this period crucially depends on joint stiffness regulation.

To identity the mechanics of stiffness regulation, Tchkhaidze (1970) and Lukirskaya (1965) conducted a comparative analysis of muscle activity and the

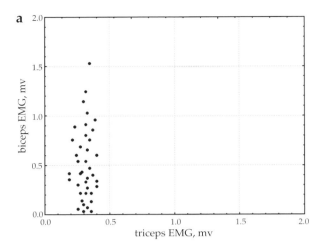

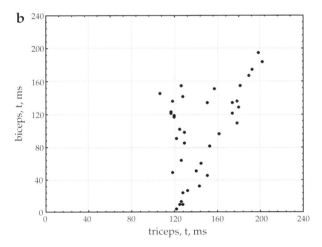

Figure 8.11. *Parameters of electrical activity in biceps and triceps during a volleyball stroke. (a) Mean EMG amplitude; (b) Period of activity.*

mechanical characteristics of such movement. During a tennis stroke, three types of muscle-antagonists activity can operate in the wrist: 1) short and strong reciprocal activity (Fig. 8.10a); 2) strong and short simultaneous activity (Fig. 8.10b); and 3) weak and long simultaneous activity (Fig. 8.10c). The first two characterize the wrist activities of experienced players; the third activity is found only in beginners.

In highly-skilled players, the roles of muscle-antagonists are finely differentiated. During a volleyball stroke, the triceps (extensor of the elbow) play the role of agonist and the biceps (flexor of the elbow) are the antagonist. The triceps rotate the forearm 100 m/s before the stroke actually occurs. Most of this forearm velocity is acquired from rotating more proximal segments of the body. Therefore, the triceps cannot add much energy. To the contrary, in order to regulate energy flow the biceps are activated exactly at the

moment of the stroke. Biceps activity varies significantly depending on the vagaries of game situations. As a consequence, the activity of the triceps is rather stable while the activity of the biceps is more variable (Fig. 8.11a). Similarly, the temporal period of muscular activity involved is twice as long in the biceps than it is in the triceps (Fig. 8.11b). No statistically-significant correlation, however, was found between bicep and tricep activities (Ivanova 1991).

Unlike this fine regulation of the reciprocal activities of specific arm muscles, the entire kinematic chain of the body remains stable and reliable. Such control is manifested, in particular, in the high correlation of the electrical activities (EMG) of wrist flexors and extensors under various movement parameters: 1) Wrist flexor switching is highly correlated with the moment of maximum of ground reaction force ($r = 0.99$); 2) EMG length of time and EMG frequency of wrist flexor are correlated both with forearm acceleration and a pushing force ($r = 0.69$); 3) EMG amplitude of wrist extensor is correlated with acceleration of the forearm ($r = 0.72$) (Ivanova 1991).

Discussion

The organization of an exactly-coordinated stroke is a complex biomechanical task. The main difficulties in achieving desired motor control concern the organization of impulse transmission from one segment to another and, therefore, the combination of appropriate muscles able to provide the necessary moment of force. A high degree of coordinated movement, which only comes after a long period of motor learning, manifests itself in a recurrent series of kinematic movements provided by flexible and dynamic muscular interactions operating at different levels of the motor system.

The process of learning a highly-coordinated stroke requires several stages. Stage one involves a simplification of the motor system by reducing its number of degrees of freedom. During the second stage, the number of segments involved in the stroke increases and several muscles are combined into an integrated functional unit, i.e. a muscle-antagonist group able to generate short and timely efforts which together contribute, with minimal energy loss, to the overall force of the stroke. Finally, the third stage of this learning process involves developing well-tuned sensor corrections, which can allow for the automatic use of various energy resources within the motor system. At this stage, the exactness of impulse transmission from different body segments to the ball is provided by well-developed anticipatory muscle activity (see Biryukova & Bril 2002 for review of Bernstein's theoretical basis of tool use).

The mechanics of motor organization for a tennis stroke are probably not all that different than those involved in stone knapping, as described elsewhere in this volume (e.g. Biryukova *et al.*; Bril *et al.*). Compared to stone knappers of lesser skill, expert knappers employ the greatest number of arm joints in their activities. As well, expert knappers have the most stable kinematic pattern and the highest degree of the coordination between arm joints (Biryukova *et al.* this volume). These results are in keeping with the characteristics described above for highly-skilled tennis players.

The example of motor organization in a tennis stroke shows that for multi-joint coordination, nervous control is extremely complex. From a mechanical point of view, the complexity of the human and the primate arm is similar: each can be considered a mechanical system consisting of three rigid bodies (arm, forearm, hand) with seven degrees of freedom (three in the shoulder, two in the elbow. two in the wrist joint; see Biryukova *et al.* this volume). The differences between human and primate motor-control systems concern the levels at which the central nervous system controls movement. Following Bernstein's classification, there are four levels in the construction of movement: muscle tone (A); muscular-articular links (B); space (C); and actions (D). According to this classification, it may be hypothesized that for the first two levels (A and B) there is no difference between human and primate. When climbing or jumping, primates demonstrate inter-joint coordination which is even more perfect than it is in humans. Similarly, there are no differences in terms of space (C), since primates are capable of performing precise movements in 3-dimensional space, for example when cracking nuts. The differences between human and primate motor control occur at the level of actions (D), defined as a sequence of movements directed toward understanding and solving a problem. Major corrections in muscular actions originate from continuous and meaningful observation, for example, in the ability to assess whether the gradual application of some muscular action to solve a motor task is proceeding correctly, or whether some movement is doing exactly what is required according to the meaning given to that task.

It may be difficult for a chimpanzee to perform the necessarily continuous and meaningful assessment of their muscular operations needed to produce a desired final shape for a stone roughout. At the same time, if links in the operational chain are missing or their order is mixed up, one will also fail to solve their problem. For primates, the crucial difficulties seem to be a lack of adaptive flexibility in their body of operational chains, as well as in their being unable to anticipate different kinds of muscular needs (both abilities are necessary for the success of any motor task under fluctuating environmental circumstances) (Bernstein 1996). And this is why it is quite difficult to imagine a chimpanzee ever playing tennis or any other human sport.

Acknowledgements

The author is grateful to Blandine Bril for fruitful suggestions when editing the manuscript, to Elena Biryukova for the translation from Russian to English. The help from Ivan Biryukov for editing the figures is sincerely appreciated.

References

Bernstein, N.A., 1923. A study in the biomechanics of the stroke using light recording, in *Proceedings of Central Institute of Work,* vol. 1(1). Moscow, 19–79. [In Russian.]

Bernstein, N.A., 1926. *Biomechanics for Instructors*. Moscow: Novaia Moskva. [In Russian.]

Bernstein, N.A., 1990. *The Physiology of Movements and Activity*. Moscow: Nauka. [In Russian.]

Bernstein, N.A., 1996. On dexterity and its development, in *Dexterity and its Development*, eds. M.L. Latash & M.T. Turvey. Mahwah (NJ): Lawrence Erlbaum Associates Inc.

Biryukova, E.V. & B. Bril, 2002. Bernstein et le geste technique, in *Revue d'Anthropologie des Connaissances. Le geste technique. Reflexions methodologiques et anthropologiques. Technologies/Ideologies/Pratiques*, eds. B. Bril & V. Roux. Ramonville Saint-Agne: Editions Eres, 49–68.

Donskoi, D.D., 1995. *The Structure of Movement*. Moscow: State Institute of Physical Culture. [In Russian.]

Dorokhov, S.I., 1983. A Methodology for the Elementary Education of the Kicking Task, based on a Biomechanical Analysis. Unpublished PhD thesis. St Petersburg. [In Russian.]

Fetisova, S.L., 1978. A biomechanical study of the volleyball serve, in *Proceedings of P.F. Lesgaft State Academy of Physical Culture*. St Petersburg: P.F. Lesgaft State Academy, 26–37. [In Russian.]

Golenko, V.A., 1973. A study of the kinematic structure of the tennis serve. *Theory and Practice of Physical Culture* 3, 16. [In Russian.]

Groppel, J., I.S. Shin, I. Tomas & J. Gregory, 1987. Tension impact of midsized and oversized tennis rackets. *International Journal of Sport Biomechanics* 3, 40–46.

Ivanova, G.P., 1972. The peculiarities of biodynamics and the control of stroke movements, in *Proceedings of P.F. Lesgaft State Academy of Physical Culture*. St Petersburg: P.F. Lesgaft State Academy, 106–15. [In Russian.]

Ivanova, G.P., 1991. The Biomechanics of Stroke Interactions in Sports. Unpublished Doctoral dissertation. St. Petersburg. [In Russian.]

Knudsonn, D. & S. White, 1989. Forces on the hand in the tennis forehand drive: application of force sensing resistors. *International Journal of Sport Biomechanics* 5(3), 324–31.

Lukirskaya, G.P., 1965. Comparative biomechanical characteristics of the structure of the tennis stroke. *Theory and Practice of Physical Culture* 11, 37–47. [In Russian.]

Lukirskaya, G.P., 1967 About the functioning of muscle-antagonists during the stroke movement (the example of the tennis stroke), in *Problems of Sport Physiology*. Moscow: Physical Culture and Sport, 37–42. [In Russian.]

Pershin, A.N., 1987. The Biomechanical Basis of Technical Tool Use while Learning a Stroke. Unpublished PhD thesis, St Petersburg [In Russian.]

Tchkhaidze, L.V., 1970. *About the Control of Human Movement*. Moscow: Physical Culture and Sport. [In Russian.]

Thelen, E., D. Corbetta & J.P. Spencer, 1996. Development of reaching during the first year: role of movement speed. *Journal of Experimental Physiology: Human Perception and Performance* 22(5), 1059–76.

Tutevitch, V.N., 1969. *A Theory of Throwing in Sports*. Moscow: Physical Culture and Sport. [In Russian.]

Chapter 9

Action Dynamics in Tool Use

Ad W. Smitsman, Ralf F.A. Cox & Raoul M. Bongers

The present chapter addresses the question what enabled humans over the history of mankind and developing children today to increasingly take advantage of opportunities for action that objects provide for using them as tools. Scientists often mainly attribute the evolution of tool use in mankind and its development in young children to the emergence of a more advanced computational brain that enables development of means end insight and the formation of blueprints for the planning and control of complexly-nested sequences of action as occur in human tool use. The present chapter argues that a too exclusive focus on the mind at the cost of the rest of the body grossly oversimplifies what tool use entails, and creates an untenable dichotomy between the brain and the rest of the body. The chapter elaborates on how our understanding of tools is grounded and born from our capacity to act by firstly showing that it is this capacity, and more specifically the need and opportunity to enhance it, when it falls short for a task, that motivates tool use. This opportunity exists because objects can modify the geometrical, dynamical and sensitive properties of the body for action needed for a task, and will do so when the individual can assemble postures and movements that make the object a tool. Secondly the chapter discusses the action parameters that need to be regulated for making an object a tool. Finally the chapter presents a dynamical approach on planning that is not based on blueprints but takes into account the dynamical interplay during the action between brain, sensory and motor variables when action proceeds. Such interplay is needed to make the different parts of the body communicate and the planning future directed, as well as flexible, in that it can take advantage of upcoming circumstances that are fortuitous for the task performance.

Tool use by humans has evolved into a complex skill originating more than 2.5 million years ago. Around that time hominins for the first time began to use stones as hammers and anvils, not just for cracking nuts, but for knapping stones into sharp-edged flakes (Roche this volume). In human children tool use develops by the end of the first year of life, although it can be seen earlier (Lockman 2000). By the end of the first year of life, however, reaching and grasping have been sufficiently developed to manipulate objects. In addition, postural control in sitting and walking is then at a stage that it enables the child to free their hands for using objects in instrumental ways (Smitsman & Bongers 2003; Corbetta this volume). As we will argue later on, it is important that motor milestones such as postural stability have first to be accomplished before tool use arises, .

What led our hominin ancestors to discover the possibility of using stones to knap other stones instead of just using them to crack nuts as their ancestors did? What enabled young children to discover the opportunities to use objects as tools in increasingly complex ways? Today, an endless variety of tools are available in the different artefacts and technologies that surround humans in modern societies.

Although the question of evolution and development are not strictly similar, they are related. Both address change, the emergence of novel forms of behaviour. Unfortunately, we cannot directly observe what happened millions of years ago, but we can observe tool use in developing children. The developmental question is more easily studied and may provide valuable insights into the question of evolution. Both questions have intrigued scientists for centuries and they remain a puzzle. The questions are intriguing, because they lie at the core of our understanding of human intelligence, human culture and technology and their evolution over time. Human tool use expresses newly-emerging possibilities for action and interaction that arose for hominins and still arise for young children. The practice of using tools evolved over time and shaped the human-action repertoire, intelligence, technology, language, social relationships and culture and was in turn shaped by each of these. They co-evolved over thousands of years and mutually influenced one another.

As is the case with all intriguing questions, simple answers are not readily available. We may hint at some answers, however, by observing human tool use in its fragile beginnings as well as in its more fully-skilled form. To start with the latter, when we observe skilled human tool use, for instance, in knapping stones, carpeting or forging, we observe an action that encompasses a rather elaborate and complexly-nested sequence of activities. Several perception–action cycles of bodily postures and movements smoothly ordered over time and space progressively change an object from its originally raw form into a nicely-shaped artefact. The final shape of the artefact may have been intended from the beginning, but it may also arise more or less spontaneously when the work proceeds. Certainly not all of its details will have been intended. A smaller or larger portion of it emerges from the action itself. The artefact expresses the craftsmanship of the tool user. It arises as the result of a complex set of relationships of bodily components, tool, object and surrounding surfaces and substances, which the tool user was capable of maintaining over time and space. The artefact and its quality, in a manner of speaking, grow out of these relationships.

Because the products of tool use result from the relationships a tool user was able to maintain, the primary question for understanding tool use and its evolution and development concern those relationships. The relationships at least involve the body of the tool user, the tool object and the target object the tool user worked on. Often other surrounding surfaces and substances are involved as well. What enables a tool user to coordinate and control such relationships? All actions rest on relationships that are maintained over time between components that involve the body as well as surrounding surfaces and tasks. Moreover,

they mostly consist of several nested perception–action cycles that extend over time and space. Is the answer in the case of tool use and tool making any different from actions that do not involve the use of an implement, such as in reaching, grasping and manipulating objects using just the hands? Do new challenges arise for the coordination and control of action when an implement complements the body, as is the case in tool use? Tool use is widespread among the animal kingdom and not only present in hominins or humans. Given these observations, the answer should be negative. Nevertheless, it has become tempting for many scientists to answer this question in the affirmative in the case of humans. The complexity of the relationships in the case of humans and the number and heterogeneity of components involved have led researchers to suggest that new capabilities were needed for human tool use to evolve. Remarkably the new capacities that were held responsible for human tool use were exclusively attributed to the brain ignoring the rest of the body, which also evolved. They concerned planning and decision-making, and were also held responsible for the emergence of language (Greenfield 1991) and human social interaction. The later capabilities supposedly also emerged in hominins about 2.5 million years ago and in young children after the first year of life (Lockman this volume; Stout this volume).

It cannot be denied that mental capacities are important in human tool use and that changes with respect to those capacities in humans and young children greatly contribute to their developing skills of tool use and tool making. But to understand what tool use and tool making involve and even how the mind may contribute to them, we have to realize that they are actions in the first place. All actions consist of bodily postures and movements (Reed 1982; 1988). These postures and movements can involve the whole body, or just a sub-system of it, and it is these that transform a hand-held object into a tool and regulate the relationships that are needed for tool use. When we take a closer look at it from an action perspective, it becomes questionable even whether the mind or the brain is privileged. Other parts of the body are of importance as well. The human hands and digits are extremely suitable to tool manipulation. Manipulation also requires a stable platform which is provided by the trunk and legs. Activities have to be controlled to succeed which requires the concerted effort of sensory systems connected to action. In case of visual control, a stable gaze is required, which also involves the trunk and legs as well as the head. Bodily activities not only determine whether an object will become a tool but also the kind of tool the object will be. A stick can be used for hitting, piercing and even writing in the sand.

Each involves a different pattern of motions, different grips, and different places where the object will be grasped. The problem with focusing too exclusively on the mind at the cost of the rest of the body is that it grossly oversimplifies what is going on in tool use.

Tool use as an action

A generally agreed-upon definition of tool use and tool making (which often includes tool use) is that they extend a person's capacity for action. Tool use — and as its extension tool making — enables tasks that otherwise would be impossible or difficult to achieve for an individual. However, the question of why such is the case has hardly been addressed. It awaits specification of what composes an individual's capacity to act, and how and when it is extended in tool use. Smitsman (1997) and Smitsman & Bongers (2003) argue that a capacity is not extended solely because a person 'understands' that an object provides means for a task, or more generally, means–end relationships, a cognitive accomplishment that scientists generally consider to be a prerequisite and at the core of human tool use (Piaget 1954; Willatts 1990). The reason why this understanding does not extend a person's capacity to act, or at least will be insufficient for that purpose is trivially simple. A person may perceive another person using an object as a means to an end and understand that objects can be used this way without being able to extend his or her capacity for action in the same way. To comprehend why and how objects may aid individuals to act, we first need to address what composes the capacity to act and when and why it may fall short. We need insight into what composes the capacity to understand why and how tool use and tool making may extend that capacity.

Action and, more specifically, the capacity to act are determined by opportunities and limitations of the body relative to a particular environment and task. For each individual the body forms a rich source of resources, as well as the environment and the task. Bodily resources have to be defined with respect to the geometric (size and shape), dynamic (active and passive forces) and information gathering (perceiving) properties or constraints of the body. Environmental resources, also called affordances (Gibson 1979/1986), can be defined in a similar way, that is, relative to the bodily resources. The same can be done for task properties. Tools are part of the environmental resources. Actors mobilize these resources for a task by means of bodily postures and movements. Action falls short when bodily resources do not fit environmental and task constraints or when no stable postures and movements are available to mobilize them. One can reach no further in space than the arm movement and body posture allows one to do. The reaching range varies from standing on a surface to sitting in a comfortable armchair or lying on the ground. While standing, the range will be reduced when the surface becomes sloped and even more so when it also becomes slippery. Tool use shows that the boundary of action is not limited to the body, but flexible and can be extended. Attaching implements temporarily to the body can extend this boundary. This is because implements instantaneously modify the bodily resources that can be mobilized for a task. Hands that hold sticks of some length provide reaching devices that increase the reaching range. However, the increment is not purely geometrical, because postures and movements are also needed to increase the range of reaching. Because a hand-held stick also modifies the passive forces that act on arms, trunk and legs, postural adaptations are needed to counteract these forces. These adaptations again may reduce the increased reaching range, or even worse perturb the system such that reaching becomes impossible to achieve, depending on the load and inertial forces that act on the system.

The example shows that bodily modifications are needed to extend a capacity for action, and that objects attached to the body will do so. In addition, it shows that such modifications are only useful when the individual can exploit them, which requires stable postures and movements of the body that can be adapted to the changes that occur for the system. Finally, it shows that the change occurs irrespective of what the individual understands about the tool object. Rather, understanding arises from finding out how to exploit the change in resources. Knowing how to take advantage of modifications arising with respect to bodily resources for action, thus involves more than a purely mental kind of understanding of new means that may be available in tool objects. It is an understanding that is not dissociated from the bodily organizations that exploit tool objects.

Tool use as well as tool making exploit a fact of nature: that resources for action are not static but dynamic; they change over time. Bodily changes are common in nature. They take place when the individual grows up, ages or more or less haphazardly, for instance, when accidents occur. In fact such changes provide the underlying dynamics of evolutionary and developmental processes. This is common feat well known among scientists (see Sameroff 1983; Gottlieb 1992; Thelen & Smith 1994; Smitsman & Bongers 2003). Less well realized is that any object that is implemented to the body will do the same on a shorter time scale. Implements set the stage for tool use by modifying the geometry, dynamics and information-gathering characteristics (Smitsman 1997; Smitsman & Bongers 2003). Tool use can and could arise in individual's who are able to explore and discover possibilities that take advantage of such changes. When we accept that an individual's capacity for action is not limited just to the boundary of its skin, but can be extended instantaneously by environmental affordances as tools, we may begin to understand what tool use and tool making entails and also how they could and can evolve and how this evolution will contribute to the evolution of human action and technology.

What enables a person to mobilize stable organizations of postures and movements amidst changes of his/her body's geometry, dynamics and perceiving qualities? It should be noticed beforehand that changes have to be within the scale of the individual's action system. A stone that is too heavy or too large and cannot be lifted or held will never become a tool. There are at least three answers to the above question. The first one is that action is not prefixed but dynamically organized at different levels and time scales, taking advantage of whatever is available for a task at the time. The second reason is the available degrees of freedom. There is an enormous reservoir of degrees of freedom not used in daily actions, leaving room for new different organizations when circumstances require. Species may differ in this respect. The third reason is that action is prospective. It is prospective in the sense that its organization over time not only senses what happens to the system and the relationship of the system with the environment, but also senses and prepares what has to happen to make action proceed in an intended direction. In all this, the relationship with the environment is of central significance for the way action is and becomes organized over time. The system cannot survive without that relationship.

In the following section we will discuss the prospective side of action in case of tool use in more detail, borrowing from our research.

Anticipating new goals

We have seen that any object attached to a limb, for instance the hand, changes the limb with respect to its geometry, dynamics and information-gathering sensitivity. Because the limb is part of a larger system, the changes are not limited to the limb alone, but affect the whole system. The change, however, does not only affect the body but also the relationship of the body with the environment. The end-effector that relates the system with the environment is no longer the limb, but a tool object. The relationship of tool object and the environment now defines the goal of the action. Parameters that need to be regulated to ascertain those

goals are defined by that relationship. New opportunities for action arise, depending on whether and how the individual can negotiate the changes of the body with respect to a task and an environment. Look at the very simple example of holding a stick of some length, shape and weight while standing on both feet in an upright posture. Holding the stick means that environmental targets can be poked at and hit from a larger distance and with different force. Poking and hitting require bodily postures, movements and locations to execute them. A location is needed that agrees with the increased 'arm length', as well as arm and body postures and movements to control poking or hitting. Therefore, an individual's selection of the location determines the distance at which bodily postures and arm movements allow the person to extend the stick and control the contact that the tool object will make with a target. A location at too short a distance will lead to awkward, poorly-controlled arm and body movements. They can even make it impossible to touch the target with the tip, when the arm has to extend too far backward and the body needs to lean too far into the same direction, to compensate for the overshoot of the stick. The opposite happens for a distance too far away from the target. In short, the location should not only define the new geometry of the modified prehensile system, but also its dynamics, i.e. the changed pattern of forces that need to be controlled by arm and body postures and movements to perform the task. This means that the location should differ, depending on whether a heavy stick is held or a light one, whether the mass is equally or unequally distributed over the stick and whether the target is very small or relatively large in size. It should also differ depending on the task that is performed. Wagman & Carello (2001) showed that tool users grasp an object at a different position for tasks such as poking or hitting in order to take advantage of the inertial properties of the stick, that have a different meaning in these both tasks.

In a series of studies (Bongers 2001; Bongers *et al.* 2003) we investigated whether children of about 2 to 4 years old and adults take advantage of the new properties that arise when the prehensile system has been changed by holding a stick. We also studied how they take advantage of these changes in the way they organize the action. In different studies, we varied stick length, the weight of the stick and the way this weight was distributed over the stick, for instance, heavy at the tip, in the middle, or at the fist. Finally, we varied the size of the target in order to study the effects of task constraints. The task was a very simple one: we asked the participants to push an object to the side with the tip of the stick. The object was located at a table or at a small platform at about elbow height (Fig. 9.1). To do so, participants needed to walk a few steps forward towards the target, with the stick held upwards at about 45 degrees to the horizontal plane of the floor. They had to stop and stand still on a location at a distance to the target that allowed them to perform the task in a controlled way. Results showed that at all ages, participants selected a location that agreed with the change in the length of the arm due to the stick. Thus, they determined the change in geometry of the system and were able to take advantage of it. With respect to the change in dynamics, however, results were more complicated and differed for adults and young children. This indicates that taking full advantage of a modified system is a complicated task that may require years of prac-

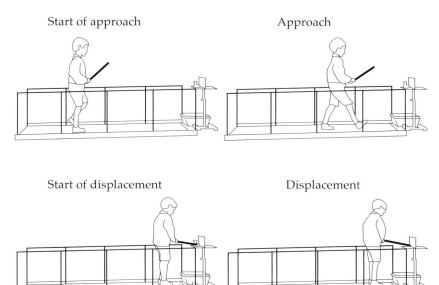

Figure 9.1. *Schematic representation of the task used by Bongers (2001) and Bongers* et al. *(2003).*

tice, even for a simple task as the one we studied. In adults the location where participants stopped, agreed with the change in postures and movements needed to counteract the changed pattern of forced induced by the mass variation of the stick. In young children such effects were not found. Postural changes in young children indicated that at these ages, children are sensitive to variation in dynamics as a consequence of holding sticks of varying length, mass and mass distribution. The way they organized the arm and body posture on touching the object with the tip of the stick clearly indicated such sensitivity. They were just not able to negotiate the changes in dynamics, in stopping at a position that agreed with the postural adaptations they needed. Moreover, when sticks became too heavy, too long or too inert by the load at the tip, they began to show defects in following the instructions. Apparently, in conditions in which the changed pattern of forces began to perturb their action, they needed to explore new ways of performing the task. It is highly unlikely that they did not understand the instructions, given that they were perfectly able to follow them for lighter and shorter sticks.

Interestingly, the way the variation in dynamics affected the action, strongly suggested that it was not a comfortable arm and body posture — for instance, reducing the load at joints — which determined the place to stop, but regulation of the relationship of tool object and target. For instance, touching and displacing a small object on a small platform at midair with

the tip of a stick, requires control of the variability of the stick at its tip. Too high a variability may become problematic especially for small targets, longer sticks and sticks that are heavy at the fist and light at the tip. Shortening the reaching distance by a less-stretched arm and a more upright body posture can reduce the variability. This strategy was exactly what we found in adults with respect to the location they selected, as well as with respect to the way postures and movements were organized when targets became small.

There has been little research done of the kind discussed above. To summarize, however, results indicate that even young children can take advantage of changes with respect to their bodily resources for actions that occur when a tool object is held. Not all changes can be negotiated immediately. Some changes — in our study changes in dynamics — may require a lengthy period of exploration and practice to negotiate them and to plan the action accordingly. The results show that the relationship with the environment determines the way the action will be planned and organized. This relationship has been changed as a consequence of holding a tool object. Even young children are aware of this change and their changed capacity that results from holding an object. However, to organize the action in a way that fully exploits the new opportunities that came with the tool object, may take a lengthy period of time given that even 4-year-old children, who already have some years of practice in carrying sticks, were not able to do what adults did.

Action parameters in tool use

An object gets its meaning as a tool from the way it modifies an action system *relative* to an environmental target. For instance, there exist all kind of tools for hitting. Each of them may afford a percussion movement of a type we see, for instance, in nailing, drumming and stone knapping. This movement enables a person to effectively transfer energy to the target object. The movement that is made, however, as well as the tool object that is needed for the movement, differs depending on the target that is hit and the event that should take place with respect to its surfaces. In nailing, transfer of energy to the top of a nail drives the nail into another surface. In case of stone knapping, energy directed to the surface of a stone on a particular location knaps flakes of the stone and changes its shape. The tool function as well as the behavioural organizations that underlie it, derive from the relationship that is required for the tool + target system. An individual's attention should be directed to this relationship in order to discover what a tool and target may mean for action and to learn how to take advantage of it.

How can we describe the relationship that determines the system of tool and target and that an individual needs to establish and maintain by his/her postures and movements? A precise description is needed for studying tool use as well as tool making. A description of a tool as a means to an end, as is often done, will be insufficient. It does not clarify what the end precisely involves and what is needed to make the tool object the means to ascertain this end. To define the system that we want to describe, we take the situation that a tool object has been attached to a limb (e.g. the hand) and forms the new end-effector, as most often is the case.[1] In this situation the body or a limb no longer forms the interface with the environment. Thus, the new relationship that now forms the goal of the action is a relationship between an object attached to the body and another object or a surface, the target of the action. Often, shortly, the tool object is described as the tool, but one should realize that the object becomes a tool by the way action unfolds over time, which includes the grip and other postures and movements to attach the object to the body and to exploit its properties. Hands are particularly suited for this purpose and erect locomotion or sitting further supports its realization.

At an abstract level a tool-use situation manifests itself as something we would like to call a *topology* or *topological structure* (Smitsman & Bongers 2003), a notion that originally belongs to mathematics. The topological structure pinpoints the meaningful relationship that obviously exists between the constituents of a tool-use situation (tool, target and their surrounding). This relationship can be expressed by the basic topological terms neighbourhood, connectedness and continuity that correspond to the actual nearness and possible physical connection of the constituents and the possibility of a useful tooling action, respectively. By this, the three notions capture the essentials of tool use. The topology therefore determines whether a particular constitution of a tool and target will be a means to an end and which means it will be. Given that tool objects and target objects are spatial entities, of which the relationship changes over time, as is the case with hand-held tools, a topology can be defined by a set of *relative geometrical parameters* and *relative dynamical parameters*. Because the topology is based on a tool and a target, which mutually imply one another, the parameters are relative parameters. Describing tool use and tool making in terms of the regulation of a set of relative parameters reveals the action and perception dynamics approach to this kind of human endeavour — one of the central themes of this chapter.

Among the most frequently-involved relative geometrical parameters in a general tool-use task are the parameters of relative distance, relative orientation, relative size and relative shape. Important relative dynamical parameters are relative linear and rotational motion, relative inertial properties and various relative material properties like friction, viscosity, elasticity, hardness and plasticity.[2] Note that material properties are relative too. Our ancestors selected stone, wood or steel of a type suited to the purpose it was used for to make tools (e.g. furniture, houses, ships and weapons). In modern times, much of the technological research is directed at the innovation of the relative material properties of our tools. The parameters do not necessarily have to be independent and in most cases they are not. Altering the size and shape of objects, for example, will most definitely change their inertial properties.[3] Of course, these alterations are only possible if certain relative material parameters (e.g. friction and plasticity) are within particular ranges of values. The important point is that the set of all the relative geometrical and dynamical parameters together pinpoints the abstract topological structure that tool use can entail.

The relative geometrical and dynamical parameters like relative distance, relative orientation and relative linear and rotational motion have a direct relationship with their counterparts from physics, viz. the distance and (solid) angles between the objects and their linear and angular momentum, respectively. Although this connection is quite obvious and direct, it is important to keep in mind that they are not necessarily the same. All these parameters are defined as properties of the tool + target system as a whole, on the scale of the observer. There is no need for a representation of absolute properties of objects in this context. The topological structure is perceived directly in the sense of ecological reality and the parameters have relevance for action of the organism in a particular tool-use situation. This means that the abstract topological structure presents itself to the tool user or tool maker in a specific pattern of these parameters and ranges of parameter values or patterns of values.

The parameters and their values differ for different kinds of tool objects and for different tooling operations with the same object. They, for instance, distinguish nailing, drumming and stone knapping from one another, but also stone knapping from cutting. Tool objects and target objects embody opportunities with respect to those parameters by their properties relative to one another and may be more or less suited for a particular tooling operation depending on the opportunities they can make available. Often different objects can be used for the same tooling operation and the same object can be used for different tooling operations. The kinds of tool an object can become in a particular task and for a particular target, depends on the specific values for the relative parameters it can make available.

The parameters from the set, that is relevant in a particular setting, can be either constraints (fixed) or parameters that have to be regulated (free). Perceptual sensitivity to their values is crucial in both cases (Bernstein 1967). That this is true for the constraint parameters as well may be contra-intuitive, given that they cannot be regulated. Still their values (of tool relative to target) have to be within particular ranges, in order to make tool use successful. When, for instance, an object has a convex blade, it can become a tool for scooping and transporting food when regulation of its relative orientation and distance leads to the proper patterns for scooping and transporting. To make regulation possible, in ordinary spoons, the handle extends the longitudinal axis of the blade and is not placed perpendicular to this axis. In this example other parameters like the relative shape and size and the coefficients of friction and viscosity can not be regulated. They are determined by the fixed properties of the tool and target system and form constraints for the task. A change of parameter value may also create another tool. When, for instance, the convex blade has a relatively sharp edge, the same spoon that is used for scooping or transporting food may also be used for cutting, depending on how the value of the parameter of relative orientation is regulated.

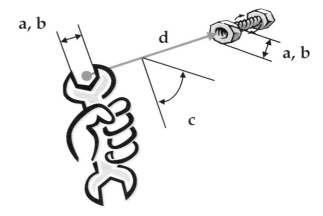

Figure 9.2. *Example of tool use: the untightening of a nut with a spanner. The relative geometrical parameters of size and shape (a, b), orientation (c) and distance (d) are indicated.*

The distinction between constraints and parameters that have to be regulated is not a principal one, but depends on the task that is performed and the phase of the task. Some tools are designed so that the parameters can become constraints in some phases, while they can be regulated in other phases. For example, the size and shape of the head of a spanner relative to a nut have to be within particular ranges of values, otherwise enclosure of the nut by the tool is not possible, making screwing impossible (Fig. 9.2). The two parameters are fixed, forming constraints in this tool-use situation. Their values cannot be changed, that is the tool user cannot regulate them and so has no control over these potential degrees of freedom. Nonetheless, the tool user does have to be sensitive to their values in order to choose the right tool for the job. Another way to solve the problem, besides choosing another spanner is to use a pair of pliers or a wrench to un-tighten the nut. In that case, the parameters of relative size and shape become free to regulate providing more flexibility to the tool user. With this new system of tool and target (i.e. pliers or wrench and nut), more degrees of freedom are made available.

To elaborate some more on the importance of the concept of the relative geometrical and dynamical parameters in the context of this workshop, consider the example of stone knapping in early man. This is a clear case of a task that entails both tool use and tool making in a symbiotic relationship. The stone knapper is making a stone tool, while using other stone tools. Moreover, preceding the actual stone knapping, the selection of appropriate stones to knap and for knapping with, forms an important part of the entire tool-making and tool-using activity. Choosing these stones badly can render the whole enterprise unsuccessful. The stone knapper is looking for a stone of roughly the 'right' size and shape, and in particular of the right material properties. An experienced eye can distinguish from each other different stone types with different material properties. Stones are generally inhomogeneous and anisotropic in their material properties, which largely determine the way the stone will split and the way flakes will come off. To increase the chance of producing a useful new tool from a roughly-shaped stone, the stone knapper has to be sensitive to these parameters. After a suitable stone to knap, and one for knapping with, is chosen, the process of tool using and tool making proceeds to the next level. The action of stone knapping will require sensitivity of the stone knapper to a more extended set of parameters. The stones' inhomogeneous and anisotropic properties are fixed now and the material properties of the stones become constraint parameters. This does not mean that these parameters lose their importance; they still have to be dealt with, although they cannot be regulated anymore. To make use of them or to diminish their disturbing influence, the stone knapper has to monitor them and arrange his actions for regulating the other parameters in a suitable way, accordingly. Among the parameters the stone knapper has to regulate are relative distance and orientation and relative motion (linear and rotational) of the knapping stone (tool) and rough 'tool-becoming' stone (target) system. The distance and motion of the knapping stone to the tool-becoming stone has to be constantly regulated into percussion-like movement patterns, while monitoring the relative orientation in doing so. The relative orientation and motion of the two stones determine, under conditions of fixed material properties, the way the flakes will come off and so the way the new stone tool will become shaped. In the case of stone knapping, the parameter of relative motion is functionally equal to the motion of the stone that is knapped with. This is, of course, because in the action of stone knapping the tool-becoming stone is in a steady position on the stone knapper's lap in order to establish a firm base. The parameter of relative orientation, however, is actively regulated by the stone knapper by manipulating both of the stones. He is constantly rotating and rearranging the two stones after every one or two strokes, under continuous inspection of the inhomogeneous and anisotropic properties of the tool-becoming stone.

A description of tool use in terms of a limited set of parameters enables us to relate tool use and tool making in an insightful and coherent way to one another. As the example above clearly shows, the parameters that are constraints in the phase of the actual stone knapping were regulated in the phase of exploring and became fixed by the choice of a suitable stone. The same set of parameters, however, was involved in both phases. This illustrates the connection between tool use and tool making. They form two processes that are embedded in the same abstract space. One usually precedes the other in time, making parameters fixed while leaving others free for the tool user to regulate. But the processes are not really distinct; their difference is but a difference in degree, not in fundamentals. When a chimpanzee breaks a branch from a tree and takes of its leaves for termite fishing, it regulates the shape and size of the tool object. In a further phase of the task, during termite fishing, the earlier regulated parameters become constraints, and relative orientation and distance are regulated.

Researchers commonly conceive of tool use and tool making as rather different tasks, imposing different demands on the individual (see e.g. Ingold 1997). Opposite to this, Ingold has argued that this distinction is unjustifiable because it is based on a misconception of tool use and an unsupported distinction between designing and producing tools on the one hand and using the tool on the other. Moreover, in his view, designing attributed to tool making is not something higher that predominantly needs the brain as opposed to producing which 'only' requires the rest of the body. The whole body is involved in both, and both require practice. Comparable with what we have argued before, Ingold rightly asserted that, in his terms, objects become tools by practice. When we define tool use and tool making in terms of a set of relative parameters that are involved, it becomes clear that they differ only in the dimensions (i.e. which relative parameters) they control (i.e. regulate or fix) but that this distinction is not fundamental. A parameter that is controlled by the tool maker in some cases (or phases) can be controlled by the tool user in others, as mentioned before. The parameters and regulation of these are the means to ascertain an end. In tool making, regulation of these parameters leads to a particular tool that sets the stage for further tooling operations, leaving less degrees of freedom for the tool user, as more of those parameters become constraint.

Planning

As for any goal-directed action, an important question is the planning of the activities. For action to succeed, earlier activities have to prepare later ones, and present states need to set the stage for future ones. Planning concerns the fundamental property that makes action prospective or proactive. What ensures that earlier activities indeed prepare later ones? And how do the events they regulate become ordered over time (more or less smoothly) leading to the intended goal and not some other outcome? What keeps the planning on its track, or more specifically, how does a particular track arise and become more articulated in time? These intriguing questions are not easily solved, and different answers can and have been formulated for them. We will discuss these questions from a dynamical perspective that conceives of planning as being time dependent, and order as emerging out of the complexity of the many mutual influences at the lower level of the activities themselves, and by internal, environmental and task constraints (Newell 1986; 1989; see also Clark 1997). It may sound somewhat contradictory to conceive of planning as time dependent and order as emerging from the activities itself, if one assumes that the existence of a plan and steps in a preset order is what the concept of planning entails. We will not deny that such plans exist, and may be helpful in guiding action. But in order to exist, they have to arise first. We like to argue that their existence cannot be understood without also considering their emergence (Thelen & Smith 1994), both on the shorter time scale of a task that is executed, as well as on the longer time scale of experience and practice with the task and other tasks, and on the time scale of development. Processes may look very ordered and planned from the outside, but when we focus on the internal processes underlying them, they become much more chaotic. Development itself is such an ordered progression of steps or phases, without the steps being planned in advance.

Our approach differs from the (traditional) cognitive view on planning. The traditional cognitive view attributes planning to an executive function of the brain that enables people to control action on the basis of complex representations of steps or movements to take for events that occur or that one intends to realize. The planning is fed by perceptual information, but its operation stays relatively unaffected by what happens at the sensory and motor side of the system on a real time scale. This makes the system a static affair. As a consequence, control of action entails the execution of blueprints or flowcharts, instead of the dynamic interplay between perception and action at different time scales. The fact that the human brain is larger and more complexly organized compared to other hominins strongly motivates the idea of planning as computing flowcharts conceiving the brain as a kind of container that can encompass larger and more complex representations. It is also tempting to attribute the evolution of tool use in humans to this supposedly improved capacity of planning as resting on the larger representational capacity of humans compared to other hominins. Recently a more modern version of

the cognitive view on perception and action planning is introduced, based on the theory of event coding (TEC; Hommel *et al.* 2001). This new view highlights the fact that planning is not just an advanced stimulus-response process. It also states that perception and action have to be treated on an equal basis, i.e. represented in a 'common representational medium'. The cognitive codes representing perceptions and actions refer to events codes that consist of the external (distal) features of an event, and that communicate with various perceptual and motor subsystems. Although discrimination learning can lead to a more and more detailed representation of distal features (events), the representation, and with it perception and action planning, remains a static affair. Unfortunately, the TEC stays rather vague about how planning comes about and how it gets organized. Moreover, the authors specifically leave out the (hierarchical) coding of more complex events. Developmental psychologists who embrace the cognitive view conceive of planning as developing in young children in the second year of life, when the child becomes able to form more elaborate and longer mental representations of successive steps that have to be taken in problem-solving tasks (Klahr 1989; Willatts 1990; Ellis & Siegler 1997). Haith (1994) defines planning as 'future-oriented problem solving'. In this view planning is a purely mental, conscious activity, dissociated from action, that a child only 'chooses to do' in novel and difficult situations. This essentially dualistic view of planning has been earlier advocated by Piaget (1954) who also conceived of the capacity to form mental representations as the basis for the development of tool use in the child. Our different view on planning does not mean that we intend to deny the significance of the human brain for planning and the evolution of tool use. Questionable, however, is whether this contribution is in the form of flowcharts of lengthy sequences of events that need to be constructed by the brain in advance. At least two precautions are in place. The first concerns the way planning is defined. The second has to do with the tendency to attribute the evolution of tool use in humans exclusively to the brain, without considering the rest of the body that also evolved (Corbetta this volume; Steele & Uomini this volume).

Our earlier discussion on action as the basis of tool use clearly shows the significance of the human body for human tool use to evolve. In the remainder of this section we will focus on the definition of planning. Planning is not about static, purely mental mechanisms that decide for action, that is, what to do and when to do it, and that are only loosely connected to action and perception. Planning is embodied, tightly connected to action and perception, and time dependent as action and perception are themselves. Contrary to flowcharts that are made to operate mechanical and electronic devices, the units of planning for action are not events and/or activities to bring about those events. Rather these units are given by the time-dependent relationships with the environment that have to be regulated. We have argued that these relationships involve a topological structure of tool and target, or more specifically, the relative geometrical and dynamic parameters that describe this topological structure. Because a person's postures and movements actively regulate this structure, planning has to involve the body, as well as action–perception cycles, making it a dynamical system. For mechanical and electronic devices, designers have solved the problem of regulation for the large part. In tool use and tool making the individual has to solve it by his/her actions.

When action unfolds over time a more-or-less smoothly-ordered sequence of activities and events arises. One may partition this sequential order in goals and sub-goals, means and ends, or cause and effect, but does this prove that a presupposed plan or blueprint has been executed? The impression that order comes from blueprints may be especially compelling in observing skilled tool users. Indeed their behaviour shows awareness of steps they subsequently have taken and means they have used for taking these steps. Moreover, when questioning them, their answers agree with such observations and suspicions. It seems as if consciousness controlled their actions. However, there is still a problem that we have to face. Consciousness of the sequential order and even of the goals we see in those skilled activities did not exist all the time. At some moment in time they arose and subsequently they might have been further moulded by new experiences. To explain how activities and experiences can give rise to this, some other processes have to be sought. The fact that plans, and even the goals those plans serve, emerge in the cause of the action, shows that planning is a dynamic affair that continuously interacts with (perceptual) information of different modality and with the action itself. And by the way it does this, it also shows that it is often non-linear. New goals come up and may pull existing goals away, but can also make them stronger and more persistent when they become coupled to the existing goals.

The dynamic nature of planning becomes more prevalent when we take a closer look at the way activities unfold over time. The sequence of events appears less fixed and more flexible than it looks from a more distal point of view. There is not just one route to a goal, but different routes that can be taken on different occasions. Moreover, new routes come up all the time

and with them new (sub-)goals. Variability seems to be a fundamental characteristic of every action and the way it is planned (Rosenbaum *et al.* 1995). The important properties of planning are its directedness at a goal, of which one may not even be clearly aware in advance, and its flexibility in adapting to upcoming demands. Any realistic account of planning has to be founded on this dynamic nature.

Dynamic systems theory (Thelen & Smith 1994; Kelso 1995; Goldfield 1995) shows that order at a higher level emerges from constraints at a lower level in the system. In tool use and tool making the constraints concern the topological parameters combined with the opportunities to regulate them, given by the environment, the individual's body, the tools available and the task. The topological parameters form the focus of planning because all tool-use activity is regulation of one or more parameters. In our view, planning, and the sequential order we see in behaviour, emerges from the individual's attention to those parameters and their specific ranges of values and patterns when action unfolds over time. Moreover, we conceive of attention not as a static affair but as dynamic, as action itself is. The state of the planning system with respect to these parameters may vary over time due to several circumstances on multiple time scales. Some of these may have happened earlier before the action takes place (memory), some occur during the action (perception) and some may even occur later on (goal-state or intention).

Recent work of Thelen *et al.* (2001) may clarify how the dynamics that underlie planning may look like. Moreover, their work provides ways to conceptualize these dynamics not just at a theoretical or metaphorical level, but also as a starting point for precise modelling and simulation. The task they studied and subsequently modelled was an object-permanence task, originally developed by Piaget (1954). Piaget designed these tasks to assess young children's development of object permanence in the first two years of life. Roughly, object permanence concerns young children's understanding of objects as persistent entities, which have an existence independently from the child's actions and thoughts with respect to those objects. More generally, it entails children's progressive understanding of objects in space and time during the first two years of life. After Piaget, many versions of this task have seen the light. In Thelen's *et al.* version (2001), two similar containers in a rectangular block are placed in front of the child on a table, one to the right of the child's midline and one to the left. The experimenter, seated opposite to the child, repeatedly hides an object (toy) in one of those containers. After a series of hidings by the experimenter in one and the same container and subsequent recoveries by the child from that container, the experimenter switches to hiding place to the other container. The remarkable finding is that in the age of about 8 to 12 months, young children continue to search for the object in the old hiding place, although they have clearly seen the experimenter hiding the object in the new place. This error has been called the A-not-B error.

There has been considerable debate about what this object-permanence task really measures. To clarify Thelen's *et al.* viewpoint of planning, we confine the discussion to how they interpret this task. According to them the task measures a child's planning of the reach towards a particular position. They define position not as a discrete variable but as a continuous one, because in principle, the child can reach for any position that is within her reach. Geometrically, and for the task, they define the variable as the position on the axis through the two containers, perpendicular to the child's midline. Position on this axis, including the positions where the object can be hidden, gets the status of a *movement parameter* that is continuous. A reach towards a position on the axis is defined as a *motor-planning field* that is a function of the movement parameter and time. Input from different sources may activate the planning field for particular positions on this continuum. Above some critical activation level, the threshold, decisions will favour the position with the highest level of activation (Fig. 9.3). Seeing the experimenter repeatedly hiding an attractive toy at the same position will gradually build up a memory trace for that position in the child. This build up favours the child's decision to reach for that position above all other positions. On the other hand, a sudden switch of the object to a new hiding position will increase the activation level for that position, possibly even above the activation level for the old position. However, due to dynamic properties of the planning field the increased activation level for the new position may decay so fast, that at the moment of the reach its activation level is lower than that for the old position. As a consequence the child will persevere reaching to the old position instead of the new one. One prediction that follows from this model is that the error will depend highly on the time interval between the hiding event and the onset of reaching. In their model, a decay parameter describes the pace at which activation decays. Results of Thelen's *et al.* studies and of others, indeed confirm this prediction. Another result was that changes in one parameter that concerned the intrinsic dynamics of the motor-planning field would lead to qualitatively different decisions in planning leading to the presence or absence of the A-not-B error. Depending on the value of this parameter, planning would change qualitatively. It

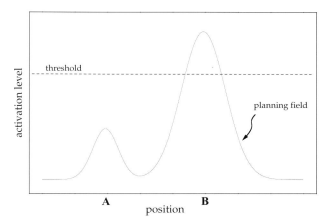

Figure 9.3. *Activation level of the planning field in the A-not-B error task. The highest activation level, above threshold, is present at the value 'B' for the movement parameter (position).*

could be fully driven by the most recent input from the setting without any memory of earlier actions, be determined by a built-up memory of earlier actions leading to perseverance in those actions, or become flexible adapted to new demands. In the later case it allows the child to shift the planning to the new hiding position, although a memory of earlier actions was build up. The parameter in their model that ensured for these qualitative shifts in planning concerned the cooperativity of the planning field. Thelen and her colleagues conceived of the cooperativity as roughly equivalent to connectivity of the neural network of the brain, which increases with age.

Extending Thelen's *et al.* dynamic field model to tool use may shed new light on the cognitive basis of tool use, that researchers such as Piaget and others (for instance Gibson 1977; Bard 1993) were looking for. At the moment we can only borrow from the dynamic field model at a metaphorical level. Nevertheless, there are several interesting features in the dynamic view of planning that are directly relevant for the processes underlying tool use. These features provide a promising starting point for studying planning of the activities (Smitsman & Bongers 2003). Before discussing them in more detail, it may be helpful to recollect what it is that we precisely want to understand. Namely how the dynamic planning of a set of parameters, driven by attention, memory and perceptual input, may lead to more or less smoothly-ordered sequences of events towards a particular end result. At this point it may be valuable and interesting to realize, that the same dynamics that are responsible for the emergence and organization of order over time, may also affect an individual's choices that turn one and the same object into different tools.

a

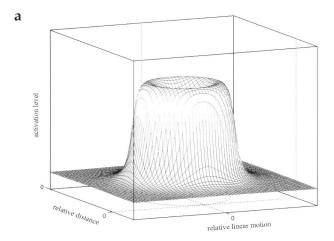

b

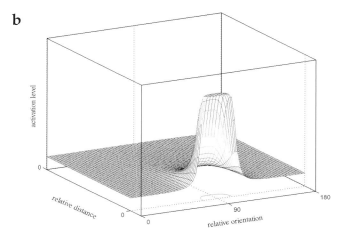

Figure 9.4. *Examples of the planning field for two-dimensional task-spaces. a) The task-space is spanned by the parameters of relative linear motion and relative distance. The activation of the planning is highest for a periodic pattern of parameter values, which is typical for a percussion movement, like in hammering or scooping. The projection of this pattern on the task-space is shown, representing the (most likely) trajectory that will be formed by the tool users action. b) The task-space is spanned by the parameters of relative orientation and relative distance. The activation of the planning is highest for a very narrow 'plateau' at 0 for the relative distance and round 90° for the relative orientation, like in cutting. The projection of the border of this plateau on the task-space is shown, representing the (most likely) region within which the tool users will execute his/her action.*

There are several valuable insights that can be borrowed from Thelen's *et al.* line of thinking and modelling work. We will confine our discussion to two of these. The first concerns the relationship between input to the planning system and decisions made

to plan the action. This relationship is modified in comparison with the (traditional) cognitive view on planning not however, by prescriptions of what to do, but by the internal dynamics of the system. These internal dynamics determines the fate of new input: whether it will decay too quickly to affect decisions, whether it will sustain over time, or whether it will become strengthened or even coupled with other input. When we conceive of the brain as a biological dynamical system, the model is more realistic with respect to its biological and neuro-anatomical properties. The second interesting property of the dynamical field model concerns the way the relevant variables for the planning system are defined, namely as variables that are continuous and directly related to action. The topological parameters in tool use can be conceived of in the same way. While in Thelen's *et al.* model there is only one parameter to deal with (simple one-dimensional task-space), in tool use, there are generally several, possibly coupled parameters involved (higher-dimensional task-space with a more complex structure). This makes the problem more complex but not fundamentally different.

To expand the above line of thinking to a tool-use setting, we have to realize that all the relevant parameters in a particular tool-use setting are always present in the task and are therefore always part of in the action. Whether they will affect the decisions to be made by the planning of the action, that is, whether they will be actively regulated, is another affair and depends on the complex interaction of a multitude of factors, including the internal dynamics of the planning system. It is important to realize that action always realizes a combination of those parameters and ranges of values for this combination, irrespective of them being part of the planning or not. Otherwise the action could only happen or be successful when everything is adequately planned, which obviously is not the case. One should also realize that although action 'selects' patterns of parameter values, all other values or patterns are in principle still covertly available in the planning, and can potentially become targets of the action, leading to more flexible use of the same tool object. The set of relevant relative geometrical and dynamical parameters can be found through a thorough task analysis of the tool-use task. They span a space in which all the available tool-use types and subtleties with that particular tool are expressed. The tool in direct relation to the target and other relevant aspects of the task (e.g. precision demands and other surrounding surfaces) defines the dimensions as well as the structure of this task-space. Different possible types of tool uses, in a particular setting, correspond to different areas in the space, which are determined by particular ranges of parameter values. Although in any particular instant in time only a definite point in the space is occupied, a whole area corresponds to a particular tool-use type. The reason for this is, of course, that there is always variability in the way action takes place. When the specific use of a tool (slightly) changes in time by the actions of the tool user, the point that is occupied in the space changes its values with respect to the dimensions of the space, accordingly. This means that over time, a trajectory through the space is formed. This trajectory formation is also the case when a tool-use type does not correspond to any specific point in a particular area, but to regularly changing parameter values within particular ranges. These correspond to the situations, in which periodic or quasi-periodic behaviour, or patterns, are the (sub-)goals of the tool-use actions. These patterns can be recognized in a significant part of all types of tool use, for example in hammering, scooping soup with a spoon, screw-driving and typing. Also, in a large number of musical instruments, repeated quasi-periodic movements can be observed during playing. Often, establishing the right (cyclic) pattern of interrelated and coupled parameter changes in time is what the planning and action of tool use is directed at. This pattern, in turn, makes it possible to establish an intended goal, by the changes it brings about. Planning is part of the action and drives an individual's movement through the task space in performing an action. It ensures that a particular trajectory will be followed and by this it controls ascertaining of an intended goal.

Our vision of planning is that of a dynamical system that has (potentially) as many degrees of freedom as there are dimensions in the aforementioned task-space. This means that, given that information of different modalities (memory, perception, intention and other) is available to be picked-up by the tool user, the planning field is a function of all these parameters. Whether and when these parameters are present in the planning, and so can actually play a regulating role in the relationship between tool, target and environment, is determined by that information, in a dynamical way. The dynamical 'solution' of all these inputs serves as an attractor of the planning field, in that it 'pulls' the planning towards particular regions in the parameter space. These regions can be points, plateaus, limit cycles or possibly even more complex types of attractors (Fig. 9.4). If a parameter is not planned for, that is, is not part of the planning, it still plays a role in the action, but is not actively regulated by the tool user. This means that the role it plays in the action is that of a constraint parameter, although its value can still change because of the way action unfolds over time.

An example may highlight the above discussion. Hitting a surface by means of a hammer head or stone implies a particular pattern of relative distance and relative linear motion to mention only a few important parameters. Input from a variety of sources may increase activation for a particular combination of these parameters and ranges or patterns of parameter values. These patterns are specific bundles of trajectories in parameter space that describe the relative geometry and dynamics of that specific tooling action. The basic activation level in terms of the planning for these trajectories increases, every time such an action is executed. At first a relatively short-living memory trace for a specific pattern will build up, when an action is executed in a particular way a number of times. When on more and more occasions this pattern is used, an attractor regime can arise that is stable on a lengthier timescale at the cost of other patterns. As another example, consider the repeated downward, orthogonal hitting of a nut, by a chimpanzee with a stone. This slowly increases the overall activation level in the animal's planning, of a trajectory corresponding to a pattern of alternating increases and decreases of relative distance in combination with an alternating ballistic and retrieving relative linear motion, in order to hit the nut with an orthogonal relative orientation until it is cracked. Other patterns of distance, orientation and motion are also possible depending on whether they can be regulated given the animal's body, the task and setting. Suppose the animal's body has been changed accidentally enabling it to more freely vary the orientation of the hammering stone. This change will lead to new input that gives way to the emergence of new patterns that slowly change the dynamic landscape (or structure) of the task-space for the planning. Not only bodily changes may affect the landscape, or how an individual moves through it, but task constraints can do the same. Increased difficulty to hit the target, owing to its relative position in space may lead to a planning that is directed at reducing the relative distance to zero at the cost of a proper regulation of relative orientation and relative motion. These examples indicate that blueprints or flowcharts are not the cause of planning, but can be the result of complex interactions of many factors that can form a dynamic landscape in the task-space for more skilled actors.

Conclusion and prospects

To summarize the above discussion, we have defined a task space that specifies how a tool object or a set of tool objects may become tools to perform a task for an individual endowed with bodily possibilities to take advantage of them. Individuals may fill in a smaller or larger part if this task space, depending on their bodily possibilities, environmental factors and so on. We have described planning as an intrinsic component of action itself and thus of these bodily possibilities, that include the brain. Planning enables the individual to regulate parameters that otherwise would be constraints and, because of this, to fill in larger parts of this space, and to move more flexibly through it. The task and the action, including its successes and failures among others form input to the planning. However, how this input interacts and affects decisions to act depends on the intrinsic dynamics of the planning. Planning is dynamically regulated. In addition, one should realize that the input itself also has its dynamics, as do the postures and movements that compose the action that feeds back on the planning.

Defining the parameters in which the planning is expressed as movement parameters, that are continuous, is not only important for understanding how particular parameters may become part of the planning, but also for understanding how actions may become smoothly ordered in time. For instance, in order to be able to use a spoon for scooping food to the mouth, it has to be grasped in a way that prepares scooping and subsequently transport of the food to and emptying it into the mouth. To make that the grip and the position where the object is held, properly prepare the subsequent actions of scooping, transporting and emptying and back again, patterns of parameter values that define the changing relationship of tool to target in each of these phases need to be targets of the planning. To make the action run smoothly, the final phase of emptying should constrain the degrees of freedom for the parameter values of relevance in the earlier phase of the action. For instance, scooping reduces the degrees of freedom for the grip on grasping the spoon and emptying does the same with respect to the degrees of freedom on scooping. It should be noted that the phases themselves do not need to be part of the planning. There is no other way to perform the action. Transporting food with a spoon is impossible without first grasping the spoon, and it becomes possible first after the spoon has been grasped. So a smooth order is a question of constraining the selection of topological parameters of relevance in earlier phase of the action by later phases. Such can only be the case when there is continuous input, with respect to these later phases, from these parameters available, to activate the planning of particular trajectories in the parameter space.

A final point we want to make is that whether a relative parameter or pattern will be present in the planning is not an all or nothing affair. It is always present in the task and action, and therefore poten-

tially in the planning, though its level of activation may vary over time. This depends on earlier experiences and a variety of input sources, which may draw an individual's attention towards or away from a parameter or a specific pattern of parameters and values for those parameters. As a consequence, its contribution in the planning depends on what is happening and what has happened before. We assume that the evolution of the brain that did take place in humans, did not lead to mental representations of longer and more complex sequences of events and activities to perform a task, but to more stability and at the same time more flexibility in the dynamics of planning. The brain co-evolved with the rest of the body. Together with environmental and task constraints it gave new input to planning and enabled humans to use tools in a new way and at new scales. These changes in combination allowed humans to evolve ever better tools and the accompanying technology. Over the course of time they became able to use those tools in the way we see today and will see tomorrow, steadily spreading through the task space, in the planning and performing of actions.

In the present chapter we have addressed the action dynamics of tool use. We are convinced that social relationships and especially the ability to imitate another person's actions, and pick up the person's perspective and/or intentions from the way he or she was using a tool, and the possibility of communicating with that person verbally and non-verbally, have significantly contributed to the evolution and development of tool use and still do so (Keller & Dixon-Keller 1999; Tomasello *et al.* 1993a,b). We are also convinced, however, that their contribution cannot properly be understood without looking at the action dynamics we have discussed that drive tool-using activities of individuals when they are using tools, and consequently must also affect the observations that are made and the communications that take place. To be successful the intention of every tool user has to be directed to the task space of using a tool and to how to move through this space in planning and organizing the action. Observations of other individuals' actions form the basis of every imitation. These observations must concern the relationship of the observed person to the task space in the way action unfolds over time. Perhaps the evolution of tool use, social relationships and language might have been driven by the same mechanism, that allowed humans to handle tools in new ways and to become more flexible in these ways, to discover to what another person's intention was and to communicate about this intention. Searching for the same mechanism contributes to parsimoniousness, which is the hallmark of science.

Notes

1. Although it will become clear that our line of thinking is much broader and can be applied to a wider range of tool-use types and even to other types of action, like grasping an object with the hand.

2. Obviously this list is not exhaustive. Heat-absorbing and heat-transporting properties, and even electromagnetic properties are important in some types of tool use as well. As for the former, think about oven gloves or a potholder. For the latter, think about the remote control, a flashlight or a pair of binoculars.

3. Relative inertial properties form a clear connection between geometrical and dynamical properties and can best be expressed in terms of the moments of mass distribution of the objects involved. The first moment of mass distribution of an object is just the objects total mass times the position of the centre of mass (its resistance to linear motion). The second moment is determined by the inertial tensor of the object (its resistance to rotational motion). Both moments are composed out of geometrical and dynamical aspects of the object.

References

Bard, K.A., 1993. Cognitive competence underlying tool use in free-ranging orang-utans, in *The Use of Tools by Human and Non-human Primates*, eds. A. Berthelet & J. Chavaillon. New York (NY): Oxford University Press, 103–14.

Bernstein, N.A., 1967. *The Co-ordination and Regulation of Movements*. Oxford: Pergamon.

Bertenthal, B.I., 1996. Origins and early development of perception, action, and representation. *Annual Review of Psychology* 47, 431–59.

Bongers, R.M., 2001. An Action Perspective on Tool Use and its Development. Unpublished thesis, KU Nijmegen.

Bongers, R.M., A.W. Smitsman & C.F. Michaels, 2003. Geometrics and dynamics of a rod determine how it is used for reaching. *Journal Motor Behaviour* 35(1), 4–22.

Chen, Z., R.P. Sanchez & T. Campbell, 1997. From beyond to within their grasp: the rudiments of analogical problem solving in 10- and 13-month-olds. *Developmental Psychology* 33, 790–801.

Clark, J.E., 1997. A dynamical systems perspective on the development of complex adaptive skill, in *Evolving Explanations of Development: Ecological Approaches to Organism-environment Systems*, eds. P. Zukow-Goldring & C. Dent-Read. Washington (DC): APA Publications, 383–406.

Ellis, S. & R.S. Siegler, 1997. Planning as a strategy choice. Why don't children plan when they should?, in *Why, How, and When do We Plan: the Developmental Psychology of Planning*, eds. S.L. Friedman & E.K. Scholnick. Hilsdale (NJ): Erlbaum, 183–208.

Gibson, J.J., 1979/1986. *The Ecological Approach to Visual Perception*. Boston (MA): Houghton-Mifflin.

Gibson, K.R., 1977. Brain structure and intelligence in macaques and human infants from a Piagetian perspective, in *Primate Bio-social Development*, eds. S. Chevalier-Skolnikoff & F.E. Poirier. New York (NY): Garland Press, 113–57.

Goldfield, E.C., 1995. *Emergent Forms: Origins and Early Development of Human Action and Perception*. New York (NY): Oxford University Press.

Gottlieb, G., 1992. *Individual Development and Evolution: the Genesis of Novel Behaviour*. New York (NY): Oxford University Press.

Greenfield, P.M., 1991. Language, tools and brain: the ontogeny and phylogeny of hierarchically organized sequential behaviour. *Behavioural and Brain Sciences* 14, 531–95.

Haith, M.M., 1994. Visual expectations as the first step towards the development of future-oriented processes, in *The Development of Future-oriented Processes*, eds. M.M. Haith, J.B. Benson, R.J. Roberts Jr & D.F. Pennington. Chicago (IL): University of Chicago Press, 11–38.

Hommel, B., J. Muesseler, G. Aschersleben & W. Prinz, 2001. The theory of event coding (TEC): a framework for perception and action planning. *Behavioral and Brain Sciences* 24, 849–937.

Ingold, T., 1997. Eight themes in the anthropology of technology. *Social analysis 1*, 106–38.

Keller, C.M. & J. Dixon-Keller, 1999. Imagery in cultural tradition and innovation. *Mind, Culture, and Activity: an International Journal* 6, 3–33.

Kelso, J.A.S., 1995. *Pattern Formation: the Self-organization of Brain and Behaviour*. Cambridge (MA): MIT Press.

Klahr, D., 1989. Information processing approaches, in *Annals of Child Development*, vol. 6: *Six Theories of Child Development: Revised Formulations and Current Issues*, ed. R. Vasta. Greenwich (CT): JAI Press, 131–85.

Lockman, J.J., 2000. A perception–action perspective on tool use development. *Child Development* 71, 137–44.

McCarty, M.E., R.K. Clifton & R.R. Collard, 1999. Problem solving in infancy: the emergence of an action plan. *Developmental Psychology* 35, 1091–101.

Newell, K.M., 1986. Constraints on the development of co-ordination, in *Motor Development in Children: Aspects of Coordination and Control*, eds. M.G. Wade & H.T.A. Whiting. Dordrecht: Martinus Nijhoff Publishers, 341–60.

Newell, K.M., 1989. On task and theory specificity. *Journal of Motor Behavior* 21, 92–6.

Piaget, J., 1954. *The Construction of Reality in the Child*. New York (NY): Basic Books.

Reed, E.S., 1982. An outline of a theory of action systems. *Journal of Motor Behaviour* 14(2), 98–134.

Reed, E.S., 1988. Applying the theory of action systems to the study of motor skills, in *Complex Movement Behaviour: the Motor Action Controversy*, eds. O.G. Meijer & K. Roth. Amsterdam: Elsevier Science Publications, 45–82.

Rosenbaum, D.A., L.D. Loukopoulos, R.G.J. Meulenbroek, J. Vaughan & S.E. Engelbrecht, 1995. Planning reaches by evaluating stored postures. *Psychological Review* 102, 28–67.

Sameroff, A.J., 1983. Developmental systems: contexts and evolution, in *Handbook of Child Psychology,* vol. 1: *History, Theory, and Methods,* ed. P.H. Mussen. New York (NY): Wiley, 237–94.

Smitsman, A.W., 1997. The development of tool use: changing boundaries between organism and environment, in *Evolving Explanations of Development: Ecological Approaches to Organism-environment Systems,* eds. C. Dent-Read & P. Zukow-Goldring. Washington (DC): APA, 301–29.

Smitsman, A.W. & R.M. Bongers, 2003. Tool use and tool making: a dynamical developmental perspective, in *Handbook of Developmental Psychology,* eds. J. Valsiner & K.J. Connolly. London: Sage, 172–94.

Thelen, E. & L.B. Smith, 1994. *A Dynamic Systems Approach to the Development of Cognition and Action.* Cambridge (MA): MIT Press.

Thelen, E., G. Schöner, C. Scheier & L. Smith, 2001. The dynamics of embodiment: a field theory of infant perseverative reaching. *Behavioural and Brain Sciences* 24, 1–86.

Tomasello, M., A.C. Kruger & H.H. Ratner, 1993a. Cultural learning. *Behavioural and Brain Sciences* 16, 495–552.

Tomasello, M., S. Savage-Rumbaugh & A.C. Kruger, 1993b. Imitative learning of actions on objects by children, chimpanzees, and enculturated chimpanzees. *Child Development* 64, 1688–705.

Wagman, J. & C. Carello, 2001. Affordances and inertial constraints on tool use. *Ecological Psychology* 13(3), 173–215.

Willatts, P., 1990. Development of problem-solving strategies in infancy, in *Children's Strategies: Contemporary Views of Cognitive Development,* ed. D.F. Bjorklund. Hillsdale (NJ): Laurence Erlbaum Associates, 23–66.

Skills Involved in Object-related Tasks in Non-human Primates

Chapter 10

A Preliminary Analysis of Nut-Cracking Movements in a Captive Chimpanzee: Adaptation to the Properties of Tools and Nuts

Julie Foucart, Blandine Bril, Satoshi Hirata, Naruki Morimura, Chiharu Houki, Yoshikazu Ueno & Tetsuro Matsuzawa

Nut cracking in chimpanzees is sometimes compared with stone knapping and presented as the starting point of human stone technology. Drawing such a parallel between these two technical skills implies that most constituents of the skills involved in stone knapping are present in nut cracking or vice versa. Is it so simple? The parallel between these two technical skills is grounded in the fact that both activities require percussive movements and may be termed 'complex'. They both involve asymmetrical, cooperative, bimanual activities, control of the strength of the hit, and a long learning process. No systematic comparative analysis of these two skills has yet been performed. We argue here that to be able to compare different technical skills adequately, one needs quantitative methods of movement analysis. In this paper, we present a preliminary quantitative analysis of nut-cracking movements in one captive adolescent male chimpanzee.

Among the variety of technical skills mastered by primates, nut cracking has often been presented as the most complex. Various characteristics of the skills involved in this behaviour have led a few primatologists and archaeologists to infer some parallels between nut cracking and stone knapping. The main argument for this position is that both techniques: 1) involve percussive movements using some sort of hammer (Marchant & McGrew this volume); and 2) are regarded as complex, mainly because they consist of an asymmetrical co-operative bimanual activity of the hands.

Boesch & Boesch (1993) concluded a paper on hand posture when using a hammer with the following speculation:

> when looking at the frequent, complex and asymmetric use of tools on which chimpanzee rely in the wild, one may ask if the tool use attributed to *Homo habilis*, such as pounding bones or stones to produce flakes … is not within the manipulative abilities of the chimpanzee's hand (Boesch & Boesch 1993, 42).

Going even further, Sugiyama & Koman (1979) present nut cracking as the starting point of human stone technology. They wrote: 'The nut-cracking behaviour using stone tools is highly suggestive of early man's stone-tool culture, although the stones were not actually manufactured purposefully' (Sugiyama & Koman 1979, 522). Boesch & Boesch (1981) further develop this idea: while early hominins used stone hammers for gathering activities, flakes could have been detached by chance.

As far as we can see, percussion is usually considered as the main component of both nut cracking and stone knapping. We wonder, however, if the similarities go any deeper. A fundamental question concerns the relevant level of analysis when comparing the two techniques, aimed at understanding the underlying necessary skills. Most studies refer to the action level. That is, nut cracking or stone knapping is described through its general components: fetching and carrying raw material (stone or nuts) and tools (hammers and anvil), holding the hammer, striking the nut or the stone, extracting the kernel or producing flakes. The posture, which is a crucial component of the action, has often been illustrated in relation to hand use. Some higher-level components such as force, energy, and amplitude of movement are occasionally referred to, but to our knowledge, only a few quantitative measures are available (Günther & Boesch 1993). We suggest here that the extent of any similarity between nut cracking and stone knapping depends on, among other levels of investigation, a precise analysis of the movements performed to crack open the nut, the type of nut to be opened and the tools utilized. A related question concerns the production of a sequence of movements, that is, the dynamics of the task.

This chapter presents a preliminary analysis of the nut-cracking movements of a captive male chimpanzee, 'Loi', from the Hayashibara Great Ape Research Institute in Okayama (Japan). After a brief review of previous work on percussive nut-cracking movements, we present the results of an analysis of the 3D reconstruction of the Loi's movements, observed when he was cracking macadamia and artificial nuts on a stone anvil which was either flat or had cavities.

Nut-cracking skill

As discussed earlier, the global act of nut cracking refers to the whole procedure for accomplishing the task. This technique involves at least two tools — a hammer and an anvil — and, although this is quite rare, a meta-tool may be used in addition to the two others (Matsuzawa 1991; 1994). The manipulative component of the nut-cracking skill refers to the activity of both hands. We restrict our analysis to the motor activity of both hands necessary to perform the percussive movements, that is, to crack open the nut. In addition, we consider how the necessary sequence of percussive movements is achieved.

A rapid overview of the literature on nut-cracking behaviour may be useful to appreciate why a precise description of the movements can help to better understand the skills involved. From previous studies, three main characteristics of nut-cracking behaviour will be outlined. First, nut cracking requires a complex, asymmetrical bimanual movement, which implies hand specialization. Second, an optimal nut-cracking action necessitates adapting: 1) the choice and use of tools to the nut; and 2) the movement. A number of studies suggest that chimpanzees are capable of all of these.

1. Complexity of action
As suggested in the previous section, nut cracking is considered to be a complex skill, as the procedure

prior to eating the kernel consists of a series of complicated actions in which each hand has a different role while working together (Fushimi *et al.* 1991; Inoue-Nakamura & Matsuzawa 1997; Matsuzawa 1994; Sugiyama 1993). Actually, each hand is specialized: one hand is used to manipulate the hammer, and the other hand for anvil, nut, and kernel manipulation. Chimpanzees observed in the wild repeatedly use the same hand for a given action (Boesch 1991; Fushimi *et al.* 1991; Matsuzawa 1994; Sugiyama *et al.* 1993). Thus, for example, if an adult chimpanzee picks up and places a nut on the anvil with the right hand, he will hold the hammer with the left hand, and once the shell is opened, picks up the kernel with the right hand. The hand specialization observed in such a sequence is stable in individuals: there is a strong and almost exclusive hand preference for the hammer manipulation. This lateralization is stable for adults but unstable during learning of nut-cracking (Sugiyama *et al.* 1993). At the population level, however, right-handedness is not more frequent than left-handedness (Sugiyama *et al.* 1993).[1] For a discussion of laterality see chapters by Byrne, Corbetta, Steel, Holder in the present volume.

In addition, nut cracking necessitates finger-precision grips. Boesch & Boesch (1993) described the different finger positions of both the percussive hand (hammer grip) and the postural hand (hand holding the nut and preventing it from moving when hit). The ability to adapt hand and finger positions to the shape, size, and weight of the hammer and/or to the shape of the anvil clearly reveals flexibility.

2. Choice and adaptation of tools
The choice of tools depends on several factors. It is first determined by the task: for nut cracking it depends on the hardness of the shell to be cracked, that in turn will influence the main characteristics of the hammer and the anvil. A hammer that is too heavy will smash the nut and kernel. If the hammer is too light, it will be more difficult to break the shell. Second, the choice depends on the availability of objects that are potentially suitable for the task. Third, an optimal choice depends on the ability of the individual to perceive the functionality of the tools relative to the task. This means that the choice of a 'good' tool necessitates perceiving the relations between the nuts' qualities, the tools' properties, and ones' own 'effectivities'[2] (Matsuzawa 1994). In other words, one must be able to perceive and use the affordances of the task (Gibson 1977; 1986; Michaels 2003; Smitsman *et al.* this volume; Stoffregen 2000).

We shall focus here on the first and third points. We omit the second one as it relates only indirectly to nut-cracking skill (see Sakura & Matsuzawa (1991) for a discussion on the role of availability of raw material on the choice of tools).

Studies suggest that chimpanzees in the wild choose both hammer and anvil according to the properties of the nut to be cracked. Observations in Bossou and in Taï clearly established the ability of chimpanzees to perceive the affordances of the task. In Taï two types of nuts — *Coula edulis* and *Panda oleosa* — are regular items in the chimpanzee diet, with panda nuts being much harder than coula nuts. Boesch & Boesch (1981) report that panda nuts are most often opened with a stone hammer, whereas for coula nuts, both wood and stone hammers may be used. In addition, when only stones are used, panda nuts require bigger, heavier and harder hammers than coula nuts. A more subtle adaptation is reported in Boesch & Boesch (1993). The choice of a hammer depends not only on the type of nut, but also on 'where' the nut is being opened: panda nuts are always opened on the ground, whereas coula may be opened either on the ground or in the trees. In this latter case, the hammer chosen is quite small; on the ground bigger hammers are chosen.

This fine adaptation of the hammer to the hardness of the nut may occur at Bossou as well, even though there is only the palm nut (*Elaeis guinensis*). Considering the weight of the hammer chosen, Sugiyama & Koman (1979) give the example of a site where two pebble hammers were almost identical in weight (750 g and 745 g). Moreover these pebbles were always held in the same way, as indicated by the striking repeated nut-cracking strikes.

Sakura & Matsuzawa (1991) have described another indicator of this capacity to adapt the choice of tool to the task ahead. They examined the use of natural stones as hammer and anvil. The analysis of the distribution of the sizes of the stones used by the chimpanzees revealed that hammers were systematically smaller than anvils. In addition, variations in hammer size were smaller than the variations for anvils. This clearly suggests that the main criterion for choosing a hammer is its size.

These authors discussed functional features that rule out the choice of a stone as an anvil: the anvil must be stable, and have a horizontal platform. In addition, depressions on the upper surface will help to stabilize the nut. Observations concerning the choice of anvil were reported, showing a similar understanding of its functions in nut cracking. The horizontality of a stone or tree-root as the main criterion for anvil selection is quite general, having been observed in Taï (Boesch & Boesch 1982) and Bossou (Sugiyama & Koman 1979). Fushimi *et al.* (1991) observed adults manipulating

the anvil stone on the ground to sit the functional surface in a horizontal position. Matsuzawa (1991; 1994) even reported a few cases of use of a meta-tool (a tool that serves as tool for another tool): to make the surface of the anvil horizontal and stable, a smaller stone was placed beneath the anvil as a wedge. The other major feature of the anvil surface relates to the immobilization of the nut. Interestingly, Sugiyama & Koman (1979) and Rahm (1971) noted that chimpanzees would use depressions on the surface following repeated use to immobilize the nut, that is to prevent the nut shifting when hit by the hammer. If, after a long period of use, the cavity is too large or covered with shell fragments that might impede its movements, the chimpanzee will move the nut to another place on the anvil or to another anvil (Boesch 1978; Boesch & Boesch 1982).

The observations summarized indicate that chimpanzees are able to apprehend *a priori* the relation between potential tools (i.e. stones or wood) and referent (i.e. palm nut, coula nut or panda nut), in other words, they recognize the function of the tool (Sakura & Matsuzawa 1991).

The ability to choose a tool that is finely adapted to the task takes a long time to develop. Fushimi *et al.* (1991) reported that in contrast to adult males who choose a heavier tool so that the number of hits necessary to open the nut is reduced, adolescent and juvenile chimpanzees sometimes choose hammers that are too light for the task.

3. Adaptation of movements
Four main aspects of posture and movement features have been occasionally considered in the literature — body posture, amplitude of movement, force produced and number of hits necessary to open the nut. As posture constrains the relative position of the hand and the nut during the movement, this aspect will be discussed first. Normally the chimpanzee sits close to the anvil, but the distance from the anvil constrains its movements. Boesch & Boesch (1984) report two categories of arm movement depending on the distance from the anvil: when the chimpanzee is close to the anvil, the movement is concentrated in the forearm; the trunk is relatively passive. In contrast, when further from the anvil, the whole body is engaged. In the latter case, the arm is quite rigid, with almost no movement of the elbow joint. Females make much smaller movements that males, using the elbow technique, while males make more use of large movements of the trunk and head associated with a rigid elbow. Boesch & Boesch (1984) repeatedly emphasize that females' movements are more efficient than males, probably for several reasons (less concentration for

males, more motor difficulties, and cognitive differences in adaptation).

The efficiency of the movements will depend on different factors, in particular in amplitude and force control. Very few quantitative data exist, but interesting general information has been drawn from behavioural observations. The amplitude of the movement used to crack open palm nuts with a stone hammer has been estimated to vary between 5 and 20 cm (Sugiyama & Koman 1979), while Fushimi et al. (1991) give an estimated range of 10 to 40 cm. Fushimi et al. (1991) emphasize the importance of fine-tuning of force to produce an efficient hit, which is to open the shell without smashing the kernel. The amplitude of the movement influences the force produced by the movement of the hammer. Other elements, however, such as trajectory, velocity, acceleration and weight of the hammer are also important. To our knowledge, only one study included quantitative estimations of such parameters of striking movements (Günther & Boesch 1993). The aim of that study was very different from ours: determining the total energy expenditure of a wild chimpanzee during nut-cracking activity (from fetching the nut and tools to ingesting the kernel) during an entire day. Our study focuses on adaptation of the movement. Günther & Boesch (1993) give quantitative estimates of amplitude of the hammer displacement, velocity at impact and kinetic energy. We will see that their estimated values are quite different from ours, but taking into account the differences in weights of the hammer and amplitude of the movements, the results are quite coherent.

Those authors and others have called attention to the precise control of forces required to open nuts without smashing them. Boesch & Boesch (1981; 1982; 1984) observed that when they open panda nuts (*Panda oleosa*) chimpanzees in Taï perform powerful hits at the beginning of the opening procedure, more gentle and precise ones afterwards. They also mention that males seem to have difficulties in controlling their strength. In order to estimate the strength of these two kinds of hits, they noted the position of the hammer in relation to the chimpanzee's chest, for a crude estimate of the amplitude of the movement. For example, a movement starting when the hand is positioned below the chest is considered typical of controlled and subtle hits. Unfortunately, those authors ignored the weight of the hammer, so there was no indication of the force produced during the strike. Fushimi et al. (1991) also described the necessary fine-tuning of force for producing an efficient hit. They observed one infant chimpanzee who typically failed to open palm nuts; they suggested that she was unable to adequately control force.

The last frequently-studied parameter is the number of hits necessary to open the nut. In Bossou, Sugiyama & Koman (1979) reported an average of 2.84 hits to crack open a palm nut. In two different studies, Boesch & Boesch (1981; 1984) performed a two-level comparison, males and females on the one hand, coula and panda nuts on the other hand. As panda-nut shells are much harder than coula nuts, the number of hits per nut — when cracked on the ground — was significantly higher for panda nut (8.75 for males vs 6.35 for females and 14.58 for males vs 16.96 for females respectively in the 1981 study; 7.02 vs 6.26 and 22.3 vs 17.3 in the 1984 study). The results from these different studies are consistent as palm nuts are less hard than coula nuts, which in turn are less hard than panda nuts.

More interesting perhaps is the analysis of data concerning adolescent and juveniles, showing a considerably higher number of hits per nut compared with adults (especially for juveniles), showing how long it takes to learn to adapt the movements to the nut properties.

Discussion

Most of the data reported here come from wild chimpanzees communities observed in West Africa. Each study brings some valuable information about this technique in terms of action and movement. Unfortunately, owing to the difficulties of studying action and movement in 'natural' conditions, none of them gives a complete picture. In addition, the recording techniques presently available do not yet allow precise measurement of the movements of the apes outside the laboratory. Consequently, at present, a precise measure of the many characteristics of the manipulation involved in nut cracking can be undertaken only in captivity. We present here the results of a preliminary study done in captivity.

The experiment was carried out after a preliminary 2D analysis performed from video records by T. Matsuzawa, concerning wild chimpanzees in Bossou (Guinea) and captive ones at the Primate Research Institute (Inuyama, Japan).

A nut-cracking experiment

In this section we present preliminary data on the striking movements performed when a chimpanzee is about to crack open a nutshell to extract the reward (kernel or fruit). Our objective was to test the feasibility of a 3D analysis of such movements in chimpanzees. While there exist quite sophisticated methods for recording upper limb movements in humans (see Biryukova et al. this volume), the problem is much

Figure 10.1. *a) Artificial nuts and b) macadamia nuts.*

trickier with non-human primates as subjects. For example, any attempt to stick markers on the skin would fail, as the chimpanzee would immediately remove them.

Materials and methods
The experiment was performed at the Hayashibara Great Ape Research Institute (GARI, Okayama, Japan), with a 7.5-year-old captive male chimpanzee named 'Loi'. Loi acquired the nut-cracking technique in June 2002, after a long period of training. The experiment was conducted in an indoor experimental area. There was no one else present but the experimenter and Loi.

In order to assess the flexibility and adaptiveness of Loi's behaviour, the task was based on two varieties of nuts and two different anvil-tools.

Protocol
Two nut-cracking sessions took place in December 2002. Two tools were provided, a stone hammer and a stone anvil. The type of anvil supplied was different in each session: for the first session it had a flat surface; while for the second session, the surface had a few artificial cavities.

During each session Loi cracked open 20 nuts — 10 macadamia nuts and 10 'artificial' nuts. The nuts were given one by one, alternately. The session stopped once the 20 nuts had been opened.

The macadamia nuts weight about 6 g and are 25 mm in diameter. Their shell is about 2.7 mm thick. The artificial nuts were made of two plastic parts joined by a metal belt. To make them as attractive as real nuts, they contained a fruit as reward (see Fig. 10.1). These two types of nuts have regularly been used at GARI; opening such nuts was familiar to Loi.

The hammer was a stone hammer, weighing 443 g; its dimensions were 8 cm long, 7.7 cm wide, and 5.2 cm high. The anvil was a round stone — with a diameter of 35 cm, and a height of 7 cm. One side was flat; the

Figure 10.2. *Localization of the dots selected for the movement reconstruction.*

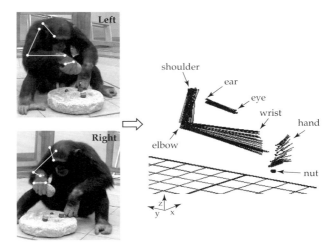

Figure 10.3. *3D movement reconstruction.*

other was curved with two big artificial cavities and 13 small ones. The big cavities were about 50 mm in diameter and 15 mm in depth (at the deepest spot). The small ones were about 18 mm in diameter and 10 mm deep.

Loi sat on the floor with the anvil in between his legs (see Fig. 10.2).

Movement recording and reconstruction
Both sessions were recorded using two fixed digital video cameras (sampling rate 60 hz) positioned right and left in front of Loi. In addition a block of stone 39 cm high (gradated every 5 cm), 10 cm wide and 19 cm large was used to calibrate the space.

The 3D reconstruction of the upper-limb movement was performed using Kihopsys software[3],

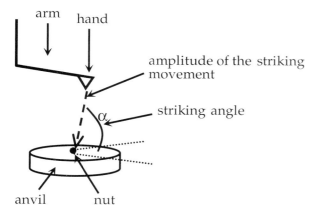

Figure 10.4. *Parameters concerning the elementary hand movement: amplitude of the striking movement and striking angle.*

through the following steps:

1. Select the specific body locations necessary for the 3D reconstruction. As Loi held the stone hammer with the right hand, the right upper limb was used. Eight points were selected (see Fig. 10.2): two on the head: right eye (1), right ear (2); five on the right arm: shoulder (3), elbow (4), wrist (5), hand 6 and 7 (junction between the hand and the first phalanx of the little finger (6) and the first phalanx of the index finger (7)); in addition the nut (8) was included.
2. Synchronization of the two cameras was done a-posteriori: the record of each sequence of movements corresponding to one nut was transferred to computer and a frame-by-frame analysis was performed to record the position of each point.
3. Based on the calibration frame, the reconstruction of the movement in three dimensions was performed (see Fig. 10.3).
4. The position of the hand (9) was computed as the middle of the segment determined by dots 6 and 7.

Parameters
In addition to posture, two classes of parameters were selected to describe the action of cracking the nut concerning: (i) the sequence and type of movements and (ii) the basic movement (one strike).

Body posture and hand posture:
- *Body posture*: position of the body, trunk and leg while performing the action;
- *Hand posture (grip)*: position of the fingers while holding the hammer.

The sequence of movements:
- *Type of hit*: functional (large movement ending with a clear hit); not directly functional (small hit);
- *Time* necessary to open the nut (from first contact between hammer and nut, to last one), in seconds;
- *Number of hits* necessary to open the nut.

The movement (see Fig. 10.4):
- *Amplitude* (*A*) of the striking movement defined as the distance covered by the hand during the descending phase of the movement, in centimetres;
- *Striking angle* (α) formed by the trajectory of the hand and the surface of the anvil (i.e. horizontal), in degrees;
- *Temporal parameters*
  ° Duration of a striking movement (*Ts*) (movement starting when the hand starts to move upward until next contact with the nut, in milliseconds);
  ° Contact duration (*Tc*) (contact between hammer and nut until next movement of the hammer, in milliseconds));
- *Potential and kinetic energy*
  ° Potential energy (*U*) (in J) of the hammer at the start of the downward movement depends on the initial position of the hammer and on the mass of the hammer ($U = mgh$, with h vertical component of the trajectory of the hammer (in meters), m = mass of the hammer (in kilograms), $g = 9.81$ m/s^2);
  ° Kinetic energy (*K*) (in J) at time of contact of the hammer on the nut depends on its velocity and on its mass ($K = \frac{1}{2}mv^2$, with v = velocity of the hammer at time of contact (m/s));
  ° Ratio *Kinetic energy/Potential energy*: indicates the additional energy due to the chimpanzee during the movement.

Statistical analysis
An ANOVA was performed on the different parameters to test the differences between the four experimental conditions. Owing to the small sample size, a non-parametric test (Mann Whitney) was performed for energy parameters.

Results
For various reasons (Loi getting up and moving away, large shifts of the nut, lack of concentration), not all sequences have been included in the analysis. Six sequences of nut cracking were analyzed for each condition, except for the artificial nut on indented anvil where only five sequences were analyzed.

Validity of the 3D reconstruction
In order to evaluate the reliability of the 3D recon-

struction we compared the calculated length of the segment delimited by dot 6 (joint of first phalanx of the little finger and the hand) and dot 7 (joint of the first phalanx of the index finger and the hand) with the actual value. For Loi this segment measured 8.4 cm.

The ratio of the two measures was 1.07 (for session 1, the mean estimated measure was 9.32±0.084 cm, and for the second session 8.7±0.074 cm).

We consider these results to be a valid and reliable estimation.

1. Posture and grip

Loi sits on the floor, with the anvil between his legs. The right hand is used to hold the hammer and strike the nut. In contrast, the other hand usually rests on the anvil.

As the hammer is small and flat, the chimpanzee fingers cover the entire stone. So, the hammer is held only between the thumb and the length of index finger (see Fig. 10.2). The nut is struck by the part of the stone that extends beyond the 2 fingers.

2. Sequences of movements

Type of hits: Figure 10.5 gives the trajectory of the hand for a sequence of movements corresponding to each experimental situation. A quick look at these sequences shows that they display similar characteristics in three of the four experimental conditions (artificial nuts and macadamia nuts on the indented anvil; artificial nuts on the flat anvil): regular amplitude and timing of the strikes. When using a flat anvil for macadamia nuts, however, Loi shifts to a completely different strategy. The succession of movements is quite erratic in amplitude and timing. Small irregular movements precede large amplitude hits. In addition, the behavioural data (from the videos) shows that while the large amplitude movement always completes the action (ends hitting the nuts), this is not always with small movements.

Number of full hits: The mean number of large strikes necessary to crack open a nut is significantly higher, more than twice as much, for artificial than for macadamia nuts in both anvil conditions (flat anvil: 11.7 and 4 strikes respectively for artificial and macadamia nuts, $F_{(1/10)} = 44.66$, $p < .001$ - anvil with cavities: 15.6

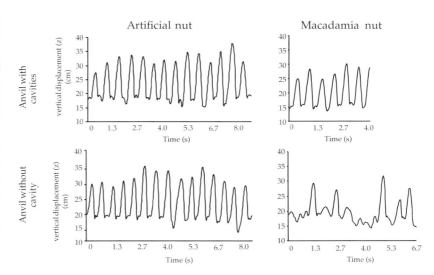

Figure 10.5. *Examples of the vertical displacement (z) of the hand to crack open one nut, for each experimental condition. Each peak represents a hit.*

Table 10.1. *Mean number of hits necessary to open one nut.*

	Anvil without cavity	Anvil with cavities	Mean:
Artificial nuts	11.7±1.3 hits/nut	15.6±3.2 hits/nut	**13.5±1.5 hits/nut**
Macadamia nuts	4±0.5 hits/nut	6.8±1.4 hits/nut	**5.4±0.8 hits/nut**
Mean:	**7.8±1.4 hits/nut**	**10.8±2 hits/nut**	

and 6.8 respectively, $F_{(1/9)} = 12.57$, $p < 0.01$) (see Table 10.1).

The number of strikes, however, does not differ in the two anvil conditions for artificial nuts (see Table 10.1). In contrast, there is a small difference in the case of macadamia nuts, with fewer strikes on the flat anvil ($F_{(1/10)} = 5.62$, $p < 0.05$).

The small number of strikes in the case of macadamia nut cracked on the flat anvil, is based on large movements only. The number of small strikes is approximately the same (4±1.2 on average per nut).

Time necessary to open a nut: It takes significantly more time to open an artificial nut than a macadamia nut, (8.9 s vs 5 s, $F_{(1/21)} = 11.55$, $p < 0.01$) (see Table 10.2). When the indented anvil is used, the time required to open artificial nuts is higher than for macadamia nuts (10.5 s vs 4.3 s) ($F_{(1/9)} = 10.34$, $p < 0.05$). On the other hand, there are no significant differences when the flat anvil is used.

The type of anvil has no effect on the latency to open a nut, regardless of the type of nut (see Table 10.2).

3. Striking movement

The parameters concerning the basic movements are calculated only for large strikes.

Table 10.2. *Mean time necessary to open one nut (seconds).*

	Anvil without cavity	Anvil with cavities	Mean:
Artificial nuts	7.6±0.8 s	10.5±2.4 s	**8.9±1.1 s**
Macadamia nuts	5.7±1.1 s	4.3±1.1 s	**5±0.7 s**
Mean:	**6.6±0.7 s**	**7.1±1.5 s**	

Table 10.3. *Mean amplitude of the striking movement (centimetres).*

	Anvil without cavity	Anvil with cavities	Mean:
Artificial nuts	13.3±0.7 cm	13.3±1.3 cm	**13.3±0.6 cm**
Macadamia nuts	11.6±0.97 cm	12.3±1.4 cm	**11.9±0.7 cm**
Mean:	**12.4±0.6 cm**	**12.7±0.8 cm**	

Table 10.4. *Mean striking angle formed by the trajectory of the hand and the anvil plane.*

	Anvil without cavity	Anvil with cavities	Mean:
Artificial nuts	72.3±1.9°	64.8±3.8°	**68.9±2.1°**
Macadamia nuts	71.1±3.3°	64.2±2.1°	**67.6±2°**
Mean:	**71.7±1.6°**	**64.4±1.7°**	

Table 10.5. *Mean duration of a striking movement (milliseconds).*

	Anvil without cavity	Anvil with cavities	Mean:
Artificial nuts	467±29 ms	446±22 ms	**457±16 ms**
Macadamia nuts	459±31 ms	423±29 ms	**441±19 ms**
Mean:	**463±18 ms**	**433±16 ms**	**449±12 ms**

Table 10.6. *Mean contact duration (time of contact of hammer and nut between two movements of the hammer) (milliseconds).*

	Anvil without cavity	Anvil with cavities	Mean:
Artificial nuts	164±12 ms	153±12 ms	**159±8 ms**
Macadamia nuts	218±38 ms	143±8 ms	**180±21 ms**
Mean:	**191±19 ms**	**147±6 ms**	

Amplitude: The amplitude of large hand movements varies in average between 11.6 cm for striking macadamia nuts on the flat anvil, and 13.3 cm for artificial nuts on the anvil with cavities. These differences, however, are not statistically significant (see Table 10.3).

In the case of macadamia nuts cracked on the flat anvil, small amplitude hits are more than four times smaller than large movements, 2.5±0.6 cm vs 11.6±0.97 cm respectively ($F_{(1/10)}$ = 90.42, $p < 0.01$).

Striking angle: The striking angle does not differ for artificial and macadamia nuts (see Table 10.4). A comparison along the anvil dimension shows a smaller angle when nuts are cracked on the anvil with cavity; the angle values are 64° vs 72° ($F_{(1/21)}$ = 11.49, $p < 0.01$).

This means that the hand trajectory is more vertical with a flat anvil.

Striking duration: The duration of a strike is 449 ms on average; there is no difference between conditions (see Table 10.5).

Contact duration: The duration of contact with the nut, that is the time span between two movements, varies from 143 ms to 218 ms. The longer duration occurs with macadamia nuts on the flat anvil. There is a significant difference between the two anvil conditions ($F_{(1/21)}$ = 5.33, $p < 0.05$) mainly due to the macadamia nuts (see Table 10.6). For the macadamia nuts, the mean contact duration between the hammer and the nut after a hit is greater on the flat anvil than on the indented one ($F_{(1/10)}$ = 5.81, $p < 0.05$) (see Table 10.6). In contrast, for the artificial nuts, the contact duration does not differ significantly according to the anvil.

The type of nut has no effect on the contact time, whichever anvil is used.

Potential and kinetic energy: Owing to the low sampling rate, it was quite difficult to estimate the velocity at time of contact as the time of contact falls somewhere in between the last two recorded positions of the hand. Consequently, we computed these values on a truncated trajectory based on the last position of the hammer before contact. This calculation minimizes the values of kinetic and potential energy, but makes sure that the computation for both is correct. In addition, we discarded all movements when this position cut off the trajectory by more than one-third.

For all conditions, the kinetic energy was significantly greater than potential energy (0.668±0.02 J and 0.388±0.009 J respectively; $U = 2051$, $p < 0.001$) (see Table 10.7).

The ratio between kinetic and potential energy, does not differ significantly according to the nut. However, this ratio is slightly greater when a flat anvil is used ($U = 2497$, $p = 0.054$) and is due mainly to macadamia nuts (1.861±0.126 J (on the flat anvil) vs 1.627±0.077 J (on the anvil with cavities)) (see Table 10.8).

Discussion

The experiment and analysis reported here, although preliminary, confirm that video recordings from at least two cameras, allow precise analysis of upper-arm movements in chimpanzees' nut-cracking actions. Such an analysis provides complementary ways to approach and to analyze adaptability of chimpanzees' actions to environmental conditions. In this experiment, one male chimpanzee was observed cracking two types of nut on two different anvils, using only one hammer. A frame-by-frame analysis of the displacement of the different segments of the upper limb was performed, allowing a 3D reconstruction of the movements. Precise measures of kinematics were conducted, including length and direction of the hand trajectory, potential and kinetic energy. Beyond methodological issues, the main focus of this paper was to test if chimpanzees' adaptation to the specificity of the task was reflected in the striking movement itself. Several studies have shown that chimpanzees in the wild choose their pounding tools in order to meet task constraints: the size, weight and hardness of the hammer chosen depend of the hardness of the nutshell. A related question is the following: does the chimpanzee have the capacity of flexible movement to adapt to the characteristics of the nuts or of the tools? Or are the movements mainly determined by the tools?

Our results clearly show that the nut cracking behaviour of the chimpanzee Loi is flexible and adapted to the specificity of the task, at the level of action: striking strategy and sequence of strikes. It is less clear, however, that Loi adapts his movement — *stricto sensu* — to the characteristics of the task — i.e. variation in amplitude or force — in the different conditions.

Adaptation to action constraints

One of the main differences between conditions is the very specific striking strategy applied to the macadamia nut when a flat anvil is used. In all three conditions (artificial nuts with both types of anvil, and macadamia nuts cracked on an anvil with cavity), the sequence of strikes is quite homogeneous, with large hits performed at a regular pace. When cracking macadamia nuts on the flat anvil, large hits are fewer and small 'non-functional' hits are performed in between. This radical change in strategy may reflect the optimal solution of anticipating the slippery consequence of a strike, which may cause the nut to shift away. When

Table 10.7. *Mean values of kinetic and potential energies for each experimental condition (in J.).*

Nuts	Anvil	Kinetic energy	Potential energy
Macadamia nuts	Anvil without cavity	0.578±0.068	0.310±0.027
Macadamia nuts	Anvil with cavities	0.584±0.06	0.363±0.031
Artificial nuts	Anvil without cavity	0.739±0.03	0.421±0.014
Artificial nuts	Anvil with cavities	0.662±0.034	0.394±0.015
	Mean:	0.668±0.02	0.388±0.009

Table 10.8. *Mean ratio between kinetic and potential energy (= K / U).*

	Anvil without cavity	Anvil with cavities	Mean:
Artificial nuts	1.775±0.057	1.699±0.071	1.739±0.045
Macadamia nuts	1.861±0.126	1.627±0.077	1.739±0.072
Mean:	1.798±0.052	1.678±0.054	

an indented anvil is used, the nut stabilized in the cavity solves this problem. Here, the small hits seem to be intended to ensure the stability of the nut. After the hammer hits the nut, it rests on the fruit for longer than in the other conditions. Is this long contact a way to stabilize the nut after the destabilizing strike? In addition, the direction of the hammer trajectory — more vertical when the flat anvil is used for both macadamia and artificial nuts — strongly suggests that the chimpanzee attempts to control nut stability to ensure the success of a large hit.

Control at the movement level

The calculation of the kinetic energy compared with potential energy was aimed at indicating to what extent the ape was able to control the forces of the hits. If the chimpanzee's aim was just to pound the hammer on the nut, relying exclusively on forces due to the mass and trajectory of the hammer, the kinetic energy at contact would be equal to the potential energy at the time of the highest position of the hammer. The energy ratio we computed suggests that kinetic energy is more than 60 per cent greater than potential energy. Knowing that our computation is done on a shorter trajectory than the real one, the kinetic energy value is minimized. Consequently we may consider the real value of this ratio to be higher. Günther & Boesch (1993) estimated in the case of coula nuts that the kinetic energy was over twice as high as potential energy. The results presented here are quite concordant with theirs.

A final argument in favour of the capacity to tailor movements to comply with the task: with a flat-surface anvil, the ratio is greater than with an indented anvil. This means that in the former case the chimpanzee deploys slightly more muscular energy.

This strategy could reduce the number of strikes necessary and consequently reduce the probability of the nut shifting and perhaps being lost. The highest value of the ratio kinetic energy:potential energy appears when striking macadamia nuts on the flat anvil. This result, even if not statistically significant, supports the idea that Loi has the capacity to finely adapt his movement to the situation.

In the present study, artificial nuts were more difficult to open, than macadamia nuts.[4] This may explain that more strikes are necessary to open macadamia nuts. It would be interesting, however, to have some kind of quantification of the hardness of the shell. Boesch & Boesch (1982) computed the impulse needed to crack different types of nuts ($I = m\sqrt{2gh}$, where m = mass of the hammer, g = gravity acceleration, h = vertical component of the trajectory of the hammer). The impulse indexes the attributes of a passive strike necessary to crack open the nut. The computation of such an index (or of the potential energy) is a way to determine the relationship between the weight of the hammer and the length of its vertical trajectory. It gives an overall picture of the optimal passive strike for a specific nut. A comparison between the choice of tools and the performed strike reveals the real capacity for adaptation of the chimpanzee.

If the present results are valid — and once again, these results are preliminary and need confirmation — one can ask why, in the case of artificial nuts that are supposed to be harder than macadamia, the chimpanzee does not increase either the amplitude of its movement or the kinetic energy produced. An increase in kinetic energy would lead to fewer striking movements performed. Does this mean that the chimpanzee is unable to fine-tune his movement — which seems contradictory to what has been discussed in the previous paragraph — or that there is no need to reduce the number of strikes? Indeed, the laboratory situation is far removed from the wild, where survival may depend on saving energy expenditure. On the other hand, an increase in kinetic energy could be more costly than an increase in the number of strikes.

Conclusion

The 3D analysis of Loi's nut-cracking movements confirms the capacity for tool adaptation and flexibility in chimpanzees. This adaptation, however, appears mainly at the level of action — type and sequence of strikes. Loi's action strategy is adapted to the properties of the tool (flat surface of the anvil or anvil with cavities) and of the nut properties. Unfortunately, in this experiment only one type of hammer was given to the chimpanzee. As the literature is rich in observations showing that chimpanzees do choose the hammer according to the nut properties, which means that they probably 'anticipate' the characteristics of the action to be performed, it might be possible that they have the capacity to adjust their movement to the properties of the hammer (i.e. its weight). This is clearly the next issue to address. In addition, we need data from more than one chimpanzee to confirm these preliminary results.[5]

Does such an analysis support the often-proposed parallel between nut cracking and flake knapping? Wynn & McGrew (1989), scrutinizing Oldowan tools and chimpanzees' tools suggested that neither general motor patterns nor cognitive demands of either type of tool activity were unique. In sum, 'the minimum competence needed to produce Oldowan tools and site is that of an ape adaptive grade' (Wynn & McGrew 1989, 384). They explicitly state, however, that chimpanzees do not have the ability required to control either contingency plans or more than one variable at a time. Even if nut-cracking implies an asymmetrical hand specialization, the whole sequence of movements required is quite repetitive. Only one variable has to be controlled at a time and casual encounter is rare. The direction of the movements stays the same during the whole sequence of strikes. Only one dimension is considered at a time. The actions are performed in sequence.

Two main differences with nut cracking suggest that stone knapping differs considerably in terms of complexity. The conchoidal fracture imposes not only an asymmetrical use of the hands, but also the simultaneous control of at least two variables (see Pelegrin this volume). The knapper must simultaneously control the orientation of the stone and the trajectory of the hammer, as well as the characteristics of the hammer movement (trajectory and velocity). The reciprocal orientation of the core and the trajectory of the hammer requires a very precise tuning to obtain a conchoidal fracture. In addition, this reciprocal orientation varies continuously during the sequence of strikes.

We believe these differences between the two techniques — nut cracking and stone knapping — are crucial. The central question here relates to the definition of adaptation and flexibility. How can we define a certain degree of flexibility, of adaptation, of complexity? Even if chimpanzees are capable of the most complex behaviours, the ability to produce flakes — involving a conchoidal fracture — seems beyond their capacities.

Acknowledgements

We would like to very sincerely thank James Anderson for his comments and careful reading of our chapter; Lena Biryukova and Rémi Goasdoué for their suggestions for data analysis.

This research was funded by the French Ministère délégué à la recherche et aux nouvelles Technologie (ACI TTT P7802 n° 02 2 0440) and partly by the Ministry of Education, Culture, Sports, Science, and Technology of Japan (a grant for the Biodiversity Research of the 21st Century COE, A14).

Notes

1. A chimpanzee holding the hammer with the right hand is considered right-handed, while one holding it with the left hand is considered left-handed.
2. The effectivities refers to the invariant properties of the organism. 'Effectivities are the way the actor could use the biomechanical characteristics of its body to act on the world' (van Leeuwen *et al.* 1994, 176).
3. This software has been written by Gilles Dietrich (Université Paris 5).
4. The difficulties of opening an artificial nut is not that they are harder than macadamia nuts; in order to open an artificial nut the chimpanzee has to hit it in a way that the joint of the two plastic compartments and the metal ring will successfully come undone. The problem is not just of power.
5. An experiment was performed at GARi in January 2005. Data are under analysis.

References

Boesch, C., 1978. Nouvelles observations sur les chimpanzés de la forêt de Taï (Côte-d'Ivoire). *La Terre et la Vie* 32, 195–201.

Boesch, C., 1991. Handedness in wild chimpanzees. *International Journal of Primatology* 12, 541–58.

Boesch, C. & H. Boesch, 1981. Sex differences in the use of natural hammers by wild chimpanzees: a preliminary report. *Journal of Human Evolution* 10, 585–93.

Boesch, C. & H. Boesch, 1982. Optimisation of nut-cracking with natural hammers by wild chimpanzees. *Behaviour* 83, 265–86.

Boesch, C. & H. Boesch, 1984. Possible causes of sex differences in the use of natural hammers by wild chimpanzees. *Journal of Human Evolution* 13, 415–40.

Boesch, C. & H. Boesch, 1993. Different hand postures for pounding nuts with natural hammers by wild chimpanzees, in *Hands of Primates*, eds. H. Preuschoft & D.J. Chivers. Vienna: Springer-Verlag, 31–43.

Fushimi, T., O. Sakura, T. Matsuzawa, H. Ohno & Y. Sugiyama, 1991. Nut-cracking behavior of wild chimpanzees (*Pan troglodytes*) in Bossou, Guinea (West Africa), in *Primatology Today*, eds. A. Ehara, T. Kimura, O. Takenaka & M. Iwamoto. Amsterdam: Elsevier Science B.V., 695–6.

Gibson, J.J., 1977. The theory of affordance, in *Perceiving, Acting, and Knowing*, ed. J. Bransford. Hillsdale (NJ): Lawrence Erlbaum Associates, 67–82.

Gibson, J.J., 1986. *The Ecological Approach to Visual Perception*. Hillsdale (NJ): Lawrence Erlbaum Associates. (First published in 1979.)

Günther, M.M. & C. Boesch, 1993. Energetic cost of nut-cracking behaviour in wild chimpanzees, in *Hands of Primates*, eds. H. Preuschoft & D.J. Chivers. Vienna: Springer-Verlag, 109–29.

Inoue-Nakamura, N. & T. Matsuzawa, 1997. Development of stone tool use by wild chimpanzees (*Pan troglodytes*). *Journal of Comparative Psychology* 111, 159–73.

Matsuzawa, T., 1991. Nesting cups and metatools in chimpanzees. *Behavioral and Brain Sciences* 14, 570–71.

Matsuzawa, T., 1994. Field experiments on use of stone tools by chimpanzees in the wild, in *Chimpanzee Cultures*, eds. R.W. Wrangham, W. McGrew, F.B.M. de Waal & P.G. Heltne. Cambridge (MA): Harvard University Press, 351–70.

Michaels, C.F., 2003. Affordances: four points of debates. *Ecological Psychology* 15, 135–48.

Rahm, U., 1971. L'emploi d'outils par les chimpanzés de l'ouest de la Côte-d'Ivoire. *Terre et Vie* 25, 506–9.

Sakura, O. & T. Matsuzawa, 1991. Flexibility of wild chimpanzee nut-cracking behavior using stone hammers and anvils: an experimental analysis. *Ethology* 87, 237–48.

Stoffregen, T.A., 2000. Affordance and events. *Ecological Psychology* 12, 1–28.

Sugiyama, Y., 1993. Local variation of tools and tool use among wild chimpanzee populations, in *The Use of Tools by Human and Non-human Primates*, eds. A. Berthelet & J. Chavaillon. Oxford: Clarendon Press, 175–87.

Sugiyama, Y. & J. Koman, 1979. Tool-using and making behavior in wild chimpanzees at Bossou, Guinea. *Primates* 20, 513–24.

Sugiyama, Y., T. Fushimi, O. Sakura & T. Matsuzawa, 1993. Hand preference and tool use in wild chimpanzees. *Primates* 34, 151–9.

van Leeuwen, L., A. Smitsman & C. van Leeuwen, 1994. Affordances, perceptual complexity and the development of tool use. *Journal of Experimental Psychology: Human Perception and Performance* 20, 174–91.

Wynn, T. & W.C. McGrew, 1989. An ape's view of the oldowan. *Man* 24, 383–98.

Chapter 11

The Maker not the Tool:
the Cognitive Significance of Great Ape Manual Skills

Richard W. Byrne

Tool use by chimpanzees has attracted disproportionate attention among primatologists, because of an understandable wish to comprehend the evolutionary origins of hominin tool use. In archaeology and palaeoanthropology, a focus on made-objects is inevitable: there is nothing else to study. However, it is evidently object-directed manual skills, enabling the objects to be made, that are critical in understanding the evolutionary origins of stone-tool manufacture. In this chapter I review object-directed manual skills in living great apes, making comparison where possible with hominin abilities that can be inferred from the archaeological record. To this end, 'translations' of terminology between the research traditions are offered. Much of the evidence comes from observation of apes gathering plants that present physical problems for handling and consumption, in addition to the more patchy data from tool use in captivity and the field. The living great apes, like ourselves, build up novel hierarchical structures involving regular sequences of elementary actions, showing co-ordinated manual role differentiation, in modular organizations with the option of iterating subroutines. Further, great apes appear able to use imitation of skilled practitioners as one source of information for this process, implying some ability to 'see' below the surface level of action and understand the motor planning of other individuals; however, that process does not necessarily involve understanding cause-and-effect or the intentions of other individuals. Finally I consider whether a living non-human ape could effectively knap stone, and if not, what competence is lacking.

Only two years after Louis Leakey (1961) defined Man's origin as the point at which an ape-like creature first made tools to 'a regular and set pattern', Jane Goodall (1963) published her evidence that the chimpanzees of Gombe did just that. The 40 years that followed have seen many attempts to sharpen definitions — of human, of tool, and of what counts as a regular and set pattern — to avoid the unfortunate syllogism that these facts point toward, and to gain a better understanding of the origins and development of tool making in humans. We now know that the chimpanzee *Pan troglodytes* is not alone among living great apes in making tools (e.g. Fox *et al.* 1999), that chimpanzees make many different types of tool for different purposes (Boesch & Boesch 1990; Goodall 1986; Nishida 1986), and that the styles of tool making differ between chimpanzee communities (McGrew 1992; McGrew *et al.* 1979). Meanwhile, archaeological evidence has pushed the origins of flaked stone tools way back (Roche *et al.* 1999), beyond the comfortable period when tall, large-brained ancestral humans lived over much of the Old World, to African strata in which the few hominin bones are of small animals with chimpanzee-sized brains, species not even classified in the genus *Homo*. These facts may seem to encourage 'continuity' theorizing, until the tools themselves are examined. The fact is, there is a big difference between the most elaborate chimpanzee tool, a green twig stripped of its leaves, and the 2.3 Mya stone tools showing organized sequential detachment of flakes. Put bluntly, any of us can make any chimpanzee tool, without training and in a few seconds, but stone knapping is an esoteric and difficult skill which excites admiration and awe even today. No living ape has learnt to remove a flake in the way hominins could even at 2.3 Mya (Toth *et al.* 1993; Wright 1972). Are all efforts to understand pre-hominin origins of human tool making doomed to disappointment?

Part of the difficulty with answering this question is the difference in evidence from living great apes and extinct hominins. Behavioural observation of apes allows us to identify tools made from grass, vine and woody material, tools that entirely comprise chimpanzee tool manufacture; but we see only a snapshot in time, lacking any historical record (or even definite fossils of chimpanzee ancestors). The only *stone* tool use by chimpanzees, for cracking nuts (Boesch & Boesch 1990; Sugiyama & Koman 1979), involves selection of found objects, thus leaving no archaeological record except small piles of rocks. Conversely, the archaeological record of early hominins entirely omits tools made of plant material, which presumably these creatures were at least as well able to fashion as are modern chimpanzees; but this is compensated by a rich time-series of tools, some associated with bones of particular hominin species. If we insist on parity by ignoring tools made of non-fossilizing plant material, tool making becomes once more 'uniquely human': but ignoring evidence is no way to make progress. (Unfortunately, just this approach remains frequent in more popular treatments of human origins.) Even when direct comparison between tools of apes and hominins *has* been made, it has inevitably been at a highly abstract level; and claims have been controversial (McGrew 1987; Wynn & McGrew 1989). This paper will argue for another way: let us back off from this close-focus upon tools, stone or otherwise, and concentrate instead on their psychological significance.

Surely the reason that for hundreds of years scholars have been content to define our species as 'Man the Tool-maker' is not because of any special symbolic meaning of tools, but the fact that making tools is smart. Finding a delicately-flaked stone arrowhead in the ground is exciting to most people because of what it tells them about the mind of the tool-maker. The real significance of the earliest stone tools in the fossil record is the deductions they allow us to make about the cognitive psychology of long-extinct hominins. The slight change of emphasis immediately enables progress: we *can* compare two-million-year-old hominins and modern chimpanzees on the metric of psychological capacity, no matter where our evidence for those capacities comes from. The lesson has perhaps been better grasped by palaeoarchaeologists — who have long attempted to reconstruct behaviour from the use of debitage, flaking sequences, cut marks on bones, disposition of tools on floors and so on — than by primatologists, held in thrall by the tyranny of the tool as detached object. Chimpanzees are the only ape species commonly to make tools in the wild, and this has led to an inordinate concentration on the chimpanzee, much puzzlement about the relative lack of tools in other great apes (e.g. McGrew 1989), and theories that awkwardly postulate the secondary loss of tool-making abilities in apes other than chimpanzees (e.g. Parker & Gibson 1979). Let us instead concentrate our analyses upon the *process*: of tool making, tool using, or any comparably skilled manual activities. This brings immediate advantages

from the point of view of the evolutionary psychologist. Study is no longer restricted to species that make tools (which effectively meant to one species of ape, the chimpanzee), but can be widened to any species that uses its hands or equivalent effector organs in interesting ways: even raccoons, squirrels and parrots. That will allow more genuinely comparative study. For reconstructing the evolution of human psychology, by examining the manual dexterity and flexibility of non-human primates, starting with the great apes, we have some prospect of gaining important clues to the evolutionary origin of technological skill. One aim of the current paper, then, is to present a brief overview of the *object-directed manual skills of the living great apes*, as presently known, in order that palaeoarchaeologists may make informed comparisons with the corresponding manual skills they deduce from the fossil record.

An additional problem in making productive comparisons between skills of living apes and extinct hominins is that the two traditions of study have proceeded independently, and each has needed to use technical terms. Often, wishing to avoid cumbersome jargon, researchers have recruited everyday words and given them new, operational definitions. Unfortunately, the same words may have been given very different definitions, a problem sometimes further compounded by slightly different everyday meanings in English and French. For instance, 'technique' has been defined as 'the practical manner of accomplishing a particular task' (Inizan *et al.* 1999), and 'an ordered sequence of elements of manual skill, coordinated so that the whole performance serves to {accomplish a purpose}' (Byrne & Byrne 1993). These definitions may not sound incompatible, but in reality it is clear that Inizan *et al.* use the term for how a local purpose is achieved, such as whether a stone hammer or a soft hammer is used for percussion flaking, whereas Byrne & Byrne use it to describe the overall organization of a task: almost the exact reverse. These terms are understood perfectly by cognate researchers, but as soon as the two traditions attempt to talk to each other, problems are likely to arise. To make any sort of worthwhile comparison, it is first necessary to make terms mutually comprehensible. A secondary aim of this paper, then, is to provide an approximate *translation of terminology* to allow better communication between cognitive archaeology and cognitive primatology. Thus, whenever I introduce and define a term used by primatologists to describe great ape manual capacities, I will attempt to provide the equivalent term that has been used to describe equivalent behaviour within knapping (Bril *et al.* 2000; Inizan *et al.* 1999; Roux 2000).

Although I will not ignore the tool making and tool use unique to the chimpanzee (and to one tool-using population of Sumatran orangutan *Pongo abelii*, a population which is now probably extinct), I will concentrate on the preparation of 'hard-to-process' plants for consumption, a task that confronts all apes to a greater or lesser extent. My terminology was developed originally while working with mountain gorillas *Gorilla beringei* engaged in terrestrial herb feeding. Research employed both real-time observations in the field (Byrne & Byrne 1991; 1993), and more detailed analysis of video records of gorilla behaviour in the laboratory (Byrne *et al.* 2001a,b). The definitions were subsequently refined through extension to chimpanzees, where difficult fruit processing was also examined (Corp & Byrne 2002a,b); and to describe the compensations employed by snare-injured chimpanzees and gorillas who cope with these challenging feeding tasks (Byrne & Stokes 2002; Stokes & Byrne 2001). Comparable work has begun on the Bornean orangutan *Pongo pygmaeus* (Russon 1998).

Manual challenges of plants

In this paper, the emphasis will be on plants which present special difficulties, and the impression might be gained that most foods of great apes are hard to process, or that apes are specialists on the more intractable plants found within their ranges. Compared with their closest feeding competitors, the Old World monkeys, there may be some truth in this view (Byrne 1997); however, great apes do of course avoid difficulties when they can. Most strikingly, chimpanzees and western gorillas relish figs *Ficus* spp. (Wrangham *et al.* 1993). Because of the fig's unusual pollination method, its fruits normally contain living fig wasps and thus provide protein as well as sugars. In regions of high density and year-round availability of figs, availability of this balanced diet means that chimpanzees are able to avoid many of the problematic foods they must eat elsewhere. For instance, at Budongo and Kibale, Uganda, chimpanzees do not feed on social insects and so no individuals in these populations engage in regular tool use. The abundance of figs in the ranges of some chimpanzee populations is therefore rather an annoyance for cognitive psychologists! Because it is precisely when they are engaged with manually-challenging foods that we see the cognitive capacities of apes most clearly displayed, fleshy fruits provide little useful information about manual skills. Even within leaf-eating tasks, we have found that it is only the physically-'defended' leaves which reveal many of the manual capacities of most interest for comparison with hominin abilities, including an overall hierarchical task organization (Corp & Byrne 2002a).

Some of the plant-processing tasks that elicit complex manual strategies from great apes are tasks readily comprehensible to Europeans and Americans who — like myself — are already familiar with the some of challenges they would present for handling. This is the case because the plants eaten by some great apes, such as mountain gorillas, are plants of the temperate zone and as such are matched by closely-related forms in the Holarctic. For instance, the nettle *Laportea alatipes*, like the nettles familiar to northern Europeans, is more or less covered by stinging hairs. The sting mechanism only activates as the leaf matures, so the topmost immature leaves on a stem are relatively safe to touch. Stings are found all over mature leaves, the leaf underside is less protected than the edges or upper surface. Worst to touch are the stems, both that of the leaf (the petiole) or the main upright stem, which are densely covered by stings. As children sometimes discover by trial and error, but are often told, a firm grip is less painful, because the sting mechanism is delicate and can often be crushed before it triggers; conversely, a light touch can be very unpleasant. (Hence the English phrase, 'grasping the nettle'.) For the mountain gorillas of Karisoke, Rwanda, *Laportea* leaves are one of the four most frequent plant items in the diet (Watts 1984). This is not surprising since they are rich in protein and low in indigestible lignin (Waterman *et al.* 1983). The reactions of young gorillas, however, show that they find contact with nettle plants painful and aversive, just as humans do (pers. obs.). Other plants of similar importance in gorilla diet, like the thistle *Carduus nyassanus* and the bedstraw *Galium ruwenzoriense* share the same genus and the same difficulties for handling as common wayside plants of late summer in Europe and America. *Galium* is a clambering plant, adapted to this way of growing by numerous minute hooks on the edges of leaf and stem; these hooks hinder swallowing, and could easily trigger choking. Like all the terrestrial herbs staple to gorilla diet, *Carduus* is highly nutritious, but it is defended from animals by long, tough spines on the leaves and the winged extensions of the stem.

Chimpanzees are restricted to tropical zones, and the challenges they face in plant handling are less familiar. Two plants in particular have been found to test the manual abilities of chimpanzees. These are the leaves of *Broussonettia papyrifera*, a Southeast Asian tree introduced to Budongo, Uganda, in a failed attempt to establish paper making. Its leaves are covered on one side with woolly hairs that, like the hooks of *Galium*, make swallowing difficult (Stokes 1999; Stokes & Byrne 2001), and *Saba florida*, a vine whose baseball-sized fruits are delicious and high in sugars, but which are difficult to open neatly enough to gain the flesh (Corp & Byrne 2002b). Orangutans have attracted far less study than chimpanzees or mountain gorillas (though even less has yet been possible with western gorillas *Gorilla gorilla* or bonobos *Pan paniscus*, whose manual skills in the wild remain sadly unexplored). However, orangutans' approach to the problem of obtaining the nutritious meristem of new leaves of the palm *Borassodendron borneensis*, defended by razor-sharp edges of the surrounding leaf petioles, shows many parallels with the manual skills of African great apes (Russon 1998).

The smallest functional units of action

Suppose a leaf needs to be folded, as is the case when a gorilla eats nettle (because folding wraps a whole bundle of stinging nettle leaves and exposes only the relatively sting-free leaf underside). There are many ways for an ape to do it. Holding with precision grips of thumb and first finger of a different hand at either end, one hand may be rotated until the leaf is folded, then the thumb of the other hand moved to hold both leaf ends; or, holding only one end of the leaf with a scissor grip of digits 2 and 3 (Christel 1993; Marzke & Wullstein 1995; Napier 1961), the index finger of the other hand can push the leaf tip over until it can be held by opposition of thumb against the two fingers; and so on. There are literally dozens of ways of achieving this single function (Byrne & Byrne 1993). They presumably vary in efficiency, for instance in how quickly the job can be done, whether the method is reliable in every case, and whether the hand can simultaneously be used for another purpose — perhaps retaining already-folded leaves to add to the bundle. In a sense, however, the variation is unimportant compared to the fact that any of the alternatives allow the job to be done. (Although practically-inclined readers may be interested to know that for a gorilla, much the most popular and apparently efficient method is to fold a bundle of nettle leaves over the thumb of the hand grasping the bundle with a power grip, using a tip-to-tip precision grip of the complementary hand, then re-grasp the folded bundle with the thumb over which it was folded.)

Distinguishing every variant that differed in the digits involved and the overall form of movements made, we found that gorillas employ a very large number these elementary units of action, which we called *elements*. For instance, in gorillas eating the pith and leaves of *Carduus* thistle, we found 222 elements in detailed analysis of data from 14 individuals processing up to 40 handfuls of thistle (Byrne *et*

al. 2001b). Moreover, we showed that this count had by no means reached asymptote, and the same was true for other plant-processing tasks. Such variation may have rather little significance in terms of the overall range of tasks which can be tackled, and in any case we had no way in the field of measuring the mechanical efficiency of each variant, or charting the changes in motor proficiency during development. Instead, we 'lumped' elements that resulted in the same change made to the plant material. For thistle, there were 46 *functionally-distinct elements*, and this estimate was found to be much closer to asymptote. When the functionally distinct elements for two other leaf-processing tasks were combined (Byrne & Byrne 1993), we found a total set of 53. This approach offers a simple way of comparing tasks in their manual complexity at a relatively elemental level (Byrne *et al.* 2001b); when a similar analysis has been performed for other great apes, it will be possible to compare species and populations that use their skills for very different tasks.

Our *functionally distinct element* is probably closest to the term *elementary gesture* used in the analysis of knapped stone (Bril *et al.* 2000), although it is perhaps more conservative in potentially lumping together very different ways for achieving the general effect with the plant material. (In practice, because we think that this lowest level of variation in ape data is mainly a matter of trivial differences in grips and the specific fingers involved, we would suspect that counts of elements from human and ape might reasonably be compared.)

Presumably, in both living ape and hominin, the mode of effect and practical use of each functionally distinct element of action are mostly discovered by trial and error, but sometimes imitation may also be valuable. Anecdotal evidence suggests this is sometimes the case in gorillas (Byrne 1999, 343–5). Mountain gorillas forage out of visual contact with other adults; only as an infant does a gorilla have the chance to watch closely while another individual is feeding: its own mother. At adolescence, all female gorillas leave their natal group and move away to join another group, sometimes moving more than once. However, a female joining a group whose range is in a different habitat to that in which she grew up has no opportunity to learn locally-appropriate skills by imitation. Intriguingly one such female, Picasso, whose natal range did not include nettle, never learnt the 'folding' described at the start of this section. Moreover, her juvenile offspring also failed to learn the trick. Perhaps folding is difficult to discover without a model to copy, and until one of Picasso's descendants gets a lucky break and either discovers folding for itself or sees another gorilla doing it, they may be in for a painful time eating nettle leaves.

Coordination of the hand

Most manual actions of monkeys are carried out with a single hand, and often the other hand is in use simultaneously to support the body. The more upright body-carriage of great apes allows bimanual use of the hands, particularly if the animal is in the sitting posture favoured by gorillas. In addition, the mobile lips of great apes, especially the chimpanzee, mean that the mouth can sometimes be used almost as a 'third hand'. Most obviously, two hands can be used jointly to apply double the force to an object. Such symmetrical bimanual use of the hand is presumably relatively straightforward for the brain to program. In contrast, *asymmetric bimanual action*, in which the two hands are used in different and complementary ways (and for this reason it is sometimes called 'complementary bimanual action'), likely demands considerable neural flexibility. Asymmetric bimanual processing displays what has been called manual role differentiation (Elliott & Connolly 1984), in which the two hands must separately achieve different functions in different ways, yet be coordinated together both in space and time. As an example, consider how asymmetric bimanual action is central to a gorilla's processing of nettle to eat. In processing a single plant, four different uses of asymmetric bimanual hand action may be employed: if the ground is soft, in order for the leaves to be efficiently stripped off the stem the other hand will be needed to support the stem base securely; then, it is essential that the two hands can be opposed to twist-off or tear-apart the leaf blades from the petioles, which are discarded; next, any debris that contaminates the bundle will be picked out, with delicate use of tip-to-tip precision grip of one hand while the other loosely retains the bundle; finally, the folding of the leaves to encase the parcel in a single leaf underside crucially depends on asymmetric bimanual action. The assignment of hand to role is highly lateralized: a gorilla that uses the right hand to hold the leaf-bundle and the left to fold it over will hardly ever reverse these roles. For a given task, and a given animal, the asymmetry in manual action is highly stable.

Asymmetric bimanual hand use with manual role differentiation is apparently rare or absent in monkey species (but see Boinski *et al.* 2001), yet it has been widely reported in great apes (e.g. Boesch & Boesch 1990; Byrne & Byrne 1991; Byrne *et al.* 2001a; Fox *et al.* 1999; Russon 1998; see also Fragaszy 1998). The importance of this ability for chimpanzees, when they crack nuts with hammer and anvil, can clearly be seen in Boesch & Boesch's (1993) analysis of hand posture in this task.

Coordination can also occur within a single hand, if the digits can be controlled independently. This *digit role differentiation* is probably impossible for most mammals, including monkeys, and certainly has not been described until recently (Byrne *et al.* 2001a). Once again, however, it may well be rather routine for great apes. For instance, nettle processing would be inefficient if each plant had to be dealt with separately: often the plants are rather small and yield few leaf blades to eat, especially from the perspective of a huge silverback male gorilla. However, in fact it is routine to see a part-processed bundle of leaves retained in part of the hand (either digits 2 and 3, or 4 and 5, are commonly used), while a new plant is processed to the same stage (Byrne & Byrne 1991). The accumulation may take place (1) once the leaves of a stem have been stripped off in a compact whorl; or (2) it may be delayed until leaf petioles have also been detached, thus allowing the iteration of a longer sequence of processing actions. Either way, the facility enables the edible part of several plants to be accumulated, and critically relies on digit role differentiation (Byrne *et al.* 2001a). All the main food plants of mountain gorillas are processed in ways that rely on this within-the-hand accumulation (Byrne & Byrne 1991), illustrating the importance of digit role differentiation for this species. The ability has not been studied in other great apes, but a review by Fragaszy (1998) points out it may be important to them also: for instance, nut-cracking chimpanzees hold intact nuts in the same hand that they use to position and support a nut on an anvil for striking.

Within writing on stone knapping, little has been made of the importance of bimanual asymmetric coordination between the hands and digit role differentiation within the hand: perhaps, because these abilities are so familiar in our own species that their absence is unimaginable in other hominins. Bimanual asymmetric coordination would appear to be absolutely essential for any skilled stone working to take place, and digit role differentiation — while perhaps not essential — is certainly used routinely when a stone's position is adjusted within the hand by a modern stone knapper.

So far, we have considered skill at what has been called the 'action level' (Byrne & Russon 1998). Effectiveness at this level is a matter of (1) how well an action is carried out, the gradual increase in *efficiency of motor movement* that comes with long practice (something that cannot be effectively studied in observational studies of wild animals, although it is a prominent part of discussions of skill in humans e.g.

Welford 1968); (2) the *size of repertoire* of functionally-distinct elements of action, providing both different ways of achieving effects (in stone knapping parlance, different *techniques* to achieve a similar end: Inizan *et al.* 1999) and alternative ways of achieving a single effect. Having several alternative ways to achieve the same purpose sounds like unnecessary redundancy, but for an animal that may need to forage in tall trees while safely supporting its bulk, the option to carry out a normally bimanual action with one hand may be critical. This sort of flexibility also confers an unexpected benefit on great apes: the chance to survive after maiming of the hands, which sadly occurs in many areas of Africa as a consequence of snares set by humans. Young apes are highly curious, and liable to explore novel objects with their hands, with grim consequences (Stokes *et al.* 1999). Not all die of their injuries, however, and those that survive have been found to show quite remarkable accommodations to their severe disablement (Byrne & Stokes 2002; 2003; Stokes & Byrne 2001), using a very different range of action elements to achieve the same functions as their able-bodied counterparts, but nevertheless achieving comparable feeding efficiency.

To deal with complex manual problems, however, another type of skill is also required: the ability to build up programmes of goal-directed action out of constituent elements of action, and it is to this ability we turn next.

Building up elements into hierarchical organization

In principle, the organization of a programme of goal-directed actions might be *linear*: a string of elements, joined together into a chain of actions whose sequential application achieves the desired effect. This possibility has great attraction to psychologists within the learning theory tradition, because of the computational simplicity or 'parsimony' of the associative process needed to construct linear strings. (Indeed, the assumption that associative chaining could account for all human behaviour was central to the doctrine of behaviourism.) Imitative learning of string-like structures of action — called 'action-level imitation' by Byrne & Russon 1998 — can be accommodated by an associative process, with some modification of the basic theory (Heyes & Ray 2000).

No doubt, some animals can only acquire novel complex behaviour by action-level imitation, producing an undifferentiated linear sequence of actions; many animals probably do so frequently; and even humans certainly do so sometimes. Consider, for instance, the ability to mimic the style and mannerisms

of another person that some comics use to devastating satirical effect. More significantly, we may copy in a linear fashion when we cannot 'see below the surface' of a smooth performance to understand its organization, and in the process of imitation we may gain more insight into that organization.

However, it is now thoroughly accepted within psychology that human skills are normally *hierarchically* organized (Chomsky 1959; Miller *et al.* 1960; Newell & Simon 1972), and that this applies at every point from tying shoelaces to constructing a novel sentence. Increasingly, there is evidence that the manual skills of great apes also show hierarchical organization: they are structured more like a branching tree than a linear chain, and large branches or small twigs can be dealt with as units, allowing great flexibility. Gorillas, for instance, are able both to *omit* parts of an otherwise rather standardized sequence of actions, if there is no need on occasion to perform one particular action, or alternatively to *repeat* a section of the normal program iteratively to a criterion (Byrne & Byrne 1993). The section of program repeated, and thus treated as a single module, may be short or quite long. (A *program* in this context is an organized sequence of motor actions used to process potential food into a form suitable for ingestion; a *module* is a section of a program that can be treated as an independent unit, for instance by repetition, omission or use in a different program altogether.) In nettle eating, the whole sequence of *pull a stem into range, hold the base while the other hand strips up the stem, grasp the petioles to twist or lever them off the leaf blades* may be repeated, while already-processed leaf blades are retained in the lower fingers of one hand, showing that this sequence can form a module. This allows a gorilla to accumulate a larger handful of nettle leaves to eat. Modules which achieve a common function may be *shared* between two otherwise very different programs. And unlike the 'fixed action patterns' of classical ethology, a gorilla's program for dealing with plant food can be *interrupted* — provided the interruption occurs at a module boundary — and resumed smoothly later, allowing individuals often to stop mid-process, scan the environment, interact vocally with others, etc. before continuing to process the same handful. Orangutans also organize their motor planning in a hierarchical way (Byrne & Russon 1998; Russon 1998), as do chimpanzees (Stokes & Byrne 2001).

Hierarchical organization of learned behaviour is likely common to all great apes (the manual behaviour of the bonobo has not yet been studied under natural conditions, but in captivity the species appears to have similar manual abilities to the chimpanzee). The ability to schedule novel hierarchical structures, themselves composed of smaller, familiar components, means that great apes have *generative* manual skill (Case 1985; Corballis 1991): a limited range of basic motor components can be combined in many different ways to produce a potentially unlimited range of skills. Most animals, even other non-human primates, show no such generative ability in their actions: essentially, their motor repertoires are fixed, and all that can be learnt is in under what circumstances to use an action, and how firmly or gently it should be applied. The fact that the living apes, our closest relatives, show generativity in manual skills is significant for two reasons. Most relevant to this chapter, generative manual ability is an important precursor of hominin tool construction; but in addition, it means that the closest to syntax in the natural behaviour of great apes is in their hand action, not their voices (which are restricted to a fixed and presumably innate repertoire of signals: Marler & Tenaza 1977). Hierarchically-organized structures of manual action, in which the constituent modules are themselves built up out of more elementary action components, have been called *techniques* in primate work, a very different usage from that of archaeology. The closest equivalent in archaeology is probably the *plan of action* (Bril *et al.* 2000), or *method* (Inizan *et al.* 1999). The term *sequential organization* has also been used, but it is important to realize that in knapping as in ape plant preparation the organization is hierarchical, not simply a linear sequence.

The pattern of variance in the gorilla data (i.e. *idiosyncratic* at low levels of description, such as the precise form of elements or the manual laterality, but highly *standardized* at the level of the overall structure) has been used to argue for the importance of program-level imitation in acquisition (Byrne 1998; Byrne & Byrne 1993; Byrne & Russon 1998). In *program-level imitation* the imitator 'sees' and copies the underlying planning structure, but may well use its own way of achieving many of the actions copied (Note that slavish copying of low-level manual elements may well be inefficient, whereas trial-and-error exploration often efficiently homes in on the optimum.) The idea that apes can learn by program-level imitation has been subsequently supported by analysis of the behaviour of disabled chimpanzees in the wild (Byrne & Stokes 2002; Stokes & Byrne 2001). Young apes are highly curious, and vulnerable to disabling and often fatal injuries when they explore snares set to catch other animals. Nevertheless, some survive, and go on to manage to eat foods which require complex processing. If their normal skills developed solely by individual exploration, one would expect highly-idiosyncratic techniques to be acquired by disabled animals. However, if imitation is necessary to acquire

a skilled technique, and the only available model (the mother) is able-bodied, then hers is the technique that must perforce be acquired. The latter pattern was found: disabled apes use the same overall method as able-bodied ones, working round the local problems caused by their disablement.

In program-level imitation, what is essential is the opportunity to watch a skilled performer at work *for a long time*: only then can statistical regularities in the behaviour betray the underlying planning structure (Byrne 2002; 2003). Young apes have abundant opportunities of this kind, and perhaps the same was true of the children of hominin knappers. Teaching, in contrast, may be less important when great apes learn elaborate motor skills. Active demonstration was seen only twice in an 11-year project on the acquisition of chimpanzee nut cracking (Boesch 1991b) and has not been noted again since. None at all was seen in a study of acquisition of *Saba florida* processing, the most complex plant feeding task for the Mahale, Tanzania, chimpanzee population (Corp & Byrne 2002b). Instead, both studies noted that the behaviour of mother chimpanzees makes many opportunities available to their infants that may have beneficial consequences for their learning. In particular, mothers allow infants and juveniles to watch them closely, scrounge food, and interact with aspects of their own food preparation (e.g. stone tools). However, Corp & Byrne questioned whether the mothers intend (or are adapted to produce) an effect upon learning. They noted that despite repeated begging by infants below one year, mothers do not share *Saba florida* pith, while when the infant is over one year they share readily, even sometimes offering the pith. This pattern is more consistent with a nutritional effect: below a year, lactation cannot be replaced or reduced by supplemental pith feeding, whereas the infant is presumably at least as well able to learn about the task.

Could a living great ape learn to knap stone?

Living great apes evidently possess many manual skills that are directly comparable to those of hominin stone knappers. Their hands are surprisingly dextrous, allowing a range of precision as well as power grips (especially in the gorilla, whose relatively long thumb and short fingers are most similar in proportion to those of modern humans). A large range of differentiated manual actions are performed, specific to functions required for particular tasks. This gives ample testament to apes' ability to learn novel motor actions, including deftly-coordinated bimanual actions, in which the two hands take complementary roles simultaneously. In addition, fingers can be independently manipulated, allowing a single hand to carry out two different functions at once: for instance, picking up a small object while retaining a tight bundle of stems in other fingers. Dependent upon the flexibility of motor learning in all great apes, the extensive repertoire of manual actions for achieving different functions seems to be learnt mainly by individual exploration and trial and error, because the fine details vary idiosyncratically across the population. However, chains of different actions can be built up into complex programs, at least five steps in length, and these more elaborate constructions are learnt partly by imitation. The process of constructing action sequences from smaller components is hierarchical, allowing flexibility in response to environmental need, efficient modular organization, and enlargement of the repertoire in a generative and 'productive' way. These abilities would appear to allow the rudiments of stone knapping to be done, although certainly would not be sufficient to account for the stone tools of early modern humans, which show clear evidence of being made to a preconceived plan.[1]

So, why do living apes *not* make stone tools? Before jumping to conclusions about cognitive limitations, it may be worth noting that most living apes do not make tools at all, although there is little doubt they are capable of doing so, and readily do in captivity when given tasks experimentally (McGrew 1989). It is evident that bonobos, gorillas, almost all orangutans, and some populations of chimpanzees, have no reason in the wild to embark on tool making: they manage just fine in their environment without needing tools. (Some part of the reason for this is no doubt the absence of tasks for which a tool is a suitable solution, but much more often it will be due to the availability of alternative, simpler sources of the same nutrients.) Might modern apes be capable of knapping? Experimental studies in captivity suggest that the answer is probably no. Both an orangutan and a bonobo have learned to flake a stone in order to obtain a sharp flake (Toth *et al.* 1993; Wright 1972). The orangutan, however, was extensively trained by the experimenter, and had the advantage that the core was held in place artificially for it. The bonobo, a 'language'-trained ape, was simply shown simple knapping by the experimenter, and presented with a task that depended on cutting a rope. Rather than knap a hand-held rock, it preferred to throw the rock at the hard ground: this was effective in shattering the rock, and the bonobo then carefully selected a sharp flake to use. Since this was in fact effective, and the ape clearly understood the cause-and-effect of sharp flakes and cutting, it is hard to know what to make of its 'failure' to knap in classic hominin fashion: if you

can invent a safe and effective method, why bother to imitate a riskier and trickier one?

Alternatively, it may very well be that no living great ape is capable of learning the motor skill involved in aiming a *powerful and accurate* blow at an object held in the other hand: it is the combination that may be beyond them, because there is no doubt that living apes have both great limb power and delicate precision ability, in separate contexts (Goodall 1986). Some evidence for this conjecture comes from manual laterality, which appears to develop mainly in the context of 'difficult' tasks.[2] All the skilled plant preparation of the mountain gorilla is highly lateralized at the individual level (Byrne & Byrne 1991). Most of the natural manual behaviour of chimpanzees, like that of monkeys, lacks clear lateralization: in captivity, individual lateral preferences are found with repetitive tasks, but their significance — both statistical and functional — is controversial (Marchant & McGrew 1996; McGrew & Marchant 2001; Warren 1980). The exceptions to this generalization, cases where chimpanzees do develop strong individual lateralization in the wild, are mostly tasks that require skilled use of tools or aimed percussion of objects (Boesch 1991a; McGrew & Marchant 1996; McGrew *et al.* 1999; Sugiyama *et al.* 1993). For this reason, lateral specialization has often been associated with skilled tool use (e.g. McGrew & Marchant 1996). Alternatively, Byrne & Byrne (1991; Byrne *et al.* 2001) noted the cognitive complexity of asymmetric bimanual coordination, also a feature of those chimpanzee tasks eliciting individual laterality, and — crucially — found in all the highly-lateralized but non tool-using gorilla activities. Byrne & Byrne suggested that it was instead asymmetric bimanual coordination that benefited from strong lateralization: when the two hands need to take distinctively different roles in a single task, it pays not to switch roles between left and right hands. The correlation with tool use and percussion is a coincidence of the particular chimpanzee tasks that needed bimanual coordination.

Humans, of course, also show population-level manual laterality, 'handedness', and this has generally been assumed to be critical to the highest echelons of manual skill, as for instance in writing. It is therefore intriguing that gorilla leaf-eating tasks — which are more complex in various ways than pith-extraction tasks — show weak but statistically-significant population right-handedness (Byrne & Byrne 1991; Byrne *et al.* 2001a). Gorillas are more likely to be lateralized so that precise actions are performed right-handed, with the left hand as a support. Could it be that manual role differentiation not only predisposes apes towards strong laterality, but also benefits from an inherited population bias towards particular hand assignment — right-handed precision? This speculation is supported by Hopkins's (1995) study of an asymmetric bimanual task in captivity, where strong individual laterality and significant population right-handedness were found, whereas no population effects had been detected in wild chimpanzee tasks. Now, however, population-level manual laterality has at last been found in wild chimpanzees, when eating *Saba florida* (Corp & Byrne 2004), with females showing right- and males left-handedness. Importantly for the present discussion, this task requires both great *power* (to tear open the hard fruits), and delicate *precision* (to remove flesh without loss), in close alternation. If the expressed laterality is a sign of difficulty for the apes, it may well be beyond the capability of a modern chimpanzee, gorilla or orangutan, to exert the combination of power and precise aim in a single task that is required to knap stone.

Notes

1. It is controversial whether some or all of the stone tools of earlier hominins would also require the ability to envisage the finished product in advance and so guide the entire process of flaking. For most pre-sapiens tools, variation in types is extensive and no advance plan is evident. In contrast, the Acheulean hand-axe and the Levallois flake are relatively standardized, suggesting a real plan (Mithen 1996). However, Davidson (2002; Davidson & Noble 1993) interprets these distinctive forms more prosaically. He argues that much of the 'standardization' of the hand-axe reflects selection by modern archaeologists, and that in fact the distribution of ancient bifaces includes a wide range of forms. Moreover, he suggests that the desired product was usually the flakes not the final core, which thus represents the leftover stone from which no more flakes can be detached. Dibble (1987; 1989) earlier suggested that much of the patterning in artefacts of the French Mousterian can be explained in terms of the processes of reduction, given differential availability of raw materials. Davidson goes further, interpreting the large, 'final' flake of the Levallois technique as a (failed) attempt to open up the core to allow more detachments (i.e. produce an acute angle at its edge), making the point that in the cases where this was successful the core would have been flaked further, so the evidence necessarily no longer exists. Needless to say, these views are not accepted by many researchers, but resolution of this controversy will require new evidence.
2. It is not really clear in what aspect of the tasks these difficulties reside. McGrew and colleagues (1999) argue that laterality makes for increased neural efficiency, and support this with evidence that more highly lateralized chimpanzees are quicker at processing. However, Byrne & Byrne (1991), who showed the same correlation in

gorillas, noted that hand preference inevitably meant an asymmetry in practice, and more practice will anyway lead to greater efficiency.

References

Boesch, C., 1991a. Handedness in wild chimpanzees. *International Journal of Primatology* 12, 541–58.

Boesch, C., 1991b. Teaching among wild chimpanzees. *Animal Behaviour* 41, 530–32.

Boesch, C. & H. Boesch, 1990. Tool use and tool making in wild chimpanzees. *Folia Primatologica* 54, 86–99.

Boesch, C. & H. Boesch, 1993. Different hand postures for pounding nuts with natural hammers by wild chimpanzees, in *Hands of Primates*, eds. H. Preuschoft & D.J. Chivers. New York (NY): Springer-Verlag, 31–41.

Boinski, S., R. Quatrone & H. Swartz, 2001. Substrate and tool use among brown capuchins in Suriname: ecological contexts and cognitive bases. *American Anthropologist* 102, 741–61.

Bril, B., V. Roux & G. Dietrich, 2000. Skills involved in the knapping of chalcedony beads: motor and cognitive characteristics of a complex situated action, in *Cornaline de l'Inde: des pratiques techniques de Cambay aux techno-systemes de l'Indus*, ed. V. Roux. Paris: Editions de la Maison des sciences de l'homme, 207–329. [English cd-rom.]

Byrne, R.W., 1997. The technical intelligence hypothesis: an additional evolutionary stimulus to intelligence?, in *Machiavellian Intelligence II: Extensions and Evaluations*, eds. A. Whiten & R.W. Byrne. Cambridge: Cambridge University Press, 289–311.

Byrne, R.W., 1998. Imitation: the contributions of priming and program-level copying, in *Intersubjective Communication and Emotion in Early Ontogeny*, ed. S. Braten. Cambridge: Cambridge University Press, 228–44.

Byrne, R.W., 1999. Cognition in great ape ecology: skill-learning ability opens up foraging opportunities. *Symposia of the Zoological Society of London* 72, 333–50.

Byrne, R.W., 2002. Imitation of complex novel actions: what does the evidence from animals mean? *Advances in the Study of Behavior* 31, 77–105.

Byrne, R.W., 2003. Imitation as behaviour parsing. *Philosophical Transactions of the Royal Society of London (B)* 358, 529–36.

Byrne, R.W. & J.M. Byrne, 1991. Hand preferences in the skilled gathering tasks of mountain gorillas (*Gorilla g. beringei*). *Cortex* 27, 521–46.

Byrne, R.W. & J.M. Byrne, 1993. Complex leaf-gathering skills of mountain gorillas (*Gorilla g. berengei*): variability and standardization. *American Journal of Primatology* 31, 241–61.

Byrne, R.W. & A. Russon, 1998. Learning by imitation: a hierarchical approach. *Behavioral and Brain Sciences* 21(5), 667–721.

Byrne, R.W. & E.J. Stokes, 2002. Effects of manual disability on feeding skills in gorillas and chimpanzees: a cognitive analysis. *International Journal of Primatology* 23, 539–54.

Byrne, R.W. & E.J. Stokes, 2003. Can monkeys malinger?, in *Malingering & Illness Deception*, eds. P. Halligan, C. Bass & D. Oakley. Oxford: Oxford University Press, 52–65.

Byrne, R.W., N. Corp & J.M. Byrne, 2001a. Manual dexterity in the gorilla: bimanual and digit role differentiation in a natural task. *Animal Cognition* 4, 347–61.

Byrne, R.W., N. Corp & J.M. Byrne, 2001b. Estimating the complexity of animal behaviour: How mountain gorillas eat thistles. *Behaviour* 138, 525–57.

Case, R., 1985. *Intellectual Development: Birth to Adulthood*. New York (NY): Academic Press.

Chomsky, N., 1959. Review of Skinner 1957. *Language* 35, 26–58.

Christel, M., 1993. Grasping techniques and hand preferences in Hominoidea, in *Hands of Primates*, eds. H. Preuschoft & D.J. Chivers. New York (NY): Springer Verlag, 91–108.

Corballis, M.C., 1991. *The Lopsided Ape*. Oxford: Oxford University Press.

Corp, N. & R.W. Byrne, 2002a. Leaf processing of wild chimpanzees: physically defended leaves reveal complex manual skills. *Ethology* 108, 1–24.

Corp, N. & R.W. Byrne, 2002b. The ontogeny of manual skill in wild chimpanzees: evidence from feeding on the fruit of *Saba florida*. *Behaviour* 139, 137–68.

Corp, N. & R.W. Byrne, 2004. Sex differences in chimpanzee handedness. *American Journal of Physical Anthropology* 123, 62–8.

Davidson, I., 2002. The 'finished artefact fallacy': Acheulean handaxes and language origins, in *Transitions to Language*, ed. A. Wray. Oxford: Oxford University Press, 180–203.

Davidson, I. & W. Noble, 1993. Tools, humans and evolution: the relevance of the Upper Palaeolithic, in *Tools, Language and Intelligence: Evolutionary Implications*, eds. T. Ingold & K. Gibson. Cambridge: Cambridge University Press, 363–88.

Dibble, H., 1987. Reduction sequences in the manufacture of Mousterian implements of France, in *The Pleistocene Old World: Regional Perspectives*, ed. O. Soffer. New York (NY): Plenum Press, 33–45.

Dibble, H., 1989. The implications of stone tool types for the presence of language during the Middle Paleolithic, in *The Human Revolution: Behavioral and Biological Perspectives on the Origins of Modern Humans*, vol. 1, eds. P. Mellars & C. Stringer. Edinburgh: Edinburgh University Press, 415–32.

Elliott, J.M. & K.J. Connolly, 1984. A classification of manipulative hand movements. *Developmental Medicine & Child Neurology* 26, 283–96.

Fox, E., A. Sitompul & C.P. van Schaik, 1999. Intelligent tool use in wild Sumatran orangutans, in *The Mentality of Gorillas and Orangutans*, eds. S.T. Parker, H.L. Miles & R.W. Mitchell. Cambridge: Cambridge University Press, 99–116.

Fragaszy, D.M., 1998. How non-human primates use their hands, in *The Psychobiology of the Hand*, ed. K.J. Connolly. Cambridge: Mac Keith Press, 77–96.

Goodall, J., 1963. Feeding behaviour of wild chimpanzees: a preliminary report. *Symposia of the Zoological Society of London* 10, 39–48.

Goodall, J., 1986. *The Chimpanzees of Gombe: Patterns of Behavior*. Cambridge (MA): Harvard University Press.

Heyes, C.M. & E.D. Ray, 2000. What is the significance of imitation in animals? *Advances in the Study of Behavior* 29, 215–45.

Hopkins, W.D., 1995. Hand preferences for a coordinated bimanual task in 110 chimpanzees (*Pan troglodytes*): cross-sectional analysis. *Journal of Comparative Psychology* 109, 291–7.

Inizan, M.-L., M. Reduron-Ballinger, H. Roche & J. Tixier, 1999. *Technology and Terminology of Knapped Stone*. Nanterre: CREP.

Leakey, L., 1961. *The Progress and Evolution of Man in Africa*. London: Oxford University Press.

Marchant, L.F. & W.C. McGrew, 1996. Laterality of limb function in wild chimpanzees of Gombe National Park: comprehensive study of spontaneous activities. *Journal of Human Evolution* 30, 427–43.

Marler, P. & R. Tenaza, 1977. Signalling behaviour of apes with special reference to vocalization, in *How Animals Communicate*, ed. T. Sebeok. Bloomington (IN): Indiana University Press, 965–1033.

Marzke, M.W. & K.L. Wullstein, 1995. Chimpanzee and human grips: a new classification with a focus on evolutionary morphology. *International Journal of Primatology* 17(1), 117–39.

McGrew, W.C., 1987. Tools to get food: the subsistants of the Tasmanian Aboriginies and Tanzanian chimpanzees compared. *Journal of Anthropological Research* 43, 247–58.

McGrew, W.C., 1989. Why is ape tool use so confusing?, in *Comparative Socioecology: the Behavioural Ecology of Humans and Other Mammals*, eds. V. Standen & R.A. Foley. Oxford: Blackwell Scientific Publications, 457–72.

McGrew, W.C., 1992. *Chimpanzee Material Culture: Implications for Human Evolution*. Cambridge: Cambridge University Press.

McGrew, W.C. & L.F. Marchant, 1996. On which side of the apes? Ethological study of laterality of hand use, in *Great Ape Societies*, eds. W.C. McGrew, L.F. Marchant & T. Nishida. Cambridge: Cambridge University Press, 255–72.

McGrew, W.C. & L.F. Marchant, 2001. Ethological study of manual laterality in the chimpanzees of the Mahale Mountains, Tanzania. *Behaviour* 138, 329–58.

McGrew, W.C., L.F. Marchant, R.W. Wrangham & H. Klein, 1999. Manual laterality in anvil use: wild chimpanzees cracking *Strychnos* fruits. *Laterality* 4, 79–87.

McGrew, W.C., C.E.G. Tutin & P.J. Baldwin, 1979. Chimpanzees, tools, and termites: cross-cultural comparison of Senegal, Tanzania, and Rio Muni. *Man* 14, 185–214.

Miller, G.A., E. Galanter & K. Pribram, 1960. *Plans and the Structure of Behavior*. New York (NY): Holt, Rinehart and Winston.

Mithen, S., 1996. *The Prehistory of the Mind: the Cognitive Origins of Art and Science*. London: Thames & Hudson.

Napier, J.R., 1961. Prehensility and opposability in the hands of primates. *Symposia of the Zoological Society of London*

5, 115–32.

Newell, A. & H.A. Simon, 1972. *Human Problem Solving.* New York (NY): Prentice-Hall.

Nishida, T., 1986. Local traditions and cultural transmission, in *Primate Societies*, eds. B.B. Smuts, D.L. Cheney, R.M. Seyfarth, R.W. Wrangham & T.T. Struhsaker. Chicago (IL) & London: University of Chicago Press, 462–74.

Parker, S.T. & K.R. Gibson, 1979. A developmental model for the evolution of language and intelligence in early hominids. *The Behavioural and Brain Sciences* 2, 367–408.

Roche, H., A. Delagnes, J.-P. Brugal, C. Feibel, M. Kibunjia, V. Mourre & P.-J. Texier, 1999. Early hominid stone production and technical skill 2.34 Myr ago in West Turkana, Kenya. *Nature* 399, 57–60.

Roux, V. (ed.), 2000. *Cornaline de l'Inde: des pratiques techniques de Cambay aux techno-systemes de l'Indus.* Paris: Editions de la Maison des sciences de l'homme. [English cd-rom.]

Russon, A.E., 1998. The nature and evolution of intelligence in orangutans (*Pongo pygmaeus*). *Primates* 39(4), 485–503.

Stokes, E.J., 1999. Feeding Skills and the Effect of Injury on Wild Chimpanzees. Unpublished PhD, University of St Andrews, Scotland.

Stokes, E.J. & R.W. Byrne, 2001. Cognitive capacities for behavioural flexibility in wild chimpanzees (*Pan troglodytes*): the effect of snare injury on complex manual food processing. *Animal Cognition* 4, 11–28.

Stokes, E.J., D. Quiatt & V. Reynolds, 1999. Snare injuries to chimpanzees (*Pan troglodytes*) at 10 study sites in East and West Africa. *American Journal of Primatology* 49, 104–5.

Sugiyama, Y. & J. Koman, 1979. Tool-using and tool-making behaviour in wild chimpanzees at Bossou, Guinea. *Primates* 20, 513–24.

Sugiyama, Y., T. Fushimi, O. Sakura & T. Matsuzawa, 1993. Hand preference and tool use in wild chimpanzees. *Primates* 34, 151–9.

Toth, N., K.D. Schick, E.S. Savage-Rumbaugh, R.A. Sevcik & D.M. Rumbaugh, 1993. Pan the tool-maker: investigations into the stone-tool-making and tool-using capabilities of a bonobo (*Pan paniscus*). *Journal of Archaeological Science* 20, 81–91.

Warren, J.M., 1980. Handedness and laterality in humans and other animals. *Physiological Psychology* 8, 351–9.

Waterman, P.G., G.M. Choo, A.L. Vedder & D. Watts, 1983. Digestibility, digestion-inhibitors and nutrients and herbaceous foliage and green stems from an African montane flora and comparison with other tropical flora. *Oecologia* 60, 244–9.

Watts, D.P., 1984. Composition and variability of mountain gorilla diets in the central Virungas. *American Journal of Primatology* 7, 323–56.

Welford, A.T., 1968. *Fundamentals of Skill.* London: Methuen.

Wrangham, R.W., N.L. Conklin, G. Etot, J. Obua, K.D. Hunt, M.D. Hauser & A.P. Clark, 1993. The value of figs to chimpanzees. *International Journal of Primatology* 14, 243–56.

Wright, R.V.S., 1972. Imitative learning of a flaked-tool technology: the case of an orang-utan. *Mankind* 8, 296–306.

Wynn, T. & W.C. McGrew, 1989. An ape's view of the Oldowan. *Man* 24, 383–98.

Chapter 12

Capuchins as Stone-knappers?:
an Evaluation of the Evidence

Sarah E. Cummins-Sebree & Dorothy M. Fragaszy

Comparisons of tool-using behaviours in human and non-human primates can help answer this question: is stone knapping a uniquely hominin behaviour? More specifically, comparisons between humans, apes, and capuchins may allow us to determine whether certain tool-using capabilities (including propensities to knap stone) are the result of divergent or convergent evolution. We review findings from our lab and those of others with capuchin monkeys to generate a set of possible requirements for stone knapping to develop in a primate species based on a perception–action model. We also speculate on the likelihood that a population of tufted capuchins (Cebus apella) *could spontaneously develop these skills.*

The hand is the cutting edge of the mind.
(Jacob Bronowski)

For many centuries, the ability to use tools was considered to be a uniquely human behaviour, something that divided humans from the rest of the animals. However, as Beck (1980) documented compellingly, we are not the only animal species that uses tools. Many species, from fish to mammals, use tools, but the position of humans at the top of the mountain is hardly challenged by non-human species. Other animals typically use an object as a tool in one or a few specific situations, and their actions with tools lack the variety and complexity of human actions. This leads to an evolutionary conundrum. How can we understand tool use (by humans) as the outcome of a continuous evolutionary process if we see only its discontinuous nature with respect to tool use by other species? This is where studies of tool use in non-human primates can help. A few species of non-human primates commonly use tools for varied purposes and in flexible ways; these include two species of great apes, orangutans (*Pongo pygmaeus*) and chimpanzees (*Pan troglodytes*) and one genus of monkeys, capuchins (*Cebus*) (Boesch & Boesch-Achermann 2000; Matsuzawa 2001; Tomasello & Call 1997; Visalberghi & Fragaszy 1999; in press). Both chimpanzees and capuchins sometimes use stones as pounding tools. Pounding with a stone

can be seen as a precursor to stone knapping; consequently, these taxa are of the most interest with respect to the purposes of this volume.

The primary goal of the international workshop that led to this volume was to determine in what sense stone knapping is a uniquely hominin behaviour. To do this, we must answer a set of related questions about tool-using actions in other species, and particularly about their use of stones as pounding or cutting tools. First, do other primates exhibit behaviours similar to stone knapping, in form or consequence? Second, if they do not, could they develop such behaviour under appropriate conditions? If so, what constitutes appropriate conditions? In this chapter, we examine these questions with respect to the capuchin monkey (*Cebus*), and particularly with respect to tufted capuchins (*Cebus apella*), the species studied most extensively in captivity. Capuchins, from Central and South America, are phylogenetically far removed from the great apes and humans, as Old World (African and Asian) and New World (American) primates last shared a common ancestor an estimated 40 million years ago (Jones *et al.*1992). Capuchins are much smaller (average adult body weight, ~3 kg) than apes and are more arboreal than chimpanzees (Fragaszy *et al.* 2004). Yet, they are alone among monkeys that use objects (including stones) as pounding and cutting tools, the first step in stone knapping.

Studying tool-using behaviours in capuchin monkeys gives us a unique opportunity to study the origins of tool use. Because of their phylogenetic distance from great apes and humans, capuchins allow us to investigate *convergent* evolution (i.e. how certain ecological conditions can promote the evolution of similar traits in species that are not closely related: Raven & Johnson 1992) of tool-using abilities. If we study only the great apes, and the great apes exhibit certain types of tool-using abilities that are similar to simple human tool use, it is difficult to determine the evolutionary trajectory of those behaviours: is the similarity a result of common descent or convergent evolution? In contrast, similarities in tool-using behaviours between capuchins and anthropoids (humans and apes) can be safely laid at the feet of convergent evolution. No other monkeys show the proclivities to manipulate objects and to use tools that capuchins do (Fragaszy *et al.* 2004). This activity is not a primitive trait, shared between capuchins and anthropoids through common ancestry.

Capuchins also provide an opportunity to examine the ontogeny of tool use. These monkeys, like humans and apes, develop skill through practice at managing the movement of objects, producing appropriate forces, achieving precision placement, etc. in tool-using situations (Cummins-Sebree & Fragaszy in prep.). Like humans and apes, they pass through a lengthy period of juvenescence in which the basic elements of manual activity are present but skill in manual action is developing, and young individuals develop problem-solving skills, including the use of tools, in a supportive social context (Fragaszy *et al.* 2002; 2004; Resende *et al.* 2003). Thus they provide an independent model of development of skilled tool use in highly-social individuals.

In this chapter, we briefly review characteristics of capuchin monkeys that impact their use of objects as tools. Then we review what is known about capuchins' tool use, with emphasis on stone tools, from observations of wild and semi-free ranging monkeys and studies with captive monkeys. We evaluate this evidence from a perception–action viewpoint (Gibson 1979; Lockman 2000; Smitsman 1997; Smitsman *et al.* this volume); that is, in relation to the requirements to produce spatial and force relations between objects and the individual's ability to discover and to make use of appropriate affordances to meet these requirements. Finally, we evaluate capuchins' behavioural characteristics in relation to hypothesized requirements for stone knapping as these are understood for humans. We shall see that capuchins have some potentially advantageous characteristics for stone knapping, but face many significant constraints that humans do not,

or that humans overcome through growth and persistence. Thus capuchins' actions with stones, although impressive in some respects, are not likely to extend spontaneously to stone knapping. Whether knapping might be instantiated in capuchins through carefully-scaffolded learning remains to be determined.

Capuchin monkeys: the tool users of the New World

Fragaszy *et al.* (2004) provide a comprehensive review of the behavioural biology of the capuchin monkeys; we touch here only on highlights that in our opinion are most relevant to skilled use of stones as tools. These include manual dexterity, proclivity to combine objects and surfaces in action, and tendency toward terrestriality. Capuchin monkeys are well known for their manipulative and destructive style of foraging, in which they use their hands to search for hidden foods and extract small objects from embedding surfaces or from husks, shells, or other protective coverings (e.g. Boinski *et al.* 2001; Christel & Fragaszy 2000; Fragaszy & Adams-Curtis 1991; Janson & Boinski 1992; Panger 1998). Capuchins are the only New World monkey genus known to use a precision grip, including thumb-forefinger opposition (Christel & Fragaszy 2000; Costello & Fragaszy 1988). Precision grips and other aspects of individuated digit control afford greater dexterity than the whole-hand grips used by other New World monkeys. They also imply haptic sensitivity to force and friction during action, although these aspects of manual function have not been studied. Manual actions are used to explore objects in other ways as well: Visalberghi & Néel (2003) describe how capuchin monkeys lifted nuts in their hands and tapped the shells with their fingers to evaluate whether the shell merited opening (contained nut meat) or not (were empty). Capuchin monkeys explore objects with their hands using similar actions as do humans (Lacreuse & Fragaszy 1997). Altogether, they appear to have sufficient manual dexterity to knap stone.

Capuchin monkeys discover how to use objects as tools through persistent exploratory actions with objects, including actions that combine objects and surfaces. Capuchins of all ages forcefully bang objects against surfaces in a very common form of exploration, just as do human children (Fragaszy & Adams-Curtis 1991; compare with Lockman this volume). Exploratory banging supports discovery of how to use an object to pound something else for effect; capuchins readily discover that they can use a hard object to break open something less strong.

Using stones as tools virtually requires a terrestrial habit (Fragaszy *et al.* 2004; Visalberghi 1997).

Banging something against a surface is easiest if the surface is solid and stationary, for postural reasons and also for precision of striking (a moving target is more challenging). The ground is an ideal fixed (often flat) solid surface; a swaying tree limb is not. If a pounding tool is dropped on the ground, the actor can retrieve it readily. If a pounding tool is dropped from the top of a tree, retrieving it is more problematic. Finally, finding a hard object to use to pound is more likely on the ground than up in a tree. For all these reasons, highly-arboreal animals, no matter what other characteristics they may have, are unlikely to use stones as tools. Capuchins, although primarily arboreal, spend substantial amounts of time on the ground when food is to be found there more readily than elsewhere and when risks of predation are offset by access to resources (Fragaszy 1990; Rose 1994). Thus, they are occasionally in the right place to discover the value of pounding objects against a surface using another object (i.e. hammering).

In sum, capuchins exhibit the necessary prerequisites to use stones as pounding tools: they are dexterous, they produce pounding actions commonly in exploratory and instrumental situations, and they spend time on the ground when conditions favour doing so. Thus it should come as no surprise that capuchins in captive conditions routinely use stones and other hard objects as pounding tools. Until very recently, however, we had limited evidence that capuchins in nature did so. Fernandes (1991) reported the first direct observation of a capuchin monkey hammering; it used a piece of oyster shell to pound open an oyster still fixed to the substrate. It is illuminating that the food was embedded in the ground. But this case concerned a single individual. A better-studied circumstance concerns capuchin monkeys in Tietê Ecological Park, São Paulo, Brazil. These monkeys live in a habitat devoid of natural predators, and they are provisioned well with pelleted food and fruit, so food is abundant. Palms (*Syagrus romanzoffiana*) are also abundant, and the monkeys relish the small nuts of these palms. They cannot bite these hard nuts open; they can only open them by banging the nuts with a stone against a hard surface (such as another stone). Fortunately for the monkeys, loose stones are abundant in this park, the nuts are abundant on the ground, and the monkeys collect nuts and bring them to anvil sites near the trees under which the nuts are collected. The monkeys devote much time and energy to opening palm nuts by banging them with stones against the anvil surface (Mannu 2002; Ottoni & Mannu 2001; Resende *et al.* 2003). Very recently, Oxford (2003) and Fragaszy *et al.* (in review) document that wild monkeys in the cerrado woodland of Piauí,

Brazil, where palm-fruit clusters grow directly from the ground, routinely use stones to pound open palm nuts. Like the monkeys in Tietê Ecological Reserve, the monkeys in Piauí go to the ground to collect palm nuts, transport them to an anvil site, and use a stone to pound them open on the anvil surface. Systematic observation of the monkeys in Piauí is just beginning, but already this population has confirmed that some wild capuchins use stone tools routinely in a manner and context superficially similar to that reported for wild chimpanzees in west Africa (e.g. Matsuzawa 2001; Boesch & Boesch-Achermann 2000).

Capuchins' actions with stone tools

Capuchins in captivity use sticks to probe, sweep, and pound; cups to hold liquids, paper towels to absorb water, and stones to pound (e.g. Anderson & Henneman 1994; Westergaard & Fragaszy 1987; Westergaard *et al.* 1995; Westergaard & Suomi 1993; 1994; 1995; see Fragaszy *et al.* 2004 for a comprehensive review). Although we have extensive descriptions of successful use of different tools, and know something about the facilitative role of social context for younger animals in particular (Resende *et al.* 2003; Visalberghi & Fragaszy 1990; 1996; Westergaard & Fragaszy 1987), we know almost nothing about the biomechanical or kinematic aspects of tool use, nor about the acquisition of skilled action. Thus we cannot yet compare capuchins to other species in these domains. We are, however, beginning to understand the range of situations they can manage in using objects, and we review some of the relevant findings in this domain later in this chapter.

Experimental studies shed some light on capuchins' aptitude for using stone tools and for modifying stones. Studies of capuchins using a tool to pound something open have been conducted in four laboratories. The first reports documented that capuchins used stones to pound open loose nuts (Anderson 1990; Antinucci & Visalberghi 1986) or a metal object to pound open nuts fixed to a surface (Fragaszy & Visalberghi 1989), confirming earlier anecdotal reports going back hundreds of years, to Erasmus Darwin (Darwin 1794) and others. More germane to the topic of stone knapping, Westergaard and colleagues conducted a series of studies on capuchins using and modifying stones for different purposes (Westergaard & Suomi 1993; 1994; 1995; Westergaard *et al.* 1995). For example, Westergaard & Suomi (1995) presented capuchins with a variety of objects (including stones) that could be used as pestles for grinding sugar cane. Seven of 18 capuchins used a stone to grind and pound the sugar cane; the percentage of tool-using bouts per individual involving stone pestles ranged from 24 per cent to 82 per cent. Some of the monkeys also combined food biscuits with the sugar cane, adding the biscuits into the test apparatus between bouts of grinding. The monkeys modified stick pestles using their teeth and hands, leading the authors to conclude that manual and dental actions can produce artefacts that are similar in appearance to those left on stick tools by early hominins. However, they did not modify stone pestles.

Westergaard & Suomi (1997) found that capuchins transferred stone tools and food across groups. Two groups of capuchins were given different items: one group received stones (sharpened quartzite), while the other group received a container of hazelnuts (a desirable food item for capuchins) with an acetate lid. The cages of the two groups were pushed together so that the monkeys could transfer food and/or stones. Over 100 times across 64 trials (out of 68), monkeys in the second group obtained stones provided by the first group, and three capuchins in the second group used those stones to cut through the acetate lid to get the hazelnuts. Capuchins in the second group 'provided' food to the first group by giving or by leaving the nuts within arm's length in 62 of 68 trials for a total of 192 food transfers. These behaviours indicate that capuchins are capable of 'sharing' food and tools, as seen in chimpanzees (Savage-Rumbaugh et al. 1978; Matsuzawa 2001). The process by which food and stones moved between cages was primarily passive, enabled by individuals in the two groups approaching their common cage walls in a tolerant manner and leaving objects within reach of their neighbours. Tolerance of nearby others while feeding is characteristic of capuchins, most particularly of adults towards infants and juveniles less than two years old (Fragaszy et al. 1997; 2004).

Westergaard & Suomi (1994) investigated the extent to which capuchin monkeys modified stones and later used those as cutting tools. When provided with quartzite stones, six of eleven capuchins used three actions that produced stone flakes (sharp debris). The three actions consisted of: a) pounding the stone against a stable, stationary surface; b) striking the stone against a portable, but stabilized stone surface (i.e., a stone positioned on a perch); and c) pounding one stone in hand to another stone in the other hand. Two individuals used the third technique, the one we consider most like stone-knapping. Westergaard & Suomi also provided the capuchins with stones and a container of syrup with a sheet of clear acetate covering the opening of the container. Three monkeys used the stones without modification to cut or strike open the acetate covering. Two monkeys used two stones in combination (as a 'chisel and hammer') to open the acetate. One capuchin attempted to use larger stones to cut the acetate; when this failed, he struck stones to

other stones in ten bouts, producing flakes and sharp cores that he then used to cut through the acetate.

In a second study of stone flaking, Westergaard & Sumoi (1995) provided seventeen capuchins from the groups in the previous study with quartzite stones over a four-week period and monitored their actions with those stones. Eleven capuchins used five techniques to modify stones presented to them: throwing a stone onto a surface, pounding a stone with a piece of wood, striking a stone against the caging material, striking one stone against another positioned on a surface, and striking a stone in hand to another stone in hand. The capuchins produced almost 300 flakes, and 93 per cent of the flaked cores contained at least one sharp edge. The experimenters removed the stones and flakes, and one week later gave the monkeys a collection of cores and flakes, along with a lidded container holding peanut butter. Three capuchins that used stones to cut in the previous study also used the flakes and sharp cores to cut into the container of peanut butter.

Westergaard's studies provide evidence that capuchins can modify stones using species-typical pounding behaviours and that they will use the sharpened edges produced through their actions. Both of these behaviours are precursors to stone knapping. However, we cannot assume that capuchins modified the stones intentionally, as is implied in human stone knapping. Moreover, the cores the monkeys created were crude at best. Figures show only a few clean breaks per core, and the cores do not resemble well-knapped stones (see Bril et al. this volume; Pelegrin this volume). Stone knapping implies hitting a core stone with a percussor stone to produce a conchoidal fracture (Pelegrin this volume). At the present time, we have no evidence that capuchins produce conchoidal fractures. Thus in several fundamental respects, capuchins' actions do not merit the label of 'stone knapping'. Nevertheless, their actions provide an interesting counterpoint to human stone knapping in other ways. We consider these facets of their actions next.

Components of stone-knapping: How do capuchins measure up?

Components of action important for stone knapping in humans include stable upright postural, bimanual coordination (one hand to strike and the other to resist the strike), specialized roles for each hand, appropriate positioning of the stones in each hand, and application of appropriate force with the percussor to the core on the right part of the core and at the appropriate angle. Selection of stones and their positioning in the hands precede and follow these actions. Clearly there are many steps to get to the point where striking one stone with another will reliably produce a useful outcome, as many chapters in this volume attest. Capuchins most obviously possess one of the fundamental components of knapping, that is, applying force with an object held in the hand or hands to another object or surface (basic percussive striking). This, as we have seen, is a common element in their foraging repertoire and their exploratory behaviour. But what of other elements of action more specific to knapping? Below we reconsider capuchins' actions in the various studies of pounding with stones, and other tool-using situations, with respect to the action components of stone knapping.

Bimanual coordination, manual laterality, postural stability, and force requirements

As Corbetta (this volume) pointed out, infants' bimanual capabilities increase concurrently with postural stability, and so does their ability to solve object-related problems, such as opening a container or (much later) knapping stones. Increased postural stability is also linked to an increase in the strength of lateral preference for the acting hand (see Corbetta for humans, Holder for non-human primates, this volume). Bimanual activity with portable objects is a general capability of non-human primates. It appears in infant capuchin monkeys reared with their mothers from the third month of life, just a few weeks after unimanual activity is evident (Adams-Curtis et al. 2001), and capuchin monkeys commonly use both hands in manipulation from infancy onward. Even in infancy they exhibit differentiated roles for the two hands in bimanual manipulation (Adams-Curtis et al. 2001), and such activity is common throughout their lives. The prehensile tail of capuchin monkeys is an important support for bimanual activity; it provides postural stability from many positions other than vertically upright. Capuchins have a much wider range of stable postures than do humans or apes, thanks to their prehensile tails (e.g. Bergeson 1996; Youlatos 1999). Thus, demands for bimanual action and postural stability do not limit capuchins' opportunities to knap stone.

The evidence to date suggests that capuchins often show no particular lateral bias in simple reaching or other ubiquitous activities (such as which limb is used to initiate locomotion), but they readily exhibit individual biases when performing finely modulated movements with the hands or when dealing with strong postural demands, such as maintaining a bipedal stance (Anderson et al. 1996; Panger 1998;

Westergaard et al. 1997; 1998a). As a general rule, the more demanding the task with regard to posture or dexterity, the stronger are individual biases, suggesting that individual bias arises from practice with the task (e.g. Fragaszy & Mitchell 1990; Limongelli et al. 1994; Spinozzi & Cacchiarelli 2000; Spinozzi & Truppa 1999; 2002). However, there is no consistent direction of asymmetry across the (small) populations. For example, Westergaard & Suomi (1993) report that eight of fourteen capuchin monkeys that used a stone to crack open a nut preferentially used the left hand; four preferentially used the right hand, and the other two exhibited no bias. This mixed outcome (in terms of direction of bias across individuals) is typical of studies assessing manual preferences in non-human primates.

A group-wide directional bias for the use of one hand has been found in more than one group of capuchins, but only in tasks with a high demand for fine spatial positioning and repositioning of the fingers and incorporating a strong haptic component. The tasks in question involved locating and prehending seeds placed in crevices of irregularly-shaped objects, discriminating seeds from similarly-shaped pieces of tinfoil, or searching for grapes buried in wood shavings or under water and discriminating them from stones of similar size and shape. A left-hand bias was evident in three groups of capuchin monkeys in these conditions (64 monkeys, three studies combined: Lacreuse & Fragaszy 1999; Parr et al. 1997; Spinozzi & Cacchiarelli 2000). Forty-two of the monkeys preferred left or right hands equally often when they picked up small pieces of food, whether they could see their hands or not, suggesting that reliance on touch alone is not sufficient to induce consistent use of the left hand (Lacreuse & Fragaszy 1999; Spinozzi & Cacchiarelli 2000).

Maintaining a bipedal stance without the use of the tail as an anchor is posturally demanding for capuchins. Spinozzi and colleagues (1998) measured preferences for the acting hand in a group of capuchins in reaching and retrieval tasks requiring quadrupedal and bipedal postures. A unimanual task entailed simple reaching for food, while the bimanual task required the monkeys to retrieve food from a plastic tube. Both tasks were presented close to or on the ground and higher off the ground. The capuchins did not exhibit hand preferences in the quadrupedal-unimanual condition, but they did exhibit a group-level right-hand preference for the upright-unimanual and both bimanual conditions. The strength of hand preference increased across conditions in the following pattern: quadrupedal-unimanual, upright-unimanual, upright-bimanual, and a bimanual pattern induced by placing the tube 5 cm from the ground. In this situation the monkeys adopted a crouched position in which the torso touched the ground while the hands manipulated the tube.

For most manually-skilled individuals, hand preference is evident for the acting hand (see chapter by Holder this volume). In tasks requiring the use of tools, capuchins may exhibit individual hand preferences for the acting hand, although not a population-level preference (Anderson *et al.* 1996; Cummins-Sebree & Fragaszy 2005; in prep.; McGrew & Marchant 1997; Westergaard *et al.* 1998a). A hand preference for the acting hand may aid the acquisition of skill in stone-knapping, perhaps by supporting the development of a routinized motor pattern for efficiently striking the core stone (Wilson 1998). A routinized pattern might support more efficient perceptual learning that leads to each hand adjusting striking force or resistive force and positioning for optimal outcomes. Capuchins can develop strong manual preferences, but they rarely are as lateralized as humans for skilled manual action. This characteristic mitigates against the development of skilled knapping.

We do not have any information on the forces that capuchins can produce through percussion. Given that they are much smaller than humans (remember, an average adult capuchin weighs a mere 3 kg), we cannot expect them to generate equivalent kinetic force. Their smaller hands can hold smaller stones, and they generate a much smaller moment arm when striking. The physics of this arrangement clearly limit the force they can produce compared to humans. The force required to flake a stone does not scale with its weight, but with its hardness and crystalline structure. Thus capuchins are at a stiff disadvantage compared to larger-bodied primates with respect to flaking stones by manual action alone.

Knapping stone skillfully requires precise positioning of the percussor and core stones with respect to each other, skill that takes humans a long time to acquire (Roux *et al.* 1995). Can capuchins master this kind of haptic-kinesthetic-visual coordination of action? We do not know; we have no evidence bearing on this issue. We do, however, have experimental evidence bearing on the more general theme of capuchins' abilities to produce and modify spatial and force relations between objects and surfaces in other situations. We review some of these studies to illustrate capuchins' capabilities in this general domain.

Sliding an object across an irregular surface

Consider first the challenge of using a tool to move an object across a surface. If the surface is smooth and continuous, then sliding the object is straightforward.

If there is a hole or a barrier along the projected path of retrieval, however, one must use the tool to manoeuvre the desired object around the aberration. For example, suppose a group of children are playing a baseball game in a fenced yard. The ball rolls under the fence and out of a child's reach; however, his or her baseball bat is sufficiently long to rake in the ball. If the ground between the ball and the child is fairly smooth and continuous, then the child may retrieve the ball with little effort. But suppose there are bumps or hollows along the potential trajectory for retrieving the ball. In that case the child must attend to the surface features and manoeuvre the bat so that the ball does not fall into a hollow or become lodged behind a bump.

We wanted to know if capuchins could detect and avoid surface aberrations when retrieving food with a tool (Cummins-Sebree & Fragaszy in prep.). The design of our study was inspired by one reported by Povinelli (2000) with chimpanzees, although our theoretical perspective, the details of our procedure, and our interpretation of our findings differ substantially from his. Povinelli's (2000) aim was to determine if the chimpanzees would select, in advance of action, a tool and a platform that did not contain a hole *vs* an identical tool on a platform that had a hole in front of the desired food item. According to Povinelli, if the chimpanzees understood the causal relations governing the movement of the food by the tool, and the fate of the food when it fell into the hole, they would select the tool and platform that did not contain the hole. If they did not have a 'concept of causality', then they would choose between the platforms at random. In this task, the platforms were constructed with vertical walls on three sides, the blade of the hoe tool was wider than the hole, and the only movement that could be made with the hoe was a straight pull towards the body (i.e. no horizontal movement of the tool was allowed). Povinelli found that the chimpanzees initially chose at random between the two platforms and tools, although several individuals quickly developed a preference for the platform with no hole.

We interpreted the chimpanzees' actions as reflecting their ability to detect through action the relevant properties of the surfaces. Accordingly, we arranged our study to provide different opportunities to learn about the surfaces through action. We presented capuchins with three types of platforms (plain, containing a hole, or containing a barrier) in a dichotomous choice task in three phases of testing. We measured the frequency of choices made in selecting the platform from which to retrieve a food treat, as well as success in retrieving the treats. Working from a perception–action model, we predicted that capuchins would not initially attend to a hole in a platform in

Figure 12.1. *Phase 1: our subject chooses to retrieve food from the plain platform instead of from the hole platform and is successful.*

Figure 12.2. *Phase 2: our subject chooses to retrieve food from the barrier platform instead of from the hole platform and is successful.*

the early phase of testing, and thus would not avoid it when attempting to retrieve a treat with the tool. Consequently, the capuchins would be less successful at using the hoe tool on the platform with a hole than on the platform with a barrier, where the treat could be moved behind the barrier but could still be retrieved through persistent efforts. We hypothesized, however, that our subjects would avoid a barrier on a platform early in testing, because the barrier would be more visually salient than the hole, and because the monkey could more reliably gain information about a solid obstacle by striking it with the tool than it could gain information about the hole by swiping across it. We also predicted that as the capuchins progressed through testing, they would learn to attend to the hole and to modulate their actions with the tool when moving food past the hole.

Four adult male tufted capuchin monkeys (*Cebus apella*) participated in this task. We constructed two dark gray PVC platforms to present to the monkeys that each contained a hole in the centre of the front quarter. We could place a PVC block below the hole to yield a plain, continuous platform, or above the hole to yield a platform with a barrier (see Figs. 12.1–12.3). We provided a hoe to be used as a tool to retrieve small pieces of dried fruit and oat cereal. The design of our apparatus allowed movement of the hoe tool horizontally and vertically, and the blade of the hoe could fall into the hole.

We divided testing into three phases. For all phases, we presented a food treat at the centre of each of two platforms so that the treat would be in view but behind either the hole or the barrier. The hoe was placed in the centre, between the two platforms, so that the handle was within the monkey's reach. In

Figure 12.3. *Phase 3: our subject successfully maneuvers food from around a barrier.*

Phase 1, we presented the plain platform and either the hole platform or the barrier platform (see Fig. 12.1). In Phase 2, we presented the hole and barrier platforms together (see Fig. 12.2). In Phase 3, we presented two similar platforms with either the holes or the barriers (see Fig. 12.3). Our dependent variables were choice of platform and success at retrieving the food.

In Phase 1, none of the four capuchins preferred the plain platform over the hole platform, and their rate of success suffered when they chose the hole platform. Two of the four capuchins, however, preferred the plain platform when it was paired with the barrier platform, and their success rates were higher accordingly. In Phase 2, one subject preferred the barrier platform to the hole platform, and he succeeded at retrieving his treats at above-chance levels. Two of the other three capuchins chose the hole platform more often than the barrier platform, even though they continued to lose the treat into the hole more often than they were able to retrieve it. By Phase 3, two of the four subjects mastered using the hoe to retrieve the treat around both the barriers and the holes, while one subject continued to perform at chance levels. The fourth subject chose the platform on his right and used his left hand for almost all trials, regardless of which platform was on his right.

We suggest that capuchins can detect barriers on surfaces more readily than they can detect holes in the same type of surfaces. Moreover, the monkeys can move a desired object past a barrier more easily than past a hole. This is sensible, not only because of the visual salience of barriers, but also because of proprioceptive information the monkey produces when it contacts the barrier with the hoe. The hole is less visually salient, although the hole can provide proprioceptive information about the surface if the blade falls into it (which occurred often for our capuchins). Also, repeated attempts at retrieval are possible when the treat touches the barrier but not when the treat contacts the hole. Thus, for several reasons, the monkeys learned to manage moving past barriers more quickly than past holes.

Managing multiple relations concurrently

Monitoring the position of the food relative to the hole and the tool simultaneously demands joint attention to two dynamic spatial relations external to the actor's body: the relation between the hoe and the food, and between the food and the hole. These relations are dynamic because the position of the food changes over time, and thus its relation to both hoe and hole change over time as well. Thus capuchins' management of this problem is impressive. Stone knapping also requires managing multiple simultaneous dynamic spatial relations, in this case, minimally, between the two stones and between each stone and each hand. This aspect of stone knapping would not, by itself, prevent capuchins from achieving basic success at the task. We do not know if capuchins can also concurrently monitor the position of objects in the hand to achieve specific points of contact between objects, or what kinds of practice support learning to do this. This aspect of using objects as tools challenges young children (Lockman 2000) and it challenges adult human stone knappers with years of experience (Roux et al. 1995).

Selecting a tool and positioning it

To knap stones to yield sharp flakes and core stones, one must select percussor and core stones of appropriate material, and of appropriate size, shape and mass for the actor. Capuchins' choices of stones for pounding have not been studied. Capuchins' choices, however, have been studied in other kinds of tool-using tasks. The results of these other studies bear on the general question of attention to affordances of objects. We use affordance here to mean the usefulness of an object for a particular user and a particular use. For example, suppose a child's ball has rolled underneath the sofa and he or she cannot reach it directly. To retrieve it, the child would need to use an object long enough to make contact with the ball, as well as thin enough to be held comfortably in the hand. The tool should also be light in weight but rigid enough to transfer the force of the child's swipe to the ball so that ball would move from underneath the couch. Though the tool could be of various shapes, one that is shaped like a hook may work well because the ball could be manoeuvred within the crook of the hook. Other properties of the selected tool may not be important, such as its colour, texture, or familiarity.

We conducted a series of experiments to determine what properties guided tufted capuchins' selection of tools to retrieve food treats (Cummins-Sebree & Fragaszy 2005). We presented our subjects with hook tools differing in colour, shape, texture, and size, and in their orientation to a food treat (i.e. the crook surrounding the food, or the food outside the crook) in a dichotomous choice task. We measured frequency of choices of the various tools, as well as success in using the tools to retrieve food treats. This set of experiments was a replication of a study done by Hauser (1997) in which he provided these same types of tools to cotton-top tamarins (*Saguinus oedipus*), another New World primate species that, unlike capuchins, is not known for their object-manipulation skills. We predicted that the capuchins would select tools based on their shape and size, but not on their size or texture; we also expected the capuchins to choose tools that minimized the actions required to pull the treat within reach (i.e. select tools that contained the food within the crook). In situations in which the treat resided outside the crooks of both tools, we predicted the capuchins would attempt to realign a tool and occasionally succeed at using the tool in this manner. By modulating their behaviour, the capuchins would learn how to use particular tools.

Six adult male tufted capuchin monkeys (*Cebus apella*) participated in this task. We constructed the hook tools from flexible copper tubing. We used wire to make 'bumps' and punctured holes into the tubing to provide different textures, and we painted them different colours. The tools were placed two at a time on a plain PVC platform, along with food treats (dried fruit and oat cereal).

We administered a training session, followed by three experimental phases. In the training session, we presented each subject with two blue hooks (similar to candy canes in appearance); one hook contained the treat within the crook, while another treat lay outside the crook of the other hook. In Experiment 1, we presented two tools that differed in one of four properties from the original blue hooks: colour, shape, texture or size. For Experiment 2, we presented each subject with two novel tools that differed in the location of the treat; some tools contained the treat within the crook ('possible'), while others did not have the treat within the crook, and thus required additional manipulation to retrieve the treat ('convertible'). These tools could differ dramatically in colour, shape, and texture from the original blue cane (see Fig. 12.4). In Experiment 3, we presented tools that were 'possible' tools in Experiment 2 as 'convertible' tools, along with novel tools in the 'possible' orientation. Our dependent variables were choice of tool and success at retrieving the food.

In Experiment 1, the capuchins did not exhibit a preference for hook tools based on colour, shape, texture, or size. However, the monkeys preferred 'possible' tools to 'convertible' tools when they were paired together in Experiments 2 and 3, regardless of the familiarity of the tool. When 'convertible' tools were chosen, the capuchins often attempted to reposition those tools to retrieve the treat, and they occasionally were successful at doing so. Though they did not often succeed with 'convertible' tools, their success with those tools increased from 2 retrievals out of 24 attempts in Experiment 2 (8 per cent) to 13 retrievals out of 35 attempts in Experiment 3 (37 per cent). For further details see Cummins-Sebree & Fragaszy (2005).

The performance of the tufted capuchins differed in some ways from the cotton-top tamarins' performance (Hauser 1997). The tamarins chose tools based on their shape and size, but not on their colour or texture, while the capuchins showed no preferences based on those properties. Like capuchins, tamarins chose 'possible' tools more often than 'convertible' tools when paired together. However, when a 'convertible' tool was chosen, the tamarins never attempted to realign the tool so that the treat could be retrieved (Hauser pers. comm.). Thus, the tamarins never succeeded at retrieving food with a 'convertible' tool. On the other hand, the capuchins attempted to reposition 'convertible' tools, and they were occasionally successful when doing so. We predict that the capuchins' success rates with those tools would increase if given additional opportunities to manipulate them in this task.

We suggest that the differences in performance between the two species are due to their differing

Figure 12.4. *Experiment 2: our subject chooses a 'possible' tool instead of a 'convertible' tool to retrieve food and is successful.*

propensities for object manipulation and their ability to modulate actions with their arms and hands, and thus with the tool. It seems the tamarins find it more challenging to alter their action when pulling in a hook. Tufted capuchins manipulate objects more often and in more varied ways, and they modulate actions with objects more flexibly than tamarins can. As seen in the increased success with convertible tools between Experiments 3 and 4, the capuchins were learning to modulate their actions to align an appropriate part of the tool-object to the treat. They clearly did not achieve full skill in using oddly-shaped objects to pull in food, but they were on their way. Overall, these findings suggest that capuchins are attentive to the properties of objects and vary their actions to explore and to exploit varying objects. These characteristics are necessary for learning to knap stones.

Conclusions

We consider the following characteristics as potentially enabling capuchins' discovery that stones can be modified through action to improve their functionality: a) good postural stability while seated or standing bipedally (often aided by their prehensile tails), freeing the hands for action; b) aptitude for bimanual action, especially role-differentiated bimanual action; c) ubiquitous pounding of objects on substrates as a species-typical perception-action routine used in foraging and exploration; d) common discovery of tool use, especially incorporating percussion; and e) terrestrial habits. We see continuity between human and non-human primates in these features of action related to stone-knapping. Indeed, features (a) to (d) are the same features that provide ontogenetic continuity in human stone knapping, as laid out in other chapters in this volume. Capuchins are very small, however, compared to humans, and therefore they cannot produce the same kinetic forces by their strikes as can humans. This characteristic mitigates against capuchins modifying stones in the same ways as humans.

Skilled stone knapping involves selection, planning, and integration of multiple relational demands in action. We have only a little evidence suggesting that capuchins can manage these aspects of knapping to the level required for effective knapping. We have seen that capuchins can monitor two dynamic relations simultaneously while using a hoe tool in one hand to slide food across a discontinuous surface. We also have shown that they can modulate their movements to become more skilled at positioning the familiar hoe and to reposition novel variably-shaped objects to use them to sweep in food. Thus they plan action with objects and integrate multiple spatial, force, and temporal relations in these actions to some extent. But we have not examined capuchins' abilities to modulate actions of the two hands in an integrated task requiring precise positioning and production of force, as occurs in knapping, nor have we examined any aspect of planning in tool use situations beyond selection of a single object to use in a given circumstance, or a sequence of actions to gain a specific tool (e.g. Westergaard *et al.* 1998b).

Given our current understanding of capuchins' flexibility in other manipulation tasks, and their rate of mastering various tasks incorporating multiple relations, we predict that capuchins could master the basic elements of knapping through carefully-scaffolded learning experiences, although most likely they would require far more practice for improvement at each aspect than do adult humans. But they are unlikely, unless perhaps they devote a lifetime to knapping under expert tutelage, to match a moderately-skilled human knapper in any aspect of skill. Capuchins generate the same kinds of information for learning through action that humans do, but they seem to learn from their actions or recognize the significance of various information less slowly and less richly than humans, and they modulate their actions through a smaller range than do humans. The human advantage is cumulative and synthetic: we do not possess any single proclivity or action capability relevant to stone knapping that capuchins do not possess, but we are better at every single step, and/or acquire skill in each domain more quickly, so that we can master additional levels of integration, cope with variations more

quickly, modulate our movements more precisely, etc. Rapidly-improving action skills enable detection and focused attention to relevant properties of the stones, to their position in the hand, and so forth, and therefore to what we recognize collectively as planning. In other words, embodied cognition in humans is vastly richer than in capuchins, and we believe this is what supports stone knapping (and many other familiar skills) in humans (and explains its absence in other species). Capuchins show us how fundamental action is to the human condition.

Acknowledgements

We would like to thank Drs Valentine Roux and Blandine Bril for inviting us to contribute to such an exciting and comprehensive volume on what may make stone knapping a unique hominin ability. We would also like to thank Ron Davis and his staff at the Instrument Shop at the University of Georgia for their skill in constructing much of the materials used in our studies. We greatly appreciate the help we have had from many of our undergraduate assistants throughout our studies, including Amy Fuller, Jennifer Hohman, Michelle Smith, and countless others who have assisted us. Research completed at the University of Georgia and described in this chapter was made possible by Grant HD6016 from the National Institutes of Health, USA to Georgia State University.

References

Adams-Curtis, L.E., D. Fragaszy & N. England, 2001. Prehension in infant capuchins (*Cebus apella*) from six weeks to twenty-four weeks: video analysis of form and symmetry. *American Journal of Primatology* 52, 55–60.

Anderson, J.R., 1990. Use of objects as hammers to open nuts by capuchin monkeys (*Cebus apella*). *Folia Primatologica* 54, 138–45.

Anderson, J.R. & M.-C. Henneman, 1994. Solutions to a tool-use problem in a pair of *Cebus apella*. *Mammalia* 58, 351–61.

Anderson, J.R., C. Degiorgio, C. Lamarque & J. Fagot, 1996. A multi-task assessment of hand lateralization in capuchin monkey (*Cebus apella*). *Primates* 37, 97–103.

Antinucci, F. & E. Visalberghi, 1986. Tool use in *Cebus apella*: a case study. *International Journal of Primatology* 7, 351–63.

Beck, B.B., 1980. *Animal Tool Behavior: the Use and Manufacture of Tools by Animals*. New York (NY): Garland Press.

Bergeson, D., 1996. The Positional Behavior and Prehensile Tail Use of *Alouatta palliata*, *Ateles geoffroyi*, and *Cebus capucinus*. Unpublished PhD thesis, Washington University, St Louis.

Boesch, C. & H. Boesch-Achermann, 2000. *The Chimpanzees of the Taï Forest*. Oxford: Oxford University Press.

Boinski, S., R.P. Quatrone & H. Swartz, 2001. Substrate and tool use by brown capuchins in Suriname: ecological contexts and cognitive bases. *American Anthropologist* 102, 741–61.

Boinski, S., K.S. Quatrone, L. Selvaggi, M. Henry, C.M. Stickler & L.M. Rose, 2003. Skilled foraging actions by brown capuchins in Suriname: are these socially supported and transmitted behavior?, in *Traditions in Non-human Animals: Models and Evidence*, eds. D.M. Fragaszy & S. Perry. Cambridge: Cambridge University Press, 365–90.

Christel, M.I. & D. Fragaszy, 2000. Manual function in *Cebus apella*: digital mobility, preshaping, and endurance in repetitive grasping. *International Journal of Primatology* 21, 697–719.

Costello, M.B. & D.M. Fragaszy, 1988. Prehension in *Cebus* and *Saimiri*, part I: Grip type and hand preference. *American Journal of Primatology* 15, 235–45.

Cummins-Sebree, S.E. & D.M. Fragaszy, 2005. Choosing and using tools: capuchins (*Cebus apella*) use a different metric than tamarins (*Saguinus oedipus*). *Journal of Comparative Psychology* 119, 210–19.

Cummins-Sebree, S.E. & D.M. Fragaszy, in prep. Capuchins can detect surface aberrations in a tool-use task.

Darwin, E., 1794. *Zoonomia or Laws of Organic Life*. London: J. Johnson.

Fernandes, E.B.M., 1991. Tool use and predation of oysters (*Crassostrea rhizophorae*) by the tufted capuchin, *Cebus apella apella*, in brackish water mangrove swamp. *Primates* 32, 529–31.

Fragaszy, D.M., 1990. Sex and age differences in the organization of behavior in wedge-capped capuchins, *Cebus olivaceus*. *Behavioral Ecology* 1, 81–94.

Fragaszy, D.M. & L.E. Adams-Curtis, 1991. Generative aspects of manipulation in tufted capuchin monkeys (*Cebus apella*). *Journal of Comparative Psychology* 105, 387–97.

Fragaszy, D.M. & S.R. Mitchell, 1990. Hand preference and performance on unimanual and bimanual tasks in capuchin monkeys (*Cebus apella*). *Journal of Comparative Psychology* 104, 275–82.

Fragaszy, D.M. & E. Visalberghi, 1989. Social influences on the acquisition of tool-using behaviors in tufted capuchin monkeys (*Cebus apella*). *Journal of Comparative Psychology* 103, 159–70.

Fragaszy, D.M. & E. Visalberghi, 1990. Social processes affecting the appearance of innovative behaviors in capuchin monkeys. *Folia Primatologica* 54, 155–65.

Fragaszy, D.M., J.M. Feuerstein & D. Mitra, 1997. Transfers of food from adults to infants in tufted capuchins (*Cebus apella*). *Journal of Comparative Psychology* 111, 194–200.

Fragaszy, D., K. Landau & K. Leighty, 2002. Inducing Traditions in Captive Capuchins, part I. Presented at the Biannual Meeting of the International Primatological Society, Beijing, China (August, 2002).

Fragaszy, D.M., E. Visalberghi & L. Fedigan, 2004. *The Complete Capuchin: the Biology of a Genus*. Cambridge: Cambridge University Press.

Gibson, J.J., 1979. *The Ecological Approach to Visual Perception*. Boston (MA): Houghton Mifflin.

Hauser, M.D., 1997. Artifactual kinds and functional design features: what a primate understands without language. *Cognition* 64, 285–308.

Janson, C.H. & S. Boinski, 1992. Morphological and behavioral adaptations for foraging in generalist primates: the case of the *Cebines*. *American Journal of Physical Anthropology* 88, 483–98.

Jones, S., R. Martin & D. Pilbeam, 1992. *The Cambridge Encyclopedia of Human Evolution*. Cambridge: Cambridge University Press.

Lacreuse, A. & D.M. Fragaszy, 1997. Manual exploratory procedures and asymmetries for a haptic search task: a comparison between capuchins (*Cebus apella*) and humans. *Laterality* 2, 247–66.

Lacreuse, A. & D. Fragaszy, 1999. Left hand preferences in capuchins (*Cebus apella*): role of spatial demands in manual activity. *Laterality* 4, 65–78.

Limongelli, L., M.G. Sonetti & E. Visalberghi, 1994. Hand preference of tufted capuchins (*Cebus apella*) in tool-using tasks, in *Current Primatology*, vol. III: *Behavioural Neuroscience, Physiology and Reproduction*, eds. J.R. Anderson, J.J. Roeder, B. Thierry & N. Herrenschmidt. Strasbourg: Université Louis Pasteur, 9–15.

Lockman, J.J., 2000. A perception–action perspective on tool use development. *Child Development* 71, 137–44.

Mannu, M., 2002. O uso espontâneo de ferramentas por macacos-prego (*Cebus apella*) em condições de semi-liberdade: Desçrição e demografia. Unpublished doctoral dissertation, University of São Paulo.

Matsuzawa, T., 2001. Primate foundations of human intelligence: a view of tool use in non-human primates and fossil hominids, in *Primate Origins of Human Cognition and Behavior*, eds. T. Matsuzawa. New York (NY): Springer-Verlag Publishing, 3–25.

McGrew, W.C. & L.F. Marchant, 1997. Using the tools at hand: manual laterality and elementary technology in *Cebus* spp. and *Pan* spp. *International Journal of Primatology* 18, 787–810.

Ottoni, E.B. & M. Mannu, 2001. Semi-free ranging tufted capuchin monkeys (*Cebus apella*) spontaneously use tools to crack open nuts. *International Journal of Primatology* 22, 347–58.

Oxford, P., 2003. Cracking monkeys. *BBC Wildlife* 21(2), 26–9.

Panger, M., 1998. Object-use in free-ranging white-faced capuchins (*Cebus capucinus*) in Costa Rica. *American Journal of Physical Anthropology* 106, 311–21.

Parr, L., W. Hopkins & F. de Waal, 1997. Haptic discrimination in capuchin monkeys: evidence of manual specialization. *Neuropsychologia* 35, 143–52.

Povinelli, D.J., 2000. *Folk Physics for Apes*. New York (NY): Oxford University Press.

Raven, P.H. & G.B. Johnson, 1992. *Biology*. 3rd edition. St Louis (MO): Mosby –Year Book, Inc.

Resende, B., P. Izar & E. Ottoni, 2003. Interaction between social play and nutcracking behavior in semifree tufted capuchin monkeys (*Cebus apella*). *Revista de Etologia* 5, 198–9.

Rose, L.M., 1994. Sex differences in diet and foraging behavior in white-faced capuchins (*Cebus capucinus*). *International Journal of Primatology* 15, 95–114.

Roux, V., B. Bril & G. Dietrich, 1995. Skills and learning difficulties involved in stone knapping: the case of stone-bead knapping in Khambhat, India. *World Archeology* 27, 63–87.

Savage-Rumbaugh, S.E., D.M. Rumbaugh & S. Boysen, 1978. Linguistically mediated tool use and exchange by chimpanzees (*Pan troglodytes*). *Behavioral and Brain Sciences* 1, 539–54.

Smitsman, A.W., 1997. The development of tool use: changing boundaries between organism and environment, in *Evolving Explanations of Development*, eds. C. Dent-Reed & P. Zukow-Goldring. Washington (DC): American Psychological Association, 301–29.

Spinozzi, G. & B. Cacchiarelli, 2000. Manual laterality in haptic and visual reaching tasks by tufted capuchin monkeys (*Cebus apella*): an association between hand preference and hand accuracy for food discrimination. *Neuropsychologia* 38, 1685–92.

Spinozzi, G. & V. Truppa, 1999. Hand preference in different tasks by tufted capuchin monkeys *Cebus apella*. *International Journal of Primatology* 20, 827–49.

Spinozzi, G. & V. Truppa, 2002. Problem-solving strategies and hand preferences for a multicomponent task by tufted capuchins (*Cebus apella*). *International Journal of Primatology* 23, 621–38.

Spinozzi, G., M.G. Castorina & V. Truppa, 1998. Hand preferences in unimanual and coordinated-bimanual tasks by tufted capuchin monkeys (*Cebus apella*). *Journal of Comparative Psychology* 112, 183–91.

Tomasello, M. & J. Call, 1997. *Primate Cognition*. New York (NY): Oxford University Press.

Visalberghi, E., 1997. Success and understanding in cognitive tasks: a comparison between *Cebus apella* and *Pan troglodytes*. *International Journal of Primatology* 18, 811–30.

Visalberghi, E. & D.M. Fragaszy, 1990. Do monkeys ape?, in *'Language' and Intelligence in Monkeys and Apes: Comparative Developmental Perspectives*, eds. S. Parker & K. Gibson. Cambridge: Cambridge University Press, 247–73.

Visalberghi, E. & D.M. Fragaszy, 1996. Pedagogy and imitation in monkeys: yes, no, or maybe?, in *The Handbook of Education and Human Development*, eds. D.R. Olson & N. Torrance. Cambridge (MA): Blackwell, 277–301.

Visalberghi, E. & D. Fragaszy, 1999. Tool use by monkeys and apes, in *The Biology of Behavior*, eds. P.P. Bateson & E. Alleva. Rome: Institute del la Enciclopedia Italia Treccani, IV, 209–18.

Visalberghi, E. & D. Fragaszy, in press. Tool use: a challenge for capuchins, a challenge for us, in *Comparative Cognition: Experimental Explorations of Animal Intelligence*, eds. E. Wasserman & T. Zentall. Oxford: Oxford University Press.

Visalberghi, E. & C. Néel, 2003. Tufted capuchins (*Cebus apella*) use of sound and weight to optimise their choice between full and empty nuts. *Ecological Psychology* 15, 215–28.

Westergaard, G.C. & D.M. Fragaszy, 1987. The manufacture and use of tools by capuchin monkeys (*Cebus apella*). *Journal of Comparative Psychology* 101, 159–68.

Westergaard, G.C. & S.J. Suomi, 1993. Hand preferences in the use of nut-cracking tools by tufted capuchin monkeys (*Cebus apella*). *Folia Primatologica* 61, 38–42.

Westergaard, G.C. & S.J. Suomi, 1994. A simple stone-tool technology in monkeys. *Journal of Human Evolution* 27, 399–404.

Westergaard, G.C. & S.J. Suomi, 1995. The stone tools of capuchins (*Cebus apella*). *International Journal of Primatology* 16, 1017–24.

Westergaard, G.C. & S.J. Suomi, 1997. Transfer of tools and food between groups of tufted capuchins (*Cebus paella*). *American Journal of Primatology* 43, 33–41.

Westergaard, G.C., J.A. Greene, M.A. Babitz & S.J. Suomi, 1995. Pestle use and modification by tufted capuchins (*Cebus apella*). *International Journal of Primatology* 16, 643–51.

Westergaard, G.C., A.L. Lundquist, H.E. Kuhn & S.J. Suomi, 1997. Ant-gathering with tools by captive tufted capuchins (*Cebus apella*). *International Journal of Primatology* 18, 95–104.

Westergaard, G.C., H.E. Kuhn & S.J. Suomi, 1998a. Laterality of hand function in tufted capuchin monkeys (*Cebus apella*): comparison between tool use actions and spontaneous non-tool actions. *Ethology* 104, 119–25.

Westergaard, G.C., C.L.T.J. Chavanne & S.J. Suomi, 1998b. Token-mediated tool-use by tufted capuchin monkey (*Cebus apella*). *Animal Cognition* 1, 101–6.

Wilson, F.R., 1998. *The Hand: How its Use Shapes the Brain, Language, and Human Culture*. New York (NY): Pantheon Books.

Youlatos, D., 1999. Tail-use in capuchin monkeys. *Neotropical primates* 7, 16–20.

Part II

Stone Knapping:
the Necessary Conditions for the Required Skills

Section A

The Bio-behavioural System

Chapter 13

Dynamic Interactions between Posture, Handedness, and Bimanual Coordination in Human Infants: Why Stone Knapping might be a Uniquely Hominin Behaviour

Daniela Corbetta

In this chapter, we present an evolutionary scenario that may have contributed to the development of stone-knapping skills in early hominins. This scenario relies on findings in human infants and non-human primates revealing that preferred patterns of two-handed coordination and hand preference are dynamically linked to preferred patterns of locomotion. Specifically, these findings show that stronger handedness and stable bimanual coordination are better achieved when an upright posture is adopted, or when bipedal locomotion has become the preferred mode of locomotion (as opposed to quadrupedal locomotion). We relate these findings to some major postural adaptations that followed the emergence of bipedalism in early hominins. We argue that these bipedal postural adaptations that occurred during early human prehistory have contributed to create favourable bio-behavioural conditions from which stone-knapping skills have evolved.

The emergence of stone-tool manufacture during the Palaeolithic marked an important and unique transition in human evolution. Not only did its appearance in our prehistoric ancestry unquestionably reflect the development of novel cognitive and motor competencies, but it also paved the way to a wide array of future skills and technological developments that were utilized in conjunction with hunting, food handling, and other tool production, to cite a few examples. How did such crucial tool-manufacturing skills emerge? What were the conditions or circumstances that led to the appearance of such a remarkable technological advance? Can we trace the origins of stone-knapping skills to other crucial events or critical transitions in human evolution that took place prior to the emergence of stone knapping? And why should stone knapping be considered a uniquely hominin behaviour?

In this chapter, we attempt to answer to these questions by delineating an *evolutionary scenario* that may have taken place early during the Pliocene — prior to the emergence of stone knapping — and may have contributed to create *favourable bio-behavioural conditions* from which stone-knapping skills

in early hominins may have evolved. In particular, we report evidence suggesting that these *favourable bio-behavioural conditions* may have originated from and gradually formed following the emergence and adoption of the upright bipedal posture about 6 to 4 million years ago.

Rooting the origins of stone-knapping skills to the emergence of bipedalism is not new. Several authors already proposed many evolutionary accounts linking the development of novel manual functions, manual specialization, and tool use to the transition and adoption of upright locomotion in early hominins (see for example Corballis 1991; Frost 1980; Hewes 1961; 1964; Hunt 1994; Leroi-Gourhan 1964; Lewin 1998; Lovejoy 1981; MacNeilage *et al.* 1987; Marshack 1984; Marzke 1996). One common denominator of these previous accounts rests on the underlying assumption that adopting the bipedal posture allowed freeing the hands from their locomotor's role, which in turn set the stage for developing increasingly-sophisticated manual skills, and thereby promoting novel societal activities and tool manufacture. Here, we elaborate on this link between the emergence of

PREMISE

Stone knapping requires the development of stable
dynamic interactions between three behavioural components

Fine bimanual
coordination

Stable
posture

Clear
division of labour

Stability at all three levels must be met in order to attain *stable
dynamic interactions* between these cooperating behavioural levels

Figure 13.1. *The three cooperating behavioural components underlying
the act of stone knapping. (Picture of stone knapper is from Roux (2000),
reprinted with permission.)*

the erect posture and the development of sophisticated
manual skills. In particular, we use recent findings
from research in human development and non-human
primates to provide a mechanistic account for why the
transition to upright locomotion may have been such
a significant trigger in the formation of finer manual
coordination and the development of stone knapping
in human prehistory.

Our account rests on one fundamental premise:
to perform precise two-handed movements — such as
hitting a stone repeatedly at specific controlled angles
to shape it into a tool — one must have developed
stable dynamic interactions between three fundamental
and necessary behavioural components (see Fig. 13.1).
First, one must have developed a steady posture, in
order to provide a firm and balanced anchorage to
such dexterous and ballistic manual activities. *Second,*
one must have established clear hand preferences (or
stable division of role between hands) in order to use
manual actions in a complementary fashion, according
to their respective specialized functions (e.g. holding
and hitting). And *third,* one must have the potential
to achieve fine bimanual coordination between hands
in order to time, sequence, and modulate the action of
each hand in concert and in relation to one another. This
fundamental premise requires thus, that stability at all
three levels must be met in order to attain overall *stable
dynamic interactions* between these cooperating behavioural levels. Such stable interactions between posture,

handedness, and coordination are
necessary to allow the development
and achievement of finely-controlled
and sophisticated bimanual tasks such
as knapping a stone. Here we report
data suggesting that such interactive
stability between body/trunk, arms
coordination, and laterality can be
achieved specifically following the
emergence and adoption of the erect
posture.

To support our thesis, we rely on
findings with human infants and non-
human primates showing congruent
interactions between posture and
manual laterality in tasks requiring
reaching and two-handed coordination. *First,* we present data from our
own research on the development of
bimanual coordination, hand preference, and transitions in posture and
locomotion in human infants during
their first year of life. We show that
the stability of two-handed coordination and the lateral organization of
the upper limbs change as infants learn to sit, crawl
and walk. Of particular interest, we report results
depicting that the establishment of clear directions in
hand preferences and specializations begins to form
steadily and strengthens following the emergence of
upright locomotion.

Second, we review recent findings in non-human
primates' laterality and posture, which similarly reveal
that solving manual tasks while in an upright position
leads to greater indexes of hand preference compared
to solving the same tasks while in a quadrupedal
position. Together, the human infant and non-human
primate studies congruently reveal that specific patterns of manual coordination and lateralization are
dynamically linked to the adoption of particular and
preferred postural locomotor's modes. Specifically,
they reveal that bipedal forms of locomotion facilitate
the formation and organization of stable lateralized
bimanual coordination, whereas quadrupedal forms
do not lead to comparable behavioural outcomes.

Finally, we draw some parallels between these
findings and some archaeological artefacts in human
prehistory. We discuss the implications of this body
of evidence for human evolution and elaborate on
the possible underlying brain mechanisms that may
account for the body/trunk and arm interactions observed in human infants and non-human primates.
We propose, from an evolutionary perspective, that
such mechanisms may have played a significant role

following the emergence and adoption of the erect posture in early hominins, providing critical bio-behavioural foundations upon which stable dynamic interactions between body/trunk and arm activity have developed. We also argue that stone knapping may have evolved to a degree of fine and sophisticated manual specialization only in hominins, because only hominins truly adopted and maintained a fully-erect posture as their preferred mode of locomotion and postural organization.

Part I: Handedness, bimanual coordination, and postural transitions in human infants

In the first year of life, human infants develop an impressive array of fundamental motor skills in a very short time. From about the age of four months, infants begin to control their arms and hands to perform voluntary behaviours such as reaching for and manipulating objects. Shortly after, they learn to sit on their own, and next, they become increasingly mobile, first by crawling on their belly or four limbs, and then by adopting an erect posture and walking. This rapid developmental succession offers unique opportunities to study how newly-emerging behaviours interact and are integrated with other formerly-acquired skills. For example, one can ask how newly-emerging modes of locomotion interrelate with previously-acquired manual skills.

In recent years, my colleagues and I engaged in a series of longitudinal studies with human infants with the specific purpose to capture and study changes in manual activity as a function of early locomotion development. We wanted to investigate whether the development of early hand preference and two-handed coordination over the first year of life revealed identifiable periods of transition in manual coordination. We also wanted to determine whether these observed transitions in hand preference and coordination were linked to successive postural reorganizations as infants learned to sit, crawl, and walk. We were interested in studying this question because we knew from previous research that human handedness and manual coordination are quite unstable in early development (Carlson & Harris 1985; Corbetta & Thelen 1996; 1999; Gesell & Ames 1947; McManus et al. 1988). Handedness, in particular, becomes a strong, lasting, and easily identifiable behavioural asymmetry from early childhood. However, during infancy, preferred hand use tends to shift and alternate between hands numerous times before settling into a preferred direction (Corbetta & Thelen 1996; 1999; Gesell & Ames 1947). This is especially true during the months following the emergence of reaching for objects. As a result of these findings, researchers argued that hand

preference can remain unstable up to three years old and beyond, despite infants' growing proficiency at manipulating objects (Gesell & Ames 1947; McManus et al. 1988).

The question that really interested us was why infants' early manual preferences fluctuated so much between left-, right-, and two-handed use before settling into a preferred direction. Some preliminary observations suggested that these fluctuations might have been related to postural reorganizations as infants acquired new fundamental motor milestones (Corbetta & Thelen 1996; 1999). In that work, we noted that infants' initial and apparent preferred manual biases dissipated when they began to crawl on hands-and-knees, and that bimanual coupling in reaching returned when infants began to walk upright on their own. Nonetheless, because these early observations were performed with a very small infant sample, we were uncertain of the generalizability of our findings. The research we review in the next sections reflects our follow-up attempts to assess more systematically and more reliably whether successive postural reorganizations and manual activities occurring over the first year of life interact with one another over developmental time. Most of the findings summarized here have already been published in two reports (Corbetta & Bojczyk 2002; Corbetta & Thelen 2002). These previous publications provide a more thorough review of some of the developmental issues discussed here.

Coordination and hand preference in pre-locomotor infants: establishing a baseline

All the longitudinal studies we summarize hereafter were performed using a task commonly known in developmental psychology as the 'object-retrieval task'. In this task, infants first watch an experimenter place an attractive toy inside a container; then, after a short time, the infants are allowed to retrieve the toy. The container we adopted for our studies was a plastic box equipped with a hinged lid (see Fig. 13.2). Once closed, the lid of the box would not lock, such that infants could manage to open it. For the young infants, one major difficulty of this task resided in discovering how to coordinate and sequence the movements to open the lid, hold it open with one hand, while retrieving the toy inside the box with the other hand as illustrated on Figure 13.2. Indeed, previous research demonstrated that before the age of eight months, infants usually fail at retrieving the toy from such boxes, precisely because they have difficulties at coordinating and using their hands differentially (Bojczyk & Corbetta 2004; Bruner 1970; Diamond 1991; Fagard & Pezé 1997). One goal of our research was to document the movement strategies that the infants

Figure 13.2. *The object-retrieval task used in the developmental studies reported in this chapter.*

used to retrieve the toy out of the container as they learned to master the task.

This task offered a number of advantages for addressing our developmental questions. First, by using infants younger than eight months and by following them over time, we were able to document progress in interlimb coordination and manual preference, and determine when infants would learn to sequence and differentiate their hands' activities effectively to retrieve the toy out of the box. Second, because this task required differential and complementary two-handed coordination to retrieve the toy, it allowed us to document, within and between sessions, whether infants used consistent, stable hand roles to perform each particular movement phase in the object retrieval process. Finally, because this is a task that infants enjoy performing until early in their second year of life, it was possible to use it with older infants as well in order to assess whether coordination and division of hand roles would change as infants became increasingly mobile.

In this section, we report findings from an initial study that we performed with pre-locomotor infants who were 6^1/$_2$ months old at the time they were recruited. Because none of these infants were crawling or were in any way mobile at the onset of the study, they provided us with a behavioural baseline of coordination skills and manual preferences existing prior to the emergence of any form of self-produced locomotion. This longitudinal sample comprised a total of twelve infants. They came to our Infant Motor Development Laboratory at Purdue University every week for a period of two to three months, depending on infants' individual rate of learning in solving the task. Every week, we screened

their sitting abilities and assessed their mobility skills to detect eventual changes in their overall capacity to control their body and move around. Also, every week, infants were exposed to the object-retrieval task using the same procedure as follows (see also Bojczyk & Corbetta 2004 for more details on the procedure).

At their arrival to the laboratory, infants were comfortably seated on a specially-designed infant seat that provided stability and support to the trunk, while leaving the infant's arms free to move. An experimenter placed in front of the child a small table, the top surface of which reached the infant waist level. The testing box was then placed open, on top of the table, and out of the infant's reach. Testing began with the experimenter facing the infant from the other side of the table, and showing the child a colourful and attractive rattle. The experimenter put the attractive rattle in the box and closed the lid while the infant watched. Next, the experimenter closed the box and pushed it toward the infant's reaching space at midline, and the child was given one minute to retrieve the toy. If the infant successfully retrieved the toy, or failed to retrieve the toy within that one-minute time window, the box would be pulled back, and a new trial would be performed. Infants were exposed to a total of six trials each week. At each new trial, the experimenter used a new rattle to maintain the infants' attention and interest in the task whether they succeeded or not at retrieving the toy. All rattles used in the study were easily graspable with one hand and were symmetrically shaped. They were also always placed at the centre of the box to prevent any biases that could have influenced infants' choice of hand use. Finally, all infants were followed over time every week until they were able to retrieve the toy out of the box using bimanual complementary strategies with good timing between hands (as illustrated on Fig. 13.2) and were able to maintain that level of performance on five out six trials over three consecutive weeks. When that behavioural criterion was met we ended our weekly observations for that infant.

In our analyses, we categorized infant's coordination responses: 1) as *failure*, when infants did not succeed in taking the toy out of the box within the one-minute exposure to the task; 2) as *unimanual*, when they used the same hand to open the box and retrieve the toy; and 3) as *bimanual with weak or good timing*, when they used both hands in a complemen-

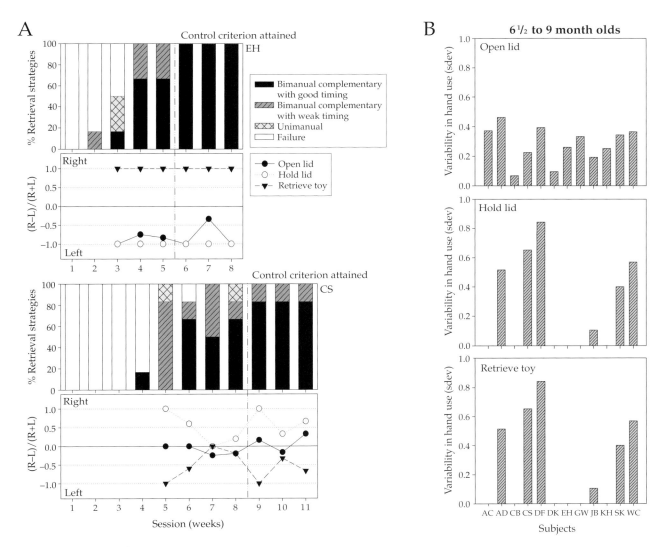

Figure 13.3. *A) Exemplars of developmentally-stable (top) and relatively-stable (bottom) patterns of hand use in two young non-crawling infants, EH and CS, while learning to solve the object retrieval task across the consecutive weekly sessions. Each bar graph reports the rate of success and type of bimanual patterns used to retrieve the toy from the box as a function of the weekly sessions. The line graphs underneath the bar graphs report which hand was used by these infants for opening the box, holding the lid, and retrieving the toy during the same developmental period. B) Overall variability in hand use for opening the box, holding the lid, and retrieving the toy computed over the entire study sessions for each individual infant in the $6^1/_2$- to 9-months-old group.*

tary fashion to open the box and hold the lid open with one hand, while retrieving the toy with the other hand (good or weak timing depended on the level of coordination interference between hands). Additionally, for the unimanual and bimanual behavioural categories, we coded which hand(s) — right, left, or both — were used for opening the lid, holding the lid, and retrieving the toy (see also Corbetta & Thelen 2002).

Figure 13.3A reports the developmental changes in bimanual coordination and division of hand roles over the session time in two exemplar infants, EH and

CS, until they reached the end of study criterion. The stacked bars on top report the frequency of coordination categories used by the infants to retrieve the object out of the box as a function of the consecutive sessions. The corresponding line graphs below report for each session a frequency index of preferred hand use for each movement phase in retrieving the object, namely, which hand was used for opening the lid, for holding the lid open, and for retrieving the toy.

The stacked bars on Figure 13.3A show that both infants failed initially. Within a few sessions, however, and after they managed to retrieve the toy out of the box once (on week two for EH and on week four for CS), they both developed effective interlimb coordination with good timing in a few weeks. The corresponding line graphs reveal that despite early timing difficulties in coordination before attaining criterion, both infants displayed quite clear division of hand roles over time. The straight lines in EH's graph indicate that she was very consistent, within and between sessions, at opening and holding the lid with her left hand, while retrieving the toy with her right hand. CS's fluctuating lines reveal that he was a bit more variable in his hand use, but preferred hand use was still identifiable over the session time; CS opened the box with two hands, then, most of the time, held the lid with his right hand while retrieving the toy with his left hand.

EH's and CS's performances on the object retrieval task were typical of what most infants did in this study. All infants acquired two-handed coordination with good timing within $1^1/_2$ to $2^1/_2$ months from the onset of the study (Bojczyk & Corbetta 2004) and all infants displayed and maintained relatively identifiable preferred hand use and division of hand roles throughout the study. Figure 13.3B reports the overall index of variability in hand use across sessions by infant and by movement phases during object retrieval. These data show that for the movement phases that required complementary activity (i.e. holding the lid while retrieving the toy), seven out of the twelve infants displayed no or very little variability in hand use over time. Like EH, on Figure 13.3A, these infants consistently used the same hand to hold the lid and the opposite hand to retrieve the toy throughout the study.

The five other infants on Figure 13.3B, with greater variability bars for holding and retrieving, were more like infant CS. Over session time, these infants tended to display identifiable preferred hand uses for holding the lid and retrieving the toy, but their preferred hand uses were not as consistent and as steady as for the seven other infants. Indeed, these five infants sometimes alternated hand roles within and between sessions, similar to CS on Figure 13.3A.

We were curious to find out if these differences in performance variability were related to the emergence of self-produced locomotion. We were aware that some infants began to crawl on hands-and-knees before they attained our good timing movement criterion. Thus, we looked at our records of postural screening that we performed every week to assess which and when infants began to become mobile. We found that the seven infants, who displayed consistent preferred hand use over time, only averaged 2.2 weeks of crawling experience before they reached the

end of study criterion. The five infants, who displayed more variable hand use over time, displayed 7.8 weeks of crawling experience before the end of the study. These findings were interesting because, consistent with a previous study (Corbetta & Thelen 1999), they indicated that a decline in preferred hand use could be associated with the emergence of crawling. To verify such hypothesis, we embarked on a similar study, however with crawling infants aged eight to thirteen months old. We predicted that these infants should not show preferred hand biases.

Coordination and hand preference in crawling and walking infants

Human infants become mobile around eight to nine months old. First, they begin to crawl on their belly or hands-and-knees, then, as they are able to move closer to the furniture in their home environment, they pull up to stand and begin to cruise in an upright position using the furniture as their support to reach other places (see Gabbard 2004). Eventually, they will let go of the furniture and take their first independent steps. In performing a second study with infants aged eight to thirteen months old, we wanted to track these progressive changes in self-produced locomotion and determine if they were matching changes in hand preference and coordination in reaching and object-retrieval tasks. In particular, we wanted to investigate whether infants' preferred hand use would dissipate during their crawling period as suggested by our previous studies, and we wanted to assess whether hand preference would eventually reappear once infants would adopt an upright posture and become independent walkers.

To address these goals, we followed ten infants — again on a weekly basis — from the time they were about eight months old, up to the time they walked independently for about two months (Corbetta & Bojczyk 2002). At every session and similarly to the previous study: 1) we screened each infant's posture and locomotor progresses; 2) we tested their bimanual coordination skills and hand preference with the same object-retrieval task while they were seated in an infant chair; and 3) we asked them to reach for small one-handed and large two-handed objects at midline also while seated. Additionally, when infants began to walk independently, we enticed them to traverse a 3-m-long surface in order to capture their walking cadence and identify their arm positions during walking. Indeed, young walkers who have precarious balance control tend to walk keeping their arms up, in a high guard position. As they gain balance control, they eventually lower their arms along their body sides. We tracked arm position during walking because we hypothesized that hand preference might reemerge when infants would

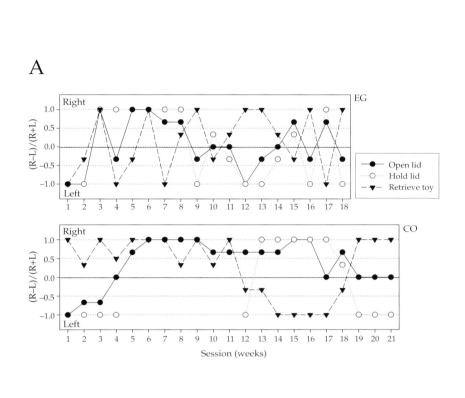

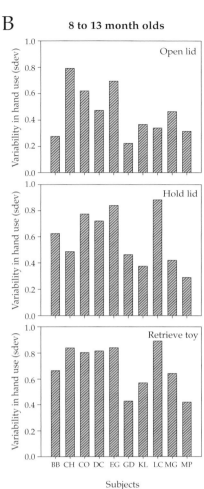

Figure 13.4. *A) Exemplars of developmentally-unstable patterns of hand use in two older crawling infants, EG and CO, while solving the object-retrieval task during consecutive weekly sessions. B) Overall variability in hand use for opening the box, holding the lid, and retrieving the toy computed over the entire study sessions for each individual infant in the eight- to thirteen-month-old group.*

lower their arms and display better balance control in upright locomotion. Additionally, change in arm height during progress in walking proficiency could easily be matched to the patterns of coordination and hand preference displayed by the infants over the same developmental period. Below, we first report data in preferred hand use in relation to hands-and-knees crawling, and then we discuss interlimb coordination changes in relation to the onset of upright locomotion.

a) Does hand preference dissipate when infants are crawling?
Most infants from this study were crawling or began to crawl on hands-and-knees shortly after they were recruited. These infants were also able to retrieve the toy out the box from the first sessions and, on average, they achieved coordination using bimanual complementary patterns with good timing within three to four weeks from the onset of the study (Corbetta &

Bojczyk 2002). Were their movement patterns showing a clear and steady division of hand roles as the infants in the previous group?

Figure 13.4A reports the developmental changes in hand use over the session time in two exemplar infants, EG and CO, for the portions of the task involving opening of the lid, holding the lid, and retrieving the toy. Figure 13.4B reports the overall index of variability in hand use over the different successive sessions by infant and by movement phases for the whole group. Although these infants did not have difficulties retrieving the toy out of the box successfully from the first session, they displayed much more variable movement patterns in regard to hand preference than the previous group of infants. The data from both infants EG and CO clearly illustrate that they did not adopt consistent preferred hand use over time for any of the movement phases. Both EG and CO changed and shifted hand use

Reaching for Small Objects
Lid Opening

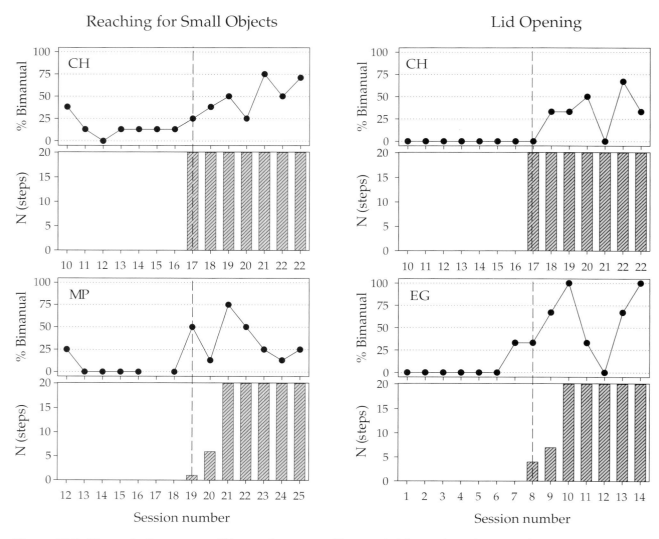

Figure 13.5. *Change in the per cent of bimanual responses (line graphs) for reaching for small objects (left panel) and opening the lid of the box (right panel) in three infants, MP, CH, and EG, during seven weeks prior to the emergence of upright locomotion and seven weeks following the onset of upright locomotion. The bar graphs represent the number of independent steps that infants performed each week before and after beginning to walk.*

almost continuously within and between sessions for most of the duration of the study. The overall indexes of hand-use variability per infant displayed in Figure 13.4B reveal that all infants in this group produced much more variable hand-use responses over time. Statistical analyses comparing response variability between this group and the previous group of younger infants confirmed that hand use in this older group was significantly more variable in all movement phases than in the previous group of non-crawling infants (Unpaired *t*-tests for: Opening, $t(20) = 2.65$, $p < .01$; Holding, $t(20) = 2.81$, $p < .01$; Retrieving, $t(20) = 3.86, p < .001$). In sum, the findings from this second study were consistent with our prediction that hand preference tends to dissipate when infants begin to crawl on

hands and knees (see also Corbetta & Thelen 2002). What happens when infants abandon crawling as a preferred mode of locomotion, adopt an upright posture and begin to walk independently? Would hand preference and steady division of hand roles reemerge?

b) Hand preference and the onset of upright locomotion infants
Because we tracked infants' postural progression on a regular basis, we were able to identify for each infant the exact week during which they began to produce their first unsupported independent steps. Here we present data illustrating how response patterns in reaching and object retrieval changed around the walking transition. Note, however, that the story here is a

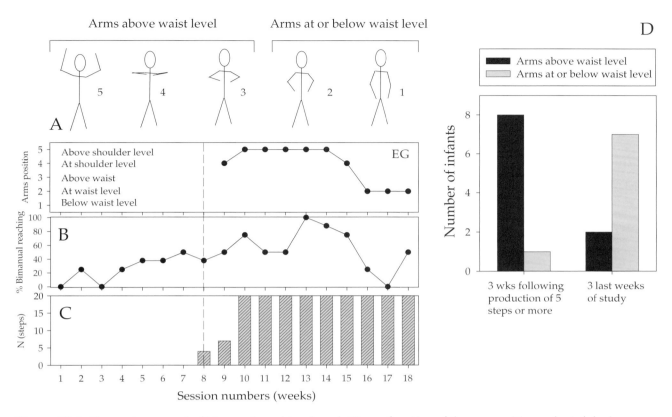

Figure 13.6. *Change in per cent of bimanual reaching (graph B) as a function of the arm positions adopted during walking (graph A) in one infant, EG, during the entire period of the study. Graph C displays the session at which walking emerged and reports following progress in walking as frequency of steps. Graph D reports the number of infants who held their arms above or below waist level while walking during three weeks following the onset of walking and the three last weeks of the study.*

little bit more complicated because of task interactions that occurred with this postural transition. In particular, we found that changes in upper-arm coordination differed depending on whether the task involved *simple reaching* or *bimanual complementary hand roles*.

Infants performed *simple reaching* tasks when they extended their arms to attain an object presented at their midline or when they aimed for the lid of the box to open it. Either task could be performed successfully with either one- or two-handed symmetrical movements. We observed that prior to walking, infants tended to use one hand for reaching for small toys or for opening the lid of the box. However, when they began to walk independently, infants began to use more symmetrical two-handed movements for performing the same tasks. This increase in bimanual coupling occurred right around the transition of independent walking and lasted between four to ten weeks depending on the infants (Corbetta & Bojczyk 2002).

This increase in bimanual coupling for reaching for small objects and for opening the lid is depicted in Figure 13.5 as a function of walking onset for four in-

dividual infants. The line graphs describe the percent of bimanual responses per session produced during a 7-week period prior to the emergence of independent upright locomotion and during the next seven-week period following the emergence of independent walking. The bar graphs below indicate the sessions at which infants began to walk and how many independent steps they produced thereafter. As shown, on average, infants displayed a relatively greater rate of two-handed reaching after walking onset, relative to prior to walking onset. This increase in bimanual coupling in reaching and lid opening following walking onset resulted in statistically-significant differences for each task when measured on the whole group of ten infants (see full report in Corbetta & Bojczyk 2002).

These two-handed responses in reaching began to decline when infants became relatively stable walkers and were more proficient at controlling their upright balance. Recall that we monitored progress in balance control by capturing infant's arm height position in relation to their body. Usually, when infants begin to perform their first steps, they tend to maintain their

195

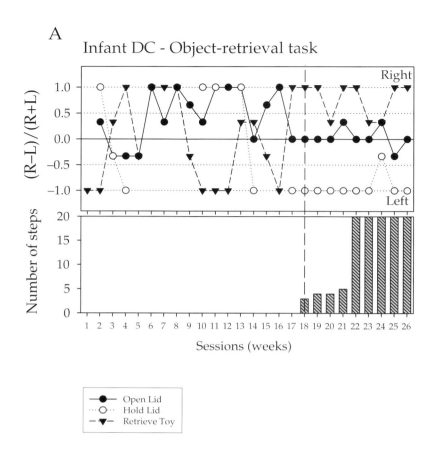

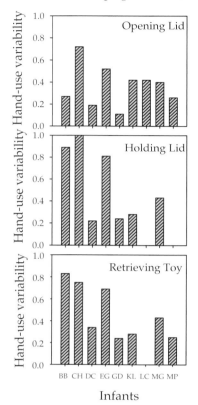

Figure 13.7. *A) Exemplar of patterns of hand use of one infant, DC, while solving the object-retrieval task throughout the consecutive weekly sessions (top graph). These patterns of coordination are displayed as a function of the emergence of walking (bottom graph). B) Overall variability in hand use for opening the box, holding the lid, and retrieving the toy computed for each individual infant in the eight- to thirteen-month-old group for the post-locomotor period only.*

arms in a high guard position. Their arms are up, at or above shoulder level as illustrated in the stick figures 5 and 4 in Figure 13.6A. But as infants become better walkers and are more proficient at controlling their equilibrium, they tend to lower their arms along the sides of their body. Interestingly, we discovered that infants also began to resume more frequent one-handed reaching patterns once they began to lower their arms during walking and displayed better upright balance control. An example of that developmental change is illustrated in Figure 13.6, for one infant, EG. Figure 13.6 overlays on top of each other and as a function of session time: a) the developmental changes in arm position during walking; b) the developmental changes in bimanual reaching for small objects; and c) the number of independent steps performed at the different sessions. This figure shows that when this infant, EG, began to lower her arms along her body sides during the last three weeks of the study, her bimanual coupling in reaching also began to decline. When we compared

the arm position of the different infants during the three first weeks following walking onset and the last three weeks of the study, we noticed a similar shift (see Fig. 13.6D). This shift in arm position during walking was statistically significant and was accompanied by a lower rate of two-handed reaching in most infants (see Corbetta & Bojczyk 2002).

These data support our general hypothesis that the organization of the upper-arm system interacts dynamically with the formation and acquisition of novel postural configurations as infants learn to develop new modes of locomotion. With the onset of early walking, the manual-coordination pattern that emerged was one of upper-arm coupling, while the one we described previously with the appearance of hands-and-knees crawling was one of alternated hand use. Yet, as we mentioned earlier, the demands of the tasks also played a role in this developmental scenario. We observed an increase in upper-arm coupling in simple reaching with walking because reaching can still be successfully achieved with two-handed symmetrical responses. But what happens when the task requires bimanual complementary activity, and bimanual coupling cannot lead to success?

Infants had to perform such bimanual *complementary activity* in the object-retrieval task when they had to hold the lid with one hand, while retrieving the toy with the other hand. Indeed, to achieve such movement patterns they needed to dissociate (not couple) the activity of each hand. We discovered that, under those specific tasks constraints, six out of the ten infants who did not display stable division of hand role prior to walking, resumed a clearer division of hand role when retrieving the object out of the box following the onset of upright locomotion and despite increased coupling in simple reaching. Figure 13.7A illustrates this developmental change in division of hand roles in object retrieval over the session time and as a function of walking onset in one infant, DC, for opening the lid, holding the lid, and retrieving the toy. Figure 13.7B reports the overall index of variability in hand use over the different successive sessions for each of the ten infants by movement phase, but for the *post-walking period only*.

Figure 13.7A reveals that, prior to walking onset, when DC was still crawling, he did not display any obvious preferred hand roles for opening, holding the lid, and retrieving the toy, as discussed earlier in this chapter. Following the emergence of upright locomotion, however, his movement patterns changed. From week 17, that is, right before he began to walk, DC began to reach for and open the lid with two hands, thus displaying more arm coupling for simple reaching. In Figure 13.7A, we can see that from week 17, the black solid line corresponding to the hand(s) used for opening the lid reached a value of zero, meaning that from that time, DC began to open the lid with two hands for several weeks in a row. Yet, following the onset of upright locomotion, he also began to adopt a clearer division of hand roles for the portion of the object retrieval task that required decoupling between hand activities. Indeed, DC's data in Figure 13.7A reveal that from week 17, again just prior to walking independently, he began to use his left hand fairly consistently for holding the lid open, while using his right hand for retrieving the toy out of the box. We detected a similar emergence of division in hand roles in five other infants. This can be seen in Figure 13.7B where the variability indexes in hand use for opening and holding the lid, and retrieving the toy, computed over *the period following the onset of upright locomotion* is reported for all ten infants. These data show that six out the ten infants notably decreased variability in hand use in object retrieval in their post-walking period compared to the same data reported in Figure

13.4B, which included hand use for the entire period of the study. This decrease in hand-use variability was not a significant one given that it occurred only in 60 per cent of our population, nonetheless, it is interesting to note that such an increase in division of hand-role stability did not have to occur for the infants to be successful at retrieving the toy. Those infants could have continued to solve the task by alternating hand roles like they did prior to walking. Moreover, there were no specific directional constraints in the task that forced them at that particular point in time to change movement organization; the change that we know has occurred during that period was the emergence of upright locomotion. This finding suggests that adopting an erect posture and developing bipedal locomotion imposed new biomechanical constraints on the motor system, which in turn may have facilitated the adoption of preferred lateralized two-handed use configurations, and favoured the establishment of preferred hand roles. However, with the present data we cannot be fully conclusive that such an interpretation is correct. To address that particular issue, and to better understand this relationship between walking and hand preference, we are currently conducting follow-up studies using advanced computer-based technology to record gait patterns, capture changes in ground-force reactions, and document arm positions during standing and early walking.

Brief discussion of the human infant data

The developmental data that we presented so far with human infants provided some evidence that postural transitions associated with the acquisition and development of early forms of locomotion interacted with the lateral organization and coordination of upper-arm activity. In particular, our data revealed that the developmental instabilities in hand preferences and coordination that are typical of early human development were not occurring randomly; rather, they fluctuated as a function of successive postural reorganizations as infants learned to sit, crawl, and walk.

We also found that a second factor played a role in pattern formation. This factor was linked to the task demands, and to whether the task required some collaboration between hands or not (this was particularly apparent in our last study on the transition to walking). Such task effects in the stability and strength of hand-use preference have been widely acknowledged by a number of researchers, especially in relation to adult and toddler populations (see for example, Fagard & Marks 2000; Oldfield 1971; Steenhuis & Bryden 1989). In early development, however, it is important to stress that these task effects may be modulated by the postural reorganizations that are taking place during the first year of life. The findings we reported here clearly revealed that even within a same highly practised task — an object-retrieval task requiring complementary hand roles at all times — forms of hand-use patterning could vary. These variations appeared to be linked to the level of posturo-locomotor achievements that were practised by the infants at the different developmental stages. Indeed, pre-locomotor infants, crawlers, and young walkers all revealed different organizational forms of hand use when solving the object-retrieval task. This suggests that postural reorganizations and the preferred modes of locomotion adopted by the infants at the different stages of their development may have to some extent interacted with the specific constraints imposed by the task. Specifically, it is plausible that the preferred mode of locomotion that infants adopted and heavily practised at certain periods of their development may have influenced in specific ways the organization and coordination of their upper-arm system (see also Corbetta & Bojczyk 2002; Corbetta & Thelen 2002). Hence, while sitting and lack of mobility may have facilitated the production of stable division of functions between hands, the emergence of crawling on hands and knees and the predominant use of alternated hand patterns during locomotion may have led infants to also alternate patterns of hand use in object retrieval and reaching.

Finally, when infants began to walk and adopted high and tightly-coupled arm positions during walking, they also increased upper arm coupling in reaching and opening the lid, as long as the task permitted arm coupling as a mean to the solution. We saw that this coupling declined when infants displayed better balance control during walking and lowered their arms along the body sides. What may happen later when infants truly overcome and master upright locomotion cannot be fully answered with our data because we did not follow infants long enough to document further changes in hand preference and coordination. Nonetheless, based on our preliminary findings on the return of lateralized division of hand roles following the onset of upright locomotion in some infants, as well as additional developmental reports from other researchers, we can hypothesize that hand preference in early childhood truly begins to form and stabilize following the transition to upright locomotion. The transition to upright locomotion is indeed the last major postural reorganization that infants need to achieve to reach a fully-erect posture and become independent walkers. Given that our data revealed systematic and coherent interactions between posture and manual organization prior to walking upright, it is possible that the absence of continuing

postural reorganizations following the emergence of the erect posture might lead to the stabilization of handedness in coordination. Some data reported by other researchers would be consistent with such interpretation. McManus and colleagues (McManus *et al.* 1988), for example, have argued that the direction of hand preference becomes clearly established around three years of age. It is interesting to note that stabilization occurs after toddlers have had time to practice and improve their upright locomotion. Recently, a study conducted by Fagard & Mark (2000) with infants aged 18 to 36 months, revealed that preferred hand use grew and increased steadily throughout this age range. Again, this is the age range during which young toddlers make steady progress in independent walking (Bril & Brenière 1992). Finally, in a study by Bonvillian *et al.* (1997), it was found that infants who developed and went through their fundamental motor milestones faster also developed a stable hand preference earlier. Together, our longitudinal data and findings from these reports are consistent with the argument that the establishment of clear directions in hand preferences and specializations of functions may begin to form steadily following the emergence of upright locomotion or after infants have attained and achieved their last major motor milestone in their progressive conquest of our species-specific erect posture.

What are the implications of such findings for human evolution? One way to expand on this question is to turn to and examine the non-human primate literature. Non-human primates can use and coordinate their hands in many ways to solve tasks requiring bimanual collaboration, but their preferred mode of locomotion is not an upright one, it is a quadrupedal one. How do our infants' data compare with the literature on non-human primates' posture, coordination, and hand preference? Can we find some regularity across species that could help us sketch an evolutionary scenario that could account for the formation of hand specialization in early hominins? To address these questions, we dedicate the next section to review compelling comparative data in non-human primates.

Part II: Handedness, bimanual coordination, and postural transitions in non-human primates

Considerable work has gone into the study of laterality in non-human primates (see for example Ward & Hopkins 1993). In particular, the question as to whether non-human primates display a species specific hand preference like humans do has been at the heart of a lively debate for many decades (see Harris 1993 for an historical account). Indeed, if handedness emerged as the result of an evolutionary process, then the origins of handedness should be traced back to the Great Apes — our genetically closest extant relatives — and potentially further down the evolutionary tree to our common ancestor with Old and New World monkeys or even prosimians. Opinions on non-human primates' laterality, however, have been quite divided. Some researchers claim that handedness is not a specific behavioural characteristic of non-human primates (e.g. Lehman 1993; Warren 1980). This view is often based on the fact that handedness can be found reliably in certain mature individuals, but systematic evidence of clear handedness at the population level is lacking. Other researchers, on the other hand, have challenged that view and have claimed that non-human primates' handedness can be found at the population level — however, this depends on the complexity of the task demands and the posture adopted while solving the task (e.g. Fagot & Vauclair 1991; MacNeilage 1991; MacNeilage et al. 1987; Vauclair & Fagot 1993).

These last researchers brought two interesting distinctions into this fascinating debate on the evolutionary origins of handedness and have stimulated a number of studies in recent years that were designed to assess the effects of task demands and posture on non-human primates' handedness. In this section, we focus on that literature because it is bearing interesting similarities with our work in human infants. We do acknowledge, however, that our review will not be exhaustive and will not touch on every aspect of non-human primates' handedness; indeed, an exhaustive review would take us away from the main purpose of this chapter.

Interactions between posture and task complexity in non-human primates

From their critical reappraisal of non-human primates' laterality, both MacNeilage et al. (1987) and Fagot & Vauclair (1991) stressed the importance of task demands and skill complexity on the expression of manual laterality. Fagot & Vauclair (1991) provided a literature review revealing that many earlier studies failed to show significant population biases in non-human primates' preferred hand use because they mainly relied on simple, low-level tasks such as *simple food reaching*, which do not require precise or sophisticated perceptual-motor adjustments. They reported that studies that relied on more complex high-level tasks requiring some level of *precision, manipulation, fine coordination,* or *dynamic body adjustments*, yielded to stronger and significant population biases in hand use. Examples of high-level tasks that Fagot & Vauclair (1991) reported involved, for instance, the precise visuospatial alignment of a window onto an aperture in order to obtain food (Fagot & Vauclair 1988a,b), the rapid visuomotor response to catch a fish (King & Landau 1993), the haptic discrimination and pushing of geometrical forms in the dark in order to receive a reward (e.g. Ettlinger 1961; Ettlinger & Moffet 1964), the manipulation of a joystick to reach a target on a computer screen (Hopkins et al. 1989), the coordination between hands to retrieve food from a hand-held tube (Hopkins et al. 2003; Spinozzi et al. 1998), or the maintenance of a vertical three-point posture on a wire netting in order to insert one hand into an opaque box and search for peanuts mixed with sand and stones (Fagot et al. 1991).

MacNeilage et al. (1987) similarly related handedness and manual specialization in non-human primates to task demands, but they also linked the origins of human right-handedness to what they called 'species-specific postural pre-adaptations' in non-human primates. As they report, these postural pre-adaptations correspond to using the right limb for postural support or vertical clinging, while using the left arm for reaching. As a result of this asymmetrical arm involvement in postural support, the right side developed greater strength and more versatile gripping configurations. MacNeilage et al. (1987) suggested that such manual specialization gave a manipulatory advantage to the right arm. This manipulatory advantage became obvious when bipedalism emerged and the right hand was freed from its role of body support.

This account now referred to as the 'Postural Origins' theory (MacNeilage 1991) and the task distinctions discussed above have both contributed to generate a new 'breed' of studies on non-human primates' handedness, which have been particularly dedicated to assessing the impact of task complexity and posture in non-human primate handedness. Many of these studies posited that task and posture, and particularly the distinction between quadrupedal and bipedal posture, mattered in relation to the expression of hand preference in non-human primates.

Most of the studies that tested the effect of posture on hand preference observed which hand individual animals used to pick food when the food was either (a) thrown on the ground or (b) located well above the ground on a shelf or was held up high through the mesh of the cage. In the first condition, on the ground, individuals were allowed to pick the food from a quadrupedal position, while in the second condition, when the food was up high, the same individuals were forced to adopt an upright stance in order to get it. Standing up to reach for the food was found to have a significant impact on the strength of hand preference in many species. Specifically, population-level biases in hand use while in the upright posture were found in Great Apes (De Vleeschouwer et al. 1995; Hopkins 1993; Hopkins *et al.* 1993; Olson *et al.* 1990; Parnell 2001), in Old World monkeys (Westergaard *et al.* 1998), in New World monkeys (Spinozzi *et al.* 1998; Westergaard *et al.* 1997), and in Prosimians (Forsythe *et al.* 1988; King & Landau 1993; Larson *et al.* 1989; Masataka 1989; Sandford *et al.* 1984). However, the direction of preferred hand use for the different groups of individuals when upright was not always consistent across these larger taxonomic groupings and within species depending on the studies. The above-mentioned studies with prosimians found that reaching for food in the upright posture triggered a left-hand population bias, while studies with Old and New World monkeys found a significant shift toward a greater use of the right hand. In Great Apes, on the contrary, some discordance in findings was reported; while some studies examining the effect of posture on hand preference found a greater use of the right hand for bipedal versus quadrupedal reaching in species such as gorillas and bonobos (Hopkins 1993; Hopkins *et al.* 1993; Olson *et al.* 1990), others reported a left-bias shift for the same species (De Vleeschouwer *et al.* 1995; Parnell 2001).

Thus, task complexity and posture both seem to have a marked effect on non-human primates hand preference. One last study uniquely investigated the interactions between task complexity and posture. Spinozzi *et al.* (1998) asked individual tufted capuchin monkeys to reach for food placed on a shelf situated at two different heights from the floor, thus, forcing the monkeys to either maintain a quadrupedal or adopt an upright posture during reaching. They also increased the task complexity by using a bimanual coordination task where the monkeys had to hold a tube hanging from the ceiling with one hand while retrieving food in the tube with the other hand through a hole. The tube, hanging at different heights from the ceilings, also constrained the monkeys to perform this bimanual task either crouched on the ground of the cage or standing upright. The authors found a significant right-hand bias for the group of monkeys in the simple reaching task when they were upright, but not when on their four limbs. When the monkeys reached in the quadrupedal posture, hand preference scores did not significantly deviate from chance. Spinozzi *et al.* (1998) additionally found a significant right-hand bias in the bimanual tasks in either postures, confirming again that upright posture alone, task complexity alone, or both upright posture and complex tasks can significantly shift preferred hand use in non-human primates.

In sum, from this body of evidence it appears that both reaching in an upright posture and solving more complex perceptual-motor tasks influence the strength of hand-use preference in a variety of non-human primate species. The direction of this increase

in hand preference, however, seems to be subject to greater variability across and within species. Why such variability in the direction of hand preference occurs is not clear, but several factors could account for it. One could be linked to the developmental histories of the animals from the different studies, and whether they were raised and observed in captivity or in the wild, leading thus to different experiences in hand use. Another possibility could be that hand-use variation is linked to the diverse contexts, tasks, and methods used to test the animals in the different studies. Finally, a last explanation could be related to varied, species-specific biomechanical constraints associated with the immediate adoption of the upright posture during reaching in the studied tasks, which *per se* could well lead to distinct preferences in hand use across species. All of those possibilities, however, remain open to further examinations.

Brief discussion of the non-human primate studies in relation to the human infant data
The above-reviewed findings on hand preference and posture reveal that the adoption of distinct postural configurations (i.e. quadrupedal versus bipedal) lead to different outcomes in regard to the strength and stability of hand use in non-human primates. These findings together with the human infant data congruently revealed that specific patterns of manual coordination and related forms of manual lateralization are dynamically linked to the adoption of particular postural configurations and preferred locomotor modes. In particular, they suggest that certain postural forms (i.e. bipedalism) facilitate the formation and organization of stable lateralized bimanual coordination, while other forms (i.e. quadrupedalism) do not lead to similarly stable behavioural outcomes. One fundamental difference, however, between humans and non-human primate species, is that humans are the only ones in the primate lineage who have truly adopted and maintained an erect posture as their preferred mode of locomotion. We propose that this fundamental difference — the fact that only human primates have adopted an upright locomotor mode — may be at the origins of the notable differences in strength and stability of hand preference that are existing between humans and non-human primates (see for example King & Landau (1993), or Westergaard *et al.* (1998) for reports or comments on human/non-human hand preference differences). In our last section, we discuss how preferred locomotor modes and the emergence of bipedalism in early hominins may have had implications for the evolution of hand preference, and the formation of sophisticated manual activities.

Conclusions and implications for human evolution

As mentioned in the introduction, rooting the origins of manual dexterity and stone-tool manufacture to the emergence of bipedalism is not a novel idea. Many authors have already acknowledged that adopting the upright posture and becoming bipedal contributed significantly to freeing the hands of our prehistoric ancestors from their locomotor role, and fostered the development of finer and more sophisticated manual skills (see Corballis 1991; Frost 1980; Hewes 1961; 1964; Leroi-Gourhan 1964; Lovejoy 1981; MacNeilage *et al.* 1987). It has also been acknowledged that the emergence of bipedalism in the Australopithecine lineage had been brought about by a number of significant anatomical changes, such as a widened pelvis and angled femurs, markers that are usually considered a direct adaptation for upright posture (Lewin 1998). Other changes, such as increased encephalization and brain asymmetries (Holloway 1996), improved manipulative hands (Marzke, 1996), and marked bone asymmetries (Steele 2000; Steele & Uomini this volume), which also occurred following the emergence of bipedalism, additionally suggest the formation of specific adaptations from novel and evolving hand activities.

The work and review presented in this chapter focused on one aspect of these changes; the possibility that the emergence of bipedalism may have created *favourable bio-behavioural conditions* for the development of such manual specializations, which in turn, may have contributed to the development of sophisticated tool-manufacturing skills. The ensemble of evidence presented in this chapter all pointed toward a greater expression of hand preference in the upright position, whereas during crawling or quadrupedal locomotion hand preference was much weaker or even lacking, depending on the tasks. We will begin by explaining how these variations in the degree of hand preference may relate to the different posturo-locomotor modes adopted.

In our previous work with infants (Corbetta & Bojczyk 2002; Corbetta & Thelen 2002), we argued that patterns of upper-arm coordination used during object manipulation can reflect practised patterns of upper-arm coordination during locomotion when the arms are also utilized to locomote. Our rationale was that the brain continuously adapts and learns to control groups of muscles as a function of sensory-motor practices and experiences. Thus, if the arms, among other activities, are heavily used for locomoting on a daily basis, it is possible that such extensive sensory-motor practice contribute to form and select specific patterns of muscle activation in the arms, which in turn will be used even during non-locomotor activities. Support

for such an interpretation can be found from a number of recent neurophysiological studies. During the past decade, there has been a growing body of literature in humans and in non-human mammals that has demonstrated that the brain changes and reorganizes itself, in particular, following specific sensory-motor experiences and motor-skill learning (Greenough *et al.* 1987; Jenkins *et al.* 1990; Karni *et al.* 1998; Kleim *et al.* 1998; Petersen *et al.* 1998). Of particular interest, studies have shown that behaviourally-driven changes in the brain can, in turn, influence specific motor performances (Dorris *et al.* 2000). Such brain reorganizations have been documented in adults, and even in human infants following the emergence and consolidation of motor milestones such as crawling (Bell & Fox 1996). And, more specifically, some studies reported that frequent practice of particular movement patterns involving muscle co-activation resulted in magnified coupled response representations in the motor cortex and greater functional coupling between hemispheres (Andres *et al.* 1999; Nudo *et al.* 1996). Such practice effects leading to greater experience-dependent representations in the cortex have been argued to increase the likelihood that the particular practised behavioural forms are selected over a range of other possible behavioural solutions (Sporns & Edelman 1993).

In the context of the findings reported in this chapter we can make the following assumptions. First, we can argue that hands-and-knees crawling and quadrupedal locomotion can hinder the expression of preferred lateral biases in manual activities precisely because quadrupedal locomotion involves the alternated and bilateral activity of the fore and hind limbs. It is interesting to note that our infant data revealed no preferred hand use trend in object manipulation during the crawling period; a period in which hands-and-knees crawling is heavily practised for several months. Quadrupedal locomotion is also the preferred mode of locomotion of non-human primates and, as reported in a large number of studies, hand preference in non-human primates is not apparent in tasks involving simple reaching. Additionally, when a preferred hand-use shift is observed in more complex tasks, the population-level shift in non-human primates is rarely as strong and as consistent in its direction as the hand preference observed in humans (King & Landau 1993; Westergaard *et al.* 1998).

Second, the same line of argument can be extended to the transition to upright locomotion. We reported that when infants begin to walk, they rely heavily on their arms for controlling balance and preventing falling. They achieve such a feat by holding their arms up high and tightly coupled. During that period, infants significantly increased coupling in reaching for objects as well, even though bimanual reaching was not needed to obtain the toys and infants were sitting and not actively walking during the reaching tasks. Again, the specific pattern of upper-arm coordination used during walking (i.e. upper-arm coupling) seemed to have generalized to other manual activities, in particular reaching and lid opening.

Finally, we observed that when infants became better walkers and did not need to rely on their arms for controlling balance, one-handed reaches and lateralized activities re-emerged. This is when the upper arms are becoming less essential to locomotion, and therefore are freed to engage in a variety of novel activities, setting the path for the development of new patterns of coordination that are not necessarily tied to locomotion. As reported, one pattern that seemed to emerge and strengthen progressively after this transition to upright locomotion was the appearance of a more consistent lateral hand usage. We argued that hand preference developed and settled in a specific direction after the *emergence and mastery* of upright locomotion because no more major postural reorganizations were occurring following the adoption of the erect posture, therefore allowing the brain to dissociate patterns of muscle activity for the arms from patterns of muscle activity specific to walking. Stronger preferred hand usage was also documented in non-human primates when tested in an upright posture. We believe, however, that a hand preference as strong as in humans has not evolved as a characteristic trait in that group of mammals, because non-human primates never adopted the upright posture for locomoting. As a result, it appears that preferred hand use in non-human primates can be observed only under specific task and postural conditions.

How can such an interpretation have implications for human evolution? We can only be speculative here and also acknowledge that many other factors may have played a role in the development of tool manufacture in early hominins (see other chapters in this book). Therefore, within the scope of this chapter, we will only refer to specific archaeological artefacts and evidence that may allow us to draw general lines of comparisons with human evolution and provide some support to our thesis.

In the introduction, we suggested that the emergence of bipedalism in human evolution may have been a catalyst of further hominin adaptations, bringing about *favourable bio-behavioural conditions* from which hand preference, fine bimanual coordination, tool manufacture and other socio-cultural changes may have evolved. It is obvious that such changes have been generally progressive throughout hominin evolution. According to our thesis — that hand preference inter-

acts with preferred locomotor forms and is particularly tied to the development of a *stable* and *fully-mastered* upright locomotion — we can speculate that hand preference may not have initially been a very strong behavioural characteristic of the earliest hominins. Hand preference may have become stronger and more established much later, in more recent generations of hominins, as they became more consistently bipedal and acquired a more erect posture. Support for this interpretation can be found in some archaeological evidence from early hominins' arm bones, particularly in the robust Australopithecine group, which suggest that these hominin species may still have partially relied on their forelimbs for locomotion (Lewin 1998). Additionally, analyses of the trunk of *Australopithecus* artefacts reveal that these prehistoric ancestors were not quite walking like modern humans do, and probably were not capable of running upright (Lewin 1998). Together, these observations suggest that although the *Australopithecus* was a bipedal hominin, its form of bipedalism may not have been altogether very stable, which might have, according to our account, limited the degree to which stable preferred hand usage might have been able to develop. More stable forms of bipedalism may have emerged in the next generation of hominins, in the *Homo* lineage. *Homo habilis,* not only seemed to have fully adopted the erect posture for locomoting, but also has been linked to full control of stone knapping, making that *Homo* species 'the' stone tool maker (Campbell 1996). Additional evidence from bone asymmetries (Steele 2000) and analyses from stone-tool artefacts (Toth 1985; Steele & Uomini this volume) together suggest that hand preference may have been an established behavioural trait in this group of hominins, which would be consistent with our hypothesis that upright posture and acquired stability in upright locomotion might have played a significant role in the establishment of hand preference and the development of fine bimanual coordination. The one aspect that we have not really dwelled on in this chapter, and that remains fully open to investigations, is why the adoption of upright posture and locomotion might have triggered a population-level right-hand use in humans. Detailed analyses of the biomechanical constraints related to the upright posture may possibly shed some light onto this question. This is something that we are currently investigating in our laboratory with adults and infants in the hope to detect postural trends that could guide us toward an explanation in the near future.

References

Andres, F.G., T. Mima, A.E. Schulman, J. Dichgans, M. Hallett & C. Gerloff, 1999. Functional coupling of human cortical sensorimotor areas during bimanual skill acquisition. *Brain* 122, 855–70.

Bell, M.A. & N. Fox, 1996. Crawling experience is related to changes in cortical organization during infancy: evidence from EEG coherence. *Developmental Psychobiology* 29, 551–61.

Bojczyk, K.E. & D. Corbetta, 2004. Object retrieval in the first year of life: learning effects of task exposure and box transparency. *Developmental Psychology* 40, 54–66.

Bonvillian, J.D., H.C. Richards & T.T. Dooley, 1997. Early sign language acquisition and the development of hand preference in young children. *Brain and Language* 58, 1–22.

Bril, B. & Y. Brenière, 1992. Postural requirements and progression velocity in young children. *Journal of Motor Behaviour* 24, 105–16.

Bruner, J.S., 1970. The growth and structure of skill, in *Mechanisms of Motor Skill Development*, ed. K. Connolly. New York (NY): Academic Press, 62–94.

Campbell, B.G., 1996. An outline of human phylogeny, in *Handbook of Human Symbolic Evolution*, eds. A. Lock & C.R. Peters. New York (NY): Oxford University Press, 31–52.

Carlson, D.F. & L.J. Harris, 1985. Development of infant's hand preference for visually directed reaching: preliminary report of a longitudinal study. *Infant Mental Health Journal* 6, 158–72.

Corballis, M.C., 1991. *The Lopsided Ape: Evolution of the Generative Mind*. New York (NY): Oxford University Press.

Corbetta, D. & K.E. Bojczyk, 2002. Infants return to two-handed reaching when they are learning to walk. *Journal of Motor Behaviour* 34, 83–95.

Corbetta, D. & E. Thelen, 1996. The developmental origins of two-handed coordination: a dynamic perspective. *Journal of Experimental Psychology: Human Perception and Performance* 22, 502–22.

Corbetta, D. & E. Thelen, 1999. Lateral biases and fluctuations in infants' spontaneous arm movements and reaching. *Developmental Psychobiology* 34, 237–55.

Corbetta, D. & E. Thelen, 2002. Behavioural fluctuations and the development of manual asymmetries in infancy: contribution of the dynamic systems approach, in *Handbook of Neuropsychology*, vol. 8: *Child Neuropsychology*, part I, eds. S.J. Segalowitz & I. Rapin. Amsterdam: Elsevier Science Publishing Co., 309–28.

De Vleeschouwer, K., L. Van Elsacker & R.F. Verheyen, 1995. Effect of posture on hand preference during experimental food reaching in bonobos (*Pan paniscus*). *Journal of Comparative Psychology* 109, 203–7.

Diamond, A., 1991. Neuropsychological insights into the meaning of object concept development, in *Biology and Knowledge: Structural Constraints on Development*, eds. S. Carey & R. Gelman. Hillsdale (NJ): Erlbaum, 37–80.

Dorris, M.C., M. Paré & D.P. Munoz, 2000. Immediate neural plasticity shapes motor performance. *The Journal of Neuroscience* 20, RC52, 1–5.

Ettlinger, G., 1961. Lateral preferences in monkeys. *Behaviour* 17, 275–87.

Ettlinger, G. & A. Moffet, 1964. Lateral preferences in the monkey. *Nature* 204, 606.

Fagard, J. & A. Marks, 2000. Unimanual and bimanual tasks and the assessment of handedness in toddlers. *Developmental Science* 3, 137–47.

Fagard, J. & A. Pezé, 1997. Age changes in interlimb coupling and the development of bimanual coordination. *Journal of Motor Behaviour* 29, 199–208.

Fagot, J. & J. Vauclair, 1988a. Handedness and bimanual coordination in the lowland gorilla. *Brain, Behaviour and Evolution* 32, 89–95.

Fagot, J. & J. Vauclair, 1988b. Handedness and manual specialization in the baboon. *Neuropsychologia* 26, 795–804.

Fagot, J. & J. Vauclair, 1991. Manual laterality in nonhuman primates: a distinction between handedness and manual specialization. *Psychological Bulletin* 109, 76–89.

Fagot, J., C.M. Drea & K. Wallen, 1991. Asymmetrical hand use in rhesus monkeys (*Macaca mulatta*) in tactually and visually regulated tasks. *Journal of Comparative Psychology* 105, 260–68.

Forsythe, C., G.W. Milliken, D.K. Stafford & J.P. Ward, 1988. Posturally related variations in the hand preference of the ruffed lemur (*Varecia variegata variegata*). *Journal of Comparative Psychology* 102, 248–50.

Frost, G.T., 1980. Tool behaviour and the origins of laterality. *Journal of Human Evolution* 9, 447–59.

Gabbard, C.P., 2004. *Lifelong Motor Development*. San Francisco (CA): Benjamin Cummings.

Gesell, A. & L.B. Ames, 1947. The development of handedness. *The Journal of Genetic Psychology* 70, 155–75.

Greenough, W.G, J.E. Black & C.S. Wallace, 1987. Experience and brain development. *Child Development* 58, 539–59.

Harris, L.J., 1993. Handedness in apes and monkeys: some views from the past, in *Primate Laterality: Current Behavioural Evidence of Primate Asymmetries*, eds. J.P. Ward & W.D. Hopkins. New York (NY): Springer-Verlag, 1–41.

Hewes, G.W., 1961. Food transport and the origin of hominid bipedalism. *American Anthropologist* 63, 687–710.

Hewes, G.W., 1964. Hominid bipedalism: independent evidence for the food-carrying theory. *Science* 146, 416–18.

Holloway, R., 1996. Evolution of the human brain, in *Handbook of Human Symbolic Evolution*, eds. A. Lock & C.R. Peters. New York (NY): Oxford University Press, 74–125.

Hopkins, W.D., 1993. Posture and reaching in chimpanzees (*Pan troglodytes*) and orangutans (*Pongo pygmaeus*). *Journal of Comparative Psycholog* 107, 162–8.

Hopkins, W.D., D.A. Washburn & D.M. Rumbaugh, 1989. A note on hand use in the manipulation of a joystick by two rhesus monkeys (*Macaca mulatta*) and three chimpanzees (*Pan troglodytes*). *Journal of Comparative Psychology* 103, 91–4.

Hopkins, W.D., A.J. Bennett, S.L. Bales, J. Lee & J.P. Ward, 1993. Behavioural laterality in captive bonobos (*Pan paniscus*). *Journal of Comparative Psychology* 107, 403–10.

Hopkins, W.D., T.S. Stoinski, K.E. Lukas, S.R. Ross & M.J. Wesley, 2003. Comparative assessment of handed for a coordinated bimanual task in chimpanzees (*Pan troglodytes)*, gorillas *(Gorilla gorilla)*, and orangutans *(Pongo pygmaeus)*. *Journal of Comparative Psychology* 117, 302–8.

Hunt, K.D., 1994. The evolution of human bipedality: ecology and functional morphology. *Journal of Human Evolution* 26, 183–202.

Jenkins, W.M., M.M. Merzenich, M.T. Ochs, E. Allard & T. Guic-Robles, 1990. Functional reorganization of primary somatosensory cortex in adult owl monkeys after behaviourally controlled tactile stimulation. *Journal of Neurophysiology* 63, 82–104.

Karni, A., G. Meyer, C. Rey-Hipolito, P. Jezzard, M.M. Adams, R. Turner & L.G. Ungerleider, 1998. The acquisition of skilled motor performance: fast and slow experience-driven changes in primary motor cortex. *Proceedings of the National Academy of Sciences of the USA* 95, 861–8.

King, J.E. & V.I. Landau, 1993. Manual preferences in varieties of reaching in squirrel monkeys, in *Primate Laterality: Current Behavioural Evidence of Primate asymmetries*, eds. J.P. Ward & W.D. Hopkins. New York (NY): Springer-Verlag, 107–24.

Kleim, J.A., S. Barbay & R.J. Nudo, 1998. Functional reorganization of the rat motor cortex following motor skill learning. *Journal of Neurophysiology* 80, 3321–5.

Larson, C.F., D.L. Dodson & J.P. Ward, 1989. Hand preferences and whole-body turning biases of lesser bushbabies *(Galago senegalensis)*. *Brain, Behaviour and Evolution* 33, 261–7.

Lehman, R.A.W., 1993. Manual preference in prosimians, monkeys, and apes, in *Primate Laterality: Current Behavioural Evidence of Primate Asymmetries*, eds. J.P. Ward & W.D. Hopkins. New York (NY): Springer-Verlag, 149–81.

Leroi-Gourhan, A., 1964. *Le geste et la parole: I. Technique et langage*. Paris: Éditions Albin Michel.

Lewin, R., 1998. *Principles of Human Evolution: a Core Textbook*. Malden (MA): Blackwell Science, Inc.

Lovejoy, C.O., 1981. The origin of man. *Science* 211, 341–50.

MacNeilage, P.F., 1991. The 'postural origins' theory of primate neurobiological asymmetries, in *Biological and Behavioural Determinants of Language Development*, eds. N.A. Krasnegor, D.M. Rumbaugh, R.L. Schiefelbusch & M. Studdert-Kennedy. Hillsdale (NJ): Erlbaum, 165–88.

MacNeilage, P.F., M.G. Studdert-Kennedy & B. Lindblom, 1987. Primate handedness reconsidered. *Behavioural and Brain Sciences* 10, 247–303.

Marshack, A., 1984. The ecology and brain of two-handed bipedalism: an analytic, cognitive and evolutionary assessment, in *Animal Cognition*, eds. H.I. Roitblat, T.G. Bever & H.S. Terrace. Hillsdale (NJ): Erlbaum, 491–511.

Marzke, M.W., 1996. Evolution of the hand and bipedality, in *Handbook of Human Symbolic Evolution*, eds. A. Lock & C.R. Peters. New York (NY): Oxford University Press, 126–54.

Masataka, N., 1989. Population level asymmetry of hand preference in lemurs. *Behaviour* 110, 244–7.

McManus, I.C., G. Sik, D.R. Cole, A.F. Mellon, J. Wong & J. Kloss, 1988. The development of handedness in children. *British Journal of Developmental Psychology* 6, 257–73.

Nudo, R.J., G.W. Milliken, W.M. Jenkins & M.M. Merzenich, 1996. Use-dependent alterations of movement representations in primary motor cortex of adult squirrel monkeys. *Journal of Neuroscience* 16, 785–807.

Oldfield, R.C., 1971. The assessment and analysis of handedness: the Edinburgh inventory. *Neuropsychologia* 9, 97–113.

Olson, D.A., J.E. Ellis & R.E. Nadler, 1990. Hand preferences in captive gorillas, orangutans and gibbons. *American Journal of Primatology* 20, 83–94.

Parnell, R.J., 2001. Hand preference for food processing in wild western lowland gorillas *(Gorilla gorilla gorilla)*. *Journal of Comparative Psychology* 115, 365–75.

Petersen, S.E., H. van Mier, J.A. Fiez & M.E. Raichle, 1998. The effects of practice on the functional anatomy of task performance. *Journal of Neurophysiology* 80, 3321–5.

Roux, V. (ed.), 2000. *Cornaline de l'Inde: des pratiques techniques de Cambay aux techno-systemes de l'Indus*. Paris: Éditions de la Maison des sciences de l'homme. (English cd-rom.)

Sandford, C., K. Guin & J.P. Ward, 1984. Posture and laterality in the bushbaby *(Galago senegalensis)*. *Brain, Behaviour and Evolution* 25, 217–24.

Spinozzi, G., M.G. Castorina & V. Truppa, 1998. Hand preferences in unimanual and coordinated-bimanual tasks in tufted capuchin monkeys *(Cebus apella)*. *Journal of Comparative Psychology* 112, 183–91.

Sporns, O. & G.M. Edelman, 1993. Solving Bernstein's problem: a proposal for the development of coordinated movement by selection. *Child Development* 64, 960–81.

Steele, J., 2000. Handedness in past human populations: skeletal markers. *Laterality* 5, 193–220.

Steenhuis, R.E. & M.P. Bryden, 1989. Different dimensions of hand preference that relate to skilled and unskilled activities. *Cortex* 25, 289–304.

Toth, N., 1985. Archaeological evidence for preferential right-handedness in the lower and middle Pleistocene, and its possible implications. *Journal of Human Evolution* 14, 607–14.

Vauclair, J. & J. Fagot, 1993. Manual specialization in gorillas and baboons, in *Primate Laterality: Current Behavioural Evidence of Primate Asymmetries*, eds. J.P. Ward & W.D. Hopkins. New York (NY): Springer-Verlag, 193–281.

Ward, J.P. & W.D. Hopkins (eds.), 1993. *Primate Laterality: Current Behavioural Evidence of Primate Asymmetries*. New York (NY): Springer-Verlag.

Warren, J.M., 1980. Handedness and laterality in humans and other animals. *Physiological Psychology* 8, 351–9.

Westergaard, G.C., H.E. Kuhn, A.L. Lundquist & S.J. Suomi, 1997. Posture and reaching in tufted capuchins *(Cebus apella)*. *Laterality* 2, 65–74.

Westergaard, G.C., H.E. Kuhn & S.J. Suomi, 1998. Bipedal posture and hand preference in humans and other primates. *Journal of Comparative Psychology* 112, 55–64.

Chapter 14

Investigating Manual Specialization in Extant and Extinct Hominins

M.K. Holder

Before addressing the question of whether or not stone knapping was a uniquely hominin behaviour, it is necessary to understand how and why a manual specialization (such as stone knapping) is acquired by individuals. A 'manual specialization' is any new manual skill, acquired over time through repeated practice, that results in an increase in strength, precision, and/or speed necessary to successfully perform that task. I describe the acquisition of motor skill, clarify the relationship between manual specialization and hand preference, and highlight methodological and theoretical problems in the interpretation of hominin manual behaviour. I suggest a cost:benefit:milieu approach to identify variables involved in the acquisition of manual specializations and to describe ranges of behavioural possibilities for an individual or a species. An investigation of hand preferences in five genera of wild African primates (Holder 1999) illustrates the usefulness of this approach.

Describing manual behaviour

Stone-tool knapping is a phrase used to describe a wide range of manual behaviour. Making a sharp cobble stone or generating a single sharp flake requires little or no skill or expertise; creating a Acheulean hand axe or Levallois core requires both highly-specialized motor skill and cognitive planning. To address when 'stone knapping' first became important for hominins, it is useful to set aside the question of what qualifies as a stone 'tool' and consider the biomechanical and neurological foundations of manual behaviour — How are motor skills acquired? What is the relationship between handedness and motor skill? How can complex manual skills be assessed in the context of phenotypic variation upon which natural selection acts?

Manual specialization

Before we can address the question of whether or not stone knapping was a uniquely hominin behaviour, we need to understand how and why living primates, both human and non-human, acquire manual specializations. By *manual specialization* I mean the acquisition of a new motor skill that first requires the optimization of biomechanical potential for the task to be successfully performed. This optimization could be an

increase in strength, in precision, and/or in speed of task performance. An example of manual specialization will help illustrate this definition.

Palm-nut cracking is a manual specialization that requires the optimization of an animal's biomechanical potential, as evidenced by a period of sustained effort, learning, and practice. Before young chimpanzees in West Africa can successfully crack open hard oil-palm nuts using stone tools, they must first increase the strength of their arm muscles (this occurs developmentally, but also through repeated practice). Secondly, they must increase the skill at which they perform this task (this occurs by learning how to combine a set of actions necessary to orient the nut, stone anvil, and hammer relative to each other, again through repeated practice, but also by observational learning). Investigators report that 5 years of practice may be required before successful completion of task, with up to 15 years to fully master the task (Fushima *et al.* 1991; Boesch 1991b; Boesch-Achermann & Boesch 1993; Boesch & Boesch 1984). Inoue-Nakamura & Matsuzawa (1997) found that while chimpanzees as young as 3.5 years old began to use stone hammer and anvil to crack palm nuts, those who do not learn to crack nuts by the age of 5 years 'will not acquire this skill in later life' (Matsuzawa 2002). This behaviour

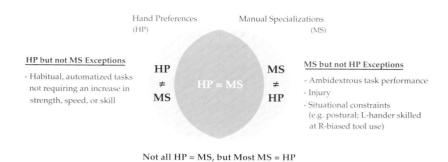

Figure 14.1. *The relationship between hand preference and manual specialization.*

is of special interest for human origins researchers because of its biomechanical similarity to knapping stone, and because archaeological and palaeobotanical evidence indicates that hominins also used stone hammers and anvils to crack hard nuts (Leakey 1971; Leakey & Roe 1994; Goren-Inbar *et al.* 2002). Among modern humans, a topically relevant example of a manual specialization requiring an increase in muscle strength, precision, and speed include the stone-adze makers of Indonesia, whose skill is acquired though apprenticeships lasting five years or more (Stout 2002; this volume).

The acquisition of manual specialization

Intact individuals of a species acquire ordinary motor skills as a dynamic developmental process, as perceptual-motor pathways develop in the brain in association with skeleto-muscular development (cf. Corbetta & Thelen 1999; Corbetta this volume). But the acquisition of a *manual specialization* depends upon conscious attention being given to various forms of feed-back (e.g. perceptual-motor, social) during extended periods of practice (Ericsson *et al.* 1993). An acquired increase in strength, precision, and speed reflects underlying changes in muscle mass and neurological function. Skills acquired over ten years can 'circumvent basic limits on working memory capacity and sequential processing' and can also 'lead to anatomical changes resulting from adaptations to intense physical activity' (Ericsson & Charness 1994). Across fields of human endeavour (music, sports, dance, touch-typing, juggling) the very 'highest levels of human performance … can only be attained after around ten years of extended, daily amounts of deliberate practice activities' (Ericsson & Lehmann 1996). Manual specialization is both a prerequisite for certain skills and the result of attaining such skills. In order to develop a manual specialization, an individual must first cognitively recognize the dynamics of the task itself and/or recognize an end goal as being attainable.

Manual specialization and hand preference

Manual specialization, as defined here, has a unique relationship with hand preference. (To briefly clarify, the term *handedness* is used to describe a population or species-level directional hand preference, such as species-level right-handedness among modern humans. For example, a species comprised of 40 per cent right-handed individuals, 40 per cent left-handed individuals, and 20 per cent ambidextrous individuals has no species-level directional handedness. Whereas a species with 80 per cent right-handed individuals, 15 per cent left-handed individuals, and 5 per cent ambidextrous individuals would be described as having species-level right-handedness. The term *hand preference* refers to an individual's left- or right-handedness.) For the present discussion I refer only to *individual* left or right manual preferences, and not *species-level* handedness. Not all tasks for which a consistent hand preference is expressed are manual specializations (see Holder 1999). Most manual specializations are performed, however, with a consistent manual preference. In other words, not all hand preferences are manual specializations, but most manual specializations are asymmetrical. While consistent hand preferences and manual specializations share much in common, they are *not* the same thing, and understanding how they differ is important for human origins research.

Most manual specializations are performed with a consistent manual preference for a simple reason. Based on biomechanical, muscular, and neurological mechanisms, if biomechanical optimization is needed, this is most likely when the manual task is practised and performed exclusively with one hand (otherwise, practice time and skill attainment is halved, being divided between the two hands). In other words, any task that requires a notable increase in existing strength, precision, and/or speed is likely to end up being performed with a preferred hand. Exceptions to this (the area labelled MS ≠ HP in Fig. 14.1) include ambidextrous task performance, injury, or situational constraints (such as left-handers who must become skilled in the use of right-biased tools).

But how do we explain those tasks for which a consistent hand preference is expressed, but which are *not* manual specializations (the area labelled HP ≠ MS in Fig. 14.1)? These tasks do *not* require additional strength, skill, or speed to execute, but are tasks that are performed routinely. Habitual tasks that have become automatized are often done with a consistent hand preference. For example, striking a match can easily be performed with either hand, but most people consistently employ a preferred hand for this task, even though it requires little strength, skill or speed to accomplish. The reason that hand preferences develop in these instances have to do with the benefits derived from *task automatization* — from not having to consciously decide which hand to use, and from being free to focus attention elsewhere than the task at hand.

Task automatization

Task automatization is when a task has been learned so well that its performance becomes 'automatic' — task performance no longer requires the conscious attention of the animal. Examples of task automatization can be observed in automobile drivers or in musicians — an adept can simultaneously talk to others or give conscious attention to matters other than the task being performed. Although the neural mechanisms underlying task automatization have yet to be fully elucidated (cf. Logan 1988; 1997), it is clear that task automatization changes the functional anatomy of the brain (Petersson *et al.* 1999). Freeing of conscious attention allows an animal to efficiently perform a task while simultaneously focusing attention on other matters, for example, on vigilance against predators or on observing social interactions. Task automatization is a meaningful benefit derived both from manual specializations and from habitual hand preferences.

Ambidexterity

A little-discussed aspect of manual behaviour that must not be neglected when considering the evolutionary development of handedness is ambidexterity. *True ambidexterity* describes an individual who can perform most tasks about equally well with either hand. *Mixed-handedness*, only mimics ambidexterity in certain situations (such as archaeological site debitage accumulation and some laterality tests), and is really a dual-specialization — the individual performs roughly half of manual tasks with one hand, and half with the other hand. So while a true ambidexter is likely to develop few strong manual specializations, a mixed-hander is likely to perform highly-specialized tasks just as well as a strongly right- or left-handed individual.

Unfortunately, little is known about ambidexterity (and mixed-handedness) because researchers studying human subjects routinely either lump ambidexters in with left-handers or disregard ambidexters entirely (e.g. Ferronato *et al.* 1974; Beukelarr & Kroonenberg 1983; Spiegler & Yeni-Komshian 1983). Even some standard handedness measures cannot distinguish between true ambidexterity and mixed-handedness because of test bias (Oldfield 1971; cf. Holder 1992).

How investigators choose to deal with ambidexterity can significantly, and predictably, skew findings of frequencies of hand preferences in populations (Holder 1992). Ambidexterity and mixed-handedness are especially problematic for human origins researchers, as I will discuss presently.

Direction versus strength of hand preference

Finally, a word about how hand preference is measured. Because modern humans are right-handed as a species (with a consistent minority of left-handers and ambidexters), primatologists, archaeologists, and human origins researchers began asking the question, 'Are other primates (or early hominins) right-handed like us?' which is an anthropomorphically-biased question with the emphasis being on the *direction*, rather than the *strength*, of manual preference (Holder 1999). In fact, the way individuals are categorized as left- or right-handed is by considering the frequency (the strength or degree) at which an individual uses one hand over the other (both within and between tasks). So there is no *a priori* reason to believe that it is the direction, rather than the strength, of asymmetry that is more relevant (cf. Flowers 1975; Roney & King 1993). Rather, evidence suggests that assessments of degree of asymmetry elucidates patterns not found when considering only direction (Johnstone *et al.* 1979; Preilowski & Leder 1985; Holder 1999). Of course, valid research considers both.

The following examples illustrate how between-task and within-task frequency (strength) of left- or right-hand use defines individual hand preference. An individual who uses her right hand for 90 per cent of her routine single-handed tasks, whose frequency of using the right hand is close to 100 per cent for most skilled tasks, would be described as strongly right-handed. An individual who uses the right hand for 70 per cent of his routine tasks, with a frequency of close to 100 per cent for skilled tasks, would be described as weakly right-handed. An individual who uses the right hand for 60 per cent of his routine tasks, but with a frequency of only 50 per cent for most skilled tasks would be described as ambidextrous. An individual who uses her right hand for 55 per cent of her routine tasks, but with a frequency of close to 100 per cent for most skilled tasks would be described as a mixed-hander. These percentages are only offered to provide examples; actual criteria for the various categories of handedness vary significantly among researchers, and are largely arbitrary delineations based on favoured theories (Holder 1992). But manual specializations, which require prolonged periods of practice to achieve, are characterized by a high frequency of within-task preferred hand use because limiting

BENEFITS	COSTS
(e.g. nutritional, social defensive, etc.)	*(e.g. time, energy, social, etc.)*
1. Sufficient influence for MS...	... with no associated cost
2. Sufficient benefit for MS...	... to eliminate costs of MS
3. Sufficient benefit for MS...	... to incur/offset costs of MS

(MS = manual specialization)

Benefits and costs may be direct or indirect, immediate or delayed

Figure 14.2. *Levels of increasing cost : benefit interactions.*

practice to one preferred hand increases the speed and level of biomechanical optimization (strength, precision, and/or speed) for the acquired skill.

A cost : benefit : milieu approach

Manual specialization: understanding causal factors

To understand what causal factors underlie the acquisition of manual specializations, we can start by investigating how and why living primates (including humans) learn manual skills within their species-typical contexts. *How* manual specializations are acquired involve an animal's development, biomechanical ability, neural processing, the specific mechanics of the given task, and the socio-environmental context. *Why* manual specializations are acquired involves discovering what *function* a given manual specialization serves (nutritional, defensive, social, etc.). In field research with five genera of African primates I have found a cost : benefit : context approach useful to identify factors or variables involved in the acquisition of manual specializations. One can expect a manual specialization to occur (minimally): 1) when specialization offers some advantage over the absence of task specialization; and 2) when the animal is either (a) free of conditions that inhibit the acquisition and/or performance of this behaviour, or (b) when the benefit of manual specialization outweighs any costs (e.g. temporal, energetic) of overcoming inhibitory conditions (Holder 1999).

While these conditions appear straightforward, the key to making this approach work in the real world is to elucidate the complex and balanced relationship between opposing forces — between variables that constrain or limit the acquisition and performance of a manual specialization and variables that favourably influence the acquisition and performance of a manual specialization. An individual is only likely to invest the time and energy in acquiring such skills when the perceived benefits either balance or outweigh associated costs, within a given context (see Fig. 14.2).

Benefits

Benefits are variables that encourage the acquisition of a manual specialization. Benefits could be immediate and/or direct (such as a new food source), delayed and/or indirect (such as increased grooming from conspecifics with whom a new food is shared). Potential benefits include nutritional, defensive, and/or social benefits. Some benefits may de differentially available to certain members of the population (e.g. male *versus* female, or body-size dependent). Some benefits may only be available to individuals during a specific developmental period. Optimization of one's ability, through a manual specialization, results in an increase in absolute strength, in precision, and/or in speed for the performance of the given task. Thus, through repeated, deliberate practice, an animal is able to learn to do things that s/he was initially unable to do.

Costs

Obvious costs associated with acquiring a manual specialization are the time and energy an animal expends in learning, practising, and performing a task. Other costs can include muscle/skeletal fatigue, a decrease in the ability to perform well with either hand (beneficial in case of injury), and a decrease in reach range (from the reach-range of both hands to the reach range of one hand, from a given posture). Costs can also be delayed or indirect, such as negative social consequences. Any constraining, limiting variable(s) that involves the physical/biomechanical, as well as cognitive, limits of an animal within the broader limits of its species-typical environment can be a cost. Just as with benefits, costs may affect members of the population differentially.

Task recognition: the cognitive aspect of manual specialization

We must also consider how an individual comes to 'recognize' both the goal of the acquired task and the strategy to achieve this goal. By definition, a manual specialization requires deliberate and repeated practice over a period of time. And often, as in the case with chimpanzee nut-cracking, an immature animal will try again and again, unsuccessfully, expending much time and energy in the process. What motivates such seemingly futile behaviour?

For immature animals, time and energy are not as precious commodities as for adults; immature animals are still being provisioned and are not held to the same social expectations as adults. Much of their time is spent in 'play behaviour', a form of social learning and practice (cf. Bekoff & Byers 1998). Some manual specializations (e.g. chimpanzee termite-fishing) might be learned by methods analogous to other types of play learning — by imitating adults and by play practising. Other, more difficult, manual specializations may require active social teaching and learning from adult to immature, as when a West African chimpanzee mother correctly re-positions a palm nut on a cracking anvil being unsuccessfully hammered by her offspring.

Still other methods of recognizing new goals and strategies to achieve them include chance discovery and/or trial-and-error problem-solving. For instance, among Taï chimpanzees, nut-cracking with a stone hammer and anvil sometimes produces stone flakes (Mercader *et al.* 2002a,b). A stray flake may either be ignored or be 'recognized' as a useful implement — but if there is no use for a sharp flake, there is no problem to be solved, and no insight to be 'recognized'. Conversely, if the benefit or goal is easily recognizable (such a new food source), then the challenge is to discover a strategy for obtaining the benefit. This is active, conscious problem-solving. Problem-solving can be accomplished through a series of trial-and-error attempts and/or through imagining a solution mentally (deductive reasoning) (cf. Köhler 1927; Kahney 1993).

Specific examples

As noted earlier, the key to using a cost : benefit : milieu approach is understanding the tasks itself and the balance between cost(s) and benefit(s) associated with the task. Some manual tasks are more difficult to acquire than others because they require a greater investment in time, energy, and deliberate practice to perform successfully. This is due to the varying levels of biomechanical optimization needed — some tasks may require only an increase in strength or in precision, while other tasks demand both. For instance, chimpanzee termite-fishing requires an increase in precision to master; chimpanzee palm nut-cracking requires an increase in both strength and precision, and takes longer to master.

As regards stone knapping, the quality of the resulting product is an important variable. Depending on the raw material type, producing a single random flake or an unspecified sharp edge on a core may require little or no manual specialization (and may be accidental, such as a flake produced as a unintentional by-product of using stone hammers and anvils to crack nuts). Producing a specific, preconceived style of flake or core reduction, however, requires recognition of the goal, or end product, in addition to an increase in manual precision (and often an increase in strength) acquired over time through deliberate practice.

Discovering why and how a single animal acquires a given manual specialization is only the first step towards understanding how evolution acts on phenotypes. Since evolution occurs when natural selection acts upon phenotypic variation, it is critical to also establish ranges of possible behaviour for a species.

Manual specializations: identifying ranges of possible behaviour within a dynamic, interactive milieu

When I speak of context for cost : benefit interactions, I mean the complete organism functioning within the species-typical milieu. It is useful to expansively define 'context' to include everything an individual animal brings to a given situation — anatomy, physiology, neurology, genetics, cognitive ability, motivation, experience, etc., *as well as* the social and environmental context, and the specific mechanics of the task in question.

There are many ways to identify ranges of possible behaviour both *within* an individual animal and *between* animals within populations. One is to investigate how variables can incur costs and benefit an individual animal's behaviour across its development and lifespan. For example, documenting how immature chimpanzees learn to use a stone hammer and anvil (Boesch 1991b; Fushima *et al.* 1991; Inoue-Nakamura & Matsuzawa 1997). Exploration of the dynamic progression of an individual's *development*, and that of manual behaviours, can reveal factors that may be influential under some conditions but not under other conditions — variables which may not be obvious when observing only adult animals, yet may be critical to understanding ranges of possible manual behaviour, especially if the goal is reconstruction of evolutionary scenarios.

Another method is to conduct case studies of the effects of natural perturbations on systems. For example, while investigating hand preference among wild primates, I was able to conduct two case studies of one-handed chimpanzees — chimps that had literally lost a hand due to snare injuries. I found that although chimpanzees with one hand forage and feed slightly more slowly than animals with two hands, and often lag behind others in a travelling party, they can survive, breed, and raise young with only one hand (Holder 1999).

Still another method is to observe how an animal's performance on a given task varies relative to changing situational conditions, both within and across individual animals. One example of a condition that is defined by the relationship between several variables — an animal's morphology, motor capabilities, and its environmental substrate — is relative postural stability. While an animal may develop a manual specialization in posturally-stable conditions, he may

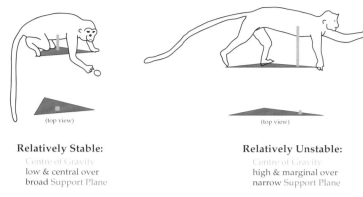

Relatively Stable:
Centre of Gravity
low & central over
broad Support Plane

Relatively Unstable:
Centre of Gravity
high & marginal over
narrow Support Plane

Figure 14.3. *Postural stability is relative.*

be less likely or unable to do so under less posturally-stable conditions, as discussed below.

Understanding how potential benefits and costs differentially affect individual animals under various conditions, or various members of a population at any one moment in time, helps identify *ranges of possible behaviours* — the phenotypic variation — upon which natural selection acts. Also, because of the incomplete nature of Palaeolithic and fossil remains, it may not be possible to deduce an exact answer to many of our evolutionary questions. In such cases, we must focus on identifying the *range* of possible answers, based on what we know about the organism, the artefacts, the context, and the principle of uniformitarianism.

Examples of a cost : benefit : milieu approach

In order to illustrate the usefulness of a cost : benefit : milieu approach, let's consider just one specific example of research derived from this perspective. Understanding modern primate manual behaviour is crucial to identify what forces of natural selection might have acted on early hominin manual behaviour. Describing how individuals typically behave in their natural environment is the first step. In a field research project (Holder 1999) I set out to describe the full range of manual behaviour for five species of wild monkeys and apes. Another objective was to identify what factors other than a presumed brain specialization might be capable of influencing and constraining primate manual asymmetry (left or right hand preference). The five species of wild African primates I observed were: redtail monkey (*Cercopithecus ascanius*), red colobus monkey (*Colobus badius*), grey-cheeked mangabey (*Cercocebus albigena* or *Lococebus a.*), and the common chimpanzee (*Pan troglodytes*) in the Kibale Forest of western Uganda. Additionally, I studied mountain gorillas (*Gorilla gorilla beringei*) in Rwanda's Parc National des Volcans. One aspect of this research was to

compare manual behaviour under varying conditions of relative postural stability. I hypothesized that postural instability would constrain, not develop, the expression of asymmetry. And I predicted that an increase in relative postural instability would lead to a *decrease* in asymmetrical manual behaviour (preferred left- or right-handedness).

Methods
By definition, 'posturally-unstable' animals fall down. 'Postural stability', therefore, is *relative* term, and is determined by the biomechanical relationship between an animal's centre of gravity and plane of postural support. The lower and more central the centre of gravity over the plane of postural support, the more stable the posture (see Fig. 14.3).

I recorded relative postural stability with a yes–no assessment of whether or not *additional postural support (from the other hand) was necessary* to extend and complete a single-handed manual task (no = relatively stable / yes = relatively unstable). Figure 14.4 illustrates the biomechanical concept of 'critical boundary' or the edge of postural stability (Mark 1987; Warren 1984) — the point at which an individual's centre of gravity is no longer balanced over the plane of postural support. Figure 14.4E illustrates my criteria for relative postural instability.

I assessed the *strength* of manual asymmetry as well as direction in wild primates, by calculating the percentage of left or right to overall manual behaviour, ranging from complete ambidexterity (50 per cent L : 50 per cent R hand use) to complete left- or right-handedness (100 per cent L or R). Although the focus of this investigation was manual preferences rather than manual specializations, the results are still relevant to this workshop's topic.

Field research findings
I tested the hypothesis that under conditions of relative postural instability, one would find less asymmetrical manual behaviour by analyzing these data by condition of relative postural stability (relatively stable vs. relatively unstable). I found that under conditions of postural instability and biomechanical constraint, animals benefit from being ambidextrous — from having either hand readily available.

Figure 14.5 shows a comparison of the strength of asymmetry (regardless of direction) for all manual tasks, for the sample of 21 redtail monkeys. The degree of asymmetry, ranging from 50 per cent (ambidextrous) to 100 per cent (complete R/L hand preference) is given for each individual. (Numbers in white are the average degree of asymmetry for each individual, for all tasks.) To test the hypothesis that under conditions of relative instability, one would find less asymmetrical behaviour, I analyzed these data by condition of relative postural stability (stable vs. unstable). Darker triangles (top) represent the average strength of asymmetry under stable conditions (no additional postural support needed to complete reach). Lighter triangles (bottom) represent the average strength of asymmetry under relatively less stable conditions (additional postural support required). The difference in strength of hand preference between these two postural conditions is striking for each individual ($p > .0001$, Student's t test). This finding was highly significant and remarkably robust, across task, sex, age, individuals, and was replicated across four species: The greater the relative postural instability, the less the manual asymmetry.

Figure 14.6 graphs the magnitude of this difference at the species level, for each of the five species studied (85 individuals; 4534 observations) for the feed/foraging task (which includes picking, lead manual processing hand, feeding). For feeding, the differences between strength of asymmetrical manual behaviour under conditions of relative postural stability (no additional postural support needed) *versus* relative postural instability (additional postural support required) were significant ($p = .001$ or greater, Student's within subjects t test for correlated/dependent samples) in all species studied except gorillas, for whom there were too few observations of additional hand support to statistically compare (civil war in Rwanda cut short data collection).

Another finding that held across all five primate species studied was that there was no evidence for *species-level* left- or right-handedness across the five genera of monkeys and apes studied. Rather, I found that animals possessed *individual* directional hand preferences, most of which were stable over time and across tasks. However, by assessing the *strength* of asymmetry regardless of direction, I showed that strength of asymmetry may be a more revealing variable than direction (had I only measured direction of hand preference, I would not have found the relationship between hand preference and relative postural stability described above, as Figure 14.6 details).

These data also show why it is inappropriate to use arboreality *per se* as a marker for postural instabil-

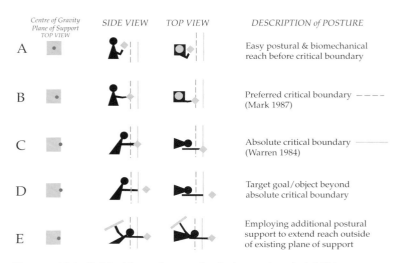

Figure 14.4. *Critical boundary and relative postural stability.*

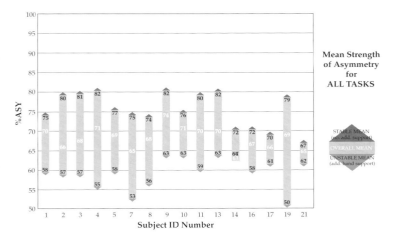

Figure 14.5. *Strength of asymmetrical hand use varies with postural stability* (Cercopithecus ascanius schmidti *(Redtail monkey)).*

ity. When strength of asymmetry between relatively stable vs less stable conditions is analyzed by condition of arboreality vs terrestrially, the relationship still holds. In other words, postural stability is defined by biomechanical rules, not by the terrestrial or arboreal substrate. I also documented how factors *other* than a presumed brain lateralization can affect the expression of manual asymmetry among wild primates — these include physical and motor development, injury, and relative postural stability. These results are detailed elsewhere (Holder 1999).

Even simple cost : benefit analyses are equally appropriate for archaeological inquiry. For example, Brantingham & Khun (2001) used a cost : benefit approach to demonstrate how Levallois core technology is 'one optimal solution to some of the potential costs associated with core reduction'. They suggested that the broad geographic distribution and persistence

211

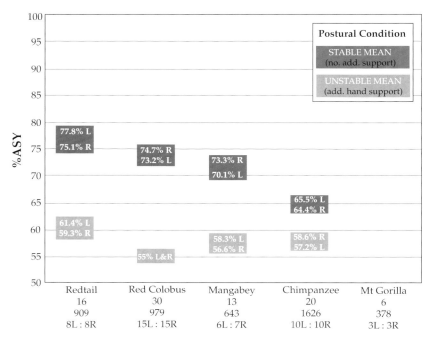

Figure 14.6. *Strength and direction of manual asymmetry by condition of relative postural stability.*

over time of this technology is based primarily on factors involving knapping efficiency and efficiency of raw material use. The attractiveness of this approach is in grounding research in the reality of the individual and the social group, and avoiding unnecessary assumptions, anthropocentric bias, and lack of alternative explanations for behaviour.

Discussion

Common problems interpreting hominin behaviour
A lack of integrative training and research underlies some of the most pervasive and serious methodological and theoretical weaknesses in the field of human origins research. Problems commonly found in attempts to reconstruct manual behaviour from the hominin record, whether from the Palaeolithic and fossil record or from extrapolating from living primates, are: 1) a failure to question assumptions, especially assumptions originating outside a researcher's area of expertise; 2) a willingness to tolerate anthropocentric bias in hypotheses; and 3) a failure to consider a range of alternative explanations (Holder & Sengelaub 1994). Thinking in terms of a cost : benefit : milieu approach would have helped researchers eliminate unnecessary assumptions such as these, minimize anthropocentric bias, and describe a range of behavioural repertoires that better reflect the real-life variations upon which selection acts.

Examples of problematic interpretation of the fossil and lithic hominin record
One assumption that human origins researchers have taken from nineteenth-century neural science is that handedness can serve as a marker for brain lateralization for language (cf. Toth 1985). A similar assumption is that an assessment of handedness can be used as 'evidence' for 'evolutionary precursors' for human language (MacNeilage *et al.* 1984). These are examples of the use of an erroneous oversimplification or assumption from one discipline being accepted without question as the foundation for research in another discipline (Holder in prep.).

Handedness is *not* a suitable method to assess brain lateralization. First, the relationship between the hand and the brain is neither simple, nor reliable, nor predictable; neurological tests indicate that most left-handers have the same left-hemispheric specialization for speech and language abilities as do right-handers (Branch *et al.* 1964; Rasmussen & Milner 1977; Szaflarski *et al.* 2002). Secondly, factors unrelated to hemispheric specialization can determine the expression of handedness; for example, cultural and social pressure, injury, intrinsic tool bias, etc. (Holder 1999). And thirdly, the definition of, and criteria for, categories of handedness are arbitrary, and this methodological problem alone can account for up to 30 per cent variation in how individuals are classified within one sample population (Martin 1952; Annett 1970, 319; Holder 1992).

In an oft-cited 1985 paper, Toth assumes that handedness can be used as a reliable marker for brain lateralization, and offers a method to assess the hand preferences of hominin tool knappers by analysis of cortical flake orientation. He concludes, based on analysis of lithic material from across continents, time periods, and hominin species, that '… there was a genetic basis for right-handedness by 1.4 to 1.9 million years ago … and this argues for the development of a profound lateralization of the hominin brain' (Toth 1985). Aside from the validity of the methodology being in doubt (Patterson & Sollberger 1986; Davidson & Noble 1996; Pobiner 1999) and the statistical problems associated with the analysis of time transgressive and taphonomically incomparable data sets, Toth failed to consider one alternative hypothesis that renders the premise of this methodology invalid — the possibility of ambidextrous and/or mixed-handed behaviour.

Not only does ambidexterity (and sometimes mixed handedness) leave no archaeological signature, it leaves *false* signatures of both left- and right-hand preferences (Holder & Sengelaub 1994; see Fig. 14.7). In an anthropocentric rush to determine whether hominins are 'like us' or not like us, we tend to frame hypotheses from our own perspective — in this case, 'were they right-handed?' in order to infer left-hemispheric specialization for speech and language (a second problematic assumption). To only consider whether or not individuals were 'left-' or 'right-handed' fails to assess the consistency of directional hand preferences across tasks (necessary to distinguish mixed-handedness), or to assess individual strength of hand preferences (necessary to distinguish ambi-dexterity) (Holder 1999).

Examples of problematic extrapolation from extant primate behaviour (human and non-human)
Similarly, few primatologists have been interested in the study of handedness *per se*; rather the interest in hand preference has been as a marker for hemispheric brain lateralization (Dimond & Harries 1984, 228; Kubota 1990, 393; Brenot 1992, 48; Rogers & Kaplan 1996, 13). A related assumption common among primate handedness researchers is that the *direction* of preference (right or left) is a more relevant variable than the *strength* of the preference. Studies of non-human primate hand preference often focus on testing for left or right preferences, sometimes disregarding variations in the strength of asymmetrical behaviour (e.g. Duel & Dunlop 1980; Hörster & Ettlinger 1985; Fagot & Vauclair 1988), which fails to consider the full range of manual behaviour, and thus limits hypotheses and possible outcomes.

Still another example of anthropocentric bias is the assumption that the conditions of arboreality or bipedality, *per se*, are 'posturally unstable' (Sanford *et al.* 1984, 223; Olson *et al.* 1990, 91; Ward *et al.* 1993, 56; De Vleechouwer & Verheyen 1995, 206). This assumption has led to a popular theory that 'postural instability' somehow leads to asymmetry (Sanford *et al.* 1984; Olson *et al.* 1990). However, as the data confirm, the definition of postural stability depends upon specific biomechanical relationships, not upon arbitrary categorization (i.e. it is common to find arbo-real and/or bipedal animals in posturally-stable states and to find quadrupedal and/or terrestrial animals in posturally-unstable states) (Holder 1999). Cost : benefit : milieu considerations can help researchers eliminate unnecessary assumptions such as these, minimize anthropocentric bias, and describe a range of behavioural repertoires that better reflect the real-life variations upon which selection acts.

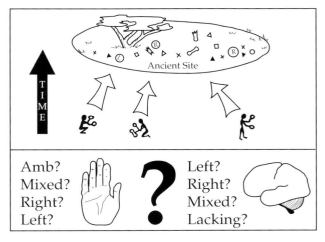

Figure 14.7. *Manual behaviour and site formation. Ambidextrous and mixed-handed behaviour leaves false 'left-' and 'right-handed' archaeological signatures. Also, hand preference is not a reliable marker for hemispheric language specialization.*

Future inquiry — What next?
Engrained in scientific inquiry is a long history of arbitrary categorization and comparison of (often false) dichotomies. Simple definitions of 'hominin' and of 'tool' weigh heavily upon the question of whether or not knapping stone was a uniquely hominin behaviour. With the plethora of recent fossil finds (White *et al.* 1994; Leakey *et al.* 2001; Haile-Selassie 2001; Senut *et al.* 2001; Ward *et al.* 2001; Brunet *et al.* 2002), the distinction between 'hominin' and 'ape' has become more, not less, complex. And documentation of living chimpanzees leaving flakes as a bi-product of stone hammer and anvil nut-cracking (Mercader *et al.* 2002a,b) shifts the emphasis away from establishing the possibility of ape 'stone knapping' (e.g. Toth *et al.* 1993) and toward comparative analyses of assemblages of small flakes and fragments between modern chimp 'sites' and ancient sites. Because be-haviour and evolutionary change usually develop along continuums, the use of dichotomous inquiry is problematic because it is overly-simplistic. That is, by limiting outcomes to either-one-or-the-other categories we constrain the range of possible findings and systematically eliminate or ignore the very data needed to resolve complex questions. (For instance, classification of handedness into right *versus* left omits the issue of ambidexterity — the very concept against which 'handedness' is defined — thereby precluding consideration of critically relevant data.) If the broad question is: '*How, why*, and *by whom* were stones knapped?', the 'by whom' question will be easier to address after first considering all the

evidence for how and why stone knapping might have occurred.

To address questions about *why* prehistoric manual specializations were acquired, we need a better understanding of comparative physiology, morphology, and environmental habitats. Specifically, what needs (nutritional, defensive, etc.) did early stone knappers meet with stone implements that would not have been possible without such innovative technology? Studies of comparative primate diet, behaviour, and ecology provide modern benchmarks from which to extrapolate likely ranges of prehistoric nutritional physiology (e.g. Leonard & Robertson 1997; Schoeninger *et al.* 2001). The challenge of reconstructing ancient environments may be approached both from what evidence remains (e.g. Sikes 1994, and Kingston *et al.* 1994 estimated the proportion of grass to woody vegetation across early hominin landscapes from the stable isotopic composition of palaeosols) and theoretical modelling (e.g. Sept 2001, modelled the palaeobotanical landscapes of early hominins by extrapolating from known ranges of the seasonal availability of modern vegetation, using modern human and non-human primate diet as benchmarks).

To address questions relating to *how* manual specializations are acquired, critical understanding comes from the fields of biomechanics, development, and learning. Studies of comparative primate skeletal structure and function compared with fossil hominin remains help define ranges of biomechanical possibilities (e.g. Marzke & Marzke 2000; Marzke this volume). Comparative cross-species behavioural studies help establish common primate behavioural responses (e.g. Holder 1999, describes common postural and manual behavioural adaptations to biomechanical constraint across varying substrata). Development and learning studies (e.g. Byrne & Byrne 1993; Inoue-Nakamura & Matsuzawa 1997; Londsdorf 2000; Matsuzawa 2002), both in the laboratory and in the field, help define developmental limitations and extrapolate ranges of primate behaviour that include the important variable of learning in skill acquisition. New methodologies, such as functional brain imaging and advances in genetics, continue to extend our knowledge of the relationship between brain, behaviour, and evolution (e.g. Obayshi *et al.* 2001; Ingman *et al.* 2000; Enard *et al.* 2002).

When addressing broad questions, one of our greatest challenges is how to encourage and implement integrative research and training. Individual disciplines remain deeply entrenched within their historical methodological approaches and theoretical perspectives, making it difficult for scholars to acquire the broad perspective necessary to fill gaps in current knowledge. Topical conferences and workshops will play an increasingly important role in helping scientists communicate and collaborate across multiple disciplines. Such communication is essential for assuring the appropriateness and validity of multi-disciplinary inquiries, and for inspiring researchers to develop better-informed theories and create new methodologies.

Acknowledgements

Merci bien to Dr Valentine Roux and Dr Blandine Bril for their integrative and artful organization of the workshop 'La Taille de la Pierre: Une Action Spécifique à l'Homme?' convened in Pont-á-Mousson, France, 21–24 November 2001. I thank Dr Frédéric Joulien for suggesting my work might contribute to the objectives of this workshop. To my fellow participants, especially Dr Daniela Corbetta, I express appreciation for their thoughtful deliberations and sharing of expertise. I am also grateful to Drs Jeanne Sept, B. Bril, and V. Roux for helpful comments on an early draft of this paper. Institutional support was provided by the Handedness Research Institute (handedness.org), the Center for the Integrative Study of Animal Behaviour, and the Department of Psychology at Indiana University.

References

Annett, M., 1970. A classification of hand preference by association analysis. *British Journal of Psychology* 61(3), 303–21.

Bekoff, M. & J.A. Byers (eds.), 1998. *Animal Play: Evolutionary, Comparative and Ecological Perspectives.* Cambridge: Cambridge University Press.

Beukelarr, L.J. & P.M. Kroonenberg, 1983. Towards a conceptualization of hand preference. *British Journal of Psychology* 74, 33–45.

Boesch, C., 1991b. Teaching among wild chimpanzees. *Animal Behaviour* 41(3), 530–32.

Boesch, C. & H. Boesch, 1984. Possible causes of sex differences in the use of natural hammers by wild chimpanzees. *Journal of Human Evolution* 13, 414–40.

Boesch-Achermann, H. & C. Boesch, 1993. Tool use in wild chimpanzees: new light from dark forests. *Current Directions in Psychological Science* 2(1), 18–21.

Branch, C., B. Milner & T. Rasumssen, 1964. Intracarotid sodium amytal for the lateralization of cerebral speech dominance: observation on 123 patients. *Journal of Neurosurgery* 21, 399–405.

Brantingham, P. J. & S.L. Khun, 2001. Constraints on Levallois core technology: a mathematical model. *Journal of Archaeological Science* 28, 747–61.

Brenot, P.H., 1992. Lateralized handedness, bipedalism and cortical specialization, in *Hands of Primates,* eds. H. Pruschoft & D.J. Chivers. New York (NY): Springer-Verlag, 45–53.

Brunet, M., F. Guy, D. Pilbeam, H.T. Mackay, A. Likius, D. Ahounta, A. Beauvilain, C. Blondel, H. Bocherens, J.-R. Boisserie, L. De Bonis, Y. Coppens, J. Dejax, C. Denys, P. Duringer, V. Eisenmann, G. Fanone, P. Fronty, D.

Geraads, T. Lehmann, F. Lihoreau, A. Louchart, A. Mahamat, G. Merceron, G. Mouchelin, O. Otero, P.P. Campomanes, M. Ponce De Leon, J.-C. Rage, M. Sapanet, M. Schuster, J. Sudre, P. Tassy, X. Valentin, P. Vignaud, L. Viriot, A. Zazzo & C. Zollikofer, 2002. A new hominin from the Upper Miocene of Chad, Central Africa. *Nature* 418, 145–51.

Byrne, R.W. & J.M.E. Byrne, 1993. Complex leaf-gathering skills of mountain gorillas (*Gorilla g. beringei*): variability and standardization. *American Journal of Primatology* 31(4), 241–61.

Corbetta, D. & E. Thelen, 1999. Lateral biases and fluctuation in infants' spontaneous arm movements and reaching. *Developmental Psychobiology* 34(4), 237–55.

Davidson, W. & I. Noble, 1996. *Human Evolution, Language, and Mind.* Cambridge: Cambridge University Press.

De Vleechouwer, L.V.E. & R.F. Verheyen, 1995. Effect of posture on hand preferences during experimental food reaching in bonobos *(Pan paniscus). Journal of Comparative Psychology* 109(2), 203–7.

Dimond, S. & R. Harries, 1984. Face touching in monkeys, apes and man: evolutionary origins and cerebral asymmetry. *Neuropsychologia* 22(2), 227–33.

Duel, R.K. & N.L. Dunlop, 1980. Hand preferences in the rhesus monkey. *Archives of Neurology* 37, 217–21.

Enard, W., M. Przeworski, S.E. Fisher, C.S.L. Lai, V. Wiebe, T. Kitano, A.P. Monaco & S. Pääbo, 2002. Molecular evolution of *FOXP2*, a gene involved in speech and language. *Nature* 418 (6900), 869–72.

Ericsson, K.A. & N. Charness, 1994. Expert performance — its structure and acquisition. *American Psychologist* 49(8), 725–47.

Ericsson K.A. & A.C. Lehmann, 1996. Expert and exceptional performance: evidence of maximal adaptation to task constraints. *Annual Review of Psychology* 47, 273–305.

Ericsson, K.A., R.T. Krampe & C. Teschromer, 1993. The role of deliberate practice in the acquisition of expert performance. *Psychological Reivew* 100(3), 363–406.

Fagot, J. & J. Vauclair, 1988. Handedness and bimanual coordination in the lowland gorilla. *Brain, Behaviour and Evolution* 32, 89–95.

Ferronato, S., D. Thomas & D. Sadava, 1974. Preferences for handedness, arm folding, and hand clasping in families. *Human Heredity* 24, 345–51.

Flowers, K., 1975. Handedness and controlled movement. *British Journal of Psychology* 66, 39–52.

Fushima, T., O. Sakura, T. Matsuzawa, H. Ono & Y. Sugiyama, 1991. Nut-cracking behaviour of wild chimpanzees *(Pan troglodytes)* in Bossou, Guinea (West Africa), in *Primatology Today,* eds. Akiyoshi Ehar, T. Kimura, O. Takenake & M. Iwamoto. Amsterdam: Elsevier Science Publications B.V., 695–6.

Goren-Inbar, N., G. Sharon, Y. Melamed & M. Kislev, 2002. Nuts, nut cracking, and pitted stones at Gesher Benot Ya'aqov, Israel. *Proceedings of the National Academy of Sciences of the USA* 99(4), 2455–60.

Haile-Selassie, Y., 2001. Late Miocene hominins from the Middle Awash, Ethopia. *Nature* 412, 178–81.

Holder, M.K., 1992. Hand Preference Questionnaires: One Gets What One Asks For. Unpublished MPhil thesis, Rutgers University, New Brunswick, NJ, USA. Online abstract: http://www.indiana.edu/~primate/92mphil.html.

Holder, M.K., 1999. Influences and Constraints on Manual Asymmetry in Wild African Primates: Reassessing Implications for the Evolution of Human Handedness and Brain Lateralization. Unpublished doctoral dissertation, Rutgers University, New Brunswick, NJ, USA. Online abstract: http://www.indiana.edu/~primate/phdabs.html.

Holder, M.K., in prep. Beyond Broca: how the historical use of handedness to assess brain lateralization impacts modern research. Manuscript in preparation.

Holder, M.K. & D. Sengelaub, 1994. Problems with the Use of Handedness as an Indicator of Brain Organization in Human Origins Research. Unpublished paper presented at the 12th Biennial Conference of the Society for Africanists Archaeologists (SAfA), Bloomington, IN, 28 April–1 May 1994.

Hörster, W. & G. Ettlinger, 1985. An association between hand preference and tactile discrimination performance in the rhesus monkey. *Neuropsychologica* 23(2), 411–13.

Ingman, M., H. Kaessmann, S. Pääbo & U. Gyllensten, 2000. Mitochondrial genome variation and the origin of modern humans. *Nature* 408, 708–13.

Inoue-Nakamura, N. & T. Matsuzawa, 1997. Development of stone tool use by wild chimpanzees (*Pan troglodytes*). *Journal of Comparative Psychology* 111(2), 159–73.

Johnstone, J., D. Galin & J. Herron, 1979. Choice of handedness measures in studies of hemispheric specialization. *International Journal of Neuroscience* (2), 71–80.

Kahney, H., 1993. *Problem-solving: Current Issues.* 2nd edition. Buckingham: Open University Press.

Kingston, J.D., B.D. Marino & A. Hill, 1994. Isotopic evidence for Neogene hominin palaeoenvironments in the Kenya rift-valley. *Science* 264 (5161), 955–9.

Köhler, W., 1927. *The Mentality of Apes.* 2nd edition. New York (NY): Harcourt Brace.

Kubota, K., 1990. Preferred hand use in the Japanese macaque troop, Arashiyama-R, during visually guided reaching for food pellets. *Primates* 31(3), 398–406.

Leakey, M.D., 1971. *Olduvai Gorge, Excavations in Beds I and II: 1960–1963.* Cambridge: Cambridge University Press.

Leakey, M.D. & D. Roe, 1994. *Olduvai Gorge, Excavations in Beds III, IV and the Masek beds: 1968–1971.* Cambridge: Cambridge University Press.

Leakey, M.G., F. Spoor, F.H. Brown, P.N. Gathogo, C. Kiarie, L.N. Leakey & I. McDougall, 2001. New hominin genus from eastern Africa shows diverse middle Pliocene lineages. *Nature* 410, 433–40.

Leonard, W.R. & M.L. Robertson, 1997. Comparative primate energetics and hominin evolution. *American Journal of Physical Anthropology* 102(2), 265–81.

Logan, G.D., 1988. Toward an instance theory of automatization. *Psychological Review* 95(4), 492–527.

Logan, G.D., 1997. Automaticity and reading: perspectives from the instance theory of automatization. *Reading & Writing Quarterly* 13(2), 123–47.

Londsdorf, E.V., 2000. Development and Acquisition of

Termite-fishing Skills in the Gombe Chimpanzees. Unpublished paper presented at 'The Apes: Challenges for the 21st Century' conference, Chicago, IL, May 2000. Online reprint retrieved 26 September, 2002 from: http://www.brookfieldzoo.org/pagegen/inc/ACLonsdorf.pdf.

MacNeilage, P.F., M.G. Studdert-Kennedy & B. Lindblom, 1984. Functional precursors of language and its lateralization. *American Journal of Physiology: Regulatory, Integrative and Comparative Physiology* 15(246), R912–14.

Mark, L.S., 1987. Perceiving the preferred critical boundary for an affordance, in *Studies in Perception and Action III*, eds. B. Bardy, R. Bootsma & Y. Guiard. Hillsdale (NJ): Erlbaum, 129–32.

Martin, K.L., 1952. Handedness: a review of the literature on the history, development and research of laterality preference. *Journal of Educational Research* 45, 527–33.

Marzke, M.W. & R.F. Marzke, 2000. Evolution of the human hand: Approaches to acquiring, analysing and interpreting the anatomical evidence. *Journal of Anatomy* 197, 121–40.

Matsuzawa, T., 2002. Chimpanzee Ai and her son Ayumu: an episode of education by master-apprenticeship, in *The Cognitive Animal: Empirical and Theoretical Perspectives on Animal Cognition*, eds. M. Bekoff, C. Allen & G.M. Burhgardt. Cambridge (MA): MIT Press, 189–95.

Mercader, J., M. Panger & C. Boesch, 2002a. Excavation of a chimpanzee stone tool site in the African rainforest. *Science* 296(5572), 1452–5.

Mercader, J., M. Panger & C. Boesch, 2002b. Chimpanzee-produced stone assemblages from the tropical forests of Tai, Cote d'Ivoire. *Journal of Human Evolution* 42 (3), A23–A24.

Obayashi, S., T. Suhara, K. Kawabe, T. Okauchi, J. Maeda, Y. Akine, H. Onoe & A. Iriki, 2001. Functional brain mapping of monkey tool use. *Neuroimage* 14(4), 853–61.

Oldfield, R.C., 1971. The assessment and analysis of handedness: the Edinburgh inventory. *Neuropsychologia* 9, 97–113.

Olson, D.A., J.E. Ellis & R.D. Nadler, 1990. Hand preferences in captive gorillas, orang-utans and gibbons. *American Journal of Primatology* 20, 83–94.

Patterson, L.W. & J.B. Sollberger, 1986. Comments on Toth's right-handedness study. *Lithic Technology* 15(3), 109–11.

Petersson, K.M., C. Elfgren & M. Ingvar, 1999. Dynamic changes in the functional anatomy of the human brain during recall of abstract designs related to practice. *Neuropyschologia* 37(5), 567–87.

Pobiner, B., 1999. The use of stone tools to determine handedness in hominins. *Current Anthropology* 40(1), 90–92.

Preilowski, B. & F. Leder, 1985. Comparative studies on laterality: hand use of a captive group of lowland gorillas, in *Bericht über den 34 Kongreß der Deutschen Gessellschaft für Psychologie in Wien 1984*, ed. D. Albert. Göttingen: Hogrefe, 550–52.

Rasmussen, T. & B. Milner, 1977. Clinical and surgical studies of the cerebral speech areas in man, in *Cerebral Localization*, eds. K.J. Zulch, O. Creutzfeldt & G.C. Galbraith.

New York (NY): Springer Verlag, 238–55.

Rogers, L.J. & G. Kaplan, 1996. Hand preferences and other lateral biases in rehabilitated orang-utans, *Pongo pygmaeus pygmaeus*. *Animal Behaviour* 51, 13–25.

Roney, L.S. & J.S. King, 1993. Postural effects on manual reaching laterality in squirrel monkeys (*Saimiri sciureus*) and cotton-top tamarians (*Saguinus oedipus*). *Journal of Comparative Psychology* 107(4), 380–85.

Sanford, C., K. Guin & J.P. Ward, 1984. Posture and laterality in the bushbaby (*Galago senegalensis*). *Brain, Behaviour, and Evolution* 25, 217–24.

Schoeninger, M.J., H.T. Bunn, S. Murray, T. Pickering & J. Moore, 2001. Meat-eating by the fourth African ape, in *Meat-eating and the Fossil Record*, eds. H.T. Bunn & C. Stanford. Oxford: Oxford University Press, 179–95.

Senut, B., M. Pickford, D. Gommery, P. Mein, K. Cheboi & Y. Coppens, 2001. First hominin from the Miocene (Lukeino Formation, Kenya). *Comptes Rendus de l'Academie des Sciences Paris* 332 (2), 137–44.

Sept, J.M., 2001. Modeling the edible landscape, in *Meat-eating and the Fossil Record*, eds. H.T. Bunn & C. Stanford. Oxford: Oxford University Press, 73–98.

Sikes, N.E., 1994. Early hominin habitat preferences in East Africa: palaeosol carbon isotopic evidence. *Journal of Human Evolution* 27(1–3), 25–45.

Spiegler, B.J. & G. Yeni-Komshian, 1983. Incidence of left-handed writing in a college population with reference to family patterns of hand preference. *Neuropsychologia* 21(6), 651–9.

Stout, D., 2002. Skill and cognition in stone tool production: an ethnographic case study from Irian Jaya. *Current Anthropology* 43(5), 693–722.

Szaflarski, J.P., J.R. Binder, E.T. Possing, K.A. McKiernan, B.D. Ward & T.A. Hammeke, 2002. Language lateralization in left-handed and ambidextrous people: fMRI data. *Neurology* 59(2), 238–44.

Toth, N., 1985. Archaeological evidence for preferential right-handedness in the lower and middle Pleistocene, and its possible implications. *Journal of Human Evolution* 14, 607–14.

Toth, N., K.D. Schick, E.S. Savage-Rumbaugh, R.A. Sevcik & D.M. Rumbaugh, 1993. Pan the tool-maker: investigations into the stone tool-making and tool-using capabilities of a bonobo (*Pan paniscus*). *Journal of Archaeological Science* 20(1), 81–91.

Ward, C.V., M.G. Leakey & A. Walker, 2001. Morphology of *Australopithecus anamensis* from Kanapoi and Allia Bay, Kenya. *Journal of Human Evolution* 41, 235–368.

Ward, J.P., G.W. Milliken & D.K. Stafford, 1993. Patterns of lateralized behaviour in prosimians, in *Primate Laterality: Current Behavioural Evidence of Primate Asymmetries*, eds. J.P. Ward & W.D. Hopkins. New York (NY): Springer-Verlag, 43–71.

Warren, W.H., 1984. Perceiving affordances: visual guidance of stair climbing. *Journal of Experimental Psychology: Human Perception and Performance* 10, 683–703.

White, T.D., G. Suwa & B. Asfaw, 1994. *Australopithecus ramidus*, a new species of hominin from Aramis, Ethopia. *Nature* 371, 306–12.

Chapter 15

Humans, Tools and Handedness

James Steele & Natalie Uomini

Precision tool use typically involves preferential use of a dominant hand in humans and some other animal species, and in humans the right hand tends to be the preferred hand. We outline conventional criteria for recognizing handedness in living subjects, and summarize some recent genetic models of the stability of human handedness as a polymorphism. We then summarize skeletal and (in greater detail) material-culture evidence for hand preference in the fossil and archaeological records. Such observations suggest that right handedness has been predominant even in early species of our own genus, although the fossil sample is exceedingly small.

The roles of the hands in tool-using tasks

Skilled tool manipulation usually falls into the category of asymmetric or differentiated bimanual activities (Guiard 1987, 487). With remarkable consistency, individuals divide the work between their two hands in a predictable and regular fashion. More specifically, one hand tends to be preferred as the one that executes an action on the object, while the other hand stabilizes the object. Most remarkably, in about eight or nine out of ten individuals it is the right hand that is selected to play the leading role (making it the dominant hand). This role typically involves finer movements, in terms of both spatial and temporal resolution (Guiard 1987, 497). The pattern is exemplified by stone knapping, where the dominant hand wields a hammerstone to strike a core that is supported by the non-dominant hand.

This pattern of population-level hand preference seems to distinguish us from other living primates, among whose populations and species it is hard to discern any such bias. Because our own right-handed bias seems to be related, via the linking mechanism of cerebral dominance, to another unique human feature (language processing: e.g. Hécaen & de Ajuriaguerra 1964; Bradshaw & Rogers 1993), an enormous volume of research has been dedicated to its understanding. In this chapter we shall introduce some aspects of the research literature in psychology and behaviour genetics, to provide context for our own archaeologi-

cal interests. We shall then discuss some skeletal and material-cultural markers of hand preference that may enable us to track the evolution of human handedness empirically.

Measurement of handedness

Handedness is measured in a variety of ways, which are either preference based or performance based (McManus 1996). Skill and preference tend to be highly correlated, although there are exceptions. Skill is usually measured by comparing the two hands in rapid aimed movement tasks such as the Annett pegboard task (Annett 1970), which measures how fast each hand can move ten pegs in a board from one row of holes to another. Handedness is assessed by calculating the relative speed advantage of the more skilled hand, and is therefore treated as a continuous variable. Preference is usually measured by questionnaires which ask about the preferred hand for each of a series of tasks, and in which the respondent indicates the strength of the preference on an ordinal scale (e.g. Always Right, Usually Right, Either, Usually Left, Always Left). Responses are usually summed into a Laterality Index by allocating values (e.g. +2, +1, 0, −1, −2) to each position on such a scale. In younger children and non-human primates, for whom a questionnaire is inappropriate, preference may instead be directly observed in a series of simple tasks.

Both measures give comparable results when used to determine broad patterns of left- and right-hand use at the population level. The preference measure has been more widely used, perhaps because it is simpler to administer. Inevitably some questionnaire items are subject to culturally-learned biases, a factor that obviously complicates interpretation of the most simple preference measure used in literate societies (the writing hand). However, there is some well-designed research using both skill and preference measures, which indicates that questionnaire responses can be analyzed and a factor identified relating to precise motor control which is impervious to cultural influences (Connolly & Bishop 1992).

One group of researchers has attempted to collect data in an ethological manner, resembling the way handedness data is collected for non-human primates such as chimpanzees. They found that human manual preference in non-tool-using tasks is less right biased than implied by the questionnaire measures (which are heavily biased towards object manipulation tasks). Marchant *et al.* (1995) tabulated hand use observed in ethnographic videos from groups of three traditional cultures (G/wi, Yanomamo, and Himba) using the kind of task classification that would be used in an ecologically-valid primate study. Examples of behavioural categories of limb movements included reaching for objects, scratching oneself, eating, and using tools. Their results evidenced a barely-discernible right hand preference for all tasks at the population level, although a stronger right-hand bias was found for tool use only (particularly where it involved a precision grip, which agrees with Guiard 1987).

Asymmetries in hand skill and movement control

In explaining the functional neurology of human handedness, most researchers take the right-hander as their prototype. Hand skill is often measured by aimed movement tasks (such as the Annett pegboard task, described above), and right-handedness is generally explained by reference to a left hemisphere advantage for fine temporal resolution of sensory input and motor output (Carson 1993). An advantage for the dominant hand is usually seen not in simple ballistic movements, but in movements of greater difficulty (in the Fitts' Law sense, Fitts 1954; also in terms of finer spatial and temporal resolution, Guiard 1987). Flowers (1975) hypothesized that in movements of greater difficulty as measured using Fitts' Index, and which imply a 'corrective mode of control', the dominant hand would have an advantage because of an underlying advantage in the rate of information transmission. Carson (1993, 481) discusses two explanations for this advantage. One is the 'feedback processing' model, which proposes that the left hemisphere is more efficient in error correction using sensory feedback. The other is the 'output vari-

ability' model, which proposes that the left hemisphere permits more precise control of net forces and force durations. There is still considerable uncertainty regarding which of these models is more valid.

There is also considerable debate regarding the level of organization at which neurophysiological asymmetry is found. A voluntary bimanual movement can be analyzed in terms of three levels of organization (Peters 1995, 201). These are Level 1 (the level at which the goal is formulated), Level 2 (the level at which 'the precisely timed commands for the initiation and termination of the movement trajectories of the two hands are issued': Peters 1995, 202), and Level 3 (the level 'which governs the final outflow of control for the particular hand that allows the hand to perform the movement as required': Peters 1995, 203). Peters (1995) favours an asymmetry in attentional processes which influences hand skill at Level 1, while Sainburg (2002) suggests that the causal agent is an asymmetry in the control of limb segment inertial dynamics which occurs downstream from the trajectory planning level. It is beyond the scope of this chapter to do more than note these debates, and point out their relevance to understanding the kinds of skilled movement control involved in the knapping gesture (e.g. Roux *et al.* 1995; Roux 2000).

Explanations of the prevalence of left- and right-handedness

The observation that other living primates do not show as strong a right-handed bias as humans at the population level (MacNeilage *et al.* 1987; Marchant & McGrew 1991; Sugiyama *et al.* 1993) has led some evolutionary psychologists to conjecture that the initial ratio of right and left-handedness was 50:50 in early hominins. If this is correct, then the present ratio of about 90:10 in humans can only have arisen subsequently through natural selection. This implies that right-handed individuals had a reproductive advantage, namely that the genes associated with right-hand dominance were positively selected for and were able to spread via Mendelian inheritance through our species. From this argument it also follows that some explanation must be given for the persistence of a small proportion of left-handers, despite this selection towards right-handedness.

There are several competing explanations for the present-day incidence of right- and left-handedness, and three of these will be detailed below. Some postulate that human right-handedness is the norm, and that left-handedness is pathological; however, there is little empirical support for such an extreme position. Others have proposed that while there are disadvantages to left-handedness, compensating advantages may accrue which are frequency-dependent. Most commonly, however, the argument is made that handedness is under partial genetic control with significant environmental modification during development. In such models, it is argued that the advantage lies with those who are moderately right-handed, but that the interaction of genetic and environmental influences produces greater phenotypic variation, ranging from left-handedness to extreme right-handedness. All such explanations have to address the empirical findings of an apparently stable underlying prevalence of about 10–15 per cent left-handedness, and of a male excess (about five males are left-handed for every four females: McManus 1996).

The most famous of the explanations which propose that left-handedness is pathological is the Geschwind-Behan-Galaburda hypothesis (Geschwind & Behan 1982; 1984; Geschwind & Galaburda 1985a,b). This proposes that individuals, by default, develop to be right-handed unless there is some testosterone-induced developmental delay in the growth of the fetal left hemisphere, causing not just left-handedness but also atypical language lateralization (and other less intuitive disorders, such as a high rate of autoimmune disease). This hypothesis has been exhaustively examined in clinical studies, and the verdict must now be that it is not supported (e.g. Bryden *et al.* 1994). Other explanations exist which relate left-handedness to developmental neurological disorders, particularly in the context of fetal growth retardation and of premature birth (Bakan 1971; Bakan *et al.*1973; Satz 1972). While such trauma, however, may account for a small fraction of left-handers whose preference is genuinely secondary to fetal brain insult, it does not seem to explain left-handedness in more than about one in twenty cases (Bishop 1984).

A second class of explanation interprets the persistence of left-handedness in low frequencies as due to some cognitive or other advantage, which counteracts any developmental disadvantages. This only works if the frequency of left-handedness stays below some critical level. The evidence for an association between developmental delay and elevated frequencies of non-right-handedness is quite strong, with some studies indicating greater risk for short stature, reduced body mass, and delayed onset of puberty (e.g. Coren & Halpern 1991; Mulligan *et al.* 2001; but see also Eaton *et al.* 1996). Claims for some specific competitive advantage associated with left-handedness are based on apparently elevated frequencies of left-handedness in certain activities and professions (Peterson & Lansky 1977; but see Wood & Aggleton 1991; Mebert & Michel 1980; Gotestam 1990). More recently, an argument for

a frequency-dependent advantage for left-handed fighting has been proposed, based on observed elevated incidences of left-handedness in interactive and combat sports (Raymond *et al.* 1996). In particular, because left-handers are in the minority, they are more successful when they fight against right-handers. Such proposals entail specific predictions about the interaction between culturally-variable selection coefficients for left-handedness, and the distribution of variance in reproductive success: higher fitness would be expected for left-handers who live in very violent societies. However, detailed genetic models to support such proposals have not yet been articulated, and until they have been, we should be wary of confusing correlation with causal explanation.

The third class of explanatory models invokes the genetic theory of a balanced polymorphism with heterozygote advantage. The single-locus theories for laterality propose that there is a gene, made up of two alleles (either one can be recessive or dominant), for left-hemisphere cerebral dominance, which causes strong right-handedness as well as language lateralization. Annett (1985; 2002) calls this the Right Shift allele (R+), and the alternative is simply an inactive allele (R–, which we will refer to here as 0). Since each person inherits one allele from each parent, there are three possible genetic combinations (genotypes): 2 R alleles (homozygous), 2 0 alleles (homozygous), or 1 R allele and one 0 allele (heterozygous). In the absence of the R gene, individuals may develop right- or left-hemisphere dominance with equal likelihood as a result of chance environmental factors during development (Annett 1985; 2002; McManus 1985; cf. Laland *et al.* 1995). The reason why we do not all have this gene is because there is an advantage for being heterozygous (R0) at this single locus. It is better to have one allele causing the 'right shift', and another allele which gives no such bias, because their interaction will tend to produce the optimal outcome — moderate left-hemisphere dominance, and thus, moderate right-handedness. Some individuals (00 homozygotes) will have a complete absence of the right-shift gene (which, cultural biases excepted, will tend to produce left-handedness in about half of the cases), and other individuals (RR homozygotes) will have a double dose of the right-shift gene (which will bias towards extreme right-handedness).

The idea of a heterozygote advantage is not new, the classic example being the malaria hypothesis for sickle-cell anaemia (Haldane 1948, cited in Durham 1991, 123). Among the populations of tropical West Africa there are three classes of haemoglobin genotypes: AA, AS, and SS. The A allele is the normal condition for haemoglobin. The recessive S allele is a mutation of the haemoglobin molecule which causes sickle-cell anaemia, but also confers resistance to malaria. People with the AA genotype have a normal (severe) reaction to malaria; people with the SS genotype have severe sickle-cell anaemia; but people with the AS genotype only show very weak sickle-cell symptoms and very low rates of malarial infection and mortality. The advantage of the AS genotype lies in the combination of normal and sickling haemoglobin. AS haemoglobin, only when infected with malaria, begins a sickling process which leads to the death of the malarial parasites. Normal AA haemoglobin does not have this capability, whereas the anti-malarial ability of SS haemoglobin is overshadowed by the high mortality caused by sickle-cell disease (Durham 1991, 106 ff. & 481).

These latter genetic models do quite well in accounting for the patterns we observe for heritability of handedness, and for the patterns observed in twinning. To date, however, the evidence for a quantifiable heterozygote advantage associated with moderate right-handedness has been equivocal. Several attempts to identify this advantage have investigated its possible behavioural origin (i.e. a cognitive advantage: Annett & Manning 1989; a link to schizophrenia: Crow *et al.* 1998; but see Nettle 2003), although there have been few if any studies of the measurable direct effects on reproductive fitness. Recent work by Yeo & Gangestad (1993; Yeo *et al.* 1993) does advance this field somewhat, although still not measuring direct fitness consequences of heterozygosity at the cerebral dominance locus. They have found that compared with moderately right-handed individuals, both left-handers and extreme right-handers have higher incidences of the minor physical anomalies that are associated with developmental instability (which is, in turn, associated with generalized homozygosity).

Skeletal correlates of handedness

To summarize our discussion so far, it seems that there is an advantage for the dominant hand in tool use that relates to an underlying efficiency in information-transfer rate in the contralateral cerebral hemisphere. This advantage is seen in the greater skill of the dominant hand when executing voluntary movement tasks with high levels of difficulty in the Fitts's Law sense, or tasks with very fine spatial and temporal resolution in the Guiard sense, and in which a corrective mode of control is indicated. It seems likely that the neurological basis of this asymmetry in skill is only weakly genetically determined, with considerable scope for environmental influence during development. Individuals vary both in their hand preference and in the degree to which one hand is more skilled than the other.

The evolutionary origins of the most commonly observed pattern, namely a left-hemisphere specialization for the executive role and consequent right-handedness, are of course matters of intense scientific interest and debate. It is beyond the scope of this paper to review such debates further, since that would require us to digress into the evolutionary anatomy of language. In this section, therefore, we shall summarize some forms of skeletal evidence enabling us to track the evolution of handedness in tool use as seen in the fossil record (see also Steele 2000, from which this three-page summary is abstracted).

Many studies in recent years have demonstrated the range of adaptive responses of the skeleton to patterns of mechanical loading *in vivo* (e.g. Carter 1987) These responses can include increases in bone strength due to increased bone density and/or cross-sectional area, increases in mechanical efficiency by shape change, and resistance to avulsion by increasing the surface area of the sites of attachment of muscles and ligaments on a bone's surface. Evidence suggests that in any particular case, the effect of muscle strength and mechanical loading on bone-mineral formation is localised to the specific site of muscle–bone interaction. Because a consistent hand preference leads to lateral asymmetry in the mechanical loading experienced by the two hands, arms and shoulders during life, we can diagnose the handedness of a deceased individual by studying right–left differences in the lifetime skeletal response to loading strains.

In humans, supporting evidence is found from a number of studies that have quantified skill and strength differences between the dominant and the non-dominant hand and arm. It is plausible that some skill differences are developmentally canalized, but that skill and strength differences are subsequently amplified by habitual patterns of use. Annett has found that in the pegboard task, the dominant hand is capable of performing with an average speed advantage over the other hand of 4.2 per cent in females and 3.4 per cent in males (Annett 1998). Other similar tasks produce larger skill asymmetries between the two hands (10–12 per cent: Tapley & Bryden 1985). It has also repeatedly been observed that in right-handed adults of both sexes, normal grip strength in the dominant hand tends to be about 10 per cent greater than the grip strength of the non-dominant hand (Thorngren & Werner 1979; Petersen *et al.* 1989; Crosby *et al.* 1994; Chau *et al.* 1998). A similar pattern of relative pinch strength between the dominant and non-dominant hand has also been reported (with the dominant hand about 10 per cent stronger than the non-dominant hand: Brorson *et al.* 1989; Bimson *et al.* 1997; Chau *et al.* 1998). Further contrasts relating to hand preference have been described for wrist extension, with the dominant side having on average about 10 per cent greater wrist extension strength (Richards *et al.* 1993). Perplexingly, however, left-handed subjects are equally likely to have a stronger grip in either hand (Crosby *et al.* 1994; Petersen *et al.* 1989); perhaps this reflects the need for left-handers to adapt their hand-use pattern to the constraints of a right-handed world. An effect of work pattern has been reported (Josty *et al.* 1997): heavy manual workers have the strongest grip and the least strength difference between the two hands, while office workers have the weakest grip and the greatest strength difference between the two hands. Light manual workers were found to be intermediate between these two groups.

The bones of the hand, arm and shoulder girdle

A repeated clinical observation is that the bones of the right hand tend to be larger than those of the left hand, as does the volume of the hand itself (Purves *et al.* 1994). This is seen in radiographs (McLeod & Coupland 1992), although in the earliest studies of side differences in the second metacarpals by Garn *et al.* (1976) and by Plato *et al.* (1980) no correlation was found with handedness (as measured either by hand preference or by grip strength). A correlation of relative hand size with handedness has been reported for right-handers, although not for left-handers (Purves *et al.* 1994). Most recently, Roy *et al.* (1994) have reported finding bilateral asymmetry of bone area in the second metacarpal correlated with hand dominance, in which handedness was assessed by the subject's own personal impressions of which handedness group they belonged to.

In right-handed adolescents and adults, muscle mass tends to be greater in the arm on the dominant side (Chhibber & Singh 1972; Schell *et al.* 1985; Neumann 1992; Taaffe *et al.* 1994). It is also well established that the right humerus and radius tend to be slightly longer and heavier than their left counterparts (Latimer & Lowrance 1965; Ruff & Jones 1981). There have been a number of recent radiographic studies of professional racquet sports players and other athletes, who may begin their training early in childhood, and whose dominant arms tend to experience unusually large mechanical loads during the playing years (Buskirk *et al.* 1956; Jones *et al.* 1977; Haapasalo *et al.* 1994; Tsuji *et al.* 1995; Kannus *et al.* 1996). These studies have concentrated on differences between the long bones of the two forelimbs in bone-mineral content, bone mineral density and cross-sectional cortical area. They repeatedly observe greater bone-mineral density and content in the long bones (humerus, radius, ulna) on the dominant side (a pattern also found, but less markedly, in normal control samples). Such modern radiographic studies converge on the finding that activity stresses produce adaptive responses in the bones of the dominant forelimb, effects that ought to be discernible as measurable asymmetries in paired skeletal elements in individuals from archaeological populations.

Asymmetrical loading patterns are also found in people without intensive sports training. Ingelmark, in an early and pioneering radiographic study (1946), found that greater forelimb length (as measured by the sum of the lengths of the humerus and radius) was correlated with the side of the preferred hand in children. In this study he classified as left-handers all children who reported the use of their left hands in at least two of seven everyday tasks. Consistent with modern behavioural data on handedness, females are also more likely than males to have longer long bones in the right forelimb. Two recent studies of tennis players and normal controls go some way to replicating, among adults, Ingelmark's finding (Krahl *et al.* 1994; Haapasalo *et al.* 1996).

Reichel *et al.* (1990), in a radiographic study of normal adults, also found a correlation between handedness and the side of greater bone-mineral density and bone width in the radius in its midshaft and distal segments. The ulna appears to be the bone with least bilateral asymmetry of the three long bones in the arm. In professional racquet sports players, the effect of prolonged unilateral loading on increase in bone-mineral content and bone mineral density in these bones is slightest at sites in the ulnar shaft and the distal ulna (Haapasalo *et al.* 1994; Kannus *et al.* 1996). Presumably this reflects its lesser role in distributing mechanical load in racquet sports. Kennedy (1983), however, has observed preferential development of the ulnar supinator crest in the right arms of males in some archaeological populations of modern humans, apparently reflecting the stresses involved in overarm throwing (as, for example, of a hunting spear).

Effects of activity on the bones of the shoulder girdle (scapula, clavicle) have been less frequently studied than they have on the long bones of the forelimb, but all these bones often show clear asymmetries related to handedness. It is usual to find a greater range of motion in the gleno-humeral joint (where the humerus articulates with the shoulder blade) on the side of the preferred hand (Bonci *et al.* 1986). In the clavicles, the right bone tends to be both shorter and more robust than the left. Mays *et al.* (1999), in a study of the clavicles from the predominantly mediaeval population of Wharram Percy, have found this same pattern and have also found a tendency for the areas of attachment of the costoclavicular ligament (the site of a feature known as the rhomboid fossa) and of the trapezoid ligament to be more developed on the right side. These authors support the hypothesis that loading of the dominant limb exerts greater axially compressive forces on the ipsilateral clavicle, leading both to shape changes (greater robusticity) and to greater development of the attachment sites of those ligaments which stabilize the clavicle within the shoulder girdle during axial compression.

These post-cranial skeletal markers of asymmetrical development in the shoulder, arm and hand appear to provide us with a very extensive tool kit for diagnosing handedness in past populations. However, a number of other processes may affect the development of asymmetry in paired skeletal elements in the forelimb and shoulder girdle, and these should also be taken into account in any such analysis (cf. Steele 2000, 213–14). These other processes include both fluctuating asymmetry, and directional asymmetries favouring growth in one member of a pair of bones when these are due to innate developmental biases and not to mechanical loading history. Pathological development of elements of one side of the body is a third potentially complicating variable.

Skeletal markers of handedness in human evolution and prehistory

If our inferences about the relationship between handedness, tool use and the adaptation of bone to loading are correct, then we would expect asymmetrical skeletal development to occur only in primate species which are extremely tool-dependent (i.e. humans, and their tool-dependent hominin ancestors). Schultz (1937) recorded asymmetries of the lengths of arm bones (humerus and radius) in a large sample of ape skeletons (including 130 gorillas, 82 chimpanzees, 8 orangutans, and 21 gibbons). In marked contrast with the 722 human skeletons in his sample, he found no tendency for the right arm to be dominant in apes as assessed by this measure. He also found that the mean degree of asymmetry (unsigned) in apes was about half that found in the arm bones of humans. These findings concur with the observation, mentioned above, that apes do not exhibit either the population-level right-handedness seen in humans, or the degree of loading of the individually-dominant side which is seen in the human bones.

If we examine skeletons of relatively recent populations from the historical period, the patterns suggest that frequencies of right- and left-handedness have been relatively stable across the centuries. Steele & Mays's (1995) study of asymmetry in the summed lengths of the humerus and radius in the medieval

Wharram Percy cemetery population found a pattern in adults very similar to that reported by Annett for the distribution of manual performance asymmetries in the modern British population, with 81 per cent showing the right-handed pattern, 3 per cent showing no significant asymmetry, and 16 per cent showing the left-handed pattern.

These frequencies of arm-length asymmetry were almost identical to those recorded by Schultz (1937) in anatomy collections in the US, where the percentages of instances falling into each of the same categories were 80:4:16 in a pooled sample of 232 Americans of European ancestry. Schultz (1937) recorded data on long-bone length asymmetries for the humerus, radius, and for both combined, partitioned by sex and also by population (his sample also included 233 Americans of African origin, 122 Alaskan Eskimo-Inuit, 118 North American Indians, and smaller samples of Chinese and of Aboriginal Australians). The overall incidence for the whole pooled sample is 79 per cent longer right arms, 3 per cent equal to measurement precision, and 18 per cent longer left arms. For all the populations for which sex information was tabulated, the females were always less likely to have longer left arms and more likely to have longer right arms (which is consistent with sexual dimorphism in the incidences of right- and left-hand preference: cf. Seddon & McManus 1991).

Moving back slightly further in time, we can also analyze skeletal samples from earlier populations of modern humans (*Homo sapiens sapiens*). Thould & Thould (1983) examined 416 adult skeletons from Romano-British Poundbury, and found that the arm bones were longer on the right side in 210 individuals and on the left in 65 (the rest were not measurably asymmetrical). A study of asymmetries in the radii in a sample of 27 individuals from three Neolithic farming sites in the Middle Elbe-Saale region, Germany, found a right-dominant pattern in 70 per cent of individuals, with 15 per cent left-handed and 15 per cent 'ambidextrous' (Reichel *et al.* 1990). However, the discriminant function used to predict handedness in this study is likely to have somewhat inflated the estimated frequencies of non-right handedness. In foraging peoples of early Holocene (Mesolithic) northern Europe, most individuals studied had longer right forelimbs, a pattern seen slightly more strongly in females (Constandse-Westermann & Newell 1989). 24 adult males had longer right arms (summed lengths of the humerus and radius), and 9 had longer left arms. For the females, the ratio was 19 with longer right arms to 5 with longer left arms.

Moving significantly further back into evolutionary time, fossil hominin remains can also be analyzed. There is only a very small number of individuals of extinct species whose skeletons are preserved in sufficient completeness to enable left–right comparisons of paired upper-limb elements. This limited evidence suggests, however, that predominant right-handedness extends back in time to at least the early members of our own genus *Homo*, around 1.6 million years ago (mya). The skeleton of the Turkana boy from Nariokotome, WT-15000 (early African *Homo erectus*, also called *Homo ergaster*), has greater development of the clavicular area of attachment of the right deltoid muscle and greater length of the right ulna, consistent with right-handedness (Walker & Leakey 1993). Asymmetry in the shafts of the humerus consistent with right-arm dominance is also prevalent in Neanderthal skeletons: of six skeletons in which the relevant measurements could be taken bilaterally, all were more robust in the right arm (Trinkaus *et al*. 1994). The Neanderthal individual buried at Le Régourdou, dated to between 75 kya and 60 kya, also shows several markers for right-handedness, such as a thicker and more curved right clavicle, ulna, radius, and humerus (Vandermeersch & Trinkaus 1995).

Material cultural markers of handedness

The skeletal evidence is very sparse for Pleistocene and earlier hominins. Technology provides another, more abundant data source. Archaeological evidence from tools and other artefacts can also be used to infer the evolution of human handedness, and is summarized first by method of estimating handedness (subjective fit in the hand; tool production including multiple flake analyses and knapping gestures; lateralized retouch; asymmetrical tool use and use-wear; teeth marks; and art including representations of tool use, engravings, cave paintings, and hand prints), and then within each method, by time period (from earliest to most recent evidence) and by material (stone, bone, wood, antler, bronze, etc.).

Subjective and early assessments
A number of early archaeologists involved in excavations have observed that certain tools fit better in the right or left hand. Nowadays archaeologists refrain from making such comments because they are seen as unscientific, but in the last century they were acceptable. For example, Gabriel de Mortillet (1890) claimed that there were more left-handers in prehistoric times, based on Neolithic double-edged scrapers from France and Switzerland. Strangely, he had previously (1883) argued for the opposite, finding that most 'hand-stones' of 'very early tribes' found in the Somme gravels were made for right-hand use (cited in Brinton 1896). Other right-hand supporting declarations were also made by Black *et al*. (1933), by Evans (1897) about handles and hafts for bronze sickles and swords in Swiss lake dwellings and English barrows (see also Wilson 1891, 138), and by Sarasin *et al*. (cited in Spenneman 1985 and Posnansky 1959).

Such subjective observations were based on an intuitive supposition of how to hold the tool, because the grips, purposes, and manners of tool use were not known. Nonetheless, it is interesting that separate researchers have made similar judgements of material from vastly distant sites both in time and space. These early assertions are therefore worth including in this review and may be worth revisiting in the future, especially now that the methods of gripping and using tools are becoming better-known. Semenov's (1964) volume is a good example of the level of detail that can be obtained in a study of use-wear in order to specify the precise kinds of hand configuration that were used to grip tools during their use. Also, recent papers by Takeoka, Phillipson, and Posnansky, which will be discussed below, do take grip position into account.

Another early argument was proposed by Dart (1949), although his ideas are now considered fanciful. He hypothesized that baboons from Sterkfontein had been hunted by tool-wielding hominins, as the crania seemed to show signs of crushing from hand-held bone weapons. These patterns, Dart suggested, indicated predominant right-handedness because a right-hander holding a tool will tend to strike the front left (if from a face-on attack), or rear right (if from a stealthy rear attack), parts of the victim's skull. Although Dart's hypothesis was developed with the scientific reasoning of his time, our current knowledge of taphonomy, as well as continuing excavations at Sterkfontein, has enabled criticisms of Dart's ideas. For example, Brain (1981, 263–4; 1994) describes the types of taphonomic processes involving carnivore gnawing and roof collapses that can produce the damage patterns observed by Dart.

Tool production
Two studies have analyzed large assemblages of flakes to find proportions of right and left flakes; they are those of Bradley & Sampson (1986), and Toth (1985). In addition, four studies look at scatters from single knapping events. Fischer (1990), Högberg (1999), Newcomer & Sieveking (1980), and Wenban-Smith (1997) present data from experiments and archaeological sites showing that the knapper's handedness produces a distinct scatter pattern on the ground. The knapping gesture also imposes constraints on accuracy and, therefore, on the homogeneity of flake-surface attributes. Three studies

have used arguments from the knapping gesture to indicate asymmetrical features on tools and flakes (Rugg & Mullane (2001), Takeoka (1991), and White (1998)). Finally, we include an anecdotal report of a left-handed knapper who was buried with his core and hammerstone in hand.

Tool production: multiple-flake analysis
An influential study by Toth (1985) proposed that right-handedness can be seen in the archaeological record by reconstructing the preferential direction of core rotation during initial flaking. The direction of rotation of the core was inferred from the presence of cortex (the outer surface of a flint nodule) on the right or left side of the dorsal surface of a flake. He studied flakes from Koobi Fora (Kenya) from a number of sites dated to between 1.9 and 1.4 mya, predominantly of the Oldowan industry, but included one Early Acheulean site (dated to between 1.4 mya and 700 kya). It is important to note that Toth's method only applies to a specific reduction strategy, namely the use of single-platform cores. This involves removing all the flakes from the same platform, in sequence. On a round cobble, this reduces the number of possible flaking locations to two: in front of the previous removal, or behind it. Toth's own replications of Karari scrapers produced 56 per cent right-biased flakes, caused by rotating the core clockwise in the left hand. He argues that this decision is dictated by 'the musculo-skeletal structure of the left hand and arm, in which the superior power of the supinators and flexors produce a preferential rotation in this direction for a stronger and more controlled turning motion (O. Lovejoy pers. comm.)' (Toth 1985, 611). The finding of 57 per cent right-oriented flakes at six Koobi Fora sites suggested that the Koobi Fora knappers, hominins from 1.6 mya, were at least as right-handed as Toth. He also studied Acheulean flakes from Ambrona (Spain), dated to 400–300 kya, and found 31 left-oriented for 48 right-oriented flakes, a R:L ratio of 61%:39%.

In a study of Acheulean handaxes from Caddington, UK (dated to 115–130 kya), Bradley & Sampson (1986) replicated biface and Levallois reduction sequences by a right-handed knapper. They classified the flakes with respect to cortex retention as well as the presence and location of relict margins. A tentative analytical method was created which yielded a handedness index of 62 per cent R for the experimental collection, and 54 per cent R for the archaeological sample. The authors interpret these results as a weaker bias towards right-handedness in Caddington compared to the experimental knapping.

Bradley & Sampson's classification according to relict margin location means that reduction sequences

are taken into account, a notion which also appears in Toth's argument although it is open to criticism. This has to do with extending the Toth method to other archaeological collections. In fact, for most types of knapping, the order of flake detachment is mostly contingent on the shape of the core or flint nodule (Patterson & Sollberger 1986; Pobiner 1999). The fact that the Karari cores were flaked from a single platform certainly allowed good serial flaking. This was demonstrated by Ludwig & Harris (1994), who confirmed that right-handers rotated the core clockwise and left-handers counterclockwise when making Karari scrapers. Therefore we must be cautious when applying Toth's method to industries whose reduction strategies were not restricted to serial flaking. With other kinds of flake production, the figures seem to approach 50:50 as the sample sizes increase (Noble & Davidson (1996), 170; Pobiner 1999; Uomini 2001).

Tool production: knapping scatters
Although there are very few high-resolution sites with *in situ* knapping scatters (e.g. Högberg 1999), they are valuable because they can reveal handedness. It has been shown experimentally that a knapper sitting on a seat produces a central concentration of debris which is skewed to the side of the knapping hand. For example, Fischer (1990) describes a series of conjoined artefacts found in place at the Trollesgave site, Denmark, near a large stone. The site is dated to 9100 BC and the artefacts are referred to the Bromme technocomplex. Fischer, a right-hander, experimentally replicated the Trollesgave blades while sitting on a similar stone seat, in the event producing a scatter which was most dense in front of his feet, fading out to the sides, and right-oriented. The archaeological scatter was also orientated to the right, located similarly in front of the stone. When sitting directly on the ground, with one leg folded and one leg straight out, a clear triangular scatter appears. Newcomer & Sieveking (1980) replicated 16 Neolithic axe roughouts at the site of Grime's Graves, UK. The left-hander, Newcomer, sitting on the ground with his right knee bent and left leg out, produced a right-skewed scatter ending abruptly where the legs were. It must be noted that there is another action which can produce a concentrated scatter: the use of a piece of hide or cloth for leg and crotch protection. The pieces which fall on the material collect into a distinct heap when they are dumped onto the ground, for example when emptying the debris or when the person stands up. It is important to note that the dumped heap looks identical whether the knapping is done sitting on the ground, on a seat, or squatting (Newcomer & Sieveking 1980). Specifically,

the manner in which the roughout was held during flaking did not seem to have much effect on the size and shape of flake scatters. When the [sheepskin] thigh pad is used, it catches the flakes as they are struck and the flakes then tend to drop in a circular heap below. Without the pad, which is difficult to use when standing or seated on the floor, the flakes are either caught in the fingers and then dropped, or allowed to shoot off freely; in either case the roughly circular shape of the scatter is recognisable. (Newcomer & Sieveking 1980, 350)

Similarly, Wenban-Smith (1997), a right-hander, sat on the ground with the left leg folded and right leg out (the inverse of Newcomer) and produced a left-skewed scatter bounded by the legs.

Tool production: knapping gesture

With respect to knapping gestures, Takeoka (1991) defines two kinds of movement which affect the position of the flake blank (or core), and thus the angle at which it receives the hammerstone blows. One is wrist abduction/adduction, the other is forearm pronation/supination. When knapping, the axis of wrist movement (if the palm is placed flat on a table, this would be a side-to-side motion of the hand) affects the direction of fracture force propagation within the core; this is the effect that the cone of percussion method exploits, although they argue for an entirely hammerstone-based cause (Rugg & Mullane 2001). Forearm rotation affects the working angle (angle between the platform and hammerstone trajectory); a more pronated wrist results in an obtuse angle (because the platform is tilted towards the body) while a more supinated wrist results in an acute angle (platform tilted away from the body). A third factor, wrist flexion/extension, affects the horizontal position of the striking platform, bringing it closer to the knapper's eyes (Takeoka 1991, 503–5).

Rugg & Mullane hypothesize that:

the angle at which the cone of percussion occurs relative to the striking platform is usually around 90 degrees, but can vary ... Because the human arm has pivot points at the shoulder, elbow and wrist, it is plausible that some blows would lead to cones of percussion that were angled to the right or left relative to the striking platform. (Rugg & Mullane 2001, 252)

Because the Hertzian cone indicates directionality, its skew should reflect the exact trajectory of the hammerstone. Rugg & Mullane experimentally validated their recognition criteria, with four left-handed knappers and four right-handers: in a blind test they were able to assign 75 per cent of those flakes that had a clear cone of percussion to the correct handedness.

The fact that right-handers produced right-skewed cones and left-handers produced left-skewed ones indicates that the tendency to skew the blow comes from either slight, unintended supination of wrist or unintended flexion at the elbow of the knapping arm. The basic knapping gesture, as described above, consists of partially pronating the wrist and simultaneously adducting the forearm, so any deviation to orient the blow towards one's body is caused by extra supination and/or flexion. These biomechanical suggestions depend on the bimanual configuration used in knapping, which is discussed below.

For simplifying purposes, we will say that knapping can be done with five general hand positions, or configurations. The first four involve holding the core against one leg and are grouped as two different techniques: Flake Support and Free Fall. We suggest these names to reflect the immediate intention for the resulting flakes. Newcomer & Sieveking (1980) refer to 'Free Fall' vs 'Deliberate placing in a heap', to distinguish ways of treating blades as they come off the core. Generally, Flake Support is used when the flake itself is the intended product, meaning the knapper wants to prevent it from falling to the ground where it might break; the core is pressed against the thigh so that the resulting flake will lie sandwiched between the core and leg. In Flake Support, the core is held either against the outer surface of the ipsilateral (same side as core hand) thigh, or the inner surface of the contralateral thigh. Conversely, Free Fall tends to be used when the flakes are waste products; in this case, the core is pressed against the leg so that the flake comes off the 'free' side of the core and falls to the ground. In Free Fall, the core is held either against the inner side of the ipsilateral thigh (flaking between the legs), or the outer side of the contralateral thigh (flaking on the outside of the body, where the knapping arm has lots of space to move).

However, these suggestions are by no means strict rules, as the shape of the flake is dictated by the way the hammer's energy is transferred. Specifically, in Flake Support, the hammer arm's trajectory is stopped by the leg, causing the energy to flow into the leg; this tends to produce curved thinning flakes. In Free Fall, the hammer arm can follow through its trajectory, resulting in the energy going through the core, producing flat thinning flakes (B. Bradley pers. comm.).

An important factor affecting knapping configuration is the technique, defined by the type of hammer (F. Sternke pers. comm.). A soft hammer (i.e. antler) requires much greater velocity, meaning one tends to knap with Free Fall so as not to smash one's leg. Hard hammers (i.e. most stones) can be wielded with less speed, so it is possible to use Flake Support. Also, when thinning a handaxe, the core is normally held in the hand or with Flake Support. This gives more control of core spatial configuration, and prevents end shock (an unpredictable accident causing the handaxe to snap in two).

Additionally, one can entirely support the core in one hand (Newcomer & Sieveking call this Freehand: 1980, 349). For large or heavy objects the forearm can be supported in turn by the ipsilateral thigh (this configuration is observed in knappers from Papua New Guinea: see Stout 2002). For small objects or when finer control is needed, the core is held in the unsupported hand, such as in the thinning stage of handaxe production.

In addition to the five mentioned above, other configurations do exist, such as holding the core between the two legs (as in indirect percussion for blade production), or holding the core against an object (anvil, tree stump, ground, etc.). It is also important to note that some methods (core-reduction strategies) make use of more than one knapping configuration. For example, making blades by direct percussion first requires making a crest, which 'is done on the outside of the thigh' (Newcomer & Sieveking 1980, 350), and second, platform preparation followed by blade removals, both 'done between the legs' (Newcomer & Sieveking 1980). In his blade experiments, Newcomer produced two distinct scatters separated by his leg, containing two different types of debitage, reflecting the use of these two configurations.

The manner of holding the core can also interact with the reduction strategy, indicating handedness. White (1998) identified four possible bimanual configurations for manufacturing twisted ovates. These bifaces exist in British sites dated to from late OIS-11 to early OIS-10 in significant proportions (20–46 per cent) at sites like Bowman's Lodge, Wansunt Pit, and Swanscombe (all three in Kent), Elveden and Foxhall Road (Suffolk), Allington Hill (Cambridgeshire), and Hitchin Lake Beds (Hertfordshire), and in France dated from OIS-12/11 to possibly OIS-8. Twisted ovates are made with a particular method, usually at the finishing stage: first, one quarter of the edge is flaked unifacially. Then the handaxe is inverted through the long axis and one quarter of the opposite face is flaked. These two sets of unifacial removals, on opposing faces, are now joined at one tip of the handaxe. Next, the piece is rotated (clockwise or counterclockwise) 180 degrees and one more quarter flaked unifacially. Finally, the piece is inverted through the long axis again and the opposite quarter is flaked, bringing the last two sets of removals to join at the other end of the handaxe. The result is a handaxe with an edge alternating four times between the two faces. This makes the profile look 'twisted' in the same way, no matter how you hold it.

For all four edges that are knapped unifacially, it is the handaxe which is rotated so that the hammer hand always knaps in the same 'active zone' of the core hand (White 1998, 99). The interpretation of handedness comes from the fact that nearly all twisted ovates have a Z-shaped profile rather than an S shape. This means that there are two possibilities for the active zone: either the area near the wrist for a right-hander, or the area near the fingers for a left-hander. (A right-hander using the fingers area, as well as a left-hander using the wrist area, would produce an S twist.) The use of the fingers area can only be justified if the prehistoric knappers were mostly left-handed, and so this possibility can be excluded, leaving only the right-handed option as an explanation of the Z-shaped profiles.

Finally, a remarkable burial was found at Hazelton North, Cotswolds, UK, dated to 5500 BP (Saville 2003). This tomb contained a male, 30–45 years old, with a flint core beneath his right elbow, and a hammerstone at the place of his left hand. The core and hammer were most likely placed into the burial after his death; they were either placed faithfully, meaning he was a left-handed knapper, or he was right-handed and they were placed incorrectly, meaning his buriers disregarded the hand he used when knapping.

Lateralized retouch
Five authors (Cornford 1986; Phillipson 2000; Semenov 1964; Blankholm 1990; Brinton 1896) describe evidence of handedness from asymmetrically-retouched tools. This asymmetry can be due to lateralized use, making it necessary to retouch the more worn side of the tool, or simply from constraints in knapping when holding the piece. Cornford (1986) describes flakes resulting from a *coup de tranchet*. The site of La Cotte de St Brelade, France has a long stratigraphy spanning the last two interglacials (from 240 kya to 122 kya). The tools were resharpened with a tranchet blow to freshen one edge of one face of the tip. These sharpening flakes were removed by right-handers in proportions ranging from 77 per cent to 91 per cent, from oldest to youngest layers of the site. Further evidence comes from the use of bone retouchers (Semenov 1964, 163). The artefacts come from Middle Palaeolithic (Kiik-Koba and Teshik-Tash) to Upper Palaeolithic (Kostenki 1) sites in Russia, dated to 37–34 kya. Semenov indicates dents on the convex side of bone retouchers which met at an angle of 75–85 degrees to the long axis, suggesting they were used by right-handers. Blankholm (1990) also found lateralized retouch on microlithic armatures of the Maglemosian industry (9.5–8 kyr BP) in southern Scandinavia. These lanceolates and triangles were mostly retouched on the left side, in

proportions from 50 per cent to 100 per cent, and this was not due to any functional constraints. Phillipson (2000 and pers. comm.) notes a site containing chert scrapers at Aksum, Ethiopia, dated to the fifth to sixth centuries AD, which are asymmetrical in shape. They consistently have one spurred corner, usually on the left, and which Phillipson attributes to habitual use in the right hand. An early study of North American Indian tools by Brinton (1896) measured three asymmetrical criteria: offset point asymmetry, side of lateral retouch, and blade 'twisting'. He found about two-thirds more right-handed features than left-handed ones in undated blades of chert and jasper (Ohio), chert, quartz, and jasper (Wisconsin), and argillite, jasper, quartz, and black chert (New Jersey).

Use and use-wear
Two authors examined the traces left on stone tools by use, specifically scrapers and flakes (Frame 1986; Semenov 1964). Three authors include specific constraints about grips in their analysis (Takeoka 1991; Phillipson 1997; Posnansky 1959). Two authors and colleagues studied use-wear from a rotating motion (Keeley 1977; Cahen *et al.* 1979; Cahen & Keeley 1980; Spenneman 1987). Roosevelt (1974) describes asymmetrical wear on wooden spoons. Gerharz & Spenneman (1985), along with Wilson (1885; 1886; 1891), report evidence of use-wear and use patterns from bronze sickles. Three authors point to the necessity of hiring left-handed miners in Roman times.

The La Cotte artefacts were examined for microscopic use-wear traces to determine handedness by another technique. Frame (1986, in the Cornford volume) inspected the striation orientation and bands of polish from working wood, hide, or other materials on long sharpening flakes. Of 18 right-asymmetrical sharpening flakes, 4 had oblique rightward marks, 1 left, and the remainder either perpendicular, parallel, or multidirectional. Of 4 left-asymmetrical flakes, 2 had traces of moving leftward, 1 perpendicular, and 1 multidirectional. Frame proposed that these marks, in relation to the working edge indicating the direction of tool use, showed they were preferentially used by right-handers.

Semenov (1964, 87f.), in his volume on use-wear, described the mechanism for asymmetrical scraper wear. The scrapers were used on hide, without handles, simply held in the hand. Because the tool is held 'with its axis at an angle of 75–80 degrees to the skin surface', by implication, there is a constraint on simultaneous abduction of the upper arm and pronation of the wrist/forearm (in orienting the tool-using hand perpendicular to the surface being worked). This implies that force is more efficiently exerted when the

arm is less abducted and the forearm less pronated. Semenov counted that about 80 per cent of end-scrapers are worn on the right side. His data include Russian (Kostenki 1, Timonovka, Mezin, Suponevo, Sakajia) as well as other Upper Palaeolithic sites. Takeoka (1991) further argued from scraper usage, with the assumption that the scraper was pulled towards one's body, the ventral surface at the front. In this motion, the thumb is pressed against the ventral surface, fingers supporting the dorsal surface. Takeoka argued that the working edges of the scrapers are mostly located on the side of the flake that will put the proximal (thickest) end of the flake inside the cupped palm, rather than the fingers, and therefore were made for right-handers. Phillipson (1997) confirmed this effect. She scrutinized 54 handaxes and cleavers recovered by an LSB Leakey excavation in 1931 in Kenya. Their stratigraphy is dated to about 1 mya. Starting from the premise that the trailing face, not the leading face, of a used edge, would show greater signs of use, Phillipson reconstructed possible grip types for each piece. Of 54 tools, 6 (11 per cent) could be assigned to probable left-hand use, 45 to the right hand, and 3 were indeterminate. Constraints of use involve the efficient exertion of force and resistance of finger and hand muscles:

> rotation of the wrist without shifting fingers permits the concave edge to be used as a pull scraper. (Phillipson 1997, 180)

Some implements had more than one working edge, and so by implication were held in several different ways:

> These positions would have allowed for a number of types of force to be exerted in several directions with the tool, depending upon exactly how the hand was placed. A line of force from the working edge through the central mass of the tool to the base of the palm of the hand, for example, permits steady pressure to be applied while the fingers are partially freed to rotate the tool in subtle scooping, twisting or scraping motions. A grasp in which the handaxe is compressed between the tips of the fingers and the palm of the hand is needed to prevent loss of control when it is used for heavy cutting or sawing in a direction parallel to the utilized edge. The shock of chopping or digging motions is best absorbed by the front of the palm of the hand or the base of the fingers, although a posture with the fingers well spread and the force falling somewhat further forward is also effective. (Phillipson 1997, 174)

Furthermore, an asymmetrical weight distribution on the tool can facilitate use:

> a hand-hold was provided by a retained area of the original cortex or a flake striking platform on an otherwise bifacially worked specimen. In most instances this more rounded area was associated

with an asymmetric bulge on one or both faces of the handaxe which fit comfortably into the concavity of the user's grasp and greatly facilitated the controlled manipulation of the tool. (Phillipson 1997, 174)

This latter statement, like the next one below, is an example of how to reconcile the nineteenth-century subjective observations mentioned above with the rigorous scientific approach preferred today. A similar observation on the use-constraining effects of asymmetrical weight distribution in the artefact was made by Posnansky (1959), in studying a collection of Early to Middle Acheulean handaxes from the Trent Valley (UK) and 118 handaxes from the Furze Platt site (UK). He states:

it is found that the displacement of the weight away from the cutting edge, which a non-central median ridge implies, increases the efficiency for cutting. (Posnansky 1959, 42)

Like Phillipson, Posnansky tested the handaxes for ease of use in either hand, assuming a cutting function. Specifically, 'the most efficient method of cutting is one in which the butt of the tool is held in the palm of the hand with the fingers splayed around the blunter of the two edges and the flat face of the tool faces the inner cut face' (Posnansky 1959, 43). Of 40 complete tools in the Turton collection, 35 per cent were found to better accommodate the right hand, 12.5 per cent the left hand, and 52.5 per cent either hand. Two independent observers found similar proportions: they assigned the following respective proportions to the same handaxes 37.5 per cent-15 per cent-47.5 per cent and 22.5 per cent-10 per cent-67.5 per cent.

Keeley (1977) describes a biface from Clacton (200 kya) with microscopic use-wear showing it was used with a vertical rotating motion, such as boring holes, in a clockwise direction. Keeley's argument implies that greater torque forces are exerted during wrist supination (clockwise for a right-hander) than pronation. Indeed, supination produces more torque than pronation (Sellers 2004), and this is the reasoning behind the design of screws: they must be screwed in clockwise, which exploits the stronger supinating torque of the right hand. The mode of prehension is not specified, but a tool being vertically rotated can be held either with the elbow up and palm facing outward (screwdriver grip), or with the elbow down and palm inward (stabbing grip). This presupposes that whatever the grip on the tool, people grind in a direction outward from the centre. In a screwdriver grip, the wrist must produce mainly supinating forces, while grinding with a stabbing grip, the wrist produces mainly extensor forces. Both of these could reflect a preference to supinating/extension rather than pronation/flexion (which would be the forces

required if the grinding motion went inward). Cahen *et al.* (1979) confirm this constraint:

Although a back-and-forth turning of the borer is efficient when the borer is hand-held, the outward turn of the wrist is more powerful. Experimental observations have shown that the return stroke in the weaker, inward direction is usually accompanied by a slackening of the vertical pressure. (Cahen *et al.* 1979, 668).

In other words, boring is usually done with a back-and-forth motion, but the outward stroke produces the bulk of the striations. In addition, microwear polish and edge damage indicate the principal direction of turning:

Generally speaking, microwear polish forms on the aspect of edge ridges and projections facing toward the principal direction of turning, while utilization damage is created most heavily (sometimes only) on the aspect facing away. (Cahen *et al.* 1979, 681, in reply to objections from Newcomer and Odell).

Using the same analysis method, Cahen and colleagues (1979; Cahen & Keeley 1980) studied flint tools from Meer. This Belgian site was excavated in the 1960s and 70s, and is dated to 9 kyr BP. The lithic assemblage is characterized by Tjonger points, which are backed blades used in projectiles. They examined the use-wear on 31 tools which had been used for boring holes in, and engraving, bone and antler. These thick-bitted borers are called becs. The becs were grouped according to which flint block they could be refitted to; there were 6 refit groups in this sample. 21 becs had been used clockwise and 3 counterclockwise. These three becs were all knapped from the same block, suggesting they were made and used by a single person. The authors conclude that the main knapping scatter, called Concentration IV, was produced by at least two people, one of whom was left-handed (Cahen *et al.* 1979, 671).

Another study using the marks from rotating motions was made by Spenneman (1984a), who examined Swiss and German Neolithic bone, antler, and stone grinding tools. These tools display striations running from the top left to bottom right (for a right-hander) and top right to bottom left for a left-hander. The sites are all dated to between 4050 and 2900 BC, contain 19.4 per cent (of 31) left-handed tools at Burgerroth, Germany, 19.6 per cent (of 51) at Bodman, Germany and 6.3 per cent (of 597) at Twann, Switzerland.

Roosevelt (1974) examined a series of wooden and bone spoons and spatulas from northern Chile. They come from the Chiu Chiu site and are dated to AD 1000–1500. Roosevelt also created an experimental set of wooden spoons used, right-handedly, to stir and scoop food in a coarse ceramic bowl, and these showed lateral wear on the distal end. The archaeological spoons consisted of 76 determinable tools, of which 48 were right worn, 4 left worn, and 26 bilaterally worn. Because the archaeological and experimental spoons show identical wear patterns, their usage for mixing food as well as pigment and snuff was confirmed. Bone and wooden spatulas were also probably used with the concave part facing toward the user and the handle slightly angled (not vertical), as this is the most effective way to hold them (Roosevelt 1974, 102). This implies particular constraints on combinations of motor acts when performing a stirring or ladling motion.

Spenneman (1987, 22) offers some suggestions for identifying use-wear in adzes:

> In general, the movement of a hafted adze blade is not vertical but oblique in relation to the operator's body. This is due to the nature of the ball joint between the shoulder blade and the humerus. This angle is more oblique if the adze is held in one hand, than when held in both. In case of a right-handed individual, the movement runs from top left to bottom right (as viewed by the worker). ... Due to this slightly oblique movement the edge of the stone adze does not hit the worked material in an optimal manner, one end of the edge making contact earlier than the other.

In application of these constraints, Gerharz & Spenneman (1985) describe two bronze farming tools from northern Ethiopia showing use by left-handers. The tools can be related typologically to industries around 1000 BC, although direct dating of the site disagrees. Several cast adzes from Yeha, a site contemporary with Haoulti, have asymmetrical use-wear. The upper face is more worn on the right corner, indicating it was used by a left-hander. Another adze from the same site shows right-handed use, as do two other adzes from other northern Ethiopian sites. Furthermore, one cast sickle from Haoulti, dated to between 300 BC and AD 100, is worn from intensive use. It was made for a left-hander because it has a strengthening rib running along the upper face, and the upper face was hafted on the left, meaning it was held in the left hand. The authors report finding, among 8000 bronze sickles, only four other left-handed sickles (two German ones, one Hungarian and one Romanian).

The use of left-handed workers has been documented in Roman times, in the context of mining. Röder (1957) describes the Roman mines for tuff (consolidated ash) in the Pellenz, Brohl Valley, Rheinland (Germany), in which there were usually 3 left-handers for 2 right-handers (3:2), or even 2:1. The workers used rods to dig out the walls of the mines, making vertical walls. The left walls were straightened by right-handers, and the right walls had to be straightened by left-handers (Bedon 1984, 158). In the Gallo-Roman mine at Saint-Boil (France, 1st century AD), the rectangular blocks had to be carved out by two miners working together, one of each handedness (Monthel 2002, 96). The biomechanical constraints of working close to a wall with a mining rod meant that the proportions of right and left handed miners had to be carefully selected; these should be visible in the written records that some miners kept of their workers (G. Monthel pers. comm.).

Cut marks on teeth

Three studies have studied the marks left on Neanderthals' anterior dentition by using stone tools to cut meat held between the teeth. This is ethnographically common (Semenov 1964, 104):

> Generally pastoral or hunting people (like the nomads of Mongolia, Tibet, Abysinnia and other countries) eat such meat with a knife in one hand. Meat is normally cut into strips, and baked or cured in this form. Then each person takes a piece and, holding one end in his teeth, cuts it free with a quick movement of the knife at his mouth, repeating the operation until the whole strip has been consumed. The cutting is done upwards from below. We have seen this done among Nenetz reindeer herdsmen in the Kanin peninsula in 1928.

The striations on Neanderthal and pre-Neanderthal hominins' teeth were examined by Bermúdez de Castro *et al.* (1988) and by Fox & Frayer (1997). In addition, the Boxgrove hominid has similar marks on its two teeth. If one dislikes the idea of using the teeth as tools (e.g. Bax & Ungar 1999, who explicitly reject a connection between handedness and striation orientation), there is also the interesting possibility that these marks were made by chipping flint with the teeth, an action which has been observed in Plains Indians (USA) and Australian Aborigines (Hester 1973).

Bermúdez de Castro *et al.* (1988) reported on striations found on the front teeth of *Homo heidelbergensis* individuals from the Sima de los Huesos site (Atapuerca, Spain) (19 teeth, comprising 4 individuals and 10 unassigned teeth), the La Quina 5 Neanderthal (2 teeth), one isolated tooth from Cova Negra, Hortus (several anterior teeth from 5 individuals), and include published data on Saint Brais (1 isolated tooth), Angles-sur-l'Anglin (1 isolated tooth), and the Shanidar 2 Neanderthal (2 teeth). Rough dates for these fossils are as follows: Atapuerca about 300 kya; La Quina 35–30 kya (a French cave with artefacts from a Mousterian area and an Aurignacian-Châtelperronian area); Cova Negra 120–35 kya (a Spanish cave with many stone tools, faunal, and Neanderthal remains); Hortus 60–55 kya (a French cave with many Neanderthal remains and stone tools); St Brais 50–40 kya (a Swiss cave); Angles-sur-l'Anglin 14–13 kya (a middle Magdalenian rock shelter with paintings); Shanidar 60 kya (a Neanderthal cave burial in Iraq).

For comparison, a prognathic mouth-guard with fake enamel Neanderthal teeth was worn by a right-hander. The experimental procedure involved holding a piece of meat between the front teeth and cutting off bite-sized pieces with flint flakes. The experimenter made striation patterns consistent with a right-handed downward motion from left to right (when viewed from the front), matching those on the fossil teeth. All of the fossil samples (except Angles, which has horizontal marks, and Hortus VIII) show striations pointing downward to the right. The teeth from Hortus VIII has inversely oriented striations, suggesting this individual was a left-hander.

The authors state that 'in the experimental study, the action that would produce striations as in scheme C [consistent with a right-handed operator cutting leftwards] was uncomfortable and felt less efficient' (p. 410). This implies that it would be equally uncomfortable and inefficient for a left-hander to cut rightwards, and therefore the observed rightward fossil striations preclude a left-handed product. The inefficiency of the right-handed leftward motion implies a constraint on simultaneous pronation at the wrist and extension of the forearm. A right-hander cutting from below (as described by Semenov) would produce pattern D on his/her teeth, consistent with a left-hander cutting leftward from above. But Bermúdez de Castro et al. (1988) did not observe pattern D in the fossils, suggesting the cutting was done downwards by right-handers. Furthermore, the authors identified partial Hertzian cones in the striations which indicate a downward cutting direction.

Fox & Frayer (1997) studied the teeth of Krapina Neanderthals, which also show striations consistent with cutting meat held between the teeth. Six of the thirteen individuals above age thirteen were found to display rightwards scratches, with one showing leftwards scratches. The remaining six individuals showed no predominant pattern (judged by the 50 per cent mark). Fox & Frayer also include published data from Kabwe and Tabun individuals, who also have right-handed striations. Further evidence comes from the two Boxgrove (400 kya) hominin teeth, which both came from the same mouth and were adjacent bottom front teeth, and show similar striations. They also indicate right-handed cutting with flint (Pitts & Roberts 1997, 265).

In total, these three studies reveal only 2 left-handed hominins for 19 right-handers. The number of individuals of unknown or indeterminate handedness is 7 in these studies, but we might assume that the proportion of right to left (10.5 per cent) is roughly similar in the indeterminate samples.

Art

Upper Palaeolithic and later art is a further source of evidence for handedness. One suggestion is that the paintings and engravings are easier to read, and therefore were made, with a light source coming from above on the left side (Delluc & Delluc 1993, 44); meaning the artists held their torch in the left hand because they needed to use their right hand to draw and engrave. Other forms of evidence are images of people using their hands, engraved pebbles whose characteristic traces show the direction of engraving, the drawing of animal silhouettes, and the proportions of handprints and hand stencils made with the right and left hands.

Representations of lateralized tool use

Five studies have counted the number of depictions of right- and left-handed tool use in works of art. Uhrbrock (1973) made an extensive review of laterality depicted in paintings, sculptures, medallions, coins, and stamps. He reports higher proportions of left-facing profiles on US coins and medallions, but more right-facing profiles on European coins and medallions dating from 600 BC to AD 1964. Painted portraits are also slightly more likely to depict right-facing people. Depictions of tool use in sculptures, columns, and drawings from the Renaissance to modern times show right- and left-handedness, and representations of the Madonna holding her Child frequently show her holding him on her left side (Uhrbrock 1973). This might reflect either a conscious choice of the painter/sculptor, or the need for right-handed mothers to keep their dominant hand free. Another review was made by Coren & Porac (1977), who tabulated 1180 instances of unimanual tool and weapon use depicted in drawings, paintings, and sculptures from Europe, Asia, Africa, and America, spanning the time 15,000 BC to AD 1950. 92.6 per cent of these images portrayed right-hand use, remaining significantly consistent across geographical areas and time periods. Other such studies are described by Spenneman (1984a, 613); Dennis (1958) studied Egyptian paintings in tombs and found 7.5 per cent ($n = 120$) left-handed actions in the 2500 BC-dated sample, and 4.76 per cent ($n = 191$) left-handed depictions in the more recent sample. An assessment of hand use depictions was made by Spenneman (1984b), for a decorated Buddhist pyramid in Central Java which was constructed between the eight and tenth centuries AD. Spenneman studied 1504 scenes (none depicting the Buddha). These reliefs depict 14,892 people, 1085 of which are using their hands unimanually. Most (926 = 83.5 per cent) were simply holding an object, and only 153 (= 16.52 per cent) were performing a skilled action. The unskilled actions include leaning on a stick, holding a horse, a sword, a flower, axe, fan, umbrella, or reaching for something. The skilled actions include playing an instrument, manipulating food, riding an elephant, and using a weapon such as a sword, knife, bow and arrow, or spear. The right to left ratio for skilled actions was found to be 137:16 (89.5 per cent right-handed), while the ratio for unskilled actions was 578:348 (62.4 per cent right). Spenneman takes these figures to reflect reality, and rejects the possibility of artistic stylization, as the pyramid shows no signs of mirror-image symmetry or 'other kind of arts-connected constraint' (p. 165). It is possible, however, that such a constraint existed in the totem poles studied by Marrion & Rosenblood (1986). They examined 110 depictions of hand use in carved standing poles (nineteenth to twentieth century) used for houses and totems in the Kwakiutl Indian areas off the west coast of British Columbia. They found 20 per cent right-handedness, 24 per cent left-handedness, and 56 per cent simultaneous use of both hands.

Engravings

D'Errico (1992, 100, 99) reports on four possible ways of configuring the two hands and arms, derived from his experimental replications of engraved Azilian pebbles at Rochedane, le Mas d'Azil, and Pagès, France. The Azilian culture was Mesolithic, between 11 kya and 8 kya. D'Errico showed (1988) that the engravings were made working towards oneself, and therefore they tend to produce the frequently-observed pattern of right to left juxtaposition. Observing the clockwise direction of turning while working the pebbles, he notes that 'in all the engravings with two opposed series the surface was rotated 180 degrees between one series and the next' (1992, 100). This is a similar constraint to that mentioned by White (1998) for the working of twisted ovates. Studying the grooves with scanning electron microscopy, d'Errico (1988) showed that a right-hander engraving from left to right creates a groove which is compacted along the edge closest to the user. Drawing from top to bottom, the compact area runs along the left side (1988, 172–6). The incisions on the 27 Azilian pebbles are consistent with having been made from left to right by a right-hander.

Profile drawing

There have been many suggestions that, when drawing a person or animal in profile, a right-hander tends to draw the face to the left, and a left-hander facing right. Proponents of this hypothesis include Wilson (1885, 132; 1891, 33), Breuil (1952), Leroi-Gourhan (1965), Perelló (1970, 141), Alter (1989), and Willcox (1991, 146). One of the earliest mentions is from J.S. 1870 (cited in Uhrbrock 1973, 28), who wrote

> Most boys know that it is easier to draw a profile with the face looking toward the left hand; yet on looking over the hieroglyphs in the British Museum the faces will be generally found toward the right.

Alter (1989) made an experimental study of 231 subjects (19 L handers and 148 R) who were asked to quickly draw six shapes (bicycle, dog, bus, face profile, airplane, pitcher). The results showed consistent J-distributions in the location of the leading feature (i.e. the 'direction' of the drawing). Namely, the direction was strongly correlated with handedness, with most subjects consistently directional and a sharp drop-off to weaker and weaker consistency. Like Wilson, Perelló (1970) confirms this tendency to draw leading features on the side contralateral to the drawing hand:

> We have observed that when right-handed children draw man or animal faces, these faces always look left. On the contrary, left-handed children draw faces looking right. (Perello 1970, 141)

The only one so far to argue for more left-facing (and hence more right-handed artists), Wilson (1886, 17) refers to hieroglyphs at Palenque (Mexico, Mayan site), in which 'most' of the animals are depicted looking to the left.

On the opposite side, some argue that prehistoric painters were more left-handed than nowadays, or ambidextrous. This is the case of Perelló, Breuil, Leroi-Gourhan, and Willcox. Breuil (1952) reported finding 50.56 per cent right-oriented profiles in European cave art (*n* = 720) (cited in Willcox 1991). Similarly, Leroi-Gourhan (1965) reported 58.9 per cent right-oriented profiles in European cave art (cited in Willcox 1991). Perelló found, in the Spanish cave of Altamira, equal numbers of right- and left-facing bison (Perello 1970, 142). From these and other references (books on cave art, etc.) Perelló agrees with the high proportions of left-handers among prehistoric 'artists'. André Leroi-Gourhan (1965, cited in Willcox) found 58.9 per cent right-facing animals, as did Breuil (1952), who found 50.56 per cent right-facing profiles (Breuil (1952). From a survey of several site records, Willcox (1991) found figures ranging from 53 per cent to 64 per cent right-facing animals in South African, San, and nearby rock art. He speculates that the right hemisphere's superiority in face/pattern recognition, colour perception, and other visual abilities causes a higher proportion of left-handers to be artists, and agrees that the African data supports greater prehistoric left-handedness than in living San bushmen. Pales, cited in Delluc &

Delluc (1993, 44) also found more animals facing to the right, and concluded there must have been more left-handers in prehistory.

Handprints and hand stencils
A substantial body of literature has been published on counts of right and left handprints and stencils in caves. As these are frequent throughout the world, easy to count, and were directly created by the hands of actual prehistoric people, they contribute valuable data. There are three ways of making representations of hands in caves or rock shelters: 1) by dipping the hand in paint, or painting a motif onto the hand, then pressing the hand against the wall; 2) by putting the hand on the wall and spraying, or outlining, or dabbing paint around it; 3) by drawing a hand, either stylized or realistic-looking. The first method results in positive handprints, the second method produces negative hand stencils, and the third will not be considered here because it is disconnected from any real, actual human hand.

Handedness can be interpreted through these images if we make the basic assumption that the non-dominant hand was preferentially placed on the wall, and that it was placed palm down. If the dominant hand was needed to hold the paint palette, the blowing tube, the candle or torch (since most cave paintings were made beyond the light of day), or anything else, then the nondominant hand would naturally have been the one selected to press against the wall. When using a blowing tube to spray pigment, the implied biomechanical constraint is that the dominant hand (the one with more precise control) will hold the tube, leaving the nondominant hand free to be painted on. Without a tube, one mixes pigment powder with water and/or saliva and sprays it directly from the mouth. It may be necessary to hold a container of pigment, for which the dominant hand might be used. Even without holding anything in the other hand, it appears more natural to press the nondominant hand against the wall (see below Gilabert pers. comm.; Faurie & Raymond 2004).

For positive prints, there is no question that the palm must have been down, since the skin on the back of the hand has its own distinctive pattern which is not that of a palm print. For negative images or stencils, in which we only see the outline of the hand, it is possible to distinguish between palm up and palm down by several methods: the clarity of the outline, the spreading angle between fingers, the presence of the forearm, and the position of the hands on the cave wall. Gradín (1994, 153) explains that a distinct contour can only be achieved with the palm down; the back of the hand cannot be applied with enough pres-

sure on the wall to make a tight seal. In discussing the practice of making fingers look deliberately distorted (such as missing fingers), Walsh (1983, 4) indicates that some Australian Aborigines avoided the underspray problem 'either by greasing the hand to make it fit close to the surface, or by placing the back of the hand against the rock and then holding the fingers down'. Barrière & Sueres (1993, 52) conducted experiments showing that a dorsal hand position, even with the fingers held down, produces this invasive pigment in between the fingers due to the lack of a tight seal, and furthermore that the hand cannot reach its maximum spread of fingers when it is dorsally placed. This is one way to rule out the possibility of faking missing fingers: the maximal spread between fingers cannot be faked if the fingers are bent. Kirchner (1959), from her own experiments, concluded it was possible to replicate, with clear outlines, the Gargas hands (with missing fingers) by bending the fingers.

In addition, the very position and angle of handprints can rule out the use of one hand. First, the height above ground (usually eye-level: Henneberg & Mathers 1994) constrains the angle at which the elbow can bend. Second, if part of the outline of the forearm is present, then it is clear which hand was used; but even without the forearm, some left hand stencils with a bent wrist coming from the left side (see for example the frieze of 21 aligned hands at Gua Ham, Borneo: Fage & Chazine 2001) can only have been made with the left hand palm down. This kind of wrist-bending can be seen in many photographs of hand stencils around the world, and seems to be a natural effect of trying to make a vertical hand stencil (because the distance required to blow pigment from one's own mouth is around 40 cm (Barrière & Sueres 1993, 49) the elbow must bend outward from the body). Furthermore, it appears more natural for a right-hander to place the left hand against the wall. It has been observed by one right-handed painter with four years' experience making hand stencils, that it feels more comfortable and natural to press the left hand against a wall (C. Gilabert pers. comm.). This is because the body must twist slightly to position the left hand on the wall while leaving the correct distance between mouth and wall. This seems to imply some sort of biomechanical preference on torso twisting.

Barrière & Sueres (1993, 50) give two examples from Gargas Cave (France, Gravettian era, 26–21 kya) that would have been impossible to make with the right palm up. One stencil is a hand placed horizontally with the wrist to the left, located 2 m above the ground in a narrow niche. In order for the right hand to be used palm up, the person would have had to hang upside-down while a second person sprayed the pigment, and yet the niche was only big enough for one person. The second example is a left hand with the arm extending to the elbow, oriented 45 degrees to the right, located beneath a sloping wall.

The techniques and methods for making negative and positive hand images have been extensively studied experimentally (e.g. Ringot 2002). The technique used 30,000 years ago can be determined by microscopic features of the pigment on the cave wall, such as degree of pigment invasion into the porous surface, the size of pigment particles, and their distribution (Clot *et al.* 1995). These authors identified three techniques used at Gargas, for different colours of pigment. For red and yellow, and black carbon-based pigment stencils, liquid paint was applied by spraying from the mouth. For black manganese stencils, the pigment was applied by dabbing with a brush or piece of fur (Clot *et al.* 1995, 231).

Paunero (1992, 53), in a study aiming to replicate the negative hands (or stencils) at Cañadón de Los Toldos, Patagonia, experimentally tested numerous variables in order to create the negative hand painting process which gives results 'most closely approximating the observed archaeological reality'. He tested the technique in which paint is directly sprayed from the mouth. The variables were: paint density, velocity of application, quantity of air, distance between the mouth and hand, temperature of the paint, basal area (area covered by sprayed paint), angle of dispersion (indicates the amplitude of spraying), angle of mouth position (measured from 0 degrees for the horizontal to the direction of spraying). He concluded that the Patagonian hand stencils at Cañadón de Los Toldos were made with mouth spraying.

The method of spraying with a tube was experimentally tested by Faurie & Raymond (2004). They tested 179 naive subjects for throwing hand, and instructed them to make a negative hand using a pen which sprays ink when blown into, mimicking the technique of prehistoric painting with a tube. Finally the subjects were asked which was their writing hand. Although most subjects held the tube in the same hand as the throwing and writing hand — making stencils of the opposite hand, as expected — a surprising number of right-handers made right-hand stencils (17 per cent). In contrast, only one left-hander made a left-hand stencil. These results suggest that the archaeological record should show more right-hand stencils than expected, if a certain proportion of right-handers are adding their right-hand outlines to the total of right hand outlines produced by left-handers. Furthermore, it can be deduced that the actual number of right stencils indicates the very maximum possible number of left-handed people, since some of

the images could have been produced by right-handers. Thus the number of left-handers can be estimated from the number of right stencils, if 93 per cent of right stencils were made by left-handers. Conversely, nearly 100 per cent of left stencils can be attributed to right-handers. Compared with the summed data from Europe, Faurie & Raymond's proportions are almost identical to those of several European caves, suggesting that similar proportions of right- and left-handers existed in the last 10 kya. Aside from the assumption that painters only painted their own hands, Faurie & Raymond are also based on the supposition that negative hands were painted with a blowing tube. (Barrière & Sueres 1993, 50 describe a single painting event in Gargas, two adult hands framing a pair of child's hands, which implies they were painted hands-free, unless a third person held the tube. The evidence for spraying directly from the mouth suggests that the use of a tube must not be taken for granted).

Taking into account the assumptions that the preferred way of making hand images was palm-down placing of the nondominant hand, we can now turn to the archaeological data. The oldest cave paintings are currently in Chauvet Cave (France), and are dated to 32–30 kya (Valladas *et al.* 2001; Clottes n.d. website).

In the Cosquer cave (France, dated to 27–19 kya: Valladas *et al.* 2001), Clottes & Courtin (n.d. website) counted 54 negative hand stencils and one positive print. The proportion of left and right hands is unclear, but there is a panel with 8 left stencils sprayed in black.

Delluc & Delluc (1993, 34–5) review the literature from France and Spain, finding majorities of left hands everywhere: 17 caves with 319 hands yield 228 left hands for 52 right hands. In Kirchner's study (1959, 110) on hand representations in the Franco-Cantabrian area, combined with data from the rest of prehistoric Europe and ethnographic data from Australia and the Americas, she counted 304 left-hand stencils for 71 right, and 83 right-hand prints for 15 left-hand prints. This makes a total of 473 hands, consisting of 82 per cent right-handedness and 18 per cent left-handedness. Kühn (1955) had already counted 9 right- and 35 left-hand stencils at the site of El Castillo, in Spain.

In a study of several caves on the Nullarbor Plain, Australia, Lane & Richards (1966, 46) report that 'the majority' of stencils are left hands. The stencils are found in Murrawijinie Cave Numbers 1 and 3, Knowles Cave, and Abrakurrie Cave. The dates given for nearby Koonalda Cave are 13,700 and 18,200 ya.

Fage and colleagues (Fage & Chazine 2001; Fage *et al.* 2002) report on recent discoveries in Kalimantan, Borneo. There are 1500 hands in 26 caves, which have been dated to about 9900 ya (Plagnes *et al.* 2003). The sample taken from a calcite drapery covering a hand stencil at Gua Saleh was dated to 9870 ya, so the image must predate the drapery. Total hand stencil counts for one of the caves, Gua Tewet level 1, are 189. Of these, 114 are left hands, 50 right hands, and 25 indeterminate. This follows the general pattern of about two-thirds left hands to one-third right hands in all the Kalimantan caves (L.-H. Fage pers. comm.). The magnificent frieze at Gua Ham, for example, is made of 21 aligned hands, of which 20 are left and 1 right. The only exception is in one section of the 'Tree of Life' in Gua Tewet, consisting of 20 right and 2 left hands. The uniqueness of Borneo's hand images are the composition of interconnected 'trees' of hands, connected with lines, and decorated with symbols painted onto the palms.

Gradín (1994, 153) studied the Río Pinturas (Painted River) region of cave art in Central Patagonia. Hand stencils date to at least 9 kya and extend to 5300 ya. Two caves, Cueva de Las Manos and Cueva Grande of the Arroyo Feo, yielded counts of 329 left hands to 31 right ones, and 97 left hands for 2 right hands, respectively.

Greer & Greer (1999, 60) report on 708 rock-art sites in Montana, USA. These caves, bluff faces and rock shelters can be dated as beginning in the Middle Archaic period (3000 BC) and extending to AD 1400. The majority are positive prints (only 7 hand stencils exist). There are 429 identifiable prints with respect to laterality; 317 (74 per cent) are right hands and 112 (26 per cent) are left hands.

Gunn (1998) describes two rock-art complexes in the Levy Ranges, Australia, Kulpi Mara and Irtikiri. They have unique patterned handprints which were made by first painting patterns onto one hand, then pressing the painted hand onto the rock surface. In 7 sites there are 109 patterned handprints, 84 hand stencils, and 7 handprints. Reliable counts reveal 4:1 right to left prints, 1:4 right to left stencils, and generally more left- than right-patterned prints. Gunn proposes this latter fact reveals the tendency for right-handers to paint with the right hand onto the left. Suggested dates for these sites are fairly recent, i.e. within the last 2000 years, although one shelter was occupied in the last 30 kya.

Conclusions

We shall conclude by discussing the question that structured this symposium — namely, is knapping stone a uniquely hominin behaviour? It seems that humans routinely use a single 'preferred' hand to play the leading role in tool use, and that nearly nine times out of ten the choice is of the right hand. As we have

mentioned, and as is discussed by other contributors to this volume, there is only weak and inconclusive evidence for a similar population-level bias towards the right hand in the tool-using behaviours of other living primates. This suggests that there may also be something unique about the organization of the neural substrate that controls these voluntary manual actions. If we analyze the skeletal and material cultural evidence for a population-level bias towards right-handedness, we see that the bias is consistently observed in the remains of anatomically modern human populations, and that there is a limited quantity of evidence which consistently indicates that such a bias also existed among the earlier members of our own genus. Whether this reflects selection for tool-making and tool-using capacities, or selection for some other adaptive capacity, is unfortunately beyond the scope of this paper.

Although the study of human handedness certainly opens an intriguing window onto the past, and onto the evolution of human tool making and tool use, there are other questions about hand skill which also need to be asked. It is logically quite possible that the evolution of handedness addresses only a part of the problem of the evolution of skill and complexity in the *chaîne opératoire*. If the evolution of a bias towards right-handedness preceded the evolution of a fully-modern capacity for complex serial order in planning and executing tool-making and tool-using actions, then we may be over-estimating the significance of handedness as an evolutionary marker of 'left hemisphere' executive functions of a fully human kind, including linguistic ability. An integrated assessment of both dimensions of the organization of skilled tool-using actions in the archaeological record is thus long overdue. For some handedness researchers this could amount to 'thinking the unthinkable'; but thinking the unthinkable is always a stimulating (if unsettling) exercise.

References

Alter, I., 1989. A cerebral origin for 'directionality'. *Neuropsychologia* 27(4), 563–73.

Annett, M., 1970. The growth of manual preference and speed. *British Journal of Psychology* 61, 545–58.

Annett, M., 1985. *Left, Right, Hand and Brain: the Right Shift Theory*. London: Lawrence Erlbaum Associates.

Annett, M., 1998. The stability of handedness, in *The Psychobiology of the Hand*, ed. K.J. Connolly. (Clinics in Developmental Medicine 147.) Cambridge: Cambridge University Press, 63–76.

Annett, M., 2002. *Handedness and Brain Asymmetry: the Right Shift Theory*. Hove (UK): Psychology Press.

Annett, M. & M. Manning, 1989. The disadvantages of

dextrality for intelligence. *British Journal of Psychology* 80, 213–26.

Bakan, P., 1971. Handedness and birth order. *Nature* 229, 195.

Bakan, P., G. Dibb & P. Reed, 1973. Handedness and birth stress. *Neuropsychologia* 11, 363–6.

Barrière, C. & M. Sueres, 1993. Les mains de Gargas. *Les dossiers d'archéologie* 178 (Jan), 46–55.

Bax, J.S. & P.S. Ungar, 1999. Incisor labial wear striations in modern humans and their implications for handedness in Middle and Late Pleistocene hominids. *International Journal of Osteoarchaeology* 9(3), 189–98.

Bedon, R., 1984. *Carrières et Carriers de la Gaule Romaine.* Paris: Picard.

Bermúdez de Castro, J.M., T.G. Bromage & Y. Fernández-Jalvo, 1988. Buccal striations on fossil human anterior teeth: evidence of handedness in the middle and early Upper Pleistocene. *Journal of Human Evolution* 17(4), 403–12.

Bimson, B., J. Ottevanger, N. Roberts, G. Macho, D. Percy & G.H. Whitehouse, 1997. Hominid thumb strength predicted by high resolution magnetic resonance imaging. *Magnetic Resonance Imaging* 15, 899–908.

Bishop, D.V.M., 1984. Using non-preferred hand skill to investigate pathological left handedness in an unselected population. *Developmental Medicine and Child Neurology* 26, 214–26.

Black, D., C.C. Young, W.C. Pei & T. de Chardin, 1933. Fossil man in China. *Mem Geological Survey of China,* Series A, no. 11.

Blankholm, H.P., 1990. Stylistic analysis of Maglemosian microlithic armatures in southern Scandinavia: an essay, in *Contributions to the Mesolithic in Europe,* eds. P.M. Vermeersch & P. van Peer. Leuven: Leuven University Press, 239–57.

Bonci, C.M., F.J. Hensal & J.S. Torg, 1986. A preliminary study on the measurement of static and dynamic motion at the glenohumeral joint. *American Journal of Sports Medicine* 14, 12–17.

Bradley, B. & C.G. Sampson, 1986. Analysis by replication of two Acheulian artefact assemblages, in *Stone Age Prehistory,* eds. G.N. Bailey & P. Callow. Cambridge: Cambridge University Press, 29–45.

Bradshaw, J.L. & L.J. Rogers, 1993. *The Evolution of Lateral Asymmetries, Language, Tool Use, and Intellect.* San Diego (CA): Academic Press.

Brain, C.K., 1981. *The Hunters or the Hunted? An Introduction to African Cave Taphonomy.* Chicago (IL) & London: University of Chicago Press.

Brain, C.K., 1994. The Swartkrans Palaeontological Research Project in perspective: results and conclusions. *South African Journal of Science* 90 (Apr), 220–23.

Breuil, H., 1952. *Four Hundred Centuries of Cave Art.* (English edition.) Montignac.

Brinton, D.G., 1896. Left-handedness in North American Aboriginal art. *American Anthropologist* IX (May), 175–81.

Brorson, H., C.O. Werner & K.G. Thorngren, 1989. Normal pinch strength. *Acta Orthopaedica Scandinavica* 60, 66–8.

Bryden, M.P., I.C. McManus & M.B. Bulman-Fleming, 1994. Evaluating the empirical support for the Geschwind-Behan-Galaburda model of cerebral lateralization. *Brain and Cognition* 26, 103–67.

Buskirk, E.R., K.L. Andersen & J. Brozek, 1956. Unilateral activity and bone and muscle development in the forearm. *The Research Quarterly* 27, 127–31.

Cahen, D. & L.H. Keeley, 1980. Not less than two, not more than three. *World Archaeology* 12(2), 166–80.

Cahen D., L.H. Keeley & F.L. van Noten, 1979. Stone tools, toolkits, and human behavior in prehistory. *Current Anthropology* 20(4), 661–83.

Carson, R.G., 1993. Manual asymmetries: old problems and new directions. *Human Movement Science* 12, 479–506.

Carter, D.R., 1987. Mechanical loading history and skeletal biology. *Journal of Biomechanics* 20, 1095–109.

Chau, N., E. Remy, D. Petry, P. Huguenin, E. Bourgkard & J.M. André, 1998. Asymmetry correction equations for hand volume, grip and pinch strengths in healthy working people. *European Journal of Epidemiology* 14, 71–7.

Chhibber, S.R. & I. Singh, 1972. Asymmetry in muscle weight in the human upper limbs. *Acta Anatomica* 81, 462–65.

Clot A., M. Menu & P. Walter, 1995. Manières de peindres des mains à Gargas et Tibiran (Hautes-Pyrénées). *L'anthropologie* 99 (2/3), 221–35.

Clottes, J., n.d. La Grotte Chauvet. http://www.culture.gouv.fr/culture/arcnat/chauvet/fr/index.html [accessed 27 April 2004].

Clottes, J. & J. Courtin, n.d. La Grotte Cosquer. http://www.culture.gouv.fr/culture/archeosm/fr/fr-medit-prehist.htm [accessed 27 April 2004].

Connolly, K.J. & D.V.M. Bishop, 1992. The measurement of handedness: a cross-cultural comparison of samples from England and Papua New Guinea. *Neuropsychologia* 30, 13–26.

Constandse-Westermann, T.S. & R.R. Newell, 1989. Limb lateralization and social stratification in western European Mesolithic societies, in *People and Culture in Change,* ed. I. Hershkovitz. (British Archaeological Reports, International Series 508.) Oxford: BAR, 405–33.

Coren, S. & D. Halpern, 1991. Left-handedness: a marker for decreased survival fitness. *Psychological Bulletin* 109, 90–106.

Coren, S. & C. Porac, 1977. Fifty centuries of right-handedness: the historical record. *Science* 198, 631–2.

Cornford, J.M., 1986. Specialized resharpening techniques and evidence of handedness, in *La Cotte de St Brelade 1961–1978: Excavations by C.B.M. McBurney,* eds. P. Callow & J.M. Cornford. Norwich: Geo Books, 337–51 & 413–14.

Crosby, C.A., M.A. Wehbe & B. Mawr, 1994. Hand strength: normative values. *Journal of Hand Surgery* [American Volume] 19, 665–70.

Crow, T.J., L.R. Crow, D.J. Done & S.J. Leask, 1998. Relative hand skill predicts academic ability: global deficits at the point of hemispheric indecision. *Neuropsychologia* 36, 1275–882.

Dart, R.A., 1949. The predatory implemental technique of Australopithecus. *American Journal of Physical Anthropology* 7(1), 1–38.

de Mortillet, G., 1883. *Le préhistorique: origine et antiquité de l'homme*. Paris: C. Reinwald.

de Mortillet, G., 1890. Formation des variétés. Albinisme et gauchissement. *Bulletins de la Société d'Anthropologie de Paris* 1(4), 570–80.

Delluc, B. & G. Delluc, 1993. Images de la main dans notre préhistoire. *Les dossiers d'archéologie* 178 (Jan), 32–45.

Dennis, W., 1958. Early graphic evidence of dextrality in man. *Perceptual and Motor Skills* 8, 147–9.

d'Errico, F., 1988. A study of Upper Palaeolithic and Epipalaeolithic engraved pebbles, in *Scanning Electron Microscopy in Archaeology*, ed. S.L. Olsen. (British Archaeological Reports, International Series 452.) Oxford: BAR, 169–84.

d'Errico, F., 1992. Technology, motion, and the meaning of Epipaleolithic art. *Current Anthropology* 33(1), 94–109.

Durham, W.H., 1991. *Coevolution: Genes, Culture, and Human Diversity*. Stanford (CA): StanfordUniversity Press.

Eaton, W.O., J.G. Chipperfield, K.F.W. Ritchot & J.H. Kostiuk, 1996. Is a maturational lag associated with left-handedness? A research note. *Journal of Child Psychology and Psychiatry and Allied Disciplines* 37, 613–17.

Evans, J., 1897. *The Ancient Stone Implements, Weapons and Ornaments of Great Britain*. London: Longmans, Green, and Co.

Fage, L.-H. & J.-M. Chazine, 2001. L'art pariétal des grottes de Kalimantan (Indonésie). Bilan de dix années de prospection. Découvertes récentes de juin 2001 et perspectives de protection, in Publication du Congrès Suisse de Spéléologie, Genève, 2001. Also available on *Le Kalimanthrope*, http://www.kalimanthrope.com [date accessed 27.04.2004].

Fage, L.-H., J.-M. Chazine & P. Setiawan, 2002. The rock art of Kalimantan. *Ligabue Magazine*, Dec. http://www.ligabue.it/eng/magazine.asp

Faurie, C. & M. Raymond, 2004. Handedness frequency over more than ten thousand years. *Proceedings of the Royal Society of London B* (suppl.), 271, 543–5.

Fischer, A., 1990. On being a pupil of a flintknapper of 11,000 years ago, in *The Big Puzzle: International Symposium on Refitting Stone Artefacts*, eds. E. Cziesla, S. Eickhoff, N. Arts & D. Winter. (SMA 1.) Bonn: Holos Verlag, 447–64.

Fitts, P.M., 1954. The information capacity of the human motor system in controlling the amplitude of movement. *Journal of Experimental Psychology* 47, 381–91.

Flowers, K., 1975. Handedness and controlled movement. *British Journal of Psychology* 66, 39–52.

Fox, C.L. & D.W. Frayer, 1997. Non-dietary marks in the anterior dentition of the Krapina Neanderthals. *International Journal of Osteoarchaeology* 7(2), 133–49.

Frame, H., 1986. Microscopic use-wear traces, in *La Cotte de St Brelade 1961–1978: Excavations by C.B.M. McBurney.*, eds. P. Callow & J.M. Cornford. Norwich: Geo Books, 353–64.

Garn, S.M., G.H. Mayor & H.A. Shaw, 1976. Paradoxical bilateral asymmetry in bone size and bone mass in the hand. *American Journal of Physical Anthropology* 45, 209–10.

Gerharz, R.R. & D.R. Spenneman, 1985. Northern Ethiopian bronze implements for left-handed individuals. *Azania* 20, 163–7.

Geschwind, N. & P. Behan, 1982. Left-handedness: association with immune disease, migraine and developmental learning disorder. *Proceedings of the National Academy of Sciences of the USA* 79, 5097–100.

Geschwind, N. & P. Behan, 1984. Laterality, hormones and immunity, in *Cerebral Dominance, the Biological Foundation*, eds. N. Geschwind & A.M. Galaburda. Cambridge (MA): Harvard University Press, 211–24.

Geschwind, N. & A.M. Galaburda, 1985a. Cerebral lateralization. Biological mechanisms, associations, and pathology: a hypothesis and a program for research. *Archives of Neurology* 42, 428–59; 521–52; 634–54.

Geschwind, N. & A.M. Galaburda, 1985b. *Cerebral Lateralization. Biological Mechanisms. Associations and Pathology*. Cambridge (MA): MIT Press.

Gotestam, K.O., 1990. Lefthandedness among students of architecture and music. *Perceptual and Motor Skills* 70, 1323–7; comments on pp. 1345–6.

Gradín, C.J., 1994. L'art rupestre dans la Patagonie argentine/Rock art in Argentine Patagonia. *L'Anthropologie* 98(1), 149–72.

Greer, M. & J. Greer, 1999. Handprints in Montana rock art. *Plains Anthropologist* 44(167), 59–71.

Guiard, Y., 1987. Asymmetric division of labor in human skilled bimanual action: the kinematic chain as a model. *Journal of Motor Behavior* 19(4), 486–517.

Gunn, R.G., 1998. Patterned hand prints: a unique form from central Australia. *Rock Art Research* 15(2), 75–80.

Haapasalo, H., P. Kannus, H. Sievanen, A. Heinonen, P. Oja, & I. Vuori, 1994. Long-term unilateral loading and bone mineral density and content in female squash players. *Calcified Tissue International* 54, 249–55.

Haapasalo, H., H. Sievanen, P. Kannus, A. Heinonen, P. Oja & I. Vuori, 1996. Dimensions and estimated mechanical characteristics of the humerus after long-term tennis loading. *Journal of Bone and Mineral Research* 11, 864–72.

Haldane, J.B.S., 1948. The rate of mutation of human genes. *Hereditus* (suppl.), 267–73.

Hécaen, H. & J. de Ajuriaguerra, 1964. *Left-handedness: Manual Superiority and Cerebral Dominance*. Trans. E. Ponder. New York (NY): Grune & Stratton.

Henneberg, M. & K. Mathers, 1994. Reconstruction of body height, age and sex from handprints. *South African Journal of Science* 90(Aug/Sep), 493–6.

Hester, T.R., 1973. A supplementary note on flint-chipping with the teeth. *Newsletter of Lithic Technology* 2(1–2), Jan–May, 23.

Hinckley, K., R. Pausch, D. Proffitt, J. Patten & N. Kassell, 1997. Cooperative Bimanual Action. Paper presented at ACM CHI '97 conference on human factors in computing systems, Atlanta, 22–7 Mar. Html version available at: http://www.acm.org/sigs/sigchi/chi97/proceedings/paper/kh.htm [DOI: http://doi.acm.org/10.1145/258549.258571].

Humans, Tools and Handedness

Högberg, A., 1999. Child and adult at a knapping area. A technological flake analysis of the manufacture of a Neolithic square sectioned axe and a child's flintknapping activities on an assemblage excavated as part of the Öresund Fixed Link Project. *Acta Archaeologica* 70(1), 79–106.

Ingelmark, B.E., 1946. Über die Längenasymmetrien der Extremitäten und ihren Zusammenhang mit der Rechts-Linkshändigkeit. *Uppsala Läkareförenings Förhandlingar* N.F. 52, 17–82.

J.S., 1870. Right-handedness. *Nature* 1, 605.

Jones, H.H., J.D. Priest, W.C. Hayes, C.C. Tichenor & D.A. Nagel, 1977. Humeral hypertrophy in response to exercise. *Journal of Bone and Joint Surgery* [American Volume] 59, 204–8.

Josty, I.C., M.P. Tyler, P.C. Shewell & A.H. Roberts, 1997. Grip and pinch strength variations in different types of workers. *Journal of Hand Surgery* [British Volume] 22, 266–9.

Kannus, P., H. Haapasalo, M. Sankelo, H. Sievanen, M. Pasanen, A. Heinonen, P. Oja & I. Vuori, 1996. Effect of starting age of physical activity on bone mass in the dominant arm of tennis and squash players. *Annals of Internal Medicine* 123, 27–31.

Keeley, L.H., 1977. The functions of Paleolithic flint tools. *Scientific American* 237, 108–26.

Kennedy, K.A.R., 1983. Morphological variation in ulnar supinator crests and fossae as identification markers of occupational stress. *Journal of Forensic Science* 28, 871–6.

Kirchner, L., 1959. *Jungpaläolitische Handdarstellungen der Franko-kantabrischen Felsbilderzone: Ein Versuch ihrer Deutung unter Berücksichtigung ethnographischer Parallelen.* Göppingen: Werner-Muller Verlag.

Krahl, H., U. Michaelis, H.G. Pieper, G. Quack & M. Montag, 1994. Stimulation of bone growth through sports. A radiologic investigation of the upper extremities in professional tennis players. *American Journal of Sports Medicine* 22, 751–7.

Kühn H., 1955. *On the Track of Prehistoric Man.* New York (NY): Random House.

Laland, K.N., J. Kumm, J.D. Van Horn & M.W. Feldman, 1995. A gene-culture model of human handedness. *Behavior Genetics* 25, 433–45.

Lane, E.A. & A.M. Richards 1966. Hand paintings in caves. with special reference to Aboriginal hand stencils from caves on the Nullarbor Plain, Southern Australia. *Helictite* January, 33–50.

Latimer, H.B. & E.W. Lowrance, 1965. Bilateral asymmetry in weight and in length of human bones. *The Anatomical Record* 152, 217–24.

Leroi-Gourhan, A., 1965. *Préhistoire de l'art occidental.* Paris.

Ludwig, B.V. & J.W.K. Harris, 1994. Handedness and Knapping Skill: their Effects on Plio-Pleistocene Lithic Assemblage Variability. Theme paper presented at the WAC-3 Conference, New Delhi (December).

MacNeilage, P.F., M.G. Studdert-Kennedy & B. Lindblom, 1987. Primate handedness reconsidered. *Behavioral and Brain Sciences* 10(2), 247–63; References on pp. 298–303.

Marchant, L.F. & W.C. McGrew, 1991. Laterality of function in apes: a meta-analysis of methods. *Journal of Human Evolution* 20, 425–38.

Marchant, L.F., W.C. McGrew & I. Eibl-Eibesfeldt, 1995. Is human handedness universal? Ethological analyses from three traditional cultures. *Ethology* 101, 239–58.

Marrion, L.V. & L.K. Rosenblood, 1986. Handedness in the Kwakiutl totem poles: an exception to 50 centuries of right-handedness. *Perceptual and Motor Skills* 62, 755–9.

Mays, S., J. Steele & M. Ford, 1999. Directional asymmetry in the human clavicle. *International Journal of Osteoarchaeology* 9(1), Jan/Feb, 18–28.

McGrew, W.C. & L.F. Marchant, 1997. On the other hand: current issues in and meta-analysis of the behavioral laterality of hand function in nonhuman primates. *Yearbook of Physical Anthropology* 40, 201–32.

McLeod, D.R. & S.G. Coupland, 1992. Asymmetry quantification utilizing hand radiographs. *American Journal of Medical Genetics* 44, 321–5.

McManus, I.C., 1985. *Handedness, Language Dominance, and Aphasia: a Genetic Model.* (Psychological Medicine Monograph Supplement 8.) Cambridge: Cambridge University Press.

McManus, I.C., 1996. Handedness, in *The Blackwell Dictionary of Neuropsychology,* eds. J.G. Beaumont, P.M. Kenealy & M.J.C. Rogers. Oxford: Blackwell, 367–76.

Mebert, C.J. & G.F. Michel, 1980. Handedness in artists, in *The Neuropsychology of Left-handedness,* ed. J. Herron. New York (NY): Academic Press, 273–9.

Monthel, G., 2002. La carrière gallo-romaine de Saint-Boil (Saône-et-Loire). *Gallia* 59, 89–204.

Mulligan J., R.J. Stratford, B.J.R. Bailey, E.S. McCaughey & P.R. Betts, 2001. Hormones and handedness. *Hormone Research* 56, 51–7.

Nettle, D., 2003. Hand laterality and cognitive ability: a multiple regression approach. *Brain and Cognition* 52, 390–98.

Neumann, S., 1992. Händigkeit im Vergleich zur Asymmetrie der oberen Extremität. *Zeitschrift für Morphologie und Anthropologie* 79, 183–95.

Newcomer, M.H. & G. de G. Sieveking, 1980. Experimental flake scatter-patterns: a new interpretative technique. *Journal of Field Archaeology* 7(3) Autumn, 345–52.

Noble, W. & I. Davidson, 1996. *Human Evolution, Language and Mind: a Psychological and Archaeological Inquiry.* Cambridge: Cambridge University Press.

Patterson, L.W. & J.B. Sollberger, 1986. Comments on Toth's right-handedness study. *Lithic Technology* 15, 109–11.

Paunero, R.S., 1992. Manos pintadas en negativo: un ensayo de experimentación. *Revista de Estudios Regionales (Mendoza)* 9, 47–66.

Perelló, J., 1970. Digressions on the biological foundations of language. *Journal of Communication Disorders* 3(2), 140–50.

Peters, M., 1995. Handedness and its relation to other indices of cerebral lateralization, in *Brain Asymmetry,* eds. R.J. Davidson & K. Hugdahl. Cambridge (MA): MIT Press, 183–214.

Petersen, P., M. Petrick, H. Connor & D. Conklin, 1989.

Grip strength and hand dominance: challenging the 10% rule. *American Journal of Occupational Therapy* 43, 444–7.

Peterson, J.M. & L.M. Lansky, 1977. Left-handedness among architects: partial replication and some new data. *Perceptual and Motor Skills* 45, 1216–18.

Phillipson, L., 1997. Edge modification as an indicator of function and handedness of Acheulian handaxes from Kariandusi, Kenya. *Lithic Technology* 22(2), 171–83.

Phillipson, L., 2000. Askumite lithic industries. *African Archaeological Review* 17(2), 49–63.

Pitts, M. & M. Roberts, 1997. *Fairweather Eden: Life in Britain Half a Million Years Ago as Revealed by the Excavations at Boxgrove*. London: Century.

Plagnes, V., C. Causse, M. Fontugne, H. Valladas, J.-M. Chazine & L.-H. Fage, 2003. Cross dating (Th/U-^{14}C) of calcite covering prehistoric paintings in Borneo. *Quaternary Research* 60(2), 172–9.

Plato, C.C., J.L. Wood & A.H. Norris, 1980. Bilateral asymmetry in bone measurements of the hand and lateral dominance. *American Journal of Physical Anthropology* 52, 27–31.

Pobiner, B.L., 1999. The use of stone tools to determine handedness in hominids. *Current Anthropology* 40(1), 90–92.

Posnansky M., 1959. Some functional considerations on the handaxe. *Man* 59 (March), 42–4.

Purves, D., L.E. White & T.J. Andrews, 1994. Manual asymmetry and handedness. *Proceedings of the National Academy of Sciences of the USA* 91, 5030–32.

Raymond, M., D. Pontier, A.-B. Dufour & A.P. Møller, 1996. Frequency-dependent maintenance of left handedness in humans. *Proceedings of the Royal Society of London* B 263, 1627–33.

Reichel, H., H. Runge & H. Bruchaus, 1990. Die Seitendifferenz des Mineralgehaltes und der Breite am Radius und ihre Bedeutung für die Händigkeitsbestimmung an Skelettmaterial. *Zeitschrift für Morphologie und Anthropologie* 78, 217–27.

Richards, R.R., R. Gordon & D. Beaton, 1993. Measurement of wrist, metacarpophalangeal joint, and thumb extension strength in a normal population. *Journal of Hand Surgery* [American Volume] 18A, 253–61.

Ringot, J.-L., 2002. Der Steinzeitmensch als Sprayer? Neue Hypothese zum Farbauftrag der Steinzeitmalerei, in *Experimentelle Archäologie in Europa*, ed. Europäische Vereinigung zur Förderung der Experimentellen Archäologie. Oldenburg: Isensee Verlag, 65–9.

Röder, J., 1957. Die antiken Tuffsteinbrüche der Pellenz. *Bonner Jahrbücher* 157, 213–71 & plates 21–9.

Roosevelt, A.C., 1974. Handedness in prehistory: a study of tools from ancient Chile. *Indian Notes* 9, 98–109.

Roux, V. (ed.), 2000. *Cornaline de l'Inde. Des pratiques techniques de Cambay aux techno-systèmes de l'Indus*. Paris: Editions de la Maison des Sciences de l'Homme.

Roux, V., B. Bril & G. Dietrich, 1995. Skills and learning difficulties involved in stone knapping: The case of stone-bead knapping in Khambhat, India. *World Archaeology* 27, 63–87.

Roy, T.A., C.B. Ruff & C.C. Plato, 1994. Hand dominance

and bilateral asymmetry in the structure of the second metacarpal. *American Journal of Physical Anthropology* 94, 203–11.

Ruff, C.B. & H.H. Jones, 1981. Bilateral asymmetry in cortical bone of the humerus and tibia - sex and age factors. *Human Biology* 53, 69–86.

Rugg, G. & M. Mullane, 2001. Inferring handedness from lithic evidence. *Laterality* 6(3), 247–59.

Rust, A., 1973/74. Handwerkliches Können und Lebensweise des Steinzeitmenschen. *Mannheimer Forum* 2, 193–247.

Sainburg, R.L., 2002. Evidence for a dynamic-dominance hypothesis of handedness. *Experimental Brain Research* 142, 241–58.

Satz, P., 1972. Pathological left-handedness: an explanatory model. *Cortex* 8, 121–35.

Saville, A., 2003. Entombed with the tools of his trade. *British Archaeology* 72 (Sep), 46.

Schell, L.M., F.E. Johnston, D.R. Smith & A.M. Paolone, 1985. Directional asymmetry of body dimensions among white adolescents. *American Journal of Physical Anthropology* 67, 317–22.

Schultz, A.H., 1937. Proportions, variability, and asymmetries of the long bones of the limbs and the clavicles in man and apes. *Human Biology* 9, 281–328.

Seddon, B.M. & I.C. McManus, 1991. The Incidence of Left-handedness: a Meta-analysis. Unpublished manuscript.

Sellers, B., 2004. Functional Anatomy of the Upper Limb. http://homepage.mac.com/wis/personal/lectures/musculoskeletal/upperlimb.pdf

Semenov, S.A., 1964. *Prehistoric Technology*. Transl. M.W. Thompson. London: Cory, Adams, & Mackay.

Spenneman, D.H.R., 1984a. Handedness data on the European Neolithic. *Neuropsychologia* 22(5), 613–15.

Spenneman, D.H.R., 1984b. Right- and left-handedness in early Southeast Asia: the graphic evidence of the Borobudur. *Bijdragen tot de Taal- Land en Volkenkunde* 140(1), 163–6.

Spenneman, D.H.R., 1985. On the origins and development of handedness in humans: some remarks on past and current theories. *Homo* 36, 121–41.

Spenneman, D.H.R., 1987. On the use-wear of stone adzes and axes and its implication for the assessment of humans' handedness. *Lithic Technology* 16, 22–7.

Steele, J., 2000. Handedness in past human populations: skeletal markers. *Laterality* 5(3), 193–220.

Steele, J. & S. Mays, 1995. Handedness and directional asymmetry in the long bones of the human upper limb. *International Journal of Osteoarchaeology* 5(1), 39–49.

Stout, D., 2002. Skill and cognition in stone tool production: an ethnographic case study from Irian Jaya. *Current Anthropology* 43(5) (Dec), 693–722.

Sugiyama, Y., T. Fushimi, O. Sakura & T. Matsuzawa, 1993. Hand preference and tool use in wild chimpanzees. *Primates* 34(2),151–9.

Taaffe, D.R., B. Lewis & R. Marcus, 1994. Quantifying the effect of hand preference on upper limb bone mineral and soft tissue composition in young and elderly women by dual-energy X-ray absorptiometry. *Clinical*

Physiology 14, 393–404.

Takeoka, T., 1991. Développement de la latéralité examinée à partir de l'analyse de la pierre taillée du paléolithique. *Journal of the Anthropological Society of Nippon* 99(4), 497–516.

Tapley, S. & M. Bryden, 1985. A group test for the assessment of performance between the hands. *Neuropsychologia* 23, 215–21.

Thorngren, K.-G. & C.O. Werner, 1979. Normal grip strength. *Acta Orthopaedica Scandinavica* 50, 255–9.

Thould, A.K. & B.T. Thould, 1983. Arthritis in Roman Britain. *British Medical Journal* 287, 1909–11.

Toth, N., 1985. Archaeological evidence for preferential right-handedness in the Lower and Middle Pleistocene, and its possible implications. *Journal of Human Evolution* 14 (6 Sep), 607–14.

Trinkaus, E., S.E. Churchill & C.B. Ruff, 1994. Postcranial robusticity in *Homo*, II: humeral bilateral asymmetry and bone plasticity. *American Journal of Physical Anthropology* 93, 1–34.

Tsuji, S., N. Tsunoda, H. Yata, F. Katsukawa, S. Onishi & H. Yamazaki, 1995. Relation between grip strength and radial bone mineral density in young athletes. *Archives of Physical Medicine and Rehabilitation* 76, 234–8.

Uhrbrock, R.S., 1973. Laterality in art. *Journal of Aesthetics & Art Criticism* 32(1), 27–35.

Uomini, N.T., 2001. Lithic Indicators of Handedness: Assessment of Methodologies and the Evolution of Laterality in Hominids. Unpublished MSc dissertation, Department of Anthropology, University of Durham.

Valladas, H., J. Clottes, J.-M. Geneste, M.A. Garcia, M. Arnold, H. Cachier & N. Tisnérat-Laborde, 2001. Evolution of prehistoric cave art. *Nature* 413, 479.

Vandermeersch, B. & E. Trinkaus, 1995. The postcranial remains of the Régourdou 1 Neandertal: the shoulder and arm remains. *Journal of Human Evolution* 284, 39–76.

Walker, A. & R. Leakey, 1993. The postcranial bones, in *The Nariokotome* Homo erectus *Skeleton*, eds. A. Walker & R. Leakey. Cambridge (MA): Harvard University Press, 95–160.

Walsh, G.L., 1983. Composite stencil art: elemental or specialised? *Australian Aboriginal Studies* 2, 34–44.

Wenban-Smith, F.F., 1997. Raiders of the lost part. Book review. *Lithics* 17/18, 87–90.

White M.J., 1998. Twisted ovate bifaces in the British Lower Palaeolithic: some observations and implications, in *Stone Age Archaeology: Essays in Honour of John Wymer,* eds. N. Ashton, F. Healy & P. Pettitt. (Oxbow Monograph 102, Lithic Studies Society Occasional Paper 6.) Oxford: Oxbow.

Willcox, A.R., 1991. Prehistoric handedness, in *Rock Art – the Way Ahead: Proceedings of the South African Rock Art Research Association First International Rock Art Conference, Conservation, Recording, and Study, 25–31 August 1991, Cathedral Peak Hotel, Natal Drakensberg, R.S.A,* eds. S.A. Pager, B.K. Swartz & A.R. Willcox. (SARARA Occasional Paper 1.) Johannesburg: Parkhurst, 146–51.

Wilson, D., 1885. Palaeolithic dexterity. *Transactions of the Royal Society of Canada* 7(2), 119–33.

Wilson, D., 1886. The right hand and left-handedness. *Transactions of the Royal Society of Canada* 8(2), 1–41.

Wilson, D., 1891. *The Right Hand: Left-handedness.* London: Macmillan.

Wood, B., 2002. Hominid revelations from Chad. *Nature* 418 (11 July), 133–5.

Wood, C.J. & J.P. Aggleton, 1991. Occupation and handedness: an examination of architects and mail survey biases. *Canadian Journal of Psychology* 45, 395–404.

Yeo, R.A. & S.W. Gangestad, 1993. Developmental origins of variation in human preference. *Genetica* 89, 281–96.

Yeo, R.A., S.W. Gangestad & W.F. Daniel, 1993. Hand preference and developmental instability. *Psychobiology* 21, 161–8.

Section B

Somatic and Neural Substrate

Chapter 16

Who made Stone Tools?

Mary W. Marzke

Identifying tool makers in the fossil record depends upon our ability to find a pattern of hand-functional capabilities and stress markers that are specific to the requirements for controlling stones and for accommodating stresses associated with tool-making activities. This pattern must be specific enough to stone-tool making to be discriminated in the fossil record from patterns associated with retrieving and processing foods with the hands by non-human primates.

A comparative, multi-faceted study that is attempting to discern such a tool-making pattern is reported here. A distinctive pattern of features has been found in the modern human hand, which is consistent with requirements of stone-tool making for bimanual percussion using firm precision grips of stones, and also with the large external and internal forces on the hand bones that accompany these activities. Some elements of the pattern are shared with other primates, and are being studied in connection with stresses required by extractive and forceful feeding on tough vegetation and fauna, as well as with tool making.

Early hominin fossil bones currently available for comparative functional analysis are virtually inscrutable, because different combinations of bones are found at each site and the small number of bones in each sample is insufficient for positively identifying integrated morphological patterns that suggest tool-making capabilities and stresses. Recent advances in the comparative quantitative analysis of bone, joint and muscle parameters are, however, facilitating the identification of multiple indicators of functional capabilities for tool making throughout the modern hand. These studies should prove more informative as more fossil hominin hand bones are discovered.

The question of who made stone tools is raised by the existence of two or more early hominin species at the same level as stone tools, as long ago as the earliest known tools in Africa at 2.6 Myr BP. It is of interest to determine whether all the species were making tools, or whether there were perhaps variations among them in the kinds of tools used and/or manufactured.

The most direct potential source of evidence regarding this question are the hand bones of these fossil hominin species. The bone shapes and internal structure provide clues to the magnitude and kinds of stresses that were associated with habitual uses of the hands. Joint surface topography reflects potential joint ranges of motion and loading capabilities. Muscle attachment areas may in some cases serve as guides to the relative sizes of muscles, and skeletal contours in the region of tendon attachments may indicate relative lengths of tendon moment arms. The interpretation of these skeletal clues to hand functions and behaviours requires detailed knowledge of grips, joint movements and muscle recruitment associated with habitual manipulative behaviours of living humans and non-human species. It also requires an understanding of the morphological features that facilitate these functions and that accommodate the internal and external loads associated with the behaviours.

Our interdisciplinary research group has applied an interrelated set of approaches to obtaining such knowledge and understanding. These approaches include: 1) analysis of hand grips, movements and muscle recruitment associated with the use and manufacture of prehistoric tools, using electromyography (EMG), videotapes and load cells; 2) observation of hand grips and movements used in feeding and tool activities by captive and wild non-human species; 3) comparison of bone shapes and joint morphology among species, including 3D analysis of curvature, areas and orientation angles of mutual joint surfaces; and 4) comparison of muscle parameters among species, involving measurements in cadaver specimens of joint ranges of motion, tendon excursion, hand muscle cross-sectional areas, tendon moment arms and muscle torque potential. We are studying the resulting findings in order to discern possible links between specific behaviours, hand functions and hand morphology. The findings are reviewed briefly below, followed by a discussion of their implications for fossil hominin tool-making capabilities.

Figure 16.1. *Human three-jaw chuck grip (A, right hand), cradle grip (A, left hand), pad-to-side (key) grip (B, right hand) and power-squeeze grip (B, left hand).*

Findings

Grips required for the manufacture and use of early hominin tools

The first step in attempting to relate hand morphology to the manipulation of stone, bone and wood tools is to make these tools and to use them. Even without applying sophisticated techniques, one may gain an appreciation of skills required and stresses on the hand, for example in striking a large stone core with a hammerstone. Do you smash your fingers? Does the strike dislodge the stones from your hands? How do you reorient the core quickly for successive strikes along the edge? Or try striking an object on the ground with a large long bone or a heavy piece of wood. How do you anchor the tool in your hand and how do you accelerate it? You quickly find that grips must be very forceful in these activities to maintain control of the objects. Each hand alone must be able to secure these firm grips. Another requirement is that the grips leave the working edges of the tools well exposed, to avoid injury to the hand.

Systematic biomechanical studies performed on archaeologists who have learned to replicate prehistoric tools show that there are a limited number of grips that satisfy these requirements (Marzke *et al.*1998). The findings are as follows. During hard hammer percussion removal of flakes from stone cores in Oldowan tool manufacture, the spherical hammerstones are invariably held and manoeuvred by a 'three-jaw chuck grip' (Fig. 16.1A), in which the thumb, index and third finger pads cup the stone, buttressed in some cases by the flexed fourth and fifth fingers. (This is also the grip used for throwing stones.) Large stone cores from which flakes are removed are frequently controlled by what we call a 'cradle grip' (Fig. 16.1A), in which the core is cradled by the upwardly-facing palmar pads of the four fingers and secured by the opposed pad of the thumb. As the core becomes smaller with the removal of flakes by the hammerstone, it is shifted away from the palm by the thumb and finger pads, or may be held between the thumb and the side of the index finger by the grip we use for holding key when we unlock a door. All these grips assure continued exposure of the working edges of the stones.

Precision handling plays an important role during the activity, reorienting the core for the succession of strikes by the hammerstone. This involves translation, fine rotation and shifting of the stones by the pliable pads on the palmar aspect of the distal phalanges (see Fig. 16.2 for anatomical terminology).

Flakes removed from the cores for use in activities such as cutting meat require strong pinch by the thumb and index finger, generally between the thumb and the side of the index finger with a 'key' pinch (Fig. 16.1B), which is the strongest form of pinch grip (Chao *et al.* 1989).

All cylindrical tools (for example, long bones and sticks) are held by the squeeze form of power grip (the grip we use for modern hammers and tennis rackets), in which the tool is squeezed by the convergent sides of the palm and by the thumb against the flexed fingers (Fig. 16.1B, left hand). The thumb is either wrapped around the tool and the flexed fingers or held next to the index finger in line with the long axis of the tool.

Chimpanzee grips of foods and tools

Chimpanzees do not appear to share with humans the forceful precision grips that resist large external forces (Marzke & Wullstein 1996; Marzke 1997; Marzke & Marzke 2000). Their feeding behaviours are similar to tool making in requiring that part of the manipu-

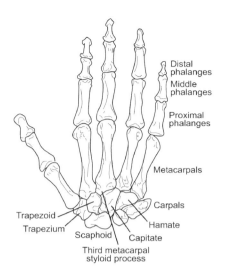

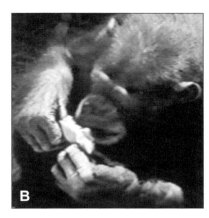

Figure 16.3. *Chimpanzee cup grip by two hands, aided by a foot (A) and pad-to-side hold grip (B) by two hands (video captures).*

Figure 16.2. *Human hand skeleton, viewed from the back.*

lated object be exposed, in this case for biting. While humans expose the working edges of large stones by pinching them tightly between the thumb and finger pads of a single hand, the chimpanzees support foods in the upturned palm and curved fingers of one hand, buttressed by the second hand in a similar posture and in some cases by one foot as well, when the teeth pull on the food (Fig. 16.3A). The grip of smaller pieces of food between the thumb and the side of the index finger is also regularly supplemented against resistance by a similar grip by the other hand (Fig. 16.3B). The strongest one-handed grip appears to be one in which an object is held in the V-shaped webbed pocket between the thumb and the flexed index finger, the way humans frequently hold an apple against the pull of the teeth (Reece *et al.* 2000). However, even this grip is not strong enough against substantial resistance. One possible explanation for the difference between chimpanzees and humans in the strength of these one-handed precision grips is the relatively low potential torque of the thumb muscles (Marzke *et al.* 1999).

It is not surprising that Kanzi, the bonobo trained to remove flakes from stone cores with a hammerstone (Toth *et al.* 1993), was more successful removing the flakes when he threw the core on the floor than when he struck the core (held in one hand) with a hammerstone held by the other.

Skeletal correlates of joint movements and stresses associated with human forceful precision grips and the power-squeeze grip

Humans have a distinctive pattern of joint morphology involving metacarpals II–V and the carpal bones (Fig. 16.2). This pattern facilitates the postures that secure the grips of hammerstones, stone cores, and cylindrical bone, wood and antler tools.

In the human index finger metacarpal there is a complex of features at the base and the distal end that facilitates rotation of the index finger pad toward the fifth finger pad as it flexes and deviates (abducts) toward the thumb (Fig. 16.4A; Marzke 1983; 1997). This rotation (called 'pronation') aligns the full friction surface of the index finger pad with the curved surface of spherical objects (see, for example, the position of the index finger of the right hand on the hammerstone in Fig. 16.1A), and also allows greater alignment of the lateral side of the index finger with the thumb pad in the grip of small objects (such as sharp flakes) between these two surfaces (see Fig. 16.1B). An important component of this complex is the orientation of the joint surface between the trapezium (the wrist bone at the base of the thumb) and the second metacarpal near the coronal and transverse planes (Fig. 16.5). A recent 3D comparative quantitative analysis of this joint shows that modern humans are significantly different from chimpanzees and gorillas in the orientation of this surface (Fig. 16.5), which lies in the sagittal plane in these species (Tocheri *et al.* 2003). Orientation of the blunt medial second metacarpal surface and its mutual capitate surface near the transverse plane complements the orientation of the joint between the lateral second metacarpal surface and the trapezium (Fig. 16.6), also facilitating pronation. Humans are also distinctive in the shape of the joint between the second metacarpal and the base of the proximal phalanx of the index finger. This joint, like the joint at the base of the metacarpal, allows pronation of the finger when it flexes and abducts.

A complementary morphological complex is found at the base and distal end of the fifth metacarpal. A proportionately large joint at the metacarpal base

 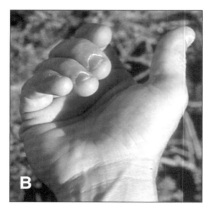 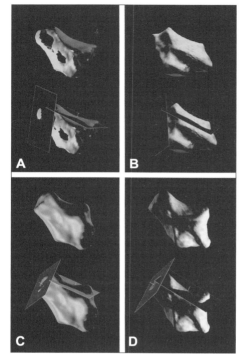

Figure 16.4. *Human hand with index finger pronated (A) for the three-jaw chuck grip of a spherical object and supinated (B) for the power squeeze grip of a cylindrical object.*

(Fig. 16.6; Marzke *et al.* 1992), together with medial bevelling of the metacarpal head, facilitate rotation of the fifth finger pad toward the thumb and index finger pads. This rotation (called 'supination'; see Fig. 16.4B) enhances accommodation of the friction pad to varying shapes of objects, secures grips of large objects between the thumb and all the fingers, and is essential to the distinctively human power squeeze grip, in which the fifth finger anchors cylindrical tools in the palm, in opposition to the thumb (see Fig. 16.1B, left hand).

The third metacarpal head has a distinctive radial orientation toward the thumb, which brings the palmar surface of the third finger into opposition to the thumb when the finger flexes (Susman 1979). This orientation complements the index finger features, facilitating cupping of spherical objects such as hammerstones and stone missiles by the thumb, index and third fingers (Marzke 1997).

Recently it has been discovered that humans are clearly distinguishable from the great apes in having a significantly larger relative joint surface area on the trapezium for the first metacarpal and the scaphoid (Tocheri *et al.* 2005; see Fig. 16.2). This is an important joint for accommodating the large axial loads from the thumb in manipulative behaviour. In contrast, the great apes have a significantly larger relative joint surface areas on the trapezoid for the medial second metacarpal and the scaphoid. This reflects the large loads that are transmitted through the base of the index finger in locomotion. These differences between humans and the great apes highlight the trend in humans toward manipulative behaviour involving forceful grips by the thumb and fingers.

Thumb-joint morphology involving the first metacarpal is not so clearly distinctive of humans. The reasons for this lie in the competing purposes

Figure 16.5. *3D models of the trapezium: A) Homo habilis; B) Gorilla gorilla; C) Australopithecus afarensis; D) and a modern human, Homo sapiens. Least-square planes generated from the laser scans are shown below each trapezium, one plane for the joint surface for the first (thumb) metacarpal (superior margin in these views) and the other for the second (index finger) metacarpal surface (at the left side of the figures). Note the difference between the gorilla and human in the orientation of the plane for the second metacarpal surface. The surface in the gorilla lies in the sagittal plane, whereas it lies between the coronal and transverse planes in the human. The orientation in* Homo habilis *recalls that of the gorilla, whereas in A. afarensis it is more similar to the human orientation. (For more information about the images, see Tocheri* et al. *2003, fig. 9.)*

which the joint must serve, in both apes and humans. For example, our stereophotogrammetric study has shown that there is significantly less curvature of the mutual first metacarpal and trapezial surfaces in humans than in chimpanzees (Marzke 1997; Marzke *et al.* 2002). The advantage to humans is that there is less locking by the proximal anterior beak of the metacarpal against the convex anterior surface of the trapezium, so that the metacarpal is able to move further across the trapezium in opposition to the fourth and fifth fingers in order to secure the cradle grip of large objects. (Examples of such objects include the stone preforms from which flakes are removed with the hammerstone.) However, this morphology is also a liability in strong pinch grips between the thumb and the pad or side of the index finger, which tend to force the metacarpal dorsally and off the side of the trapezium (Eaton & Dray 1982). The curved trapeziometacarpal joint in chimpanzees is compatible with their frequent use of pinch grips between the thumb and the side of the index finger, but it constrains opposition of the thumb to the fifth finger. Thus, curvature differences between the two species both may be the results of compromises.

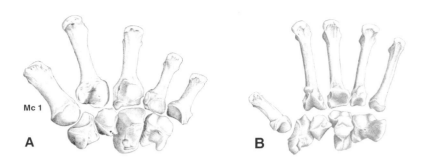

Figure 16.6. *Carpometacarpal region of a human hand (A) compared with the same region in a chimpanzee (B). The joints are separated so that the bases of the metacarpals may be viewed as well as the full distal surfaces of the carpal (wrist) bones with which they articulate. Note the proximal blunt surface on the second metacarpal for the distally-oriented surface at the lateral side of the capitate in the human. Differences between the species can also be seen in the size of the fifth carpometacarpal joint relative to the size of the fourth.*

In this respect, it is interesting to note that curvature of the trapezial joint surface for the first metacarpal in a sample of anubis baboons (*Papio anubis*) is significantly different from the human joint in its bone curvature, but not in the curvature of the articular cartilage that covers the bone (Su *et al.* 2002). This finding cautions physical anthropologists to systematically measure joint surface curvature with the cartilage as well as after cartilage removal, and to keep in mind the absence of evidence for articular cartilage topography when inferring joint movement capabilities from the bones of fossil species.

Although gorilla trapezia have not yet been included in quantitative analyses of first metacarpal joint surface topography, Lewis (1989) has noted that the surface appears to be more flat than in chimpanzees, and thus to approach humans in its topography.

Overall, humans do not appear to be unique in the general topography of their trapeziometacarpal joint. In fact, their topography may be primitive for catarrhines. The important point with regard to tool-making capabilities is that the shared human pattern is compatible with requirements for forceful precision gripping of stones, and does form part of a total hand pattern that characterizes humans.

A genuinely distinctive set of skeletal and ligamentous features associated with the third metacarpal is essential in counteracting forces toward the centre of the palm with the repeated striking motions of the hammerstone during flake removal. The hammerstone strikes on the core are directing reaction forces toward the heads of the second and third metacarpals, since the hammerstone is held by the thumb, index and third rays of the hand in the three-jaw chuck grip. This direction of reaction forces would thus tend to tilt the third metacarpal head dorsally, leading to a tendency for the third metacarpal base to slide forward. A styloid process at the dorsal base of the metacarpal (seen

in Fig. 16.2) and a pair of ligaments from two sides of the wrist that converge to anchor the palmar base of the metacarpal (Fig. 16.1; Marzke & Marzke 1987) act to prevent this hyperextension and counteract base subluxation.

Another distinctive pattern, consisting of relatively large joint sizes and robust bones in the human thumb and fifth finger regions (Marzke *et al.* 1992), is consistent with the strong muscle contraction in forceful grips described by Chao *et al.* (1976) and by Cooney & Chao (1977). Our EMG experiments show that the thumb and fifth finger are subjected to strong and repeated contraction of the intrinsic and extrinsic muscles during hard hammer percussion manufacture of tools. One would therefore predict that the hands of early hominin tool makers would have become adapted to this pattern of loading, with proportionately robust first and fifth metacarpals and relatively large joint surfaces involving these metacarpals.

Percussive forces associated with the hammerstone removal of flakes from stone cores, and with striking of objects with cylindrical bone, wood and antler tools, would appear to generate large, rather damaging reaction forces on the hand. However, I have recently examined the size of these forces with Jiping He, PhD, Department of Bioengineering, Arizona State University, by placing load cells on the stones where the hand grasps the tool. The forces at the time the tool strikes the target are not so large as had been predicted (Marzke & He unpublished). The most likely reason may be gleaned from the EMG signals recorded concurrently with the sound of the strike of the hammerstone on the core, which is obtained with a microphone. The signals are consistently lower at strike compared with signals

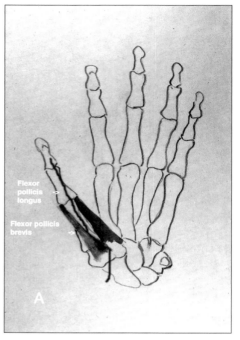

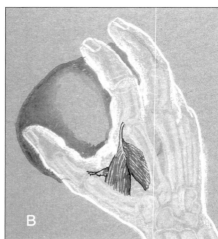

muscle activity is recorded simultaneously with the wrist, thumb and finger movements caused by contraction of the muscles. Videotapes have been used to record these movements. One of the most interesting results of these experiments is the very strong recruitment of muscles that flex and rotate the joints of the fifth finger and pull the finger into opposition to the thumb when the hand cups tools in cradle and power-squeeze grips. The fifth finger has rarely been considered in discussions of the evolutionary morphology of the hand, yet our EMG evidence suggests that the joints and bones of this finger are likely to have shapes and internal structure reflecting stresses and movements associated with the strong and habitual use of these muscles. The intrinsic muscles of the thumb and index finger also

Figure 16.7. *The human flexor pollicis brevis and flexor pollicis longus muscles (labeled) and the more medial oblique adductor pollicis muscle (A) and the human first dorsal interosseous muscle (B) showing its extensive origin along the first (thumb) metacarpal. The transverse portion of the adductor pollicis muscle can be seen in B on its course to the proximal phalanx of the thumb in B.*

prior to and/or following strike (Marzke *et al.* 1998). It appears that the tool maker or tool user is loosening the grasp of the tool at the moment when the reaction force from target contact would be greatest. The relaxation of grasp is brief enough that it does not allow displacement of the tool.

Skeletal correlates of muscle functions associated with human forceful precision grips and the power-squeeze grip

Now that several necessary skeletal correlates of these grips have been discussed, we turn to the question of what makes these human grips so strong as to be able to resist displacement of the tools from the hands, by the large external forces associated with flake removal using hammerstones and with pounding using cylindrical tools. This question has been addressed by two related sets of experiments. The first set has monitored muscle recruitment during these activities, using electromyography (EMG) to identify the muscles that are most strongly and repeatedly engaged in each activity (Marzke *et al.* 1998). The second set has compared the mechanics of the strongly-recruited muscles across species.

For the EMG experiments, fine wire electrodes are inserted into muscles of the hand and wrist. The

contract at high levels, particularly a group of three muscles that function together in moving and then stabilizing the trapeziometacarpal joint at the base of the thumb, during its opposition to the fingers. These are the oblique portion of the adductor pollicis muscle, the superficial head of the flexor pollicis brevis muscle, and the first dorsal interosseous muscle (Fig. 16.7). The first dorsal interosseous muscle also abducts and pronates the index finger. We found (as did Hamrick *et al.* 1998) that strong contraction of the extrinsic flexor pollicis longus muscle (Fig. 16.7A) is elicited primarily by the power-squeeze grip of cylindrical tools.

Muscles that were strongly recruited during prehistoric tool-making and tool-using experiments have been examined in a second set of studies, which compares humans and chimpanzees in muscle potential for exerting torque at the hand and wrist joints. Since potential torque is the product of a muscle's force potential and the moment arm of its tendon, we estimated these parameters in cadavers of chimpanzees and compared the estimates with those for humans (Marzke *et al.* 1999). Force potential is proportional to the physiological cross-sectional area of the muscle, and this area is determined by measuring the length of the fibers at three locations and the volume of the muscle, then dividing the volume by the mean fiber length. Moment arm is estimated from simultaneous measurements of tendon excursion and changes in the angle of the joint crossed by the tendon, during passive movements of the cadaver hands.

Humans were found to have a significant advantage over chimpanzees in most intrinsic thumb tendon moment arm lengths, for both flexion/extension movements and side-to-side abduction/adduction movements. They are thus are able to generate greater muscle torque with relatively less energy (Marzke *et al.* 1999). This ability is very likely to have become important for humans, as tool manipulation increasingly required repeated contraction of the thumb muscles at high levels. It still remains to identify the 3D skeletal topographical features that contribute to the tendon moment arm differences between humans and chimpanzees. These features may serve as important signals of relative hand-muscle leverage in fossil species. It is of course important also to compare tendon moment arms among a larger sample of species.

Among the possible reasons for this human advantage in intrinsic muscles may be that intrinsic muscles that cross the trapeziometacarpal joint at the base of the thumb serve twin functions. They not only move the thumb bones, they also stabilize this basal joint, while extrinsic muscles move the more distal interphalangeal joints. An important contributor to the stabilizing function is the lateral belly of the first dorsal interosseous muscle, which in humans attaches to the thumb metacarpal as well as to the index finger metacarpal and lateral base of the proximal phalanx (Fig. 16.7B). It is thus in a position to balance the pull of intrinsic muscles at the other side of the trapeziometacarpal joint (the short flexor muscle and the oblique portion of the adductor pollicis muscle: Fig. 16.7A) while the extrinsic muscles (flexor pollicis longus, Fig. 16.7A and extensor pollicis longus) flex and extend the tip of the thumb (Brand & Hollister 1999). The origin of the lateral belly of the first dorsal interosseous muscle in humans is distinctive in the long average distal extent and large size of the markings associated with its attachment on the first metacarpal (Jacofsky 2002). Thus a large human-like marking for the muscle in a fossil hominin hand may reflect a high level of recruitment of this muscle in manipulative activities.

We also studied carefully the results of our measurements of the human flexor pollicis longus muscle. This muscle is distinctive in its high frequency of independence of the long deep flexor muscle to the index finger, and in the asymmetry of its attachment to the distal phalanx of the thumb (Shrewsbury *et al.* 2003). The muscle and its tendon are independent in approximately 70 per cent of humans (Lindburg &

Comstock 1979), whereas in other mammals, including non-human primates, connections between the two muscles are regularly found among the fibers or tendons. The reason for its more frequent independence in humans may be that repetitive recruitment of the deep muscles to the thumb and index finger during human manipulative behaviour leads to inflammation in the carpal canal if the tendons are connected (Kozin *et al.* 1998; Lombardi *et al.* 1988). This effect of tendon connections may have become a liability as humans became increasingly dependent upon forceful, repetitive manipulation of tools (Shrewsbury *et al.* 2003).

Unfortunately the degree of flexor pollicis longus independence of the other deep flexors is not reflected in bone. However, the insertion of the flexor pollicis longus muscle is marked on the distal phalanx of the thumb by a gable-shaped crest, which in most humans is longer on the radial than on the ulnar limb of the gable. This asymmetry of attachment reflects disproportionate emphasis on the fibers of the flexor pollicis longus muscle that draw the thumb into pronation with flexion. The elongated radial limb of the crest is consistent with other features of distal pollical phalanx indicating an emphasis on strong interphalangeal joint pronation toward the finger pads in manipulatory activities (Shrewsbury *et al.* 2003).

The systematic study by Shrewsbury *et al.* (2003) did not reveal any evidence to support the assumption in the anthropological literature that a depression at the palmar base of the distal thumb phalanx reflects flexor pollicis longus muscle size or independence.

Who made stone tools?

As set forth in the previous sections, we have found clear evidence throughout the human hand for a pattern of morphology that is both distinctive of humans and consistent with the movement capabilities and stresses associated with the manufacture of stone tools. Few individual elements of the pattern may prove to be unique to humans, but the combination of elements that facilitates the movements and accommodates the internal and external forces associated with stone-tool making is comprehensive in scope. In our view, compelling evidence in fossil hand bones for grip capabilities compatible with stone-tool making, and for stresses on the bones and joints associated with forceful precision grips and hard hammer percussion flake removal with two hands would need to include most of the following combination of elements: 1) thumb/finger proportions that permit manipulation of stones by the thumb and finger pads; 2) carpometacarpal and metacarpophalangeal joint topography that

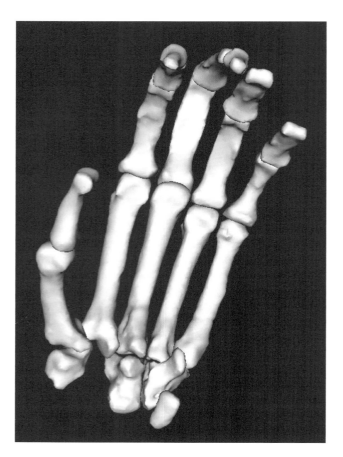

Figure 16.8. *A composite set of* Australopithecus afarensis *hand bones, modelled by W.L. Buford from computerized tomography scans of casts provided by the Institute of Human Origins. Use of mirror images allows for the assemblage of an almost complete hand.*

allows cupping of the hand in accommodation to the shapes of the stones; 3) skeletal features at the thumb joints that maximize the moment arms of the intrinsic and extrinsic thumb muscles; 4) a third metacarpal styloid process; 5) a relatively robust fifth metacarpal; and 6) skeletal markings on the thumb bones reflecting asymmetric pull of the flexor pollicis longus muscle and strong recruitment of the first dorsal interosseous muscle. Taken together, this suite of features would reflect the distinctively human ability to hold a stone tightly in each hand by the thumb and finger pads, allowing the working edges to be exposed and resisting displacement of the stones when they are struck, an ability that appears to be essential to the effective, repeated removal of flakes from a stone core by a hammerstone.

Regarding item 6, the relative size and extent of the attachment area on the first metacarpal for the first dorsal interosseous muscle may prove to be one of the most significant signals of stresses on the thumb associated with tool-making activities in fossil hands. This is not a feature whose presence alone is indicative of modern human-like thumb function, but a relatively high degree of its development may prove to be informative. Gorillas share with humans an attachment of the muscle to the first metacarpal, but the attachment does not reach the large size and extent of the muscle seen in many humans.

With regard to item five, the fifth finger has emerged from the experiments as an important contributor to the security of human grips involved in tool making. The intrinsic muscles of this finger are strongly recruited when the finger resists displacement of the stone core during flake removal and when it buttresses the other fingers holding the hammerstone. Evidence of a saddle joint at the fifth carpometacarpal joint in a fossil species would indicate the ability to oppose the full palmar aspect of the fifth finger to the thumb through rotation of the fifth metacarpal toward the thumb metacarpal. A relatively robust fifth metacarpal would reflect large internal forces associated with strong contraction of the intrinsic and extrinsic fifth finger muscles that would have secured grips involving the thumb and fifth fingers.

How well do specimens from our current collection of the fossil record exhibit the features of the tool-making suite?

It must be noted that the number of early hominin fossil bones from levels with stone tools is very small, and the different combinations of bones from each site renders inter-site comparison virtually impossible. Nevertheless, sufficient evidence exists to make the inquiry highly instructive.

Hadar

A composite set of well-preserved hand bones from *Australopithecus afarensis* from Hadar (Bush *et al.* 1982; see Fig. 16.8) exhibits an interesting mosaic of features. The bones pre-date the earliest current evidence for stone-tool manufacture by approximately 600 ky. It is therefore perhaps not surprising that the fifth metacarpal lacks the relative robusticity and the distinctively human saddle joint at its base, both of which would be expected if it had been strongly and repeatedly recruited and stressed during stone-tool making with the cradle grip and pounding with the power-squeeze grip of cylindrical tools (Marzke 1983; 1997; Marzke *et al.* 1992).

Consistent with this limitation to fifth finger rotation and apparent lack of large manipulative stresses is the chimpanzee-like topography of the trapeziometacarpal joint. The RMS (root mean square) curvature of the trapezium falls directly at the chimpanzee mean, and the metacarpal curvature is very close to the chimpanzee mean (Marzke *et al.* 2002). This topography similarly stabilized the thumb metacarpal for grips with the index finger, but limited excursion of the thumb over the full distance to opposition with the fifth finger, which is essential to the control of large objects by the cradle grip.

There is evidence for an origin of the first dorsal interosseous muscle along the shaft of the first metacarpal of *A. afarensis*, but the marking is significantly smaller than in modern humans. (Jacofsky pers. comm.). The small size of this origin implies a lower level of internal loading of the thumb by muscles acting on the metacarpophalangeal and interphalangeal joints than in most modern humans (Jacofsky pers. comm.).

While the two margins of the hand might imply chimpanzee-like behaviour, the morphology of the bones and joints involving the index finger strongly recalls certain distinctive aspects of modern human morphology. The topography of the index metacarpal joints with the wrist bones (Fig. 16.5) and with the proximal phalanx would have facilitated pronation with abduction and flexion that enhances the three-jaw chuck grip of round stones and the grip of flakes between the thumb and the side of the index finger (Marzke 1983; Marzke 1997; Tocheri *et al.* 2003). The thumb was apparently long enough relative to the fingers to control objects with the palmar pads of the index and third fingers (Marzke 1983). The chimpanzee-like trapeziometacarpal joint morphology would actually have lent stability to these grips.

The overall pattern suggests a hand that was used effectively for manipulating spherical stones, possibly as hammers for nut-pounding and as missiles for dispersing intruders or stunning small prey. The human-like index finger mobility, paired with chimpanzee-like thumb base stability, was a marriage of advantages that probably formed a central element of *A. afarensis* manipulative behaviour.

It is interesting to note that the third metacarpal lacks a proximal styloid process but probably did have a human-like palmar stabilizing ligament, judging by the groove near the hook of the hamate bone that accommodates the ligament in modern humans (Marzke & Marzke 1987).

Three sets of hand bones, as well as three isolated bones (a capitate, a thumb metacarpal and a fifth metacarpal), are known from a later time range (*c.* 2.5–1.75 mya) at Sterkfontein and Swartkrans in southern Africa and at Olduvai in East Africa, during which two, or possibly three genera coexisted in Africa. The Sterkfontein set, found in Member 4, includes metacarpals 2–5. The fifth metacarpal in this

set is the most robust of the finger metacarpals, as in modern humans, indicating that it was probably subjected to large loads. Presumably the loading was manipulative, since bones of the trunk and hindlimb indicate that Sterkfontein hominins were bipedal. A styloid process on the proximal dorsoradial corner of the third metacarpal also may reflect loading at a level similar to that in modern humans (Ricklan 1987).

Swartkrans and Sterkfontein

Evidence for large stresses on the thumb consistent with forceful manipulative behaviours has been found in both metacarpals from Swartkrans (SK 84 and SKX 5020) by Jacofsky (2002). These fossils are contemporary with stone and possible bone tools. A well-marked area of origin on the first metacarpal for the first dorsal interosseous muscle reflects forceful manipulative behaviours involving the thumb, consistent with manufacture and use of stone tools (Jacofsky 2002).

Olduvai

Hand bones of a juvenile individual from Bed I, Olduvai (O.H.7), contemporary with stone tools, include a trapezium and the distal phalanx of the thumb. A striking feature of this hand is a trapezial surface for the thumb metacarpal whose RMS curvature is approximately 1 standard deviation unit below the mean for modern humans (Marzke *et al.* 2002). This relatively flat topography of the surface is in marked contrast to the *Australopithecus afarensis* trapezium, whose RMS curvature, like that of chimpanzees, is significantly greater than in modern humans. The relatively flat surface in the Olduvai individual would have been unstable in forceful pinch grips between the thumb and index finger. However, it would have allowed ample excursion of the metacarpal toward the fifth finger. Unfortunately bones of the fifth finger were not recovered, so it is impossible to speculate on capabilities for gripping large objects by convergence of the thumb and fifth finger metacarpals.

The facet on the Olduvai trapezium for the second metacarpal was oriented in the sagittal plane, as it is in gorillas and chimpanzees (Fig. 16.5). It therefore would not have facilitated rotation of the metacarpal in cupping of the thumb, index and third fingers around spherical objects such as stones for throwing and pounding (Tocheri *et al.* 2003). This orientation contrasts with the orientation of the facet in *A. afarensis* (Fig. 16.5), which recalls that of humans and complements morphology elsewhere in the second carpometacarpal and metacarpophalangeal joints that facilitates pronation of the index finger (Tocheri *et al.* 2003).

The relatively broad O.H.7 pollical distal phalangeal tuberosity ('apical tuft') recalls that of modern humans. However, since baboons share this feature with humans (Shrewsbury *et al.* 2003), it is not a reliable predictor of tool-making capabilities.

Flexor pollicis longus muscle size cannot be inferred from the size of the fossa at the proximal volar aspect of this fossil distal phalanx as it has in the past, because the tendon does not insert in this fossa (Shrewsbury *et al.* 2003).

In summary, there are elements of modern human hand morphology in the Sterkfontein and Swartkrans hand bones that indicate a level of stresses on the hand associated with modern human manipulative behaviour. Unfortunately the evidence comes from the ulnar side of the Sterkfontein hand and the radial side of the Swartkrans hand, without complementary elements to provide a more comprehensive view of the potential range of grips and manipulative behaviours in either group. The morphology and potential functions of the Olduvai hand bones have become increasingly enigmatic with new studies of the available bones. Currently there is no compelling evidence for a pattern of modern human-like tool-making capabilities and stresses in the available bones.

Who used cylindrical bone and wood tools?

Our comparative studies have indicated that some aspects of hand morphology may distinguish among tool-using capabilities as well as between some tool-using and some tool-making capabilities. The use of a cylindrical bone or branch held diagonally across the palm may deliver substantial blows to animal and vegetable foods when it is held firmly by a power squeeze grip and brought into line with the forearm through ulnar deviation of the wrist. In this position it serves as an extension of the forearm, increasing the leverage and acceleration of the tool. A fifth carpometacarpal saddle joint, permitting convergence of the fifth metacarpal with the thumb metacarpal, is fundamental to the anchoring of this grip. EMG analyses of muscle recruitment during these activities highlight the intensity of both thumb and fifth finger muscle recruitment. It is thus interesting that the *A. afarensis* hand lacks evidence for this human tool-using capability, whereas it does exhibit evidence for other tool-using capabilities involving the thumb, index and third fingers that distinguish humans from non-human species.

The relatively robust Sterkfontein fifth metacarpal is consistent with loading associated with the power squeeze grip (Marzke *et al.* 1992). Bones that would throw light on this capability are not available for the Swartkrans or Olduvai species.

Can capabilities and stresses associated with stone-tool making be differentiated in hand morphology from those associated with feeding on tough vegetation?

Mountain gorillas emerged from the presentation, videotapes and discussions at this conference by R. Byrne (this volume) as a crucial species for the functional analysis of fossil hominin hands. The forcefulness with which celery and other vegetation is dislodged and then broken by the two hands for ingestion puts into relief the importance of considering food retrieval and processing as potentially significant factors in explaining bone and joint shape and robusticity in fossil hominin hands. It is interesting to note that the relatively flat topography of the joint at the base of the thumb of the Olduvai hand is approached by the gorilla trapezial surface (Lewis 1989). The middle phalanges of the hand also recall those of juvenile gorillas (Susman & Creel 1979). In addition, gorillas were also the only catarrhines found by Jacofsky (2002) to have a first dorsal interosseous muscle attachment along the shaft of the first metacarpal. This attachment area did not reach the extent or size of area found in many humans, but it suggests that the thumb is exerting a substantial amount of force during manipulative activities. The shared occurrence of this feature in humans and gorillas encourages us to explore more thoroughly the stresses at the base of the thumb associated with retrieving and processing of vegetation. There is a strong likelihood that stresses associated with extractive, forceful retrieval and processing of tough vegetation and fauna may have been a factor in the evolution of features in ancestral hominin hands that were preadapted to the requirement of forceful precision grips in tool making.

Have we been asking the right questions regarding the hand?

There have been four unfortunate and interrelated trends in comparative studies that have constrained insights into the relationships of hominin hand and tool evolution. One has been the tendency to focus almost exclusively on the functional morphology and behavioural recruitment of isolated bones and joints for which there is evidence in the early hominin fossil record. The hope, and expectation has been that clear signals of modern human-like behaviour might be found in these restricted joint regions. Unfortunately, an understanding of the functioning and potential recruitment of one region of the hand can rarely predict functioning and recruitment of other regions with which it interacts in manipulative behaviour. Since very few bones have been recovered from early hominin species, and still fewer bones have counterparts among more than one species, there has been relatively little consideration of functioning among kinematic and morphological links in the forearm, wrist and hand, and within the wrist and hand.

Second, assumptions that there are unique features in the human hand, which by their uniqueness imply adaptation to unique human tool-making behaviour, have not been adequately tested. Some that have been tested have fallen by the wayside. For example, our relatively broad distal pollical ungual tuberosity ('apical tuft') and possession of pollical distal phalangeal ungula spines, are not unique to humans (Shrewsbury et al. 2003), nor is our relatively large pollical metacarpal head (Hamrick & Inouye 1995; Ohman et al. 1995). However, our research is revealing features that occur in higher frequencies among humans than in other species (see, for example, Marzke et al. 1992 and Jacofsky 2002), and a pattern of features that seems to be unique (e.g. Marzke 1997; Shrewsbury et al. 2003). The pattern is becoming more clear as we examine an increasingly wide range of species in their hand behaviours, morphology and functions. Single morphological signals of tool making are unlikely to exist, but carefully identified and analyzed patterns of high-frequency human features may provide signposts to evolutionary stages in hominin tool-using and tool-making capabilities and stresses on the hand.

Third, the drive to identify tool makers in the fossil record has overwhelmed judicious consideration of the full range of manipulative and locomotor activities that might explain patterns of hand morphology in the fossil hominin species. Food manipulation is such a fundamental aspect of hand recruitment in primates, as well as in many other mammals, that hand functions and structure in relation to this behaviour should be as strong a focus of research as hand recruitment in locomotion. Species of particular interest are those that use the hand in forceful food extraction, such as the gorillas, capuchins (Fragaszy 1998), and sea otters (which pound shellfish on stones balanced on their chests, to attain the edible portions). Locomotor stresses on the fingers and wrist have been emphasized in comparative studies of the hand, but locomotor stresses on the thumb have barely been explored. It is possible that some aspects of thumb morphology shared by certain fossil hominins and gorillas and baboons might find at least a partial explanation in locomotor behaviour similar to that of some of these non-human primate groups.

The fourth, related trend has been an overemphasis on comparisons of modern and fossil hominin hands with that of our closest living relative, the chim-

panzee. Our research has led to the conclusion that the chimpanzee hand is in fact quite highly derived in structure. The thumb is specialized at the carpometacarpal joint for stability, compatible with grips between the thumb and the side of the index finger (Marzke 1997; Marzke et al. 2002), and is the most divergent of several species compared with humans in morphology of the distal phalanx (Shrewsbury et al. 2003). Baboons (Shrewsbury in press; Su et al. 2002), gorillas (Tocheri et al. 2003) and perhaps capuchin monkeys may prove to be more relevant and interesting models for early hominin hand functions and behaviours.

What evidence is there in the forearm, arm, trunk and hindlimbs for tool use and tool making?

Bipedality freed our hands from locomotion, but hand function in human manipulative behaviour is not independent of the trunk and hindlimb. It is well known by professionals in sports and in sports medicine that trunk and hindlimb movements enhance the force and acceleration of tools held in the hand or thrown by the hand. Watch, for example, the knee flexion and trunk rotation, together with movements at the shoulder, elbow and wrist that generate the high-speed serves of tennis players. Failure to recruit movements at all these joint regions may focus debilitatingly large stresses on the remaining joints that are recruited. This knowledge points us toward regions of fossil hominin morphological link systems that should be examined in the search for patterns reflective of tool use in throwing, clubbing and digging. For example, evidence for the ability of A. afarensis to control movements of the trunk in bipedal posture reflects a potential for trunk use in the enhancement of tool-using as well as bipedal locomotor capabilities (Marzke 1986; Marzke et al. 1988).

What are the motor and sensory neurological requirements for manipulative behaviour?

The neurological basis of the ability of rhesus monkeys to move the fingers independently of one another has been illustrated with elegant experiments reported by Maier et al. (this volume). These monkeys have a more direct connection with motor neurons to the hand, via the corticospinal tract, than do squirrel monkeys with which they have been compared. Dexterity is also illustrated by the preparation of nettles for ingestion by the gorillas described by Byrne (this volume), and is described by Boesch & Boesch-Achermann (2000) for chimpanzee nut-cracking. This latter ability is consistent with the finding of a dexterity index in chimpanzees (measured by independence of finger action) comparable to that of humans (Kuypers 1981). Cebus monkeys have a larger corticospinal tract compared with their close relatives, the squirrel monkeys, consistent with their dextrous manipulative behaviours (Fragaszy 1998).

These studies are just at their beginning stages, regarding the questions of hand function and tool use. It is hoped that these and other provocative windows on neurological aspects of manipulative behaviour in non-human primates will draw students interested in the evolution of manipulative behaviour into comparative studies of neural control of manipulation, and of the multiple sensory systems that modulate precision gripping and power grasping of objects by humans and non-human primates.

Conclusion and challenges for the future

The major hurdle in identifying early hominin stone-tool makers in the fossil record is to identify a pattern of skeletal clues to the behaviours that distinguish human hand use in stone-tool making from hand use in tool manipulation and food retrieval and processing of other species. This chapter has attempted to draw together clues to the form that this pattern takes. Identifying the pattern requires, first, the comparison of humans with a wide range of non-human species in manipulative behaviour. These species should include close-living relatives as well as less closely related species with shared manipulative behaviours. Second, further comparative EMG and movement analyses of both the shared and the species-distinctive behaviours are needed, to target joint and muscle functions essential to the respective species behaviours. Third, morphological features that facilitate or, in some cases reflect responses to, the species' hand functions should be discerned through continued kinematic and biomechanical analyses of hand functions associated with both the shared and distinctive behaviours of the species.

The preliminary results of our participation in this process of investigation have been reported in this chapter. A pattern of skeletal clues to tool-making capabilities in fossil hominin hands has been proposed, based upon a limited application of the comprehensive behavioural/functional/morphological approach. The approach has tested, and in some cases dismissed, previous assumptions of relationships between fossil hand morphology and tool-making capabilities (some of them made by this author as well as by others). It has also introduced a new set of morphological predictors of these capabilities for future testing.

A sample of metacarpals 2–5 from Sterkfontein and two thumb metacarpals from Swartkrans exhibit features that reflect a level of first and fifth metacarpal stresses found so far only in human hands. The pattern of Olduvai hand-bone morphology does not provide compelling evidence for human-like grip capabilities associated with stone-tool making.

New techniques for comparative quantitative analyses of bone and joint surface topography are accelerating progress in this research (Marzke & Marzke 2000; Tocheri et al. 2003), but these will need to be applied with a view toward creative, integrative and objective approaches to understanding the complex functioning of the link system involving the hand in locomotion and manipulative behaviour.

Acknowledgements

The author is grateful to R.L. Linscheid, M.D., K.-N. An, PhD and the staff at the Orthopedic Biomechanics Laboratory, Mayo Clinic for their sustained support of, and contributions to the research reported here. Drawings were kindly provided by D. To (Fig. 16.6) and R.L. Linscheid, M.D. (Fig. 16.7B), and S. Selkirk provided technical assistance with the figures. W.L. Buford, PhD, Department of Orthopaedic Surgery and Rehabilitation, University of Texas Medical Branch, Galveston, created the model of the *A. afarensis* hand (Fig. 16.8). Thanks also to R.F. Marzke, PhD, who has contributed substantially to all aspects of the research. The work has been supported in part by the National Science Foundation (Grant IIS-9980166).

References

Boesch, C. & H. Boesch-Achermann, 2000. *The Chimpanzees of the Taï Forest*. Oxford: Oxford University Press.

Brand, P.W. & A. Hollister, 1999. *Clinical Mechanics of the Hand*. 3rd edition. St Louis (MI): Mosby Year Book.

Bush, M.E., C.O. Lovejoy, D.C. Johanson & Y. Coppens, 1982. Hominid carpal, metacarpal, and phalangeal bones recovered from the Hadar formation: 1974–1977 collections. *American Journal of Physical Anthropology* 57, 651–77.

Chao, E.Y.S., J.D. Opgrande & F.E. Axmear, 1976. Three-dimensional force analysis of finger joints in selected isometric hand functions. *Journal of Biomechanics* 9, 387–96.

Chao, E.Y.S., K.-N. An, W.P. Cooney III & R.L. Linscheid, 1989. *Biomechanics of the Hand*. Singapore: World Scientific.

Cooney, W.P. & E.Y.S. Chao, 1977. Biomechanical analysis of static forces in the thumb during hand function. *Journal of Bone and Joint Surgery* 59-A, 27–36.

Eaton, R.G. & G.J. Dray, 1982. Dislocations and ligament injuries in the digits, in *Operative Hand Surgery*, ed. D.P. Green, vol. 1. New York (NY): Churchill Livingstone, 637–68.

Fragaszy, D., 1998. How non-human primates use their hands, in *The Psychobiology of the Hand*, ed. K.J. Connolly. Cambridge: Cambridge University Press, 77–96.

Hamrick, M.W. & S.E. Inouye, 1995. Thumbs, tools and early humans. *Science* 286, 587.

Hamrick, M.W., S.E. Churchill, D. Schmitt & W.L. Hylander, 1998. EMG of the human flexor pollicis longus muscle: implications for the evolution of hominid tool use. *Journal of Human Evolution* 34, 123–36.

Jacofsky, M.C., 2002. Variation in Morphology and Musculoskeletal Stress Marker Expression of the First Dorsal Interosseous Muscle in Catarrhines. MA paper, Arizona State University.

Kozin, S.H., A.T. Bishop & W.P. Cooney, 1998. Tendinitis of the wrist, in *The Wrist*, vol. 2, eds. W.P. Cooney, R.L. Linscheid & J.H. Dobyns. St Louis (MI): Mosby, 1181–96.

Kuypers, H.G.J.M., 1981. Anatomy of the descending pathways, in *Handbook of Physiology: the Nervous System II*, eds. J.M. Brookhart & V.B. Mountcastle. Bethesda (MD): American Physiological Society, 597–666.

Lewis, O.J., 1989. *Functional Morphology of the Evolving Hand and Foot*. Oxford: Clarendon Press.

Linburg, R.M. & B.E. Comstock, 1979. Anomalous tendon slips from the flexor pollicis longus to the digitorum profundus. *Journal of Hand Surgery* (Am) 4, 79–83.

Lombardi, R.M., M.B. Wood & R.L. Linscheid, 1988. Symptomatic restrictive thumb-index flexor tenosynovitis: incidence of musculotendinous anomalies and results of treatment. *Journal of Hand Surgery* (Am) 13, 325–38.

Marzke, M.W., 1983. Joint function and grips of the *Australopithecus afarensis* hand, with special reference to the region of the capitate. *Journal of Human Evolution* 12, 197–211.

Marzke, M.W., 1986. Tool use and the evolution of hominid hands and bipedality, in *Primate Evolution*, eds. J.G. Else & P.G. Lee. Cambridge: Cambridge University Press, 203–9.

Marzke, MW., 1997. Precision grips, hand morphology and tools. *American Journal of Physical Anthropology* 102, 91–110.

Marzke, M.W. & R.F. Marzke, 1987. The third metacarpal styloid process in humans: Origins and functions. *American Journal of Physical Anthropology* 73, 415–31.

Marzke, M.W. & R.F. Marzke, 2000. Evolution of the human hand: approaches to acquiring, analysing and interpreting the anatomical evidence. *Journal of Anatomy* 197, 121–40.

Marzke M.W. & K.L. Wullstein, 1996. Chimpanzee and human grips: a new classification with a focus on evolutionary morphology. *International Journal of Primatology* 17, 117–39.

Marzke, M.W., J. Longhill & S.A. Rasmussen, 1988. Gluteus maximus function and the origin of hominid bipedality. *American Journal of Physical Anthropology* 77, 519–28.

Marzke, M.W., K.L. Wullstein & S.F. Viegas, 1992. Evolution of the power (squeeze) grip and its morphological correlates in hominids. *American Journal of Physical Anthropology* 89, 283–98.

Marzke, M.W., N. Toth, K. Schick, S. Reece, B. Steinberg, K. Hunt & R.L. Linscheid, 1998. EMG study of hand muscle recruitment during hard hammer percussion of Oldowan tools. *American Journal of Physical Anthropology* 105, 315–32.

Marzke, M.W., R.F. Marzke, R.L. Linscheid, P. Smutz, B. Steinberg, S. Reece & K.-N. An, 1999. Chimpanzee muscle cross-sections, moment arms and potential torques, and comparisons with humans. *American Journal of Physical Anthropology* 110, 163–78.

Marzke, M.W., R.F. Marzke, R.L. Linscheid & S.P. Reece, 2002. Trapeziometacarpal Joint Curvature Variation among Humans, Chimpanzees and Fossil Ancestral Species. Poster presented at the 57th annual meeting of the American Society for Surgery of the Hand, Phoenix, Arizona.

Ohman, J.C., M. Slanina, G. Baker & R.P. Mensforth, 1995. Thumbs, tools and early humans. *Science* 268, 587–9.

Reece, S., M.W. Marzke, L.F. Marchant & W.C. McGrew, 2000. Food object manipulation by chimpanzees in Mahale Mountains National Park. *American Journal of Physical Anthropology* Supplement 30, 259–60.

Ricklan, D.E., 1987. Functional anatomy of the hand of *Australopithecus africanus*. *Journal of Human Evolution* 16, 643–64.

Shrewsbury, M.M., M.W. Marzke, R.L. Linscheid & S.P. Reece, 2003. Comparative morphology of the pollical distal phalanx. *American Journal of Physical Anthropology* 121, 30–47.

Su, B.W., M.F. Koff, T.S. Protopsaltis, K.P. Chang, V. Sarwahi, V., A.L. Coon, E.S. Connolly Jr, V.C. Mow, M.W. Marzke & M.P. Rosenwasser, 2002. Comparative Topography of the Carpometacarpal Joint (CMC) of Baboons (*Papio anubis*). Poster presented at the 57th annual meeting of the American Society for Surgery of the Hand, Phoenix, Arizona.

Susman, R.L., 1979. Comparative and functional morphology of hominoid fingers. *American Journal of Physical Anthropology* 50, 215–36.

Susman, R.L. & N. Creel, 1979. Functional and morphological affinities of the subadult hand (OH7) from Olduvai Gorge. *American Journal of Physical Anthropology* 51, 311–32.

Tocheri, M.W., M.W. Marzke, D. Liu, M. Bae, G.P. Jones, R.C. Williams & A. Razdan, 2003. Functional capabilities of modern and fossil hominid hands. *American Journal of Physical Anthropology* 122, 101–12.

Tocheri, M.W., A. Razdan, R.C. Williams & M.W. Marzke, 2005. A 3D quantitative comparison of trapezium and trapezoid relative articular and nonarticular surface areas in modern humans and great apes. *Journal of Human Evolution*.

Toth, N., K.D. Schick, S. Savage-Rumbaugh, R.A. Sevcik & D.M. Rumbaugh, 1993. Pan the tool-maker: investigations into the stone tool-making and tool-using capabilities of a bonobo (*Pan paniscus*). *Journal of Archaeological Science* 20, 81–91.

Chapter 17

The Importance of Direct vs Indirect Corticospinal Connections for Dexterity and their Evolution

Marc A. Maier, Peter A. Kirkwood,
Katsumi Nakajima & Roger N. Lemon

To gain a better understanding of the neural systems that might contribute towards dexterity and tool use in primates, we compared the excitatory neural influence of direct projections from motor areas of the cerebral cortex on upper-limb motoneurones with the more indirect influences that are transmitted through a system of propriospinal neurones (PNs) located in the upper cervical spinal cord (C3–C4 level). We considered four species with increasing dexterity: cat, squirrel monkey, macaque monkey and Homo, *and attempted to relate the phylogenetic development of these two neuronal systems, which are both implicated in the control of upper-limb movements, to the evolution of manual dexterity. Our findings suggest that a more advanced dexterity across species correlates (1) positively with the strength of the direct corticomotoneuronal (CM) system and (2) negatively with the strength of the indirect PN-mediated excitatory transmission. We predict that in humans, where the CM system is most highly developed, the C3–C4 PN system is unlikely to be responsible for any significant transmission of cortical commands. We argue that the existence of CM connections is a necessary and sufficient precondition for dexterity, but is not sufficient for tool use and tool manufacturing.*

The old but not out-dated philosophical question of what differentiates human beings from animals is particularly difficult to answer in regard to non-human primates and our extinct predecessors. If hominins are indeed categorically different from non-human primates, how have they become so, and if they are not, what would be the (ethical) implications of any gradual differences (Ferry & Vincent 2001). Many different individual (anatomical, physiological, behavioural) and social traits have been regarded as characteristic features of human beings, one of them being the high degree of manual dexterity. More recent evidence, however, shows that human manual skills are not radically superior to those of non-human primates in terms of movement performance, i.e. judged on movement parameters such as force, speed, precision and versatility, though they are obviously different in the cognitive domain of goal achievement, planning and learning (e.g. Byrne & Byrne 1993). So, if dexterity does not make the difference, maybe the next higher level does, i.e. tool use; but this skill does not seem to represent a categorical difference either: there are non-human primates and other species that use tools (e.g. Boesch & Boesch 1993). It seems that the big gap appeared with the manufacturing of tools: although the genus of our first ancestor, who used his hands for the manufacturing of formal stone and pebble tools, has not yet been definitely established, it is clear that early *Homo* developed stone tools to a degree never before observed in extant non-human primates.

This kind of dextrous behaviour, however, goes beyond the strict definition of what constitutes a motor skill, and needs to be viewed in terms of purposeful, goal-oriented and problem-solving motor behaviour. Indeed, the surprisingly long period between the emergence of fully-upright stance and gait (more than

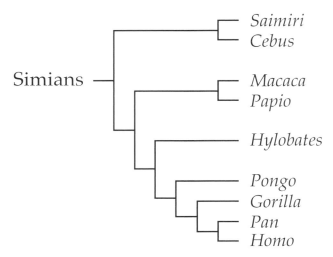

Figure 17.1. *Phylogenetic relation between selected primate species (based on Purvis 1995; see also Table 17.1).* Saimiri *and* Cebus *are New World monkeys and belong to the family Ceboidea.* Macaca *and* Papio *are Old World monkeys and belong to the family Cercopithecoidea.* Hylobates *form their own family.* Pongo, Gorilla, Pan *(apes) and* Homo *belong to the family Hominoidea.*

1 million years) and that of tool manufacturing indicates that brain evolution did not only optimize motor skills, but also the cognitive abilities required for tool use and tool manufacturing (Wiesendanger 1999).

This chapter focuses on issues of brain evolution and manual dexterity as a motor skill in four species: cat, squirrel monkey, macaque monkey, and *Homo*. We will discuss the neural basis of manual dexterity in terms of the phylogenetic development of two neural systems: i) the corticospinal system; and ii) the propriospinal system, as assessed by an inter-species comparison. The phylogenetic relation among these and some other primate species (see Table 17.1) is shown in Figure 17.1. We will finally speculate on the relation between the evolution of these systems and the development of tool use and tool manufacturing.

Relation between manual dexterity and brain evolution

In order to establish a relation between the degree of manual dexterity and the phylogenetic development of particular neural structures, several factors need to be taken into account, three of which will be discussed: the *morphological* (skeletal) development of the hand, which must attain a minimal degree of complexity to provide the mechanical substrate for a dextrous apparatus; the evolution of *behavioural* dexterity as a skill; and the evolution of the *neural structures* which control this apparatus.

Hand morphology

A minimal level of mechanical complexity and of degrees of freedom seems to be necessary for dextrous object manipulation. The particular anatomy of the human hand provides sufficient degrees of freedom to achieve a high degree of dexterity. Thus the question arises (Napier 1980): What are the crucial features of hand morphology to provide the mechanical substrate for manual skills, and where in primate evolution have they been realized? Several variables have been identified:

1. the proportionality between thumb length and index finger length varies substantially in primate species and affects the ability to grip and control objects. In humans this ratio is 0.67, and decreases to about 0.4 in monkeys, with intermediate scores for gorilla (0.54) and chimpanzee (0.47);
2. the variability in shape and arrangement of carpal and metacarpal bones (Lewis 1989);
3. the shape of the distal phalanges (Smith 1995; Marzke *et al.* 1998) and other features.

One of the main interests of comparative hand morphology is to deduce the manual capabilities of early hominins from fossil records: Was *Homo habilis* the maker of the Oldowan stone tools (Leakey *et al.* 1964; Napier 1962); What morphological features would prove beneficial for the manufacturing and use of those and other tools (Marzke 1997); and Could an ape have made those tools? (Toth *et al.* 1993). However, several problems make a reliable answer unlikely:

1. The relationship of hand morphology to functional, i.e. manipulative, skills is not clear. In particular, bony fossils do not necessarily give enough information on muscular morphology to deduce the dextrous potential of a hand. For example, differences in terms of maximal torque and control of movement direction have been established between the human and chimpanzee hand muscles (Marzke *et al.* 1999).
2. The notorious scarcity of fossil records contemporaneous with stone tools (Marzke & Marzke 2000) precludes any statistical evidence to date.
3. The evolution of morphology and the necessary neural control may not have been concomitant, which underlines the importance of intermediary variables, such as the neural control of the hand or the control of the proximal upper limb, in order to causally link morphology to dextrous behaviour.

To what degree the morphology of the human hand provides an advantage over that of the monkey's or the great ape's hand is an open but important question. If the morphology were of minor importance, this would mean that the dextrous skills of *Homo* are mainly due to an increased refinement of sensorimotor control, and thus a monkey hand, equipped with a human control system, could achieve human-like dexterity. If, however, the morphology were of major importance, the morphological limits of the monkey hand would not allow for human-like dexterity, regardless of the sophistication of the neural control. Varying degrees of morphological and behavioural differences between monkey, ape and human dextrous activities have been reported, however, these do not correspond with phylogenetic continuity (Christel *et al.* 1998; Christel & Billard 2002; Maier 1993).

Measures of dexterity

The index of dexterity, developed by Napier (1961), which ranges from 1, (defined as 'fused or restrained digits'), up to 7, (defined as 'opposable thumb, capable of precision grip in opposition to each finger') has been widely used. This index describes the ability to perform a precision grip and it combines anatomical and behavioural components; however, it is not without controversy: not only has the assignment of particular values to some species been challenged, but also the validity of the index as a whole. With the advent of more sophisticated movement analysis, particular cases of incorrect assignments have been noted: the rat should, according to some authors, have a rank of 4 or 5 rather than 3 (Whishaw & Gorny 1994; Whishaw & Coles 1996). The cat, too, seems to merit a higher index of 4 rather than the originally assigned 2 (Boczek-Funcke *et al.* 1998). Among primates, the great apes were originally given an index of 6, but it now seems clear that they have a remarkably wide manual repertoire and should be assigned an index of 7 (Christel 1993; Marzke & Wullstein 1996; Byrne *et al.* 2001b). Equally, two species of New World monkeys (*Cebus* and *Saimiri*) had been assigned an index of 5, based on the fact that they did not have a truly opposable thumb. More recent evidence, however, indicates that *Cebus* has a well-developed grip repertoire, including precision grip between index and thumb and would merit an index of 6 (Costello & Fragaszy 1988; Antinucci & Visalbergi 1986). Thus, it is unclear to what extent the original index is still valid; it seems evident that it needs updating.

Some even argue that the index of dexterity needs to be replaced by an altogether new index (Iwaniuk *et al.* 1999). In particular, the non-dissociation of anatomical and behavioural variables is problematic: the fact that in more than 1 million years there were only minor changes in hand morphology, but at the same time an astonishing increase in manual capability (Wiesendanger 1999), raises the question of which neuronal structures have improved the control and

the use of the hand. An answer could be found more easily, if we were able to dissociate anatomical from behavioural variables of dexterity.

To quantify manipulative abilities, complementary tests have already been proposed and used: the index of dexterity, essentially a classification of grip types, was extended by Marzke & Wullstein (1996), who proposed a more elaborate differentiation of grips (see also Christel 1993) by including further variables, such as the force in precision grips, the ability to translate and rotate objects in the hand ('precision handling') and the grip used for grasping cylindrical objects (tools). Furthermore, the index of dexterity is a purely unimanual measure that focuses on the functional differentiation of grips and single digits, whereas manipulative actions often involve bimanual skills, where each hand may have a different function ('bimanual role differentiation': see Byrne & Byrne 1993; Byrne *et al.* 2001b). There is a clear need for a measure that incorporates degrees of bimanual dextrous behaviour, as required, for example, in stone knapping. A measure of 'bimanual asymmetric coordination' (BAC) was used by van Schaik *et al.* (1999), and a more general measure of manipulative patterns during object handling was developed in an experimental set-up by Torigoe (1985), in which a knotted rope and a wooden cube were used. In summary, the different and complementary measures of manual dexterity have to be unified in such a way that distinctive and overlapping abilities in grip repertoire, digit differentiation as well as bimanual role differentiation, can be quantitatively and adequately described. Ideally, one would like to be able to dissociate morphological traits, i.e. variables that determine the maximal (potential) degree of anatomical dexterity, from functional variables (skills), i.e. those that quantify the degree of the executed behavioural dexterity

Brain structure and dextrous function

An optimal compromise between the maximal use of all possible mechanical degrees of freedom and the efficiency of their control, as well as adaptability and flexibility, are the essential characteristics of a sophisticated sensorimotor control. All neural motor commands, whatever their origin, must pass through the final common pathway, constituted by the motor unit, which represents the last element of neural control over muscle activity. Therefore, when we ask which brain structures were relevant for the development of manual dexterity, the systems impinging directly onto spinal motoneurones, i.e. the monosynaptic premotoneuronal (first-order) systems, seem, at first, to be of prime importance. Then, on closer examination, the second-order systems (i.e. with disynaptic access to motoneurones, such as motor-cortical interneurones acting on corticomotoneuronal cells) that control the actual premotor systems seem to be implicated as well, and the same goes for third-order systems and so on. However, since there are several first-order systems with functionally-different roles, the importance of second-order systems depends indirectly on whatever first-order system they act upon, which explains the pivotal role of the premotor systems. Furthermore, owing to relatively easy experimental access, first-order systems have been studied most extensively — not only in terms of connectivity, their defining feature, but also in terms of activity. Below we will discuss the functional implications of two of the premotor systems for manual dexterity.

Premotoneuronal systems
Motoneurones are integrators; whether or not they discharge and cause movement depends upon the integration of the many thousands of excitatory and inhibitory influences converging on them. Spinal motoneurones receive inputs from a variety of premotor systems and the question therefore arises, which of these systems is most important for providing a high degree of manual dexterity. *A priori*, each one of these systems, or any combination of them could form the neural basis of dexterity. Among these are the corticospinal as well as several non-cortical descending systems with direct connections onto motoneurones, including the reticulo-, vestibulo- and rubro-spinal neurones, all of which seem to vary phylogenetically (Nudo & Masterton 1989; Kuypers 1981). In addition, local spinal systems, such as the propriospinal neurones (located in segments remote from the motoneurone) and segmental interneurones (in the same segment) converge on motoneurones. Finally a wide range of primary sensory afferents, bringing information from peripheral sensory receptors, also terminate on these same motoneurones. Descending inputs from supraspinal motor structures to motoneurones vary in size, but in general they are rather small; the exceptions seem to be some of the direct corticomotoneuronal inputs to motoneurones that supply the intrinsic hand muscles in primates (Baldissera *et al.* 1981; Lemon *et al.* 2004).

A clue towards identifying the most likely candidates among the premotor systems lies once again in their connectivity: some of the systems can be excluded, because their input source is not pertinent and/or because they project to particular groups of motoneurones not implicated in manual dexterity, such as the vestibulo- and reticulo-spinal systems with descending connections that mainly influence axial muscles (i.e. spine) and are concerned with postural

control. Sensory afferents impinging directly onto motoneurones are implicated in reflex activity. The spinal segmental interneurones integrate information from various sources, in particular from all the other premotor systems mentioned (i.e. cortical, subcortical and peripheral). This leaves us with several candidate systems for the control of upper-limb movements: the propriospinal and in particular the cortico- and the rubro-spinal system. All three pathways convey direct excitation to upper-limb motoneurones and the latter two in particular to motoneurones supplying hand muscles. In terms of output, these three systems are organized in parallel, however, there is a hierarchy in terms of input: the corticospinal system provides input to the rubrospinal and propriospinal neurones but not *vice versa*. Furthermore, cortico- and rubro-spinal action bypasses possible segmental and propriospinal reflex activity based on peripheral afferents.

During primate evolution there has been a remarkable increase in the relative size of the cortex (Jerison 1973; Barton & Harvey 2000; Falk & Gibson 2001) and a parallel growth of the area of the cortex contributing to the corticospinal tract (Nudo & Masterton 1990). In contrast, the size of the magnocellular part of the red nucleus, which gives rise to the rubrospinal tract, seems to regress during primate evolution (Nathan & Smith 1982) and suggests a diminishing importance for dexterity. The segmental spinal circuitry also underwent phylogenetic changes, especially that of the distal forelimb, perhaps so that the mechanical degrees of freedom of the forelimb could be used for actions other than locomotion (Illert & Kümmel 1999).

In the following, we will discuss the implications of the phylogenetic variation of two premotoneuronal systems: the corticospinal and the propriospinal system (Fig. 17.2). The corticospinal system needs to be considered as prime candidate for providing the ability to perform relatively independent finger movements, the hallmark of manual dexterity. Although the propriospinal system is not considered to be of major importance for manual dexterity, it shares a feature common to many subcortical premotor systems: it receives input from the corticospinal system, thus providing a disynaptic link to motoneurones, as do the rubrospinal and the segmental interneuronal systems. Therefore, from the viewpoint of *cortical* transmission of excitation to motoneurones, there is only one *direct* monosynaptic pathway and there are several *indirect*, disynaptic pathways. By a comparison of the cortico- and proprio-spinal system, we will provide evidence that the phylogenetic development favours direct rather than indirect cortical control over motoneurones.

The classic case: the corticospinal system: the direct pathway
A high degree of manual dexterity is generally attributed to a well-developed corticospinal system (Wiesendanger 1981). Two factors highlight the relation between the corticospinal tract (CST) and skilful hand movements: i) the emergence of dextrous behaviour in parallel with the ontogenetic development of the CST (Armand *et al.* 1994; 1997); and ii) the phylogenetic development of the CST and the emergence of dextrous skills. Heffner & Masterton (1975) determined the relation between different anatomical features of the CST and digital dexterity and concluded that the length of the CST fibres (termination in more and more caudal spinal segments) and their depth (depth of penetration within the segmental laminae) correlated positively with the degree of dexterity exhibited by 69 different mammalian species. Furthermore, from a study in species theoretically linked to man's ancestral lineage, they concluded that length and depth of CST, as well as the degree of dexterity, culminated in *Homo* (Heffner & Masterton 1983). Recently, however, based on methodological grounds, such as a biased sample (over-representation of primates) or the presence of non-independent observations due to ancestry (Iwaniuk *et al.* 1999), the reliability of these data has been questioned. A re-analysis of the Heffner & Masterton (1983) data, based on comparative statistics, revealed that only fibre length, and not fibre depth, correlated significantly with the degree of dexterity (Iwaniuk *et al.* 1999).

It is important to point out that, just as new studies have questioned some of the ranking of dexterity in some species (see above), there is also an urgent need for proper quantitative and comparative neuroanatomical studies, so that the correlations, first attempted by Heffner & Masterton, can be carried out with greater confidence. In this light, the study of Bortoff & Strick (1993) takes on additional significance: their work clearly demonstrated that corticomotoneuronal projections to hand motoneurones were far more dense and widespread in the dextrous *Cebus* monkey than in the squirrel monkey (*Saimiri*). This reinforced the view of earlier investigators as to the importance of this projection for dextrous skills (Phillips & Porter 1977; Kuypers 1978; Porter & Lemon 1993). As has been first suggested by Bernhard & Bohm (1954), the direct CM component of the CST, i.e. the direct monosynaptic excitatory connections between cortical neurones and spinal motoneurones, might be of particular importance for achieving control of independent finger movements. There is clear supporting evidence for this suggestion: experimental lesions of the CST (Lawrence & Kuypers 1968; Hepp-Reymond 1988) have shown particular deficits in independent digit

movements, the severity of which varies according to the species. In the same line, Kuypers (1978) suggested a predominant involvement of the CM connections in the 'fractionation', the selective spatio-temporal activation, of distal muscles. Evidence for the pivotal role of the CM system for primate dexterity has since been provided in the behaving monkey by Fetz & Cheney (1980), Lemon *et al.* (1986), Bennett & Lemon (1996), McKiernan *et al.* (1998), Baker *et al.* (2001).

The significance of CST length is less clear, but one might speculate that CM connections for the lower limb in monkey (Jankowska *et al.* 1975) and humans (Palmer & Ashby 1992; Nielsen & Petersen 1995) may provide selective activation of foot muscles needed for controlling the high demands posed on bipedal stance and gait.

What is the appropriate measure?
This controversy on the apparently missing link between phylogenetic evolution and functional importance of the CM system might be resolved by clearly distinguishing between anatomical *projections* and physiological *connections* in the CNS. Although projections and connections are related, they are not strictly identical. Although projections are a prerogative for functional significance, they alone are not sufficient: synaptic connections are needed to achieve a functional link. Projections may make direct connections with a motoneurone anywhere on its large dendritic tree; since, for most motoneurones, this extends well beyond the boundaries of lamina IX (the classical description of that part of the spinal grey in which the motor nuclei are located), projections outside lamina IX could still provide monosynaptic input to motoneurones (Bortoff & Strick 1993; Maier *et al.* 1997).

Functional connections can be excitatory or inhibitory and they can vary (at least to some degree) independently from projection strength. The amplitude of the compound excitatory post-synaptic potential (EPSP) in motoneurones, evoked by the stimulation of the entire tract, is an estimate of the efficacy or strength of a monosynaptic input. Classically, intracellular recordings of postsynaptic effects in identified motoneurones after stimulation of the contralateral pyramidal tract (PT) allows for the quantification of the compound EPSP of the corticomotoneuronal system (Fig. 17.2). For these kinds of recordings, we and others have used the adult cat or monkey under chloralose-anaesthesia and neuromuscular paralysis. The compound EPSP is, in our view, a more appropriate, because more direct, measure of the efficacy than the density of a projection. In the following we will compare the occurrence and amplitude of compound EPSPs in three species: the cat, the squirrel monkey

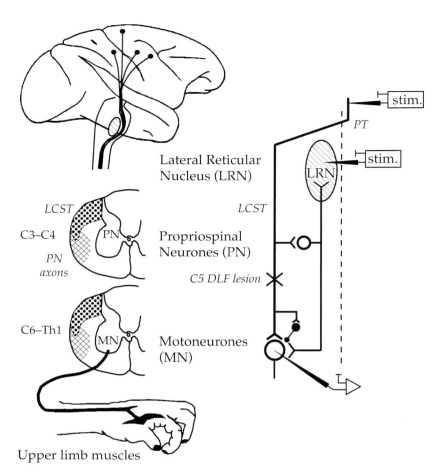

Figure 17.2. *Schematic diagram of corticospinal and propriospinal pathways to upper-limb motoneurones in the primate. Left: schematic anatomical location of the neural structures implicated. From top: Cortex and brain stem (with lateral reticular nucleus [hatched]), two spinal segments: the upper containing propriospinal neurones, the lower containing motoneurones that activate hand and digit muscles. Terms in Italics indicate fibre tracts at the spinal level: lateral corticospinal tract, LCST [dotted]; fibre tract composed of propriospinal axons [crosshatched]. Right: schematic diagram of the connectivity and experimental procedures. Corticospinal projections originate in several cortical motor areas, pass the brain stem and cross the midline (where they form the lateral corticospinal tract, LCST) and terminate monosynaptically on spinal interneurones and motoneurones in the segments C6–Th1. Collaterals of corticospinal neurones may provide inputs to propriospinal neurones (PN) located in spinal segments C3–C4. These PNs have descending monosynaptic connections to motoneurones as well as ascending branches to the lateral reticular nucleus (LRN) in the brainstem. Experiments consisted in either stimulating the corticospinal tract (in the medullary pyramidal tract, PT) or in stimulating the PNs (in the LRN). Effects on motoneurones were assessed by intracellular recordings in identified upper-limb alpha motoneurones. The di- or oligosynaptic C3–C4 PN-mediated effects after PT simulation were identified by making a lesion in the dorsolateral funiculus at C5, which should abolish the corticospinal segmental input but leave intact the corticospinal input to PNs as well as the more caudally-situated PN axons that connect to motoneurones.*

(*Saimiri sciureus*) and the macaque monkey (*Macacca fascicularis*) and relate them to estimates in man. Several problems may arise in cross-species comparison of these features and caution must be taken (discussed in Maier *et al.* 1998; Lemon *et al.* 2004). In particular, as has been repeatedly confirmed for the corticomotoneuronal system, there is a gradient for larger EPSPs in hand motoneurones compared to upper-limb motoneurones (factor of about 1.3–1.5: Clough *et al.* 1968; Porter & Lemon 1993). There are also variations with motoneurone types (supplying fast or slow motor units). Thus, the average amplitude depends on the sample of motoneurones and might be biased. Furthermore, the compound EPSP may provide an estimate of the upper limit or maximal strength of connections, but it does not indicate the actual efficacy during a particular, naturally-executed behaviour. However, this objection also applies to estimates of the importance of anatomically-identified projections or connections. The difficulty of estimating the importance of a given input during actual behaviour is attested by the sparse literature. Cheney *et al.* (1991) tried to calculate the importance of the facilitatory CM input to wrist muscles in the behaving monkey and arrived at an upper estimate of 60 per cent of the total drive.

The efficacy of corticomotoneuronal (CM) excitation in four species

The cat does not have any corticomotoneuronal connections, its CST provides inputs to interneurones exclusively (Kuypers 1981; Baldissera *et al.* 1981). In the squirrel monkey, 79 per cent (23/29) of upper-limb motoneurones showed CM-EPSPs after single PT stimulation (Fig. 17.3A), characterized by brief segmental delays (<1.1 ms) and a mean amplitude of only 0.6±0.3 mV (Nakajima *et al.* 2000). Their amplitude varied in different motoneurones from 0.3 to 1.6 mV. In comparison, in the macaque monkey, 73 per cent (84/110) of upper-limb motoneurones showed CM-EPSPs with a larger mean amplitude of 1.9±1.0 mV (Fig. 17.3B, min 0.5 mV, max 4.5 mV: Maier *et al.* 1998). In the baboon, a similar mean value of 1.9 mV was found (Clough *et al.* 1968). No values are available for apes. In humans, it is possible to estimate the size of the EPSP underlying the motor-unit activation after transcranial electrical stimulation. de Noordhout *et al.* (1999) provided evidence for EPSPs in the order of at least 4–5 mV in human hand and finger muscles.

We conclude from these data on occurrence and amplitude of compound EPSPs that there is a gradient in the efficacy of monosynaptic excitation over these four species: it is absent in the cat, weak in the squirrel monkey, stronger in the macaque and strongest in humans.

A new case: the proprio-spinal system — an indirect cortical pathway
In the cat, the C3–C4 propriospinal system has been thoroughly investigated (e.g. Alstermark & Lundberg 1992) and represents an important pathway, mediating cortical, rubral, collicular and reticular control of the forelimb via interneurones located in the spinal segments C3 and C4. The propriospinal neurones (PNs: Fig. 17.2) have monosynaptic descending connections to forelimb motoneurones as well as ascending branches to the lateral reticular nucleus (LRN), a structure which projects to the cerebellum. The descending axons travel in the ventral part of the lateral funiculus, thus, a C5 lesion of the dorso-lateral funiculus cuts the fibers of the lateral CST and interrupts most of the direct corticospinal input to the lower segments where the motoneurones are located: this includes the monosynaptic motoneuronal and the segmental interneuronal input. This lesion, however, leaves intact the disynaptic, indirect pathway from the lateral CST to the motoneurones via the PNs located above the lesion, and this C5 lesion has been used to good effect for the study of the propriospinal system. In order to ensure that PNs, which mediate corticospinal inputs to motoneurones, discharge and thus provide oligosynaptic excitation, it is often necessary to use repetitive stimulation. After a dorso-lateral C5 lesion, the size of the disynaptic (or oligosynaptic) compound EPSP after repetitive stimulation of the PT should thus indicate the efficacy of the PN system in exciting upper-limb motoneurones due to cortical input.

The efficacy of propriospinal (PN) transmission: input from the cortex
In the cat, virtually all upper-limb motoneurones show disynaptic excitation after a C5 lesion (Alstermark &

Lundberg 1992) with a mean amplitude of about 3-4 mV (Alstermark & Sasaki 1986). In the squirrel monkey (Fig. 17.3C), oligosynaptic C3–C4 transmission was found in most motoneurones (86 per cent, 32/37) with a lower mean amplitude of 1.2±0.6 mV (Nakajima *et al.* 2000). In the macaque (Fig. 17.3D), however, the result was strikingly different. The occurrence of oligosynaptic effects was much weaker (18 per cent, 16/88) and the amplitude of the EPSPs even smaller (0.9±0.5 mV) than in the squirrel monkey (Maier *et al.* 1998). In humans, Pierrot-Desilligny and colleagues interpreted their measurements of non-monosynaptic excitation in cortical pathways to upper-limb motoneurones as evidence for the existence of a PN system in humans (Pierrot-Desilligny 1996). This interpretation relies particularly on an increasing central delay the more caudal the motor nuclei is from the presumed C3–C4 PNs (Pauvert *et al.* 1998). However, the existence and efficacy of excitatory PN transmission in man remains to be determined. Evidence from transcranial magnetic stimulation (TMS) in humans points toward rather weak excitatory transmission: transmission is seen only when TMS is very precisely coupled with rather precise stimulation of particular peripheral inputs, which probably converge on common PN systems. Stronger TMS may even switch excitation of PNs to inhibition (Nicolas *et al.* 2001). In animals where PN transmission is well developed (e.g. cat or squirrel monkey), such effects have not been reported.

We suggest from these data that the efficacy of C3–C4 propriospinal transmission of excitation to upper-limb motoneurones shows a clear gradient over three species: it is strong in the cat, intermediate in the squirrel monkey, and weak in the macaque. By extrapolating this gradient, we hypothesize that in humans the indirect transmission of cortical excitation through a PN system will be weak.

The efficacy of propriospinal (PN) excitation: input from the brain stem
The validity of these conclusions, however, has been questioned by Alstermark *et al.* (1999), who repeated the experiments in the macaque, but this time following systemic administration of strychnine, an antagonist to glycine (one of the main inhibitory neurotransmitters). Showing a much higher occurrence of oligosynaptic effects under these conditions of reduced inhibition, they argued that the weaker transmission in the macaque was not due to a change in connectivity, but due to stronger inhibition of PNs than in the cat. A detailed discussion on the issue of various forms of inhibition within the propriospinal pathway and its implications for assessing its efficacy can be found in Kirkwood *et al.* (2002).

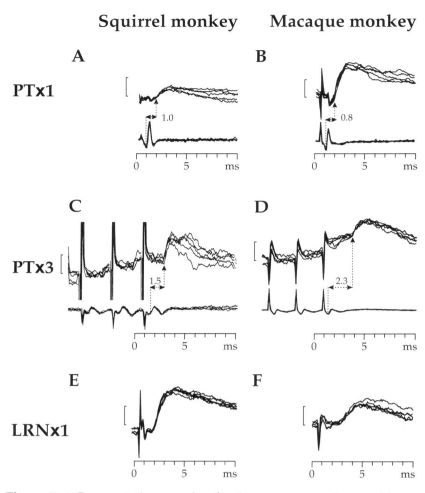

Squirrel monkey   Macaque monkey

A   **B**

PTx1

1.0   0.8

C   **D**

PTx3

1.5   2.3

E   **F**

LRNx1

Figure 17.3. *Representative examples of excitatory postsynaptic potentials (EPSPs) in identified forelimb motoneurones in squirrel monkey and macaque monkey: A, B) Comparison of squirrel monkey (A) and macaque monkey (B) CM-EPSP after a single shock to the pyramidal tract (PT×1) in the intact animal. EPSPs with monosynaptic segmental latencies are usually smaller in squirrel monkey; C, D) Comparison of squirrel monkey (C) and macaque monkey (D) PN-EPSP after a triple shock to the pyramidal tract (PT×3) in the C5-lesioned animal. The PN-mediated, di- or oligosynaptic EPSPs are usually larger in squirrel monkey; E, F) Comparison of squirrel monkey (E) and macaque monkey (F) LRN-EPSP after a single shock to the lateral reticular nucleus (LRN×1) in the C5-lesioned animal. The EPSPs, probably mediated by stimulation of the ascending branch of the PN axon, are usually larger in squirrel monkey. A–D) top trace: five superimposed traces of EPSPs; bottom trace: corresponding PT volley evoked by the PT stimulation and recorded on the surface of the spinal cord at the segment of the intracellular recording. Note largely-reduced PT volley after the C5 DLF lesion; A–F) Stimulation strength: 200 μA, calibration bar: 1 mV. (B, D, F: previously unpublished data from Maier et al. 1998; A, C, E: from Nakajima et al. 2000.)*

A way to resolve this issue may be through stimulation of the ipsilateral LRN (Fig. 17.2), which antidromically activates most of the ascending PN axons and gives rise to monosynaptic EPSPs in motoneurones,

mediated by the descending PN axon (Alstermark *et al.* 1981). These EPSPs should be indicative of the efficacy of the PN-motoneurone connection, independent of any inhibition provided by the PT stimulation. In the cat, these EPSPs were seen in the large majority of motoneurones and had an average amplitude in the order of 5 mV, larger than the oligosynaptic EPSPs evoked by repetitive PT stimulation (Alstermark *et al.* 1981). In the squirrel monkey, these monosynaptic LRN-EPSPs were seen in 94 per cent (34/36) of the motoneurones after the C5 lesion and had a mean amplitude of 1.7±0.8 mV (Fig. 17.3E). In the macaque, the occurrence was clearly lower with 75 per cent (67/89) and the amplitude with a mean of 1.2±0.7 mV significantly weaker (Fig. 17.3F).

These results from the stimulation of the LRN support our view that transmission through the PN system is relatively weak, probably due to relatively weak PN-motoneurone synapses. Furthermore, there is a gradient for LRN-EPSPs across species similar to the one found for PN-mediated effects from stimulation of the PT. This finding does not exclude additional inhibition of PNs themselves by cortical inputs.

Comparison of CM-, PN- and LRN-EPSPs

On their own, neither occurrence nor amplitude of postsynaptic effects estimates the efficacy of a synaptic link to a population of motoneurones. A highly-efficient and functional synaptic linkage is characterized by a strong link to most or all of the target neurones, i.e. by a high amplitude and frequent occurrence. The multiplication of amplitude and occurrence provides a single measure, which allows a direct comparison of the efficacy of functional synaptic linkage across species. We normalized this measure with respect to the species with a maximal efficacy for the PN (cat) and for the CM system (*Homo*), which revealed quite dramatic differences (Fig. 17.4A): using *Homo* as reference for the CM system (100 per cent efficacy), there is a categorical difference between cat and primates, the former lacking this direct connection (0 per cent). Within primates, the efficacy of CM-EPSPs increases from ~15 per cent for the squirrel monkey, to ~50 per cent for the macaque, and to 100 per cent for *Homo*, i.e. by a factor of ~7–8 between *Saimiri* and humans. For the indirect, PN-mediated cortical transmission (Fig. 17.4B) the trend is even stronger: compared to the cat (100 per cent), the macaque showed an efficacy of ~5 per cent, i.e. a difference in occurrence by a factor of ~4 and a smaller amplitude by a factor of ~5, resulting, in terms of decline of the efficacy of transmission, in an overall factor of around 20 (or 5 per cent). A similar line of reasoning arrives at an efficacy of 25 per cent for the squirrel monkey. This gradient is confirmed by taking into account the occurrence and amplitude of LRN-EPSPs (Fig. 17.4C). In the squirrel monkey the efficacy drops to ~30 per cent and in the macaque to ~20 per cent.

In conclusion, there are important species-related differences in the organization of the corticospinal and propriospinal transmission to upper limb motoneurones. There is a relative increase in the importance of the *direct* CM system from the cat, over the squirrel monkey, to the macaque and to humans, and a parallel decrease of excitatory *indirect* transmission via the PN system from the cat, over the squirrel monkey to the macaque (Nakajima *et al.* 2000). By extrapolating these two gradients we would predict that in humans the transmission through the CM system is most important and the parallel transmission via the PN system relatively unimportant.

We speculated that these changes in relative influence of the CM and PN systems are related to differences in dextrous manipulation. Taking into account a modified index of dexterity (cf. discussion above), cat, squirrel monkey, macaque and humans would respectively have an index of 4, 5, 6 and 7. Table 17.1, which lists the index of dexterity as well as the efficacy of motoneurone excitation of the

A **Proportion and amplitude of CM-EPSPs**

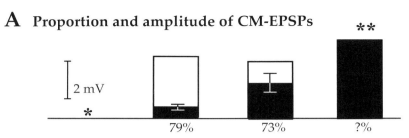

B **Proportion and amplitude of PT evoked PN-EPSPs**

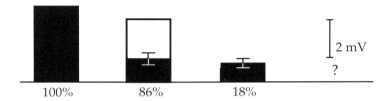

C **Proportion and amplitude of LRN evoked PN-EPSPs**

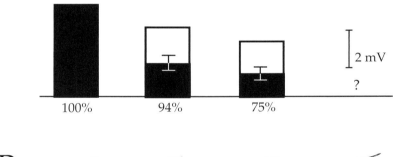

D

Dexterity index

CAT   SQUIRREL MONKEY   MACAQUE MONKEY   GREAT APES + HUMANS

Figure 17.4. *Contribution of corticomotoneuronal (CM) and propriospinal (PN) excitation to upper-limb motoneurones in cat, squirrel monkey, macaque monkey and human: A–C) Proportion of motoneurones (open box) in per cent and mean amplitude (black box) ±SD in mV for (from left to right): cat, squirrel monkey, macaque monkey and human. A) Proportion and amplitude of monosynaptic CM-EPSPs; B) Proportion and amplitude of di- and oligosynaptic PN-EPSPs after a C5 lesion of the dorsolateral funiculus and evoked PT stimulation; C) Proportion and amplitude of monosynaptic LRN-EPSPs (data from Maier* et al. *1998 and Nakajima* et al. *2000); D) Index of dexterity for the four species.*

CM and PN systems for selected species, shows a clear qualitative relation between increasing dexterity and efficacy of the CM system, and, on the other hand, a negative relation between dexterity and efficacy of the PN system. For the CM system, this is in line with the original assumption of Bernhard & Bohm (1954), Kuypers (1981) and Heffner & Masterton (1983), which, however, relies on the efficacy of transmission as measured by the occurrence and amplitude of the compound EPSP rather than on anatomical evidence. Furthermore, as cited above, there is plenty of supporting evidence for the importance of the CM system in dextrous manipulation based on recordings during voluntary movements in the macaque (Porter & Lemon 1993).

Our hypothesis for the PN system, although based on a similar criterion, is new, but there is as yet no positive anatomical or behavioural neurophysiological evidence in the monkey. However, other parallel and indirect descending pathways receiving cortical input, such as the rubrospinal tract, also have been shown to decrease in importance during phylogeny compared to the corticospinal system (Nathan & Smith 1982). It thus seems that spinal segmental and propriospinal networks as well as brain-stem centres for upper-limb movement control are not only supervised by cortical motor areas, but their excitatory drive to motoneurones are increasingly weakened in favour of direct CM access. We assume that forelimb reaching, where the PN system plays a major role in the cat (Alstermark & Lundberg 1992), has, in part, been taken over in primates by the CM system, which controls manual dexterity and may as well control the aspects of reaching needed to support stable, distal grasp and manipulation. In heuristic terms, it would be surprising if reaching (hitting) would be independent of manipulation. However, in human prehension two kinematic components have been described: the transport and the grasp phase (Paulignan *et al.* 1990), but a strict dissociation in kinematic terms could not be demonstrated, implying a common or at least interdependent neural control at an as yet undetermined level (e.g. Paulignan *et al.* 1991). A candidate for that link is the CM system, which is particularly well developed for the distal control of the hand and the digits, but is by no means exclusively dedicated to the control of hand muscles (McKiernan *et al.* 1998). We may extend this argument and even postulate a role of the CM system in the control of distal hind limb muscles during upright stance in relation with dexterity, so that reactive forces due to upper limb manipulation can be counteracted by the fine control of foot muscles in a predictive rather than in a reflex manner. This may partially explain the relation between the length of the CST and dexterity observed by Heffner & Masterton (1983) and confirmed by Iwaniuk *et al.* (1999). One may further speculate that early hominins, in terms of efficacy of CM and PN systems, may have occupied an intermediate position between *Homo sapiens* and apes, all of them, in terms of dexterity, upscale in comparison to the macaque.

Relation between manual dexterity and tool use

How is the development of dexterity and its neural substrate related to tool use? In non-human primates and particularly in the great apes, tool use has been reported in various behavioural contexts: for intimidation and defence, for social display, for grooming and for feeding. Tool use in the wild, however, appears in only few non-human primate species and even then not population-wide. We will focus on feeding tools, i.e. hand-held (solid) objects to modify food items or to facilitate feeding: the use of (knapped) stones falls within this category. Table 17.1 lists the use of feeding tools observed in selected primate species in the wild (or in captivity) (taken from van Schaik *et al.* 1999). Clearly there is a general trend between the degree of development of the CM system and the degree of tool use: species with and index of 6 or 7 seem to have high enough dextrous skills to use feeding tools. This does not prevent primates with lower indices from using tools in other ways, such as throwing of objects. A similar and statistically-significant dependence of tool use on the presence of manual dexterity, based on a far larger sample of primate species, was found by van Schaik *et al.* (1999). Thus, in absence of a counter example, having an index of at least 6 may be a necessary condition for manual use of feeding tools in primates. However, this list shows that a dexterity index between 6 and 7 does not allow any prediction about the prevalence of tool use: for example among primates with an index of 6 and a CM system, such as *Cebus* and *Hylobates*, the former does show tool use (Westergaard & Suomi 1997) but the latter does not. Therefore an index of 6 may be necessary, but is not sufficient for tool use. The same holds for an index of 7 (if one accepts tool use in the wild only). However, tool use in the wild is not habitual nor customary among monkeys (McGrew & Marchant 1997), and only in great apes has tool use been reported as regular in some of their populations (e.g. Inoue-Nakamura & Matsuzawa 1997).

Since there is obviously no *strict* relation between the use of feeding tools and dexterity, i.e. between the size of the manual repertoire targeted at purposeful manual actions and dextrous capability, other variables seem to play crucial roles, in particular cognitive, social and ecological variables. Not only motor skills, but also cognitive skills, are needed to learn how to use an existing object as a more efficient tool for feeding than the hand alone.

This is where second- and higher-order motor systems may very well play a crucial role: the CST and the CM system do not by themselves create motor commands, but they provide the descending output system for the primary motor cortex and higher-order motor areas (Rizzolatti *et al.* 1998).

In order to use the motor skills of a dextrous hand for prehension, exploration and manipulation, other modalities, such as somatosensory (Johansson 1996) and visual information, need to be integrated (Jeannerod *et al.* 1995; Johansson *et al.* 2001). Hands deprived of the somatic modality, such as in deafferented patients (Rothwell *et al.* 1982), perform poorly even under visual guidance (Johansson *et al.* 1992), and without any vision at all, no prehension is possible. The integration of multisensorial information is linked to the development of the association cortices rather than to that of the motor cortex (Paillard 1993). Higher-order visual areas (Wise *et al.* 1997) provide rich connections, particularly to the secondary motor areas, and tactile areas (Jones 1986) provide connections to the primary and secondary motor cortex.

Table 17.1. *Comparison between behavioural variables of dexterity and neurophysiological measures.*

Genus	Primate family	Index of dexterity	BAC *	Use of feeding tools*	Manufacture of tools*	CM excitation **	PN excitation **
Carnivora:							
Cat		4		No	No	No: 0%	Y: 100%
Primates:							
Saimiri	A	5	0	No	No	Y: 15%	Y: 25%
Cebus	A	5	2	Y	No	Y	?
Macaca	B	6	2	Y	No	Y: 50%	Y: 5%
Papio	B	6	2	Y	No	Y: 50%#	
Hylobates	C	6		No Captivity:Y	?	?	?
Pongo	D	7	1	Y	Y	Y	?
Gorilla	D	7	3	No Captivity:Y	No Captivity:Y	Y	?
Pan	D	7	2	Y	Y	Y	?
Homo	D	7+ ***	3	Y	Y	Y: 100%	?

Primate family: A) Ceboidea; B) Cercopithecoidea; C) Hylobatidae; D) Hominoidea (apes and humans: see Fig. 17.1 for phylogenetic relation).

* BAC [bimanual asymmetric coordination]; Use and Manufacture of feeding tools in the wild (No, Y: Yes) taken from van Schaik *et al.* (1999).

** Efficacy in terms of [occurrence × amplitude of EPSPs]. CM: 4–5 mV = 100% assumed in *Homo*; PN: 100% in cat.

*** 7+ for *Homo*: see Marzke & Wullstein (1996)

from data of Clough *et al.* (1968)

Using microneurographic recordings, Johansson and colleagues have established that cutaneous afferents provide information on physical properties as well as on transient slips of objects held in precision grip. These slips often occur without awareness and are corrected automatically based on these afferent signals. The sharp increase in grip force to counter the slips occur non-voluntarily, i.e. much faster than the human reaction time (~65 ms) would allow, and is in the order of transcortical long-loop reflexes. CM cell activity was shown to be causally involved in transcortical stretch-reflex activity (Cheney & Fetz 1984), at least for long-loop reflexes of proprioceptive origin. The pivotal role of M1 may not only stem from the monosynaptic connections to motoneurones which bypass the spinal reflexes, but also from the ability to combine higher order (voluntary) information with reflex-like actions in one common system. This does not exclude the involvement of other systems in the processing of multisensorial information for updating and correcting movements, such as the cerebellum, which also undergoes phylogenetic changes (Barton & Harvey 2000).

Thus, the development of the CM system in primates seems more strongly related to dexterity than to tool use. This suggests that the existence of direct corticomotoneuronal connections is, in terms of neural structures, a necessary and sufficient precondition for a high degree of primate manual dexterity, but that dexterity alone is not a sufficient condition for tool use.

Relation between tool use and tool manufacturing

How is the development of tool use in non-human primates related to object manipulation and tool manufacturing? Table 17.1 lists the manufacturing of feeding tools (taken from van Schaik *et al.* 1999). Tool manufacturing is restricted to great apes, who all have an index of dexterity of 7, a highly-developed CM system and who (at least in captivity) use tools. Again, these conditions may be necessary for tool manufacturing, but the presence of these elements is not sufficient to predict manufacturing of feeding tools in the wild: among the great apes with an index of 7, *Pan* and *Pongo* both show tool use and tool manufacturing, but *Gorilla* does not (van Schaik *et al.* 1999).

The cognitive requirements for the manufacturing of a specific tool for later use in feeding are certainly different from those of using an existing tool to acquire food. The former necessitates the representation of the goal, a hierarchical planning of sub-goals that eventually leads to the ultimate goal, which goes way beyond the multisensorial information processing needed to exploit the manual skills discussed above. It may be that the general cognitive abilities (intelligence) of monkeys are insufficient for tool manufacturing, whereas those of the great apes are just about adequate for rudimentary production of tools. The origins of the different cognitive abilities between monkeys and great apes are not known, but it is clear that particular learning abilities, such as a prolonged attention span, a high potential for representation of goals, means and time (action sequences, strategy), and memorization are needed, so that problem-solving tasks requiring manual dexterity can be accomplished (McGrew 1992).

How can tool manufacturing be acquired and maintained? Acquisition probably depends on the general cognitive abilities needed in different forms of learning and on social variables. Learning by invention, i.e. a non-premeditated and accidental action based on trial and error, which leads directly to an advantage in feeding might not require much intelligence, but it calls for sufficient exploratory behaviour and the availability of suitable objects. Invention does not seem to be common among great apes (Kummer & Goodall 1985), and the learning of tool manufacturing through insight definitely requires more complex cognitive abilities, such as the capacity to link several hierarchically-organized actions (Byrne & Russon 1998; Byrne *et al.* 2001a) and a representation of the not yet existing tool including its desired effect on another object (food) (Povinelli 2000). Only great apes, (but not monkeys) are known to show an understanding of the physical relation between objects (Visalberghi *et al.* 1995; Fox *et al.* 1999) and only they manufacture tools. To what degree the manufacturing of stone tools (i.e. unintentionally flaked stones) by great apes may approach those of early hominins is currently debated (e.g. Roche *et al.* 1999 *vs* Mercader *et al.* 2002).

However, any new skill, in whatever way acquired, needs transmission from the individual to the population if it is to be maintained. Learning through imitation, which requires a minimum of cognitive skills, occurs predominantly in great apes (Fragaszy & Visalberghi 1989; Byrne 1995), and there is clear evidence that they emulate and imitate (Whiten 1998; Byrne & Russon 1998). Social learning rather than independent discovery or simple maturation predominates in great apes (Tomasello & Call 1997; Boesch 1996), indicating that the social organization within a species in terms of tolerance and gregariousness influences transmission so that tool use and manufacturing can occur (van Schaik *et al.* 1999; Inoue-Nakamura & Matsuzawa 1997). Finally, ecological variables play a role as well: the diet and food resources vary among apes and therefore the advantage or need for tool manufacturing might be smaller or greater. Tool use and manufacturing in great apes is also adapted to the local habitat (Whiten *et al.* 1999; Mercader *et al.* 2002). In captivity, great apes and monkeys learn tool use and manufacturing to a degree not observed in the wild (Tomasello & Call 1997). This may in part explain the variety of material cultures within and between the great ape species (Humle & Matsuzawa 2001; Povinelli 2000) as well as in early *Homo*.

Acknowledgements

This work was carried out with support from the Wellcome Trust and the International Spinal Cord Trust.

Annexe: abbreviations

BAC: Bimanual Asymmetric Coordination. A behavioural measure of bimanual integration developed by van Schaik *et al.* (1999).

CM: CorticoMotoneuronal. A subpopulation among corticospinal neurones (forming the CST), which have monosynaptic connections to spinal motoneurones.

CM-EPSP: EPSP (in the motoneurone) after stimulation of the PT, mediated by CM connections.

CST: CorticoSpinal Tract. An ensemble of axons arising from cortical neurons (in motor and somatosensory areas) and passing to the spinal cord, where they connect to spinal interneurones or, if they originate from CM cells, to spinal motoneurones.

C3, C4, C5: spinal cord, cervical level, cervical segment 3, 4, 5.

EPSP: Excitatory PostSynaptic Potential. Excitatory potential evoked in the postsynaptic cell. The EPSP is mediated by postsynaptic receptors activated by neurotransmitters released by the presynaptic neurone. EPSPs increase the probability that the (postsynaptic) cell will fire action potentials (be excited). The larger the amplitude of the EPSP, the higher will be the probability of firing.

LRN: Lateral Reticular Nucleus. A brain stem nucleus that projects to the cerebellum and receives input from PNs.

LRN-EPSP: EPSP (in the motoneurone) after stimulation in the LRN.

M1: primary motor cortex. A motor cortical area that contains many neurones contributing to the CST.

PN: Propriospinal Neurone. Neurones located in the cervical segments C3 and C4 of the spinal cord, receiving inputs from various brain regions (including the motor cortex via the CST) and having monosynaptic connections to spinal motoneurones (as well as to the LRN).

PT: Pyramidal Tract. A part of the CST located in the brain stem (i.e. in the medullary pyramid).

TMS: Transcranial Magnetic Stimulation.

References

Alstermark, B. & A. Lundberg, 1992. The C3–C4 propriospinal system: target-reaching and food-taking, in *Muscle Afferents and Spinal Control of Movement*, eds. L. Jami, E. Pierrot-Deseilligny & D. Zytnicki. Oxford: Pergamon Press, 327–54.

Alstermark, B. & S. Sasaki, 1986. Integration in descending motor pathways controlling the forelimb in the cat, 14: Differential projection to fast and slow motoneurones from excitatory C3–C4 propriospinal neurones. *Experimental Brain Research* 63, 530–42.

Alstermark, B., S. Lindström, A. Lundberg & E. Sybirska, 1981. Integration in descending motor pathways controlling the forelimb in the cat; 8: Ascending projection to the lateral reticular nucleus from C3–C4 propriospinal neurones also projecting to forelimb motoneurones. *Experimental Brain Research* 42, 282–98.

Alstermark, B., T. Isa, Y. Ohki & Y. Saito, 1999. Disynaptic pyramidal excitation in forelimb motoneurons mediated via C(3)–C(4) propriospinal neurons in the *Macaca fuscata*. *Journal of Neurophysiology* 82(6), 3580–85.

Antinucci, F. & E. Visalberghi, 1986. Tool use in *Cebus apella*: a case study. *International Journal of Primatology* 7, 351–63.

Armand, J., S.A. Edgley, R.N. Lemon & E. Olivier, 1994. Protracted postnatal development of corticospinal projections from the primary motor cortex to hand motoneurones in the macaque monkey. *Experimental Brain Research* 101, 178–82.

Armand, J., E. Olivier, S.A. Edgley & R.N. Lemon, 1997. Postnatal development of corticospinal projections from motor cortex to the cervical enlargement in the macaque monkey. *Journal of Neuroscience* 17, 251–66.

Baker, S.N., R. Spinks, A. Jackson & R.N. Lemon, 2001. Synchronization in monkey motor cortex during a precision grip task, I: Task-dependent modulation in single-unit synchrony. *Journal of Neurophysiology* 85(2), 869–85.

Baldissera, F., H. Hultborn & M. Illert, 1981. Integration in spinal neural systems, in *Handbook of Physiology: the Nervous System*, vol. II, eds. J.M. Brookhart & V.B. Mountcastle. Bethesda (MD): American Physiological Society, 509–95.

Barton, R.A. & P.H. Harvey, 2000. Mosaic evolution of brain structure in mammals. *Nature* 405, 1055–8.

Bennett, K.M.B. & R.N. Lemon, 1996. Corticomotoneuronal contribution to the fractionation of muscle activity during precision grip in the monkey. *Journal of Neurophysiology* 75, 1826–42.

Bernhard, C.G. & E. Bohm, 1954. Cortical representation and functional significance of the corticomotoneuronal system. *Archives of Neurology and Psychiatry* 72, 473–502.

Boczek-Funcke, A., J.P. Kuhtz-Buschbeck, J. Raethjen, B. Paschmeyer & M. Illert, 1998. Shaping of the cat paw for food taking and object manipulation: an X-ray analysis. *European Journal of Neuroscience* 10(12), 3885–97.

Boesch, C., 1996. The emergence of cultures among wild chimpanzees. *Proceedings of the British Academy* 88, 251–68.

Boesch, C. & H. Boesch, 1993. Different hand postures for pounding nuts with natural hammers by wild chimpanzees, in *Hands of Primates*, eds. H. Preuschoft & D.J. Chivers. New York (NY): Springer Verlag, 31–43.

Bortoff, G.A. & P.L. Strick, 1993. Corticospinal terminations in two New-World primates: further evidence that corticomotoneuronal connections provide part of the neural substrate for manual dexterity. *Journal of Neuroscience* 13, 5105–18.

Byrne, R.W., 1995. *The Thinking Ape: Evolutionary Origins of Intelligence*. Oxford: Oxford University Press.

Byrne, R.W. & J.M.E. Byrne, 1993. Complex leaf gathering skills in mountain gorillas (*Gorilla g. beringei*): variability and standardization. *American Journal of Primatology* 31, 241–61.

Byrne, R.W. & A.E. Russon, 1998. Learning by imitation: a hierarchical approach. *The Behavioral and Brain Sciences* 21, 667–721.

Byrne, R.W., N. Corp & J.M.E. Byrne, 2001a. Estimating the complexity of animal behaviour: how mountain gorillas eat thistles. *Behaviour* 138, 525–57.

Byrne, R.W., N. Corp & J.M.E. Byrne, 2001b. Manual dexterity in the gorilla: bimanual and digit role differentiation in a natural task. *Animal Cognition* 4, 347–61.

Cheney, P.D. & E.E. Fetz, 1984. Corticomotoneuronal cells contribute to long-latency stretch reflexes in the rhesus monkey. *Journal of Physiology* 349, 249–72.

Cheney, P.D., E.E. Fetz & K. Mewes, 1991. Neural mechanisms underlying corticospinal and rubrospinal control of limb movements. *Progress in Brain Research* 87, 213–52.

Christel, M.I., 1993. Grasping techniques and hand preferences in Hominoidea, in *Hands of Primates*, eds. H. Preuschoft & D.J. Chivers. Berlin: Springer, 91–108.

Christel, M.I. & A. Billard, 2002. Comparison between macaques' and humans' kinematics of prehension: the role of morphological differences and control mechanisms. *Behavourial Brain Research* 131, 169–84.

Christel, M.I., S. Kitzel & C. Niemitz, 1998. How precisely do bonobos (*Pan paniscus*) grasp small objects? *International Journal of Primatology* 19, 165–94.

Clough, J.F.M., D. Kernell & C.G. Phillips, 1968. The distribution of monosynaptic excitation from the pyramidal tract and from primary spindle afferents to motoneurones of the baboon's hand and forearm. *Journal of Physiology* 198, 145–66.

Costello, M.B. & D.M. Fragaszy, 1988. Prehension in *Cebus* and *Saimiri*, 1: Grip type and hand preference. *American Journal of Primatology* 15, 235–45.

de Noordhout, A.M., G. Rapisarda, D. Bogacz, P. Gerard, V. De Pasqua, G. Pennisi & P.J. Delwaide, 1999. Corticomotoneuronal synaptic connections in normal man: an electrophysiological study. *Brain* 122, 1327–40.

Falk, D. & K.R. Gibson (eds.), 2001. *Evolutionary Anatomy of the Primate Cerebral Cortex*. Cambridge: Cambridge University Press.

Ferry, L. & J.-D. Vincent, 2001. *Qu'est-ce que l'homme*? Paris: Poches Odile Jacob.

Fetz, E.E. & P.D. Cheney, 1980. Postspike facilitation of forelimb muscle activity by primate corticomotoneuronal cell. *Journal of Neurophysics* 44, 751–72.

Fox, E.A., A.F. Sitompul & C.P. van Schaik, 1999. Intelligent tool use in wild Sumatran orang-utans, in *The Mentality of Gorillas and Orangutans*, eds. S.T. Parker, L. Liles & R. Mitchell. Cambridge: Cambridge University Press, 99–116.

Fragaszy, D.M. & E. Visalberghi, 1989. Social influences on the acquisition of tool-using behaviors in tufted capuchin monkeys (*Cebus apella*). *Journal of Comparative Psychology* 103(2), 159–70.

Heffner, R.S. & R.B. Masterton, 1975. Variation in the form of the pyramidal tract and its relationship to digital dexterity. *Brain, Behavior and Evolution* 12, 161–200.

Heffner, R.S. & R.B. Masterton, 1983. The role of the corticospinal tract in the evolution of human digital dexterity. *Brain, Behavior and Evolution* 23, 165–83.

Hepp-Reymond, M.-C., 1988. Functional organization of motor cortex and its participation in voluntary movements, in *Comparative Primate Biology*, vol. 4, eds. H.D. Steklis & J. Erwin. New York (NY): Alan Liss, 501–624.

Humle, T. & T. Matsuzawa, 2001. Behavioural diversity among the wild chimpanzee populations of Bossou and neighbouring areas, Guinea and Cote d'Ivoire, West Africa: a preliminary report. *Folia Primatol* (Basel) 72(2), 57–68.

Illert, M. & H. Kümmel, 1999. Reflex pathways from large muscle spindle afferents and recurrent axon collaterals to motoneurones of wrist and digit muscles: a comparison in cats, monkeys and humans. *Experimental Brain Research* 128, 13–19.

Inoue-Nakamura, N. & T. Matsuzawa, 1997. Development of stone tool use by wild chimpanzees (*Pan troglodytes*). *Journal of Comparative Psychology* 111, 159–73.

Iwaniuk, A.N., S.M. Pellis & I.Q. Whishaw, 1999. Is digital dexterity really related to corticospinal projections?: a re-analysis of the Heffner and Masterton data set using modern comparative statistics. *Behavourial Brain Research* 101(2), 173–87.

Jankowska, E., Y. Padel & R. Tanaka, 1975. Projections of pyramidal tract cells to alpha-motoneurones innervating hind-limb muscles in the monkey. *Journal of Physiology* 249(3), 637–67.

Jeannerod, M., M.A. Arbib, G. Rizzolatti & H. Sakata, 1995. Grasping objects: the cortical mechanisms of visuomotor transformation. *Trends in Neuroscience* 18(7), 314–20.

Jerison, H.J., 1973. *Evolution of the Brain and Intelligence*. New York (NY): Academic Press.

Johansson, R.S., 1996. Sensory control of dextrous manipulation in humans, in *Hand and Brain*, eds. A.M. Wing, P. Haggard & J.R. Flanagan. London: Academic Press, 381–414.

Johansson, R.S., C. Hager & L. Backstrom, 1992. Somatosensory control of precision grip during unpredictable pulling loads; III: Impairments during digital anesthesia. *Experimental Brain Research* 89(1), 204–13.

Johansson, R.S., G. Westling, A. Backstrom & J.R. Flanagan, 2001. Eye–hand coordination in object manipulation. *Journal of Neuroscience* 21(17), 6917–32.

Jones, E.G., 1986. Connectivity of the primate sensory-motor cortex, in *Cereberal Cortex*, vol. 5, eds. E.G. Jones & A. Peters. New York (NY): Plenum Press, 113–83.

Kirkwood, P.A., M.A. Maier & R.N. Lemon, 2002. Interspecies comparisons for the C3–C4 propriospinal system: unresolved issues. *Advances in Experimental Medicine and Biology* 508, 299–308.

Kummer, H. & J. Goodall, 1985. Conditions of innovative behaviour in primates. *Philosophical Transactions of the Royal Society of London* Series B 308, 203–14.

Kuypers, H.G.J.M., 1978. The organization of the motor system in primates, in *Recent Advances in Primatology*, vol. 1, eds. D.J. Chivres & J. Herbert. New York (NY): Academic Press, 623–34.

Kuypers, H.G.J.M., 1981. Anatomy of the descending pathways, in *Handbook of Physiology: the Nervous System*, vol. II, eds. J.M. Brookhart & V.B. Mountcastle. Bethesda (MD): American Physiological Society, 597–666.

Lawrence, D.G. & H.G.J.M. Kuypers, 1968. The functional organization of the motor system in the monkey, I: The effects of bilateral pyramidal lesions. *Brain* 91, 1–14.

Leakey, L.S.B., P.V. Tobias & J. Napier, 1964. A new species of the genus *Homo* from Olduvai Gorge. *Nature* 202, 7–9.

Lemon, R.N., G.W.H. Mantel & R.B. Muir, 1986. Corticospinal facilitation of hand muscles during voluntary movement in the conscious monkey. *Journal of Physiology* 381, 497–527.

Lemon, R.N., P.A. Kirkwood, M.A. Maier, K. Nakajima & P. Nathan, 2004. Direct and indirect pathways for corticospinal control of upper limb motoneurones in the primate. *Progress in Brain Research* 143, 263–79.

Lewis, O.J., 1989. *Functional Morphology of the Evolving Hand and Foot*. Oxford: Clarendon Press.

Maier, M.A., E. Olivier, S.N. Baker, P.A. Kirkwood, T. Morris & R.N. Lemon, 1997. Direct and indirect corticospinal control of arm and hand motoneurons in the squirrel monkey (*Saimiri sciureus*). *Journal of Neurophysiology* 78, 721–33.

Maier, M.A., M. Illert, P.A. Kirkwood, J. Nielsen & R.N. Lemon, 1998. Does a C3–C4 propriospinal system transmit corticospinal excitation in the primate? An investigation in the macaque monkey. *Journal of Physiology* 511, 191–212.

Maier, W., 1993. Adaptations in the hands of cercopithecoids and callitrichids, in *Hands of Primates*, eds. H. Preushoft & D.J Chivers. New York (NY): Springer-Verlag, 191–8.

Marzke, M.W., 1997. Precision grips, hand morphology and tools. *American Journal of Physical Anthropology* 102, 91–110.

Marzke, M.W. & R.F. Marzke, 2000. Evolution of the human hand: approaches to acquiring, analysing and interpreting the anatomical evidence. *Journal of Anatomy* 197, 121–40.

Marzke, M.W. & K.L. Wullstein, 1996. Chimpanzee and human grips: a new classification with a focus on evolutionary morphulogy. *International Journal of Primatology* 17, 117–39.

Marzke, M.W., N. Toth, K. Schick, S. Reece, B. Steinberg & K. Hunt, 1998. EMG study of human hand muscle recruitment during hard hammer percussion manufacture of Oldowan tools. *American Journal of Physical Anthropology* 105, 315–32.

Marzke, M.W., R.F. Marzke, R.L. Linscheid, P. Smutz, B. Steinberg, S. Reece & K.N. An, 1999. Chimpanzee thumb muscle cross sections, moment arms and potential torques, and comparisons with humans. *American Journal of Physical Anthropology* 110, 163–78.

McGrew, W.C., 1992. *Chimpanzee Material Culture*. Cambridge: Cambridge University Press.

McGrew, W.C. & L.F. Marchant, 1997. Using the tools at hand: manual laterality and elementary tchnology in *Cebus* spp. and *Pan* spp. *International Journal of Primatology* 18, 787–810.

McKiernan, B.J., K. Marcario, J.H. Karrer & P.D. Cheney, 1998. Corticomotoneuronal postspike effects in shoulder, elbow, wrist, digit and intrinsic hand muscles during a reach and prehension task. *Journal of Neurophysiology* 84, 698–709.

Mercader, J., M. Panger & C. Boesch, 2002. Excavation of a chimpanzee stone tool site in the African rainforest. *Science* 296(5572), 1452–5.

Nakajima, K., M.A. Maier, P.A. Kirkwood & R.N. Lemon, 2000. Striking differences in transmission of corticospinal excitation to upper limb motoneurons in two primate species. *Journal of Neurophysiology* 84, 698–709.

Napier, J.R., 1961. Prehensility and opposability in the hands of primates. *Journal of Bone Joint Surgery* 38B, 902–13.

Napier, J.R., 1962. The evolution of the hand. *Scientific American* 207, 56–62.

Napier, J.R., 1980. *Hands*. London: George Allen & Unwin.

Nathan, P.W. & M.C. Smith, 1982. The rubrospinal and central tegmental tracts in man. *Brain* 105, 223–69.

Nicolas, G., V. Marchand-Pauvert, D. Burke & E. Pierrot-Deseilligny, 2001. Corticospinal excitation of presumed cervical propriospinal neurones and its reversal to inhibition in humans. *Journal of Physiology* 533, 903–19.

Nielsen, J. & N. Petersen, 1995. Evidence favouring different descending pathways to soleus motoneurones activated by magnetic brain stimulation in man. *Journal of Physiology* 486, 779–88.

Nudo, R.J. & R.B. Masterton, 1989. Descending pathways to the spinal cord, II: Quantitative study of the tectospinal tract in 23 mammals. *Journal of Comparative Neurology* 286(1), 96–119.

Nudo, R.J. & R.B. Masterton, 1990. Descending pathways to the spinal cord, IV: Some factors related to the amount of cortex devoted to the corticospinal tract. *Journal of Comparative Neurology* 296(4), 584–97.

Paillard, J., 1993. The hand and the tool. the functional architecture of human technical skills, in *The Use of Tools by Human and Non-human Primates*, eds. A. Berthelet & J. Chavaillon. Oxford: Clarendon, 37–46.

Palmer, E. & P. Ashby, 1992. Corticospinal projections to upper limb motoneurones in humans. *Journal of Physiology* 448, 397–412.

Paulignan, Y., C. MacKenzie, R. Marteniuk & M. Jeannerod, 1990. The coupling of arm and finger movements during prehension. *Experimental Brain Research* 79(2), 431–5.

Paulignan, Y., M. Jeannerod, C. MacKenzie & R. Marteniuk, 1991. Selective perturbation of visual input during prehension movements. 2. The effects of changing object size. *Experimental Brain Research* 87(2), 407–20.

Pauvert, V., E. Pierrot-Desilligny & J.C. Rothwell, 1998. Role of spinal premotoneurones in mediating corticospinal input to forearm motoneurones in man. *Journal of Physiology* 508, 310–12.

Phillips, C.G. & R. Porter, 1977. *Corticospinal Neurones, their Role in Movement*. (Monographs of the Physiological Society 34.) London: Academic Press.

Pierrot-Desilligny, E., 1996. Transmission of the cortical command for human voluntary movement through cervical premotoneurones. *Progress in Neurobiology* 48, 489–517.

Porter, R. & R.N. Lemon, 1993. *Corticospinal Function and Voluntary Movement*. Oxford: Oxford University Press.

Povinelli, D., 2000. *Folk Physics for Apes*. Oxford: Oxford University Press.

Purvis, A., 1995. A composite estimate of the primate phylogeny. *Philosophical Transactions of the Royal Society of London*, Series B 348, 405–21.

Rizzolatti, G., G. Luppino & M. Matelli, 1998. The organization of the cortical motor system: new concepts. *Electroencephal Clinical Neurophysiology* 106, 283–96.

Roche, H., A. Delagnes, J.P. Brugal, C. Feibel, M. Kibunjia, V. Mourre & P.J. Texier, 1999. Early hominid stone tool production and technical skill 2.34 Myr ago in West Turkana, Kenya. *Nature* 399(6731), 57–60.

Rothwell, J.C., M.M. Traub, B.L. Day, J.A. Obeso, P.K. Thomas & C.D. Marsden, 1982. Manual motor performance in a deafferented man. *Brain* 105, 515–42.

Smith, S.L., 1995. Pattern profile analysis of hominid and chimpanzee hand bones. *American Journal of Physical Anthropology* 96, 283–300.

Tomasello, M. & J. Call, 1997. *Primate Cognition*. New York (NY): Oxford University Press.

Torigoe, T., 1985. Comparison of object manipulation among 74 species of nonhuman primates. *Primates* 26, 182–94.

Toth, N., K.D. Schick, E.S. Savage-Rumbaugh, R.A. Sevcik & D.M. Rumbaugh, 1993. Pan the tool-maker: investigations into the stone tool-making and tool-using capabilities of a bonobo (*Pan paniscus*). *Journal of Archaeological Science* 20, 81–91.

van Schaik, C.P., R.O. Deaner & M.Y. Merrill, 1999. The conditions for tool use in primates: implications for the evolution of material culture. *Journal of Human Evolution* 36, 719–41.

Visalberghi, E., D.M. Fragaszy & S. Savage-Rumbaugh, 1995. Performance in a tool-using task by common chimpanzees (*Pan troglodytes*), bonobos (*Pan paniscus*), an orangutan (*Pongo pygmaeus*), and capuchin monkeys (*Cebus apella*). *Journal of Comparative Psychology* 109(1), 52–60.

Westergaard, G.C. & S.J. Suomi, 1997. Capuchin monkey (*Cebus apella*) grips for the use of stone tools. *American Journal of Physical Anthropology* 103, 131–5.

Whishaw, I.Q. & B.L.K. Coles, 1996. Varieties of paw and digit movement during spontaneous food handling in rats: posture, bimanual coordination, preferences and the effect of forelimb cortex lesions. *Behavioural Brain Research* 77, 135–48.

Whishaw, I.Q. & B. Gorny, 1994. Arpeggio and fractionated digit movements used in prehension by rats. *Behavioural Brain Research* 60, 15–24.

Whiten, A., 1998. Imitation of the sequential structure of actions by chimpanzees (*Pan troglodytes*). *Journal of Comparative Psychology* 112(3), 270–81.

Whiten, A., J. Goodall, W.C. McGrew, T. Nishida, V. Reynolds, Y. Sugiyama, C.E. Tutin, R.W. Wrangham & C. Boesch, 1999. Cultures in chimpanzees. *Nature* 399(6737), 682–5.

Wiesendanger, M., 1981. The pyramidal tract: its structure and functional considerations, in *Handbook of Behavioral Neurobiology*, vol. 5, eds. A.L. Towe & E.S. Luschei. New York (NY): Plenum Press, 401–91.

Wiesendanger, M., 1999. Manual dexterity and the making of tools: an introduction from an evolutionary perspective. *Experimental Brain Research* 128, 1–5.

Wise, S.P., D. Boussaoud, P.B. Hohnson & R. Caminiti, 1997. Premotor and parietal cortex: corticocortical connectivity and combinatorial computations. *Annual Review of Neuroscience* 20, 25–42.

Chapter 18

Neural Foundations of Perception and Action in Stone Knapping

Dietrich Stout

Conventional archaeological, ethological and psychological approaches to understanding the origins and evolution of human tool use employ a representational perspective that emphasizes underlying cognitive mechanisms rather than overt performance. This perspective has yielded important progress in understanding the conceptual foundations of tool use and in revealing the impressive mental capacities of non-human primates, but does not address the full range of mental behaviours involved in effective action in the real world. This has led to an underestimation of the uniqueness and potential evolutionary significance of early (Oldowan) stone knapping. A perception–action approach to tool use instead emphasizes the dynamic activity of the organism-plus-environment system, investigated through the detailed empirical observation of real world behaviour. Recent (Stout et al. 2000) and ongoing experimental work using Positron Emission Tomography (PET) to examine brain activation during simple Mode I or 'Oldowan-style' stone knapping provides an excellent opportunity to explore the application of this perspective in human evolutionary studies. PET provides concrete information about task-related brain activity on an intermediate spatial and temporal scale that is useful in forging a link between dynamic behavioural processes and the (relatively) static anatomical substrates that are the medium of biological evolution. Preliminary results from this research corroborate the conceptual simplicity of Mode I knapping, but reveal the unusually demanding perceptual-motor processes involved.

The production of knapped stone artefacts has traditionally been viewed as a uniquely hominin behaviour that exerted a major formative influence in human evolution (Oakley 1954; Washburn 1960; Leakey *et al.* 1964). More recently, however, a growing appreciation of the tool-making and tool-using capacities of modern non-human primates (Goodall 1964; Boesch & Boesch 1990; McGrew 1992; Schick *et al.* 1999), together with a reassessment of the technical sophistication of early stone tools (Toth 1985), has led many to conclude that 'toolmaking *per se* cannot have constituted the main "adaptive wedge" driving the evolution of hands, brains and behaviour in early *Homo*' (Potts 1993).

On the other hand, the intuitive conviction that stone knapping is somehow special remains hard to dismiss. After all, hominins are the only animals ever to have engaged in this behaviour in a natural setting. Can it be that this uniquely hominin behaviour is merely a 'variation on the theme' of an ape adaptive grade (Wynn & McGrew 1989, 384)? The way in which this question is answered depends quite a bit on the theoretical perspective that is adopted. This chapter explores the potential application of a *perception–action* perspective to the question of stone knapping in human evolution, especially in relation to recent functional brain-imaging research (Stout *et al.* 2000) on the subject.

The 'representational' perspective

Archaeologists and primatologists considering the psychological implications of tool behaviour commonly adopt a *representational* approach to cognition. In this view, cognition is an abstract, internal construction of the brain, much like the computation carried out by a digital computer. Actual sensation and action are seen as little more than peripheral input/output channels for the mental work carried out by the 'central processing unit'.

Informed by this representational view of mind, Palaeolithic archaeologists have commonly defined the sophistication of lithic technologies in terms of the abstract mental (Clark 1996) or procedural (Gowlett 1984) 'templates' needed to achieve the 'imposition of arbitrary form' (Holloway 1969) during tool production. Comparative investigations of primate tool use similarly focus on the issue of 'causal understanding' and the mental representation it is thought to imply (Tomasello & Call 1997). In fact, mental representation is the primary criterion used by Parker & Gibson (1977) to define 'intelligent' tool use.

The representational perspective tends to produce an essentialist view of tool behaviour. For example, McGrew (1992) uses the taxonomies of Beck (1980) and Oswalt (1976) to describe tool manufacture in terms of abstract *operational features* like *detachment*, *conjunction*, and *reduction*. Other researchers (Chevalier-Skolnikoff 1983; Poti 1996; Parker & Mckinney 1999) use (neo)Piagetian developmental stages to provide similarly abstract descriptions. In each case, the descriptive categories are intended to capture the essential cognitive (computational) operations underlying superficially variable tool-making behaviours.

From this perspective, Oldowan knapping and ape tool behaviour are quite similar. However, it might be argued that an exclusive focus on cognitive 'essence' tends to gloss over important differences in the actual performance of tool behaviours. Although valuable, the representational perspective on tool use does not exhaust the range of psychologically-meaningful comparisons to be made.

The 'perception–action' perspective

One way to more fully explore the range of such comparisons is to adopt an alternative, *perception–action* perspective on stone knapping. This perspective, which finds its origins in the ecological perception theory of Gibson (1950; 1979) and the dynamic biomechanics of Bernstein (1967; 1996), seeks to 'ground' psychological theory in real-world situations and behaviours, and views variability as a primary focus of study rather than as an undesirable source of 'noise' (Reed & Bril 1996).

In the representational paradigm, variable real-world behaviours are merely imperfect reflections of an essential world of formal cognitive operations. In contrast, the perception–action perspective sees cognition as concretely embodied in performance. In this view, perception and action are not simply peripheral input/output channels, but are themselves the stuff of which cognition is made.

The perception–action perspective has been applied to the problem of tool behaviour by a number of researchers (e.g. Smitsman 1997; Lockman 2000; Bongers 2001). In this body of work, the fundamentally-interesting property of a tool is not its representation by some kind of 'causal understanding' but rather its potential to alter the possibilities for action in an environment. What is unique about tools is that they alter environmental possibilities (*affordances*) by changing the properties of an organism's effectors (*effectivities*). Because tools allow actors to modify affordance–effectivity relationships (Bongers 2001), the foundations of tool use lie in the ability to detect the action possibilities afforded by relations between objects (Lockman 2000). What separates this ecological view from a typical representational account is that the detection of such affordances is considered to occur on the basis of environmental information that is directly perceptible rather than internally constructed.

A perception–action perspective sees tool-using capabilities and understanding as arising dynamically from experience rather than devolving from an abstract internal system of formal cognitive computations. Although the broader implications of the dynamical paradigm for cognitive science remain controversial (e.g. Bechtel 1998; Dennett 1993; van Gelder 1998) this approach has much to recommend it in the particular case of stone knapping.

Many archaeologists have noted the perceptual-motor skill evident in the earliest stone tools (Ludwig & Harris 1998; Semaw 2000; Ambrose 2001). As suggested by Bril *et al.* (this volume; Roux & David this volume) the uniqueness of Oldowan technology may be embodied more in the sophistication of the elementary knapping gestures employed than in the presence of abstract spatial and procedural representations. Work with the stone-bead knappers of Cambay (Roux *et al.* 1995; Bril *et al.* 2000) reveals that, in practice, mastery of the forces involved in individual flake removals is an essential pre-requisite for the emergence of effective knapping plans. Such plans are not abstract and inflexible templates imposed from above, but rather outgrowths from a practical understanding (*savior-faire*) of knapping processes and potentials.

274

This understanding arises, not from abstract Euclidean representations or formal computational procedures, but from direct experiential knowledge of flaking dynamics. In other words, it arises from the acquired ability to perceive relevant affordances.

Perception and action in human evolutionary studies

Despite the overall theoretical suitability of a perception-action approach to stone-tool making and use, there are two major difficulties to be overcome in its application to human-evolutionary studies. To begin with, there is the nature of the Palaeolithic archaeological record itself. The modified stones and bones that constitute Early Stone Age (ESA) archaeological sites present only static and isolated glimpses of behaviour. In stark contrast, the perception–action approach requires detailed, real-time observations of behaviour in its natural context.

The solution is actualistic research in the modern world. Although the complexities and pitfalls of argument by analogy must be respected, the actualistic approach provides the researcher with relevant phenomena that may be observed and manipulated in real-time. Actualistic research with stone tools promises insight into the ways in which stone knapping is situated within real-world social and cultural contexts (Stout 2002; this volume), as well as into the behavioural dynamics (Roux *et al.* 1995; Bril *et al.* 2000) and neural (Stout *et al.* 2000) and somatic (Marzke *et al.* 1998) substrates of stone-knapping skill.

The second major obstacle in applying a perception–action perspective to human-evolutionary studies arises from a perceived conflict between dynamic and structural modes of explanation. Human origins researchers are primarily concerned with understanding human 'biocultural' evolution, a process in which 'behaviour and structure form an interacting complex, with change in one affecting the other' (Washburn 1960). Those specifically interested in cognition focus on the evolutionary relationships between hominin behaviour and brain structure (especially size). In contrast, students of modern human perception and action seek dynamic explanations of behaviour and its development in individuals. The emphasis is on understanding the way in which the system changes over time and how its various states relate to each other, rather than describing the internal structure that defines any one particular state (van Gelder 1998).

The problem is that, while human-origins researchers need mechanistic, structural explanations in order to understand how behaviour relates to biological evolution, perception–action theorists operate at the more holistic level of dynamic organization.

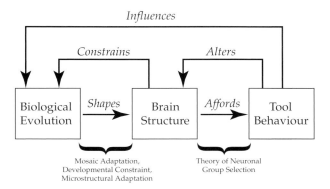

Figure 18.1. *Analytical levels and relationships in the evolution of tool behaviour (flow chart of interacting levels).*

Fortunately, and despite a superficial 'appearance of tension', these two levels of explanation are actually complementary (Bechtel 1998). The trick lies in recognizing the causal relationships between levels (Fig. 18.1). Although this task is far from accomplished, Thelen & Smith (1994) advocate Edelman's (1987; 1989) Theory of Neuronal Group Selection (TNGS) as an important step in the right direction.

Theoretical integration

The TNGS differs from many more conventional descriptions of brain function in its emphasis on dynamic patterns of neuronal activity rather than static, anatomically-defined neuronal networks. Nevertheless, it recognizes that neuroanatomical structure, itself a product of dynamic developmental processes, is an essential substrate:

> the brains of richly endowed organisms show a structure unique among all known physical objects … Even in biological systems such as jungles or food webs, where complex parallel dynamics occur in the exchange of signals, comparable *preexisting* structural pathways of this type cannot be found. (Edelman 1989, 64).

This preexisting structure results from the action of evolved developmental processes in a particular ontogenetic environment. Although the complexities of these evolutionary, structural and functional relationships (Fig. 18.1) can be daunting, the TNGS nevertheless points toward ways in which palaeoanthropological interest in evolving brain structure might be integrated with psychological perspectives on the dynamics of perception and action.

Positron emission tomography as a research tool in human origins

The functional brain-imaging technique of Positron Emission Tomography (PET) offers unique opportunities for human-origins researchers to examine the patterns of neuronal activity associated with evolutionarily-significant behaviours. It is exactly the kind of actualistic research tool that is needed to facilitate the application of perception–action perspectives in human-evolutionary studies. Although the temporal resolution of PET is not such that it can reveal the fine-grained dynamics of neuronal activation (Segalowitz 2000) during knapping, it can reveal global patterns. This is an important beginning in the attempt to relate structure and process in an evolutionarily meaningful way.

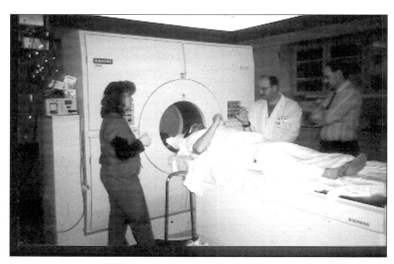

Figure 18.2. *Subject from pilot study.*

Table 18.1. *Knapping-related activations from the pilot study (Stout et al. 2000).*

Location no.	Centroid location	Functional attribution	Side	Talairach Coordinates (X,Y,Z)	Volume (mm³)	Mean Z value
1	Superior parietal (Brodmann Area 7)	Dorsal 'where' visual pathway	left	21, –49, 56	6948	5.75
2			right	–30, –53, 61	1948	5.16
3	Central sulcus (Brodmann Areas 1 & 4)	Primary motor and somatosensory processing	left	33, –26, 52	8042	5.24
4	Postcentral gyrus (Brodmann Area 1)	Primary somatosensory processing	right	–39, –26, 56	5889	5.10
5	Cerebellum (hemisphere)	Motor planning and initiation	left	10, –37, –18	1002	5.22
6			right	–37, –51, –25	604	4.82
7	Cerebellum (vermis)	Motor coordination	right	–3, –53, –9	1082	5.07
8	Fusiform gyrus (Brodmann Area 37)	Ventral 'what' visual pathway	right	–24, –53, –9	1287	5.05

PET experimental design and interpretation

The immediate objective of PET research is to identify the patterns of brain activation that are associated with particular behaviours. PET images can provide this information, but must be properly interpreted in light of the effects of background or *baseline* (Gusnard & Raichle 2001) brain activity. In living subjects, neuronal activity is obviously ongoing throughout the brain at any given time. What researchers are really interested in is the way in which this pattern of activity changes during behaviour. For this reason, PET images collected during an experimental task are always compared with images collected during a control condition. It is the statistically-significant differences (*activations*) revealed by these image *subtractions* that are actually interpreted.

The meaning of brain activations thus depends as much on the nature of the control condition as it does on the experimental task itself. In a typical PET experiment, a control task is designed that replicates the experimental task as closely as possible, excepting only those narrowly-defined aspects of behaviour that are under investigation. This is done in order to isolate changes in activation patterns that are specific to the behaviour of interest.

The PET research

The pilot study

In February of 1997 a single-subject pilot study was performed in order to more concretely assess the utility of PET as a research tool in human-evolutionary studies. Results from this study (Stout *et al.* 2000) not only confirmed the practicality and value of the technique, but also suggested specific hypotheses and methodological improvements for further research. These were incorporated into a six-subject follow-up study that is now in the data analysis stage.

Methods

In the pilot study an H₂¹⁵O water tracer[1] was used in order to examine patterns of brain activation during simple (Mode I or 'Oldowan-style')

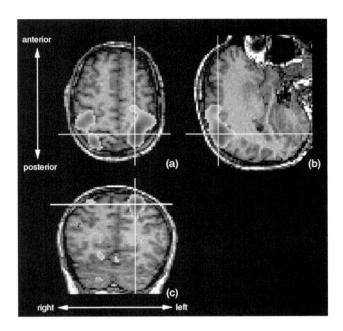

Figure 18.3. *Activation of pericentral cortex in the pilot study (Stout* et al. *2000).*

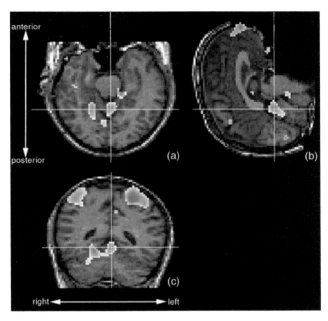

Figure 18.4. *Activation of cerebellum in the pilot study (Stout* et al. *2000).*

flake production. The subject of the study was Nicholas Toth, an experienced Palaeolithic archaeologist and experimental stone knapper with over 20 years knapping experience. Results of the pilot study should thus be viewed in light of the subject's prior experience and may not reflect the brain activation that would occur in less-experienced subjects performing the same tasks.

As described by (Stout *et al.* 2000), activation images were collected using a Siemens 951/31R whole body PET scanner. Due to the relatively short half-life of ^{15}O, all experimental tasks were performed with the subject lying prone on the scanner bed (Fig. 18.2). The control task consisted of the subject visually focusing on a roughly spherical cobble held aloft using both hands. This condition was intended to reflect a normal, baseline state of brain activation, including visual stimulation. Numerous studies cited by Gusnard & Raichle (2001) indicate that, outside the visual cortices, passive visual inspection is associated with typical 'resting' or baseline activation patterns. The knapping task consisted of the (right-handed) subject removing flakes from a core held in the left hand using a hammerstone held in the right hand. Because image data were being collected during actual task performance, movement of the subject's head had to be minimized. For this reason, knapping was done at approximately 'half-strength'. Despite this, flakes were removed from the core.

Pilot results
Subtraction of the control task from the knapping

task revealed large volumes of significant activation during knapping. For convenience, the results of the Region of Interest (ROI) analysis reported in Stout *et al.* (2000) are re-presented here in Table 18.1. As these results show, knapping-related activations are centred in the primary motor and somatosensory cortices surrounding the central sulcus, the superior parietal lobule, the cerebellum and the fusiform gyrus of the right inferior temporal lobe.

More qualitative examination of the images reveals a large contiguous volume of activation in the left cerebral hemisphere, extending from the posterior parietal to the anterior bank of the central sulcus (Fig. 18.3). A similar pattern is visible in the right parietal, although the generally lower level of activation yields a clear separation between the anterior (peri-central) and posterior (superior parietal) volumes. In the cerebellum (Fig. 18.4), activation may be seen in the central vermis and in both hemispheres. There is a small volume of activation in the right fusiform (Fig. 18.3) but, as noted by Stout *et al.* (2000), caution is required in interpreting the more marginal results from this single subject study. With the exception of the fusiform gyrus, activation in all of these regions is of consistently greater significance/extent in the left hemisphere compared with the right. In general terms, the activations observed in the pilot study suggest that the brain structures most active during Mode I stone knapping are those associated with visuomotor performance rather than more internally-directed mental behaviours like im-

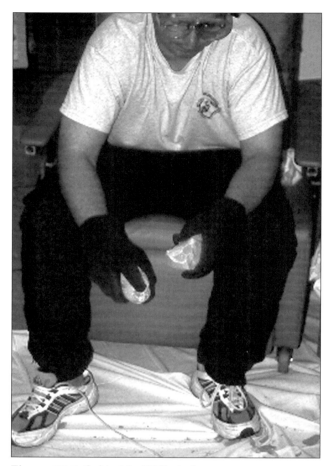

Figure 18.5. *Subject in FDG study.*

agery or planning.

Ongoing research

Results from the pilot study may now be augmented through comparison with preliminary results from the ongoing follow-up research. This research effects an increase in sample size ($n = 6$) as well a number of other important methodological improvements. Although the image data from the follow-up research are still being analyzed, sufficient work has been done for a preliminary, qualitative assessment and comparison with the pilot study.

Methodological improvements

The major achievement of the pilot study was to demonstrate the utility and practicality of PET as a research tool in human origins. The study also provided a valuable opportunity to develop and refine research methods for use in follow-up research.

In the pilot study, a relatively 'minimalistic' control task (visual inspection) was used. Happily, the results obtained were sufficiently robust as to encourage the use of more elaborate control tasks in

follow-up research. By using control tasks that more closely approximate the experimental knapping task, it should be possible to more narrowly define neural demands specific to knapping. In the ongoing follow-up research, the control task consisted of striking together two cobbles without attempting to produce flakes. This activity involved vigorous physical activity and visual guidance closely analogous, but not identical, to that involved in stone knapping.

Also important in isolating the specific neural demands of stone knapping is selection of an appropriate radionuclide tracer. The use in the pilot study of $H_2^{15}O$, with its relatively short half-life, required that all task be performed within confines of the scanner (Fig. 18.2). As a result, the subject was in an unnatural position (prone) and had to minimize the vigorous movements that are a natural part of knapping. Both of these factors could easily affect the neural demands of the task. Furthermore, the limited timeframe and physical constraints of the scanning situation did not allow for the unfolding of a natural knapping plan, which might (hypothetically) involve multiple generations of contingent flake removals.

In the follow-up research, the more slowly decaying glucose analog FDG ([18]flouro-2-deoxyglucose) was employed. This tracer is taken up by metabolically active neurons over a period of 40 minutes, after which time its distribution in the brain is 'fixed' and may be imaged at any point until the isotope decays. Thus, images are collected of an activity *after* it is completed. Although the use of FDG further decreases the temporal resolution of PET to 40 minutes, it allows for much more naturalistic task conditions. Thus, experimental subjects in the follow-up research performed control and experimental knapping tasks comfortably seated in a chair (Fig. 18.5), and were able to engage in a full range of knapping actions, from core and hammerstone selection to full-force percussion and (potentially) exhaustive core reduction. The images produced indicate the time-averaged neuronal demands of sustained knapping activity in a naturalistic setting. Insofar as this experimental arrangement better reflects knapping as an everyday human activity, an additional level of ecological validity is achieved.

Preliminary results

Despite the substantial differences in experimental design outlined above, preliminary evaluation of results from the follow-up research largely corroborates the findings of the pilot study. Bilateral activation of the primary somatosensory and motor cortex surrounding the central sulcus and of the cerebellar hemispheres is clearly evident. Somewhat less intense bilateral activation of the superior parietal lobule also appears to be present, but will need to be confirmed in more thorough analysis. The follow-up research thus provides at least provisional corroboration for all of the major knapping-related activations observed in the pilot study. More conclusive evaluation of the anterior extent of activation into the secondary motor areas of the frontal lobe, as well as of possible activations elsewhere in the cerebrum, will have to await further analysis.

One striking divergence of the follow-up results from those of the pilot study is, however, readily apparent. This is the robust and extensive activation of occipital visual cortices. The activation clearly encompasses the primary (striate) visual cortex (V1) surrounding the calcharine fissure and likely extends into the secondary visual cortices (V2, V3, V4 and V5) of Brodmann's area 19. The exact reason underlying this major difference between pilot and follow-up results is not clear, but the strong activation of the occipital evident from the improved sample size and experimental conditions of the follow-up research nevertheless provides powerful evidence of its involvement in supporting knapping activity.

Functional interpretation

Taken together, the pilot and preliminary follow-up results reveal those large-scale neuroanatomical structures that are exceptionally active during stone knapping. Ongoing analysis will ultimately refine this course-grained picture, and will most likely implicate additional structures. For the time being, however, it is safe to say that stone knapping involves activation of a network of structures commonly associated with visuomotor performance. This network extends in cerebral cortex from at least the primary motor cortex (M1) of the precentral gyrus, posteriorly through the primary somatosensory cortex (S1) of the postcentral gyrus and the polymodal cortex (Roland 1993) of the superior parietal lobule, to the primary and secondary visual cortices of the occipital lobe (Fig. 18.6). It also includes the sub-cortical cerebellar hemispheres and vermis. Involvement

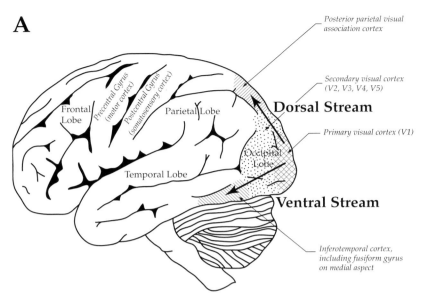

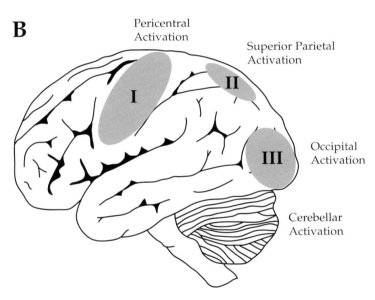

Figure 18.6. *Knapping-related activations and relevant functional neuroanatomy.*

of the 'remote' visual cortex of the inferotemporal fusiform gyrus remains equivocal at present.

Dynamic cognition and functional localization
These activation data provide a static 'snapshot' view of brain activity during stone knapping. There is the danger, as Segalowitz (2000, 164) points out, that 'by focusing on average activation values, we are prone to the classic error in neuropsychology theory … of simply attributing complex cognitive processes to "centers" rather than dynamic parallel networks'. In fact, the dynamical hypothesis in cognitive science

stipulates that mental behaviour is embodied in the continuous evolution of states through time rather than in 'simple transformations of static structures' (van Gelder 1998, 621). In Edelman's (1987) *Theory of Neuronal Groups Selection (TNGS)*, mental functions like categorization and memory are achieved through population-level correlations in the activity of dynamically-variable groups of neurons. They do not arise from the passage of signals along fixed neuronal networks. Nevertheless, the modal structure and organization evident in larger-scale brain regions is an essential substrate.

It is at this larger spatial and temporal scale that PET images provide insight. PET images do not explain *how* neuronal activity contributes to mental behaviour, but they do indicate *where* this activity takes place. To study behaviour using the static images of PET is not necessarily to reduce complex process to simple anatomy, it is merely to focus on a particular level of spatiotemporal organization. To put it bluntly, 'Neuropsychology is not a danger to ecological psychology' (Pickering 2001, 148). The level at which PET works may or may not be the appropriate one to address particular psychological questions, but it is well suited for use in human-evolutionary studies.

The neuropsychology of stone knapping

One way in which PET evidence may be used in human origins research is to provide a general neuropsychological characterization of stone knapping behaviour. As shown in Figure 18.6, currently available imaging evidence indicates that Mode I or Oldowan-style stone knapping is associated with activation in the four main areas: 1) pericentral cortex; 2) the superior parietal lobule; 3) the occipital lobe; and 4) the cerebellum. The first three of these are components of the *dorsal stream* of cortical visuomotor control (Milner & Goodale 1995), while the cerebellum is a classic subcortical motor structure. Considered individually, each of these regions or structures is well known for its association with perceptual-motor action.

Pericentral cortex

The 'pericentral' cortex surrounding the central sulcus includes the primary motor cortex (M1) of the precentral gyrus and the primary somatosensory cortex (S1) of the postcentral gyrus. M1 is commonly considered to be a motor 'output' structure responsible for the execution of movement. M1 receives afferent stimulation from diverse brain regions, including S1, frontal 'motor planning' areas, thalamus and cerebellum. In turn, it sends efferent impulses directly to the motoneurons of the spinal cord. In this way, neuronal activity in M1 is tightly coupled with movements of the limbs. In

fact, the seminal work of Georgopoulos and colleagues (1982; 1984; Brown *et al.* 1989) has demonstrated the relationship between population-level neuronal activity in M1 and the direction of limb movements. More recent work (Pascual-Leone *et al.* 1994; Sanes & Donoghue 2000) has also begun to reveal the dynamic reorganization of somatotopic neuronal groups in M1 that occurs during motor learning. The elevated activity in M1 during knapping as compared to simple percussion likely reflects the demands of mapping the faster and more accurate actions involved.

Like M1, primary somatosensory cortex (S1) is characterized by relatively direct connections to the somatic periphery. Neurons in S1 receive afferent connections from the ventral posterior lateral (VPL) nucleus of the thalamus, a relay nucleus for impulses from the sensory receptors of the skin and joints. Thus it is not surprising to find that S1 is activated during vibration of the fingers (Fox & Applegate 1988), tactile shape discrimination (Roland 1985) and movements in extra personal space (Roland *et al.* 1980). The coactivation of S1 and M1 during knapping illustrates the general indivisibility of perception from action in *ecologically valid* (Kotchoubey 2001) behaviour, as well as the exceptional sensorimotor demands of the knapping task.

Superior parietal lobule

Activation of the superior parietal lobule is a particularly interesting result of the PET research. This region consists of *polymodal* association cortex, and supports mappings between diverse visual, somatosensory, auditory, vestibular and motivational signals. Anatomically, this region differs from primary sensorimotor regions in that it is dominated by intracortical, rather than subcortical or peripheral, connections.

The superior parietal lobule includes Brodmann's areas 5 and 7. Area 5 receives major afferent connections from neighbouring somatosensory cortex in the postcentral gyrus, as well as the vestibular (balance and orientation) system, the premotor areas of the frontal lobe, and the limbic (motivation and emotion) system (Kandel *et al.* 1991). It sends efferent connections back to the premotor cortices as well as on to the more posterior area 7. Area 7, in addition to receiving inputs from area 5, is reciprocally connected with the visual cortices of the occipital lobe and receives afferent connections from the auditory cortex of Brodmann's area 22 in the superior temporal gyrus. Area 7 sends efferent fibers to the frontal premotor cortices and to the cerebellar hemispheres. As a result of these connectional arrangements, the superior parietal lobule is a critical anatomical substrate supporting the dynamic coupling between multiple modes of sensory perception and motor action. Its heightened activation during Oldowan-style stone knapping clearly reflects on the complexity and elaboration of the polymodal mappings involved in the perception-through-action of knapping-related affordances.

Occipital lobe

The occipital lobe is composed of the primary (V1) and secondary (V2, V3, V4 & V5) visual cortices of Brodmann's areas 17, 18 and 19. V1 receives signals from the retina via the lateral geniculate nucleus and shares major reciprocal connections with the secondary visual cortices. These 'higher order' visual areas are massively interconnected both amongst themselves and with the more remote visual areas of the superior parietal and inferior temporal.

According to Edelman's (1989) Reentrant Cortical Integration (RCI) model of vision, reentrant mapping between these thoroughly interconnected regions integrates various visual attributes to produce basic perceptual phenomena like the recognition of contours. Conventional computational accounts similarly emphasize the role of the occipital cortices in creating representations of the fundamental components of visual stimuli, including colour, edges, orientation and motion. Increased occipital activity during stone knapping results from the focused visual attention required by the task (Brefczynski & DeYoe 1999), and reflects the sensitive dependence of this behaviour on details of the visual environment.

Cerebellum

The cerebellum consists of three main functional divisions, the *vestibulocerebellum*, *spinocerebellum* and *cerebrocerebellum*. Of these, the spinocerebellum and cerebrocerebellum are clearly activated during stone knapping. The centrally-located spinocerebellum receives most of its input from the spinal cord, and sends efferent fibers via two deep cerebellar nuclei (fastigial and interposed) to the descending motor pathways of the brain stem. This spino-cerebellar loop allows for detailed mapping between cerebellar activity and ongoing movement. The spinocerebellum also sends signals via the thalamus to primary motor cortex, allowing for integration at multiple levels. Activity in the spinocerebellum is thought to be linked to muscle tone and the smooth execution of movement (Kandel *et al.* 1991).

The cerebrocerebellum includes the lateral portions of the cerebellar hemispheres and is reciprocally connected with large areas of cerebral cortex, including premotor, motor, somatosensory and posterior parietal regions. It is thought to play an important role in the precise timing of complex multi-joint movements (Kandel *et al.* 1991).

Edelman (1989), on the other hand, characterizes the cerebellum as an 'organ of succession' responsible for the temporal coordination of global perceptual-motor mappings. As in more traditional views, regulation of motor timing is seen as a central function of the cerebellum. The difference is that Edelman further interprets the cerebellum as a 'modulating device' facilitating the categorization and perception of temporally defined motor synergies.

The distributed system

Considered as a whole, the brain regions activated during Oldowan-style stone knapping provide a distributed structural medium for the dynamic processes that implement behaviour. Individual regions display preexisting patterns of internal organization and external connectivity that both facilitate and constrain aspects of signal transmission and reentrant mapping. The massive interconnection of these regions supports the globally integrated, polymodal mapping of the knapping action by neuronal activity. The sustained activity observed in this distributed system, although revealed by static PET images, conforms with the expected behaviour of a system in which reentrant mapping is achieved through synchronized activity in spatially-distributed areas (Tallon-Baudry *et al.* 2001; Martinez *et al.* 2001). The fact that the level of this sustained activity exceeds that seen in an active perceptual-motor control task reflects the complexity of stone-knapping behaviour and indicates the exceptional physiological demands on the brain that are associated with it.

Implications for human origins

The PET research presented here reveals the neural substrates of Oldowan-style knapping in modern humans. In order for these actualistic results to be useful in human-evolutionary studies, some form of analogy must be made with the actual Oldowan knapping done by Plio-Pleistocene hominins. One level at which such an analogy may be made is that of the broad mental demands of the task. The basis of this analogy is the argument that similar behaviours imply similar mental processes even though the size and organization of the neural substrate may vary.

Psychological interpretation

Although it is easy to go overboard in attributing particular mental processes to discrete neural 'centres', different mental behaviours certainly are instantiated by different patterns of activity in the brain. PET reveals only the spatial dimensions of these differences, but is nevertheless capable of differentiating broad classes of mental behaviour (e.g. Roland 1993). As pointed out by Thelen & Smith (1994), thinking about an action is as much a behaviour as is performing the action, it is simply a *different* behaviour. The spatial distribution of activation during stone knapping, and particularly the absence of activation in the frontal and temporal association cortices, makes it clear that the most salient mental demands of Mode I knapping have to do with execution rather than conceptualization. PET research with modern humans cannot indicate the absolute perceptual-motor or conceptual capacities that were required of Oldowan toolmakers, but it does reveal the relative emphasis placed on these different kinds of mental behaviour.

Evolutionary interpretation

Modern PET images may also be used to identify brain regions that are relatively more likely to have been the focus of evolutionary selection relating to stone knapping ability. Those areas that experience the greatest physiological stress (i.e. activation) during knapping in modern humans are also the ones most likely to have experienced evolutionary pressure in the past. Conversely, structures not activated in modern humans may be considered much less likely to have been the direct focus of knapping-related selection. PET research with modern humans cannot directly reveal ancestral conditions, but does define at least one point along the evolutionary trajectory under investigation.

Unfortunately, interpretation of the PET evidence is hampered by our limited knowledge regarding the patterns and processes of human brain evolution. Very little is actually known about how brain structure has changed during hominin evolution, let alone about how this change came about. Adaptive processes that may have played an important role include mosaic changes in regional brain size (e.g. Holloway 1979; Armstrong 1982; Barton 1998; Dunbar 1998), coordinated overall brain expansion (Finlay & Darlington 1995; Finlay *et al.* 2001), and microstructural adaptation of neuronal organization (Nimchinsky *et al.* 1999; Preuss *et al.* 1999; Buxhoeveden *et al.* 2001). Given our limited knowledge, multiple alternatives must be entertained in interpreting the PET evidence.

Mosaic evolution

If we assume a simple process of mosaic brain evolution, we might expect that those brain regions most heavily taxed by knapping activities would have experienced preferential expansion. Although comparative data about the size of these regions is difficult to come by, this simple hypothesis does not appear to be supported. While the posterior parietal

area in humans does indeed appear to have expanded (Passingham 1975; Holloway 1983), and the relative size of the cerebellum is controversial (Deacon 1997; Rilling & Insel 1999; Semendeferi & Damasio 2000), the primary visual, somatosensory and motor areas that are so heavily activated during stone knapping are actually among the least expanded portions of the human brain. It does not currently appear that the distributed network of structures associated with Mode 1 knapping was a unitary focus for mosaic brain enlargement. Although interpretations may change somewhat with further analysis, any relationship that is ultimately discerned between Oldowan knapping and mosaic brain expansion will be a relatively complex one.

Coordinated evolution

On the other hand, there is the possibility that selection on individual brain structures may have produced coordinated enlargement of the whole brain, as suggested by the developmental constraint hypothesis of Finlay & Darlington (1995). In this case, modest expansion of one or more of the structures supporting knapping behaviour could easily have contributed to the broader pattern of overall brain enlargement seen in human evolution. Unfortunately, this particular evolutionary relationship is not very testable because the constraint hypothesis predicts the same result (overall brain enlargement) from selection relating to any given behavioural capacity. The PET evidence confirms that stone knapping places relatively intense physiological demands on the brain, and so could have contributed to selection on brain size, but does not demonstrate that it actually did.

Microstructural evolution

Perhaps more interesting in light of currently-available evidence is the possible existence of microstructural adaptations relating to stone-knapping ability. As we have seen, stone knapping activates a string of structures from the occipital visual cortices through the superior parietal and into frontal motor cortex. This corresponds quite closely to what has been commonly thought of as the *dorsal stream* of visual processing.

The existence of two streams of visual processing (dorsal and ventral) in the primate cerebral cortex was first proposed by Ungerleider & Mishkin (1982), who differentiated between a dorsal 'where' stream involved in the perception of location and motion and a ventral 'what' stream implicated in the perception of object characteristics like form and colour. More recent work has stressed the role of the dorsal stream in visuomotor control (Milner & Goodale 1995) and in perception-for-action on relatively short time scales (Green 2001).

Although the anatomical segregation between visual streams does not appear to be as rigid as some (Livingstone & Hubel 1988) had hypothesized, there clearly are parallel neuronal networks that respond preferentially to stimulus components such as motion, contrast and colour. In the case of the dorsal stream, there is a loose continuity all the way from the fast acting, motion-sensitive *parasol cells* of the retina, through the *magnocellular layers* of the lateral geniculate and the *M-stream* neurons in layer 4 of V1 to the higher-order visual-processing areas of the posterior parietal cortex. The coactivation of occipital and superior parietal cortices observed during stone knapping reflects this continuity, and indicates the importance of dorsal stream activity in knapping behaviour. It should thus be of particular interest to human origins researchers that some of the best evidence of microstructural specialization in the human brain comes from V1, and from M-stream neurons specifically.

Working with the carefully-sectioned and stained occipital lobes of 29 human and non-human primates, Preuss *et al.* (1999) found that humans display a unique arrangement of M-stream neurons and dendrites in layer 4A of primary visual cortex. Prior to the work of Preuss and colleagues, the distribution of M-related neurons in V1 was known primarily from studies of macaques, which display a characteristic honeycomb pattern of M-tissue in layer 4A. Preuss *et al.* have now shown that, although the honeycomb pattern is shared by monkeys and apes, humans display a unique mesh-like architecture in layer 4A that results in a much greater representation of M-tissue.

Preuss and colleagues suggest that this derived characteristic of human visual cortex may represent an augmentation of the M-stream in humans. Given the level of dorsal stream activity observed during stone knapping, it is quite plausible that a hominin M-stream specialization relating to motion perception could have either contributed to the initial emergence of stone knapping or been part of an adaptive response to its later spread. Such specializations of primary visual cortex would also be expected to have cascading effects on higher levels of the visual system, which receive most of their input from V1 (Preuss *et al.* 1999).

Summary and conclusions

Over the past 75 years, research into the tool behaviour of modern apes has dramatically expanded our appreciation for the mental capacities of our closest relatives (Köhler 1925; Goodall 1964; McGrew 1992; Matsuzawa 1996). By elevating our estimations of apes, this research has also contributed to a reduction

in the perceived uniqueness of the earliest knapped stone tools (e.g. Wynn & McGrew 1989). For the most part, however, students of tool behaviour in both modern apes and prehistoric hominins have focused on underlying cognitive mechanisms rather than on actual performance. This focus results from a representational perspective concerned less with what an individual does than with how the individual conceives of what he or she does (Smitsman 1997). Although the conceptual simplicity of Oldowan stone knapping has been well described (Wynn & McGrew 1989), a perception–action perspective on tool use opens the door to additional avenues of investigation.

A perception–action perspective sees tool use as the dynamic product of an integrated organisms-plus-environment system rather than as the unilateral expression of static internal concepts. This perspective is particularly useful in dealing with the issues of motor skill and practical understanding that are so important to a full description of stone-knapping behaviour. Although the application of this perspective to the evidence and questions commonly held by human origins researchers is a non-trivial undertaking, the empirical observations of functional brain structure provided by PET make it an ideal actualistic research tool.

In the preliminary research presented here, PET was used to compare brain activity during Oldowan-style (Mode I) stone knapping to that during less-elaborate control tasks. The results provide further corroboration for the view that Mode I knapping is not especially demanding in the conventional conceptual or cognitive sense. However, activations seen in motor, somatosensory, superior parietal and visual cortices and in the cerebellum indicate that it *is* an especially demanding perceptual-motor task. The mental demands of stone knapping may lie more with execution than conceptualization, but they are no less real or unique because of this.

The activations observed during stone knapping also suggest potential evolutionary relationships. Although currently available brain volume data do not reveal any simple relationship between the distributed network that supports knapping and mosaic patterns of human-brain expansion, the observed activation would be consistent with a contribution to coordinated overall brain enlargement. At the microstructural level, there is clear evidence of a uniquely human adaptation in the dorsal stream of cortical visual processing. It is a plausible hypothesis for further investigation that this adaptation may have in some way either contributed to or arisen from the development of stone knapping in human evolution.

Note

1. $H_2{}^{15}O$ is a radionuclide tracer consisting of water molecules that incorporate the radioactive oxygen isotope ^{15}O. It is carried by blood vessels in the brain and produces activation data that reflect the sensitive response of blood flow to changes in local neuronal metabolism (Roland 1993).

Acknowledgements

I would like to thank Nicholas Toth and Kathy Schick for the inspiration for the PET research presented here, as well as for advice and assistance in its execution. This research also would not have been possible without the participation and efforts of the experimental subjects. My thanks go to Julie Stout and David Kareken for assistance in data analysis, Gary Hutchins and Rich Fain for help with experimental design and execution, and PET Technologists Kevin Perry and Susan Geiger. Funding for the pilot research of Stout *et al.* (2000) was provided by the Center for Research into the Anthropological Foundations of Technology (CRAFT) at Indiana University, the office of Research and the University Graduate School at Indiana University, and the Indiana University School of Medicine. Funding for the ongoing follow-up research comes from the National Science Foundation (Award # BCS-0105265), the L.S.B. Leakey Foundation, and CRAFT. My attendance at the Knapping Stone workshop was supported by a David C. Skomp Fellowship from Department of Anthropology, Indiana University, Bloomington.

References

Ambrose, S.H., 2001. Paleolithic technology and human evolution. *Science* 291, 1748–53.

Armstrong, E., 1982. Mosaic evolution in the primate brain, in *Primate Brain Evolution*, eds. E. Armstrong & D. Falk. New York (NY): Plenum Press, 131–62.

Barton, R.A., 1998. Visual specialization and brain evolution in primates. *Proceedings of the Royal Society of London* 265, 1933–7.

Bechtel, W., 1998. Dynamicists versus computationalists: wither mechanists? *Behavioral and Brain Sciences* 21(5), 629.

Beck, B.B., 1980. *Animal Tool Behavior: the Use and Manufacture of Tools by Animals*. New York (NY): Garland STPM Press.

Bernstein, N., 1967. *Coordination and Regulation of Movement*. New York (NY): Pergamon Press.

Bernstein, N., 1996. On dexterity and its development, in *Dexterity and its Development*, trans. M.L. Latash. Mahwah (NJ): Lawrence Erlbaum Associates, 3–246.

Boesch, C. & H. Boesch, 1990. Tool use and tool making in wild chimpanzees. *Folia Primatologica* 54, 86–99.

Bongers, R., 2001. An Action Perspective on Tool Use and its Development. Unpublished PhD dissertation, University of Nijmegen.

Brefczynski, J.A. & E.A. DeYoe, 1999. A physiological correlate of the 'spotlight' of visual attention. *Nature Neuroscience* 2(4), 370–74.

Bril, B., V. Roux & G. Dietrich, 2000. Skills involved in the knapping of chalcedony beads: motor and cognitive characteristics of a complex situated action, in *Cornaline de l'Inde: des pratiques techniques de Cambay aux techno-systemes de l'Indus*, ed. V. Roux. Paris: Editions de la Maison des sciences de l'homme, 207–329. [English cd-rom.]

Chevalier-Skolnikoff, S., 1983. Sensorimotor development in orangutans and other primates. *Journal of Human Evolution* 12, 545–61.

Clark, J.D., 1996. Decision-making and variability in the Acheulean, in *Aspects of African Archaeology: Papers from the 10th Congress of the PanAfrican Association for Prehistory and Related studies*, eds. G. Pwiti & R. Soper. Harare: University of Zimbabwe Publications.

Deacon, T.W., 1997. *The Symbolic Species: the Co-evolution of Language and the Brain*. New York (NY): W.W. Norton.

Dennett, D., 1993. Review of F. Varela, E. Thompson & E. Rosch, 'The Embodied Mind: Cognitive Science and Human Experience'. *American Journal of Psychology* 106, 121–6.

Dunbar, R.I.M., 1998. The social brain hypothesis. *Evolutionary Anthropology* 7, 178–92.

Edelman, G.M., 1987. *Neural Darwinism*. New York (NY): Basic Books.

Edelman, G.M., 1989. *The Remembered Present: a Biological Theory of Consciousness*. New York (NY): Basic Books.

Finlay, B. & R. Darlington, 1995. Linked regularities in the development and evolution of mammalian brains. *Science* 268, 1578–84.

Finlay, B., R. Darlington & N. Nicastro, 2001. Developmental structure in brain evolution. *Behavioral and Brain Sciences* 24, 263–308.

Fox, P.T. & C.N. Applegate, 1988. Right-hemispheric dominance for somatosensory processing in humans. *Society of Neuroscience Abstracts* 14, 760.

Georgopolous, A.P., J.F. Kalska, R. Caminiti & J.T. Massey, 1982. On the relations between the direction of two-dimensional arm movements and cell discharge in primary motor cortex. *Journal of Neuroscience* 2, 1527–37.

Georgopolous, A.P., J.F. Kalska, M.D. Crutcher, R. Caminiti & J.T. Massey, 1984. The representation of movement direction in the motor cortex: single cell and population studies, in *Dynamic Aspects of Neocortical Function*, eds. G.M. Edelman, W.E. Gall & W.M. Cowan. New York (NY): Wiley Interscience, 501–24.

Gibson, J.J., 1950. *The Perception of the Visual World*. Boston (MA): Houghton-Mifflin.

Gibson, J.J., 1979. *The Ecological Approach to Visual Perception*. Boston (MA): Houghton-Mifflin.

Goodall, J., 1964. Tool-using and aimed throwing in a community of free-living chimpanzees. *Nature* 201, 1264–6.

Gowlett, J.A.J., 1984. Mental abilities of early man: a look at some hard evidence, in *Hominid Evolution and Commu-*

nity Ecology, ed. R. Foley. New York (NY): Academic Press, 167–92.

Green, P.R., 2001. The relation between perception and action: what should neuroscience learn from psychology? *Ecological Psychology* 13(2), 117–22.

Gusnard, D.A. & M.E. Raichle, 2001. Searching for a baseline: functional imaging and the resting human brain. *Nature Reviews Neuroscience* 2(October), 685–94.

Holloway, R.L., 1969. Culture: a human domain. *Current Anthropology* 10(4), 395–412.

Holloway, R.L., 1979. Brain size, allometry, and reorganization: toward a synthesis, in *Development and Evolution of Brain Size*, eds. M. Hahn, C. Jensen & B. Dudek. New York (NY): Academic Press, 59–88.

Holloway, R.L., 1983. Human brain evolution: a search for units, models and synthesis. *Canadian Journal of Anthropology* 3(2), 215–30.

Kandel, E.R., J.H. Schwartz & T.M. Jessell, 1991. *Principles of Neural Science*. Norwalk (CT): Appleton & Lange.

Köhler, W., 1925. *The Mentality of Apes*. London: Routledge & Kegan Paul.

Kotchoubey, B., 2001. About hens and eggs: perception and action, ecology and neuroscience. A reply to Michaels (2000). *Ecological Psychology* 13(2), 123–33.

Leakey, L., P. Tobias & J. Napier, 1964. A new species of the genus *Homo* from Olduvai Gorge. *Nature* 202, 7–9.

Livingstone, M.S. & D. Hubel, 1988. Segregation of form, color, movement and depth: anatomy, physiology and perception. *Science* 240, 740–49.

Lockman, J.J., 2000. A perception–action perspective on tool use development. *Child Development* 71(1), 137–44.

Ludwig, B.V. & J.W.K. Harris, 1998. Towards a technological reassessment of East African plio-pleistocene lithic assemblages, in *Early Human Behavior in the Global Context: the Rise and Diversity of the Lower Paleolithic Period*, eds. M. Petraglia & R. Korisetter. New York (NY): Routledge, 84–107.

Martinez, A., F. DiRusso, A.-V. Lourdes, M.I. Sereno, R.B. Buxton & S.A. Hillyard, 2001. Putting stimulus attention on the map: timing and localization of stimulus selection processes in striate and extrastriate visual areas. *Vision Research* 41, 1437–57.

Marzke, M.W., N. Toth, K. Schick, S. Reece, B. Steinberg, K. Hunt, R.L. Linscheid & K.-N. An, 1998. EMG study of hand muscle recruitment during hard hammer percussion manufacture of Oldowan tools. *American Journal of Physical Anthropology* 105, 315–32.

Matsuzawa, T., 1996. Chimpanzee intelligence in nature and in captivity: isomorphism of symbol use and tool use, in *Great Ape Societies*, eds. W. McGrew, L. Marchant & T. Nishida. Cambridge: Cambridge University Press, 196–209.

McGrew, W.C., 1992. *Chimpanzee Material Culture: Implications for Human Evolution*. New York (NY): Cambridge University Press.

Milner, A.D. & M.A. Goodale, 1995. *The Visual Brain in Action*. (Oxford Psychology Series 27.) Oxford: Oxford University Press.

Nimchinsky, E., E. Gillissen, J. Allman, D. Perl, J. Erwin, & P. Hof, 1999. A neuronal morphologic type unique

to humans and great apes. *Proceedings of the National Academy of Sciences of the USA* 96, 5268–73.

Oakley, K.P., 1954. Skill as a human possession, in *A History of Technology: from Early Times to Fall of Ancient Empires*, vol. 1, eds. C. Singer, E.J. Holmyard & A.R. Hall. New York (NY): Oxford University Press, 1–37.

Oswalt, W.H., 1976. *An Anthropological Analysis of Food-Getting Technology*. New York (NY): John Wiley.

Parker, S.T. & K.R. Gibson, 1977. Object manipulation, tool use and sensorimotor intellignece as feeding adaptations in *Cebus* monkeys and great apes. *Journal of Human Evolution* 6, 623–41.

Parker, S.T. & M.L. Mckinney, 1999. *Origins of Intelligence: the Evolution of Cognitive Development in Monkeys, Apes and Humans*. Baltimore (MD): Johns Hopkins University Press.

Pascual-Leone, A., J. Grafman & M. Hallett, 1994. Modulation of cortical motor output maps during development of implicit and explicit knowledge. *Science* 263, 1287–9.

Passingham, R.E., 1975. Changes in the size and organization of the brain in man and his ancestors. *Brain, Behavior and Evolution* 11, 73–90.

Pickering, J., 2001. On revising assumptions. *Ecological Psychology* 13(2), 147–61.

Poti, P., 1996. Spatial aspects of spontaneous object groupings by young chimpanzees (*Pan troglodytes*). *International Journal of Primatology* 17, 101–16.

Potts, R., 1993. Archaeological interpretations of early hominid behaviour and ecology, in *The Origin and Evolution of Humans and Humanness*, ed. D. Tab Rasmussen. Boston (MA): Jones & Bartlett Publisher, 49–74.

Preuss, T.M., H. Qi & J.H. Kaas, 1999. Distinctive compartmental organization of human primary visual cortex. *Proceedings of the National Academy of Sciences of the USA* 96(20), 11,601–6.

Reed, E.S. & B. Bril, 1996. The primacy of action in development, in *Dexterity and its Development*, eds. M.L. Latash & M.T. Turvey. Mahwah (NJ): Lawrence Erlbaum & Associates, 431–52.

Rilling, J.K. & T.R. Insel, 1999. The primate neocortex in comparative perspective using magnetic resonance imaging. *Journal of Human Evolution* 37, 191–223.

Roland, P.E., 1985. Somatosensory detection in man. *Experimental Brain Research, Supplement* 10, 93–110.

Roland, P.E., 1993. *Brain Activation*. New York (NY): Wiley-Liss.

Roland, P.E., B. Larsen, N.A. Lassen & E. Skinhöj, 1980. Supplementary motor area and other cortical areas in the organization of voluntary movements in man. *Journal of Neurophysiology*, 43, 118–36.

Roux, V., B. Bril & G. Dietrich, 1995. Skills and learning difficulties involved in stone knapping. *World Archaeology* 27(1), 63–87.

Sanes, J.N. & J.P. Donoghue, 2000. Plasticity and primary motor cortex. *Annual Review of Neuroscience* 23, 393–415.

Schick, K.D., N. Toth, G. Garufi, E.S. Savage-Rumbaugh, D. Rumbaugh & R. Sevcik, 1999. Continuing investigations into the stone tool-making and tool-using capabilities of a bonobo (*Pan paniscus*). *Journal of*

Archaeological Science 26, 821–32.

Segalowitz, S., 2000. Dynamics and variability of brain activation: searching for neural correlates of skill acquisition. *Brain and Cognition* 42, 163–5.

Semaw, S., 2000. The world's oldest stone artefacts fron Gona, Ethiopia: their implications for understanding stone technology and patterns of human evolution between 2.6–1.5 million years ago. *Journal of Archaeological Science* 27, 1197–214.

Semendeferi, K. & H. Damasio, 2000. The brain and its main anatomical subdivisions in living hominioids using magnetic resonance imaging. *Journal of Human Evolution* 38, 317–32.

Smitsman, A.W., 1997. The development of tool use : changing boundaries between the organism and environment, in *Evolving Explanations of Development: Ecological Approaches to Organism-Environment Systems*, eds. C. Dent-Read & P. Zukow-Goldring. Washington (DC): American Psychological Association, 301–31.

Stout, D., 2002. Skill and cognition in stone tool production: an ethnographic case study from Irian Jaya. *Current Anthropology* 45(3), 693–722.

Stout, D., N. Toth, K. Schick, J. Stout & G. Hutchins, 2000. Stone tool-making and brain activation: Position Emission Tomography (PET) studies. *Journal of Archaeological Science* 27, 1215–23.

Tallon-Baudry, C., O. Bertrand & C. Fischer, 2001. Oscillatory synchrony between human extrastriate areas during visual short-term memory maintenance. *Journal of Neuroscience* 21(RC177), 1–5.

Thelen, E. & L. Smith, 1994. *A Dynamic Systems Approach to the Development of Cognition and Action*. Cambridge (MA): MIT Press/Bradford Books.

Tomasello, M. & J. Call, 1997. *Primate Cognition*. New York (NY): Oxford University Press.

Toth, N., 1985. The Oldowan reassessed: a close look at early stone artifacts. *Journal of Archaeological Science* 12, 101–20.

Ungerleider, L.G. & M. Mishkin, 1982. Two cortical visual systems, in *Analysis of Visual Behaviour*, eds. D.J. Ingle, M.A. Goodale & R.J.W. Mansfield. Cambridge (MA): MIT Press, 549–86.

van Gelder, T., 1998. The dynamical hypothesis in cognitive science. *Behavioral and Brain Sciences* 21, 615–65.

Visalberghi, E., D. Fragaszy & S. Savage-Rumbaugh, 1995. Performance in a tool-using task by common chimpanzees (*Pan troglodytes*), bonobos (*Pan paniscus*), an orangutan (*Pongo pygmaeus*) and capuchin monkeys (*Cebus apella*). *Journal of Comparative Psychology* 109, 52–60.

Washburn, S.L., 1960. Tools and human evolution. *Scientific American* 203(3), 63–75.

Wynn, T. & W.C. McGrew, 1989. An ape's view of the Oldowan. *Man* 24, 383–98.

Chapter 19

Three-dimensional Analysis of Tool-use Gestures in Apraxic Patients

Stéphane Jacobs, Nezha Bennis & Agnès Roby-Brami

Studying tool-use gestures and their impairment in humans might be a relevant way to provide an answer to the question of whether tool use is specific to human beings. In this paper, we introduce the topic of apraxia and of the cerebral control of tool-use gestures. Apraxia is a higher motor disorder that impairs the control of learned/skilled movements, such as tool-use gestures. Our hypothesis is that the impairment of apraxic patients might be due to difficulties in integrating the working point of the tool in the movement. To this end, we first present a non-exhaustive review of the literature on apraxia and the cerebral control of actions and complex gestures. Then, we present several studies on tool use, addressing the question of how the brain concretely controls these particular gestures. A three-dimensional analysis of tool-use gestures was performed in apraxic and non-apraxic subjects. We studied the kinematics of the tool with regard to those of the hand. We observed an impairment in capitalizing on the tool's mechanical properties during the hammering action. This difficulty was shared by both the apraxic and non-apraxic patients. Therefore, this impairment might not be specific to apraxia, but seems to be specific to tool-use gestures in their full context of performance (i.e. with both tool and object). The topic of stone knapping raises a series of questions about the specificity of complex gestures involving tool use in hominins. This question has been considered with regard to evolution, human development, and comparative ethology. A complementary approach is provided by the clinical observation of specific disorders that may affect praxis, i.e. tool use and complex gestures, following cerebral injury in adult humans.

Introduction to apraxia and to the control of tool use
Literature review
In the first part, we present neuropsychological theories on the organization of the control of complex gestures and actions, raised by the study of apraxia.

Then, we introduce some of the teachings concerning hemispheric specialization provided by the study of apraxia.

Apraxia: definition and concepts
Definition: Limb apraxia is a higher-order impairment of motor control, affecting the performance of learned and/or skilled movements. Impairment of gesturing should be termed apraxia only if it cannot be explained by a primary sensory or motor deficit, a language comprehension deficit or dementia (Geschwind 1975). However, apraxia may be superimposed on such primary deficits.

First theoretical work: A first and influential theory on the praxis system's organization was elaborated through Liepmann's work, at the beginning of the twentieth century. Liepmann observed that, in right-handed individuals, *bilateral* limb apraxia typically occurs following left hemisphere damage, particularly damage to the left parietal lobe (Liepmann 1905). Therefore, he proposed that the left hemisphere in right-handers is 'dominant' for praxis control. According to Liepmann's suggestions, the praxis system relies on the storage of some kind of representation of learned movements in the left parietal lobe. These representations contain the spatial and temporal attributes of learned movements.

Based on this hypothesis, Liepmann distinguished between two main types of apraxic disorders: *ideational apraxia* and *ideomotor apraxia*. *Ideational apraxia* is the consequence of damage to the movements' representations. Ideational apraxic patients have lost the knowledge of learned movements. *Ideomotor apraxia* results from the disconnection of the representations of intact movements from the structures responsible for their transformation into specific sequences of motor commands. Thus, ideomotor apraxic patients know *what* to do, but they no longer know *how* to do it.

Current theoretical framework: The legacy of Liepmann's work has been prominent for several decades. However, the classification of apraxic disorders into *ideational* and *ideomotor* apraxia does not account for all the clinical aspects of apraxia. In order to improve our understanding of the praxis system, recent authors have proposed different models, designed to better reflect the reality of apraxic disorders and the diversity of symptom groupings.

First, Roy & Square (1985) postulated that the control of gestures is divided into two subsystems: a *conceptual system*, and a *production system*.

The *conceptual system* is assumed to encompass three types of knowledge related to a given known action: i) knowledge of the sequential organization of the action. This concerns complex goal-directed actions, such as lighting a candle with a match: the subject has to take a match from its box, scratch it, and then apply the flame to the candle's wick; ii) knowledge of the action, whatever the context, where appropriate tools[1] and objects[2] can be incorporated (for example: knowing what the hammering action involves, knowing that a hammer is usually used to perform this action, and knowing what mechanical properties the tool used for hammering must have to allow to perform the action correctly: it has to have a flat surface, and be strong and heavy enough). This kind of knowledge helps solve the mechanical problems encountered when the usual tool is not available, i.e. choosing an appropriate alternative tool, which has the necessary mechanical properties to reach the goal. This implies that the person is able to link the structure of an object to its potential functions, in other words to take advantage of the *affordances* (Gibson 1977) of an object; iii) the knowledge of tools and objects in terms of their functions

and the actions they serve (for example: a hammer is used to drive a nail into a material).

The *production system* is assumed to be responsible for the execution of the action. It would contain sensory motor knowledge of actions, and the perceptual-motor processes required to organize and execute the action.

This model helps interpret apraxic disorders in terms of dysfunctions of the *conceptual* and/or *production system*. Impairment to the *conceptual system* may give rise to different kinds of errors. Damage to the knowledge of actions itself may lead to errors in tasks that require associating a tool with an action (i.e. choosing an appropriate tool to perform an action, or performing an appropriate action with the tool presented (De Renzi 1989; Ochipa *et al.* 1992), or in tasks that do not require actual manipulation of the tool, such as describing the use of a tool, or tasks of 'gesture reception' (i.e. judging whether actions performed by the examiner are correct or not: Bergego *et al.* 1994). Knowledge of the sequential organization of actions also may be altered, leading to inversions or omissions of stages in the sequence to be followed, and thus to difficulties in performing complex sequential actions (Lehmkuhl & Poeck 1981). Finally, the ability to infer potential functions of the structure of a tool may be altered (Goldenberg & Hagmann 1998).

Impairment of the *production system*, on the other hand, would be characterized by a disturbance in the quality of the execution of actions. Despite the deterioration of movement production, the content of the action may remain recognizable and appropriate with regard to the stimulus. In contrast to damage to the conceptual system, tasks that do not require the actual use of a tool, such as a description of an action or 'gesture reception', would be spared. A case of selective impairment of the production system is documented in Rapcsak *et al.* (1995).

Although Roy & Square's model provides further insight into the organization of the praxis system, it still does not account for all the major clinical profiles apraxic patients might show. In particular, patients may show dissociations between elicitation modalities, i.e. impairment or preservation of gesture production depending on the way the gesture is elicited by the examiner (i.e. verbal command, showing a tool, demonstrating a gesture, etc.). Rothi and colleagues (1991; 1997) elaborated a more detailed neuropsychological model in order to better account for major dissociations (see Fig. 19.1). It provides a useful theoretical framework for interpreting apraxic disorders, and for trying to understand the organization of the praxis system.

This model was inspired by the models classically used to study the language system. It postulates the existence of an *action semantic system*, on which the comprehension and production of meaningful gestures rely, and which could be the equivalent of the *conceptual system* in Roy & Square's model (1985). Upstream of this semantic system different entries represent the various sensorial modalities by which a gesture can be elicited in experimental conditions: auditory or visual modality. The stimulus is analyzed *via* structures that make it possible to compare and match it with known stimuli (*input lexicons, object recognition system*). If the stimulus is recognized, the semantic representation of the action/object is activated, the appropriate action is retrieved through an *output action lexicon*, and the motor response is elicited. This pathway can be referred to as the *semantic* or the *lexical pathway*. In addition to this *semantic pathway*, a *non-lexical* or *non-semantic pathway* is assumed to account for the special case of gesture imitation. Indeed, it has been observed in apraxic patients that gesture imitation might be spared when spontaneous gesture production (i.e.

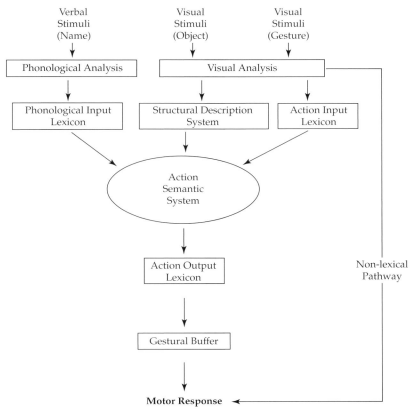

Figure 19.1. *Neuropsychological model of limb praxis, according to Rothi* et al. *(1991; 1997).*

to a verbal command, or in response to seeing an object) is impaired. Then, the model assumes that, if the demonstrated gesture is not recognized by the *action input lexicon*, a meaningless gesture can be directly 'translated' into the appropriate motor commands. In the case of impairment of the semantic system, known meaningful gestures may thus be imitated through this pathway.

The model of Rothi and colleagues (1991; 1997) accounts for the dissociations observed in apraxic patients, between different elicitation modalities of gestures. It also accounts for the dissociations observed between spontaneous gesture production and gesture imitation. (For a comparison of clinical profiles observed in patients and the model's predictions, see Cubelli *et al.* 2000.)

Then, building such theoretical neuropsychological models provides a helpful framework to explore the organization of the praxis system, and to understand the nature of praxic disorders. It should be noted, however, that this kind of model does not take into account the neuroanatomical substrate of the praxis system. Indeed, precise regions of the brain have yet not been identified as being responsible for a

given part of the praxis system, as has been done for the language system, for example. It is known that the left parietal lobe (in right-handers) plays a crucial role in praxis, but patients suffering from lesions in other brain areas, in particular the left frontal lobe, might also show apraxic disorders.

It remains clear, however, that in right-handers apraxia typically occurs following left-brain lesions, which leads us to consider that the left hemisphere of right-handers seems to be specialized for praxis control.

Apraxia and hemispheric specialization
Lateralization of praxis: As mentioned above, the fact that apraxia is typically associated with a lesion to the left hemisphere in right-handers suggests that the control of skilled movements is lateralized, and conducted by the left hemisphere in right-handers. Other evidence supporting this lateralization of praxis has been provided by functional brain-imaging studies, which show specific activation of left parietal and dorso-frontal areas in right-handers when pantomiming tool-use gestures regardless of the hand used (Moll *et al.* 2000; Choi *et al.* 2001).

However, this 'dominance' of the left hemisphere might not be absolute, and the right hemisphere might still be involved in the control of praxis. Indeed, it appears that the dominance of the left hemisphere for the control of gestures relies mainly on the context of execution, and on the cognitive demands of the task (Leiguarda & Marsden 2000).

Using precise analysis of errors committed by stroke patients, with regard to the type of movements performed (i.e. transitive[3] versus intransitive movements), some authors attempted to determine the respective roles of both hemispheres in the control of praxis. Haaland & Flaherty (1984) suggested that intransitive gestures might be equally disturbed in non-apraxic right-brain-damaged patients and in ideomotor apraxic patients. This would mean that the dominance of the left hemisphere might concern more the performance of transitive gestures. Additionally, several studies suggested that this dominance might be more crucial when these gestures are performed outside their natural context, in the clinical or experimental setting (Rapcsak et al. 1993; Schnider et al. 1997).

According to several studies, the left hemisphere might also be in charge of movement sequencing, which may be altered in apraxia. Indeed, left-hemisphere damaged patients are impaired in movement sequencing, both when movement selection does (Roy & Square 1994) and does not involve memory (Harrington & Haaland 1992). It has been proposed that impairment in the sequencing of movement might reflect damage to the process of motor attention, which is involved in the preparation of the next movement to be executed, and which is controlled by the left hemisphere (Rushworth et al. 1997). Impairment in this process in left hemisphere-damaged patients would generate a difficulty in shifting the focus of motor attention from one movement in the sequence to the next, producing errors in movement sequencing.

Therefore, it remains fully accepted that the left hemisphere of right-handers is crucial and responsible for the main features of the movement. However, the right hemisphere is still believed to be involved in more specific aspects of praxic control, such as limb configuration and timing (Hanna-Pladdy et al. 2001).

Links with other hemispheric specialization: One of the most obvious behavioural asymmetries in humans is the predominant right-hand preference. Since the muscles of the upper limb are controlled by the contralateral cerebral hemisphere, this behavioural asymmetry should reflect functional brain asymmetries.

Among other theories (see a brief review in Heilman 1997), it has been proposed that the left cerebral dominance for praxis might be the basis of this hand preference. Thus, right-hand preference might rest on the fact that the right hand, controlled by the contralateral (left) hemisphere, has direct access to the representations of movements when learning or performing a manual skill, unlike the left hand.

However, the link between hand preference and cerebral dominance for praxis is not absolute. Indeed, some studies reported atypical cerebral dominance for praxis in individuals. One showed unilateral (left) apraxia following right-brain damage, suggesting that each hemisphere controlled praxis for the contralateral upper limb in this patient (Heilman et al. 1986). Others showed bilateral apraxia induced by right-brain damage, suggesting that their right hemisphere was dominant for the control of praxis (crossed dominance) (Heilman et al. 1986; Rapcsak et al. 1987; Berthier et al. 1987; Marchetti & Della Sala 1997; Raymer et al. 1999). Thus, although dominance of the left hemisphere for praxis in right-handers seems to be the rule, the degree of lateralization may vary from subject to subject, leading to cases of equipotentiality of the two hemispheres for praxis (De Renzi 1989), or even to cases of crossed dominance (Marchetti & Della Sala 1997).

Another well-known cerebral asymmetry in humans concerns the control of language: in right-handers, the left hemisphere is in charge of the main features of language. It has been thought for a long time that language control was closely related to control of praxis, since apraxia and aphasia (i.e. troubles in language due to central damage) are often associated in stroke patients. However, double dissociation between apraxia and aphasia (i.e. aphasic patients without apraxia, and apraxic patients without aphasia) has been observed. Furthermore, dominance for praxis seems to be more strongly related to hand preference than dominance for language (see a review in Marchetti & Della Sala 1997). Indeed, several studies report right-handed patients showing apraxia but not aphasia following a left hemisphere lesion, and left-handed patients showing the same profile following a right-hemisphere lesion. Thus, in these individuals, the cerebral hemisphere dominant for hand preference, was also dominant for praxis, but not for language. In addition, right-handed patients with a lesion to the corpus callosum, a cerebral structure that allows communication between the two hemispheres, have been described, showing a left dominance for praxis and a right dominance for language (review in Marchetti & Della Sala 1997). Cases showing crossed dominance for praxis but not for language exist, but seem to be much rarer (Marchetti & Della Sala 1997).

It is interesting to note that the possibility of dissociation between the control of praxis and language raises the question of whether these two systems share a common semantic system. This point is still in dispute, and will not be discussed further in this text.

In conclusion, praxis, as well as language, is lateralized in humans. This suggests that one part of the brain evolved during the process of hominization, in order to specifically control the most complex aspects of actions, including tool use. This process is not strictly linked to the control of language. Lateralization for the control of praxis and language in apes and late hominins is a matter that was extensively debated during the workshop. Neuropsychological observations of apraxic patients are obviously relevant to this topic.

How does the brain concretely control tool-use gestures?

The neuropsychological models presented above provide a framework for interpreting apraxic disorders and for trying to understand how the brain controls actions and complex gestures. However, as already mentioned, they do not take into account the underlying mechanisms, in terms of physiology and motor control. Neuropsychological concepts such as *movement representations*, that are supposed to contain sensory and motor information about movements, remain an abstract 'black box'.

The question of how the motor system concretely controls complex gestures, such as tool use, must still be elucidated. It may be addressed in different ways. One way is to identify the cortical brain areas involved in the control of tool use, through electrophysiological methods, for example. Another way is to use biomechanical methods to precisely describe these gestures at the behavioural level, and to try to determine which parameters of the movements might be crucial to the motor system to control. In this section, we briefly present studies illustrating these two ways of studying tool use.

Electrophysiological studies

In the particular case of tool use, the brain has to consider the tool as a means to perform an action. Therefore, the motor system has to integrate the tool as a functional extension of the limb during the movement.

Evidence of this integration of the tool as a functional extension of the limb comes from neurophysiological studies in awake monkeys, using cortical recordings. Iriki *et al.* (1996) recorded the activity of specific neurons of the parietal lobe, called *bimodal neurons*. The particularity of these neurons is that they show two superimposed receptor fields,[4] for visual and somaesthetic stimuli. The receptor fields of the neurons recorded in this study were located on the upper limb (mainly on the hand), or in the peri-personal space, defined as the space within the hand-reaching distance. Iriki and colleagues recorded the activity of these bimodal neurons while monkeys were being trained to use a rake to retrieve food placed out of reach of their hands. After practice, the authors observed a re-mapping of the bimodal neurons' visual receptor fields, that is an extension of the visual receptor field to include the entire tool, or to cover the enlarged accessible space (i.e. tool-reaching distance). This extension was transient and, more interestingly, occurred only if the rake had been used recently to perform an action (i.e. to retrieve food). Indeed, when the monkey simply held the rake, without using it, there was no alteration of the bimodal neurons' receptor fields.

Re-mapping of peri-personal space through tool use has also been described in humans by Berti & Frassinetti (2000) and Farnè & Làdavas (2000). These studies included only right-handed patients suffering from lesions in the right parietal lobe, using their right upper limb. These results show that the human left parietal cortex is involved in integrating the tool as a functional extension of the right upper limb when performing an action using this tool. To our knowledge, this property has not been observed for the right parietal lobe in right-handers, and cannot be tested, for clinical reasons. Therefore, the question of whether this property of left parietal neurons may or may not account for the dominance of the left hemisphere for praxis in right-handers, remains unsolved.

Biomechanical analysis of tool-use gestures

This second approach may be used to precisely describe tool use in healthy participants, in order to try to identify the parameters that might be directly controlled by the cerebral motor system. One prominent contribution to the understanding of the control of complex movement has been provided by the work of Bernstein (1967) (see also Biryukova & Bril 2002 for a review of Bernstein's approach). Bernstein developed and used some of the first biomechanical methods to study human complex movements in the three dimensions of space. In particular, he worked on technical gestures such as hammering. He posited that in this kind of movement, the point controlled by the system might be the head of the hammer, which is the working point[5] of the tool, and not the hand, as might be intuitively believed. Indeed, he observed that during a hammering sequence, the trajectory of the head of the hammer was much more regular in space than that of any part of the limb, suggesting that the most important element for the system and for the efficiency of the action is the trajectory of the working point of the tool.

These methods may also be used to compare the behaviour of patients suffering from central motor troubles to that of healthy participants. Poizner and colleagues developed a method to analyze movements in the three dimensions of space (Poizner *et al.* 1990), and used it to compare the performance of tool-use gestures between apraxic and non-apraxic individuals, both in pantomime (with or without the real tool in the hand) and in actual execution conditions (with the actual tool in the hand, and the target object available). They observed several abnormalities in the execution of gestures in apraxic patients, either for spatial characteristics (movement path, selection of the space plan of movement), or inter-joint coordination during movement. They also observed a disruption of the spatio-temporal coupling usually observed in non-apraxic individuals (Poizner *et al.* 1990; 1995; 1998; Clark *et al.* 1994).

Kinematic analysis of tool use in apraxic patients

Preliminary results
As seen above, biomechanical analysis is helpful in describing normal tool-use gestures, as well as in objectively identifying alterations of these gestures in apraxic individuals.

However, the question of whether these alterations directly identify the parameters controlled by the motor system, or are the consequence of the disruption of the control of another specific parameter, remains unsolved. As posited by Bernstein (1967) in the case of tool-use gestures, the final goal of the motor system might be to control the working point of the tool, which is the actual effector of the action. Therefore, it is conceivable that the main impairment of apraxic individuals might be a difficulty in integrating the working point of the real or imagined (in case of pantomimes) tool into the movement. In this preliminary work, we aimed to study how the tool is integrated in the movement by non-apraxic and apraxic individuals, in order to try to determine whether this parameter is altered in apraxic patients.

Methods
Participants
Seven right-handed apraxic patients were recruited for this study. All had sustained a stroke-induced cerebral injury and were examined at the chronic stage of their disease, at least one month following stroke. Six of them suffered from an extensive cortical lesion of the left hemisphere, including the parietal lobe. The seventh suffered from a lesion affecting the left fronto-temporal area, sparing the left parietal lobe. Five of the apraxic patients also had a right hemiplegia, a typical consequence of damage to left primary motor areas. The

impairment of tool use was objectively assessed by the means of a simple test. Individuals were asked to pantomime the use of seven familiar tools (i.e. tooth brush, screw driver, hammer, pen, scissors, razor, knife), with the actual tool in their left hand. The tool was placed in front of the subject, without any particular orientation. Five qualitative criteria were used for scoring: quality of reaching, quality of handling, tool orientation, tool use, and perseverations. Based on a global evaluation of these five criteria, a score from 0 to 3 was assigned to each of the seven tool-use performances: completely wrong (0), recognizable (1), approximate (1), perfect (3). The maximum score was 21.

Two control groups were also included. The first, referred to as the healthy participants group, was composed of six right-handed healthy participants, with no neurological, psychiatric or orthopaedic history, and age-matched with the apraxic patients. Since apraxic patients were impaired in the use of their right arm, the healthy participants performed all the tasks with their left arm, for the sake of comparison. In addition, they were administered the tool-use test mentioned above, in order to establish reference scores, to which the scores of apraxic patients would be compared.

The second control group, referred to as the control patients group, was composed of four right-handed right hemiparetic individuals, who suffered from a left hemisphere lesion, but did not show apraxia. All had sustained a stroke-induced cerebral injury and were examined at the chronic stage of their disease, at least two months after stroke. Some of them showed aphasia, but their comprehension was sufficient to understand the examiner's instructions. They also performed all tasks with their left arm, and were administered the tool-use test, in order to objectively confirm that they showed no difficulty in using tools. These patients were recruited in order to test the effect of left-brain damage, independently of apraxia.

The demographic and clinical data concerning the participants are summarized in Table 19.1.

Data acquisition
Movements were recorded using a Fastrack Polhemus system, which recorded the position and orientation of two electromagnetic sensors in the three dimensions of space, with respect to a source. The orientation is given by three Euler's angles: azimuth, pitch and roll (Fig. 19.2). Recording frequency was 60 Hz for each sensor. This experimental device is not restricting and thus makes it possible to record gestures that are as natural as possible.

For each task, the movements were recorded with two sensors: one was placed on the left hand of the subject (middle of the third metacarpal bone),

Table 19.1. *Subjects' demographic and clinical data.*

Subject group	Subject	Age	Sex	Lesion location	Time since lesion occurred	Tool-use test score
Apraxic	BON	49	F	left frontal, temporal, parietal and occipital lobes	18 months	6/21
	DAV	31	F	left fronto-parietal region	5 months and 3 weeks	13/21
	GOL	78	F	left parieto-occipital region	5 months	5/21
	MUD	52	F	left temporo-frontal region	3 months and 3 weeks	9/21
	SAL	73	M	left fronto-parietal region and insula	3 months and 2 weeks	2/21
	TOE	47	F	left temporo-parietal region	7 months	16/21
	TOM	65	M	left temporo-parietal region	1 month	10/21
Hemiparetic	BAU	79	M	deep and superficial left middle cerebral artery area	6 months and 3 weeks	18/21
	CHE	67	F	left deep temporo-parietal region	2 months	19/21
	NAR	73	M	subcortical (internal capsule, thalamus)	3 months and 2 weeks	20/21
	WAR	55	M	left middle cerebral artery area	5 months and 2 weeks	19/21
Healthy	AGN	47	F	--	--	20/21
	BER	48	M	--	--	21/21
	MIC	55	F	--	--	19/21
	NEZ	35	F	--	--	19/21
	PIE	73	M	--	--	20/21
	ROL	58	M	--	--	19/21

and a second was placed on the tool itself, in order to record the trajectory of the working point of the tool during the movements, with regard to the hand.

Task description and protocol
The subject sat at a table, with the electromagnetic source of the Fastrack Polhemus system attached to the underside of the table.

For each task, the examiner imposed one way (always the same) of handling the tool. There were two reasons for this: first, it provided a way to standardize the tasks from one subject to another. Second, handling the tool in the proper way helps apraxic patients to perform a more correct movement (Sirigu *et al.* 1995). The position of the participant with regard to the table (shoulder 30 cm from the table) and the position of the object on the table were also standardized, so that all the individuals were in the same posture to perform the movements. The individuals performed each task twice (2×15s) with the *tool* and its target (the *object*).

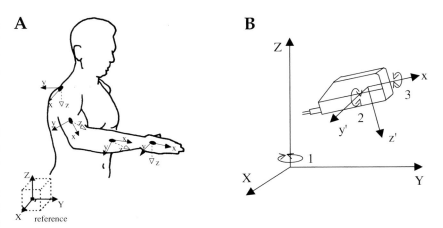

Figure 19.2. *Fastrack Polhemus System: A) layout of four electromagnetic sensors on the upper limb, and orientation in 3-D space with regard to the steady source frame of reference; B) Euler's angles: sketch of a sensor with its own reference x'y'z', in the steady frame of reference of the source (XYZ). The azimuth corresponds to the rotation around the Z-axis of the source frame of reference (1), while pitch and roll are defined as the rotation around y' (2) and x' (3) axis, respectively, of the sensor's frame of reference.*

Each participant performed three tasks, involving a tool and an object:
• *Hammering*: a wooden hammer (length: 22 cm; weight: 65 g) (*tool*) was used to hit a fixed wooden nail (*object*), partially sunk into a piece of wood,

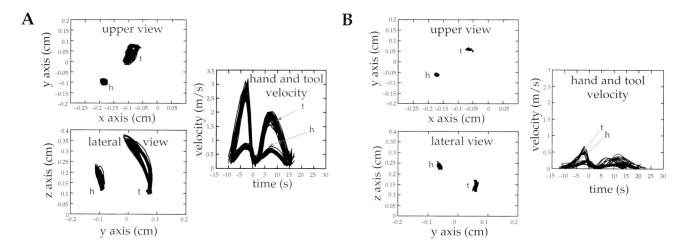

Figure 19.3. *Trajectory and segmented velocity profile of the hand (h) and the working point of the hammer (t). A segment consists of a downward and an upward movement of the hand and the tool: A) healthy subject BER; B) apraxic patient BON. Trajectories are shown from the upper and lateral views on the left side, and velocity profile on the right side. The axes are those of the source steady frame of reference.*

with the instruction to hit it as if to drive it into the table.

- *Turning*: a wooden spoon (length: 31.5 cm; weight: 34 g) (*tool*) was used to pretend to stir a soup in a bowl (*object*). The direction of the rotation was not imposed.
- *Slicing*: a bread knife (length: 29 cm; weight: 100 g) (*tool*) was used to slice a stick of fresh bread (*object*).

Data analysis
The path and tangential velocity of the hand and of the tool's working point were analyzed. Tangential velocity was calculated by derivation.

We considered that the location of the working point was the centre of the percussion surface for the hammer, the extremity of the head for the spoon, and the middle of the cutting edge for the bread knife. The coordinates of this working point were calculated with regard to the magnetic centre of the sensor placed on the tool.

Using velocity profiles, we segmented each movement of *hammering* and *slicing* into elementary movements. The *turning* movement was also segmented, using a rotational velocity profile, computed as a variation velocity of the azimuth signal, which was more regular than the tangential velocity profile. The azimuth variation velocity was calculated through derivation of the azimuth signal.

We analyzed the position and orientation of the hand and of the tool at certain instants of the movements, which will be detailed for each of the three tasks.

All values studied were analyzed using statistical

tests (ANOVA, Tukey-Kramer *post hoc* test ($\alpha = 0.05$), and correlation).

Results
Tool-use test
The scores are presented in Table 19.1. The mean score for healthy participants was 19.67/21±0.816 (standard deviation). Scores inferior to two standard deviations below the healthy participants' mean were considered pathological. The scores of apraxic patients ranged from 2/21 to 16/21 (mean 8.71±4.82 sd). Thus, all apraxic patients showed impairment in tool use. Control patients showed scores comparable to those of the healthy participants (mean 19±0.82 sd, ranging from 18 to 20), confirming they were not impaired in tool use.

Tasks
Hammering will be analyzed in a more detailed way than the two other tasks, since it is the most relevant with regard to the topic addressed at the workshop.

Hammering: One apraxic patient (SAL) was not able to properly perform this task, even when the examiner demonstrated the movement. Data for hammering will be presented for the remaining six apraxic patients.

The sequence of hammering was segmented into single percussion movements, each segment corresponding to a downward and an upward movement of the hand and the hammer. Figure 19.3A shows the upper and lateral views of the trajectories of the hand and the tool's working point, and their velocity profiles, for a healthy subject (BER). Trajectories were regular and superimposed from one segment to the next. The trajectory of the hand was linear, short and vertical. The trajectory of the tool was wider, curved, and less vertical, with a posterior–anterior downward slope. The velocity profile was also regular and superimposed from one segment to another. It was composed of two bell-shaped curves. The first corresponded to the downward movement, leading to the percussion of the hammer on the nail, and the second to the upward movement, preparing the hand and the hammer for the next strike.

The minimum between the two curves represented the time of percussion. The velocity of the tool was much greater than that of the hand (about three times greater). Velocity was also greater during the downward movement than during the upward movement.

The apraxic patients showed two kinds of behaviour for this task: the performance of two of them (MUD and TOM) was like that of the healthy participants, while the others behaved as shown in Figure 19.3B (patient BON). The trajectories of both the hand and the tool were vertical, much shorter than those observed in healthy participants, and there was no difference in amplitude between them. The velocity of the tool and the hand were similar and much lower than those observed for healthy participants. The velocity profiles and trajectories were less regular and superimposed from one segment of the movement to the next.

The main quantitative difference between the healthy participants and the apraxic patients was the ratio of tool velocity to hand velocity. The healthy participants showed a velocity amplification of the head of the hammer compared to the hand, which was much lower, if present, in the apraxic patients. Figure 19.4 represents this speed amplification for each group of individuals, during the downward percussion movement.

Mean velocity amplification was 3.54±0.82 (sd) for the healthy participants, 2.63±1 (sd) for the apraxic patients, and 1.8±0.47 (sd) for the control patients. The group effect was significant (ANOVA: $F_{(29.2)}$ = 10.73; $p = 0.0003$), and the Tukey-Kramer *post-hoc* test revealed a significant difference between the healthy participants and the apraxic patients, and between the healthy participants and the control patients, but not between the apraxic patients and the control patients. Considering the apraxic individuals, as mentioned above, MUD and TOM (the two highest circles) behaved like the healthy participants. The others obtained lower results (DAV, BON) or results comparable to those of an older healthy individual (patient TOE, subject PIE). The control patients were comparable to the apraxic patients; only one of them

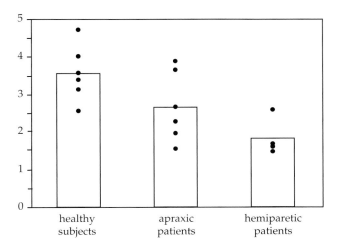

Figure 19.4. *Ratio of tool velocity to hand velocity for each group of subjects. Bar height indicates the group mean performance, while circles correspond to individual subjects.*

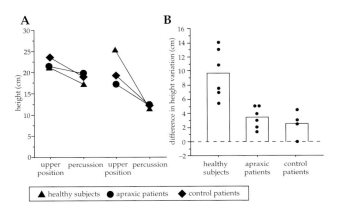

Figure 19.5. *Analysis of the evolution of the height of hand and tool during the downward percussion movement: A) height at initial position and percussion, for hand and tool; B) difference of height variation during the downward percussion movement between the tool and the hand. Bar height indicates the group mean performance, while circles correspond to individual subjects.*

(NAR, the highest circle) performed like the healthy participants.

The variations of the height of the hand and the tool during the downward percussion movement were analyzed to determine the origin of this velocity amplification. Height variation of the hand between the upper position and percussion was comparable for the three groups, whereas it was much greater in the healthy participants for the tool (Fig. 19.5A). The difference in height variation between the tool and the hand during the downward percussion movement re-

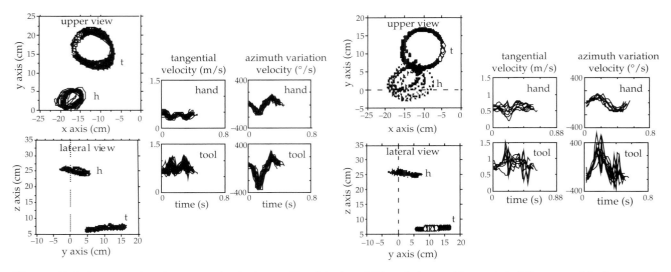

Figure 19.6. *Segmented trajectory and velocity profile of the hand (h) and the working point of the spoon (t). A segment consists of a revolution of the hand and the tool: A) healthy subject BER; B) apraxic patient BON). Trajectories are shown from the upper and lateral views on the left side, and velocity profile on the right side. White circles on the trajectory upper view are segmentation points corresponding to the minimum rotational velocity. The axes are those of the source steady frame of reference.*

flects a rotation of the hand-tool complex in the plane defined by the hand and the tool. This variation was much greater in the healthy participants (9.7 cm±3.8 (sd)) than in the patients (apraxic patients: 3.4 cm±1.5 (sd); control patients: 2.5 cm±1.8 (sd)) (Fig. 19.5B). The group effect was highly significant (ANOVA: F(29.2) = 23; p <0.0001), and the Tukey-Kramer *post-hoc* test revealed a significant difference between the healthy participants and the apraxic patients, and between the healthy participants and the control patients, but not between the apraxic patients and the control patients.

It is clear that this rotation of the hand-tool complex in the hand-tool plane was not the only source of velocity amplification. Indeed, some healthy individuals used an additional rotation of the hand-tool complex in a plane perpendicular to the hand-tool plane. This rotation increased the length of the path covered by the extremity of the hammer, and consequently, its velocity.

Turning: Figure 19.6 presents the upper and lateral views of the trajectories of the hand and the spoon, as well as their velocity profiles. As the velocity profile was quite irregular, even for the healthy participants, we chose to segment this movement using the rotational velocity, which was more regular. Each segment corresponded to a complete lap.

There was no major difference between the three groups. The trajectory of the tool was more regular than that of the hand, well superimposed from one segment to the next. It is noticeable on the lateral view that the spoon's trajectory was more planar in the apraxic patients. This reflects the fact that the apraxic patients used the bowl's surface (side and bottom) as a guide for the spoon, in order to perform the most regular movement as possible. This is probably why the profiles of velocity and azimuth variation velocity were less regular in the apraxic patients.

Further analysis of this movement was difficult, because of the wide range of different strategies used to perform this task, which varied between 'beating eggs' and 'stirring soup', depending on the subject. Thus, detailed quantitative comparison between individuals, even within a group, was not performed.

Slicing: This movement was divided into segments corresponding to a forward and backward movement of the hand and the knife. Figure 19.7 represents the upper and lateral views of the trajectories of the hand and the knife, and their velocity profiles. In the healthy participants, the velocity profile of both the hand and the tool consisted of two bell-shaped curves, the first corresponding to the forward movement and the second to the backward movement. In the apraxic patients, the trajectories were comparable to those observed in the healthy participants. On the other hand, the velocity profiles were much less regular and superimposed from one segment to the next, even though the two phases were distinguishable.

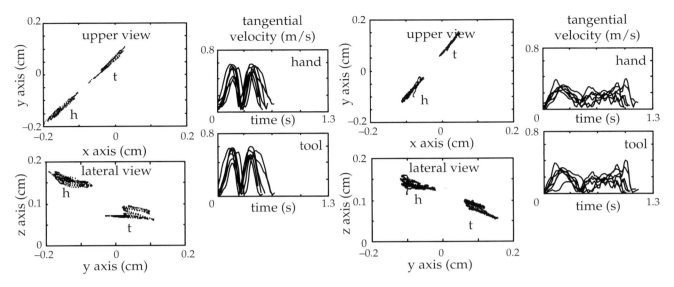

Figure 19.7. *Trajectory and segmented velocity profile of the hand (h) and the working point of the knife (t). A segment consists of a forward and a backward movement of the hand and the tool: A) healthy subject BER; B) apraxic patient BON. Trajectories are shown from the upper and lateral views on the left side, and velocity profile on the right side. The axes are those of the source steady frame of reference.*

Discussion

In this study, we attempted to determine whether the apraxic patients showed specific impairment when actually performing qualitatively correct tool-use gestures in full context.

First, it has to be mentioned that we did not find any significant difference between the apraxic patients and the control patients (i.e. left brain lesioned individuals without apraxia). This suggests that the behaviour observed for the patient groups in this study might not be specific to apraxia, but might rather be a consequence of left brain damage.

The first observation of the patients' behaviour in this study is that their movements were slowed according to the severity of their global impairment. This motor slowing in stroke patients is well-known clinically (Roby-Brami *et al.* 1997). This phenomenon was also present in the oldest healthy participants, but to a much smaller degree.

We observed impairments that are more specific to tool-use actions. First, in the turning and slicing tasks, the patients were able to achieve the goal of the task, and produced movements which were qualitatively comparable to those of the healthy participants. However, the velocity profiles in the patients were much more irregular, particularly for the slicing task. We suggest that this reflects a lack of anticipation of the resistance of the bread, showing difficulty in adapting the action to the mechanical properties of the task. Second, the turning task shows that the patients

used the bowl's inner surface to guide the extremity of the spoon. This observation suggests that they use the mechanical cues and constraints provided by the task in order to perform it as correctly as possible. Then, we suggest that the beneficial role of the context for task execution by apraxic patients depends, at least partly, on the mechanical cues and constraints.

In the hammering task, the healthy participants produced a rotation in space of the hand-tool complex, resulting in velocity amplification for the extremity of the tool compared to the hand. The consequence of this velocity amplification is a gain in energy for the extremity of the hammer, which makes percussion more efficient. It is noticeable that the value of this velocity amplification was quite variable within the group of healthy participants. This variability may be explained by the difference in the levels of expertise between individuals. However, another explanation must be considered: perhaps all individuals did not perform the same goal-directed action. Knowing that the nail would not sink into the table, two behaviours are conceivable: either pretend to drive the nail into the table or just hit the nail as a fixed target. The first action requires percussion that is as efficient as possible, whereas the second does not. The individuals were asked to hit the nail *as if* they wanted to drive it into the table. However, some might have produced the second action, and therefore did not need to produce the velocity gain for the hammer with regard to the hand. However, even though the task might have not been sufficiently standardized, the difference between the healthy participants and the patients remains significant. The velocity amplification observed in the healthy participants was dramatically reduced in most of the apraxic and control patients: they just barely translated the hand-tool complex in space, instead of rotating it, making percussion much less efficient.

This velocity amplification increases the energy of the extremity of the hammer, thereby increasing the efficiency of the percussion. Considering this, we suggest that it might reflect the ability to capitalize on the tool's mechanical properties to produce the most efficient hammering action possible. The fact that it was so dramatically reduced in patients might reflect an inability to integrate the hammer's mechanical properties into the movement.

All these observations together suggest a global difficulty in adapting the action to the mechanical environment of the task, that is in performing a efficient movement: neither the apraxic patients nor the control patients are able to capitalize on the tool's mechanical properties in order to optimize the efficiency of the action (*hammering*), or to anticipate the resistance that the action's recipient might oppose to the tool used (*slicing*). Only in the case of strong mechanical cues and spatial constraints are they capable to perform a correct tool-use gesture (*turning*).

These difficulties, in particular observed in hammering, seem to indicate an impairment that is specific to the execution of tool-use gestures in full context. However, since both the control patients and the apraxic patients suffered from this impairment, it does not seem to be specific to apraxia. The neuroanatomical basis of this difficulty remains unclear, but our observations suggest that it might be related to a lesion of the dorsal area of the left parietal cortex, which is spared in the apraxic patients MUD and TOM, and in the control patient NAR. However, this must be confirmed by further analysis of the correlation between behaviour and lesion location.

Notes

1. Tool: means by which the action is performed.
2. Object: recipient of the action.
3. Movements that involve the use of a tool (transitive) versus those that do not (intransitive).
4. The receptor field of a neuron corresponds to the region of space in which an appropriate sensorial stimulus induces a response from the neuron.
5. The working point of a tool represents the actual end-effector of the action. In the case of a hammer, it would be the centre of the percussion face of the head of the hammer (not its centre of gravity).

Acknowledgements

We thank Professor B. Bussel and M. Combeaud, who helped recruit patients and manage experiments. S. Jacobs holds a grant from the French Ministry of Research (Cognitique). A. Roby-Brami is supported by INSERM. This work was supported by a grant from the French Ministère délégué à la recherche et aux nouvelles Technologie (ACI Cognitique L103).

References

Bergego, C., P. Pradat-Diehl, C. Taillefer & H. Migeot, 1994. Evaluation et rééducation de l'apraxie d'utilisation des objets, in *L'apraxie*. Marseille: Solal, 214–23.

Bernstein, N., 1967. *The Coordination and Regulation of Movements*. Oxford: Pergamon.

Berthier, M., S. Starkstein & R. Leiguarda, 1987. Behavioral effects of damage to the right insula and surrounding regions. *Cortex* 23(4), 668–73.

Berti, A. & F. Frassinetti, 2000. When far becomes near: remapping of space by tool use. *Journal of Cognitive Neuroscience* 12(3), 415–20.

Biryukova, L. & B. Bril, 2002. Bernstein et le geste technique. *Technologies, Idéologies, Pratiques: Revue d'Anthropologie des Connaissances* 14(2), 49–68.

Choi, S.H., D.L. Na, E. Kang, K.M. Lee, S.W. Lee & D.G. Na, 2001. Functional magnetic resonance imaging during pantomiming tool-use gestures. *Experimental Brain Research* 139(3), 311–17.

Clark, M., A. Merians, A. Kothari, H. Poizner, B. Macauley, L. Rothi & K. Heilman, 1994. Spatial planning deficits in limb apraxia. *Brain* 117, 1093–106.

Cubelli, R., C. Marchetti, G. Boscolo & S. Della Sala, 2000. Cognition in action: testing a model of limb apraxia. *Brain and Cognition* 44(2), 144–65.

De Renzi, E., 1989. Apraxia, in *Handbook of Neuropsychology*, vol. 2, eds. F. Boller & J. Grafman. Amsterdam: Elsevier, 245–63.

Farne, A. & E. Lèdavas, 2000. Dynamic size-change of hand peripersonal space following tool use. *Neuroreport* 11(8), 1645–9.

Geschwind, N., 1975. The apraxias: neural mechanisms of disorders of learned movement. *American Scientist* 63(2),188–95.

Gibson, J.J., 1977. The theory of affordance, in *Perceiving, Acting, and Knowing*, eds. R.E. Shaw & J. Bransford. Hillsdale (NJ): Lawrence Erlbaum Associates, 67–82.

Goldenberg, G. & S. Hagmann, 1998. Tool use and mechanical problem solving in apraxia. *Neuropsychologia* 36(7), 581–9.

Haaland, K. & D. Flaherty, 1984. The different types of limb apraxia errors made by patients with left vs. right hemisphere damage. *Brain and Cognition* 3, 370–84.

Hanna-Pladdy, B., S.K. Daniels, M.A. Fieselman, K. Thompson, J.J. Vasterling, K.M. Heilman & A.L. Foundas, 2001. Praxis lateralization: errors in right and left hemisphere stroke. *Cortex* 37(2), 219–30.

Harrington, D.L. & K.Y. Haaland, 1992. Motor sequencing

with left hemisphere damage. Are some cognitive deficits specific to limb apraxia? *Brain* 115(3), 857–74.

Heilman, K.M., 1997. Handedness, in *Apraxia: the Neuropsychology of Action*, eds. L.J.G. Rothi & K.M. Heilman. Erlbaum: Taylor & Francis, 19–24.

Heilman, K.M., L.G. Rothi, L. Mack, T. Feinberg & R.T. Watson, 1986. Apraxia after a superior parietal lesion. *Cortex* 22(1), 141–50.

Iriki, A., M. Tanaka & Y. Iwamura, 1996. Coding of modified body schema during tool use by macaque postcentral neurones. *Neuroreport* 7(14), 2325–30.

Lehmkuhl, G. & K. Poeck, 1981. A disturbance in the conceptual organization of actions in patients with ideational apraxia. *Cortex* 17, 153–8.

Leiguarda, R. & C. Marsden, 2000. Limb apraxias: higher-order disorders of sensorimotor integration. *Brain* 123(5), 860–79.

Liepmann, H., 1905. Die linke Hemisphare und das Handeln. *Münchener Medizinische Wochenschrift*, 48–9.

Marchetti, C. & S. Della Sala, 1997. On crossed apraxia. Description of a right-handed apraxic patient with right supplementary motor area damage. *Cortex* 33(2), 341–54.

Moll, J., R. de Oliveira-Souza, L.J. Passman, F.C. Cunha, F. Souza-Lima & P.A. Andreiuolo, 2000. Functional MRI correlates of real and imagined tool-use pantomimes. *Neurology* 54(6), 1331–6.

Ochipa, C., L. Rothi & K. Heilman, 1992. Conceptual apraxia in Alzheimer's disease. *Brain* 115, 1061–71.

Poizner, H., L. Mack, M. Verfaellie, L. Rothi & K. Heilman, 1990. Three-dimensional computergraphic analysis of apraxia. *Brain* 113, 85–101.

Poizner, H., M. Clark, A. Merians, B. Macauley, L. Rothi & K. Heilman, 1995. Joint coordination deficits in limb apraxia. *Brain* 118, 227–42.

Poizner, H., A. Merians, M. Clark, B. Macauley, L. Rothi & K. Heilman, 1998. Left hemispheric specialization for learned, skilled, and purposeful action. *Neuropsychology* 12(2), 163–82.

Rapcsak, S.Z., L.J. Gonzalez Rothi & K.M. Heilman, 1987.

Apraxia in a patient with atypical cerebral dominance. *Brain and Cognition* 6(4), 450–63.

Rapcsak, S.Z., C. Ochipa, P.M. Beeson & A.B. Rubens, 1993. Praxis and the right hemisphere. *Brain and Cognition* 23(2), 181–202.

Rapcsak, S.Z., C. Ochipa, K.C. Anderson & H. Poizner, 1995. Progressive ideomotor apraxia: evidence for a selective impairment of the action production system. *Brain and Cognition* 27(2), 213–36.

Raymer, A.M., A.S. Merians, J.C. Adair, R.L. Schwartz, D.J. Williamson, L.J. Rothi, H. Poizner & K.M. Heilman, 1999. Crossed apraxia: implications for handedness. *Cortex* 35(2), 183–99.

Roby-Brami, A., S. Fuchs, M. Mokhtari & B. Bussel, 1997. Reaching and grasping strategies in hemiparetic patients. *Motor Control* 1, 72–91.

Rothi, L., C. Ochipa & K. Heilman, 1991. A cognitive neuropsychological model of limb praxis. *Cognitive Neuropsychology* 8(6), 443–58.

Rothi, L., C. Ochipa & K.M. Heilman, 1997. A cognitive neuropsychological model of limb praxis, in *Apraxia: the Neuropsychology of Action*, eds. L. Rothi & K.M. Heilman. Erlbaum: Taylor & Francis, 29–49.

Roy, E.A. & P. Square, 1985. Common considerations in the studies on limb, verbal and oral apraxia, in *Neuropsychological Studies of Apraxia and Related Disorders*, ed. E. Roy. Amsterdam: North Holland, 111–62.

Roy, E. & P. Square, 1994. Neuropsychology of movement sequencing disorders and apraxia, in *Neuropsychology*, ed. D. Zaidel. San Diego (CA): Academic Press, 183–218.

Rushworth, M.F., P.D. Nixon, S. Renowden, D.T. Wade & R.E. Passingham, 1997. The left parietal cortex and motor attention. *Neuropsychologia* 35(9), 1261–73.

Schnider, A., R.E. Hanlon, D.N. Alexander & D.F. Benson, 1997. Ideomotor apraxia: behavioral dimensions and neuroanatomical basis. *Brain and Language* 58(1), 125–36.

Sirigu, A., L. Cohen, J.R. Duhamel, B. Pillon, B. Dubois & Y. Agid, 1995. A selective impairment of hand posture for object utilization in apraxia. *Cortex* 31(1), 41–55.

Part III

'Actualizing' Conditions for Innovation in Stone Knapping

Chapter 20

Transfer According to the Means in Human Infants: the Secret to Generative Tool-use?

Emily W. Bushnell, Jason Sidman & Amy E. Brugger

This paper focuses on the cognitive skills and abilities involved in tool using and tool making, and an analogy is drawn between the behaviour of developing infants and scenarios which may have occurred among hominins 2–3 million years ago. It begins with a review of the developmental and comparative literature on several cognitive capacities central to making and using tools, including the ability to project into the future, the ability to differentiate and relate means to ends, and the ability to imitate object-directed skills. Original research with human infants is presented which builds on this prior literature and establishes that infants attend to the model's causal actions in demonstrations of means–ends behaviours and furthermore are able to transfer these actions learned by imitation to novel circumstances. An important implication of these results is that such transfer increases the probability of discovering useful new means–ends behaviours even without full causal understanding or 'insight'. Thus transfer of the means may be a significant source for invention of new behaviours during an intermediate phase of causal cognition. The paper closes with the speculation that a parallel process of transfer according to the means could also have operated in evolutionary time and been a part of how human technology progressed from the original case of stone knapping.

Making and using tools requires a unique confluence of anatomical features, neuro-motor skills, intellectual capacities, and social and environmental circumstances. Many of these prerequisites are addressed in the various contributions to this volume, which targets the prototypical instance of tool use and manufacture, knapping stone. As psychologists, our focus and expertise is on the cognitive skills and abilities demanded by such activities. For example, to make and use even the simplest kind of tool requires at least intention, memory, learning, foresight, attention, and sequencing (Schick & Toth 1993; Wynn & McGrew 1989). More advanced technologies may additionally require mental imagery, categorization, decision-making, evaluation, and spatial concepts such as symmetry and balance (Corballis 1999). Any early hominin or proto-human who systematically made and used stone tools must therefore have possessed these mental faculties, and thus archaeological finds of stone tools can serve as benchmarks helping to characterize the evolution of intelligence.

The cognitive prerequisites for using tools have also been emphasized in analyses of child development. The logic, as for the hominin above, is that in order to effectively exploit objects in particular ways, a child must possess the cognitive abilities entailed. Therefore, the development of tool using in individuals will be paced by cognitive development, among other things, and conversely what children are able to do with objects can serve to diagnose their level of cognitive maturity. This reasoning is the basis for several standard assessments of infant growth and development, for example the Uzgiris-Hunt Ordinal Scales of Psychological Development (Uzgiris & Hunt 1975) and the Bayley Scales of Infant Development (Bayley 1969).

The difference between the early hominin and the child, of course, is that the child is here and now and can be confronted empirically with various object tasks and situations. Suites and sequences of abilities with objects can be firmly established and conditions which promote these can be identified. These developmental findings in turn may be useful to scientists working to define how technologies such as flint knapping first arose in humans and why they exist only in humans. While we do not think that ontogeny necessarily recapitulates phylogeny, the cognitive problems posed by acquiring and executing object-directed skills and the potential set of solutions to these challenges are similar in many respects for children and early hominins. Like infants in particular, early hominins presumably did not have access to symbolic instructional media (i.e. language, diagrams, etc.), but they did operate in a rich social milieu and in an environment 'cluttered' with objects. Furthermore, given that the 'final state' for both the developing child and the evolving hominin is the same, namely the cognitively-mature modern human, there are only so many intermediate states of cognition that are logically possible. Thus, those which can be empirically documented in the case of the developing child are worth considering as perhaps applicable to the evolving hominin as well.

Drawing out this analogy between the cognitive status of developing infants and scenarios which may have occurred among hominins 2–3 million years ago is our general strategy in this chapter. We will first briefly review the infant and comparative literature on several cognitive capacities central to making and using tools, including the ability to project into the future, the ability to differentiate and relate means to ends, and the ability to imitate object-directed skills. We will then present some of our own research with infants which builds on this prior literature and examines the phenomenon of generalization or 'transfer' of imitated actions. Finally, we will elaborate on an important implication of the results of our research, and outline how a parallel process might conceivably have operated in evolutionary time. Our goals are to advance what is known about infants' object-directed skills and the development of tool use, and with that knowledge to provoke healthy speculation about how and why human technology may have realized and then progressed beyond the original case of stone knapping.

Cognitive capacities central to making and using tools

Future-oriented thinking

We begin by noting that both tool using and tool making are clearly means–ends behaviours. In each case, an action or sequence of actions is performed at one time in order to bring about a particular product or event moments, hours, or even days later. An important cognitive component of means–ends behaviour is future-oriented thinking or 'foresight', the ability to run time forward mentally and 'see' an end state before it has occurred. Indeed, looking ahead in the mind to a particular end state, that is needing it or wanting it, may be thought of as the stimulus which prompts performing the initial action or means in the first place. In some sense, any operant behaviour emitted to obtain a reinforcement involves future-oriented thinking, but with tool using and tool making, the ends do not necessarily follow the means so immediately or directly; large spans of time and numerous other events may intervene. With early stone knapping, for example, a certain type of strike (at a given angle, with a given force, etc.) may have been prompted by the desire to have a certain edge just moments later, but selecting the core with an eye to producing that same edge may have occurred at a remote site and thus hours or more in advance. Similarly, producing the edge and perhaps carrying it around would have been predicated on the intention or need to use it at some point in the future well beyond the next instant, perhaps even at some indeterminate point in the future.

This parameter of the span of time to which one can look ahead has been emphasized by both anthropologists and developmental psychologists. For example, Boesch & Boesch (1983) observed that chimpanzees in the Taï forest carry nuts and stones with which to crack them open to anvil sites as far as 500 metres away and often out of sight from the starting place. Because transport distance equates to travel time, this behaviour implies a certain ability to look ahead to a future ends or goal-state. Meanwhile, Visalberghi (1993) found that capuchin monkeys did not traverse even to an adjacent room to fetch a tool for obtaining food at the starting place, implying a rather short time span for planning. In comparison, Wynn & McGrew (1989) noted that the makers/users of Oldowan tools carried stone to work-sites as far as 6 kilometres away from its source, implying perhaps a longer time span of prospective thinking than the chimpanzees show. Of course there are other factors involved in these behaviours as well, such as spatial-memory capacities, the natural ecology in which different species live, the availability of alternative food sources, and so forth, but if we set these aside or presume them constant for a moment, a pattern seems to emerge. Namely, the closer a primate species is to modern-day humans, evolutionarily speaking, the longer the span of future-oriented thinking it shows. The makers/users of Odowan tools could apparently plan further ahead than chimpanzees, who in turn can evidently plan further ahead than capuchins.

The same pattern of an expanding time frame for planning is observed over the course of early development. For example, at the simplest level of thinking ahead over a matter of a few seconds, Canfield & Haith (1991) found that 3-month-old infants learned to anticipate the reappearance of visual stimuli over a greater number of steps and thus a longer time frame than 2-month-olds could anticipate. Similarly, with a more complicated task involving manual skills, Willatts (1999) found that 7-month-olds were able to intentionally pull on a cloth in order to retrieve a toy resting on it, provided the toy was at the near end of the cloth and thus could be retrieved immediately with the initial pulling act. However, 8-month-olds intentionally pulled on the cloth even when the toy was at the far end and thus required several tugs and more time to reel in. With a related pull-to-obtain task, Boudreau & Bushnell (2000) likewise documented that older infants can 'look ahead' through several steps and over a time-frame of about 10 seconds as they commenced a manual task.

Perhaps the clearest demonstration of the developmental increase in time span which can be accommodated between means and ends comes from some clever work by McCarty *et al.* (1999). These researchers examined how infants approached a spoon loaded with food which was placed at different orientations in front of them. They observed that with older and older infants, adjustments in gripping the spoon to successfully get food in the mouth were made progressively earlier and earlier in the sequence of actions. The youngest infants, 9-month-olds, frequently grasped the bowl of the spoon and only switched to grasp the handle after they had put the handle in the mouth and received no food. Fourteen-month-olds adjusted their grips 'mid-stream'; they grasped the spoon's handle but sometimes with the thumb pointed away from the bowl and then shifted the spoon to the other hand to achieve the optimal grip as they moved the spoon to the mouth. Finally, 19-month-olds selected which hand to use or whether to grasp the handle over-handed or under-handed right at the start of the trial, so that they could put the spoon in the mouth smoothly from there, with no further adjustments. In short, McCarty *et al.*'s results showed that with their initial approach to grasping the spoon, older infants planned further ahead toward the aim of feeding themselves than younger infants.

Thus in the context of several different tasks — anticipatory looking, pulling one thing in to obtain another, and using a spoon to transport food — developmental psychologists have found that older infants were able to look ahead across more action steps, greater distances, and longer time intervals than

younger infants. This developmental pattern parallels the one observed earlier within primate and hominin evolution. In both cases, as the human species evolved and also as the human infant develops, the cognitive ability to run time forward from an active means to a desired ends seems to expand, and individuals can look ahead farther and farther into the future to regulate concurrent manual behaviour. Similar changes in brain anatomy and functioning might be responsible for these parallel improvements in future-oriented thinking, or it is also possible that altogether different factors mediate the evolutionary and developmental trends. Either way, though, the types of tool-using and tool-making skills logically possible at particular values of this looking-ahead parameter would be similarly constrained. Thus, as we argued earlier, it may be instructive for understanding the underpinnings of seminal behaviours such as stone knapping to examine the tool-using and object-manipulation abilities of infants.

Understanding physical causality
Comparative and evolutionary considerations
Even more than the span of time over which ends can be seen from their means, anthropologists and developmentalists have emphasized appreciating the *connection* between means and their ends as a critical cognitive component for object-directed skills and tool using. As Tomasello (1999) clarifies, anticipating what end state will follow a particular means is not the same as knowing 'why' that particular means leads to that end state, that is, appreciating the causal forces and spatial relationships which ensure that it will be so. Although the former can be learned from repeated experiences, the latter may facilitate faster learning, the repair of failed attempts, the construction of new or substitute means in the absence of the initial one, and so on.

Accordingly, anthropologists have focused on causal understanding as an important distinction between species which use tools flexibly and frequently and those which use tools rigidly, in narrow contexts, and in highly-rehearsed ways. For example, although they readily learn to do so in captivity (see Cummins-Sebree & Fragaszy this volume), capuchin monkeys rarely use tools in the wild, whereas chimpanzees use a variety of tools and some 15 per cent of their food processing in the wild involves tool use (Matsuzawa 1994). Laboratory research also supports this cognitive distinction between apes and monkeys. In their extensive review of the experimental literature on primates and tool using, Tomasello & Call (1997, 95) concluded that 'apes may have a deeper causal understanding of tool-use tasks than monkeys'. Byrne (1995, 98) likewise concluded that 'all the great apes, but probably no other animals, can comprehend the simple cause-and-effect relationships that govern the use of objects to solve problems'. Most telling in Byrne's analysis is the variety of errors that capuchins made when confronted with novel variations on a task they had mastered. They used sticks which were too short and too thick to poke a peanut out of a transparent tube, for example, whereas chimpanzees solved these extraction tasks insightfully (without trial-and-error). Importantly, the solutions to these tasks required the actor to *create* a certain spatial relationship; with pull-to-obtain problems where the presence or absence of the necessary spatial support is visible, capuchins as well as chimpanzees performed successfully. Thus the ability to mentally represent relations between objects may be a critical difference between monkeys and apes so far as causal understanding is concerned.

When multiple relations must be represented, however, even apes seem to be challenged. Byrne (1995) points out that despite the range of tools they use in the wild, chimps do not make any tools by adding one item to another (as a shaped stone and a stick are added to make a spear, for instance). Likewise, although they do modify objects to use as tools, they do not make any tools which are used for making another tool (as humans make knifes in order to sharpen digging sticks, for example). Similarly, Tomasello & Call (1997, 95) note that when a trap component is added to the tube-extraction task mentioned earlier, thus requiring an additional relation to be represented, 'apes are far from perfect, (and) require many trials for learning in some variations'. Furthermore, once they learn the appropriate strategy for avoiding the trap, they persist in using it even when the spatial arrangement is changed and no longer demands it. Mature modern humans solve all of these tasks, of course (they invented them!), and so the ability to represent not just object relations but sequences and hierarchies of object relations may be a critical difference between apes and humans with regard to causal understanding.

Thus, as with the time-span for prospective thinking, we again see a sort of scaling from monkey to chimpanzee to human, so far as causal understanding goes. Monkeys (in particular capuchins) do not seem to appreciate mechanical, cause-and-effect relations, except perhaps when they are transparent in the visible layout of objects. Apes (in particular chimpanzees) may appreciate simple causal relations, but are not able to manage sequential or embedded strings of them, which humans in turn can master. Where on this rough continuum the earliest stone knappers might lie is something of an open question. Obviously, cloth-pulling and tube-extraction tasks cannot

be posed to extinct species, and there is disagreement in the literature concerning the level of understanding with which the earliest Oldowan artefacts were made. Some have pointed to the lack of symmetry and retouching in these tools as an indication that there was no real intended design; thus Wynn & McGrew (1989) and Toth (1985) argue that Oldowan tools require no more than the ape 'grade' of intelligence. On the basis of more recent evidence, however, others argue that even Oldowan tools betray multi-step planning and complex intentionality in their making (see Roche this volume). Still others have questioned whether the heralded Acheulean handaxe really represents any cognitive advance over the earlier Oldowan tools (see Davidson & Noble 1993). Without the opportunity to observe these ancient artefacts in the making, these issues may be very difficult to resolve. However, it seems fair to say that at some point in evolutionary time between now and the days of our common ancestor with apes, there was a level of causal understanding intermediate to those of modern chimpanzees and modern humans.

Understanding physical causality: developmental considerations
As a window on what such an intermediate level of causal understanding might be, we now turn to the field of child development, where an incremental achievement of causal understanding has also been examined and outlined. Indeed, many of the tasks used in the primate studies cited above were employed first to test babies and children. The seminal work here is that of the pre-eminent developmental psychologist, Jean Piaget (1952; 1954), who thoroughly dissected the means–ends abilities of infants and charted their emergence and development through careful observations of his own three children during the first two years of life. According to Piaget, an important transition occurs at about 8 months of age, when infants begin to differentiate the means from the ends in their causal activities with objects. Prior to this transition, these activities are experienced as unanalyzed and unordered wholes. Seeing the effect (e.g. instigated by someone else) is as likely to provoke the infant to act as the infant's action is to create the effect, in a phenomenon Piaget labelled the secondary circular reaction. In novel situations, infants' haphazard behaviour may fortuitously produce effects, and they may then experience a sense of efficacy and systematically repeat the precipitating actions. However, Piaget argued that even while they deliberately repeat effective actions, young infants are unaware of the particular spatial and temporal relations which mediate between their actions and an effect. Thus their sense of

causal agency is largely 'phenomenalistic' or magical, and their efforts to recreate effects may often prove to be irrational and ineffective. A true understanding of causality, according to Piaget, is implied only when the infant intentionally acts in a deliberate fashion so as to reliably and efficiently obtain a desired outcome. This level of understanding is betrayed by premeditated actions before an effect has been observed, for example, and by systematic searching for a cause upon observing an unprompted effect.

The developmental difference described by Piaget (1952; 1954) and his emphasis on intentionality or prior expectation are supported by the results of Willatts's (1999) empirical work with cloth-pulling, mentioned earlier in the context of prospective thinking. In addition to the distance effects discussed there, Willatts also found that although 6-month-olds and 8-month-olds were equally likely to retrieve a toy by pulling in the cloth it was on, their behaviour was qualitatively different. Six-month-olds' retrieval of the toy was often an unexpected 'side-effect' of grasping the cloth to play with it (the cloth). In contrast to 8-month-olds, they did not maintain fixation on the toy as they pulled the cloth, and they showed longer time intervals between contacting the cloth and contacting the toy, filling this time with shaking the cloth, mouthing it, etc. before 'noticing' the now within-reach toy and grasping for it. Even more telling, 6-month-olds were just as likely to pull on a cloth when there was no toy on it as when there was a toy, whereas 8-month-olds pulled the cloth more frequently when a toy was there. For the older infants, pulling on the cloth was a deliberate means to an end (obtaining the toy), but for the younger infants pulling on the cloth was a behaviour in and of itself, which then fortuitously brought a toy within reach if one happened to be there.

Thus understanding the means to an end as such in effective activities is a developmental achievement that unfolds during infancy in humans. Moreover, the emergence of causal understanding is not an all-or-none phenomenon, but is affected by the same spatial transparency and embedding factors which are relevant in analyses of nonhuman primates' causal understanding. Both Bates et al. (1980) and also van Leeuwen et al. (1994) found that infants were more likely to systematically use various tools to obtain a goal toy if the tool was presented in spatial contact with the toy; only older children systematically used the tools when they were not initially in contact with the toy and the children had to generate this contact themselves. Similarly, both van Leeuwen et al. (1994) and Bushnell & Boudreau (1998) have discussed the parameter of 'complexity' in children's tool use and the understanding which mediates it. Bushnell

& Boudreau, for example, discuss several instances where children can successfully control each component of a tool-using task, but are unable to perform effectively when these must be nested together. For the purpose of comparing both across-species and across-age (within humans) then, causal understanding appears to be very domain-specific; an individual can 'have' it with regard to one kind or level of problem and not with regard to others.

For any particular means–ends task, though, an important developmental question (and evolutionary one too, we suppose) is not so much when the transition to causal understanding occurs for an individual or a species, but how it occurs, that is, what drives the change that takes place. Piaget argued that, somewhat ironically, it is the very haphazard, unintentional behaviours of the pre-causal infant which blossom into goal-directed actions that qualify as genuine means to ends on the part of older infants. Through acting frequently and variably with objects, and attending to the consequences of these activities, infants become sensitive to the relevant spatial and temporal contingencies and internalize them as causal knowledge. Thus acting comes first; within any given task domain, infants initially behave so as to cause effects without knowing how or why their actions do so.

In contrast to Piaget, others maintain that infants understand aspects of causality well before they act either haphazardly or systematically in means–ends tasks. For instance, some researchers argue that very young infants understand principles of spatial support (Baillargeon 1994) and human agency (Leslie 1984; Woodward 1998); although they do not act on this knowledge, they evidence it by looking longer at visual displays which violate the principles in question. These researchers suggest that casual understanding is either present innately or derived very early in life through applying general learning mechanisms to numerous observations of everyday events and other people's actions on objects. Young infants perform unsystematically in tasks such as Willatt's cloth pulling because of limitations on attention, inabilities to inhibit pre-potent behaviours, and difficulties coordinating their knowledge with motor behaviour. As soon as these ancillary problems are resolved, infants' behaviour in means-ends tasks shows itself to be intentional and predicated on causal understanding which was present all along.

Although the debate just outlined continues, two recent direct comparisons of infants' performance on means–ends tasks and their independently-assessed understanding of the same tasks seem to support Piaget's original suggestion that successful acting precedes causal understanding. Schlesinger & Langer

(1999) presented some infants with several different object-retrieval tasks similar to those employed by Willatts (1999). Other groups of infants were shown visual displays of 'possible' and 'impossible' toy retrievals in the same task contexts. The researchers found that infants were able to perform each task effectively at a younger age than that at which they showed comprehension of the corresponding visual displays. For instance, as in Willatt's studies, 8-month-olds systematically pulled on a cloth to retrieve a toy when the toy was on the cloth but not when it was beside it. However, they did not also look longer at displays where a toy came forward even though it was not in spatial contact with the cloth; only 12-month-olds showed a reaction to these 'impossible' displays. The authors concluded from results such as this that within each task domain, causal action precedes causal 'perception' or understanding.

Woodward & Sommerville (2002) conducted a similar study but employed a within-subject design. They tested the same individual infants in both a cloth-pulling task and a looking paradigm designed to assess their interpretation of someone else's cloth-pulling. The results showed that only those infants who intentionally pulled cloths to retrieve toys themselves seemed to recognize the toy as the actor's goal in the looking paradigm. Conversely, infants whose performance in the cloth-pulling task was disorganized and not systematically related to the toy's position seemed to interpret the cloth as the actor's goal in the looking paradigm. These results along with those of Schlesinger & Langer (1999) suggest that infants do not understanding why pulling a cloth makes the toy obtainable, that is, they do not appreciate the spatial relation between the cloth and the toy, until after they are able to effectively pull cloths to obtain toys! Thus in development, causal understanding may be formulated in a *post hoc* fashion, derived from a kind of reflection upon or 'noticing' the outcomes of one's successful behaviours.

Understanding physical causality: a conundrum
The developmental sequence just discussed highlights a subtle but important distinction between 'intentionally' in the lay sense and 'with intentionality' in the stricter Piagetian sense. To whit, one can perform an action (the means) intentionally, that is purposefully and with every expectation that a certain result (the ends) will ensue, but still without Piaget's intentionality or true understanding of the mechanical relations which link the means to the ends. This is the intermediate position of the infants observed by Schlesinger and Langer (1999) and Woodward & Sommerville (2002), where the infants could perform effectively on

certain problems but could not yet perceive effective solutions.

It is possible that this same seemingly backwards sequencing of causal understanding and performing means–ends behaviours might also apply across species or evolutionarily. Both Byrne (1999) and Tomasello (1999), for instance, conclude in their reviews of the primate literature that although chimpanzees certainly use tools purposefully and effectively (intentionally), they may not understand (have intentionality) the dynamic, physical relations among the objects in their instances of tool use. This failure to understand would prohibit chimpanzees from readily inventing new tools and uses for them, and indeed technological advances are slow to accumulate in primate cultures and require multiple trials to learn in the lab. Along these lines, Byrne (1995) has qualified the quintessential instance of causal understanding on the part of non-human primates, and suggests that Kohler's chimpanzee Sultan may have played at joining sticks together before the famous occasion on which he did so to obtain out-of-reach bananas. That is, Sultan's intelligent behaviour may have been a case of noticing after the fact of performing rather than genuine 'insight' or performing *de novo* predicated on causal understanding. Similarly, some have characterized the earliest tool making of hominins as '*ad hoc*' or executed effectively but without full understanding of the spatial and mechanical factors involved (Wynn & McGrew 1989; Mithen 1996), although this interpretation is vigorously disputed by others (Pelegrin this volume) and would be difficult to establish (or not) with only artefacts as evidence.

In any event, the possibility that an infant or an ape or even an early hominin might systematically and purposefully engage in a means–ends behaviour without understanding why or how it works seems paradoxical. Why would they do so? This state of affairs — observed in the case of infants, suspected in the case of apes, and posed here for the sake of argument in the case of early hominins — demands that *something other than* causal understanding must sustain and support the initial instances of systematic means–ends behaviour. If understanding comes from noticing and reflecting after doing, then the doing must be predicated on other grounds. What could such other grounds be?

One mechanism which could maintain effective behaviour without cause–effect understanding is operant conditioning. However, this is only plausible if the effective action or 'means' (unknown as such) is likely to occur spontaneously and then also 'happens' to lead to a positive outcome relatively frequently. These conditions are readily met for certain support relations. For example, grasping a cloth just to mouth or attain it will inevitably bring anything resting on the cloth closer and perhaps within reach for the infant. In contrast, the odds of finding a nut sitting on a rock and happening to strike it with another rock are much lower than those for grasping a colourful cloth. Similarly, it would require quite a rare confluence of events for breaking one rock with another to coincidentally be followed by a rewarding consequence and thus learned by conditioning processes.

As an alternative to conditioning, Lockman (2000; this volume) has suggested that many behaviours which ultimately become functional may originate in infants' explorations of objects' perceptual properties or 'affordances'. For instance, towards the end of the first year infants frequently engage in banging objects against surfaces, presumably for the pleasure of making noise. In the course of this activity, they become sensitive to properties such as the weight of objects and the compliance of surfaces. They also master the motor elements of hammering, becoming adept at aiming, at controlling the angle between the object and the surface, at varying the force of the stroke, and so forth. These skills are then available to be easily incorporated into functional hammering later on. Similarly, lateral hand movements initially practised in the context of exploring textures (see Lederman & Klatzky 1987; Bushnell & Boudreau 1991) may become incorporated into scribbling with crayons and ultimately into writing. In these examples, particular actions which eventually are involved in tool-using and means-ends behaviours are initially sustained by perceptual feedback. Once actions are perfected and objects become familiar in this context, the cognitive 'leap' to imagining them in functional roles may be minimal. Indeed, with such practice and familiarity, straight-forward causal relations may literally be 'seen' in a quasi-perceptual process, as opposed to worked out thoughtfully. This process is further described by Cummins-Sebree & Fragaszy (this volume), who propose it as the likely foundation for capuchin's solutions to simple obtaining problems.

Imitation of goal-directed activities
A final and very viable mechanism which could support early instances of means–ends behaviour without causal understanding is imitation, or more broadly, observational learning. Intuitively, children and adults alike routinely exploit many objects without understanding how or why they physically work, and almost always, they have seen someone older or more knowledgeable demonstrate the activity beforehand. Operating complex machines such as cars, telephones, and microwave ovens come to mind as cases in point. Empirically, there are many reports in the literature of children learning means–ends behaviours by

imitation. For example, with regard to tool using in particular, Bushnell & Boudreau (1998) and also Chen & Siegler (2000) found that although toddlers hardly ever spontaneously tried to use novel tools to obtain out-of-reach toys, they readily and successfully did so after seeing a model demonstrate using the tools. Similarly, van Leeuwen et al. (1994) found that following a demonstration, children were able to succeed with more complex tool/goal configurations than they could manage spontaneously. These results highlight the 'added value' of imitation for acquiring skills, above and beyond whatever exploratory tendencies and elementary causal knowledge children might bring to the task themselves. Even preverbal infants can imitate highly unconventional, novel actions toward objects, actions which they never exhibit while exploring the objects on their own (Meltzoff 1988). Indeed, imitation is so pervasive among children and at such early ages that Meltzoff & Moore (1989; 1994; 1999) have proposed an innate 'Active Intermodal Mapping' mechanism which permits even newborns to relate postures and movements they see in others to their own proprioceptively-experienced postures and movements.

The importance of imitative abilities to tool use has also been acknowledged in conceptions of the evolution of culture and technology. For example, Tomasello (1999) has emphasized that imitation permits new strategies discovered by especially intelligent individuals or through rare and fortuitous circumstances to accumulate, distribute, and be maintained within a group and across generations. He calls this important consequence of imitation the 'ratchet' effect; there is no slippage with the loss of knowledgeable individuals. Even more to the point, Merlin Donald (1991) has argued that a broad capacity to re-enact events was the first major evolutionary transition that set the cognition of hominins truly apart from that of apes some two million years ago. Among other things, this 'mimetic' ability allowed for the perfection and transmission of tool-using and tool-making skills, even in the absence of symbolic communication systems (language).

To Donald's position, some would immediately counter that other animals and especially non-human primates are capable of imitation. Certainly to the extent that some present-day apes use tools and other complex manual skills in their foraging, juveniles seem to acquire these abilities through observing adults execute them. Matsuzawa (1994) has described in some detail how young chimpanzees learn to crack nuts with stone hammers in the context of adults engaged in nut cracking, and Byrne (1999; this volume; Byrne & Byrne 1993) has similarly analyzed how young gorillas learn to manipulate particular plant foods from observing their mothers feeding. However, in the same breath these researchers also grant that the imitative abilities of nonhuman primates are qualitatively different from those of human infants. For instance, Byrne (1999) stresses that apes have usually seen repeated demonstrations — that is, in the hundreds — before they begin to copy a modelled action sequence. In contrast, humans including infants often successfully imitate object-directed actions after just a single demonstration. Byrne suggests that ape imitation may be mediated by a statistical learning process that involves motor priming; human imitation on the other hand may be mediated by more abstract mental representations and understandings of actions.

Want & Harris (2002) have recently provided another approach to distinguishing different qualities of imitation. In a comprehensive review aimed at both comparative and developmental psychologists, they scrutinized imitative behaviour and decomposed it into smaller constituent components. Following other analyses, they note that a given instance of reproduced behaviour could be the result of the imitator's attraction to the stimulus itself (stimulus enhancement), the imitator's attraction to the location of the observed behaviour (local enhancement), the reproduction of only the means (mimicry) or of only the ends (goal emulation) without consideration of the other, or the intentional linking of an observed means to achieve a desired end (true imitation). Want & Harris close with the suggestion that a set of criteria and also further research based on these separable components may facilitate both across-species and across-age comparisons with regard to imitative abilities.

Some researchers have already begun to evaluate imitative behaviours in light of Want & Harris's scheme. For example, Tomasello (1999) thinks a critical difference between apes and humans is that human children attend to and duplicate the model's precise actions or 'means' in means–ends behaviours, while apes only seem to learn what end results are possible from demonstrations. Thus, strictly speaking, apes do not imitate but instead only 'emulate' the model by recreating the observed effect in their own way. Tomasello and colleagues have documented this distinction in several studies directly comparing the behaviour of chimpanzees and human children when both were shown means–ends activities such as retrieving toys with a rake or a reel (Tomasello et al. 1993; Nagell et al. 1993). Children (and also enculturated chimpanzees) were more likely to imitate the experimenter's methods than mother-raised chimps were; the chimps often employed alternative means and either achieved the ends by some different route or failed to achieve the ends.

Tomasello (1999) and also Meltzoff (1995) have identified another way in which ape and human imitation may differ as well. Here they maintain that human children are uniquely successful at imitating because they are able to appreciate other people's intentions as they manipulate objects. Children inherently understand that other people are 'like me', and thus predicate their own manipulations of objects on the assumption that objects will do 'for me' what I have seen them do 'for' other people, if I act on them in the same way. Bard & Vauclair (1984) have also emphasized a social distinction between apes and humans with regard to object manipulations and the potential for imitation. In some direct comparisons, they found that in contrast to human adults, ape adults did not attend to their infants' activities with objects or attempt to facilitate and structure them in any way.

Any or all of these differences in the imitative process — concerning the number of demonstrations required, concerning whether the means as compared to the ends is attended to, and concerning the social aspects of the imitative context — may be important to technological differences between apes and humans. If imitation is a uniquely efficient and prepotent learning mechanism among humans, then rare inventions devised by an individual and spurious occurrences observed in nature can be 'seized upon' in a way that is not possible with more laborious and halting imitative abilities. Thus, technological advances can accumulate and rapidly spread through groups and across generations, as indeed they do within human cultures and today in our 'global village'. Note that with the vehicle of imitation, this dispersal effect is not dependent on deep causal (physical) understanding on anyone's part. By interpolation then, and without questioning their level of causal understanding, one could speculate that an advance in one or more of these special features of imitation was integral to hominins moving beyond the 'ape grade' and sustaining the seminal behaviour of stone knapping.

We would like to highlight yet another potentially-distinctive attribute of human imitative abilities that might have technological implications. This has to do with the fact that individuals learning through imitation do not limit themselves to acting with just the one object they saw demonstrated or to just the one purpose for which they saw it used. Instead, they generalize the learned behaviours to other similar objects and to analogous problem situations. People not only imitate but also adapt, improve, extend, and expand upon the goal-directed actions of others, or as the saying goes, they 'build better mouse-traps'. Even young children seem to abstract something more general from the imitative context and then generalize or 'transfer' it to other circumstances. This extension of activities learned through imitation may be part of what makes human tool-using so defining and productive, along with or instead of an advanced understanding of causality. Our current research on infant development focuses on this special transfer ability. In the following section, we describe several studies which document that young children not only attend to and imitate the means, as per Tomasello (1999), but also transfer the means to other novel objects and thereby 'invent' new goal-directed activities.

Research on transfer according to the means in human infants

Attention to the means during demonstrations

Our first approach to investigating transfer from instances of imitation was to simply look at what infants attend to while they observe demonstrations of object-directed actions (Brugger & Bushnell 1999). We showed 15- and 21-month-old infants mechanical toys which an adult model operated by manipulating a handle at one end. After seeing the demonstration, infants were given a turn to operate each toy themselves. The special feature of this study was that at least some versions of the toys were unusually long. For example, with the 'frog' toy, the handle at one end of a wooden base was some 80 cm away from a toy frog at the other end; the frog jumped back and forth when the handle was moved in and out. The extra length of the toys made it easy to see what the child looked at during the experimenter's demonstration, whether toward the experimenter's hands and their movements (i.e. the means) or toward the toy animal at the other end and its movements (i.e. the ends). Seeing how the model manipulated the handle would be necessary in order to 'imitate' rather than 'emulate' with these toys, following the distinction discussed earlier.

The results were that, first of all, the older children were generally more successful at making the toys work. As is shown in Table 20.1, this was true for each of the three toys used, that is, regardless of whether pressing, pulling, or turning was the critical action to perform. Overall, 21-month-olds reproduced the demonstrated effect by operating the handle on nearly 80 per cent of their trials, whereas 15-month-olds did so on only about one-third of theirs.

To further analyze these results, we broke the trials down according to whether the infant looked at the animal moving and also at the model's hands operating the handle during the demonstration or instead looked only at the animal moving. As might be expected, success was clearly predicated on having looked at the model's hands during the demonstra-

Table 20.1. *Numbers of infants at each age who were successful or not at operating the toys.*

	Press		Pull		Turn	
	Dog toy		Frog toy		Cow toy	
	Yes	No	Yes	No	Yes	No
15-month olds	14	24	11	16	7	26
21-month olds	17	5	16	7	16	2

tion. Infants who looked at the model's hands were usually successful at working the toy themselves, while infants who did not look at the model's hands during the demonstration were almost never successful at working the toy themselves. This was true for the younger as well as for the older infants, suggesting that the motor demands of operating the handles were not too difficult for the 15-month-olds. Instead, the principal age difference was that older infants looked at the model's hands on almost every occasion, whereas younger infants failed to do so about 40 per cent of the time. This difference in attending to the means was the main reason why the younger infants were less successful at making the toys work overall.

These results reinforce the distinction that Tomasello (1999) and Want & Harris (2002) have made between imitating the means and emulating the ends, and furthermore, they suggest that this distinction is relevant developmentally as well as between species. Only infants who looked at the model's hands were successful at working the toys themselves, and older infants looked at the model's hands more consistently than younger infants did. Looking to the hands by older infants may reflect an emerging understanding of physical causality or alternatively of social agency; either way, there is a cognitive 'burden' on the imitative learner— the infant has to know what to look for in a demonstration in order to benefit from it. It would be interesting to observe the gaze patterns of non-human primates during demonstrations with analogous 'long' objects where the means is performed at some distance from the ends. Perhaps the capacity to attend to the means despite the attraction of a perceptually salient ends originated with early hominins and was integral to their tool-making and tool-using skills.

Transfer according to the means with similar objects

In a subsequent study, we further examined the role of attention to the means during imitative learning and also began to explicitly address the question of transferring imitated behaviour beyond the initial learning situation (Sidman *et al.* 2001). In this work, we used a standard transfer design which in effect pitted attention to the means against attention to the ends. This allowed us to examine which aspect of an imitated behaviour — the means or the ends — might govern infants' later behaviour with a new toy.

The participants were 14- to 16-month-old infants, and each baby was first shown how to work two novel mechanical toys. As in the previous study, each toy had a handle on one end which could be manipulated in a certain way to move an animal mounted elsewhere on the toy. There were two kinds of handles (a faucet and a D-ring) and two ways that each of these could be manipulated (by pulling in and out and by turning in the fronto-parallel plane).There were also two different animals (a bird and a dog), and each of these could either jump up and down or spin around when the handle was manipulated. Each infant learned how to work a toy configured with one combination of these components and another toy configured with the alternative components. For example, an infant might first be shown how to *turn* the *D-ring* to make the *dog jump*, and then next shown how to *pull* the *faucet* to make the *bird spin*. For these learning trials, an experimenter demonstrated how to work the toy, and then offered the infant turns until he or she had successfully made the animal move.

After the infant had learned to work the two demonstration toys, a third object was brought out and offered to the infant with no demonstration. This test object was a hybrid of the first two; it had the handle of one demonstration object and the toy animal of the other. The question of interest was how the infant would try to work the test object, whether by turning or by pulling; that is, would they act on the test toy according to how they had acted before with that kind of handle (the means) or according to how they had acted before with that kind of animal (the ends).

The primary results are shown on Table 20.2. As can be seen, most infants acted on the test toy according to the means. If the test toy had the handle they had learned to pull earlier, they were more likely to pull than turn on the test trial, even though they had also learned earlier to move that particular animal by turning. These results suggest that similarity of the

Table 20.2. *Infants' performance according to means-driven or ends-driven behaviours.*

Action on test	Pull handle and turn toy	Turn handle and pull toy
Pulled	9	3
Turned	3	5

means, rather than similarity of the ends, governed motor transfer for these infants. Additional analyses showed that infants also tended to act on the test toy with the motor behaviour (pulling or turning) they were most proficient with during the learning phase and with the one they had used most recently.

What is common to all of the strategies implied by the results is that the causal action itself is central, as opposed to the effect that is to be produced. Infants' transfer to the test toy was governed by the part of the object they had previously acted on, by the action they were most skilful at, and/or by the action they had most recently performed. The action was learned and practised in the context of imitating the experimenter with a particular toy, but infants seemed to abstract the action from this specific context and then apply it readily to another toy. As in the first study, attention to the means was evidently critical to infants' imitative behaviour, and in this case it also drove their subsequent interactions with a new toy which they had not seen demonstrated.

Transfer according to the means with dissimilar objects

We proceeded to investigate this transfer of learned means in another study (Bushnell & Sidman 2002), this time with more diverse objects and distinctive effects, in order to determine how far removed from the imitation context the means can be taken. In this study, we used two sets of three toys each. In one set, each toy could be activated by pressing a large blue button, and in the other, each toy could be activated by pulling on a white knob. Except that they had the same press-button or pull-knob, the toys in each set were otherwise different in colour, size, shape, and the nature of the effect they yielded — one toy made a song play, another made some balls spin, the third made a dog bark and wag its tail, and so forth.

The participants were again 14- to 16-month-old infants, and as before, each infant was first shown how to work two of the toys from a given (i.e. pressing or pulling) set. With each learning toy, an experimenter demonstrated how to work the toy, gave it to the baby for a turn, and then repeated this exchange once again. After these imitative turns with two of the toys, the third toy from the same action set was brought out and offered to the baby without any demonstration. The significant question was what the babies would do with the novel toy on this third or 'test' trial. Each baby had also been offered (with no demonstration) a toy from the alternative action set even before the learning trials began. These 'baseline' trials were included to see what infants would do with the stimulus toys spontaneously, in particular whether they could

Table 20.3. *Numbers of infants who successfully activated the toys in the baseline and test conditions.*

	Baseline	Test
Pull toys	3 (of 11)	8 (of 11)
Press toys	1 (of 11)	11 (of 11)
Total	**4 (of 22)**	**19 (of 22)**

discover the toys' cause–effect characteristics on their own, prior to demonstrations of any kind.

The results are shown in Table 20.3, which summarizes the infants' success at activating the toys on the baseline trials and on the corresponding test trials. As Table 20.3 shows, babies rarely managed to activate the toys on the baseline trials, although they typically did explore the toys and even touched the perceptually salient press-buttons and pull-knobs. However, on the test trials, almost all of the infants activated the toys successfully; furthermore, they often did so right away, within 3–4 seconds of being given the toy. That is, infants usually went straight for the test toy's button or knob and manipulated it in the same way (i.e. pressing or pulling) that had been effective with the demonstration toys. It is important to emphasize that this behaviour is not just the most obvious or easy thing to do with these toys, because on the baseline trials, babies almost never acted toward the same toys in this way. They clearly learned the effective action from imitating the experimenter with the first two toys, and then they just as clearly extended that action to the third toy which they had not seen demonstrated.

We had observed transfer of a learned means to a new toy in the previous study also; however, in the present case, the test toy was substantially different from either of the training toys. It was unlike them in colour, size, shape, the nature and number of discernable parts, and so forth, and there was nothing about it to suggest it would yield an effect like those of the training toys (which indeed it did not, it yielded a different effect). Only the manipulandum and the action required to operate it — that is, the means — were similar across the several toys; infants must have remembered this from the imitation trials and then carried it over to the new object.

Transferring the means: a proposed intermediate level of causal understanding

What we would like to emphasize from our work with infants is the apparent abstraction or disentangling of the pressing and pulling actions from the particular objects and effects for which they were first performed. From the imitation trials, infants seemed to learn not

only how to play with those individual objects, but also that pressing buttons or pulling knobs is a generic 'way to make things happen'. Of course this does not reflect a real understanding of causality or any knowledge of how the toys worked in the intuitive physics sense. That is, we do not suppose that from the learning trials babies had come to understand the mechanics of springs or levers, so that when the novel toy came out, they could actually foresee what would happen if they pressed the button or pulled the knob. In most cases the mechanisms were hidden or actually electronic, so this kind of genuine insight would have been impossible for anyone, never mind for 15-month-olds. But at the same time, the infants seemed to have learned more than just that buttons are for pressing or knobs for pulling. Our impression is that on the test trials, they expected acting on the novel toy to have some sort of effect, although they did not (and could not) know exactly what it would be. It is almost as though in the infant's mind there was a blank slot to be filled in, in a kind of action–effect or means–ends frame.

In future research, we are planning to further investigate this frame-and-slot interpretation for early transfer. For example, we will observe the behaviour of infants when the test toy is 'broken', so that unlike the demonstration toys, pressing and pulling produces no effect and thus violates the presumed expectation for one. We will also observe infants' choice behaviour after demonstrations with one toy where an action leads to an effect and another where an action leads to no effect. But for now, if one accepts the frame-and-slot idea on speculation, an important implication from it is the opportunity for invention it affords.

As an analogy, consider the 'verb island' (Tomasello 1999) or 'pivot word' (Braine 1976) constructions that children produce at a certain stage in language acquisition. In these constructions, a certain key word is followed (or preceded) by any one of a whole class of words, as when a child uses the pivot term 'give' in combination with 'cookie', 'ball', 'hug', 'book' or any of the various content words he or she knows and might want an instance of. Such constructions are thought to reflect something less than genuine syntactic categories or sentence predicates, but they do grant the child an important measure of generativity which was not present before. In the prior phase, utterances consist of single word labels and so-called unanalyzed routines such as 'gimmeakiss' (but never 'gimme' anything else). These routines are highly context-dependent and impenetrable, and children's language at this point is somewhat imitative and robotic. However, when the pivot word strategy emerges, the child is suddenly a creative speaker, producing novel

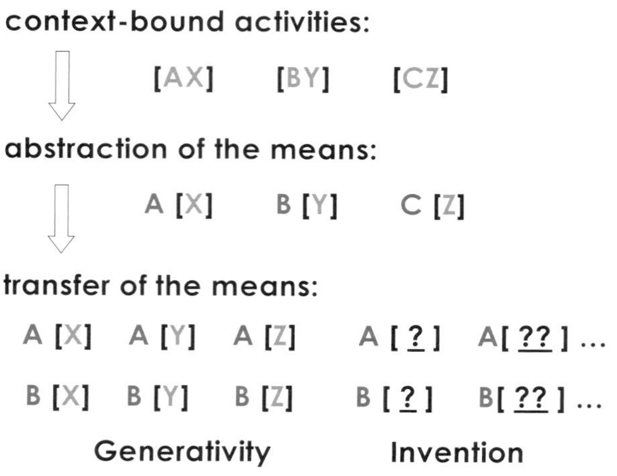

context-bound activities:

⬇

     [AX]   [BY]   [CZ]

abstraction of the means:

⬇

     A [X]   B [Y]   C [Z]

transfer of the means:

A [X] A [Y] A [Z]   A [**?**] A[**??**] ...

B [X] B [Y] B [Z]   B [**?**] B[**??**] ...

     Generativity   **Invention**

Figure 20.1. *Schematic depiction of the proposed developmental and perhaps evolutionary sequence, culminating in a generative action-grammar which enhances the discovery of new means–ends relationships.*

two-word utterances left and right and 'on the fly'. With this immature grammatical device, the child is in control of an infinitely expandable repertoire of expressible meanings.

We think that the transfer phenomenon we observed with our mechanical toys may represent the same kind of intermediate step but quantum leap with regard to children's means–ends activities with objects. Initially, effective actions and the objects to which they are applied may be inseparably bound together, essentially by conditioning processes, and the infant's goal-directed activities are limited to these learned responses and to the contexts in which they were learned. For example, Rovee-Collier and colleagues (Butler & Rovee-Collier 1989; Hayne *et al.* 1986; Rovee-Collier *et al.* 1985) have found that young infants easily learn a leg-kicking response which activates a mobile, but if even quite subtle aspects of the context or the mobile's elements are changed, infants do not generalize the kicking response to activate the new mobile. When an infant is able to abstract a means from its situational substrate, however, it becomes an entity in its own right and may be stored in an inventory of ways to make things happen. A particular action, say pressing or pulling, now plays the role of a pivot word. It is a sort of 'free radical' with the potential to combine with many objects, sometimes to no good effect at all and sometimes to produce exciting new effects. Thus because of this free-wheeling transfer, the odds of fortuitously discovering new means–ends relationships increase dramatically and further development is catalyzed. This hypothetical sequence and the generativity it permits are depicted in Figure 20.1.

The generalization process illustrated in Figure 20.1 is similar to developments originally described by Piaget (1952; 1954). As noted earlier, he wrote of infants first differentiating means from ends at about 8 months, and he characterized the subsequent 'stage' of cognitive development as 'the application of familiar schemata (actions) to new situations' (Piaget 1952, 212). Likewise, some have specifically defined 'play' as the free exploration of means with no particular ends in mind, and creativity and invention are supposed to arise from this aimless activity. Our contributions to this perspective are threefold. First, we have given a straightforward empirical demonstration of infants differentiating and transferring the means with our three-toy paradigm. Second, we emphasize that this process represents an intermediate stage in the development of causal cognition. When a learned action is applied to a new object, the child does not foresee or fully understand what effect will ensue, but nevertheless expects something to happen and performs the action with that ill-defined end in mind. Thus strictly speaking, transferring the means is not 'just play', with its explicitly purposeless quality. Finally, we emphasize the collaboration between adults and infants, between culture and cognition, that is involved with transferring the means. The actions which infants apply to new objects are not means they discover on their own, as Piaget might have it. They are low-probability behaviours which infants initially learn as effective actions by imitating others. But with their extraction from the learning context and application to new objects, these imitated behaviours then become the roots of individual invention, ingenuity, and problem solving. In our view, transferring the means makes for a primitive but generative action-grammar, by which individual infants can exceed what their elders have showed them.

Further speculation: transferring the means and the evolution of technology

To complete our discussion, we would like to speculate even further now and imagine a similar intermediate stage in the evolution of cognition, likewise characterized by the capacity to transfer learned means to new contexts. This conjecture rests on the several other parallels between cognitive development and evolution discussed earlier, namely with regard to future-oriented thinking, understanding connections between means and ends, advances in imitation, and so forth. As on these parameters we supposed that like infants early hominins lay somewhere between the abilities of non-human primates and modern mature humans, so we suggest they might have been positioned with respect to their capacities for invention. We have identified transfer according to the means as a potential mid-point in this regard in our work on infant development. In this final section and in what must be taken as a thought experiment, we apply this concept hypothetically to the situation of early hominins and their technology.

As a start, we know that non-human primates have at their disposal a number of purposeful and effective behaviours for attaining certain desired ends; termite fishing and nut cracking come to mind as obvious examples. Early hominins no doubt engaged in similar behaviours, including perhaps the earliest forms of using or even knapping stones as tools. These ape and early hominin behaviours presumably originated in some rare confluence of events and pressures to survive, and they are (were) sustained by their adaptive value and some form of cultural transmission such as Tomasello's (1999) emulation or Byrne's (1999) statistical learning. We suppose these activities may be the equivalent of unanalyzed routines in early language, with the causal action and its effect inseparably locked together as a unitary phenomenon, as illustrated in the top portion of Figure 20.1. Thus as with young infants' leg-kicking to mobiles, the action is not applied in other contexts and similarly the effect is not approached by other means. This state of affairs would make for a perpetuating but relatively changeless technology, as indeed some have characterized that of today's non-human primates and also that of hominins during the earliest phases of their evolution.

Following the parallel with development, we next suppose that at some point in prehistory, hominins gained the capacity to separate causal actions from their situational substrates, as exhibited by our 15-month-old research participants. Perhaps this advance was affiliated with the emergence of mimetic abilities in general (Donald 1991); like differentiating the means, imitation itself requires some sort of accessible mental representation of bodily actions. However, just when this change took place is less important for our purposes than the fact that, as in development, it would have increased the potential for invention and technological progress enormously. As is illustrated in the lower portion of Figure 20.1, with transfer according to the means, familiar means may be recombined with other familiar ends, to generate alternative ways of accomplishing something, say in the face of altered circumstances. Thus a hominin capable of transferring the means might strike an insect instead of a nut with a stone, for instance, and thereby 'invent' a more comfortable way to eat biting or pinching bugs. Conversely, he might poke a stick

into a cracked nut instead of into a termite mound, and thus discover how to glean all the nutritious bits out of the shell. Familiar means could also be applied to novel objects, leading to entirely new and unforeseen effects which then could be capitalized upon. A hominin might hit grain instead of nuts with a stone and thus invent grinding flour. He might hit a stick instead of nuts with a stone and invent tent stakes or markers. He might hit a dangerous animal or other hominin with a stone and invent weapons. He might poke a stick into a hide instead of into a termite mound and invent primitive fasteners or buttons. And so on. De Beaune (2004) has similarly outlined how transfer processes may have engendered new technological skills in human evolution and gives further examples founded in lithic analyses.

Our position is that the inventions pictured in these scenarios were not initially grounded in sophisticated means–ends analyses or detailed knowledge of physical laws such as modern-day humans possess. That level of cognition came later, with capacities that allow the recognition of specific spatial, temporal, and other constraints that define individual causal relations. Recall that in development, understanding the real 'why' of particular means–ends relations seems to come after infants have been purposefully attaining those ends with those means for some time. Instead, the innovations imagined here could have derived from a more generic and 'vague' intuition that actions which are effective in one context may also be effective in others. As with infants, we suppose that this frame-and-slot level of understanding for cause and effect prompted the hominins in question to 'try' actions learned for one purpose on other novel materials and to attend closely to what the anticipated but unspecified effect turned out to be. Occasionally it turned out to be useful, and if the action sequence was then repeated and ultimately imitated by others, a technological advance had occurred, but it was not 'intentionally' (with foresight) invented. That is, the familiar means was intentionally tried in the novel context, but the exact outcome was not predicted beforehand, only realized afterwards and from then on, deliberately repeated.

The advantage of this intermediate level of causal cognition over say trial-and-error as a source of new skills has mainly to do with the 'trials' — they are more frequent, more systematic, and applied to a wider assortment of novel materials. Thus, stone knapping itself could have originated through transfer according to the means, perhaps through a series of 'accidents' involving percussive activities such as Marchant & McGrew (this volume) describe. Later, transfer could have been involved in the refinement of knapping techniques, such as in the use of bone and antler as hammers, for preparing edges, and so forth. With transfer according to the means, progress either to the initial incidence of stone knapping or subsequently from it did not have to await low-probability and fortuitous confluences of events; these were sought out and created in a more proactive way. Accordingly, the trajectory for technological change ramped up and ultimately produced the off-scale levels of technology enjoyed by even premodern humans in comparison to other primate species.

We might finally suppose that this process of transferring the means, of 'trying' effective actions out on novel objects and materials, was most intensely engaged in by the young in any given hominin group. They were after all not preoccupied with applying those actions to already known ends in order to survive, and yet they surely observed the elders doing so. The young could have imitated the elders' activities, and in their spare time may also have transferred the causal actions to new materials and thereby occasionally discovered useful new combinations. They would then have used these improved methods routinely as they grew to become adults, and the next generation in turn would imitate and expand upon them. Out of the hands of babes.

References

Baillargeon, R., 1994. How do infants learn about the physical world? *Current Directions in Psychological Science* 3, 133–40.

Bard, K.A. & J. Vauclair, 1984. The communicative context of object manipulation in ape and human adult–infant pairs. *Journal of Human Evolution* 13, 181–90.

Bates, E., V. Carlson-Luden & I. Bretherton, 1980. Perceptual aspects of tool-using in infancy. *Infant Behavior and Development* 3, 127–40.

Bayley, N., 1969. *Manual for the Bayley Scales of Infant Development.* New York (NY): The Psychological Corporation.

Boesch, C. & H. Boesch, 1983. Optimization of nut-cracking with natural hammers by wild chimpanzees. *Behaviour* 83, 265–86.

Boudreau, J.P. & E.W. Bushnell, 2000. Spilling thoughts: configuring attentional resources in infants' goal-directed actions. *Infant Behavior and Development* 23, 543–66.

Braine, M., 1976. *Children's First Word Combinations.* (Monographs of the Society for Research in Child Development 41(1).) Oxford: Blackwell.

Brugger, A.E. & E.W. Bushnell, 1999. Imitative Strategies Employed by 15- and 21-month-old Infants for Learning to Work Novel Objects. Poster presented at the Meetings of the Society for Research in Child Development, Albuquerque, New Mexico, April 1999.

Bushnell, E.W. & J.P. Boudreau, 1991. The development of haptic perception during infancy, in *The Psychology of Touch*, eds. M.A. Heller & W. Schiff. Hillsdale (NJ): L. Erlbaum, 139–61.

Bushnell, E.W. & J.P. Boudreau, 1998. Exploring and exploiting objects with the hands during infancy, in *The Psychobiology of the Hand*, ed. K.J. Connolly. (Clinics in Developmental Medicine 147.) London: MacKeith Press, distributed by Cambridge University Press, 144–61.

Bushnell, E.W. & J. Sidman, 2002. Beyond the Information Given: Extensions of Activities Learned Through Imitation. Symposium contribution presented at the International Society for Infant Studies, Toronto, Canada, April 2002.

Butler, J. & C. Rovee-Collier, 1989. Contextual gating of memory retrieval. *Developmental Psychobiology* 22(6), 533–52.

Byrne, R.W., 1995. *The Thinking Ape: Evolutionary Origins of Intelligence.* Oxford: Oxford University Press.

Byrne, R.W., 1999. Imitation without intentionality: using string parsing to copy the organization of behaviour. *Animal Cognition* 2(2), 63–72.

Byrne, R.W. & J.M. Byrne, 1993. Complex leaf-gathering skills of mountain gorillas (*Gorilla g. beringei*): variability and standardization. *American Journal of Primatology* 31(4), 241–61.

Canfield, R.L. & M.M. Haith, 1991. Young infants' visual expectations for symmetric and asymmetric stimulus sequences. *Developmental Psychology* 27(2), 198–208.

Chen, Z. & R.S. Siegler, 2000. *Across the Great Divide: Bridging the Gap Between Understanding of Toddlers' and Older Children's Thinking.* (Monographs of the Society for Research in Child Development 65(2), v–96.) Oxford: Blackwell Publishers.

Corballis, M.C., 1999. Phylogeny from apes to humans, in *The Descent of Mind: Psychological Perspectives on Hominid Evolution*, eds. M.C. Corballis & S.E.G. Lea. Oxford & New York (NY): Oxford University Press, 40–70.

Davidson, I. & W. Noble, 1993. Tools and language in human evolution, in *Tools, Language, and Cognition in Human Evolution*, eds. K.R. Gibson & T. Ingold. Cambridge: Cambridge University Press, 363–88.

de Beaune, S.A., 2004. The invention of technology: prehistory and cognition. *Current Anthropology* 45(2), 139–62.

Donald, M., 1991. *Origins of the Modern Mind: Three Stages in the Evolution of Culture and Cognition.* Cambridge (MA): Harvard University Press.

Hayne, H., C. Greco, L. Earley, P. Griesler & C. Rovee-Collier, 1986. Ontogeny of early event memory: II. Encoding and retrieval by 2- and 3-month-olds. *Infant Behavior and Development* 9, 461–72.

Lederman, S.J. & R.L. Klatzky, 1987. Hand movements: a window into haptic object recognition. *Cognitive Psychology* 19, 342–68.

Leslie, A.M., 1984. Infant perception of a manual pick-up event. *British Journal of Developmental Psychology* 2, 19–32.

Lockman, J.J., 2000. A perception–action perspective on tool use development. *Child Development* 71(1), 137–44.

Matsuzawa, T., 1994. Field experiments on use of stone tools by chimpanzees in the wild, in *Chimpanzee Cultures*, eds. R.W. Wrangham & W.C. McGrew. Cambridge (MA): Harvard University Press, 351–70.

McCarty, M.E., R.K. Clifton & R.R. Collard, 1999. Problem solving in infancy: the emergence of an action plan. *Developmental Psychology* 35, 1091–101.

Meltzoff, A.N., 1988. Infant imitation after a 1-week delay: long-term memory for novel acts and multiple stimuli. *Developmental Psychology* 24(4), 470–76.

Meltzoff, A.N., 1995. Understanding the intentions of others: re-enactment of intended acts by 18-month-old children. *Developmental Psychology* 31(5), 838–50.

Meltzoff, A.N. & M.K. Moore, 1989. Imitation in newborn infants: exploring the range of gestures imitated and the underlying mechanisms. *Developmental Psychology* 25(6), 954–62.

Meltzoff, A.N. & M.K. Moore, 1994. Imitation, memory, and the representation of persons. *Infant Behavior & Development* 17(1), 83–99.

Meltzoff, A.N. & M.K. Moore, 1999. Persons and representation: why infant imitation is important for theories of human development, in *Imitation in Infancy*, eds. J. Nadel & G. Butterworth. Cambridge: Cambridge University Press, 9–35.

Mithen, S., 1996. *The Prehistory of the Mind: the Cognitive Origins of Art, Religion, and Science*. London: Thames & Hudson Ltd.

Nagell, K., R.S. Olguin & M. Tomasello, 1993. Processes of social learning in the tool use of chimpanzees (*Pan troglodytes*) and human children (*Homo sapiens*). *Journal of Comparative Psychology* 107(2), 174–86.

Piaget, J., 1952. *The Origins of Intelligence in Childhood*. New York (NY): International Universities Press.

Piaget, J., 1954. *The Construction of Reality in the Child*. New York (NY): Basic Books.

Rovee-Collier, C., P.C. Griesler & L.A. Earley, 1985. Contextual determinants of retrieval in three-month-old infants. *Learning & Motivation* 16(2), 139–57.

Schick, K.D. & N. Toth, 1993. *Making Silent Stones Speak*. New York (NY): Simon and Schuster.

Schlesinger, M. & J. Langer, 1999. Infants' developing expectations of possible and impossible tool-use events between ages 8 and 12 months. *Developmental Science* 2(2), 195–205.

Sidman, J., L.A. Lariviere & E.W. Bushnell, 2001. Factors Governing Infants' Transfer of Object-directed Actions. Poster presented at the meetings of the Society for Research in Child Development, Minneapolis, April, 2001.

Tomasello, M., 1999. *The Cultural Origins of Human Cognition*. Cambridge (MA): Harvard University Press.

Tomasello, M. & J. Call, 1997. *Primate Cognition*. New York (NY): Oxford University Press.

Tomasello, M., E.S. Savage-Rumbaugh & A.C. Kruger, 1993. Imitative learning of actions on objects by children, chimpanzees, and enculturated chimpanzees. *Child Development* 64(6), 1688–705.

Toth, N., 1985. The Oldowan reassessed: a close look at early stone artefacts. *Journal of Archaeological Science* 12, 101–20.

Uzgiris, I.C. & J. Hunt, 1975. *Assessment in Infancy: Ordinal Scales of Psychological Development*. Champaign (IL): University of Illinois Press.

van Leeuwen, L., A.W. Smitsman & C. van Leeuwen, 1994. Affordances, perceptual complextity, and the development of tool-use. *Journal of Experimental Psychology: Human Perception and Performance* 20, 174–91.

Visalberghi, E., 1993. Tool use in a south american monkey species: an overview of the characteristics and limits of tool use in *Cebus apella*, in *The Use of Tools by Human and Non-human Primates*, eds. A. Berthelet & J. Chavaillon. New York (NY): Oxford University Press, 118–31.

Want, S.C. & P.L. Harris, 2002. How do children ape? Applying concepts from the study of non-human primates to the developmental study of 'imitation' in children. *Developmental Science* 5, 1–41.

Willatts, P., 1999. Development of means-end behaviour in young infants: pulling a support to retrieve a distant object. *Developmental Psychology* 35, 651–67.

Woodward, A., 1998. Infants selectively encode the goal object of an actor's reach. *Cognition* 69, 1–34.

Woodward, A. & J. Sommerville, 2002. Infants' Developing Sensitivity to the Intentional Structure of Action. Symposium contribution presented at the International Conference on Infant Studies, Toronto, Canada, April 2002.

Wynn, T., & W.C. McGrew, 1989. An ape's view of the Oldowan. *Man* 24, 383–98.

Chapter 21

Tool Use from a Perception–Action Perspective: Developmental and Evolutionary Considerations

Jeffrey J. Lockman

Tool use has often been treated as a discontinuous development across phylogeny and ontogeny. Recent theoretical and empirical advances, however, suggest that the emergence of tool use across these time scales may be more continuous than previously believed. In particular, I consider how a perception–action perspective may shed new light on the psychological capacities required for the achievement of tool use. In this context, I review our research on how human infants relate objects, including objects with handles, to environmental surfaces and how parents may help infants to learn how to manipulate objects. The results of our work suggest that human infants already evidence many of the abilities that support tool use and that parents offer important support to help refine this capacity. More generally, these findings suggest that tool use, including some forms of stone knapping, may have emerged in a more gradual fashion across phylogeny and human ontogeny.

Flint knapping and other related forms of stone technology present a paradox for individuals interested in the origins of tool use. From the perspective of hominin evolution, the Palaeolithic record indicates that the earliest stone tools are indeed ancient. By current estimates, early hominins were producing stone artefacts at least two million years ago, based on archaeological evidence from the Oldowan complex (Ambrose 2001; Roche this volume; Schick & Toth 1993). Yet, speculation about the cognitive skills required to produce and employ flakes of stone for instrumental ends suggests that our evolutionary ancestors possessed relatively advanced mental capacities (e.g. Schick & Toth 1993; Wynn 1993).

Consider, for instance, the cognitive demands that have been said to underlie the production and deployment of even the most basic stone tools (Wynn 1993). The ability to strike a hammerstone on a stone core to produce an implement, which in turn is employed to accomplish some instrumental goal, may imply that some of our distant hominin relatives were able to engage in sophisticated forms of planning, problem solving, means–ends thinking and spatial reasoning — cognitive abilities that many view as uniquely human and only relatively recently evolved.

One way to resolve the apparent paradox between the early appearance of tools in the lithic record and the cognitive skills that have been postulated as underlying their production and use is to maintain that some of our hominin ancestors possessed the requisite representational abilities to accomplish these technological feats. On this view, tool use is a cognitive achievement, albeit one that occurred relatively early within the context of hominin evolution.

Such an account, however, would also need to explain the types of additional developments that underlie subsequent evolutionary advances in tool use. In this regard, investigators have invoked a variety of psychological and physical factors. These factors include increases in brain or cognitive capacity, the emergence of language, changes in the anatomy and biomechanical properties of the hand (Marzke 1997; Marzke & Marzke 2000) and the appearance of new sociocognitive capacities that enable individuals to learn from and teach others (Tomasello 1998). Undoubtedly, these factors acting in concert underlie the remarkable degree to which tool use is infused in modern-day human society. Nevertheless, this type of cognitive account implies that even our primitive hominin ancestors possessed a sophisticated cognitive substrate upon which even more advanced memory, language and sociocognitive abilities were assembled to support more complex forms of tool use.

In the current chapter, I propose an alternate approach to resolve the paradox between evidence for very early tool use in the evolutionary record and the types of advanced cognitive abilities that have been postulated as supporting the production and use of tools. The approach I advocate may also help explain a related puzzle in the tool-use literature. If tool use requires advanced cognitive skills, how can we explain the mounting evidence that non-human primates and even non-primates are capable of employing objects as tools (Beck 1980)?

In the current chapter, I suggest that debate about the evolutionary origins of tool use can be informed by considering the human ontogenesis of tool use, particularly in the first two years of life. I hasten to add that I am not advocating that ontogeny recapitulates phylogeny, a viewpoint that clearly oversimplifies the complex relation between development of an ability in an organism's lifetime and the emergence of that ability in that species' evolutionary history. Instead, I suggest that recent strides in our knowledge of how tool use develops in human infants in combination with new theoretical and empirical advances in our understanding of perception–action coupling (Gibson & Pick 2000; Gibson 1979) and infant motor development (Adolph 1997; 2002; Bertenthal & Clifton 1998; Thelen 1995), can illuminate the types of psychological capacities that are sufficient to support elementary forms of tool use.

Of course, this does not mean that these are the only kinds of psychological abilities that underlie tool use. Advanced forms of tool use and technology obviously required sophisticated cognitive skills. But I will argue that some basic forms of tool use may be less a cognitive than perceptuomotor achievement and thus not require the types of symbolic thinking abilities that many claim to be uniquely human. Moreover, this proposal has important implications for how we frame discussions about the evolution of tool use and specifically, the ways in which a tool-use behaviour like stone knapping should be viewed as a unique hominin ability.

To develop this argument, I will first discuss the traditional ways in which tool use has been conceptualized and studied in the psychological literature. Next I will review how recent theoretical and empirical discoveries have led researchers to reexamine the psychological bases of basic forms of tool use. In this context, I will review some of our own research on object manipulation in human infants. In this work, we have been examining how human infants relate objects to substrates, how infants manipulate objects attached to handles and how caregivers help teach infants to manipulate objects. Based on the results of this research, I will suggest that during human infancy, tool use develops from object-manipulation skills and thus does not depend upon the presence of advanced representational or symbolic capacities as some cognitive developmentalists have maintained (Bates 1979; Piaget 1952). More specifically, I will suggest that tool use is an outgrowth of infants' as well as non-human primates' abilities to manipulate objects and relate objects to substrates in their environments. Finally, I will consider the implications of these suggestions for discussions about the evolutionary origins of tool use.

Approaches to the study of tool use

Discontinuous models of tool use

Questions about the developmental and evolutionary origins of tool use have generated considerable controversy within and across the fields of anthropology, biology and psychology. A dominant theoretical viewpoint has been that tool use represents a discontinuous advance relative to three main behavioural time scales: phylogenesis, ontogenesis and microgenesis.

Phylogenesis

With respect to phylogenesis, many theorists have suggested that tool use is a distinctively human capacity, dependent on forms of symbolic thinking that are possessed to only a limited degree by our primate relatives (Kohler 1931; Povinelli 2000; Tomasello 1998). Even in instances where non-human primates have been shown to evidence tool use, theorists have suggested that there is something qualitatively different about the character of human and non-human primate tool use, either with respect to the initial process of discovery by which an organism learns to employ an object as a tool and/or the degree to which the organism evidences generalization to other situations requiring use of that or similar objects as a tool (e.g. Povinelli 2000).

According to this discontinuity view, the evolutionary gap between humans and non-human primates extends as well to the ways in which tool use may be a socially transmitted, particularly to the young of a species. Along these lines, some sociocultural theorists suggest that the capacity to deliberately impart culturally-specific information and the complementary capacity of children to learn from such efforts, require sociocognitive abilities that may be distinctively human (Tomasello 1998). Consistent with this viewpoint, reports that adult chimpanzees actively teach their young how to use a tool to accomplish some instrumental goal like cracking a nut have been extremely rare (Boesch 1993). More typically, investigators have reported that even though juvenile chimpanzees may spend long periods of time watching adult chimpanzees pound hammerstones on nuts to crack them open, the adults do not actively attempt to teach the juveniles the skill. Unlike humans teaching their children, adult chimpanzees do not purposefully alter their movements to simplify them nor do they attempt to intervene or adjust the less-skilled actions of their young (Inoue-Nakamura & Matsuzawa 1997; Matsuzawa 2001).

Ontogenesis

In a related vein, many investigators who focus on human ontogenesis view tool use as a discontinuous developmental achievement. According to this viewpoint, tool use depends on the emergence of qualitatively new advanced symbolic or representational reasoning abilities that are beyond the range of most infants under a year of age. Prior to this time, infants attempt to solve problems and use tools in an inefficient manner, largely through well-established sensorimotor routines and trial-and-error behaviours (Piaget 1952). Along these lines, Bates (1979) has suggested that successful tool use requires individuals to engage in a type of imagined means–ends analysis in which the individual must mentally substitute one means or object for another. The ability to do so, however, requires a symbolic or representational capacity that, at the least, is not very functional in human infants before the end of the first year. Once these representational abilities have developed, however, infants become able to approach tool use problems in a qualitatively different manner, immediately imagining solutions and applying the solutions to the real world. In short, this view suggests that tool use represents a discontinuous developmental advance, predicated on the appearance of new and more complex cognitive capacities.

Microgenesis

Finally, with respect the more limited time scale encompassing microgenetic change or learning, a related discontinuous account of tool-use behaviour has also dominated the literatures in cognitive, comparative and developmental psychology (Brown 1990; Duncker 1946; Kohler 1931). Researchers who study problem solving have routinely characterized successful tool use as requiring insight. According to this view, insight represents an abrupt change in how individuals apprehend a problem's structure or the relation amongst the elements of the problem (e.g. Kohler 1931). The visual metaphor that most often accompanies this viewpoint is a bulb lighting up inside the individual's head. A

chimp or human is said to have a flash of insight, suddenly realizing that an object may be employed in a novel manner as a tool. On this view, trial and error behaviours may precede insight, but are not considered mediators to success. Instead, insight is viewed largely as a cognitive act, the product of thinking about the relation between a problem's underlying structure and an object's function in a qualitatively new and different way (Bates 1979; Duncker 1946; Kohler 1931; Povinelli 2000; Tomasello & Call 1997).

Continuous models of tool use

Although discussions about tool use with respect to phylogenesis, ontogenesis and microgenesis have emphasized the discontinuous nature of the change that occurs across each of these time scales, recent empirical and theoretical developments have led investigators to reassess the degree to which tool use should be viewed as an altogether discontinuous advance.

Phylogenesis

Consider first discussions with respect to phylogenesis or evolutionary change. The most relevant evidence here comes from work in comparative psychology and anthropology. In recent years, investigators have documented widespread instances in which non-human primates and even non-primates employ objects in a tool-like manner to accomplish an instrumental goal or to solve problems that arise in their immediate environments (Beck 1980; Fragaszy *et al.* 2004; Goodall 1986; Hauser *et al.* 2002; McGrew 1992). If tool use is the exclusive dominion of *Homo sapiens*, how can it be that chimpanzees use sticks to extract termites or pound stones to crack nuts (e.g. Matsuzawa 2001; McGrew 1992), or that cottontail tamarin monkeys select the most appropriately-shaped tool to retrieve a lure (Hauser *et al.* 2002)? These are just a few examples from an increasing number of reports that primates and even non-primates engage in behaviours that meet criteria accepted by many as evidence for tool use.

Further, in a recent large-scale analysis of tool usage patterns in various chimpanzee communities around the world, Whiten *et al.* (1999) documented considerable variation in the types of tool use evidenced in these communities. Such variation suggests the possibility of localized cultural transmission of knowledge within a non-human species, a phenomenon that many previously believed to be exclusively human. This pattern of findings likewise challenges sociocultural views that suggest that humans are the only species who transmit knowledge about tools from one generation to the next by learning from others in their community or immediate group.

Ontogenesis and microgenesis

Recent findings in the developmental and learning literatures with humans also have begun to raise questions about the adequacy of a discontinuity approach or insight-based account of tool-use behaviour. In an investigation that combined both developmental and microgenetic approaches to the study of tool use and problem solving, Chen & Siegler (2000) reported that young children between the ages of 1½ and 3 years of age did not suddenly settle on the most adaptive strategy to solve problems involving the use of a tool to retrieve a lure. Instead, over a series of trials, children in this age range often went back and forth between more and less adaptive strategies for solving these kinds of tool-use problems. Note that this pattern of results contrasts with what we would expect from an insight-based account, which emphasizes the qualitative and discontinuous nature of developmental and/or microgenetic change. By contrast, Chen & Siegler (2000) suggest that tool-use development entails changes in the relative mix in ways of thinking about how to solve a problem.

More broadly, this conclusion is consistent with Siegler's (1996) overlapping waves theory of cognitive development. According to this approach, cognitive development is not necessarily linear. That is, children do not suddenly discover how to solve a problem and from then on, remain at that new level until they move to an even more advanced level of cognitive functioning. Instead, multiple and competing ways of thinking about and solving problems may exist simultaneously within individual children over long periods of developmental time (Siegler 1996).

Other recent work on tool-use development in human children is consistent with this conclusion about gradual and overlapping developmental change. For example, in a longitudinal study on how young children learn to use spoons, Connolly & Dalgleish (1993) observed that individual infants evidence considerable variability in how they hold a spoon at any given developmental point before one grip begins to predominate, early in the second year. Likewise, in both cross-sectional and longitudinal investigations on how preschool-aged children learn how to hold writing instruments, Greer & Lockman (1998) observed substantial within-subject variability in the grip patterns that young three-year-old children exhibited over a series of trials when these children were simply asked to trace lines on a page. Taken together, these studies, which focus on behaviour at the individual subject level, begin to suggest that tool use may emerge much more gradually over developmental and microgenetic time frames. As noted, these findings pose a challenge for insight-based or discontinuous accounts of tool-use and problem-solving development, which currently dominate the field.

Gibsonian theory and tool-use development

An additional important reason for reassessing discontinuous models of tool use stems from ideas associated with Gibsonian theory on affordances and perception–action coupling (Gibson & Pick 2000; Gibson 1979). The Gibsons make a number of important proposals about the relation between perception and action that are highly relevant for any discussion about the emergence of tool use.

First, the Gibsons take the organism–environment relation as the appropriate unit of analysis for understanding perceptuomotor functioning (Gibson 1988; Gibson & Pick 2000; Gibson 1979). This view contrasts with many traditional approaches to the study of perception and/or motor behaviour, in which the qualities of the organism alone are considered apart from the environment in which the organism behaves and has evolved.

Second, and in a related vein, the Gibsons suggest that organisms register environmental information that is geared to their physical characteristics and action capabilities. J.J. Gibson (1979) coined the term 'affordance' to denote this relation that is simultaneously objective and subjective. Organisms do not perceive the world in wholly objective terms or qualities, but with respect to self-scaled opportunities for action that enable a particular organism to function adaptively in its surroundings. Thus in an example commonly used to illustrate the affordance notion, a twig may be perceived as affording support by a bird, but not by a human being.

Third and in connection with the affordance notion, the Gibsonian approach is relatively unique in the way in which it conceptualizes the relation between perception and action. According to the Gibsonian approach, perception and action are inextricably linked: perception is designed to guide action, but action is designed to guide perception as well. Neither is primary to the other. Both function together in a completely integrated fashion, enabling organisms to behave adaptively in their environments (see also Bertenthal & Clifton 1993; Goldfield 1995). Again, this viewpoint contrasts sharply with traditional approaches that have been used to study perception or motor behaviour. In work associated with these traditional approaches, perception and action have not been linked at a theoretical level, with the implications of perception for understanding the functioning of action and vice versa remaining unexplored.

Fourth, the Gibsons maintain that the environment is rich in information that specifies affordances. In the Gibsonian view, organisms do not need to infer these properties by means of some internal process of cognitive construction or unconscious inference (Rock 1983). Instead, the relevant information is in the environment for organisms to discover. According to the Gibsons, organisms register the information directly from the environment through a process in which perception and action mutually guide one another (Gibson 1979; Gibson & Pick 2000).

Finally, even human infants may be able to register some critical affordances at, or soon after, birth (e.g. Gibson & Walker 1984). Nevertheless, the Gibsons maintain that all organisms continue to learn about other affordances as a result of active exploration and experience throughout their lives (Gibson & Pick 2000). For the human species, however, childhood constitutes a very important time frame for affordance learning. As new motor abilities come on line during the early years of life, infants and young children need to engage in a process of perceptual learning to discover the new affordances connected with each of their newly emerging motor skills. For instance, the affordances associated with the new skill of walking are not necessarily the same as those associated with crawling (Adolph 2002; Adolph et al. 1993). As I will suggest next, the notion of affordance learning has important implications for understanding the development of tool use.

Tool use from a perception–action perspective

Recently, several investigators have applied Gibsonian theory to the problem of tool use development in human children (Gibson & Pick 2000; Lockman 2000; Smitsman 1997). In an earlier paper, I argued that Gibsonian theory offers an important and rich theoretical perspective from which to consider the development of human tool use (Lockman 2000). In that paper, I argued that tool use may entail a form of affordance learning. In this view, tools change the properties of the effector organs — in this instance, the hand and arm. Accordingly, the task for the novice tool user is to discover how a given tool introduces new affordances or opportunities for action in the environment. A key implication of the Gibsonian approach is that the origins of human tool use can be found in the perception–action routines that infants employ to explore their surroundings, particularly those that arise during the course of object manipulation. Thus, tool use should not be considered an altogether discontinuous developmental advance, but an achievement that is an outgrowth of infants' efforts to explore the material world, particularly with their arms, hands and fingers.

Although I suggest that object manipulation and tool use may be developmentally linked, there are important differences between the psychological demands associated with object manipulation and tool use. During object manipulation, individuals need only relate their hands directly to the properties of the object being held. Soft, pliable objects, for instance, encourage pressing, while rough, textured ones may encourage fingering (Gibson & Walker 1984; Lockman & McHale 1989; Palmer 1989). In short, the relation that emerges through action occurs directly between the actor and the object. The individual can be said to have established a body–object relation (Lockman & Ashmead 1983; McCarty et al. 2001). In contrast, when using tools, an additional relational element is implicated. The individual not only needs to relate his or her actions to the tool, but the individual, to accomplish a desired goal, must relate the tool to another object or surface in the environment. This additional relational element has been referred to as an object–object relation (Lockman & Ashmead 1983; McCarty et al. 2001). Critically, object–object relations may significantly increase the psychological demands associated with using a tool successfully and may help to account for ontogenetic as well as phylogenetic differences in patterns of tool use (see also Matsuzawa 2001).

An additional way in which object manipulation and tool use differs is that tools typically change the properties of the arms and hands. For instance, a hammer not only extends the reach of the arm and hand, but functionally changes the end of the hand into a hard surface, suitable for pounding other objects. A spoon not only changes the reach of the arm, but functionally changes the end of the hand into a small solid bowl, enabling liquids to be held as well as transported easily. In short, tools alter the properties of the effector organs and in so doing, change our range of actions. Accordingly, the challenge for the novice tool user is to explore how a given tool introduces new affordances or opportunities for action in the environment.

Therefore, relative to traditional cognitive-based approaches to tool-use development, the Gibsonian perspective suggests a very different account of how tool use emerges in children as well as in adults. Rather than implying that tool use represents a discontinuous cognitive advance predicated on the appearance of more complex symbolic reasoning skills, the Gibsonian perspective suggests that tool use is rooted in the perception–action routines that infants perform to explore and act on their surroundings.

Further, this perspective suggests that the process by which infants learn to use tools will not be the product of a sudden insight or dependent on the emergence of newly-developed cognitive abilities. Rather, a perception–action perspective maintains that infants as well as other organisms explore tools and the new affordances that tools entail over long periods of developmental time. Successful use of the tool in one instance, however, does not necessarily guarantee successful use in subsequent instances. In this connection, Gibsonian theory implies that trial-and-error behaviours should not necessarily be taken as failures of tool use or as cognitive gaps or deficiencies. Instead, a Gibsonian perspective suggests that trial-and-error behaviours should be viewed as self-generated opportunities for perceptual learning. Accordingly, these types of behaviours need to be carefully scrutinized for what they may reveal about the processes by which individuals learn to use tools.

Social-contextual approaches to tool use

As noted, one way in which tool use in humans may differ from that evidenced by other animals, including primates, is the process by which humans learn to use tools. According to some investigators, the human propensity to use tools may be socially based (e.g. Matsuzawa 2001; Tomasello & Call 1997). That is, humans may be the only primate species in which more skilled individuals actively transmit information about tools to other, less-skilled individuals. In this regard, humans regularly teach their young and less-knowledgeable adults about tools through demonstrations and strategies that involve direct movement of the less-skilled individuals' arms and hands. Similar instances of teaching in our primate relatives are uncommon (for an exception, see Boesch 1993). Critically, these social means of transmission, along with externalized representations that describe how to use a given tool, help insure that knowledge about tools is transmitted from one human generation to the next.

The reason(s) for the difference between human and non-human primates regarding the social transmission of knowledge about tools is a matter of considerable debate (Tomasello 1998; Tomasello & Call 1997; Want & Harris 2002). Some have argued that the difference may reflect a fundamental disparity in the sociocognitive abilities of humans relative to that of our primate relatives (Tomasello & Call 1997). As discussed, humans may be the only species who possess not only a generalized capacity to learn about tool use from the behaviours of others, but also the self-awareness or meta-cognitive ability to make special adjustments in their behaviours to transmit this knowledge to less-skilled members of their species.

An alternative but related viewpoint is that although non-human primates may not spontane-

ously teach their young how to use tools, this does not necessarily mean that non-human primates are fundamentally incapable of learning from such efforts, particularly if they have been brought up in a culture where such teaching regularly occurs (e.g. Tomasello *et al.* 1993). In this view, the difference between species is more a reflection of enculturation: although humans are raised in a culture where the social transmission of knowledge is the norm, other species are not. Nevertheless, short of raising a non-human primate from birth in a human household and completely saturating the non-human primate in the ways of transmitting human culture, it may be difficult to resolve this debate.

Regardless of the answer to this controversy, a second question remains. Even if humans are the only primate species to benefit so widely from social learning, one must ask what is it about the social context that promotes learning? According to most sociocultural views of development, caregivers and other adults are said to bridge gaps in children's efforts to use particular tools, scaffolding children's fledging efforts (Rogoff 1990; Vygotsky 1978). Further, these approaches suggest that caregivers and the culture at large provide children with information that is not immediately available in the physical environment. According to these approaches, the meaning or functional significance of a culture's artefacts for the young or unskilled members of that culture are socially constructed via adult mediation.

Is this social-construction process the only way to account for the role played by caregivers in tool-use development? I have suggested that a Gibsonian or perception–action approach can also account for the role of the social context in the development of tool use and manual skills with objects, overall (Lockman in press; Lockman & McHale 1989). In a perception–action approach, however, objects are not considered impoverished stimuli. Neither do caregivers construct object meanings for their children. Rather, a perception–action approach implies that caregivers highlight information already available from objects. Caregivers may do so by demonstrating how to explore an object or tool, enabling children to see how to gain information from the artefact in a selective and efficient manner. Caregivers might also direct their children to use the object or tool in certain ways. They may do this by physically guiding children to perform an appropriate action and/or employing language to instruct children to perform a particular kind of action. Surprisingly, little is known about the strategies that human caregivers adopt to teach young children how to use tools even though these phenomena may constitute a critical difference between the tool-using capacities of humans and non-human primates (Inoue-Nakamura & Matsuzawa 1997; Tomasello 1998; Tomasello & Call 1997).

Research on early tool use from a perception–action perspective

The preceding considerations suggest that a perception–action perspective might offer a rich framework from which to consider the development of tool use. At the same time, it might challenge some commonly-held beliefs about the origins of tool use and help us understand how tool use may represent a more continuous development advance than typically believed.

In my own research, I have been studying how a percussive behaviour like banging in human infants may serve as a foundation for the emergence of such tool-use behaviours like hammering or pounding in older children. In past work with human children, banging has typically been viewed as a kind of rhythmical stereotypy. Such stereotypies in children have traditionally been considered to be simple, primitive forms of behaviour that can also be found in groups of older children and adults who are moderately to severely mentally disabled. Thelen (1979; 1981), however, has alerted us to the possibility that even simple repetitive forms of behaviours may be precursors to, or building blocks for, the development of more skilled forms of action. Thelen's proposal is consistent with other contemporary work on human motor development that suggests that 'new skills' are often assembled from existing actions and that as noted, early appearing rhythmical stereotypies may be incorporated into later developing instrumental behaviours.

Our own work has been largely motivated by the idea that tool use develops from object manipulation, particularly infants' ongoing exploratory efforts to relate objects to substrates in their surroundings. To use objects on substrates adaptively, an individual would need to take into account the *relation* between the physical characteristics of the object and the substrate and establish this relation with an appropriate action. For example, to produce noise with a hard, but not soft object, a child might bang the hard object on a thick, rigid substrate.

In the real world, however, the problem is even more complicated. Objects and substrates are typically not uniform in their properties. An individual object may vary in its physical characteristics, being composed for instance, of a smooth surface on one side, and a jagged surface on another. Likewise, substrates vary too in their physical composition. An extended substrate may suddenly change from being smooth to rough, solid to liquid, rigid to flexible. Because objects and substrates are *each* typically composed of different kinds of surfaces (defined in terms of physical composition and / or shape, extent and so on), relating objects to substrates adaptively often requires that an individual align a particular part of an object to a particular portion of a substrate. By the same token, tool use typically entails similar kinds of relational demands. On the assumption that the origins of tool use are rooted in the object-manipulation routines that infants employ to explore their environments, I suggest that understanding how infants relate objects to surfaces during object manipulation can lead to new insights about the foundations of tool use.

Our own research has been designed to elaborate this potential connection between object manipulation and tool use. As noted, we have been considering the development of object banging by infants and how this behaviour may be employed by infants for instrumental ends, including tool use. Banging is an especially interesting behaviour to examine as a precursor to tool use. Not only is it a manual behaviour that human infants exhibit early in development, but at a more general level, this behaviour is one that non-human primates employ and hominins are thought to have employed when using primitive tools (Ambrose 2001; Schick & Toth 1993). Thus understanding how infants begin to adapt related patterns of arm movements in the service of instrumental goals may suggest new ways — at the level of motor behaviour — of documenting linkages between tool-use capacities shared by humans and our primate and hominin relatives.

Banging and pounding objects
To address first the question of whether human infants indeed use banging in an instrumental fashion, Mimi Wright and I conducted a longitudinal study with a group of twenty infants, beginning at six months of age (Lockman & Wright 1989). Each infant was seen at monthly intervals, up until ten months of age. During each testing session, infants sat at a feeding table and were presented with different pairs of identical cubes on separate trials. One pair of cubes was hard, each composed of wood. One pair of cubes was soft, each composed of foam. And one pair was a mix of the two different types of surfaces: each member of the pair was half hard (wood) and half soft (foam). A primary goal of the study was to determine whether infants use banging as a way of acting on objects' affordances (Gibson & Walker 1984). In the present study, we assumed that infants would use banging to make noise, but only with certain kinds of objects, based on the object's physical composition. Additionally, we were interested in how

infants orient objects to exploit affordances unique to only certain sides of objects. This type of problem embodies the relational demands that arise in many tool-use situations. For this purpose, we examined how infants banged the mixed cubes.

Several major findings emerged. First, by eight months, infants banged the hard cubes and the mixed cubes significantly more often than the soft cubes. This result held regardless of the type of banging that infants displayed. When infants banged an object one at a time on the table surface, they did so more often when holding the hard or mixed cube than when holding the soft cube. Likewise, when infants banged the two cubes together simultaneously, they did so more often when holding the hard or mixed cubes than when holding the soft cubes. Taken together, these findings suggest that infants are using banging in an instrumental fashion to act on the affordances of the objects in their hands.

The next set of findings centred on the mixed cubes. Recall that we employed these cubes to examine whether infants exploit affordances that are unique to only certain sides of objects. Our results indicated that when infants were banging one of these objects singly, they more often oriented the cube so that the cube's hard side contacted the table surface. When infants were banging these mixed cubes together, however, they did not show evidence of appropriate object alignment. That is, they did not often orient the cubes so that the two hard sides would collide. These findings suggest that infants are beginning to align objects to surfaces, but there are important limitations to this ability based on the complexity of the alignment problem. When one side of an object needs to be oriented against a surface, infants in the second half year appear capable of exploiting the appropriate affordance relation. However, when two specific sides of objects need to be oriented and aligned with respect to one another, the relational demands appear to be beyond that of infants in the same age range. More broadly, we speculate that as infants work out these relational problems in the context of manipulating or exploring objects, they become better able to solve tool-use problems that require similar types of relational skills.

Banging or pounding handled objects

The prior study suggests that infants use banging in an instrumental fashion to exploit affordances that exist between at least one object and a surface. In these situations, infants are holding the objects directly. Tools, however, typically present an added level of complexity. Many tools can be considered compound objects composed of handles attached to the object or the tool part. A screwdriver, for instance, can be viewed as consisting of a handle attached to a thin, blunt, rigid rectangular end. Likewise, a hammer may be viewed as consisting of a handle attached to a thin or thick rigid cylindrical end. To use tools that are attached to handles, individuals must take into account how the handle functions as an extension of the object, and how displacements of the handle affect movement or positioning of the tool end. Unlike object manipulation, when individuals use tools with handles, they do not typically hold the object or tool end directly. Surprisingly, little is known about how infants begin to treat handles as extensions of objects, rather than objects in their own right. Our perception–action perspective suggests that infants' use of handled objects may be linked to efforts to use similar objects, without handles, adaptively.

To explore this possibility, we conducted a new longitudinal study on banging. We recruited a new sample of 19 infants, whom we tested monthly from eight to ten months of age (Cralley et al. 2000). During each testing session, we presented infants with the same objects that were used in the Lockman & Wright (1989) study, with the exception that the objects were now attached to long, thin handles. Thus on separate trials, infants were presented with a hammer-like object, but the properties of the mallet end of the hammer varied on each trial: mallets were either hard, soft or mixed (half hard / half soft).

Additionally, in this study and unlike the Lockman & Wright (1989) study, we also varied the properties of the surface on which infants were presented these hammer-like objects; i.e. on hard or soft table surfaces on separate trials. Thus during each session, each infant was presented six trials, for each possible hammer × surface combination. Our reason for varying the composition of the surface in this study was to examine directly whether infants take into account the *relation* between the object and substrate when they bang or pound objects. In the present experiment, we addressed this issue for objects that were attached to handles.

Overall, our results indicated that infants were able to employ handles adaptively. At all age levels, infants banged the hard hammer significantly more than the soft hammer, on the hard but not the soft table surface. Importantly, they did so when holding the hammer-like object by its handle. Thus infants distinguished between the material properties of the mallet part of the tool, even when they were not directly holding or touching this part. The result suggests that infants are treating the handle as an extension of the mallet or tool end, a critical component of effective tool use (see also McCarty et al. 2001).

Additionally, our findings indicated that infants applied a well-practised manual movement pattern when using these objects. In the present case, infants employed relatively rapid up–down arm movements or banging in a selective manner to act on the substrate, presumably to produce noise. This result is consistent with the idea that early appearing rhythmical stereotypies may be incorporated into later developing instrumental behaviours (Thelen 1979; 1981). It is also consistent with the idea that infants may employ similar actions when they manipulate objects and first begin to use tools.

Finally, our results revealed a potential limitation in infants' abilities to relate objects with handles to substrates. The limitations became apparent when infants were manipulating the mixed-mallet hammers. Although infants at all age levels more often banged the hard side of the mixed mallet on the table surface (while holding the object by its handle), infants did not vary the frequency of banging as a function of the table surface's properties (rigid or flexible). Apparently, the combined demands of orienting the mixed mallet and taking into account the table surface's properties caused difficulties for even the oldest infants in this study.

In sum, in the second half year, infants can use handled objects in an adaptive manner, appropriately relating the tool part of the object to a substrate, as long as both the tool part and substrate are uniform in terms of their physical composition. Infants encounter difficulty, however, when the relational demands are increased, as might occur when the tool part is not uniform in its physical properties and only one side/end of the tool part needs to be oriented with respect to a substrate to achieve a desired result. Our overall pattern of findings begin to suggest the conditions under which infants begin to relate objects to substrates appropriately and the types of relational demands that must be mastered by infants and possibly other creatures in order to use tools effectively.

Object manipulation and social context

Our previous studies and those of many others who have investigated object manipulation and early tool use in young human children have largely focused on how infants master this ability on their own. In the typical research study, a young child may be given an object or tool to explore — without help from a caregiver — to determine whether the child can be said to use the object in an adaptive or appropriate fashion. This type of approach is largely a legacy of Piagetian and related cognitive perspectives. By adopting these perspectives, investigators have conceptualized tool use and problem solving as a solitary activity to be mastered by the child or animal individually. Along these lines, investigators influenced by Piaget have conceptualized advances in problem solving and tool use as the result of gains in symbolic-reasoning abilities (Bates 1979; Piaget 1952). In a related vein, investigators who study problem solving and tool use in non-human primates and other animals, have often attributed success in such tasks to insight, the product of higher-order cognitive processes (e.g. Kohler 1931; Povinelli 2000).

In contrast, other investigators have alerted us to the idea that many cognitive processes, at least in humans, are inextricably embedded within the context of daily social activity (Rogoff 1990; Tomasello 1998). On this view, activities like tool use and problem solving are taught to human children by caregivers and other more skilled individuals in their immediate social milieu. According to an influential account of cognitive development, Vygotsky (1978) suggested that caregivers and other adults bridge gaps in children's attempts to solve problems and to use the tools of their culture, scaffolding children's fledgling efforts. Further, some sociocultural theorists maintain that the capacity to transmit cultural information and the complementary ability of the young of a species to learn from such efforts may require sociocognitive abilities that are uniquely human (Tomasello 1998). Consistent with this idea, reports that non-human primates actively teach their young how to use tools or objects adaptively have been exceedingly rare (Inoue-Nakamura & Matsuzawa 1997; Tomasello & Call 1997).

In our own work, we have been examining the possibility that human caregivers teach their infants how to explore objects and employ them adaptively. As noted, most past work on the development of object manipulation has neglected the possibility that this skill is transmitted socially. Instead, investigators have viewed object manipulation as either a motor skill and/or cognitive achievement, the product of either maturation (Gesell 1940) and/or learning by the child on its own (Piaget 1952).

In contrast to these viewpoints, we have proposed that the development of object manipulation may in part be a socially-mediated achievement (Lockman & McHale 1989). Further, we have argued that a perception–action approach is compatible with this idea (Lockman in press; Lockman & McHale 1989). We have suggested that when human caregivers interact with their infants either in the context of play or many daily activities, they may highlight information available from objects and in so doing, demonstrate the appropriate motor skills for gaining this information in a selective and efficient manner. Further, in some instances, human caregivers may actually take the hands of their infants and guide them to perform the appropriate behaviour, just as a sports coach might try to teach or improve a motor ability in a less-skilled individual.

Is there any evidence that human parents engage in such activities with their infants? James McHale and I investigated this possibility with mother–infant dyads. We tested pairs of mothers and their infants, by simply asking mothers to play with their infants with objects that differed along controlled physical dimensions. Infants ranged in age from six to ten months. Objects were all in the shape of pyramids, but varied along the dimensions of either texture, sound potential or colour. For the textured pyramids, the sides were composed of either different grades of sandpaper or Velcro. For the coloured pyramids, the sides were composed of different colours. And for the sounding pyramids, the pyramids contained either a bell or grains of rice, which rattled when the pyramid was shaken. By carefully controlling the composition of these objects and having them vary primarily across one dimension, we were able to determine the degree to which mothers and their infants varied their actions as a function of the objects' properties or affordances.

For our purposes here, we focus on the actions that mothers used when showing infants these objects. Our results indicated that mothers' manual actions were exquisitely tailored to the properties of these objects. With the multi-coloured objects, mothers displayed significantly more rotation of, and pointing to, individual sides of the pyramids. Rotation and pointing clearly highlight the visual characteristics of these objects. With the textured objects, mothers displayed significantly more fingering of the varied surfaces on these objects and more often touched infants with these objects, presumably so that infants might feel the different surfaces. These behaviours clearly draw attention to the tactile properties of the different textures on the objects. And with the sounding objects, mothers displayed more shaking and/or banging. These actions of course emphasize the objects' potential for producing sound.

Additionally, mothers actively directed infants to perform the appropriate exploratory action. With the textured object, for instance, mothers would drag their infants' fingers over the object to explore its texture. And with the sounding object, mothers would clasp their infants' hands to grasp the object and then shake the object with their infants. Such instances of co-action, we believe, may hold important lessons for infants regarding how to perform the action and how to obtain relevant information about the object.

Taken together, these findings suggest that caregivers may promote more appropriate forms of object manipulation in infants. In a related vein, findings by other investigators indicate that caregivers exaggerate their actions to demonstrate object properties or simple events to infants (Brand *et al.* 2002). More generally, we suggest that when caregivers either demonstrate or actively engage their infants to perform an appropriate form of object manipulation, infants are provided with just the type of rich learning environment that will promote mastery of object manipulation and tool use. Relevant information is highlighted and at times exaggerated. Irrelevant information is de-emphasized. Although we know little about the types of activities or strategies that human caregivers adopt to teach very young children how to use tools, our study on how mothers manipulate objects with their infants offers some clues. Caregivers may exaggerate actions when demonstrating tool-use behaviour to young children. Caregivers may also jointly carry out the action with their children, so that children obtain a clear sense of how the action should be performed. Although such maternal strategies may not be necessary for infants to learn how to manipulate objects that do not function as tools, we suggest that such mutual object-centred behaviours between caregivers and their infants set the stage for subsequent learning about more complex activities with objects, including tools.

It is tempting to speculate on the degree to which hominins taught their young how to use objects and perhaps simple tools. Knowledge about the ontogenetic social contexts in which object manipulation and tool use developed in different classes of hominins might shed light on the evolution of tool use, more generally. The lithic record is likely to be silent on this issue, however. Nevertheless, we suggest that because the social context in human development appears to be so important for learning to use objects and tools, the evolutionary advance entailed by human tool use and our close hominin ancestors may not just rest on advances in brain capacity associated with symbolic skills and language (see Gibson & Ingold 1993).

Conclusions

The emergence of flint knapping and other forms of stone technology raise fundamental questions about the underlying evolutionary advances entailed by the emergence of tool use. In this chapter, I have attempted to illustrate how a developmental perspective on human tool use might lead to new insights about the evolution of tool use, more generally. My argument is not that ontogeny recapitulates phylogeny. Rather I suggest that by examining the psychological skills that human infants need when they begin to engage in tool use, we can better appreciate the types of skills that are sufficient (although perhaps not necessary) to support tool use in other species, particularly our close evolutionary ancestors.

At the same time, I have tried to show that recent theoretical and empirical advances in our understanding of how tool use emerges early in human ontogenesis suggests that tool use may not require the sophisticated cognitive abilities that many have previously maintained (Bates 1979; Kohler 1931; Piaget 1952). More specifically, work on tool use from a perception–action perspective suggests that tool use may constitute a more continuous developmental achievement, building on infants' exploratory skills, particularly their abilities to manipulate objects and relate objects to substrates in their surroundings (Lockman 2000). Additionally, in humans, caregivers may play an important role in the emergence of both object manipulation and tool use, by demonstrating appropriate actions and by physically guiding infants' hands to perform these actions. From a perception–action perspective, these caregiver activities provide a rich learning environment. They constitute just the sorts of routines that infants need to perform to learn about the properties of objects and tools, particularly how objects and tools can effect change in the surrounding environment. Perhaps crucially for evolutionary accounts, these forms of teaching are rarely observed in our living primate relatives.

Taken together, these advances suggest that simple questions about whether tool use is unique or not in one species relative to others may not be the most profitable way to address the origins of tool use, either from a developmental or evolutionary perspective. Rather, we may need to reframe questions about the origins of tool use and ask in what ways or to what degree does tool use in one species differ from that seen in another *and* what ontogenetic differences across species contribute to such variation. By following this strategy, we may gain new insights into the origins of tool use, more generally.

References

Adolph, K.E., 1997. *Learning in the Development of Infant Locomotion.* (Monographs of the Society for Research in Child Development 62 (3, Serial 251).) Boston (MA): Blackwell Publishing.

Adolph, K.E., 2002. Learning to keep balance. *Advances in Child Development & Behavior* 30, 1–40.

Adolph, K.E., M.A. Eppler & E.J. Gibson, 1993. Crawling versus walking infants' perception of affordances for locomotion over sloping surfaces. *Child Development* 64, 1158–74.

Ambrose, S.H., 2001. Paleolithic technology and human evolution. *Science* 291, 1748–53.

Bates, E., 1979.The biology of symbols: some concluding thoughts, in *The Emergence of Symbols: Cognition and Communication in Infancy*, eds. E. Bates, L. Benigni, I. Bretherton, L. Camaioni & V. Volterra. New York (NY): Academic Press, 315–70.

Beck, B.B., 1980. *Animal Tool Behavior: the Use and Manufacture of Tools by Primates.* Hillsdale (NJ): Lawrence Erlbaum.

Bertenthal, B.I. & R.K. Clifton, 1998. Perception and action, in *Handbook of Child Psychology*, vol. 2: *Cognition, Perception and Language*, eds. D. Kuhn & R.S. Siegler. (W. Damon, Series ed.). New York (NY): Wiley, 51–102.

Boesch, C., 1993. Aspects of transmission of tool-use in wild chimpanzees, in *Tools, Language and Cognition in Human Evolution*, eds. K.R. Gibson & T. Ingold. New York (NY): Cambridge University Press, 171–83.

Brand, R.J., D.A. Baldwin & L.A. Ashburn, 2002. Evidence for motionese: modifications in mothers' infant-directed action. *Developmental Science* 5, 72–83.

Brown, A., 1990. Domain-specific principles affect learning and transfer in children. *Cognitive Science* 14, 107–33.

Chen, Z. & R.S. Siegler, 2000. *Across the Great Divide: Bridging the Gap Between Understanding of Toddlers' and Older Children's Thinking.* (Monographs of the Society for Research in Child Development 65 (2, Serial 261).) Boston (MA): Blackwell Publishing.

Connolly, K.J. & M. Dalgleish, 1993. Individual patterns of tool use by infants, in *Motor Development in Early and Later Childhood: Longitudinal Approaches*, eds. A.F. Kalverboer, B. Hopkins & R. Geuze. Cambridge: Cambridge University Press, 174–204.

Cralley, E.L., J. Laursen-Duarte, L. Ellman & J.J. Lockman, 2000. *Infant Tool Use.* Brighton: International Society for Infant Studies.

Duncker, K., 1946. On problem-solving. *Psychological Monographs* 58 (5), 1–112.

Fragaszy, D.M., E. Visalberghi & L. Fedigan, 2004. *The Complete Capuchin: the Biology of the Genus* Cebus. New York (NY): Cambridge University Press.

Gesell, A., 1940. *The First Five Years of Life.* New York (NY): Harper.

Gibson, E.J., 1988. Exploratory behavior in the development of perceiving, acting, and the acquiring of knowledge. *Annual Review of Psychology* 39, 1–41.

Gibson, E.J. & A.D. Pick, 2000. *An Ecological Approach to Perceptual Learning and Development.* New York (NY): Oxford University Press.

Gibson, E.J. & A.S. Walker, 1984. Development of knowledge of visual–tactual affordances of substance. *Child Development* 55, 453–60.

Gibson, E.J., G. Riccio, M.A. Schmuckler, T.A. Stoffregen, D. Rosenberg & J. Taormina, 1987. Detection of the traversability of surfaces by crawling and walking infants. *Journal of Experimental Psychology: Human Perception And Performance* 13, 533–44.

Gibson, J.J., 1979. *The Ecological Approach to Visual Perception.* Boston (MA): Houghton Mifflin.

Gibson, K.R. & T. Ingold, 1993. *Tools, Language and Cogni-*

tion in Human Evolution. New York (NY): Cambridge University Press.

Goldfield, E.C., 1995. *Emergent Forms: Origins and Early Development of Human Action and Perception*. New York (NY): Oxford University Press.

Goodall, J., 1986. *The Chimpanzees of Gombe*. Cambridge (MA): Belknap Press.

Greer, T. & J.J. Lockman, 1998. Using writing instruments: Invariances in young children and adults. *Child Development* 69, 888–902.

Hauser, M.D., L.R. Santos, G.M. Spaepen & H.E. Pearson, 2002. Problem solving, inhibition and domain-specific experience: experiments on cottontop tamarins, *Saguinus oedipus*. *Animal Behaviour* 64, 387–96.

Inoue-Nakamura, N. & T. Matsuzawa, 1997. Development of stone tool use by wild chimpanzees (*Pan troglodytes*). *Journal of Comparative Psychology* 111, 159–73.

Kohler, W., 1931. *The Mentality of Apes*. New York (NY): Vintage Press.

Lockman, J.J., 2000. A perception–action perspective on tool use development. *Child Development* 71, 137–44.

Lockman, J.J., in press. Object manipulation in context, in *Social and Cognitive Development in the Context of Individual, Social, and Cultural Factors*, eds. C. Raeff & J.B. Benson. London: Routledge.

Lockman, J.J. & D.H. Ashmead, 1983. Asynchronies in the development of manual behavior, in *Advances in Infancy Research (3)*, eds. L.W. Lipsitt & C. Rovee-Collier. Norwood (NJ): Ablex, 113–36.

Lockman, J.J. & J.P. McHale, 1989. Object manipulation in infancy: developmental and contextual determinants, in *Action in Social Context: Perspectives on Early Development*, eds. J.J. Lockman & N.L. Hazen. New York (NY): Plenum, 129–67.

Lockman, J.J. & M.H. Wright, 1989. *Relating Objects and Surfaces During Infancy: a Longitudinal Study*. Kansas City (MO): Society for Research in Child Development (April).

Marzke, M.W., 1997. Precision grips, hand morphology, and tools. *American Journal of Physical Anthropology* 102, 91–110.

Marzke, M.W. & R.F. Marzke, 2000. Evolution of the human hand: approaches to acquiring, analyzing and interpreting the anatomical evidence. *Journal of Anatomy* 197, 121–40.

Matsuzawa, T., 2001. *Primate Origins of Human Cognition and Behavior*. New York (NY): Springer-Verlag.

McCarty, M.E., R.K. Clifton & R.R. Collard, 2001. The beginnings of tool use by infants and toddlers. *Infancy* 2, 233–56.

McGrew, W. C., 1992. *Chimpanzee Material Culture*. New York

(NY): Cambridge University Press.

Palmer, C.F., 1989. The discriminating nature of infants' exploratory actions. *Developmental Psychology* 25, 885–93.

Piaget, J., 1952. *The Origins of Intelligence in Children*. New York (NY): International Universities Press.

Povinelli, D., 2000. *Folk Physics for Apes*. New York (NY): Oxford University Press.

Rock, I., 1983. *The Logic of Perception*. Cambridge (MA): MIT Press.

Rogoff, B., 1990. *Apprenticeship in Thinking: Cognitive Development in Social Context*. Oxford: Oxford University Press.

Schick, K.D. & N. Toth, 1993. *Making Silent Stones Speak*. New York (NY): Simon & Schuster.

Siegler, R.S., 1996. *Emerging Minds*. New York (NY): Oxford University Press.

Smitsman, A.W., 1997. The development of tool use: changing boundaries between organism and environment, in *Evolving Explanations of Development*, eds. C. Dent-Read & P. Zukow-Goldring. Washington (DC): American Psychological Association, 301–29.

Thelen, E., 1979. Rhythmical stereotypies in normal human infants. *Animal Behaviour* 27, 699–715.

Thelen, E., 1981. Rhythmical behavior in infancy: an ethological perspective. *Developmental Psychology* 17, 237–57.

Thelen, E., 1995. Motor development: a new synthesis. *American Psychologist* 50, 79–95.

Tomasello, M., 1998. Uniquely primate, uniquely human. *Developmental Science* 1, 1–32.

Tomasello, M. & J. Call, 1997. *Primate Cognition*. New York (NY): Oxford University Press.

Tomasello, M., E.S. Savage-Rumbaugh & A.C. Kruger, 1993. Imitative learning of actions on objects by children, chimpanzees, and enculturated chimpanzees. *Child Development* 64, 1688–705.

Vygotsky, L., 1978. *Mind in Society*. Cambridge (MA): Harvard University Press.

Want, S.C. & P.L. Harris, 2002. How do children ape? Applying concepts from the study of non-human primates to the developmental study of 'imitation' in children. *Developmental Science* 5, 1–13.

Whiten, A., J. Goodall, W.C. McGrew, T. Nishida, V. Reynolds, Y. Sugiyama, E.G. Tutin, R.W. Wrangham & C. Boesch, 1999. Culture in chimpanzees. *Nature* 399, 682–5.

Wynn, T., 1993. Layers of thinking in tool use behavior, in *Tools, Language and Cognition in Human Evolution*, eds. K.R. Gibson & T. Ingold. New York (NY): Cambridge University Press, 389–406.

Chapter 22

The Social and Cultural Context of Stone-knapping Skill Acquisition

Dietrich Stout

Modern human technological practice is an inherently social phenomenon saturated with cultural meaning. Research among the stone-adze makers of Langda village in Indonesian Propinsi Papua (Irian Jaya) (Stout 2002) illustrates the integral role that culturally-constructed values and relationships play in the acquisition and performance of sophisticated stone-knapping skills, suggesting new perspectives on prehistoric lithic technologies. The emergence of increasingly skill-intensive stone technologies over the course of human evolution implies change in the social context of skill acquisition and constitutes important evidence of hominin social cognition and cultural origins.

…there is no such thing as human nature independent of culture. (Geertz 1973)

Humans live and act in culturally-constructed environments. This construction is embodied, not merely in extensive modifications of the physical environment, but more fundamentally in the mapping of meanings and values to that environment (Ingold 1996). The historically-evolving cultural environments in which humans live shape our opportunities for action and learning at a fundamental level, providing a cumulative 'ratchet effect' that may underlie many of the distinctive cognitive skills of modern humans (Tomasello 1999). Understanding the origins and history of this uniquely human mode of cultural existence is a central question for human-evolutionary studies.

One potential source of insight into this question lies in the physical traces of proto-human behaviour, and particularly in the durable stone artefacts that dominate the archaeological record. In order to be useful, however, these artefacts must be carefully interpreted using *actualistic* models based on observable phenomena in the modern world. Artefact replication and other experimental approaches have provided valuable insights into knapping techniques, tool functions and site formation processes (review in Toth 1991) and are even beginning to elucidate the neural foundations of knapping skill (Stout *et al.* 2000; Stout this volume). However, experimental approaches are ill suited to exploring the cultural dimensions of stone knapping. For this, an ethnographic perspective is needed.

Figure 22.1. *The adze makers of Langda.*

331

Research among the stone-adze makers of Langda village (Fig. 22.1) in the central mountains of Indonesian Propinsi Papua (Irian Jaya) (Stout 2002) provides an opportunity to employ such a perspective. Obviously these modern craftsmen do not provide a direct window on the past, but they do offer a valuable example and source of inspiration for new perspectives on prehistoric stone knapping. In particular, the Langda craftsmen illustrate the pivotal role of social context in stone knapping skill acquisition. Appreciation of the social and cultural foundations of modern human knapping skill is an essential reference point when assessing the cognitive significance of prehistoric lithic technologies.

Technological practice

Although anthropologists often drawn a sharp distinction between social and technological phenomena (Ingold 1993), this is a false dichotomy. As argued by Dobres (2000, 96–7), 'Technologies are always and everywhere socially constituted' and, in fact, 'the production of matter and the production of meaning are instantiated by each other'. Technology is more than just a static collection of external objects (tools) and the internal rules (technical knowledge); it is an ongoing process of dynamic interaction between people and their social and physical environment.

Technological proficiency is a skill acquired over time through engagement with this environment. Although it is conventional to speak of the social 'transmission' of technical knowledge, this is a misnomer. Knowledge and skills are not objects to be passed around, but rather abilities to be developed. Social interaction helps to provide a supportive context (Vygotsky 1978) or *scaffolding* (Wood *et al.* 1976) for the emergence of abilities which are themselves stable and adaptive modes of interaction with the environment.

Research on the subject of *distributed cognitions* has underlined the fact that people routinely 'think in conjunction or partnership with others and with the help of culturally provided tools and implements' (Salomon 1993, xiii). In human technological practice, these 'tools and implements' may be conceptual as well as physical, including ideas regarding the potential or appropriate uses of objects (cf. Ingold 1996). Technological practice is a property emergent from the dynamic interaction of individuals in environments over time, rather than the simple expression of some set of transmitted rules.

Work on distributed cognitions generally emphasizes the flow of information between individual and environment, for example in the 'off-loading [of] mental reasoning processes as action constraints of ei-

ther physical or symbolic environments' (Pea 1993, 48). However, human cognition is more than just the dispassionate processing of information and is intimately tied with somatic sensations and emotional states (Damasio 1994; Greenspan 1996). Behavioural strategies and abilities are *situated* (Brown *et al.* 1989) in particular environmental contexts, often in ways that have more to do with emotional investment, meaning and motivation (e.g. Perret-Clermont *et al.* 1991; Fogel 1997, 417–22; and the 'mindful engagement' of Salomon *et al.* 1991, 4) than with classically 'cognitive' constraints.

As outlined in Damasio's (1994) *somatic marker hypothesis* of human cognition, emotions and associated bodily sensations help to organize experience by providing a fast and reliable system of affective categorization. So-called 'visceral reactions' to a situation drastically reduce the number of potential behavioural responses that need to be considered, and provide an affective 'weighting' to available options. When the ability to form associations between emotion and experience is compromised (as, for example, in patients with damage to the ventromedial prefrontal cortex of the brain), social skills, planning, and decision-making abilities are all drastically impaired.

Although emotion and motivation are often considered to be private and individual, they arise like other mental phenomena from the encounter with the lived-in world. In humans especially, emotional associations are shaped by social experiences and the negotiation of cultural meaning. Emotional interaction is essential for healthy mental development (Greenspan 1996), and in tragic cases where children are deprived of nurturing emotional experiences, mental health, social skills, and learning abilities are all jeopardized.

For both children and adults, the acquisition of technical skills is an evolving form of membership in a community of practice (Lave & Wenger 1991). The development of new knowledge and skills is just one part of a more general process of changing interpersonal relationships and identity that is emotionally charged and motivated. In other words, human technical learning is *meaningful* process. For this reason, the cultural construction of meaning and its influences on task-related emotional valences and attitudes must be considered as central features of human technological practice. In Langda, these and other elements may be investigated in the context of a traditional stone-knapping industry.

Skill and meaning in the Langda adze industry

Prior to the introduction and spread of metal tools, ground-stone axes and adzes were the primary heavy-duty tools of the New Guinea Highlands. These implements were used primarily to clear land, but also as all-purpose cutting tools for tasks ranging from woodworking and fiber processing to butchery. Simply put, the horticultural lifestyle of the Highlands would not have been possible without ground stone axe/adzes (Pétrequin & Pétrequin 1993). Stone axe/adzes were also of great symbolic and ceremonial importance as items of ritual exchange and bride-wealth payments, war trophies, and sacred objects (Pétrequin & Pétrequin 1993; Hampton 1999).

Currently (as of October 1999) in Langda, metal tools have replaced stone adzes for most everyday tasks. However, this transition has been a relatively recent one, and the use of stone adzes was more common as little as 10–15 years ago (Toth *et al.* 1992). Stone adzes remain an important part of the culture of Langda, for example in their continued role as an expected part of bride-wealth payments and in the contribution they make to local identity. Nevertheless, traditional patterns of production, use and exchange are clearly changing. The role of stone adzes and of their makers in Langda is in flux, but, for the time being, elements of traditional arrangements are preserved in both current practice and recent memory.

Even today and much more so in the past, the traditional value of stone adzes makes involvement in their production a potential source of both prestige and wealth. In the non-stratified societies of the New Guinea Highlands, personal stature derives from a combination of personality and social networking. Exchange is central to the development of such networks, including the expression and maintenance of group ties through ceremonial *moka* exchange (Strathern 1971) and of individual relationships through semiformal 'exchange partnerships' (Fiel 1987). Among other things, the value of stone adzes as exchange items has allowed their makers to maintain extensive social networks, contributing to their personal prestige, wealth and influence.

Due to the great value of stone adzes, the skills and raw materials needed for their production are closely regulated. Adze making is an exclusively male occupation entered through a semi-formal system of apprenticeship that is generally open only to the 'sons' of established adze makers (kinship in Langda follows a bifurcate merging or 'Omaha' system that

Figure 22.2. *The head adze maker of Langda evaluating roughouts following a communal quarrying trip to the Ey River. He is responsible for redistributing these roughouts to the men who participated.*

does not distinguish between sons and nephews). The craftsmen themselves report that adze-making skill is too valuable to teach to anyone outside close family, and each adze maker is able to recite a pedigree of past masters through whom they have inherited the tradition. The longest such list includes fourteen names stretching back to a semi-mythical progenitor of the craft, *Menminy Malyoman Balyo*.

The adze makers of Langda recognize the authority of a 'headman' who controls access to the quarry sites near the village and presides over production in general. For example, the headman regulates the distribution among the other craftsmen of blanks and rough-outs produced during communal quarrying expeditions to the river (Fig. 22.2). Hampton (1999) attributes this authority to a system of hereditary ownership over the quarry sites. Such ownership over quarries, blanks and even hammerstones is jealously guarded, even (within living memory) to the extent of using deadly force.

Apprenticeship
Traditionally, adze-making apprenticeship began at the age of 12–13. Apprenticeship typically lasted for several years, although it might take ten years or more for the highest level of skill to be achieved. According to informants, a boy might express his interest by accompanying the adze makers on quarrying trips, bringing them food while they worked and by attending to them in general. For his part, the potential master would evaluate the seriousness and commitment of the prospective student, perhaps asking him

Figure 22.3. *Adze making is a great source of pleasure for the men who participate in the craft.*

ties (birth records and exact ages are generally not available). Many children are enrolled in a primary school that has been established in the village, and the decision to pursue an apprenticeship now seems to be more commonly made later in life. Despite decreasing everyday usage, adze making continues to be a source of pride and identity for its practitioners, and motivations for entering into apprenticeship may have changed in a way which appeals more to older individuals.

Although motivation for participation may have changed somewhat, the adze makers make it clear that commitment and devotion to the craft remain highly valued. For example, one man explained that his (deceased) father was an exceptional knapper because, for him, adze making always came first. He would make time for it despite the work required by his gardens, and work long hours without eating or resting. Other adze makers similarly speak of forgetting their wives, gardens and everything else while knapping, and emphasize that a man's hand will 'grow heavy' and lose its skill without continual practice. Commitment to the craft is more, however, than just a duty or virtue. Knapping is also a great source of pleasure (Fig. 22.3), and craftsmen often call out in excitement after successful flake removals. Adze making, which is always conducted as a group exercise, is an enjoyable and meaningful social activity.

This social dimension is central, not only in the everyday conduct of the craft, but also in learning and skill acquisition by apprentices. Although each apprentice has a special relationship with his nominal 'master', he actually learns to make adzes through participation and interaction with the entire community of adze makers. In the words of one man, learning to make adzes is 'not like in school' but rather involves 'sitting together'. Overt instruction, both verbal and gestural, is commonplace but forms only one component of the social scaffold that supports skill acquisition.

Because they are participating in a group endeavour, apprentices are able to gain experience with aspects of production that would be inaccessible for them individually: they are

Figure 22.4. *An experienced craftsman offering advice to an apprentice.*

to do some flaking in order to gauge his potential. Acceptance might be indicated, among other things, by the gift of a hammerstone.

In Langda today, this pattern has changed and most apprentices appear to be in their mid-twen-

able to participate in the quarrying of suitable materials even if the they could not locate these on their own, they gain experience roughing-out blanks even if they have difficulty producing them, and they are able to practise finer knapping even if they themselves produce few usable roughouts/preforms (the Langda adze makers recognize only one intermediate stage between the blank and the finished form, covering a wide range of reduction). It is also common for more experienced knappers to help apprentices by giving advice (Fig. 22.4) about where to strike the core (and why), or even by taking and working the piece through difficult points themselves. These various forms of facilitation allow apprentices to perform beyond the unassisted level, in the optimum learning situation Vygotsky (1978) refers to as the *zone of proximal development*. At the same time, the social contexts and cultural meanings associated with adze making help to provide emotional value for practice and participation, influencing motivational, attentional and decision making processes (Damasio 1994).

Skill

Differences in knapping ability between experienced and novice craftsmen in Langda are evident in the size and proportions of adze heads (Fig. 22.5) and waste flakes produced, as well as in the strategic organization of knapping operations. As detailed elsewhere (Stout 2002), experienced knappers achieve superior results by: 1) removing longer and relatively thinner flakes allowing greater control over evolving core form; 2) manipulating local elements of core morphology (e.g. ridges, flake scars) to facilitate desired flake removals; and 3) employing more consistent and effective overall reduction strategies. The acquisition of knapping skill thus occurs at multiple levels, from the discovery of effective movement synergies for individual flake removals to perception of the affordances of changing core morphologies and the emergence of stable reduction strategies.

As illustrated by the work of Roux *et al.* (1995; Bril *et al.* 2000) with the stone-bead knappers of Cambay, India, higher-order knapping skills must emerge from mastery of elementary knapping gestures. In Cambay, superior craftsmen display a greater homogeneity of movement arising from their achievement of an optimized and stable motor state. This achievement, which takes years of practice, facilitates successful flake removals and allows for the development of more sophisticated reduction strategies that are flexible rather than stereotyped. Conceptually, less-skilled craftsmen 'know' about the necessary stages in the production of high-quality beads, but they do not comprehend them in the same experiential way as more skilled craftsmen.

A similar situation exists in Langda. Waste-flake data reveal that skilled knappers deploy more precise and effective motor synergies, reliably delivering a large amount of force to a small target. Such effective

Figure 22.5. *As illustrated by these examples, adze heads produced by skilled craftsmen (left) are longer, relatively narrower and more regular in plan form than those produced by apprentices (right).*

knapping is a specialized kind of 'action-for-perception' that allows for the discovery of otherwise inaccessible affordances of core morphology. For example, there is the dorsal ridge of the adze-head. Apprentices are aware of the need to shape this ridge but avoid working it because of the difficulty of the large platform angles typically involved. Until they have developed sufficient elementary flaking skills, apprentices are unable to gain a practical understanding of the role of the dorsal ridge in overall reduction strategies. Apprentice strategies are demonstrably less uniform and coherent than expert strategies (Stout 2002) because apprentices lack the control needed to experience and stabilize larger-scale relationships in evolving core morphologies.

Conventional approaches to stone tools and cognition (Gowlett 1992; Robson Brown 1993; Karlin & Julien 1994; Wynn 2002) generally focus on abstract planning, conceptualization and the 'imposition of arbitrary form' (Holloway 1969) rather than on the perceptual-motor skill needed for effective flake removal. Ultimately, however, the former must emerge from the latter and the strategic understanding of a skilled knapper bears little resemblance to an abstract recipe or algorithm. Preliminary investigations of brain activity during stone knapping (Stout *et al.* 2000;

Stout this volume) corroborate the predominance of externally-directed perception and action over internally-directed conceptualization. Examples from Cambay and Langda similarly illustrate the fact that, for modern humans at least, it is much more difficult and time consuming to achieve actual knapping skill than it is to develop a theoretical knowledge of the appropriate stages of reduction.

Meaning

The description of prehistoric stone-knapping technologies in terms of abstract concepts (e.g. Wynn 1989) or rule systems (e.g. Gowlett 1996) is a useful heuristic but does not address the effortful process of behavioural exploration through which actual knapping skills emerge. Much of the cognitive sophistication involved in prehistoric and pre-modern lithic technologies probably had to do with involvement in social contexts that allowed or facilitated such exploration rather than with the comprehension of a particular target form or procedural recipe.

In Langda, an elaborate system of cultural meanings provides the context for skill acquisition and execution. Adze making is a social process involving relationships between masters, peers and apprentices as well as resource owners, ancestors, mythical figures and even the personified stones themselves, not to mention the social exchange networks into which finished adzes enter. Technological practice occurs in a historically-evolved cultural environment that includes craft-related values, expectations, terminology and techniques as well as physical artefacts and locations.

As described above (p. 33 'Apprenticeship') and in Stout (2002), the social and cultural context of adze making in Langda provides an important scaffold for skill learning. Participation in the craft, and particularly movement from apprenticeship to mastery, involves changes in identity, relationships and prestige that can provide powerful motivation for practitioners. The community of adze makers also structures the learning process by providing materials and occasions for practice while restricting apprentices to tasks of appropriate difficulty. This scaffolding affords apprentices the opportunity to participate to some extent in all stages of production and to benefit from the commentary, demonstration, discussion and assistance of fellow craftsmen. Adze-making activities are conducted in social groups that provide opportunities for focused individual practice and a meaningful and enjoyable form of interaction. Situated in this context, apprentices have the opportunity and motivation to devote many hours over a period of years to the acquisition of adze-making skills that include both the shaping of stone and negotiation of the cultural environment.

Obviously, Langda provides an extreme example of an elaborate and skill-intensive stone-knapping technology. Certainly many prehistoric knapping technologies were less technically demanding, and many were probably implemented by less elaborate systems of craft-related cultural meaning and social relations. The stone-scraper technology used by hide workers in southern Ethiopia (Clark & Kurashina 1981; Brandt 1996; Weedman 2000) provides one modern example of a more 'casual' approach to stone knapping.

When it comes to the stone-tool behaviours of extinct hominin species, there is little evidence of skill and sophistication anywhere near the level seen in Langda. It is even debatable whether such behaviours were 'cultural' in the fully modern sense. Study of the modern adze-making industry of Langda will not resolve this debate but, in conjunction with studies of non-human primates, such examples of modern human skill do provide an essential point of comparison.

Stone knapping and the origins of culture

The impressive stone-knapping skills of senior adze makers in Langda are reflected in physical attributes of the tools and *debitage* that they produce. In particular, adze heads that are long but thin and narrow and waste flakes that are large and thin reflect the exercise of knapping skills acquired over years of practice (Stout 2002). Experimental replication can begin to provide similar insights into the skills indicated by proto-human stone artefacts (e.g. Callahan 1979, 35; Schick 1994, 584), and more such work is clearly needed. Future experimental research might benefit from explicit attention to the processes of knapping-skill acquisition, and from focused archaeological case studies that take raw material and technological variability fully into account.

To the extent that the knapping skills of ancient hominins can be divined, possible social and cultural implications may be considered. For example, experienced experimental knappers generally agree that the production of refined later Acheulean bifaces requires a level of skill that, even for modern humans, is attained only after substantial practice (Callahan 1979; Bradley & Sampson 1986; Edwards 2001). Contemporary Western knappers acquire this skill within academic, craft and recreational cultures (see Whittaker 1994, 60–63; Olausson 1998) that create opportunities, meaning and motivation for participation. What social (cultural?) situations might have attended the acquisition of comparable skills in archaic *Homo*?

In all prehistoric technologies, social arrangements would have had to provide sufficient opportunity for participation by learners. At a bare minimum, this requires social tolerance among conspecifics: the simple opportunity to share activity space without conflict. In fact, varying degrees of social tolerance do seem to influence the distribution of tool use across modern ape populations (van Schaik *et al.* 1999; Russon 2002). Even in the nut-cracking chimpanzees of Bossou, Guinea, a lack of adult tolerance for juveniles may inhibit skill learning beyond infancy because only infants are afforded 'opportunities to freely access stones and nuts' (Inoue-Nakamura & Matsuzawa 1997). A relatively high degree of social tolerance would have been important prerequisite for the development of increasingly diverse and skill-intensive tool behaviours during hominin evolution.

Modern human learning involves more than simple tolerance, however. In Langda, apprentices participate in a structured and meaningful community of practice that provides scaffolding and motivation for the learning process. Participation is a question of identity, and its value to the learner 'lies in *becoming* part of the community' (Lave & Wenger 1991, 111). Chimpanzee societies also scaffold learning, as in the *stimulation* and *facilitation* of infant nut cracking described by Boesch (1991), but they do not possess the same *regulative* (Ingold 1996) dimension of cultural meaning that specifies identities like teacher, learner or craftsperson.

In chimpanzees, learning is facilitated by a combination of adults' affective response to infants (tolerance) and infants' emotionally-motivated tendency to attend to, interact with and generally stay close to adults. These mechanisms of facilitation tend to break down with maturation, however, and are never elaborated into the system of meaningful social relationships and culturally-mediated identities that support human technical learning. Inoue-Nakamura & Matsuzawa (1997), for example, report that infant chimpanzees frequently emulate the nut-cracking behaviour of adults but receive little or no feedback or 'social reinforcement'. Juveniles, on the other hand, are actively denied opportunities for participation and are often chased away if they try 'to get stones and/or nuts at the side of the adults'.

Nevertheless, wild apes do engage in a range of skilled foraging activities (e.g. Byrne & Byrne 1993; Matsuzawa 1996; van Schaik *et al.* 1999) that have been loosely compared to human skills in terms of the timing, duration, and social 'transmission routes' of learning (Russon 2002). For example, many everyday human skills, like ape foraging skills, are acquired during childhood through interaction with parents (Hewlett & Cavalli-Sforza 1986). In the case of more specialized technical skills, the ten years it takes nut-cracking chimpanzees to reach 'refined' adult levels of proficiency (Matsuzawa 1996) is at least superficially reminiscent of the general '10-year rule' in human expert skill learning (Ericsson & Lehmann 1996) and the specific estimates of time to mastery provided by the Langda craftsmen. Closer consideration of such expert skill learning, however, reveals important differences between ape and human conditions.

As observed by Ericsson & Lehman (1996, 278), the fact 'that [human] experts in most domains attain their highest level of performance a decade or more *after maturation* points to the importance of extensive preparation' (italics added). Kaplan *et al.* (2000), for example, have shown that, unlike chimpanzees, human foragers do not achieve their maximal production until at least 10–15 years after maturation. In Langda adze-making apprenticeship traditionally did not even begin until around age 12. This is in striking contrast to ape skill learning, which is typically concentrated in infancy due to the changes in social relations (tolerance) that occur with maturation (Russon 2002).

Another critical difference between ape and human skill learning lies in the structure and intensity of practice. Ericsson & Lehman (1996) argue that many everyday human activities show only a weak correlation between experience and performance because such activities 'afford few opportunities for effective learning and improvement of skill'. Expert learning, in contrast, is characterized by highly-structured *deliberate practice* (Ericsson *et al.* 1993) that is often designed by a coach or teacher and requires an individual's full concentration. Such deliberate practice is exemplified in the process of knapping skill acquisition seen in Langda and is afforded by the presence of extensive social and cultural scaffolds for learning. Research is needed to better characterize the investments made by apes during foraging skill acquisition, but it seems clear that ape skills, acquired during infancy in relatively unstructured social learning environments, are more analogous to 'everyday' human skills than to expert performance.

Clear continuities thus exist between ape and human skill learning, but also important differences. Most salient of these differences is the presence in humans of intensive, socio-culturally supported expert skill learning by adults. Insofar as human intelligence is itself a form of developing expertise (Sternberg *et al.* 2000), any account of human mental evolution must deal with the emergence of this uniquely human mode of expert skill acquisition. Comparison of modern human and ape skills with those evident from prehistoric stone tools is one important method by which this question may be addressed.

Nut cracking, for example, is one of the most difficult perceptual-motor skills acquired by chimpanzees in the wild and is supported by both stimulation and facilitation of infant learning. In the absence of cultural mechanisms supporting deliberate practice and expert skill learning (as seen, for example, in 'enculturated' apes in captivity), efficient nut cracking may approximate the upper limit of skill acquisition afforded by chimpanzee societies. Research explicitly comparing chimpanzee nut-cracking and human stone-knapping skill acquisition would thus be extremely valuable.

Modern actualistic research, whether experimental, ethnographic or ethological, clearly cannot reveal the details of prehistoric social organization, but it can provide insight into some of the necessary conditions underlying particular kinds of behaviour. For example, evidence that particular pre-modern stone technologies required investments in skill acquisition appreciably beyond the levels seen in wild apes would be strongly indicative of hominin cultural elaboration. Exactly what early hominin 'proto-cultures' might have looked like is open to question. Donald (1991), for example, has suggested a pre-linguistic stage of *mimetic culture*, in which representational physical action (*mimesis*) supported 'collectively maintained customs, games, skills and representations' that served 'as the collective definition of society' (p. 173). What is clear is that the (proto) cultural foundations of expert skill acquisition would have necessarily involved the establishment of routinely *intersubjective* (Quine 1960) social relations.

Intersubjectivity, or the understanding of others as intentional agents, is the foundation of human culture and creates a medium for joint attention and action, including true pedagogy (Rogoff 1990). Intersubjective awareness transforms simple social interactions into meaningful social relationships and has been characterized by Tomasello (1999) as *the* key adaptation underlying the emergence of modern human cognitive sophistication. The constitutive sociality supported by intersubjectivity does not necessarily imply the abstract normative framework of rules and expectations seen in modern human regulative sociality (Ingold 1996), but it does offer a shared mental space for intentional learning and teaching. It is the saturation of everyday social interactions with intersubjective meaning that is lacking in modern ape societies, and which would have allowed for the invention of distinctly hominin proto-cultures and skill-intensive technological practices.

Acknowledgements

Research in Langda was funded through generous grants from the Ligabue Study and Research Center in Venice, Italy, and the Center for Research into the Anthropological Foundations of Technology (CRAFT) at Indiana University. None of this work would have been possible without the remarkable craftsmanship and cooperation of the Langda adze makers, the assistance and companionship of Daniel Balyo, and the invaluable aid of Dick and Margareet Kroneman. I would especially like to recognize the unparalleled contributions of the late Diman Balyo. I would like to thank Giancarlo Ligabue for his groundbreaking efforts in making Langda known to the archaeological community, and Nicholas Toth for both suggesting and facilitating my own trip to the plateau. My attendance at the Knapping Stone workshop was supported by a David C. Skomp Fellowship from the Department of Anthropology, Indiana University, Bloomington.

References

Boesch, C., 1991. Teaching in wild chimpanzees. *Animal Behavior* 41(3), 530–32.

Bradley, B. & C.G. Sampson, 1986. Analysis by replication of two Acheulian artefact assemblages, in *Stone Age Prehistory*, eds G.N. Bailey & P. Callow. Cambridge: Cambridge University Press, 29–45.

Brandt, S.A., 1996. The ethnoarchaeology of flaked stone tool use in southern Ethiopia, in *Aspects of African Archaeology: Papers from the 10th Congress of the PanAfrican Association for Prehistory and Related Studies*, eds. G. Pwitit & R. Soper. Harare: University of Zimbabwe Publications, 733–8.

Bril, B., V. Roux & G. Dietrich, 2000. Skills involved in the knapping of chalcedony beads: motor and cognitive characteristics of a complex situated action, in *Cornaline de l'Inde: des pratiques techniques de Cambay aux techno-systemes de l'Indus*, ed. V. Roux. Paris: Editions de la Maison des sciences de l'homme, 207–329. [English cd-rom.]

Brown, J.S., A. Collins & P. Duguid, 1989. Situated cognition and the culture of learning. *Educational Researcher* 18, 32–42.

Byrne, R.W. & J.M.E. Byrne, 1993. The complex leaf-gathering skills of mountain gorillas (*Gorilla g. beringei*): variability and standardization. *American Journal of Primatology* 31, 241–61.

Callahan, E., 1979. The basics of biface knapping in the Eastern Fluted Point Tradition: a manual for flintknappers and lithic analysts. *Archaeology of Eastern North America* 7(1), 1–172.

Clark, J.D. & H. Kurashina, 1981. A study of the work of a modern tanner in Ethiopia and its relevance for archaeological interpretation, in *Modern Material Culture: the Study of Us*, eds R.A. Gould & M.B. Schiffer. New York (NY): Academic Press, 303–43.

Damasio, A.R., 1994. *Descartes' Error: Emotion, Reason, and the Human Brain*. New York (NY): G.P. Putnam's Sons.

Dobres, M.-A., 2000. *Technology and Social Agency*. Oxford: Blackwell Publishers.

Donald, M., 1991. *Origins of the Modern Mind: Three Stages in the Evolution of Culture and Cognition*. Cambridge (MA): Harvard University Press.

Edwards, S.W., 2001. A modern knapper's assessment of the technical skills of the Late Acheulean biface workers at Kalambo Falls, in *Kalambo Falls Prehistoric Site*, vol. III, ed. J.D. Clark. Cambridge: Cambridge University Press, 605–11.

Ericsson, K.A. & A.C. Lehmann, 1996. Expert and exceptional performance: evidence of maximal adaptation to task constraints. *Annual Review of Psychology* 47, 273–305.

Ericsson, K.A., R.T. Krampe & C. Tesch-Romer, 1993. The role of deliberate practice in the acquisition of expert performance. *Psychological Review* 100(3), 363–406.

Fiel, D.K., 1987. *The Evolution of Highland Papua New Guinea Societies*. Cambridge: Cambridge University Press.

Fogel, A., 1997. 'Information, creativity, and culture', in *Evolving Explanations of Development*, eds. C. Dent-Read & P. Zukow-Goldring. Washington (DC): American Psychological Association, 413–44.

Geertz, C., 1973. *The Interpretation of Cultures*. New York (NY): Basic Books.

Gowlett, J.A.J., 1992. Early human mental abilities, in *The Cambridge Encyclopedia of Human Evolution*, eds. S. Bunney & S. Jones. Cambridge: Cambridge University Press, 341–5.

Gowlett, J.A.J., 1996. Mental abilities of early *Homo*: elements of constrain and choice in rule systems, in *Modelling the Early Human Mind*, eds. P. Mellars & K.R. Gibson. (McDonald Institute Monographs.) Cambridge: McDonald Institute for Archaeological Research, 191–216.

Greenspan, S.I., 1996. *The Growth of the Mind and the Endangered Origins of Intelligence*. Reading (MA): Addison-Wesley Publishing Company, Inc.

Hampton, O.W.B., 1999. *Culture of Stone: Sacred and Profane Uses of Stone among the Dani*. College Station (TX): Texas A & M University Press.

Hewlett, B.S. & L.L. Cavalli-Sforza, 1986. Cultural transmission among Aka pygmies. *American Anthropologist* 88, 922–34.

Holloway, R.L., 1969. Culture: a human domain. *Current Anthropology* 10(4), 395–412.

Ingold, T., 1993. Tool-use, sociality and intelligence, in *Tools, Language and Cognition in Human Evolution*, eds K.R. Gibson & T. Ingold. Cambridge: Cambridge University Press, 429–47.

Ingold, T., 1996. Social relations, human ecology, and the evolution of culture: an exploration of concepts and definitions, in *Handbook of Human Symbolic Evolution*, eds A. Lock & C.R. Peters. Oxford: Clarendon Press, 178–203.

Inoue-Nakamura, N. & T. Matsuzawa, 1997. Development of stone tool use by wild chimpanzees (*Pan troglodytes*). *Journal of Comparative Psychology* 111(2), 159–73.

Kaplan, H., K. Hill, J. Lancaster & A.M. Hurtado, 2000. A theory of human life history evolution: diet, intelligence, and longevity. *Evolutionary Anthropology* 9, 156–85.

Karlin, C. & M. Julien, 1994. Prehistoric technology: a cognitive science?, in *The Ancient Mind: Elements of a Cognitive Archaeology*, eds C. Renfrew & E.B.W. Zubrow. Cambridge: Cambridge University Press, 152–64.

Lave, J. & E. Wenger, 1991. *Situated Learning: Legitimate Peripheral Participation*. Cambridge: Cambridge University Press.

Matsuzawa, T., 1996. Chimpanzee intelligence in nature and in captivity: isomorphism of symbol use and tool use, in *Great Ape Societies*, eds. W. McGrew, L. Marchant & T. Nishida. Cambridge: Cambridge University Press, 196–209.

Olausson, D., 1998. Different strokes for different folks: possible reasons for variation in quality of knapping. *Lithic Technology* 23(2), 90–114.

Pea, R.D., 1993. Practices of distributed intelligence and designs for education, in *Distributed Cognitions: Psychological and Educational Considerations*, ed. G. Salomon. Cambridge: Cambridge University Press, 47–87.

Perret-Clermont, A.-N., J.-F. Perret & N. Bell, 1991. The social construction of meaning and cognitive activity in elementary school children, in *Perspectives on Socially Shared Cognition*, eds L.B. Resnick, J.M. Levine & S.D. Teasley. Washington (DC): American Psychological Association, 41–62.

Pétrequin, P. & A.-M. Pétrequin, 1993. From polished stone tool to sacred axe: the axes of the Danis of Irian Jaya, Indonesia, in *The Use of Tools by Human and Non-human Primates*, eds. A. Berthelet & J. Chavaillon. Oxford: Clarendon Press, 359–77.

Quine, W.V., 1960. *Word and Object*. Cambridge (MA): Harvard University Press.

Robson Brown, K., 1993. An alternative approach to cognition in the Lower Paleolithic: the modular view. *Cambridge Archaeological Journal* 3(2), 231–45.

Rogoff, B., 1990. *Apprenticeship in Thinking: Cognitive Development in Social Context*. Oxford: Oxford University Press.

Roux, V., B. Bril & G. Dietrich, 1995. Skills and learning difficulties involved in stone knapping. *World Archaeology* 27(1), 63–87.

Russon, A.E., 2002. Comparative developmental perspectives on culture: the great apes, in *Between Culture and Biology: Perspectives on Ontogenetic Development*, eds. H. Keller, Y.H. Poortinga & A. Scholmerich. Cambridge: Cambridge University Press, 30–56.

Salomon, G., 1993. Editor's introduction, in *Distributed Cognitions: Psychological and Educational Considerations*, ed. G. Salomon. Cambridge: Cambridge University Press, xi–xxi.

Salomon, G., D.N. Perkins & T. Globerson, 1991. Partners in cognition: extending human intelligence with intelligent technologies. *Educational Researcher* 20, 2–9.

Schick, K.D., 1994. The Movius line reconsidered: perspectives on the earlier Paleolithic of eastern Asia, in *Integrative Paths to the Past: Paleoanthropological Advances in Honor of F. Clark Howell*, eds. R.S. Corruccini & R.L. Ciochon. Englewood Cliffs (NJ): Prentice Hall, 2, 569–96.

Sternberg, R.J., G.B. Forsythe, J. Hedlund, J. Horvath, R.K. Wagner, W.M. Williams, S.A. Snook & E.L. Grigorenko, 2000. *Practical Intelligence in Everyday Life*. Cambridge: Cambridge University Press.

Stout, D., 2002. Skill and cognition in stone tool production:

an ethnographic case study from Irian Jaya. *Current Anthropology* 45(3), 693–722.

Stout, D., N. Toth, K. Schick, J. Stout & G. Hutchins, 2000. Stone tool-making and brain activation: Position Emission Tomography (PET) studies. *Journal of Archaeological Science* 27, 1215–23.

Strathern, A.J., 1971. *The Rope of Moka: Big-men and Ceremonial Exchange in Mount Hagen, New Guinea.* Cambridge: Cambridge University Press.

Tomasello, M., 1999. *The Cultural Origins of Human Cognition.* Cambridge (MA): Harvard University Press.

Toth, N., 1991. The importance of experimental replicative and functional studies in Palaeolithic archaeology, in *Cultural Beginnings: Approaches to Understanding Early Hominid Life-ways in the African Savanna*, ed. J.D. Clark. (Römisch-Germanisches Zentralmuseum Mainz. Forschungsinstitut für Vor- und Frühgeschichte Monographien 19.) Bonn: Dr Rudolf Habelt GMBH, 109–24.

Toth, N., D. Clark & G. Ligabue, 1992. The last stone ax makers. *Scientific American* (July), 88–93.

van Schaik, C.P., R.O. Deaner & M.Y. Merrill, 1999. The conditions for tool use in primates: implications for the evolution of material culture. *Journal of Human Evolution* 36, 719–41.

Vygotsky, L.S., 1978. *Mind in Society: the Development of Higher Psychological Process.* Cambridge (MA): Harvard University Press.

Weedman, K.J., 2000. An Ethnoarchaeological Study of Stone Scrapers among the Gamo People of Southern Ethiopia. Unpublished doctoral dissertation, University of Florida, University of Florida.

Whittaker, J.C., 1994. *Flintknapping: Making and Understanding Stone Tools.* Austin (TX): University of Texas Press.

Wood, D., J.S. Bruner & G. Ross, 1976. The role of tutoring in problem solving. *Journal of Child Psychology and Psychiatry* 17, 89–100.

Wynn, T., 1989. *The Evolution of Spatial Competence.* (Illinois Studies in Anthropology 17.) Champaign-Urbana (IL): University of Illinois Press.

Wynn, T., 2002. Archaeology and cognitive evolution. *Behavioral and Brain Sciences* 25, 389–402.

Chapter 23

Percussive Technology: Chimpanzee Baobab Smashing and the Evolutionary Modelling of Hominin Knapping

Linda F. Marchant & William C. McGrew

Hominin knapping of stone in prehistory likely did not spring full-blown, but what preceded it? Among living great apes, there is no natural flaking of stone, but there is elementary lithic technology. We report new data from Mt Assirik, Senegal, on the use of percussive technology by wild chimpanzees to process fruits of the baobab tree. The methods were 'archaeological', as only food remnants and stones but not behaviour were available. Data were analyzed from three baobab processing sites in terms of the relative location of smashed open fruits to stones of various size and condition. Results indicate that processing was by anvil alone, rather than by hammer-and-anvil. We suggest that percussive technology originated in ancestral hominoids with hard-shelled fruits being smashed against tree trunks and boughs. With greater terrestriality, anvils of stone and roots became available. To process small nuts a cognitive leap was needed to progress from object-strikes-passive-tool to active-tool-strikes-object-on-passive-tool. For some hard nuts it is necessary that both hammer and anvil be of stone. This creates the opportunity for inadvertent flaking from mishits, when stone strikes stone. This set the stage for the second major cognitive leap, that of knapping to produce a cutting edge.

It seems unlikely that hominin flaking of stone suddenly appeared, full-blown, at 2.5 million years ago at Gona in Ethiopia (Semaw *et al.* 1997). Instead of being the beginning of the evolution of hominin technology, such tools were probably just the latest stage in a long process that had much earlier origins (Panger *et al.* 2002). The usual caveat expressed about supposed earlier material culture is that previous technology was organic, and so perished and is irretrievable to archaeologists (e.g. McGrew 1992). However, this is now seen to be misguided, for several reasons. For example, not all organic material perishes as quickly as was once believed (see the replicated recovery of ancient DNA from prehistoric Neanderthal populations: Krings *et al.* 1999).

More relevant here is an intermediate grade of elementary technology: lithic technology that is not flaked. Thus, there may be objects that were used in subsistence, or self-maintenance, or even social life, that do persist, and can be recovered, but only if they can be recognized. Moreover, these objects may be modified in lawful ways that allow us to infer their function. Whether one calls them manuports or naturefacts versus artefacts, depends on definition (Joulian 1996). A prime candidate for this sort of tool is not one that presents a sharp edge or a pointed end, but one that is used to strike or receive a blow from another solid object: percussive technology.

The aims of this paper are to: 1) review percussive technology in nature among non-human species, in order to provide a sort of ecological baseline; 2) focus on a living hominoid, the chimpanzee (*Pan troglodytes*) who shows percussive technology to the greatest extent, by way of modelling the probable material culture of the Last Common Ancestor (LCA); and 3) to outline a sequence of events that could have led to the appearance of flaked-stone technology, that is, knapping, in prehistory.

Definition

Percussion, for these purposes, is the forceful, muscle-driven striking of one solid body against another. Typically, the object doing the striking is handheld, but it need not be so, since some creatures have grasping feet or gripping beaks. Typically the object being struck is stationary, but it does not have to be. Typically the goal of the act is to change the condition of one of the objects, but not the other. Therefore, the struck object is the target, and the striking object is the instrument. Finally, at least one of the objects is usually detached and therefore is portable. This definition is minimal and basic, as it means to include all cases of percussion, in human and non-human species.

The closest ethological relation may be missile technology, in which an object is thrown, rather than struck. The result may be the same, as are its key components listed below.

If we seek to deconstruct percussion, there are at least six important components:

1. Percussion is ballistic, that is, the movement once begun occurs so quickly that it cannot be modified while in progress, at least not without risk. Think of chopping wood with an axe.
2. Percussion is mass propelled through space, such that force produces greater impact than gravity alone. An axe tops a guillotine.
3. All percussion is aimed, and accuracy is usually crucial, so that wayward blows may produce poor results, or no results, or even harmful results. Think of a hammer, a nail, and a thumb–forefinger precision grip to hold the nail.
4. Related to this is eye–hand coordination. During percussion, the eyes usually fixate the target, not the striking object, regardless of which is held in the hand. Think of the game of tennis, where the ball is the focus of gaze, not the racquet.
5. Percussion typically requires a particular grip of the object held that is specific to the task, whether the grip be precision or power. Think of cracking a hen's egg with precision versus a coconut with power.
6. Finally, percussion requires motor skills, and efficient performance may require years of practice, with costs accruing to failure (Bril *et al.* this volume; Stout 2002; this volume). Think of diamond cutting as a high-risk, high-payoff enterprise.

None of the above components seems to stretch either the 'hardware' or 'software' of an ape, and so are easily imaginable in the percussive technology of a hominoid ancestral to living apes and humans (Wynn & McGrew 1989). Most of the components are probably present in other primates, and some manipulative non-primate mammals. The range of non-human percussion is reviewed in the next section.

The simplest binary taxonomy of percussive technology is anvil versus hammer (McGrew 1992, 173–6). The logic is simple: an anvil is a struck object, often fixed in the substrate. Anvils are not implements because during percussion they are not handled and remain immobile. Anvils may receive blows from the target, or may support a targeted object being struck by a hammer. Sometimes anvils may be moved, but between blows and not during percussion.

A hammer is a portable striking object, the impact of which is directed to a targeted object, usually of lesser density than itself. Often the target is supported by an anvil of greater density than itself, but this need not be so. The struck object changes state (shatters, deforms) or position.

Finally, an object can be both an anvil and a hammer at the same time. One way to crack coconuts, at least huskless ones, is to hold one in each hand and crack each against the other.

Matsuzawa (1996) derived an analytical structure of cognitively-underpinned, hierarchical processes that reflect the increasing complexity of behavioural performance related to objects. Level 0 in his scheme corresponds to direct action upon an object, e.g. cracking a nut between your teeth. (Only one external object is involved.) Level 1 corresponds to hitting a handheld nut against an anvil. (Two objects are involved.) Level 2 corresponds to using a hammer stone to hit a nut resting on an anvil. (Three objects are involved.) Level 3 corresponds to using a hammer stone to hit a nut on an anvil stone that is supported by a wedge-stone (Four objects are involved.) The wedge improves the striking surface, by making it more horizontal, through being a prop (Matsuzawa 1991). Level 3 cognition is rarely found outside of the human evolutionary line, and its first appearance there is controversial. The wedge-stone has been found in only one population of wild chimpanzees, Bossou, and the data remain sparse (Whiten *et al.* 1999).

Non-human percussion

Percussive technology is widespread among birds and mammals, but also occurs even in invertebrates, e.g. parasitic wasps seal their burrows with prey and egg inside by tamping the soil hard with a stone held in the mandibles (Beck 1980). Here a range of examples from vertebrates in nature is given, to illustrate the variety of nuances on the basic theme of percussion.

A universal of chimpanzee communication in nature is to 'drum' on the buttress roots of trees (Goodall 1968). This is done with palm or sole, and produces a long-range acoustic signal. However, it is not percussion by the definition used here, as the striking object is a body-part of the drummer. (Granted, this may seem illogical, as it rules out a bongo drummer, but rules in a snare drummer). Whether included or not, it reflects Matsuzawa's Level 0.

Male chimpanzees at Kanyawara, in Uganda's Kibale Forest, beat females with clubs of broken-off branches or saplings (Linden 2002). This is percussive weapon use. Level 1.

Thrushes of several species smash snails on stones or other comparable hard surfaces, as food processing (Henty 1986). Use of the anvil in such extractive foraging allows access to the otherwise inaccessible edible contents inside the protective shell. Level 1.

Wild Japanese monkeys at Arashiyama, near Kyoto, clack stones together, as one pattern of stone handling (Huffman 1996). Each hand holds a stone and these are repeatedly banged together, as in playing cymbals. When this is done repeatedly, the stone is recognizably modified, with many small percussion marks. The function is unknown. Level 1.

Sea otters (in California, but not Alaska) smash molluscs such as abalone against anvil stones balanced on their chests (Hall & Schaller 1969). They float supine in the kelp, and bash the shellfish held in both hands, then eat the contents. This is still Level 1, although the substrate as the otter's ventrum makes the task more reflexive.

Capuchin monkeys in arid Brazilian scrub forest crack nuts and hard-shelled fruits on boulder anvils, using hammerstones (de A. Moura & Lee 2004). Repeated blows produce a characteristic wear pattern of pitting on the boulders. This percussive technology in a New World monkey converges with that of the chimpanzee, an Old World ape (Visalberghi & McGrew 1997). Level 2.

Chimpanzees cracking nuts with stone hammers and anvils occasionally mishit and strike the anvil instead of the nut resting on it (Hannah & McGrew 1987; Hannah pers. comm.). The result can be a 'flake,' a sharp-edged, chipped-off piece of stone. If the apes went on to use these flakes, we might infer that this is Level 3 lithic tool manufacture but such use has yet to be seen.

Use of a wedge stone to prop up an anvil stone, however rare, remains the only published example of percussive technology by non-humans at Level 3. Hypothetical examples based on artefacts have also been asserted, e.g. the brush-stick of the chimpanzees of central west Africa (Sugiyama 1985). Sticks used to harvest social insect prey are apparently more efficient if their tips are frayed. This gives more surface area for the ants or termites to bite on to with their mandibles, when probed. Sugiyama hypothesized that brush sticks might be made by being pounded on anvils with hammer stones (Level 3). (Here the fourth object is the manufactured brush.) Alternatively, the ends of the sticks may become frayed by being crushed between the molar teeth, or may result inadvertently from repeated insertion of the stick into tight-fitting holes producing wear. Any of these three means may produce a usable brushstick, but the latter two would be only Level 0 or 1.

Human knapping of stone to produce flaked tools is not the same as any of these examples, yet each of them has elements that overlap with the knapping complex. There is nothing about the logical structure of anvils and hammers (and therefore of the knapping process) that is outwith the boundaries of non-human percussive technology.

Ape percussion

Of the four living species of great apes, only the chimpanzee is known to use percussive technology in nature (McGrew 1992). The main percussive task in which both behaviour and artefacts have been studied in detail is the cracking of nuts in foraging. There are two main study sites: Bossou in Guinea and Taï in Ivory Coast. At Bossou, chimpanzees use hammers and anvils of stone to crack open one species of nut, from the oil palm (Sugiyama & Koman 1979). Also, Matsuzawa (1991; 1996) has done the only experimental studies of percussive technology there, in his 'outdoor laboratory'. At Taï, chimpanzees use hammers and anvils of both wood and stone to crack open several species of nuts, not including those of the oil palm (Boesch & Boesch 1983; 1984; 1990). Taï's apes use different types of stone to crack open different species of nuts, according to the hardness of the latter (Boesch & Boesch 1983). Taï has yielded the only archaeology of percussive technology in apes, with radiocarbon dates showing that nut cracking is at least centuries old (Mercader *et al.* 2002).

No detailed studies have been done of the other main type of percussive technology, which is the use of anvils to open hard-shelled fruits. This is widespread across populations, such as cracking open the orange-sized *Strychnos* fruits at Gombe (McGrew *et al.* 1999). Whereas nut cracking is limited to rainforest populations in far West Africa, fruit smashing on anvils occurs across the complete range of habitats, from rain forest to savannas, and from Tanzania to Senegal.

All of the ape percussive technology mentioned so far targets plant parts, and the perishability of these organic items means that they will not persist in the long-term archaeological record. There is a better

Table 23.1. *Logic for determining a stone's use as hammer (H) or anvil (A), based on two variables: status (fixed vs movable) and size (big vs little). See text for details.*

		Size	
		Big	Little
	Movable	H or A	H (?)
Status			
	Fixed	A	A ?

chance for preservation of harder animal tissue, such as bone. There are some data on Taï's chimpanzees using anvils, but not hammer and anvil, to crack open the skulls of monkeys killed for food (Boesch & Boesch 1989). This processing technique allows the extraction of prized brain tissue for food.

An unusual form of percussive technology at Bossou is pestle pound (Yamakoshi & Sugiyama 1995). The chimpanzee detaches a frond from the crown of an oil palm, then uses it as a pestle. The mortar is the heart of the palm, which is nutritious but fibrously tough. By repeated pounding, the heart is reduced to a soupy, stringy pulp, which is then easily eaten.

Thus, percussive technology is common and widespread in wild chimpanzees (Whiten *et al.* 2001): Nine of 39 behavioural patterns identified as showing cultural variation across populations were percussive technology. Anvil use to pound open food items is habitual or customary in five of nine populations examined.

Surprisingly, little has been done on percussive technology in captive primates, perhaps because of concerns about the risk of encouraging weapon use. An orangutan (Wright 1972), a bonobo (Toth *et al.* 1993; Schick *et al.* 1999), and a group of capuchin monkeys (Westergaard & Suomi 1995) have been taught to make functional flakes of stone. Unpublished studies of chimpanzees show similar results (Boysen pers. comm.). The sharp-edged fragments that they produce will cut through a barrier that opens a container with a food reward. The bonobo, Kanzi, invented new ways to fracture stone, in addition to those that he was shown, and the capuchin monkeys showed five techniques for stone reduction. Clearly, more research is needed on percussive technology, apart from nut cracking, in both the wild and in captivity.

Case study: baobab smashing
Only on West African savannas does the chimpanzee co-occur with the baobab (*Adansonia digitata*, Bombacaceae). Elsewhere, habitats containing baobab are too hot and dry for apes, but humans and baboons avidly consume the fruits and seeds of this barrel-

trunked tree (Pochron 2000; Schoeninger *et al.* 2001). Baboons use their heavy teeth to open the melon-sized fruits, while humans crack them open with stones; at Mt Assirik, Senegal, the chimpanzees' technique is more like that of the humans: percussive technology.

There are two main ways to extract foodstuffs embedded in hand-shelled 'containers': one is to smash the fruit containing seeds and matrix against a hard object or substrate (= anvil only); the other is to crack the container by hitting it with one hard object while the container rests on another hard object (= hammer and anvil). Which one or both of these techniques do apes use? The simplest answer is to go to a place where apes eat baobabs and to record their food processing, that is, to collect directly behavioural data.

The other alternative is indirectly to infer the technology based on the artefacts and food remnants left behind by the processors. But can this circumstantial evidence distinguish between the two competing hypotheses? McGrew *et al.* (1988) hypothesized anvil use only but Bermejo *et al.* (1989) hypothesized hammer and anvil; neither presented behavioural evidence. Here, we present for the first time, both the complete behavioural data set (Baldwin 1979; McGrew *et al.* 2003) and the ethnoarchaeological data (this study) on the percussive technology of the chimpanzees of Assirik.

Table 23.1 gives the logic of distinguishing anvil from hammers (see Methods for details). A big, movable stone could be either hammer or anvil; nut-cracking chimpanzees elsewhere in West Africa use hammerstones (N = 172) with a median weight of 1.0–2.9 kg (Boesch & Boesch 1983, 279). A little, portable stone is likely to be a hammer; elsewhere preferred hammerstones are sized to fit one hand. A little, fixed stone cannot be a hammer, and is unlikely to be an anvil; useful anvils are usually big enough to offer a sufficient flat surface upon which to rest the container. However, a big, fixed stone can only be an anvil, and the bigger the surface, the more convenient to use. This yields certain predictions: smashed baobab fruits found more often near little stones suggests hammer use versus fruits near big stones suggests anvil use. (This assumes that a fruit shard is discarded on average nearer stones used versus not used in processing, all other things being equal.)

Materials and methods
The study was done by the two authors as members of the Miami Assirik Pan Project (MAPP) in Feb–April, 2000. Assirik is the highest point in the Parc National du Niokolo-Koba, a 9130-km² protected area in far southeastern Republique du Senegal. It is the hottest,

driest and most open site at which wild chimpanzees have been studied in the long term (McGrew *et al.* 1981). At 12°50'N and 12°45'W, Assirik's is the northern-most population of apes known in Africa. The tool-kit of Assirik's chimpanzees has 15 elements, of which baobab smashing is the only lithic pattern (Mc-Grew *et al.* 2003). The community of apes numbered about 25 (Tutin *et al.* 1983), ranged widely (Baldwin *et al.* 1982), and ate a limited diet (McGrew *et al.* 1988).

By the onset of MAPP's field season, all the accessible baobab fruits had been consumed, as the peak season for their consumption is November–January (Baldwin 1979). Thus, on the basis of informal surveying, we chose four trees for analysis, based on their having large numbers of fruit shells and stones nearby. The trees were in one of the three watersheds with permanent water that drained from Mt Assirik, about 2 km east of its summit.

Fruit
Each fruit found within 25 m of the tree was noted; those within a 10-m radius were 'assigned' to the nearest stone (see above), up to a distance of 3 m from fruit-to-stone. Fruits more than 3 m from any stone were deemed to be independent of them. To qualify as a fruit, the base of the fruit where the stem is attached had to be intact. This prevented over counting when fruits had been shattered into shards.

Each fruit was classed as having been eaten by baboons, by chimpanzees, or as unclear. Fruits eaten by baboons were much reduced and bore many bite-marks, usually incisor scrapes; those eaten by chimpanzees were often opened only enough for the contents to be extracted and bore few, if any, bite-marks. Fruits that could not be placed in either category were considered *unclear*. Two measurements were made: length (nearest cm) of fruit from stem-base to apex, and length of stem from stem-base to distal end. Stems were classed as complete or incomplete. Further characteristics were noted, when needed, e.g. if the fruit's matrix was only partly eaten.

Stone
Each stone within a 10-m radius of the tree was noted. The shortest distance (nearest 10 cm) from stone-to-trunk was measured. Stones that had one or more fruits associated with it were distinguished from those that had none (see above). Stones were classed as either **movable** (unattached and portable) or **fixed** (embedded in the ground and so not portable), and as **big** or **little** (see Table 23.1). For both types of

Table 23.2. *Numbers of stones and fruits found in association with four baobab trees at Assirik.*

Tree	No.	Stones	Fruits
Big	1	92	483
Liana	2	207	143
Open	3	81	99
Pilot	4	33	120
Total		413	845

Table 23.3. *Median distance of stone from tree (to nearest metre). Expected reflects random distribution; observed reflects actual distribution.*

Tree	<1	<2	<3	<4	<5	<6	<7	<8	<9	<10	N*
1								Obs. Exp.			68
2						Obs.		Exp.			207
3								Obs. Exp.			80
4	(no data)										(33)
Total								Obs. Exp.			355

* Differences from Table 23.2 reflect missing data or stones >10 m from tree.

stone, three perpendicular dimensions (nearest cm), were taken at their widest point: length, breadth, and height. This means that height of fixed stones was under-recorded, as part of the stone was buried. Movable stones also were weighed (nearest 100 g) by spring balance to an upper limit of 10 kg. To qualify as a stone, the product of length × breadth × height had to exceed 250 cm^3; smaller stones were ignored as being unrealistic candidates for hammer or anvil. Fixed stones with any dimension of greater than 1 m were classed as outcrops. Type of stone was classed as laterite or non-laterite.

Results
Table 23.2 shows that each of the four baobab trees had plenty of stones and eaten fruits. None of the stones yielded recognizable macroscopic remnants of fruit on their surface, thus the most direct measurement of use in fruit processing was absent. Further, in no case was a fruit shell found resting on a stone, or vice versa, so no clue to usage came from contact between fruit and stone (cf. Bermejo *et al.* 1989).

As a check of the distribution of stones on the ground, we asked if stones were found randomly distanced from the tree? If the tree's trunk is the centre of a circle with a radius of 10 m, then the area of that circle is 314 m^2 (A = π r^2). If stones occur randomly, then the median stone would be at a distance of 7–8 m from the trunk, and so gives an expected figure against which to compare the observed distribution. We predicted randomness, so no difference between observed versus expected.

Table 23.3 shows median distances for three of the four trees (as no distance data were taken at Pilot baobab). For two of the trees, the observed median distance matches the expected, and for the other, the actual median distance was less. Overall, there was no difference between observed and expected for N = 355 stones. This is reassuring.

Using the same reasoning, we expected fruits to be non-randomly distributed relative to stones, given the presumed role of stones in the fruits' processing. Thus, we predicted that fruits would be found closer to stones than expected by chance, that is, for median distance to be observed < expected. Here, the radius

was 3 m with 0.5 m bands from the stone.

Table 23.4 shows the median observed distances for all four trees to be notably less than expected distance. Accordingly, the overall average distance from fruit to stone was less than 1 metre, which coincidentally is within arm's reach for a chimpanzee. More precisely 61 per cent (387 of 636) were less than 1 m from a stone. This is also reassuring, but it does not allow us to distinguish between anvil and hammer use.

One way to tackle this is to compare degree of association of fruits with fixed versus movable stones. If movable stones (which are more likely to be hammers) more often have fruit associated with them than do fixed stones (which cannot be hammers), then this is support for the hammer-and-anvil hypothesis.

Table 23.5 shows that there is no difference between movable (35 per cent) versus fixed (34 per cent) stones with regard to fruit association. This shows no support for the hammer-and-anvil hypothesis, but neither does it support the anvil-only hypothesis, since anvils can be either fixed or movable (see Table 23.1).

If association with fruit is an indicator of stones involvement with baobab smashing, then size of stone may be revealing. If we presume that the smallest stones are most likely to be hammers and least likely to be anvils, and *vice versa*, then a high proportion of fruit association with the biggest stones would suggest anvil use, whereas a high proportion of fruit association with the smallest stones would suggest hammer use.

Table 23.6 shows that the heaviest of the four weight-classes of stone most often has fruit associated with it, and it is the only weight-class with which fruit association is the norm (at 55 per cent). This proportion is notably higher than either the lightest (29 per cent) or next lightest (28 per cent) categories. (The latter corresponds to the weight class reported to be typical for stone hammers used to crack nuts by Boesch & Boesch.)

A similar finding applies if the measure of size is volume (cm^3) instead of mass, when volume equals length × width × height of stone. Forty-two per cent of the largest stones (>10,000 cm^3) had associated fruit versus only 27 per cent of the next-smallest category (1000–4999 cm^3). This is not surprising, as volume is highly correlated with mass, especially with almost all the stones being of the same type, laterite. Thus, size of stone suggests the use of anvils and gives no support to the use of hammers.

Discussion

Many more analyses remain to be done, but the emerging picture from our data set

Table 23.4. *Median distance of fruit from nearest stone (to nearest 0.5 metre). Expected reflects random distribution; observed reflects actual distribution.*

Tree	0–0.5	0.5–1.0	1.0–1.5	1.5–2.0	2.0–2.5	2.5–3.0	N*
1			Obs.		Exp.		343
2	Obs.				Exp.		139
3		Obs.			Exp.		73
4	Obs.				Exp.		81
Total		Obs.			Exp.		636

* Differences from Table 23.2 reflect missing data or fruits >3 m from stone.

Table 23.5. *Proportion of stones (movable vs fixed) with fruit associated with them. Yes = fruit associated; No = no fruit association.*

Tree	Movable			Fixed			
	Yes	% Yes	No	Yes	% Yes	No	N*
1	25	40%	37	7	41%	10	79
2	30	29%	73	33	32%	69	205
3	14	45%	17	17	34%	33	81
4	(no data)						(33)
Total	69	35%	127	57	34%	112	365

* Differences from Table 23.2 reflect missing data.

Table 23.6. *Degree of fruit association (Yes vs No) as a function of mass of stone, in four weight classes, from lightest (<1 kg) to heaviest (>10 kg).*

Wt Class	Weight of Stone (kg)									
	< 1		1–4.9		5–9.9		>10		Total	
N	49		83		33		20		185	
Fruit assoc.	Yes	No	Yes	No	Yes	No	Yes	No	Yes	No
Freq.	14	35	23	60	12	21	11	9	60	125
% Yes	29%		28%		36%		55%		32%	

is one of anvil use, with no evidence of hammerstones being involved. How then to explain the contradictory conclusion reached by Bermejo *et al.* (1989, 70–72)? The first possibility is small sample bias: they reported only 8 small stones (range of volumes: 220–1152 cm³; range of weights: 0.5–3.0 kg) which they interpreted as hammers and 17 large stones (volume: *c.* 17,500 cm³ on average; range of weights: 10–18 kg) which they interpreted as anvils. These are small numbers upon which to generalize.

Second, they may have misunderstood the evidence. One of their photographs (p. 71) purports to show a stone hammer, but the single fruit in the frame is actually closer to a big, fixed stone anvil, which is not mentioned. Another photograph (p. 71) purports to show a hammer embedded in a baobab fruit, but the two objects are clearly lying side-by-side, with the fruit split in two.

Third, they collected their data at a different place in the Mt Assirik area than we did in the MAPP study. What Bermejo *et al.* (p. 67) called Baobab Valley in their map of the study area was at least 2 km from our four trees. Thus, micro-habitat differences could explain the different results, but their sole photograph of the habitat (p. 72) looks indiscriminable from the open woodland in which we worked.

Any or all of these three factors could explain the differing conclusions drawn by Bermejo *et al.* (1989) and ourselves.

To resolve the discrepancies between the two data sets would require a time-machine for the archaeologist, whose subjects are usually extinct, and so their behaviour is unavailable for scrutiny. For the ethologist of a living species, the ideal resource is behavioural data collected on the same subjects at the same time as the artefacts were used. The MAPP study cannot supply that, as like Bermejo *et al.* (1989), MAPP had no observations of baobab smashing.

However, the SAPP (Stirling African Primate Project) did, over a 44-month period (Feb. 1976–Dec. 1979) at Assirik, at a place to the west side of the mountain, no more than 5 km away from either of the sites mentioned above (Baldwin 1979; McGrew *et al.* 2003). Researchers found on 20 days the cracked shells of baobabs, left as remnants at feeding sites by chimpanzees. These data alone do not discriminate between the two hypotheses. On another 13 days, researchers heard the distinctive banging sounds of baobab fruits being processed. These provide aural evidence of percussion but again do not support either hypothesis.

However, on another 19 days, observers watched chimpanzees smash open baobab fruits. The results are revealing: on all 19 days, the apes showed anvil use, but in no case was the anvil a stone or a root! Instead, they used the trunk or branches of the baobab tree as the anvil and always worked arboreally. This suggests that the normative technique is not terrestrial use of stone or root anvil, and so this form of percussive technology differs from all known nut cracking by chimpanzees (e.g. Boesch & Boesch 1983). Indirect evidence of the processing of baobabs at Assirik was found for terrestrial smashing, but it was never seen directly.

This raises at least three issues of possible bias: one is that for unhabituated subjects, arboreal activity overhead (especially in leafless baobab trees) is more observable than terrestrial activity obscured by undergrowth. The strength of this bias can only be addressed with focal-subject behavioural data on habituated subjects, which will allow the true ratio of arboreal : terrestrial baobab smashing to be calculated. Another bias is that neither in Bermejo *et al.* (1989) nor in our study were the baobab trees scaled to look for indirect data on arboreal smashing there. Thus, neither team can say if arboreal smashing leaves detectable signs or not. These are missing data that require new parameters. Finally, as in nut cracking, which also shows a mixture of lithic and non-lithic technology, the long-term archaeological records from these sites will show only the lithic artefacts (Panger *et al.* 2002). As with the wooden nut-cracking hammers, the anvils of root, bough or trunk will vanish, as do all perishable, organic tools. This is a sobering reminder.

Early hominin percussion

If the earliest percussive technology used by hominins was directed to plant parts, whether nuts to be cracked, seeds to be pulverized, tubers to be pulped, lianas to be severed, bark to be stripped, and even branches to be detached, we are unlikely to recover these from the palaeontological record. They will have long since decomposed. Instead, we must rely on inorganic, e.g. phytoliths, or complex organic compounds, e.g. DNA, pollen, starch grains, etc., but only if they can be linked to hominin use. In principle, these can be recovered from the working surfaces of anvils and hammers, using scanning electron microscopy.

For animal parts, the chances are greater for recovering mineral-rich organs, such as tooth, bone, antler, that fossilize. Butchered bones are the earliest source of evidence of hominin technology; these are the slicing cut marks from flaked stone tools on ungulate long bones, attributed to *Australopithecus garhi* (de Heinzelin *et al.* 1999). The earliest evidence of surviving percussive technology, apart from flaked stone itself, is characteristic spiral fracturing of long bones that have been split open by hammer and anvil. The presumed function is extraction of bone marrow (Blumenshine & Selvaggio 1988).

For the earliest archaeological record of non-flaked technology, the evidence is of wear patterns on hammers and anvils, where pitted depressions form after innumerable blows wear down the surface. In the Near East, such depressions date to the Middle Palaeolithic, to about 800,000 years ago, and have been likened to the nut-cracking sites of chimpanzees (Goren-Inbar *et al.* 2002). It is likely that earlier examples exist but have not been recognized.

The first signs of tools made by percussion occur in Africa, with the appearance of the Oldowan in the eastern Rift Valley (Semaw *et al.* 1997). With their appearance, knapping was established as the dominant mode of lithic production in the evolution of human material culture.

'Evolutionario'

What changes in percussive technology had to occur to evolve from an anvil-using hominoid, to a hammer-and-anvil-using hominoid (LCA) to a knapping hominin? More to the point, but also much more elusively, *why* did such changes occur in evolutionary time? To answer the first question requires normative, descriptive data from artefacts (e.g. Roche *et al.* 1999; Roche this volume). To answer the second question means inferring function, that is, the results of natural selection acting on tool makers and users. We can never know for sure the intentions of extinct technologists, human or non-human, any more than we can for their living counterparts. We can but try to draw the strongest possible inferences, based on the evidence available. Therefore, an 'evolutionario' is an evolutionary scenario of events that is, at least in principle, empirically testable.

A conservative starting point was an arboreal ape that smashed hand-held, hard-shelled fruit on a natural anvil of tree trunk or bough. This is a direct, Level 1 form of percussive technology: sit in a tree, pick a fruit and crack it open, without moving from the spot. Since this occurs in living monkeys and apes and has been well-studied, it probably can also be assumed to have occurred in the LCA.

The next stage came with the shift from arboreality to increasing terrestriality. This yielded new and less precarious anvils on the ground, and in addition to roots, for the first time afforded a harder substrate: stone. This superior anvil material increased the efficiency of percussion, as well as widening the range of prey items to be cracked. We have no direct evidence of arboreality : terrestriality in Plio-Pleistocene descend-

ants of the LCA, but given the data on percussion by terrestrial capuchin monkeys and chimpanzees, the inference seems reasonable.

Some hard-shelled fruits (nuts) are too small in size to be held in the large hand of a great ape and pounded on an anvil. Not enough force can be applied to crack a small item held in a precision grip (Marzke & Wullstein 1996; Marzke 1997; this volume). A power grip is fine for smashing large fruits, but not for nuts. Most nut consumers, from palm nut vulture to baboon, crack nuts in their beaks or molars, but for an ape this is too risky of damage to the relatively thin enamel of hominoid teeth.

Thus, the stage was set for the first major cognitive leap, from anvil-only to hammer-and-anvil, and from Matsuzawa's Level 1 to Level 2. The task changed crucially from two items to three, with the addition of the active hammer addressing the target object (nut or bone), enabled by the passive substrate. The latter need be only a surface of sufficient size, orientation, and density. In nature, a root or outcrop will do as well as a log or boulder, as a striking platform. This leap was made by one or more taxa of apes but probably not all, as manifest today in the chimpanzee, but not in all populations of the species, and not at all in the bonobo or gorilla in nature.

Some nuts are soft enough to be cracked with wooden or stone hammers and anvils, e.g. *Coula edulis*, but others are so hard that only lithic technology will do, e.g. *Panda oleosa* (Boesch & Boesch 1983). Misfits of wood on wood, wood on stone, or stone on wood are inconsequential, but stone on stone may yield fragments that look like flakes (Mercader *et al.* 2002). Either a direct or glancing blow (off a spherical nut) onto a stone anvil may cause a piece of stone to fracture from the edge of a stone anvil. No actualistic etho-archaeology has been done on living apes, but the archaeological record for nut cracking at Taï yields flakes that resemble those from the Oldowan (Mercader *et al.* 2002).

No one has seen a living ape in nature use sharp-edged lithic technology, either from these inadvertent flakes from nut cracking, or from manuports of naturally-fractured stone. It can be argued that chimpanzee dentition and oral musculature are enough for any task that requires cutting, whether that be clipping by incisors or puncture or slicing by canines. The main use for cutting, in the butchery of large mammals, does not apply to apes, who eat only small to medium-sized prey, which they disassemble literally by tearing limb from limb. (Which way the evolutionary causal arrow pointed is unclear: Do apes lack cutting-edge technology because they ignore large mammals, or are apes denied large mammals because they lack a cutting-edge?)

In any event, the stage was set again for the second cognitive leap, which led to knapping. This cognitively advanced the ancestral hominin from Matsuzawa's Level 2 to Level 3. All that was needed was the transition of stone-on-stone percussion from accidental to goal-directed. At first, one can imagine a proto-knapper striking a fixed anvil with a hammerstone, but given the crucial importance of the angle of percussion, this was likely to be inefficient. But, given that some anvils used by apes are not fixed, then shifting the position of a portable anvil and thus re-orienting its surface, would be an improvement. (Chimpanzees routinely reorient the position of nuts on anvils, as cracking efficiency varies hugely from random blows to aimed blows on the nut's seams.) The logical next step is to transform a movable anvil into a handheld core, merely by picking it up and holding it appropriately.

No ape in nature has been seen to knap, for tools that are not used, need not be made. But why would a hominin, extinct or extant, take up flake production? If other selection pressures led to dental reduction, then tasks before performed by teeth would now need technological replacement. Or if longevity increased for other reasons, then individuals with dental wear or loss through ageing could 'rejuvenate' their mastication with lithic technology. Or, if resources changed, so that new potential food-items, e.g. large tubers or large animals, became available, then sharp-edged technology would enable their exploitation. All of these hypotheses are potentially testable, in the palaeontological or archaeological records. Similarly they could be tested experimentally with living apes. There is some evidence of improvement in lithic production by Kanzi, from simply fracturing stone (Toth *et al.* 1993) to targeted fragmenting of it (Schick *et al.* 1999).

Conclusions

In any event, even if some of the stages of the hypothetical progression outlined above turn out to be wrong, there is a seamless evolutionary sequence from fruit smashing to stone knapping. No leap is untenable. Further, all of the hypothesized stages are more than just-so stories, as they can be tested retrospectively in the palaeontological and archaeological records and prospectively by field observation and captive experimentation on living primates. It is no longer advisable for palaeoarchaeology to ignore primatology, any more than it is for primatology to ignore the implications of its findings for prehistory. Knapping stone may be unique to hominins, but not by much.

Acknowledgements

We thank the organizers, Valentine Roux and Blandine Bril, for their invitation to attend the workshop, 'Knapping Stone: a Uniquely Hominin Behaviour?' WCM thanks the Leverhulme Centre for Human Evolutionary Studies, University of Cambridge, for support during the writing of this manuscript. Field research was supported by L.S.B. Leakey Foundation and Phillip and Elaina Hampton Fund (Miami University).

References

Baldwin, P.J., 1979. The Natural History of the Chimpanzee (*Pan troglodytes verus*) at Mt Assirik, Senegal. Unpublished PhD Thesis, University of Stirling.

Baldwin, P.J., W.C. McGrew & C.E.G. Tutin, 1982. Wide-ranging chimpanzees at Mt. Assirik, Senegal. *International Journal of Primatology* 3, 367–85.

Beck, B.B., 1980. *Animal Tool Behavior*. New York (NY): Garland STPM Press.

Bermejo, M. & G. Illera, 1999. Tool-set for termite-fishing and honey extraction by wild chimpanzees in the Lossi Forest, Congo. *Primates* 40, 619–27.

Bermejo, M., G. Illera & J. Sabater Pi, 1989. New observations on the tool-behavior of the chimpanzees from Mt Assirik (Senegal, West Africa). *Primates* 30, 65–73.

Blumenshine, R.J. & M.M. Selvaggio, 1988. Percussion marks on bone surfaces as a new diagnostic of hominin behaviour. *Nature* 333, 763–5.

Boesch, C. & H. Boesch, 1983. Optimisation of nut cracking with natural hammers by wild chimpanzees. *Behaviour* 83, 265–86.

Boesch, C. & H. Boesch, 1984. Mental map in wild chimpanzees: an analysis of hammer transports for nut cracking. *Primates* 25, 160–70.

Boesch, C. & H. Boesch, 1989. Hunting behavior of wild chimpanzees in the Tai National Park. *American Journal of Physical Anthropology* 78, 547–73.

Boesch, C. & H. Boesch, 1990. Tool use and tool making in wild chimpanzees. *Folia Primatologica* 54, 86–99.

Boesch, C. & H. Boesch-Aschermann, 2000. *The Chimpanzees of the Taï Forest*. Oxford: Oxford University Press.

de Heinzelin, J., J.D. Clark, T. White, W. Hart, P. Renne, G. WoldeGabriel, Y. Beyene & E. Vrba, 1999. Environment and behavior of 2.5 million-year-old Bouri hominins. *Science* 284, 625–9.

de A. Moura, A.C. & P.C. Lee, 2004. Capuchin stone tool use in Caatinga dry forest. *Science* 306, 1909.

Goodall, J.L., 1968. The behaviour of free-living chimpanzees in the Gombe Stream Reserve. *Animal Behaviour Monographs* 1, 161–301.

Goren-Inbar, N., G. Sharon, Y. Melamed & M. Kisler, 2002. Nuts, nut cracking, and pitted stones at Gesher Benot Ya'aqov, Israel. *Proceedings of the National Academy of Sciences of the USA* 99, 2455–60.

Hall, K.R.L. & G.B. Schaller, 1969. Tool-using behavior of the California sea otter. *Journal of Mammalogy* 45, 287–98.

Hannah, A.C. & W.C. McGrew, 1987. Chimpanzees using

stones to crack open oil palm nuts in Liberia. *Primates* 28, 31–46.

Henty, C.J., 1986. Development of snail-smashing in song thrushes. *British Birds* 79, 277–81.

Huffman, M.A., 1996. Acquisition of innovative cultural behaviors in non-human primates: a case study of stone handling, a socially transmitted behavior in Japanese macaques, in *Social Learning in Animals: the Roots of Culture*, eds C. Heyes & B. Galef. San Diego (CA): Academic Press, 267–89.

Joulian, F., 1996. Comparing chimpanzee and early hominin techniques: some contributions to cultural and cognitive questions, in *Modelling the Human Mind*, eds. P. Mellars & K. Gibson. (McDonald Institute Monographs.) Cambridge: McDonald Institute for Archaeological Research, 173–89.

Krings, M., H. Geisert, R.W. Schmitz, H. Krainitzki & S. Pääbo, 1999. DNA sequence of the mitochondrial hypervariable region II from the Neanderthal type specimen. *Proceedings of the National Academy of Sciences of the USA* 96, 5581–5.

Linden, E., 2002. *The Octopus and the Orangutan*. New York (NY): Dutton.

Marzke, M., 1997. Precision grips, hand morphology, and tools. *American Journal of Physical Anthropology* 102, 91–100.

Marzke, M. & K. Wullstein, 1996. Chimpanzee and human grips: a new classification with a focus on evolutionary morphology. *International Journal of Primatology* 17, 117–39.

Matsuzawa, T., 1991. Nesting cups and metatools in chimpanzees. *Behavioral and Brain Sciences* 14, 570–71.

Matsuzawa, T., 1996. Chimpanzee intelligence in nature and captivity: isomorphism of symbol use and tool use, in *Great Ape Societies*, eds W.C. McGrew, L.F. Marchant, & T. Nishida. Cambridge: Cambridge University Press, 196–209.

McGrew, W.C., 1992. *Chimpanzee Material Culture: Implications for Human Evolution*. Cambridge: Cambridge University Press.

McGrew, W.C., P.J. Baldwin & C.E.G. Tutin, 1981. Chimpanzees in a hot, dry and open habitat: Mt. Assirik, Senegal, West Africa. *Journal of Human Evolution* 10, 227–44.

McGrew, W.C., P.J. Baldwin & C.E.G. Tutin, 1988. Diet of wild chimpanzees (*Pan troglodytes verus*) at Mt Assirik, Senegal. I. Composition. *American Journal of Primatology* 16, 213–26.

McGrew, W.C., L.F. Marchant, R.W. Wrangham & H. Klein, 1999. Manual laterality in anvil use: wild chimpanzees cracking *Strychnos* fruit. *Laterality* 4, 79–87.

McGrew, W.C., P.J. Baldwin, L.F. Marchant, J.D. Pruetz, S.E. Scott & C.E.G. Tutin, 2003. Ethoarchaeology and elementary technology of unhabituated chimpanzees at Assirik, Senegal, West Africa. *Palaeoanthropology* 1, 1–20.

Mercader, J., M.A. Panger & C. Boesch, 2002. Excavation of a chimpanzee stone tool site in the African rainforest. *Science* 296, 1452–5.

Panger, M.A., A.S. Brooks, B.G. Richmond & B. Wood, 2002.

Older than the Oldowan? Rethinking the emergence of hominin tool use. *Evolutionary Anthropology* 11, 235–45.

Pochron, S.T., 2000. The core dry-season diet of yellow baboons (*Papio hamadryas cynocephalus*) in Ruaha National Park, Tanzania. *Folia Primatologica* 71, 346–9.

Roche, H., A. Delagnes, J.P. Brugal, C. Feibel, M. Kibunjia, V. Mourrel & P.J. Texier, 1999. Early hominin stone tool production and technical skill 2.34 mya ago in West Turkana, Kenya. *Nature* 399, 57–60.

Schick, K., N. Toth & G. Garufi, 1999. Continuing investigations into the stone tool-making and tool-using capabilities of a bonobo (*Pan paniscus*). *Journal of Archaeological Science*, 26, 821–32.

Schoeninger, M., H.T. Bunn, S. Murray, T. Pickering & J. Moore, 2001. Meat-eating by the fourth African ape, in *Meat-Eating and Human Evolution*, eds C.B. Stanford & H.T. Bunn. Oxford: Oxford University Press, 179–95.

Semaw, S., P. Renne, J.W.K. Harris, C.S. Feibel, R.L. Bernor, N. Fesscha & K. Mowbray, 1997. 2.5-million-year-old stone tools from Gona, Ethiopia. *Nature* 385, 333–6.

Stout, D., 2002. Skill and cognition in stone tool production. *Current Anthropology* 43, 693–722.

Sugiyama, Y., 1985. The brush-stick of chimpanzees found in southwest Cameroon and their cultural characteristics. *Primates* 26, 361–74.

Sugiyama, Y. & J. Koman, 1979. Tool-using and -making behavior in wild chimpanzees at Bossou, Guinea. *Primates* 20, 513–24.

Toth, N., K. Schick, S. Savage-Rumbaugh, R. Sevick & D. Rumbaugh, 1993. Pan the tool-maker: investigations into the tool-making and tool-using capabilities of a bonobo (*Pan paniscus*). *Journal of Archaeological Science* 20, 81–91.

Tutin, C.E.G., W.C. McGrew & P.J. Baldwin, 1983. Social organizations of savanna-dwelling chimpanzees, *Pan troglodytes verus*, at Mt. Assirik, Senegal. *Primates* 24, 154–73.

Visalberghi, E. & W.C. McGrew, 1997. *Cebus* meets *Pan*. *International Journal of Primatology* 18, 677–81.

Westergaard, G.C. & S.T. Suomi, 1995. The stone tools of capuchins (*Cebus apella*). *International Journal of Primatology* 16, 1017–24.

Whiten, A., J. Goodall, W.C. McGrew, T. Nishida, V. Reynolds, T. Sugiyama, C.E.G. Tutin, R.W. Wrangham & C. Boesch, 1999. Cultures in chimpanzees. *Nature* 399, 682–5.

Whiten, A., J. Goodall, W.C. McGrew, T. Nishida, V. Reynolds, Y. Sugiyama, C.E.G. Tutin, R.W. Wrangham & C. Boesch, 2001. Charting cultural variation in chimpanzees. *Behaviour* 138, 1481–516.

Wright, R.V.A., 1972. Imitative learning of a flaked tool technology — the case of an orangutan. *Mankind* 8, 296–306.

Wynn, T.G. & W.C. McGrew, 1989. An ape's view of the Oldowan. *Man* 24, 383–98.

Yamakoshi, G. & Y. Sugiyama, 1995. Pestle-pounding behavior of wild chimpanzees at Bossou, Guinea: a newly-observed tool-using behavior. *Primates* 36, 489–500.

Part IV

Conclusion

Chapter 24

Synthesis and Speculations

Blandine Bril & Valentine Roux

Requirements for a unique tool-related task

Considering F. Boas's description of a basket-maker at work, Ingold (2001, 22) writes :

> There is no reason to doubt that the basket-maker begins to work with a pretty clear idea of what a well-woven basket should look like. She has her standards. But watching her at work, it is evident that the form of the basket emerges not from these standards but from a complex pattern of finely controlled movements.

The different studies on the skills involved in tool-related tasks (Bril *et al.*; Biryukova *et al.*; Roux & David; Winton; Ivanova; Smitsman *et al.*) have dwelled on what seems evident to Ingold, i.e. the importance of finely-controlled movements for becoming an expert in technical tasks. This importance has been assessed through a fine analysis of tool-related tasks along three levels of action: courses of action, subgoals, and elementary movements. The different authors do not deny the role played by planning in the sense of Agree & Chapman, i.e. planning as a resource. They insist on the fact that the course of action observed depends on the control of the elementary movements. It is assumed that the course of action emerges from the dynamics of the succession of elementary actions guided by the knowledge of the method that functions as a 'plan as resource'. In other words, stone knapping and, more precisely, the control of the conchoidal fracture (Pelegrin), requires a fine tuning of integrated bimanual elementary movements for further developing appropriate courses of action. This result, which can be considered as a truism by practitioners, has strong relevant implications for the understanding of human evolution. As a first step, it enables us to reconsider the specificity of stone-knapping skills when compared to the manipulative skills developed by non-human primates. In this respect, primatologists (Foucart *et al.*, Byrne, Cummins-Sebree & Fragaszy) agree upon the fact that, be they apes or monkeys, non-human primates display cognitive skills that can be compared with the ones involved in stone knapping. If non-human primates are not in a position to develop stone knapping, this is mainly because of an inability to produce the level of movement tuning required for controlling the conchoidal fracture. These movements combine precision and force, and are exerted according to a fine bimanual coordination. No ape or monkey seems able to achieve such a combination. In this regard, and contrary to what has been suggested until now, stone knapping reveals capacities that are uniquely hominin. These capacities are found at the motor level, not at the cognitive level. As stated by authors of this volume (Foucart *et al.*; Cummins-Sebree & Fragaszy), the differences between the motor capacities developed by human and non-human primates are a question of degree. Current researches on the biomechanical properties of non-human primates should permit in the future to specify more precisely these differences in degree, which entail that human and non-human primates are not able to produce the same technical actions. Also, future research on 'planning' should enable us to be more specific about the articulation between motor and planning capacities, and about how planning becomes effective as soon as the elementary movements are controlled.

Characterizing stone-knapping skills in terms of elementary movements leads next to the question of the conditions required for exerting such elementary movements. This question has been examined for the bio-behavioural system (Corbetta), the somatic (Marzke) and the neural substrate (Maier *et al.*; Stout, Jacobs *et al.*). As for the bio-behavioural system, it appears that the erect posture favours handedness and precise bimanual coordinated movements, as shown by data in infants and non-human primates. The absence of an erect posture in apes and monkeys is said to explain why they are not able to produce fine lateralized bimanual tasks. As for the somatic substrate, stone-knapping movements require a specific pattern of high-frequency human hand features (Marzke). This pattern is not found among non-human primates. Last, the neural substrate is considered from the viewpoint of the features needed for a high degree of manual dexterity and for producing tool-related tasks. An increase in dextrous manipulative behaviours is shown to be related to a larger corticospinal tract, which appears as a necessary but not sufficient condition for tool use (Maier *et al.*). In addition, stone knapping appears as an especially demanding perceptual-motor task, which can be achieved through motor, somatosensory, superior parietal and visual cortices and the cerebellum (Stout; Jacobs *et al.*). There could also be some evidence of a uniquely human adaptation in the dorsal stream of cortical visual processing (Stout).

Studies of the conditions required for stone knapping illuminate what might be the mechanisms that underpin human evolution. To begin with, let us recall that the interplay between erect posture and handedness is observed for human as well as non-human primates. In a developmental perspective, this interaction is interpreted in neural terms. The erect posture is supposed to affect the brain and improve its capacity to dissociate muscle patterns for the arms and for walking, thus favouring the development of handedness as a behavioural trait (Corbetta). For primatologists (Holder), interplay is observed between postural stability and handedness. Handedness is assumed to become effective, not because of brain specialization, but through the achievement of specialized tasks. The strong relationship in non-human primates (apes and monkeys) between postural stability, development of handedness and specialized tasks (Byrne; Holder; Cummins-Sebree & Fragaszi), leads Markze to suppose that, prior to stone knapping, the first hominins may have engaged in lateralized activities, such as extractive, forceful retrieval and processing of tough vegetation and fauna, which may have contributed to 'the evolution of features in ancestral hominin hands that were preadapted to the requirement of forceful precision grips in tool making'. The practice of lateralized activities while progressively acquiring a stable form of bipedalism possibly counted for a lot in the evolution of fine bimanual coordination, as suggested by Corbetta, and in brain micro-adaptations, as suggested by Stout. This process of evolution supposedly led to bio-behavioural systems as well as somatic and neural substrates presenting the necessary conditions for the development of the skills required by stone knapping. This process was progressive, as exemplified by the various forms of bipedalism developed by the different genus and species found during the late Pliocene. At this point, it is useful to consider whether such a progressive process, leading in time and space to the existence of different bio-behavioural systems, might not explain the variability of the earliest lithic

industries (Roche). Could the genus and species who knapped the Lokalelei 2c industries be biologically more 'advanced' in terms of posture, handedness and bimanual coordination than those responsible for the more awkward tools found for example at Gona? Could the skills developed by these 'advanced' species act as an adaptive value in the selective process that led *Homo* to become the predominant genus?

Corbetta suggests that handedness as a behavioural trait developed when the upright posture was fully adopted given the fact that a fully erect posture arguably implies brain specialization. Steele & Uomini suggest that the practice of stone knapping possibly contributed to handedness as a behavioural trait. On the basis of the studies presented in this volume, we can speculate that in a dynamic perspective entailing constant interactions between the different components that form the bio-behavioural system, it is clear that stone knapping and its technological development may have played an important role in the development of the anthropological features that characterize the line of *Homo*.

To summarize, the studies of the interactions between the different components of the non-human and human primate bio-behavioural systems enable us to propose an evolutionary scenario where the biological substrate required for stone knapping is seen as emerging from complex dynamic interactions between posture, handedness and bimanual coordination (Corbetta). These interactions were supposedly made effective through specialized activities, such as processing plants and/or fauna. In return, they had consequences in somatic and neural terms and led progressively to the biological substrate that was needed to develop the skills required by the control of the conchoidal fracture. When bipedalism stabilized and the brain specialized, handedness could develop as a behavioural trait. By that time, *Homo* was the predominant genus among hominins and lithic industries had considerably evolved.

Conditions for a uniquely hominin innovation

The conditions for the actualization of stone knapping have been examined at the individual and collective level. At the individual level, these conditions have been examined for human primates on the basis of ontogenetic data (Bushnell *et al.*; Lockman). These data, interpreted according to a dynamic-system perspective, reveal that, contrary to current views followed by primatologists (e.g. Povinelli 2000; Visalberghi & Limongelli 1996; Johnson-Frey 2003), the invention of new actions is not primarily dependant upon representational capacities combined with causal understanding, that is, a representation of the tool to be including a causal understanding of the effect of an object on another object. Invention could stem from imitating the means and exploring the properties of tools. Imitating the means is believed to govern the transfer of gestures to new situations even without a full causal understanding. In turn, the capacities required for exploring the properties of tools and relating objects to substrate and surroundings would permit new tool uses to be discovered. These capacities are not necessarily unique to human primates or great apes, as shown by capuchin monkeys, who display the cognitive capacities needed to explore and discover the properties of objects (Cummins-Sebree & Fragaszi). Examples of means imitation can also be found among non-human primates (e.g. Byrne & Russon 1998; Myowa-Yamakoshi & Matsuzawa 2000; Whiten 1998).

A capacity more specific to so-called 'human' behaviour in the process of innovating technical actions is argued to be the capacity for active teaching; this would favour the transmission of new actions by highlighting to apprentices the properties of the objects that must be taken into account to achieve a successful task (Bushnell *et al.*; Lockman). Such capacities are reported to be extremely rare among apes (Byrne). Their development is supposedly bound to the social context in which transmission occurs (Stout). More precisely, on a collective scale, it seems that the transmission of technical skills depends on the organization of the social group, when characterized in terms of sociable gregariousness (van Shaik & Pradhan 2003). An innovation such as stone knapping and its transmission among hominins would have required this degree of social tolerance between individuals.

Finally, the technological context in which the invention of stone knapping took place is considered (Marchant & McGrew). A complex percussive technology tradition is supposed to have represented a favourable context for such an invention. This hypothesis fits well into an evolutionary scenario where individual imitative and exploratory capacities possibly counted for a lot in the invention of stone knapping and its actualization, assuming the existence of prerequisites such as the biological system required for stone knapping, the dynamics underlying the phenomenon of innovation, and specific social conditions for skill transmission.

Concluding remarks

There can be little doubt that the dynamic-system approach to technological change has enabled us to design a relevant methodological framework for studying the complex phenomenon represented by such an innovation as stone knapping. As a result, the different lines of research to pursue a better understanding of human evolution are here well highlighted. They are manifold, belonging as they do to a variety of disciplinary fields. With regard to this, the dynamic system approach also emphasizes the need to combine different disciplines in order to elucidate the complex mechanisms that underpin the progressive transformation of the psychological, somatic and neural features of the primates, be it at the ontogenetic or the phylogenetic level.

Archaeological artefacts may well reflect how biological factors have influenced the characteristics of lithic industries. However, it should not be overlooked that other factors, i.e. technical, environmental or socio-cultural factors, also played a role in the evolution of these industries. Upcoming research on technological changes liable to be interpreted metaphorically as the result of dynamic interactions between different orders of components should enable us, in the future, to bring forth scenarios aimed at a better understanding of this early part of human history.

References

Byrne, R.W. & A.E. Russon, 1998. Learning by imitation: a hierarchical approach. *Behavioural & Brain Sciences* 21, 667–721.

Ingold, T., 2001. Beyond art and technology: the anthropology of skill, in *Anthropological Perspective on Technology*, ed M.B. Schiffer. Albuquerque (NM): University of New Mexico Press, 17–32.

Johnson-Frey, S.H., 2003. What's so special about human tool use? *Neuron* 39, 201–4.

Myowa-Yamakoshi, M. & T. Matsuzawa, 2000. Imitation of intentional manipulatory actions in chimpanzees (*Pan troglodytes*). *Journal of Comparative Psychology* 114, 381–91.

Povinelli, D., 2000. *Folk Physics for Apes*. Oxford: Oxford University Press.

van Schaik, C.P. & G.R. Pradhan, 2003. A model for tool-use traditions in primates: implications for the coevolution of culture and cognition. *Journal of Human Evolution* 44, 645–64.

Visalberghi, E. & L. Limongelli, 1996. Acting and understanding: tool use revisited through the minds of capuchin monkeys, in *Reaching into Thought: the Minds of the Great Apes*, eds A. Russon, K. Bard & S. Parker. Cambridge: Cambridge University Press, 57–79.

Whiten, A., 1998. Imitation of the sequential structure of actions by chimpanzees (*Pan troglodytes*). *Journal of Comparative Psychology* 112(3), 270–81.

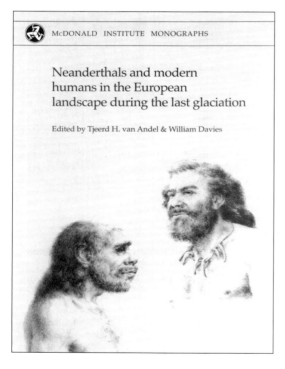